THE
COOK'S
ILLUSTRATED
COMPLETE
BOOK OF
POULTRY

THE
COOK'S
ILLUSTRATED
COMPLETE
BOOK OF
POULTRY

By the Editors of *Cook's Illustrated*

PREFACE BY CHRISTOPHER KIMBALL

ILLUSTRATIONS BY JUDY LOVE

Clarkson Potter/Publishers   New York

◆

Published by Clarkson N. Potter, Inc.,
201 East 50th Street, New York, New York 10022.
Member of the Crown Publishing Group.

Random House, Inc. New York, Toronto, London, Sydney, Auckland
www.randomhouse.com

CLARKSON N. POTTER, POTTER,
and colophon are registered trademarks of Random House, Inc.

◆

Printed in the United States of America

Design by JILL ARMUS

◆

Library of Congress Cataloging-in-Publication Data
The Cook's Illustrated complete book of poultry / by the editors of Cook's Illustrated ;
preface by Christopher Kimball ; illustrations by Judy Love.
Includes index.
1. Cookery (Poultry)   I. Cook's Illustrated.
TX750 .C68   1999
641.6′65—ddc21   98-43305
CIP

◆

ISBN 0-609-60063-X
10 9 8 7 6 5 4 3 2 1
First Edition

ACKNOWLEDGMENTS

/|\

ALL OF THE PROJECTS UNDERTAKEN BY *COOK'S ILLUSTRATED* ARE COLLECTIVE EFFORTS, THE COMBINED EXPERIENCE AND OPINIONS OF EDITORS, TEST COOKS, FOOD WRITERS, AND COOKBOOK AUTHORS ALL JOINING IN THE SEARCH FOR THE BEST COOKING METHODS.

The *Cook's Illustrated Complete Book of Poultry* is no exception.

The idea for a series of in-depth cookbooks on single subjects was initiated by our agents, Angela Miller and Coleen O'Shea; and our original executive editor, Mark Bittman, was very helpful in the planning and discussions. The idea was further refined by our editor at Clarkson Potter, Roy Finamore, who has been demanding and thoughtful, in the best tradition of great book editors. Jack Bishop, *Cook's* Senior Writer, was then asked to spearhead the project, organizing and developing recipes, as well as actually writing the book. Lauren Chattman was in charge of developing and testing many of the recipes in the pages that follow. Pam Anderson, Executive Editor of *Cook's Illustrated*, also helped shape the manuscript and is responsible for developing many of the magazine's poultry techniques and recipes.

Susan Logozzo and Anne Yamanaka organized the step-by-step photography shoot that provided artwork for the illustrator.

Photographer Jim Thomas captured more than 1,800 images on film during those long three days. Illustrator Judy Love turned these photos into the drawings you see throughout the book. Amy Klee offered her advice and keen art director's eye in helping to select drawings for the book.

Many of the recipes and techniques in this book are based on work that has appeared in *Cook's Illustrated*. We would like to thank the following authors for their contributions: Pam Anderson, Douglas Bellow, Jack Bishop, Bruce Cost, Ronnie Fein, Melissa Hamilton, Eva Katz, Stephanie Lyness, Adam Ried, Nicole Routhier, Chris Schlesinger, Stephen Schmidt, David SooHoo, John Willoughby, and Dawn Yanagihara.

CHRISTOPHER KIMBALL
Editor and Publisher

CONTENTS

/|\

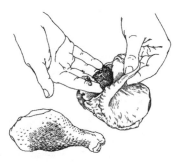

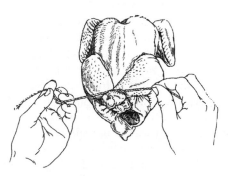

PREFACE

/|\

MY MATERNAL GRANDFATHER, DR. WHITE, HAD A FARM JUST WEST OF LEESBURG, VIRGINIA, THAT WAS POPULATED WITH AT LEAST TWO OF MOST EVERY FARM ANIMAL, INCLUDING PIGS, COWS, HORSES, BURROS, DUCKS, TURKEYS, AND, OF COURSE, CHICKENS.

A full-time farmhand, Manuel, took care of the place and his daughter, Mary Elizabeth, became good friends with my mother, Mary Alice.

They exchanged presents every Christmas, one year giving my mother a dried, blown-up pig's bladder to use as a toy, which horrified my grandmother, who was more comfortable at a dinner party back in Washington, D.C., than out on the farm. This was especially true when strong thunderstorms moved through the Blue Hills, and it took three people to close the front door because of the high winds. My grandmother was usually found hiding in a closet, waiting for the thunder and lightning to pass.

But it was the chickens that seem to have left their mark on our family. My mother owns a farm in northwest Connecticut and tends to over 150 chickens in her spare time, including silkies, who are good mothers; polish, with their distinctive topknots; austerlorps, who are big, glossy black birds, good for laying and meat; and guinea hens, who are good watchdogs but bullies, hooting and hollering if they see a hawk or stranger com-

ing. They are also known to chase other chickens, pecking out their tail feathers, hence the origin of the term "pecking order." As with all groups of animals, there is a clear hierarchy, one that is part of the daily ritual. At nighttime, when the chickens go back into the henhouse, they scramble to see who will get the top roost. It is always the birds at the top of the pecking order, the "kings of the roost," who prevail.

Over time, chickens and humans can develop quite a close relationship. My mother talks to them, calling them "girls," and if she sneezes in their presence, they take this as a sign of communication, immediately responding with a cacophony of clucking. But they also need a good deal of protection, since they are easy prey for hawks, red fox, coyotes, and raccoons. She once put a plastic owl on top of the henhouse in an effort to frighten off hawks, and the next day she came out to find a hawk perched right next to it, unfazed by the store-bought threat. But she does lose birds occasionally and takes it personally, as if a member of her extended family had been taken away. After all, as she says, "I give them garbage and they give me eggs. Even humans can't do that."

Today, however, most folks' only experience with a chicken takes place in a supermarket, where one chooses among plastic-wrapped parts from birds that were raised under less than ideal conditions. When married to imperfect cooking methods, the results are less than satisfactory. In *The Cook's Illustrated Complete Book of Poultry*, we bring you the results of thousands of hours of tests performed in our test kitchen so that you do not have to spend countless hours finding the best method for preparing game hens or the ideal method for grilling chicken parts so that both the dark and white meat end up properly cooked. Along with these master techniques and recipes, we provide a host of variations so that you can serve poultry four nights a week for a whole year and never tire.

Over the years at *Cook's Illustrated* we have found that process matters, that, when compared side by side, one method *is* actually better than another. Of course, many aspects of cooking are subjective, but there are rules. Some methods of roasting a chicken are better than others. There are techniques that effectively reduce the thick layer of fat on goose and duck, making the skin edible and the meat itself juicier. The editors of *Cook's Illustrated* have found that this process of comparing one method with another is not only enlightening but curiously entertaining as well. If you have ever wondered whether high or low heat is best for roasting turkey or whether oil or butter works best for basting, we hope that you will find your curiosity satisfied in these pages.

Of course, no cookbook is ever the last word on any topic, and as the years go by, we will discover additional methods and recipes for preparing poultry. But the editors of *Cook's Illustrated* feel confident that this book is based on a sturdy foundation of serious kitchen testing, one that we hope will both inform you and provide hundreds of recipes that are both reliable and delicious.

All the best from all of us at *Cook's Illustrated*.

CHRISTOPHER KIMBALL
Editor and Publisher

INTRODUCTION

/|\

IN LARGE PART, OWING TO THE RELATIVELY LOW COST AND FAT CONTENT OF MOST BIRDS, POULTRY HAS BECOME AMERICA'S FAVORITE "MEAT." HOWEVER, BIRDS ARE NOT NECESSARILY THE EASIEST FOODS TO COOK. UNLIKE A ROAST OR STEAK, CHICKEN AND OTHER FOWL HAVE A COMPLEX

structure that consists of a hollow cavity, bones, and meat of varying thickness. In addition, many birds have more than one kind of meat: chicken and turkey have tender white meat on the breast that is prone to overcooking, while the legs and thighs are covered with sinewy dark meat that requires longer cooking to soften properly. Finally, there is the skin, which must be crisp and brown if it is to be eaten.

Duck and goose contain an additional challenge—the fatty layer just beneath the skin that must be removed or dissolved if the birds are to be properly enjoyed. Farm-raised game birds—especially quail, squab, and pheasant—are moving into the mainstream but are so different from their wild cousins that they require a whole new set of cooking guidelines.

The thirty-eight chapters in this book take into account all these realities in order to produce foolproof recipes. Take roasting, for example. Because roasting a chicken is so different from roasting a Cornish game hen or pheasant, separate chapters deal with these issues. The book is divided into individual chapters that focus on a specific cooking

method for a specific bird or cut (such as roasted chicken, roasted duck, or broiled chicken parts), a specific dish (such as chicken soup or chicken pot pie), or an overview of an unusual cut or bird (such as duck breast, squab, or quail).

Within each chapter we have conducted dozens of tests to determine which preparations, cooking methods, serving suggestions, and flavorings work and which ones don't. Each chapter begins with an essay that explains our tests and our findings. Recipes follow, usually beginning with a master recipe that demonstrates the basic procedure, followed by variations. In effect, each chapter functions as a separate cooking lesson.

Taken as a whole, the book addresses all the important issues the modern cook is likely to encounter as he or she prepares poultry at home. As readers of our magazine know, we try to be as practical as possible when developing recipes and techniques in our test kitchen. This down-to-earth culinary philosophy translates into simple, well-conceived recipes that are easy to execute. We think you will be pleased with the results.

A GUIDE TO BUYING AND HANDLING POULTRY

GOOD POULTRY DISHES START WITH HIGH-

QUALITY, FRESH BIRDS. HOW DO YOU RECOGNIZE

A SUPERIOR BIRD AT THE SUPERMARKET AND

HOW SHOULD IT BE HANDLED AT HOME? READ ON.

THERE ARE SEVERAL TYPES of chicken in most supermarkets, each reflecting a different style of production. Mass-market chickens, such as Tyson and Perdue, aim to produce a good product at a low cost.

Kosher chickens were always popular in urban areas with large Jewish populations. In accordance with religious law, these chickens are bathed in a saltwater bath to remove blood and impurities. In effect, the chickens are brined, albeit briefly, before packaging. All kosher chickens must be grown and processed to a standardized protocol and are clearly labeled.

Many small chicken farms have returned to the animal-raising practices of the past and are now producing "free-range" chickens. Although there is no clear definition of this term, most chicken operations that allow their birds access to the outdoors use this term.

Many free-range chickens are also labeled "organic" or "natural." Again, definitions can be hazy, but most farmers that rely on organic feed and reject the use of antibiotics to treat disease in their flock are using one or both of these terms.

To make some sense of the vast array of choices, we pitted four of the leading supermarket chickens (all mass-market brands) against five specialty or premium chickens. This last group included kosher, free-range, and organic chickens, which have one thing in common—they cost more than mass-market brands.

We purchased one bird from each company and then roasted it plain, without seasonings, until the internal temperature was 160 degrees. Half of each bird was carved, and the rest was left on the carcass so panelists could judge the bird's overall appearance.

The results of our blind tasting were quite clear. The mass-market brands received uniformly negative marks. Several panelists said they would rather swear off chicken than eat these tasteless, mushy birds.

In comparison, most of the premium chickens were thoroughly enjoyed. The flavor of these birds was stronger and sometimes even a bit gamy. The texture was also firmer, but not tough. When we talked to industry experts, they offered several explanations as to why premium chickens taste so much better.

First, many small companies have invested heavily in livestock gene pool development. Some specialty companies are using French birds; others, old-fashioned American varieties known for their superior flavor. (Larger companies may be more concerned with the size of the breast or other breeding characteristics that involve keeping costs down or appealing to perceived consumer interests such as skin color.)

Second, some of the premium chickens have access to the outdoors, or at least the freedom to wander in a fairly large indoor area. Exercise is directly linked to flavor development and any hint of gaminess. The more a bird exercises, the leaner it becomes and the more flavorful (and darker) the muscles become.

Third, many small outfits take extra steps in processing (another reason for their higher cost). Bell & Evans, an East Coast brand that came out tops in our ratings, ships chickens loose on ice so that they can weep fluids and blood as they make their way from processing plant to supermarket. The net weight of each bird is reduced, so the company actually earns less for every chicken. In contrast, mass-market brands are usually shrink-wrapped at the plant and then frozen to keep moisture from accumulating in the packages. But many experts believe that a chicken must lose these fluids for stronger, meatier flavor.

Fourth, many smaller companies "grow out" their birds for eight or nine weeks, instead of slaughtering them at six or seven weeks as the industry giants do. Again, the older the bird, the more flavorful.

In sum, we think it's worth spending a little extra money to get a chicken that tastes great. In addition to Bell & Evans chickens, our panel gave high ratings to kosher chickens from Empire (which are sold nationwide); free-range, natural chickens from D'Artagnan (available in some markets mostly in the East and by mail); and free-range chickens from La Belle Rouge, which are raised without growth stimulants or antibiotics and are available in select locations around the country.

Make sure the chicken you buy is fresh. If you detect off odors—strong enough to permeate plastic wrap—or see excess liquid in the package, walk away. Since poultry is shrink-wrapped, you must rely mostly on sell dates rather than your senses. Many supermarkets put a sell-by date that is a week or more away on birds when they come into the store. Try to get a chicken that still has plenty of shelf-life left.

The size of the standard supermarket chicken (often called a broiler/fryer) varies from just under 3 pounds to 4 pounds or more. In general, we like chickens that weigh 3 to 3½ pounds, especially if we are cutting up the bird into parts for braising or frying. (Larger chickens may not fit in one pan.) While there is no reason to quibble over a few ounces when roasting a bird, we do think it's better to buy two small chickens than one large oven-roaster that weighs 6 or 7 pounds. The disparity in cooking rates for the outer layers of meat (especially on the breast) and meat near the bone is exaggerated in these oversized birds. By the time the meat near the bone is no longer bloody, the outer layers of meat are dry and unpalatable.

CORNISH GAME HENS

THIS SMALL HYBRID was developed from a small breed of Cornish chickens. Usually these birds are slaughtered at four or five weeks and weigh between 1

A NOTE ABOUT SAFETY

/\

GIVEN THE PREVALENCE OF BACTERIA IN THE POULTRY SUPPLY IN THIS COUNTRY, IT'S PROBABLY BEST TO ASSUME THAT THE BIRD YOU BUY IS CONTAMINATED. THAT MEANS YOU NEED TO FOLLOW SOME SIMPLE RULES TO MINIMIZE THE DANGER TO YOU AND YOUR FAMILY.

Keep poultry refrigerated until just before cooking. Bacteria thrive at temperatures between 40 and 140 degrees. This means leftovers should also be promptly refrigerated.

When handling poultry, make sure to wash hands, knives, cutting boards, and counters (or anything else that has come into contact with the raw bird, its juices, or your hands) with hot, soapy water. Be especially careful not to let the chicken, its juices, or your hands touch foods (like salad ingredients) that will be eaten raw.

Finally, cook poultry to an internal temperature of 160 degrees or higher to ensure that any bacteria have been killed. Note that duck breasts and game birds, especially quail and squab, taste best when cooked to medium-rare or medium—no higher than 140 or 145 degrees. There is some risk inherent in eating these birds at this temperature, although it seems that they are not plagued by safety issues as is the chicken industry. Also, note that most bacteria are killed at around 140 degrees. The recommended 160 degree cooking temperature includes a margin of error. (It also happens that chicken and turkey are not very palatable at lower temperatures.)

In the end, the decision is yours. For the greatest protection, cook all poultry to an internal temperature of 160 degrees or higher. But if you enjoy rare burgers and raw oysters, you already exchange some measure of safety for flavor. You may want to do the same thing when cooking duck breasts, squab, and quail.

and 2 pounds. Smaller birds are ideal for single servings and are preferred. Unfortunately, most game hens sold in supermarkets weigh at least 1½ pounds and are mass-market brands. These large game hens are fine split between two people. When serving many guests at a dinner party, you may want to consider poussin if small game hens are not available. Not only is the size more convenient, but the birds are likely to taste better.

POUSSIN

THESE BABY CHICKENS are slaughtered at three or four weeks, when they weigh about 1 pound, and are preferred by restaurant chefs because of their small size, which is ideal for one person. We like them because many small chicken farms raise poussin and they usually taste better than game hens, which are strictly the province of mass-market operations. Poussin are hard to find, but the trip to a specialty market or butcher is worth the effort.

TURKEY

WHEN BUYING A TURKEY, brands are rarely an option. Many markets have one kind of fresh turkey and another frozen. The fresh turkeys are better, but the real issue is size. Many cooks love the idea of roasting a 22-pound bird for the holidays. But we find that the larger the bird, the higher the likelihood that it will be overcooked. With its delicate breast meat and tougher legs, a turkey is already hard to cook. But if the bird weighs 22 pounds, it's very difficult to get the meat close to the bone cooked through without causing the outer layers to dry out.

We recommend a bird that weighs 12 to 15 pounds, gross weight. (By the time you remove the giblets and trim the neck and tail, the weight on the package label will be reduced by a pound or more.) If you are feeding a large crowd and your oven permits, think about roasting two small birds. While it is possible to roast an 18- or 20-pound bird (see page 331), never buy 20-plus-pound birds.

DUCK

THE WHOLE DUCKS SOLD in supermarkets are Pekin or Long Island ducks. Once raised on Long Island, these birds are now grown on farms around the country and the largest producer is located in Indiana, not New York. The birds weigh about 4½ pounds, perhaps 5 pounds at the most. Don't be fooled into thinking that these birds can serve five or six people. A smaller chicken serves more people. Ducks have a larger, heavier bone structure and they contain a lot more fat, much of which melts away during the roasting process. A 4½-pound duck feeds three, maybe four people. Ducks are almost always sold frozen. If you can find a fresh duck, buy it.

Other duck species are available whole if you are willing to order by mail. The Muscovy is a South American bird that is less fatty than the Pekin and has a stronger game flavor. The Moulard is the sterile offspring of a Muscovy and Pekin duck and is popular in France. These birds are often bred for the production of foie gras. Both the Muscovy and Moulard duck weigh more than Pekins, often as much as 8 pounds. Because these birds are so much leaner, they require a somewhat different cooking method. Since the Long Island duck is the breed found in supermarkets, recipes in this book have been tailored to this fattier duck.

Although whole Muscovy or Moulard duck can be hard to find, their plump breasts are often sold separately at better supermarkets and butchers. The breast meat from a Moulard is sometimes called by its French name, *magret*. This meat is usually quite plump and lean. Most duck breasts are sold whole with the skin on and can be split nicely into two halves, each weighing about 6 ounces, which is ideal for a single portion.

GOOSE

IN MANY PARTS OF EUROPE, the goose (not the turkey) is the festive bird served at holiday meals. Although goose has never caught on in this country, it is available (usually frozen) in most supermarkets, especially around the holidays. Butcher shops often sell fresh goose. A goose can range in size from 8 to 14 pounds, although 10 to 12 pounds is most common. Goose is extremely fatty, even more so than a duck. The meat itself is dark and rich, more like roast beef than chicken.

THE SCIENCE OF BRINING

/I\

IN ADDITION TO BUYING RIGHT, WE FIND THAT BRINING (SOAKING IN A SALT-AND-WATER SOLUTION) IMPROVES THE FLAVOR AND TEXTURE OF CHICKEN AND TURKEY. BRINING TRANSFORMS SO-SO CHICKEN AND TURKEY INTO SOMETHING WORTH EATING; GOOD CHICKEN AND TURKEY ONLY GETS BETTER. (OTHER BIRDS HAVE MUCH

more inherent flavor than relatively bland chicken and turkey, and we find that they don't really benefit from brining.)

We first discovered brining when researching an article on roasted turkey. Our tasters found that brining gave the roasted bird a firm, meaty texture and well-seasoned flavor. They also reported that brined turkeys are moister and juicier. We later found that brining usually improves the flavor of delicately flavored chicken as well. We use this technique throughout the book to boost flavor and improve texture when grilling chicken parts, when roasting a turkey breast, and when roasting a turkey.

The science of brining is fairly straightforward. When we started applying this technique to turkeys, we gathered some empirical data to see how brining affects pre- and postcooking weight. We started by weighing several 11-pound birds after they had been brined and found an average weight gain of almost ¾ pound. Even more impressive, we found that brined birds weighed 6 to 8 ounces more after roasting than a same-sized bird that had not been brined. Our taste buds were right: brined birds are juicier.

When we started talking to food scientists and

manufacturers, it was clear we were on to something. Salt is used in meat processing to extract proteins from muscle cells and make these proteins more viscous. They become sticky, which allows them to hold more water and make the texture of meat firmer. For example, salt gives hot dogs their plumpness. In much the same fashion, brining turkey causes a change in the structure of the proteins in the muscle and allows the meat to cook up firmer and plumper.

Salt causes protein strands to become denatured, or unwound. This is the same process that occurs when proteins are exposed to heat, acid, or alcohol. When protein strands unwind, they get tangled in one another and trap water in the matrix that forms. When these unraveled proteins are exposed to heat they gel—much like a fried egg white—and form a barrier that prevents water from leaking out of the bird as it cooks. The capillary action that draws blood out of the meat and gives it a milky-white color also helps the brining solution penetrate deep into the meat. This accounts for the pleasant salty flavor even of the inner breast meat.

It is possible to vary the strength of the brine and therefore the length of time necessary to achieve the desired effect. However, we suggest that you follow the recommendations in individual recipes. There is a fairly complex relationship among the strength of the brine, the thickness of the item being brined, and total brining time. For each recipe, we have made numerous experiments to find the optimum formula.

For instance, a super-strength brine cuts soaking time for relatively thin chicken parts, but if used with a whole turkey it would cause the exterior layers of meat to become too salty. That's why a 12-pound turkey requires a brine consisting of 2 cups of kosher salt and 2 gallons of cold water and a brining time of twelve hours. Eight chicken thighs destined for the grill need a solution made from ¾ cup kosher salt and 1 quart of water. Because the pieces are so small (at least in comparison to a whole turkey) and the brine is so concentrated, the chicken will be seasoned in just one and one-half hours.

In some cases, we have added sugar to the brine. We find that the sugar improves the flavor of chicken pieces that will be grilled. It also promotes nice caramelization of the skin. However, the sweetness is not always appropriate, especially in a roast turkey.

Finally, you may use either kosher or regular table salt in a brining solution. However, recipes were developed with coarse kosher salt so you must cut the salt in half to account for the added strength of finely ground table salt.

QUAIL

TINY QUAIL HAVE a rich flavor that is surprisingly meaty but not overly strong or gamy. Although bobwhite quail are native to this country, most commercial operations raise an Asian variety called Corturnix. They range in size from 4 to 6 ounces each. Larger quail, weighing at least 5 ounces, are easier to eat. Don't think about boning quail. It's too hard (the birds will be mangled in the process) and the meat tastes better when cooked on the bone. Plan on serving two quail per person. Quail can be ordered from most butcher shops or by mail.

SQUAB

SQUAB IS YOUNG PIGEON that cannot fly because its feathers have not developed fully. It has a dark, rich, mildly gamy flavor. Most squab weigh about 1 pound and each bird feeds one person. Domesticated squab is fairly fatty, much more so than pheasant or quail. The largest squab producer in this country is located in California's Central Valley. At the retail level, squab are sold whole or partially boned. "Boneless" squab (the leg and wing bones remain intact) weigh about 10 ounces and are ideal for sautéing or grilling. Unlike other poultry, squab is usually cooked like beef, until medium-rare.

PHEASANT

OF ALL THE GAME BIRDS, pheasant bears the greatest resemblance to chicken. While wild pheasant can be dark and overpowering, the domesticated pheasant sold by butchers is light colored and mild. Many older cooks say it reminds them of the way chicken tasted during the first half of the century, when it was mostly a local, free-range product. A whole pheasant weighs about 2½ pounds and can be cooked much like a chicken. A pheasant is ideal for two people.

A NOTE ABOUT WILD GAME: True game that is hunted bears little resemblance to the domesticated "game" available to consumers. While supermarket duck, goose, and squab are quite fatty, wild versions are so lean that the breast may need to be barded with pork fat to prevent it from drying out. The recipes in this book were tested with domesticated birds sold at supermarkets and butcher shops.

BASIC
BUTCHERING AND
CARVING

/|\

THESE GENERAL TECHNIQUES FOR BUTCHERING AND

CARVING WHOLE BIRDS ARE USED THROUGHOUT THIS

BOOK AND YOU WILL FIND THAT THEY ARE USED

REPEATEDLY IN YOUR KITCHEN IF YOU COOK A LOT OF

POULTRY. TECHNIQUES RELATED TO SPECIFIC RECIPES

ARE ILLUSTRATED IN THE APPROPRIATE CHAPTERS.

BONE STRUCTURE OF A CHICKEN

THIS ILLUSTRATION shows the bone structure of a chicken. Other birds (everything from a turkey to a quail) have a similar structure, although the exact position of some joints shifts a bit, depending on the bird.

Cutting Up a Whole Chicken

THERE ARE SEVERAL GOOD reasons to cut up chickens at home rather than buying precut parts. Butchering a whole bird yourself is cheaper than buying parts. Learning how to do it will allow you to make use of kosher and free-range chickens, which are often sold whole.

Throughout this book, there are recipes that require you to cut a whole chicken into parts. For instance, you need the back to make stock for chicken and dumplings. Other recipes simply call for a whole

chicken cut into eight parts (two breast pieces, two legs, two thighs, and two wings). You may buy these parts precut or follow our advice and cut them yourself from a whole chicken. Of course, when recipes call for a single part (such as six boneless thighs for curry), buy them precut.

Day in, day out, this is how we cut up a whole chicken for braising, grilling, broiling, and more. There are other methods, but the technique outlined here is the most useful because it follows the natural lines of the bird and is therefore easy to accomplish. When done, you will have eight pieces for cooking—two wings, two legs, two thighs, and two breasts—plus the back and wing tips, which can be used to make stock. It's a good idea to place the unused parts in a sealable plastic bag in the freezer. When you have accumulated enough, you can prepare stock without making a special trip to the market. (You may also freeze the giblets in a separate bag to make gravy.)

For butchering, we recommend using a boning knife with a 5- to 6-inch-long blade to remove the wings and leg/thigh pieces. The narrower blade is better able to follow the contours of the bird. A chef's knife can be used, but don't expect the same precision or control. However, for cutting through bone, you must use an 8- or 10-inch chef's knife. Use this heavier knife to split the breast and to sever the leg from the thigh.

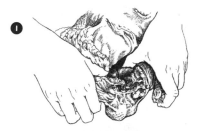

1. Most poultry companies package the giblets (the liver, heart, gizzard, and kidneys) in a paper or plastic bag. Remove this bag and look into the end of the cavity near the tail to make sure the kidneys are not still in the bird. If you see small dark red objects the size of marbles, remove them with your thumbs. Wash the bird, inside and out, under cold running water and pat it dry with paper towels.

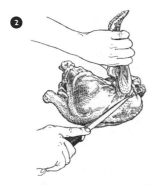

2. Turn the chicken on its side and pull the wing away from the body. Use the tip of a boning knife to cut around the joint that attaches the wing to the breast. Repeat with the second wing.

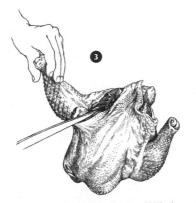

3. Turn the chicken breast side up. While pulling the leg away from the bird with one hand, use the tip of a boning knife to slice the skin between the drumstick and breast.

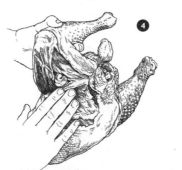

4. With one hand holding the chicken, use other hand to bend back the leg and pop out the joint that attaches the leg to the body.

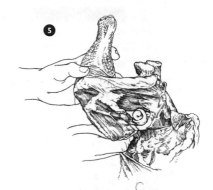

5. There is a very tender, meaty piece called the oyster, which is attached to the thigh and to the curved indentations on either side of the back. Slide your thumb into the bird at the top of the thigh. Feel for the curved indentation that is about the size of a nickel. Scrape with thumb along the bone to release this round piece of meat so that it comes away from the bird along with leg/thigh piece.

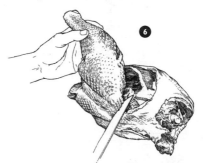

6. Holding the leg away from the body, cut around the joint to release the leg/thigh piece. Repeat to detach the other leg/thigh piece.

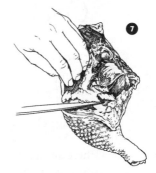

7. Place the leg/thigh piece skin side down on a cutting board. The joint that separates the leg and thigh is underneath a line of fat that divides the thigh and leg. Use a chef's knife to slice through the fat line and locate the joint. Once the joint is located, cut through to separate the leg and thigh pieces.

8. Use a chef's knife to cut between the bottom of the rib cage and the back of the bird. When you are done, the breast and back will be completely separated. Reserve the back for the making stock.

9. Starting at the tail end, use a chef's knife to cut down along one side of the breastbone (also called the keel bone because of its shape).

10. When you hit the wishbone, cut down along the side of the wishbone and use your fingers or the tip of the knife to pop it out. Repeat on the other side of the breastbone.

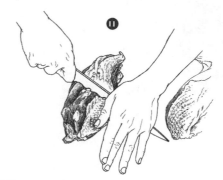

11. When you have completed steps 9 and 10, both halves of the breast will be cut from the breastbone. If you like, you can cut the breast pieces in half crosswise to make them easier to maneuver in the pan when frying or braising.

Removing Boneless Breast Meat

TO SAVE MONEY, you can create your own chicken cutlets by removing boneless meat from the breast of a whole chicken. This technique differs only slightly from that used to remove the breast with the bone in. Removing the wings, legs, and back first (see figures 1 through 8 on pages 10–12) makes this process somewhat easier.

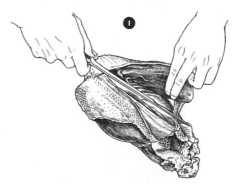

1. Using a thin-bladed boning knife, cut along either side of the breastbone, starting at the tail end and following the rib cage down and separating the meat from the bone structure.

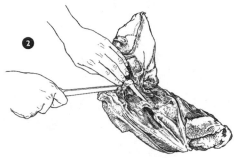

2. Expose the wing joint and cut along underneath the joint to free the breast half from the rib cage.

Boning a Chicken Thigh

USE A BONING KNIFE to create boneless thighs for stir-fries or sautés. If your market sells boneless thighs, you can use them.

1. Place the thigh skin side down and cut along one side of the thighbone, angling the knife so that it cuts slightly under the bone. Make the same cut along the other side of the bone.

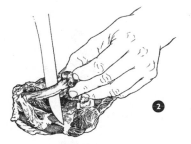

2. Slide the knife under the bone, lifting it away from the meat.

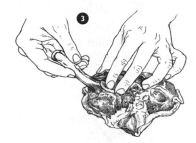

3. When the bone is completely exposed, use both hands to pull it free of the meat.

Carving a Whole Chicken

ALL BIRDS ARE EASIER to carve and will hold their juices better if they rest after being removed from the oven. We find that a chicken should rest about ten minutes before carving. Use a chef's knife to carve a chicken.

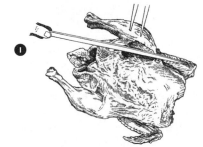

1. Start by slicing the skin between the leg and carcass.

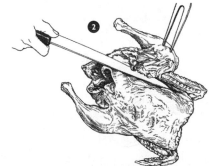

2. Pull the leg away from the carcass with a carving fork until you can see the thigh joint. Cut through the thigh joint to detach the leg. Repeat on the other side.

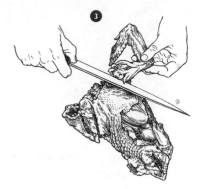

3. To remove the wing, cut into the breast next to the wing to expose the wing joint. Cut through the joint to detach the wing. Repeat on the other side.

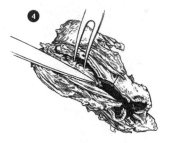

4. To remove the breasts, cut straight down along one side of the breastbone. Run the knife down along the rib cage, turning the knife out a bit when you hit the wishbone if it has not been removed before cooking (see figure 10, page 12). The entire breast should now be loosened from the carcass. Repeat on the other side.

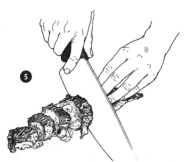

5. Slice the breast crosswise on the bias, making long, thin slices. You should get four or more slices from each breast.

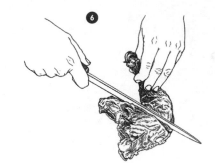

6. To separate the drumstick from the thigh, lay the piece skin side down on a cutting board. The joint is where the drumstick and thigh form the sharpest angle.

7. Leave the thigh and drumstick as they are or use a boning or paring knife to remove thigh meat from the bone. It's difficult to get neat slices, but you can get nice chunks. Cut along either side of the thighbone to remove meat. The thighbone remains in the middle piece (perfect for nibbling) and the two outer pieces are all meat.

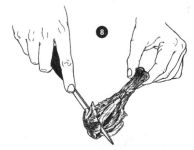

8. To remove meat from the drumstick, hold it vertically and slice off pieces.

Carving a Whole Turkey

WE PREFER TO REMOVE the entire breast half and then to slice it across the grain into relatively small pieces. This method is much easier than slicing the breast when it is still on the bird, especially for smaller turkeys. Use a sharp, 8-inch chef's knife and place the turkey on a large cutting board (slide a damp kitchen towel under the board to keep it from slipping around on the counter). The secret to easy turkey carving is to follow the contours of the bird. If you locate all the joints, you won't have to exert much pressure to separate the sections.

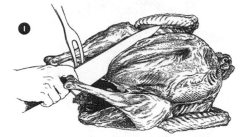

1. Remove any strings used to truss the bird. Start by slicing the skin between the meat of the breast and the leg.

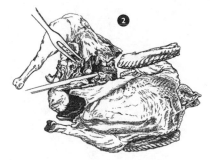

2. Continue to cut down to the joint, using a fork to pull the leg away from the bird while the tip of the knife severs the joint between the leg and breast.

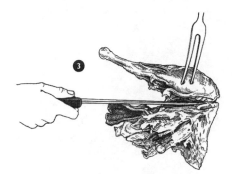

3. Place the leg/thigh piece skin side down on a cutting board. Use the blade to locate the joint between the thigh and leg. It's right where the thigh and leg form their sharpest angle. Cut through the joint. If you have properly located it, this should be easy since you are not cutting through any bone.

4. Slice medallions from the leg, turning it so you can cut all the meat off.

5. Remove the large pieces of meat from either side of the thighbone.

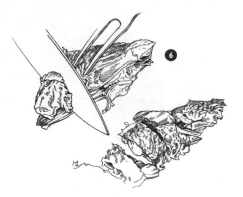

6. Slice these large thigh pieces, leaving a bit of skin attached to each slice.

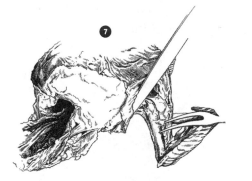

7. Use a fork to pull the wing away from the body. Cut through the joint between the wing and the breast to separate the wing from the bird.

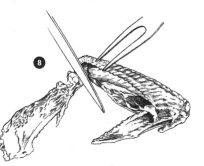

8. Cut the wing in half for easier eating.

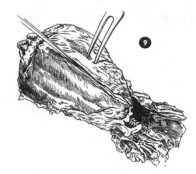

9. With the tip of your knife, cut along the length of the breastbone.

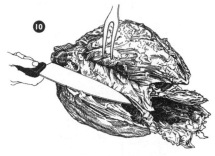

10. Angle the blade of the knife, and slice along the line of the rib cage to remove the entire breast half. Use a fork to pull the breast half away from the rib cage in a single piece.

11. Cut thin slices from the breast, slicing across the grain of the meat.

Carving a Duck

DUCK CAN BE CARVED like chicken into separate parts (wings, legs, thighs, and breasts) and served in parts as is the custom in the West. Or, you can take the meat off the leg and thighbones for an Asian-style presentation, which is easier to eat and helps to stretch one bird to feed more people. Asian cooks often cut up the back for nibbling as well. The traditional Western method is outlined below, with notes on the boneless presentation for those cooks who want to try something a bit more elaborate. Use an 8-inch chef's knife for carving a duck.

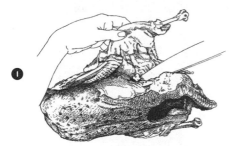

1. Cut around the leg, probing into the thigh joint with a knife to pop out the leg. The joint is much closer to the back than on a chicken. Cut down through the thigh joint to remove the leg and thigh in one piece. Repeat with the other leg.

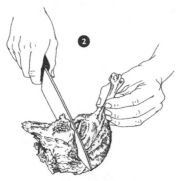

2. Hold the leg/thigh piece by the drumstick and cut through the joint between them. Serve the leg and thigh as is or split the thigh into two pieces by cutting along either side of the thighbone. Also, slice the meat off the drumstick if desired.

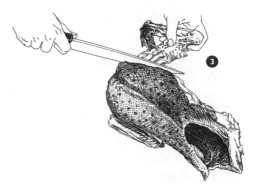

3. Pull the wing away from the body and cut around the joint to separate it from the breast. As with the leg, the joint is closer to the back than the similar joint on a chicken. Repeat with the other wing. Split the wings at the joint between the "drumstick" and doubled-boned section if desired.

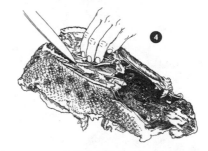

4. Starting at the tail end, slice along the side of the breastbone to remove the breast half in a single piece. When you hit the wishbone, change the angle of the knife to cut around the bone. Repeat on the other side of the bone to remove the other breast half.

5. Cut each breast half crosswise into thin slices.

Carving a Goose

CARVING A GOOSE IS similar to carving a turkey. The main difference is that the thigh on the goose is closer to the carcass and therefore a bit trickier to remove. The joint that attaches the leg/thigh to the bird is farther back than on a turkey, almost under the end of the wing. Place the bird on a large cutting board (secured with a damp towel underneath) and use an 8-inch chef's knife.

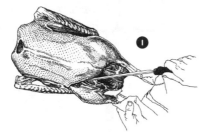

1. Start by cutting around the area where the breast and leg meet. Pull the leg away from the body (hold it with a towel rather than a fork), so that you can clearly see where the muscles meet.

2. Remove the whole leg and thigh piece, making sure you get the small, delicious, boneless piece (called the oyster) on the bird's back, next to the base of the thigh.

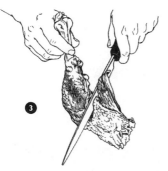

3. Hold the leg/thigh upright. Use the blade to locate the joint between the thigh and leg (it's where the leg and thigh form their sharpest angle) and cut through the joint. Slice the meat off the bones of each piece.

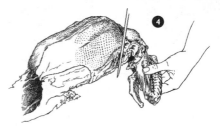

4. To remove the wing, twist it outwards to find the joint. It's tucked farther under the breast than it would be on a turkey. Slice through the joint and then cut the wing in half.

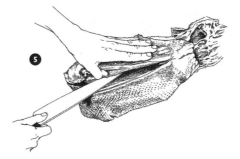

5. With the tip of your knife, cut along the entire length of the breastbone. Angle the blade of the knife and slice along the line of the rib cage to remove the entire breast half.

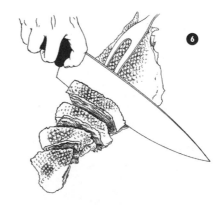

6. Cut the breast into thin pieces, slicing on the bias across the grain of the meat.

ROASTED

WHOLE

CHICKEN

/|\

A PERFECTLY ROASTED CHICKEN IS EXTRAORDINARY.

THE SKIN IS PERFECTLY CRISP AND WELL SEASONED;

THE WHITE MEAT JUICY AND TENDER, BUT WITH A

HINT OF CHEW; THE DARK MEAT FULLY COOKED ALL

THE WAY TO THE BONE. AT FIRST, ROASTING A WHOLE

CHICKEN APPEARS TO BE A SIMPLE TASK. THE MEAT IS

not tough by nature. The dark meat is relatively forgiving in terms of cooking time. The breast meat is not particularly thick, which means that the outer layers are less likely to dry out while you are attempting to cook the center of the cut properly. Yet many chickens are either grossly overcooked (the breast is dry and stringy) or so underdone that they resemble an avian version of steak tartare.

There are several challenges peculiar to chicken that must be confronted before devising the perfect roasting technique. A chicken is made up of two totally different types of meat: white and dark. The white meat is inevitably overcooked and dry even as the dark meat is still little more than raw next to the bone. The second challenge is that chicken, unlike beef, has skin, which should be nicely browned and crisp. As we found during the testing process, crisp skin is not always consistent with perfectly cooked meat. Finally, chicken is an odd amalgam of meat and bones. The drumsticks and wings stick out, the thigh meat is on the side of the bird, and the breast meat is on the top (at least when the chicken is roasted conventionally). The home cook is dealing with a complex three-dimensional structure, quite different from a brisket or a pot roast. These anatomical realities may require a more complex set of cooking instructions.

We started our tests with the most pertinent (and controversial) question: What is the best oven temperature for roasting a chicken? We find that high heat (450 degrees or more) is quick (a 3-pound bird is done in forty-five minutes) but problematic. Skin is dark and crispy, but we encounter the classic problem with high-heat meat cookery: while the dark meat is fine, the outer portion of the white meat is overcooked and on the tough side even as the internal thigh temperature registers 160 degrees. In addition, this temperature is likely to set off smoke alarms in most homes.

At the other extreme—slow and low—we tested roasting a bird in a 275-degree oven for one hour and thirty-five minutes and then raised the heat to 425 degrees for the last ten minutes to crisp up the skin— we found that the white meat was still too dry and that the skin was not nearly browned enough.

Roasting a small chicken (around 3½ pounds) at 375 degrees turns out to be the best approach. The skin becomes golden and slightly crispy. Even more important, the breast meat does not dry out as much as with the heat-high method. This is an interesting discovery. While the breast meat of chicken roasted at 450 degrees was a bit dry when the thigh registered 160 degrees, the bird roasted at 375 degrees still had juicy breast meat when the thigh registered close to 170 degrees. This extra 10 degrees in the thigh is the difference between a bloody B movie and properly cooked dark meat.

At this point in our testing we felt that a moderate heat was best, but the technique needed some refinements. The skin was not as brown or crisp as one might like. Our first thought was basting. We started with butter and basted every fifteen minutes. The results were appalling. Despite a nice brown color, the skin was chewy and greasy. The next bird was basted with oil, which turned out a crispier skin, but the color was off—a pale gold.

Basting may make sense when cooking a large piece of meat on a spit over an open fire. The outer layers would get easily overcooked, and the basting may have prevented burning or scorching. However, a small chicken in a 375-degree oven is a different matter entirely. The skin will not scorch or burn (in fact, if you leave it alone, it will cook rather nicely on its own), and the basting liquid is not going to penetrate the meat to make it more tender—juiciness has nothing to do with the external application of liquid. We brushed another bird with butter before roasting and shoved it in the oven without any further basting. This was the best method. Great color and nice crisp texture. The oven heat turned the milk solids brown and, in the process, provided added flavor. (We know that some cooks suggest placing a piece of cheesecloth soaked in melted butter over the bird during roasting. Just like frequent basting, this will produce skin that is not at all crisp. Save your cheesecloth for straining stock.)

Finally, we tested placing softened butter under the breast skin. We found that this technique delivers two benefits. First, in order to get the butter under the skin, it is necessary to carefully lift the skin off the meat. Separating the skin from the meat permits heat to get under the skin and cause it to puff and crisp better in the oven. The second benefit is to the breast meat. The butter, which can be flavored with herbs or spices, helps keep the delicate breast meat juicy, and, of course, adds flavor. We found that 2 tablespoons of softened butter under the breast skin (more if pureeing the butter with herbs or other solids) was a significant improvement. We like to melt ⅓ tablespoon of butter and brush it over the skin, especially on the legs and thighs, to help promote browning there.

We tested a few other ideas at this point. We found that trussing makes it more difficult to properly cook the inner part of the thigh—it is less exposed to heat and therefore the oven time needs to be longer. A roasting rack (see pages 32–33 for information on different types of racks) is essential for lifting the chicken off the pan surface and getting the skin crisp.

Having figured out that continuous basting and trussing are both unnecessary, we were hoping to find that the bird need not be turned, either. After all, it has always seemed to us that turning a roast in the oven was overdoing it a bit—just leave the bird alone and enjoy the cocktail hour. A couple of tests were in order.

First, we roasted a bird for twenty minutes on each side and then put it on its back. The skin was golden and crunchy, the white and dark meat perfectly cooked, and the overall presentation superb. We then tried roasting another bird breast side down for twenty minutes and then turned it breast side up. This chicken was good, but the skin was less crisp and, at the point at which the white meat was perfect, the dark meat was a bit undercooked. Thus, unfortunately, two turns proved crucial.

As this point, we also made an odd discovery. The thigh that was facing up during the second twenty minutes of roasting ended up lower in temperature than the thigh that started off facing up. At first we thought this was just a random measurement, but after four or five birds, it was clear this was a trend. After thinking about it for a few days, we hit on the problem. The thigh that starts off facing the roasting pan was facing a cold pan that reflected little heat. When the other thigh was turned face down, the pan was hot and radiating plenty of heat. So, to even things out, preheat the roasting pan.

In sum, our preferred method for roasting a chicken is quite simple:

◆ Forget trussing.
◆ Preheat the oven to 375 degrees and preheat a shallow roasting pan.
◆ Place butter under the skin and brush the bird with melted butter.
◆ Place the buttered bird on an oiled rack and set the bird and rack in the preheated roasting pan.
◆ Roast the bird on its side for 20 minutes, turn it to the other side for 20 minutes, then turn it breast side up for 20 minutes, or until the internal temperature reaches 165 to 170 degrees.

MASTER RECIPE

Easy Roasted Chicken

SERVES 4

REMOVING THE WISHBONE makes carving the breast meat easier (see figures 1 through 3, page 24). For a 3-pound chicken, shave 5 or 10 minutes off the breast-side-up roasting time. A 4- to 4½-pound bird requires 10 extra minutes with its breast side up (75 to 80 minutes total time in the oven). If using a basket or V-rack, be sure to grease it so the chicken does not stick to it. If you don't have a basket or V-rack, set the bird on an oiled flat rack and use balls of aluminum foil to keep the roasting chicken propped up on its side (see figure 5, page 24).

Oil for rack
3 tablespoons butter, softened
1 whole chicken (about 3½ pounds),
    giblets removed and reserved for
    another use, chicken rinsed and patted
    dry with paper towels
Salt and pepper

1. Place a shallow roasting pan in the oven and heat the oven to 375 degrees. Oil the rack.

2. Melt 1 tablespoon butter. Mash the remaining 2 tablespoons butter with a fork. Gently loosen the skin covering the breast. Work the softened butter under the skin so that it covers the breast meat (see figure 4, page 24). Brush the chicken with the melted butter and sprinkle liberally with salt and pepper.

3. Remove the heated pan from the oven and set the oiled rack in it. Place the chicken on the rack, wing side up (see figure 6, page 24). Pour ½ cup water over the pan bottom to prevent the drippings from burning (see figure 7, page 25). Roast 20 minutes, then rotate the chicken, other wing side up. Roast 20 minutes, then rotate the chicken, breast side up. Roast until an instant-read thermometer inserted in the breast registers 160 degrees and in the thigh registers between 165 and 170 degrees (see figures 9 and 10, page 25), 25 to 30 minutes longer.

4. Transfer the chicken to a cutting board; let rest 10 minutes. Carve (see page 13) and serve.

◆

Roasted Chicken with Garlic Croutons

DAY-OLD BREAD IS ROASTED ALONG WITH THE CHICKEN AND ITS JUICES IN THIS FRENCH RECIPE TO CREATE A CRUNCHY ALTERNATIVE TO BREAD STUFFING. THE BREAD CUBES ARE ADDED PART WAY THROUGH ROASTING AND CONTINUE TO BROWN WHILE THE CHICKEN RESTS. HAVE READY SOME THICK OVEN MITTS TO LIFT THE CHICKEN AND RACK FROM THE ROASTING PAN AND ONTO A CUTTING BOARD. **SERVES 4.**

Oil for rack
½ pound day-old country bread, cut into
    ½-inch-thick slices
3 garlic cloves, peeled and halved
3 tablespoons butter, softened
1 whole chicken (about 3½ pounds),
    giblets removed and reserved for
    another use, chicken rinsed and patted
    dry with paper towels
½ lemon
1 large bunch fresh thyme sprigs or
    ½ teaspoon dried thyme
Salt and pepper

1. Place a shallow roasting pan in the oven and heat the oven to 375 degrees. Oil the rack.

2. Rub the bread slices on both sides with 2 garlic cloves. Cut the bread into 1-inch cubes. (You should have about 5 cups.) Melt 1 tablespoon butter and set it aside. Mince the remaining garlic clove. Combine the minced garlic with the remaining 2 tablespoons butter in a small bowl. Using a fork, mash the butter and garlic until well mixed.

3. Gently loosen the skin covering the breast. Work the garlic butter under the skin so that the mixture covers the breast meat. Squeeze the juice from the lemon half into the cavity. Place the thyme inside the cavity. Brush the chicken with the melted butter and sprinkle liberally with salt and pepper.

4. Remove the heated pan from the oven and set the oiled rack in it. Place the chicken on the rack, wing side up. Roast 20 minutes, then rotate the chicken, other wing side up. Roast 20 minutes, then rotate the chicken, breast side up. Scatter the bread cubes around the rack. Continue roasting until an instant-read thermometer inserted in the breast registers 160 degrees and in the thigh registers between 165 and 170 degrees, 25 to 30 minutes longer. Transfer the chicken to a cutting board; let rest 10 minutes.

5. While chicken is resting, stir the croutons with the cooking juices. Return the pan to the oven and roast until they are golden and crisp, about 10 minutes. Carve the chicken (see page 13), arrange it on a platter with the croutons, and serve immediately.

THE TRUTH ABOUT CLAY ROASTERS

OVER THE YEARS WE HAVE TESTED CLAY ROASTERS SEVERAL TIMES AND HAVE NEVER BEEN TERRIBLY IMPRESSED. ALTHOUGH THEY HAVE THEIR ARDENT FANS, WE ARE NOT AMONG THEM. THERE ARE A NUMBER OF PROBLEMS INHERENT IN ROASTING A WHOLE CHICKEN IN ONE OF THESE DEVICES.

First, because the chicken sits in its own juices as it cooks, the skin, especially on the bottom half of the bird, is flabby and inedible. While the skin on the top half of the bird browns a bit and becomes somewhat crisp, it cannot compare to the skin on a bird that has been roasted on a rack in an open pan, as described in our master recipe.

Second, it is very hard to determine when a chicken in a clay pot is done. Clay roasters should be soaked in cold water for about fifteen minutes before being filled with the chicken, sealed, and put into the oven. The steam from the roaster is supposed to keep the chicken moist and juicy. While we found that clay roasters often do a good job of keeping the meat tender and juicy, they are perfectly capable of turning out an overcooked chicken with tough, stringy breast meat. Lifting the lid off to take the temperature of the bird causes the steam in the clay roaster to escape and defeats the purpose of using a clay roaster. The literature that came with the two clay roasters we tested suggested cooking the chicken by time. This method may or may not work; it's a crapshoot. If your oven is a bit off, the chicken is very cold when it goes in the oven, or you add more or less vegetables than the manufacturer suggests, the cooking-by-time method will not work. Cooking a chicken by temperature is our preferred method and the clay roaster makes this quite difficult.

Lastly, clay pots can crack if you expose them to sudden changes in temperature. For this reason, you must start the chicken in a cold oven. When the chicken is done, lift the chicken out of the pot and let the pot cool to room temperature before washing it.

While we do not recommend buying a clay roaster, we do have some suggestions for getting them to work better, which owners of clay pots will find helpful. First, it's better to undercook the chicken slightly, take its temperature, and then finish cooking the bird with the lid off until it reaches the desired temperature. While the chicken loses some of its juiciness, at least it won't be overcooked. Cooking with the lid off also improves the skin a bit. Second, don't flavor the bird with any butter or oil. The bird will sit in plenty of rendered chicken fat; there's no need to raise the level of fat in the pan any higher. Lastly, fill the pot with vegetables. The pots retain heat better when filled and will cook the chicken more evenly.

ROAST CHICKEN

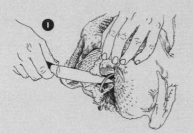

1. Removing the wishbone before roasting will make carving the chicken easier. Start by pulling back the skin at the neck and cutting underneath both sides of the wishbone to free it from the flesh.

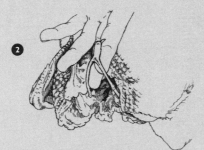

2. Loosen the top of the wishbone with your fingers and pull it away from the bird.

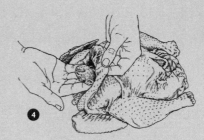

3. Holding the wishbone close to the top, twist and pull until it comes free.

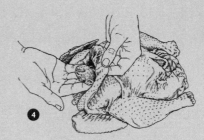

4. Placing softened butter under the skin of the breast keeps the meat juicy and helps make the skin especially crisp. Gently loosen the skin that covers the breast, being careful not to tear the skin. Work the softened butter under the skin so that it covers the breast meat.

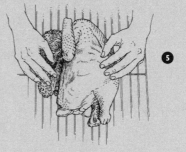

5. We recommend roasting a chicken in a basket or V-rack. If roasting the chicken on a regular flat rack, use balls of aluminum foil to keep the roasting chicken propped up on its side.

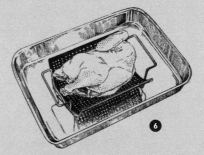

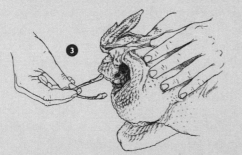

6. Start the roasting process by placing the chicken on a basket or V-rack, wing side up. You will need to turn the chicken twice, once after 20 minutes so that the other wing is facing up and again after another 20 minutes so that the breast is facing up.

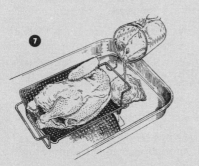

7. If not cooking vegetables along with the chicken, we find it helpful to pour ½ cup water over the pan bottom to prevent the drippings from burning and smoking. If cooking vegetables, they should absorb the pan drippings and help keep smoking to a minimum.

8. Scatter any vegetables around the perimeter of the rack. If the vegetables are placed underneath the chicken, they may not cook completely.

9. While it is possible to judge doneness in a roast chicken without a thermometer (make a cut down between the thigh and breast and make sure that the

juices run clear), an instant-read thermometer is much more precise. To accurately measure the temperature of the thigh, insert the thermometer into the thigh meat across from the breast. Make sure to avoid hitting any bone, which may throw off your reading.

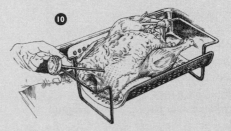

10. To measure the temperature of the breast, insert the thermometer from the neck end back into the breast without touching the rib cage or breastbone.

11. It's a good idea to measure the accuracy of your instant-read thermometer by holding the stem in boiling water. Assuming you are at sea level, the thermometer should register 212 degrees. If not, twist the small nut beneath the thermometer face with pliers until it registers the correct temperature in boiling water.

Herb-Crusted
Roasted Chicken

HERE, EGG YOLK IS USED TO HELP THE HERBS ADHERE TO THE CHICKEN SKIN AND TO FORM A DELICIOUS CRUST. BE SURE TO GREASE THE RACK VERY WELL TO AVOID LOSING THE HERB CRUST DURING TURNING. SERVES 4.

Oil for rack
2 tablespoons butter, softened
1 whole chicken (about 3½ pounds),
   giblets removed and reserved for
   another use, chicken rinsed and patted
   dry with paper towels
2 cups loosely packed fresh tarragon
   leaves
2 cups loosely packed fresh parsley leaves
2 cups loosely packed fresh dill leaves
2 egg yolks, lightly beaten
Salt and pepper

1. Place a shallow roasting pan in the oven and heat the oven to 375 degrees. Oil the rack.

2. Mash the butter with a fork. Gently loosen the skin covering the breast. Work the softened butter under the skin so that it covers the breast meat.

3. Place the herbs in the work bowl of a food processor fitted with a steel blade. Process until finely chopped. Brush the chicken all over with the egg yolks. Sprinkle liberally with salt and pepper. Sprinkle with the herb mixture and lightly pat the herbs so that the chicken is evenly coated.

4. Remove the heated pan from the oven and set the oiled rack in it. Pour ½ cup water over the pan bottom to prevent the drippings from burning. Place the chicken on the rack, wing side up. Roast 20 minutes, then rotate the chicken, other wing side up. Roast 20 minutes, then rotate the chicken, breast side up. Roast until an instant-read thermometer inserted in the breast registers 160 degrees and in the thigh registers between 165 and 170 degrees, 25 to 30 minutes longer.

5. Transfer the chicken to a cutting board; let rest 10 minutes. Carve (see page 13) and serve.

Roasted Chicken
with Fruit Compote

IN THIS VERSION OF THE MASTER RECIPE, THE CHICKEN IS SIMPLY SEASONED WITH BAY LEAVES AND ACCOMPANIED BY EITHER A RAISIN OR A DRIED APRICOT COMPOTE. SERVES 4.

Oil for rack
3 tablespoons butter, softened
1 whole chicken (about 3½ pounds),
   giblets removed and reserved for
   another use, chicken rinsed and patted
   dry with paper towels
2 bay leaves
½ lemon
Salt and pepper

1. Place a shallow roasting pan in the oven and heat the oven to 375 degrees. Oil the rack.

2. Melt 1 tablespoon butter. Mash the remaining 2 tablespoons butter with a fork. Gently loosen the skin covering the breast. Slide a bay leaf under the skin of each breast. Work the softened butter under the skin so that it covers the bay leaves and the breast meat. Squeeze the ½ lemon into the cavity and place the squeezed lemon half in the cavity also. Brush the chicken with the melted butter and sprinkle liberally with salt and pepper.

3. Remove the heated pan from the oven and set the oiled rack in it. Pour ½ cup water over the pan bottom to prevent the drippings from burning. Place the chicken on the rack, wing side up. Roast 20 minutes, then rotate the chicken, other wing side up. Roast 20 minutes, then rotate the chicken, breast side up. Roast until an instant-read thermometer inserted in the breast registers 160 degrees and in the thigh registers between 165 and 170 degrees, 25 to 30 minutes longer.

4. Transfer the chicken to a cutting board; let rest 10 minutes. Carve (see page 13) and serve with either of the following compotes.

Dried Apricot Compote with Balsamic Vinegar and Juniper Berries

JUNIPER BERRIES GIVE THIS COMPOTE A WOODSY, SLIGHTLY RESINOUS FLAVOR. LOOK FOR THEM IN THE SPICE AISLE AT BETTER SUPERMARKETS OR GOURMET STORES. USE A MORTAR AND PESTLE OR THE SIDE OF A CLEAVER OR LARGE CHEF'S KNIFE TO LIGHTLY CRUSH THE JUNIPER BERRIES. MAKES ABOUT 3 CUPS.

2½ cups dried apricots cut into ¼-inch strips
½ cup juniper berries, crushed
⅓ cup firmly packed brown sugar
½ cup balsamic vinegar
Salt and pepper

Bring the apricots, juniper berries, brown sugar, vinegar, and 2¼ cups water to a simmer in a heavy-bottomed medium saucepan. Reduce the heat to low and simmer, stirring frequently, until the apricots plump and the liquid thickens to slightly thinner than applesauce, about 20 minutes. Cool to room temperature and season with salt and pepper. Serve warm, at room temperature, or chilled.

◆

Raisin Compote with Rosemary and Thyme

USE FRESH HERBS IN THIS SWEET-AND-SOUR COMPOTE FOR MAXIMUM FLAVOR. THERE IS A LOT OF CAYENNE PEPPER; IF YOU PREFER A MILDER COMPOTE, REDUCE THE AMOUNT OF CAYENNE ACCORDINGLY. MAKES ABOUT 3 CUPS.

1 cup golden raisins
1 cup dark raisins
1 cup fresh orange juice
¼ cup fresh lemon juice
¼ cup sugar
1 teaspoon cayenne pepper
¼ cup minced fresh parsley leaves

1½ teaspoons minced fresh rosemary leaves
1½ teaspoons minced fresh thyme leaves
1 teaspoon minced fresh sage leaves
Salt and pepper

Bring the raisins, juices, sugar, cayenne pepper, and 1½ cups water to a simmer in a heavy-bottomed medium saucepan. Reduce the heat to low and simmer, stirring frequently, until raisins plump, about 15 minutes. Add the herbs; simmer about 5 minutes to blend flavors. Cool to room temperature, season with salt and pepper, then refrigerate. Serve chilled.

◆

Roasted Chicken with Rosemary and Lemon

ROSEMARY, LEMON, AND GARLIC ARE THE CLASSIC ITALIAN SEASONINGS FOR POULTRY. PLACING THE ROSEMARY AND GARLIC UNDERNEATH THE SKIN ALLOWS THE FLAVORS TO PERMEATE THE MEAT OF THE CHICKEN. LIKEWISE, PLACING A LEMON HALF IN THE CAVITY GIVES THE MEAT A LIGHT HINT OF LEMON. SERVES 4.

Oil for rack
5 tablespoons butter, softened
2 garlic cloves, coarsely chopped
2 teaspoons chopped fresh rosemary leaves
1 whole chicken (about 3½ pounds), giblets removed and reserved for another use, chicken rinsed and patted dry with paper towels
1 lemon, halved
Salt and pepper
Fresh rosemary sprigs and lemon wedges, for garnish

1. Place a shallow roasting pan in the oven and heat the oven to 375 degrees. Oil the rack.

2. Melt 1 tablespoon butter and set it aside. Combine the remaining 4 tablespoons butter, the garlic, and rosemary in the work bowl of a food processor fitted

(continued on next page)

with a steel blade. Process until smooth, scraping down the sides of the bowl as necessary.

3. Gently loosen the skin covering the breast. Work the seasoned butter under the skin so that the mixture covers the breast meat. Squeeze half of the lemon over the chicken and squeeze the other half inside the cavity. Discard one half of the lemon and place the other half inside the cavity. Brush the chicken with the melted butter and sprinkle liberally with salt and pepper.

4. Remove the heated pan from the oven and set the oiled rack in it. Pour ½ cup water over the pan bottom to prevent the drippings from burning. Place the chicken on the rack, wing side up. Roast 20 minutes, then rotate the chicken, other wing side up. Roast 20 minutes, then rotate the chicken, breast side up. Roast until an instant-read thermometer inserted in the breast registers 160 degrees and in the thigh registers between 165 and 170 degrees, 25 to 30 minutes longer.

5. Transfer the chicken to a cutting board; let rest 10 minutes. Carve (see page 13), arrange on a platter with the additional sprigs of rosemary and the lemon wedges, and serve.

◆

Cumin and Oregano Roasted Chicken with Sweet Potatoes

SWEET POTATOES CARAMELIZE BEAUTIFULLY WHEN COOKED AROUND THE CHICKEN. CUMIN AND OREGANO GIVE THE CHICKEN AND SWEET POTATOES A CARIBBEAN FLAVOR. SERVES 4.

Oil for rack
5 tablespoons butter, softened
2 tablespoons ground cumin
3 tablespoons chopped fresh oregano
   leaves
1 whole chicken (about 3½ pounds),
   giblets removed and reserved for
   another use, chicken rinsed and patted
   dry with paper towels
Salt and pepper

2 large sweet potatoes (about 1½
   pounds), peeled and cut into ¾-inch
   cubes
2 tablespoons vegetable oil
Additional oregano sprigs for garnish

1. Place a shallow roasting pan in the oven and heat the oven to 375 degrees. Oil the rack.

2. Melt 1 tablespoon butter and set it aside. Combine the remaining 4 tablespoons butter, the cumin, and 2 tablespoons oregano in the work bowl of a food processor fitted with a steel blade. Process until smooth.

3. Gently loosen the skin covering the breast. Work the seasoned butter under the skin so that the mixture covers the breast meat. Brush the chicken with the melted butter and sprinkle liberally with salt and pepper.

4. Toss the sweet potatoes with the vegetable oil, the remaining tablespoon oregano, and salt and pepper to taste in a medium bowl. Remove the heated pan from the oven and set the oiled rack in it. Scatter the seasoned potatoes around the perimeter of the rack. Place the chicken on the rack, wing side up. Roast 20 minutes, then rotate the chicken, other wing side up. Roast 20 minutes, then rotate the chicken, breast side up. Roast until an instant-read thermometer inserted in the breast registers 160 degrees and in the thigh registers between 165 and 170 degrees, 25 to 30 minutes longer.

5. Transfer the chicken to a cutting board; cover the pan with a piece of aluminum foil to keep the potatoes warm. Let the chicken rest 10 minutes. Carve the chicken (see page 13), arrange it on a platter with the potatoes, garnish with oregano sprigs, and serve.

Roasted Chicken with Sage Butter and Roasted Shiitake Mushrooms

IN THIS LUXURIOUS RECIPE, SAGE BUTTER PERFUMES THE CHICKEN MEAT AND PROVIDES A COOKING MEDIUM FOR THE SHIITAKE MUSHROOMS ADDED TOWARD THE END OF ROASTING. SERVES 4.

Oil for rack
6 tablespoons butter
1 1/2 pounds shiitake mushrooms, stems removed
Salt and pepper
20 fresh sage leaves, coarsely chopped
2 garlic cloves, coarsely chopped
1 tablespoon sherry vinegar
1 whole chicken (about 3 1/2 pounds), giblets removed and reserved for another use, chicken rinsed and patted dry with paper towels

1. Place a shallow roasting pan in the oven and heat the oven to 375 degrees. Oil the rack.

2. Melt 2 tablespoons butter. Toss the mushrooms with 1 tablespoon of the melted butter and salt and pepper to taste. Combine the remaining 4 tablespoons butter, the sage, garlic, and sherry vinegar in the work bowl of a food processor fitted with a steel blade. Process until smooth.

3. Gently loosen the skin covering the breast. Work the sage butter under the skin so that the mixture covers the breast meat. Brush the chicken with the remaining melted butter and sprinkle liberally with salt and pepper.

4. Remove the heated pan from the oven and set the oiled rack in it. Place the chicken on the rack, wing side up. Roast 20 minutes, then rotate the chicken, other wing side up. Roast 20 minutes, then rotate the chicken, breast side up. Scatter the mushrooms in the bottom of the roasting pan and toss them with any accumulated juices. Roast the chicken and mushrooms until an instant-read thermometer inserted in the breast registers 160 degrees and in the thigh registers between 165 and 170 degrees, 25 to 30 minutes longer.

5. Transfer the chicken to a cutting board; let rest 10 minutes. Toss the mushrooms with the pan juices until they are well coated and lift them from the pan with a slotted spoon. Place the mushrooms in a bowl and cover with foil. Carve the chicken (see page 13), arrange it on a platter with the mushrooms, and serve.

◆

Roasted Chicken with Asian Spices

THE SOY SAUCE AND SESAME OIL GIVE THIS CHICKEN A DEEP BROWN GLAZE, SO IT IS NOT NECESSARY TO PUT ANY BUTTER UNDERNEATH THE SKIN OF THE BREAST. FIVE-SPICE POWDER, A COMBINATION OF GROUND CINNAMON, SZECHWAN PEPPER, STAR ANISE, CLOVES, AND FENNEL, IS AVAILABLE IN THE SPICE AISLE OF THE SUPERMARKET. SERVE THIS CHICKEN WITH STEAMED WHITE RICE AND STEAMED VEGETABLES. SERVES 4.

Oil for rack
2 tablespoons Asian sesame oil
1/4 cup light soy sauce
1 garlic clove, minced
1 teaspoon minced fresh gingerroot
2 teaspoons five-spice powder
1 whole chicken (about 3 1/2 pounds), giblets removed and reserved for another use, chicken rinsed and patted dry with paper towels
Salt and pepper

1. Place a shallow roasting pan in the oven and heat the oven to 375 degrees. Oil the rack.

2. Combine the sesame oil, soy sauce, garlic, ginger, and five-spice powder in a small bowl. Brush the chicken inside and out with half of the mixture and sprinkle liberally with salt and pepper.

3. Remove the heated pan from the oven and set the oiled rack in it. Pour 1/2 cup water over the pan

(continued on next page)

bottom to prevent the drippings from burning. Place the chicken on the rack, wing side up. Roast 20 minutes, then baste the chicken with more of the soy mixture and rotate, other wing side up. Roast 20 minutes, then baste the chicken with the remaining soy mixture and rotate, breast side up. Roast until an instant-read thermometer inserted in the breast registers 160 degrees and in the thigh registers between 165 and 170 degrees, 25 to 30 minutes longer.

4. Transfer the chicken to a cutting board; let rest 10 minutes. Carve (see page 13) and serve.

◆

Roasted Chicken with Maple-Walnut Glaze

MAPLE SYRUP PRODUCES A FLAVORFUL BROWNED CRUST. THE CHOPPED WALNUTS, TOASTED DURING THE ROASTING, ADD CRUNCH AND FLAVOR. SERVES 4.

> Oil for rack
> 1 whole chicken (about 3½ pounds), giblets removed and reserved for another use, chicken rinsed and patted dry with paper towels
> 2 garlic cloves, peeled and halved
> 3 tablespoons butter, softened
> Salt and pepper
> 3 fresh thyme sprigs
> ½ cup finely chopped walnuts
> ⅓ cup maple syrup
> 1 tablespoon red wine vinegar

1. Place a shallow roasting pan in the oven and heat the oven to 375 degrees. Oil the rack.

2. Rub the chicken with the garlic cloves. Melt 1 tablespoon butter. Mash the remaining 2 tablespoons butter with a fork. Gently loosen the skin covering the breast. Work the softened butter under the skin so that it covers the breast meat. Brush the chicken with the melted butter and sprinkle liberally with salt and pepper. Place the thyme sprigs in the cavity.

3. Remove the heated pan from the oven and set the oiled rack in it. Place the chicken on the rack, wing side up. Roast 20 minutes, then rotate the chicken, other wing side up. Roast another 20 minutes.

4. While the chicken is roasting, combine the nuts, maple syrup, and vinegar in a small bowl.

5. When the chicken has been roasting a total of 40 minutes, rotate it again, breast side up. Spoon half of the glaze over the chicken. Roast for 15 minutes and brush with the rest of the glaze. Continue roasting until an instant-read thermometer inserted in the breast registers 160 degrees and in the thigh registers between 165 and 170 degrees, 10 to 15 minutes longer, basting once with the pan juices.

6. Transfer the chicken to a cutting board; let rest 10 minutes. Carve (see page 13) and serve.

◆

Roasted Chicken with Sherry-Orange Glaze

THE SUGAR IN THIS GLAZE CARAMELIZES FOR A GREAT CRUST. CUMIN AND A HINT OF HOT PEPPER BALANCE THE SWEETNESS OF THE ORANGE MARMALADE AND SHERRY. IT'S A GOOD IDEA TO BASTE THE CHICKEN ONCE OR TWICE TOWARD THE END OF ROASTING TO ENSURE THE GLAZE THICKLY COATS THE SKIN OF THE CHICKEN. SERVES 4.

> Oil for rack
> 1 whole chicken (about 3½ pounds), giblets removed and reserved for another use, chicken rinsed and patted dry with paper towels
> 2 garlic cloves, peeled and halved
> 3 tablespoons butter, softened
> Salt and pepper
> 1½ teaspoons ground cumin
> ¼ cup sherry
> ¾ cup orange marmalade
> ¾ cup fresh orange juice
> ¼ teaspoon Tabasco sauce

1. Place a shallow roasting pan in the oven and heat the oven to 375 degrees. Oil the rack.

2. Rub the chicken with the garlic cloves. Melt 1 tablespoon butter. Mash the remaining 2 tablespoons butter with a fork. Gently loosen the skin covering the breast. Work the softened butter under the skin so that it covers the breast meat. Brush the chicken with the melted butter and sprinkle liberally with salt, pepper, and ½ teaspoon cumin.

3. Remove the heated pan from the oven and set the oiled rack in it. Place the chicken on the rack, wing side up. Roast 20 minutes, then rotate the chicken, other wing side up. Roast another 20 minutes.

4. While the chicken is roasting, make the glaze. Combine the remaining teaspoon of cumin, the sherry, marmalade, and orange juice in a small saucepan. Bring to a boil, reduce the heat to medium-low, and simmer, stirring frequently until sauce is reduced to 1 cup, about 20 minutes. Remove the sauce from the heat and stir in the Tabasco.

5. When the chicken has been roasting a total of 40 minutes, rotate it again, breast side up. Brush the chicken with half of the hot glaze. Roast for 15 minutes and brush with the rest of the glaze. Continue roasting until an instant-read thermometer inserted in the breast registers 160 degrees and in the thigh registers between 165 and 170 degrees, 10 to 15 minutes longer, basting once with the pan juices.

6. Transfer the chicken to a cutting board; let rest 10 minutes. Carve (see page 13) and serve.

◆

Roasted Chicken with Garlic, Shallots, and Potatoes

ROASTING CLOVES OF UNPEELED GARLIC PREVENTS THEM FROM BURNING AND BECOMING BITTER. THE ROASTED GARLIC CLOVES, SQUEEZED OUT OF THEIR PAPERY SHELLS, ARE DELICIOUS SPREAD ON WARM GRILLED BREAD OR TOAST AS AN ACCOMPANIMENT TO THE CHICKEN, POTATOES, AND SHALLOTS. SERVES 4.

Oil for rack
16 large shallots, peeled
4 large garlic heads, separated into unpeeled cloves and tops cut off
1½ pounds small (about 1 inch in diameter) red potatoes
1 tablespoon olive oil
Salt and pepper
3 tablespoons butter, softened
1 whole chicken (about 3½ pounds), giblets removed and reserved for another use, chicken rinsed and patted dry with paper towels
8 fresh thyme sprigs

1. Place a shallow roasting pan in the oven and heat the oven to 375 degrees. Oil the rack.

2. Toss the shallots, garlic, and potatoes with the olive oil and some salt and pepper in a large bowl. Melt 1 tablespoon butter. Mash the remaining 2 tablespoons butter with a fork. Gently loosen the skin covering the breast. Work the softened butter under the skin so that it covers the breast meat. Brush the chicken with the melted butter and sprinkle liberally with salt and pepper. Place the thyme inside the cavity.

3. Remove the heated pan from the oven. Place the chicken on the rack, wing side up. Scatter the shallots, garlic, and potatoes around the perimeter of the rack. Roast 20 minutes, then rotate the chicken, other wing side up. Stir the vegetables. Roast 20 minutes, then rotate the chicken, breast side up. Stir the vegetables again. Roast until an instant-read thermometer inserted in the breast registers 160 degrees and in the thigh registers between 165 and 170 degrees, 25 to 30 minutes longer.

4. Transfer the chicken to a cutting board; cover the pan with a piece of aluminum foil to keep the vegetables warm. Let the chicken rest 10 minutes. Carve (see page 13), arrange on a platter with the shallots, garlic, and potatoes, and serve with grilled or toasted bread if desired.

BUYING A ROASTING RACK

/|\

THERE ARE FIVE BASIC TYPES OF ROASTING RACKS (SEE ILLUSTRATIONS OPPOSITE): FLAT RACKS MADE OF STAINLESS STEEL WIRES; ADJUSTABLE V-SHAPED RACKS MADE OF THIN STAINLESS STEEL WIRES; NONADJUSTABLE V-RACKS USUALLY MADE OF HEAVY STEEL WIRES THAT HAVE BEEN COVERED WITH A

nonstick coating; U-shaped basket racks made of perforated stainless steel and coated with nonstick material; and vertical roasters made of stainless steel wires (which sometimes have a nonstick coating) rising up from a metal base.

Despite the differences in design, roasting racks all get the chicken off the pan and allow heat to circulate underneath the bird. In theory, this should help promote even browning and prevent the breast meat from overcooking since it does not rest directly on the scorching hot pan, even when roasting the bird breast side down. While all the roasting racks we tested (twelve in all) do this, some are much more useful than others.

As promised, vertical racks help cut cooking times by ten minutes since the metal wires conduct heat into the cavity of the bird. However, there is a serious downside. The skin near the base of the vertical wires never becomes crisp because it is resting in the pan. Also, these racks make a tremendous mess with splattering fat everywhere in the oven.

Flat racks do not get the bird as far off the roasting pan as other types of racks and hence the breast meat tends to overcook. Also, it is nearly impossible to keep a bird wing side up, as

we prefer. You can improvise with balls of foil on either side of the bird, but this method is makeshift at best.

V-racks are a considerable improvement over flat or vertical racks. We prefer a rack with heavy-duty wires. While adjustable racks that can accommodate birds of various sizes sound good, we have found that they are generally made of lightweight stainless steel and may collapse when you turn the bird.

Our first choice is a basket or cradle rack. The chicken is held snug in the rack and the wings and legs will not dangle down as they might in a V-rack. Also, the metal surface of the basket does an excellent job of conducting heat to the skin, making it especially crisp.

A BASKET RACK is stable and solid and browns the skin more thoroughly than other racks. Its U-shaped design also cradles the chicken snugly, keeping the wings and legs close to the body.

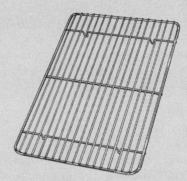

A FLAT RACK doesn't get a chicken far enough off the roasting pan and makes it difficult to roast a bird on its side.

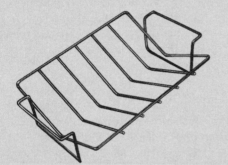

A NONADJUSTABLE V-RACK will stay put on a roasting pan. However, wings and legs may slip through the wires.

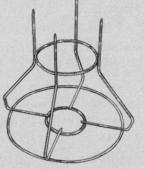

A VERTICAL RACK does a spotty job with the skin since the bottom of the bird is too close to the pan. Be prepared for a lot of splattering and a messy oven.

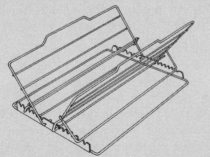

AN ADJUSTABLE V-RACK can accommodate small and large birds, but can be quite flimsy and may collapse when you turn a heavy bird.

Roasted Chicken with Jalapeños

JALAPEÑO CHILES ARE ROASTED INSIDE THE CAVITY OF THE CHICKEN TO INFUSE THE MEAT WITH FLAVOR, NOT HEAT. SERVE THE CHICKEN WITH STEAMED WHITE RICE AND BEANS AND GARNISH WITH THE CHILES. THE CHILES ARE TENDER ENOUGH TO EAT BUT MAY BE QUITE SPICY. SERVES 4.

Oil for rack
5 tablespoons butter, softened
2 garlic cloves, coarsely chopped
3 tablespoons chopped fresh cilantro leaves
1 whole chicken (about 3½ pounds),
    giblets removed and reserved for
    another use, chicken rinsed and patted
    dry with paper towels
Salt and pepper
6 jalapeño chiles

1. Place a shallow roasting pan in the oven and heat the oven to 375 degrees. Oil the rack.

2. Melt 1 tablespoon butter and set it aside. Combine the remaining 4 tablespoons of butter, the garlic, and cilantro in the work bowl of a food processor fitted with a steel blade. Process until smooth.

3. Gently loosen the skin covering the breast. Work the garlic-herb butter under the skin so that the mixture covers the breast meat. Brush the chicken with the melted butter and sprinkle liberally with salt and pepper. Place the jalapeños in the cavity.

4. Remove the heated pan from the oven and set the oiled rack in it. Pour ½ cup water over the pan bottom to prevent the drippings from burning. Place the chicken on the rack, wing side up. Roast 20 minutes, then rotate the chicken, other wing side up. Roast 20 minutes, then rotate the chicken, breast side up. Roast until an instant-read thermometer inserted in the breast registers 160 degrees and in the thigh registers between 165 and 170 degrees, 25 to 30 minutes longer.

5. Transfer the chicken to a cutting board; let rest 10 minutes. Carve (see page 13), arrange on a platter with the roasted jalapeños as garnish, and serve.

Roasted Chicken with Apples, Onions, and Potatoes

BACON TAKES THE PLACE OF BUTTER UNDER THE BREAST SKIN TO GIVE THIS CHICKEN A SLIGHTLY SMOKY FLAVOR. APPLES, ONIONS, AND POTATOES MAKE THIS A COMPLETE, FARM-STYLE MEAL. SERVES 4.

Oil for rack
2 medium onions, peeled and quartered
¾ pound small red potatoes
2 Granny Smith or other tart apples,
    peeled, cored, and cut into 8 wedges
    each
1 tablespoon vegetable oil
Salt and pepper
1 whole chicken (about 3½ pounds),
    giblets removed and reserved for
    another use, chicken rinsed and patted
    dry with paper towels
2 slices bacon
1 tablespoon butter, melted
4 fresh thyme sprigs

1. Place a shallow roasting pan in the oven and heat the oven to 375 degrees. Oil the rack.

2. Toss the onions, potatoes, and apples in a large bowl with the oil and salt and pepper to taste. Gently loosen the skin covering the chicken breast. Slide a piece of bacon under the skin of each breast. Brush the chicken with the butter and sprinkle liberally with salt and pepper. Place the thyme inside the cavity.

3. Remove the heated pan from the oven. Set the oiled rack in the pan. Place the chicken on the rack, wing side up. Scatter the vegetables around the perimeter of the rack. Roast 20 minutes, then rotate the chicken, other wing side up. Stir the vegetables. Roast 20 minutes, then rotate the chicken, breast side up. Stir the vegetables again. Roast until an instant-read thermometer inserted in the breast registers 160 degrees and in the thigh registers between 165 and 170 degrees, 25 to 30 minutes longer.

4. Transfer the chicken to a cutting board; cover the pan with a piece of aluminum foil to keep the vegetables warm. Let the chicken rest 10 minutes. Carve (see page 13), arrange on a platter with the vegetables, and serve.

◆

Roasted Chicken with Ginger Butter, Potatoes, and Onions

FOR THIS ROASTED CHICKEN, INSPIRED BY AN OLD PENN-SYLVANIA DUTCH RECIPE, GINGER BUTTER PLACED UNDER THE SKIN OF THE CHICKEN GIVES BOTH THE MEAT AND THE VEGETABLES A SPICY SWEETNESS. **SERVES 4.**

Oil for rack
1½ pounds red potatoes, cut into ¾-inch cubes
¾ pound pearl onions, peeled
1 tablespoon vegetable oil
Salt and pepper
5 tablespoons butter, softened
1 tablespoon minced fresh gingerroot
1 whole chicken (about 3½ pounds), giblets removed and reserved for another use, chicken rinsed and patted dry with paper towels

1. Place a shallow roasting pan in the oven and heat the oven to 375 degrees. Oil the rack.

2. Combine the potatoes, onions, and oil in a medium bowl. Sprinkle with salt and pepper.

3. Melt 1 tablespoon butter. Combine the remaining 4 tablespoons butter and the ginger in the work bowl of a food processor fitted with a steel blade. Process until smooth. Gently loosen the skin covering the breast. Work the ginger butter under the skin so that the mixture covers the breast meat. Brush the chicken with the melted butter and sprinkle liberally with salt and pepper.

4. Remove the heated pan from the oven and set the oiled rack in it. Place the chicken on the rack, wing side up. Scatter the potatoes and onions around the perimeter of the rack. Roast 20 minutes, then rotate the chicken, other wing side up. Stir the vegetables. Roast 20 minutes, then rotate the chicken, breast side up. Stir the vegetables again. Roast until an instant-read thermometer inserted in the breast registers 160 degrees and in the thigh registers between 165 and 170 degrees, 25 to 30 minutes longer.

5. Transfer the chicken to a cutting board; cover the pan with a piece of aluminum foil to keep the vegetables warm. Let the chicken rest 10 minutes. Carve the chicken (see page 13), arrange it on a platter with the vegetables, and serve.

◆

Roasted Chicken with Carrots, Turnips, and Onions

TURNIPS ARE A NICE ALTERNATIVE TO THE STANDARD POTATOES IN THIS RECIPE FOR CHICKEN ROASTED WITH ROOT VEGETABLES. THEIR SLIGHTLY BITTER FLAVOR IS CONTRASTED WITH THE SWEET CARROTS AND ONIONS. **SERVES 4.**

Oil for rack
3 tablespoons butter, softened
1 whole chicken (about 3½ pounds), giblets removed and reserved for another use, chicken rinsed and patted dry with paper towels
Salt and pepper
1 lemon, halved
1 small bunch dill
4 carrots, peeled and cut into 1-inch lengths
4 small turnips (about ¾ pound), peeled and cut into eighths
4 small onions, peeled and quartered
1 tablespoon vegetable oil
1 tablespoon chopped fresh dill

(continued on next page)

1. Place a shallow roasting pan in the oven and heat the oven to 375 degrees. Oil the rack.

2. Melt 1 tablespoon butter. Mash the remaining 2 tablespoons of butter with a fork. Gently loosen the skin covering the breast. Work the softened butter under the skin so that it covers the breast meat. Brush the chicken with the melted butter and sprinkle liberally with salt and pepper. Squeeze half of the lemon over the chicken and discard the shell. Squeeze the other half inside the cavity and place the shell and the dill inside the cavity.

3. Combine the carrots, turnips, and onions in a large bowl. Toss with the oil and salt and pepper to taste.

4. Remove the heated pan from the oven and set the oiled rack in it. Place the chicken on the rack, wing side up. Scatter the vegetables around the perimeter of the rack. Roast 20 minutes, then rotate the chicken, other wing side up. Stir the vegetables. Roast 20 minutes, then rotate the chicken, breast side up. Stir the vegetables again. Roast until an instant-read thermometer inserted in the breast registers 160 degrees and in the thigh registers between 165 and 170 degrees, 25 to 30 minutes longer.

5. Transfer the chicken to a cutting board; cover the pan with a piece of aluminum foil to keep the vegetables warm. Let the chicken rest 10 minutes. Carve (see page 13), arrange on a platter with the vegetables, garnish with chopped dill, and serve.

◆

Basil-Garlic Roasted Chicken with Roasted Tomatoes

BUTTER FLAVORED WITH BASIL AND GARLIC GIVES THIS CHICKEN A CRUST REMINISCENT OF PESTO. ROASTING THE TOMATOES ALONG WITH THE CHICKEN CONCENTRATES THEIR SWEETNESS. SERVES 4.

Oil for rack
5 tablespoons butter, softened
2 cups loosely packed fresh basil leaves
2 garlic cloves, coarsely chopped

1 whole chicken (about 3½ pounds), giblets removed and reserved for another use, chicken rinsed and patted dry with paper towels
Salt and pepper
8 plum tomatoes, cored and halved lengthwise
1 tablespoon olive oil

1. Place a shallow roasting pan in the oven and heat the oven to 375 degrees. Oil the rack.

2. Melt 1 tablespoon butter and set aside. Combine the remaining 4 tablespoons butter, the basil, and garlic in the work bowl of a food processor fitted with a steel blade. Process until combined. Gently loosen the skin covering the breast. Work the garlic-basil butter under the skin so that the mixture covers the breast meat. Brush the chicken with the melted butter and sprinkle liberally with salt and pepper.

3. Combine the tomatoes and oil in a medium bowl and sprinkle with salt and pepper to taste.

4. Remove the heated pan from the oven and set the oiled rack in it. Place the chicken on the rack, wing side up. Roast 20 minutes, then rotate the chicken, other wing side up. Scatter the tomatoes around the perimeter of the rack. Roast 20 minutes, then rotate the chicken, breast side up. Roast until an instant-read thermometer inserted in the breast registers 160 degrees and in the thigh registers between 165 and 170 degrees, 25 to 30 minutes longer.

5. Transfer the chicken to a cutting board; cover the pan with a piece of aluminum foil to keep the tomatoes warm. Let the chicken rest 10 minutes. Carve (see page 13), arrange on a platter with the roasted tomatoes, and serve.

ROASTED CHICKEN PARTS

SOMETIMES YOU WANT THE FLAVOR OF ROASTED

CHICKEN BUT DON'T HAVE THE HOUR OR MORE

NEEDED TO COOK A WHOLE CHICKEN. OR, MAYBE

YOUR FAMILY LIKES ROASTED CHICKEN, BUT NO

ONE WILL EAT THE WINGS AND LEGS. ROASTING

parts offers a good solution to either problem. In addition, roasting parts allows the cook to remove each piece from the oven as soon as it is done. With this method, there is no danger of the breast drying out before the thigh is cooked through.

The main challenge when roasting chicken parts is getting the skin crisp. We like to roast a whole chicken on a basket or V-rack to circulate the heat evenly around the bird and keep any part of the skin from sitting in fat or cooking juices. We assumed the same thing would hold true for parts and our tests backed up our hunch. When we roasted parts directly in the pan, the skin was more flabby than when we lifted the parts off the bottom of a roasting pan with a flat rack. You will need a roasting pan large enough to accommodate a flat rack. A 13-by-9-inch roasting pan with fairly shallow sides (about 2 inches high) and a rack that is slightly smaller works especially well.

We next turned our attention to oven heat. We started out using the same temperature we found best for roasting a whole chicken—375 degrees. Given the shorter oven time, we found that the skin did not crisp when parts were cooked at this temperature. Next, we tried 450 degrees. After setting off several smoke alarms, we realized that this super-high oven heat was going to cause pan drippings to burn. We eventually settled on 425 degrees. At this temperature, the skin was nice and crisp by the time the meat was cooked through. As an added protection against smoking, we found it useful to add ½ cup of water to

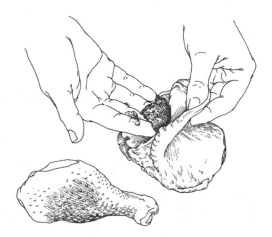

TO SEASON pieces well, we like to rub dry spice mixtures right into the skin. Wet pastes, compound butters, and pestos should go under the skin. Carefully lift the skin on each piece and rub a little of the paste into the meat with your fingers.

the roasting pan about fifteen minutes into the cooking time.

Given the configuration of chicken parts (the skin is generally on one side, bones on the other), we found no advantage in turning the chicken during the cooking process. Cooking the parts skin side up results in the crispest, brownest skin. While we found that basting actually makes skin less crisp (coating the skin with liquid and/or fat makes it soggy and slows down the crisping process), once again we clearly detected a benefit from slipping a little butter under the skin on each piece. The melting butter helps lift the skin off the meat and causes it to puff up nicely. The butter is also a good medium for herbs, spices, anchovies, chiles, and other seasonings that can flavor the meat.

Finally, as with broiled or grilled chicken parts, we like the effects of brining on parts destined for roasting. Although not essential, brining seasons the meat through to the bone and firms up the texture, making the chicken parts meatier tasting.

While we wrote recipes for one cut-up chicken, you can use the following recipes to roast 3 pounds of any combination of parts. Just remember that smaller, thinner wings and drumsticks will be done in thirty to thirty-five minutes, while thicker breasts and thighs will take forty to forty-five minutes. If you have any doubts, use an instant-read thermometer, cooking delicate breasts to 160 to 165 degrees and other parts to 165 to 170 degrees.

Roasted Chicken Parts

SERVES 4

BRINING IMPROVES THE chicken's flavor, but if you're short on time, you can skip step 1—just make sure that the chicken parts are well seasoned with salt. We've found that high heat works best on roasted parts, cooking the chicken quickly without drying it out, and producing a crisp crust. The only problem comes from the smoking fat at the bottom of the roasting pan. To avoid this nuisance, we pour ½ cup of water into the pan halfway through the cooking time.

> ¾ cup kosher salt *or* 6 tablespoons table salt, plus more to taste
> ¾ cup sugar
> 1 chicken (3 to 3½ pounds), rinsed, patted dry, and cut into 8 pieces (see "Cutting Up a Whole Chicken," page 10)
> 2 tablespoons butter, softened
> Pepper
> 1 teaspoon vegetable oil

1. If brining the chicken pieces: In a gallon-size sealable plastic bag, dissolve the ¾ cup salt and the sugar in 1 quart of water. Add the chicken, pressing out as much air as possible; seal and refrigerate until fully seasoned, about 1½ hours. Rinse the chicken pieces well and pat dry.

2. Preheat the oven to 425 degrees. With a fork, mash together the butter and salt and pepper to taste (use salt sparingly if the chicken was brined) in a small bowl. Rub the butter mixture under the skin of each chicken piece (see figure, opposite). Place a rack in a large roasting pan and transfer the chicken, skin side up, to the rack. Brush the chicken with oil and lightly season with salt and pepper.

3. Roast for 15 minutes. Add ½ cup of water to the pan to prevent excessive smoking. Cook the parts until the juices run clear, another 15 to 20 minutes for the legs and wings, 25 to 30 minutes for breasts and thighs. Remove the legs and wings to a plate when cooked through, and cover with foil to keep warm; remove the breasts and thighs when cooked through, and serve.

◆

Lemon-Herb Roasted Chicken Parts

BUTTER FLAVORED WITH LEMON ZEST GIVES ROASTED CHICKEN PARTS CRISPY SKIN AND TASTY MEAT. ANY HERB CAN BE ADDED TO THE BUTTER, BUT WE ESPECIALLY LIKE THYME OR ROSEMARY. SERVES 4.

> ¾ cup kosher salt *or* 6 tablespoons table salt, plus more to taste
> ¾ cup sugar
> 1 chicken (3 to 3½ pounds), rinsed, patted dry, and cut into 8 pieces (see "Cutting Up a Whole Chicken," page 10)
> 2 tablespoons butter, softened
> 1 tablespoon minced lemon zest
> 1 tablespoon minced fresh thyme or rosemary leaves
> Pepper
> 1 teaspoon vegetable oil

(continued on next page)

1. If brining the chicken pieces: In a gallon-size sealable plastic bag, dissolve the ¾ cup salt and the sugar in 1 quart of water. Add the chicken, pressing out as much air as possible; seal and refrigerate until fully seasoned, about 1½ hours. Rinse the chicken pieces well and pat dry.

2. Preheat the oven to 425 degrees. With a fork, mash together the butter, zest, thyme, and salt and pepper to taste (use salt sparingly if the chicken was brined) in a small bowl. Rub the butter mixture under the skin of each chicken piece (see figure, page 38). Place a rack in a large roasting pan and transfer the chicken, skin side up, to the rack. Brush the chicken with oil and lightly season with salt and pepper.

3. Roast for 15 minutes. Add ½ cup of water to the pan to prevent excessive smoking. Cook the parts until the juices run clear, another 15 to 20 minutes for the legs and wings, 25 to 30 minutes for breasts and thighs. Remove the legs and wings to a plate when cooked through, and cover with foil to keep warm; remove the breasts and thighs when cooked through, and serve.

◆

Roasted Chicken Parts with Jalapeño and Cilantro Butter

SOMETIMES WE'RE DISAPPOINTED WITH OUR SUPERMARKET'S FRESH JALAPEÑO CHILES—THEY CAN BE SO MILD THAT THEY TASTE LIKE GREEN BELL PEPPERS. ALWAYS RELIABLE, HOWEVER, ARE PICKLED JALAPEÑOS, AVAILABLE AT SUPERMARKETS ON THE SHELF WITH THE SALSAS AND NACHO FIXINGS. HERE, WE USE THEM (USE FRESH IF YOU'D LIKE) TO FLAVOR ROASTED CHICKEN PARTS. A SPRINKLING OF PAPRIKA GIVES THE SKIN SOME COLOR, BUT NO ADDED HEAT. SERVES 4.

- ¾ cup kosher salt *or* 6 tablespoons table salt, plus more to taste
- ¾ cup sugar
- 1 chicken (3 to 3½ pounds), rinsed, patted dry, and cut into 8 pieces (see "Cutting Up a Whole Chicken," page 10)

- 2 tablespoons butter, softened
- 1 tablespoon minced pickled jalapeño chile
- 1 tablespoon minced fresh cilantro leaves
- Pepper
- 1 teaspoon vegetable oil
- 1 teaspoon paprika

1. If brining the chicken pieces: In a gallon-size sealable plastic bag, dissolve the ¾ cup salt and the sugar in 1 quart of water. Add the chicken, pressing out as much air as possible; seal and refrigerate until fully seasoned, about 1½ hours. Rinse the chicken pieces well and pat dry.

2. Preheat the oven to 425 degrees. With a fork, mash together the butter, jalapeño, cilantro, and salt and pepper to taste (use salt sparingly if the chicken was brined) in a small bowl. Rub the butter mixture under the skin of each chicken piece (see figure, page 38). Place a rack in a large roasting pan and transfer the chicken, skin side up, to the rack. Brush the chicken with oil, sprinkle with paprika, and lightly season with salt and pepper.

3. Roast for 15 minutes. Add ½ cup of water to the pan to prevent excessive smoking. Cook the parts until the juices run clear, another 15 to 20 minutes for the legs and wings, 25 to 30 minutes for breasts and thighs. Remove the legs and wings to a plate when cooked through, and cover with foil to keep warm; remove the breasts and thighs when cooked through, and serve.

◆

Five-Spice Roasted Chicken Parts with Ginger Butter

WE OFTEN LIKE TO PAIR FLAVORED BUTTER UNDERNEATH THE SKIN WITH A COMPLEMENTARY DUSTING OF SPICES ON TOP. HERE, GINGER BUTTER IS MATCHED WITH FIVE-SPICE POWDER, A PRE-MIXED COMBINATION OF STAR ANISE, CLOVES, CINNAMON, FENNEL, AND SZECHWAN PEPPER. SERVES 4.

¾ cup kosher salt *or* 6 tablespoons table salt, plus more to taste

¾ cup sugar

1 chicken (3 to 3½ pounds), rinsed, patted dry, and cut into 8 pieces (see "Cutting Up a Whole Chicken," page 10)

2 tablespoons butter, softened

1 tablespoon peeled and minced fresh gingerroot

Pepper

1 teaspoon vegetable oil

1 teaspoon five-spice powder

1. If brining the chicken pieces: In a gallon-size sealable plastic bag, dissolve the ¾ cup salt and the sugar in 1 quart of water. Add the chicken, pressing out as much air as possible; seal and refrigerate until fully seasoned, about 1½ hours. Rinse the chicken pieces well and pat dry.

2. Preheat the oven to 425 degrees. With a fork, mash together the butter, ginger, and salt and pepper to taste (use salt sparingly if the chicken was brined) in a small bowl. Rub the butter mixture under the skin of each chicken piece (see figure, page 38). Place a rack in a large roasting pan and transfer the chicken, skin side up, to the rack. Brush the chicken with oil, sprinkle with the five-spice powder, and lightly season with salt and pepper.

3. Roast for 15 minutes. Add ½ cup of water to the pan to prevent excessive smoking. Cook the parts until the juices run clear, another 15 to 20 minutes for the legs and wings, 25 to 30 minutes for breasts and thighs. Remove the legs and wings to a plate when cooked through, and cover with foil to keep warm; remove the breasts and thighs when cooked through, and serve.

Cumin Roasted Chicken Parts with Oregano Butter

CUMIN AND OREGANO ARE A CLASSIC SOUTH AMERICAN FLAVOR COMBINATION. SERVE THIS CHICKEN WITH BLACK BEANS AND YELLOW RICE. SERVES 4.

¾ cup kosher salt *or* 6 tablespoons table salt, plus more to taste

¾ cup sugar

1 chicken (3 to 3½ pounds), rinsed, patted dry, and cut into 8 pieces (see "Cutting Up a Whole Chicken," page 10)

2 tablespoons butter, softened

2 garlic cloves, minced

1 tablespoon minced fresh oregano leaves

Pepper

1 teaspoon vegetable oil

1 teaspoon ground cumin

1. If brining the chicken pieces: In a gallon-size sealable plastic bag, dissolve the ¾ cup salt and the sugar in 1 quart of water. Add the chicken, pressing out as much air as possible; seal and refrigerate until fully seasoned, about 1½ hours. Rinse the chicken pieces well and pat dry.

2. Preheat the oven to 425 degrees. With a fork, mash together the butter, garlic, oregano, and salt and pepper to taste (use salt sparingly if the chicken was brined) in a small bowl. Rub the butter mixture under the skin of each chicken piece (see figure, page 38). Place a rack in a large roasting pan and transfer the chicken, skin side up, to the rack. Brush the chicken with oil, sprinkle with cumin, and lightly season with salt and pepper.

3. Roast for 15 minutes. Add ½ cup of water to the pan to prevent excessive smoking. Cook the parts until the juices run clear, another 15 to 20 minutes for the legs and wings, 25 to 30 minutes for breasts and thighs. Remove the legs and wings to a plate when cooked through, and cover with foil to keep warm; remove the breasts and thighs when cooked through, and serve.

Roasted Chicken Parts with Porcini Mushroom Paste

REHYDRATED PORCINI MUSHROOMS, COMBINED WITH BUTTER, PARSLEY, AND GARLIC, MAKE A LUXURIOUS FLAVORING FOR ROASTED CHICKEN PARTS. ORZO TOSSED WITH PARMESAN AND BASIL WOULD MAKE A NICE ACCOMPANIMENT. **SERVES 4.**

¾ cup kosher salt *or* 6 tablespoons table salt, plus more to taste
¾ cup sugar
1 chicken (3 to 3½ pounds), rinsed, patted dry, and cut into 8 pieces (see "Cutting Up a Whole Chicken," page 10)
1 ounce dried porcini mushrooms
2 tablespoons butter, softened
2 garlic cloves, minced
2 tablespoons minced fresh parsley leaves
Pepper
1 teaspoon vegetable oil

1. If brining the chicken pieces: In a gallon-size sealable plastic bag, dissolve the ¾ cup salt and the sugar in 1 quart of water. Add the chicken, pressing out as much air as possible; seal and refrigerate until fully seasoned, about 1½ hours. Rinse the chicken pieces well and pat dry.

2. Place the mushrooms in a bowl and cover with hot tap water. Let stand until the mushrooms are soft, about 20 minutes. Drain, pat dry, and finely chop the mushrooms. (Strain and reserve the soaking liquid for another use.)

3. Preheat the oven to 425 degrees. With a fork, mash together the mushrooms, butter, garlic, parsley, and salt and pepper to taste (use salt sparingly if the chicken was brined) in a small bowl. Rub the butter mixture under the skin of each chicken piece (see figure, page 38). Place a rack in a large roasting pan and transfer the chicken, skin side up, to the rack. Brush the chicken with oil and lightly season with salt and pepper.

4. Roast for 15 minutes. Add ½ cup of water to the pan to prevent excessive smoking. Cook the parts until the juices run clear, another 15 to 20 minutes for the legs and wings, 25 to 30 minutes for breasts and thighs. Remove the legs and wings to a plate when cooked through, and cover with foil to keep warm; remove the breasts and thighs when cooked through, and serve.

◆

Roasted Chicken Parts with Honey and Mustard

A HONEY-MUSTARD GLAZE BRUSHED ON HALFWAY THROUGH COOKING GIVES ROASTED CHICKEN PARTS A BEAUTIFUL, CARAMELIZED CRUST. SWEET POTATO OVEN FRIES AND MAYBE SOME WILTED SPINACH OR OTHER LEAFY GREENS COULD ROUND OUT THE MEAL. **SERVES 4.**

¾ cup kosher salt *or* 6 tablespoons table salt, plus more to taste
¾ cup sugar
1 chicken (3 to 3½ pounds), rinsed, patted dry, and cut into 8 pieces (see "Cutting Up a Whole Chicken," page 10)
¼ cup Dijon mustard
2 tablespoons honey
1 teaspoon brown sugar
2 tablespoons butter, softened
Pepper
1 teaspoon vegetable oil

1. If brining the chicken pieces: In a gallon-size sealable plastic bag, dissolve the ¾ cup salt and the sugar in 1 quart of water. Add the chicken, pressing out as much air as possible; seal and refrigerate until fully seasoned, about 1½ hours. Rinse the chicken pieces well and pat dry.

2. Preheat the oven to 425 degrees. Combine the mustard, honey, and brown sugar in a small bowl and set aside. With a fork, mash together the butter and salt and pepper to taste (use salt sparingly if the chicken was brined) in a small bowl. Rub the butter mixture under the skin of each chicken piece (see figure, page 38). Place a rack in a large roasting pan and transfer the chicken, skin side up, to the rack.

Brush the chicken with oil and lightly season with salt and pepper.

3. Roast for 15 minutes. Add ½ cup of water to the pan to prevent excessive smoking and brush the chicken with the honey mustard. Cook the parts until the juices run clear, another 15 to 20 minutes for the legs and wings, 25 to 30 minutes for breasts and thighs. Remove the legs and wings to a plate when cooked through, and cover with foil to keep warm; remove the breasts and thighs when cooked through, and serve.

◆

Roasted Chicken Parts with Rice Wine and Soy Sauce Glaze

SOY SAUCE, RICE WINE, AND HONEY MAKE A QUICK AND TASTY GLAZE. WE'VE ADDED SCALLION BUTTER UNDER THE SKIN FOR COMPLEMENTARY FLAVOR. DON'T BRUSH THE CHICKEN WITH OIL BEFORE YOU PUT IT IN THE OVEN, SINCE THIS WILL CAUSE THE THIN GLAZE TO SLIDE RIGHT OFF THE SKIN WHEN YOU TRY TO APPLY IT LATER ON. SERVES 4.

¾ cup kosher salt *or* 6 tablespoons table
  salt, plus more to taste
¾ cup sugar
1 chicken (3 to 3½ pounds), rinsed, patted
  dry, and cut into 8 pieces (see "Cutting
  Up a Whole Chicken," page 10)
1 tablespoon soy sauce
1 tablespoon rice wine
3 tablespoons honey
2 tablespoons butter, softened
2 scallions, white and light green parts,
  finely chopped
Pepper

1. If brining the chicken pieces: In a gallon-size sealable plastic bag, dissolve the ¾ cup salt and the sugar in 1 quart of water. Add the chicken, pressing out as much air as possible; seal and refrigerate until fully seasoned, about 1½ hours. Rinse the chicken pieces well and pat dry.

2. Preheat the oven to 425 degrees. Combine the soy sauce, rice wine, and honey in a small bowl and set aside. With a fork, mash together the butter, scallions, and salt and pepper to taste (use the salt sparingly if the chicken was brined) in a small bowl. Rub the butter mixture under the skin of each chicken piece (see figure, page 38). Place a rack in a large roasting pan and transfer the chicken, skin side up, to the rack.

3. Roast for 15 minutes. Add ½ cup of water to the pan to prevent excessive smoking and brush the chicken with the soy sauce mixture. Cook the parts until the juices run clear, another 15 to 20 minutes for the legs and wings, 25 to 30 minutes for breasts and thighs. Remove the legs and wings to a plate when cooked through, and cover with foil to keep warm; remove the breasts and thighs when cooked through, and serve.

Deviled Chicken Parts

A CHICKEN CLASSIC, "DEVILED" PARTS HAVE A SPICY, CRISP COATING. THEY PACK WELL FOR PICNICS. **SERVES 4.**

¾ cup kosher salt *or* 6 tablespoons table salt, plus more to taste
¾ cup sugar
1 chicken (3 to 3½ pounds), rinsed, patted dry, and cut into 8 pieces (see "Cutting Up a Whole Chicken," page 10)
2 tablespoons butter, softened
Pepper
1 tablespoon Dijon mustard
1 tablespoon white wine vinegar
¼ teaspoon cayenne pepper, or to taste
⅓ cup plain bread crumbs

1. If brining the chicken pieces: In a gallon-size sealable plastic bag, dissolve the ¾ cup salt and the sugar in 1 quart of water. Add the chicken, pressing out as much air as possible; seal and refrigerate until fully seasoned, about 1½ hours. Rinse the chicken pieces well and pat dry.

2. Preheat the oven to 425 degrees. With a fork, mash together the butter and salt and pepper to taste (use salt sparingly if the chicken was brined) in a small bowl. Rub the butter mixture under the skin of each chicken piece (see figure, page 38). Combine the mustard, vinegar, cayenne, and salt to taste in a small bowl. Rub the mixture all over the chicken pieces. Sprinkle the skin side of each piece of chicken with bread crumbs and press to adhere. Place a rack in a large roasting pan and transfer the chicken, skin side up, to the rack.

3. Roast for 15 minutes. Add ½ cup of water to the pan to prevent excessive smoking. Cook the parts until the juices run clear, another 15 to 20 minutes for the legs and wings, 25 to 30 minutes for breasts and thighs. Remove the legs and wings to a plate when cooked through, and cover with foil to keep warm; remove the breasts and thighs when cooked through, and serve.

Barbecue-Roasted Chicken Parts

BARBECUE SAUCE GIVES ROASTED CHICKEN A LITTLE BIT OF AN OUTDOORSY FLAVOR. COOK UP ONE OF OUR BARBECUE SAUCE RECIPES (SEE PAGES 164–166) OR CHOOSE YOUR FAVORITE SAUCE. WE BRUSH THE SAUCE ON IN THE MIDDLE OF COOKING, WHEN WE ADD THE WATER TO THE PAN. THIS GIVES THE SKIN TIME TO CRISP UP A LITTLE BIT BEFORE IT IS COVERED. **SERVES 4.**

¾ cup kosher salt *or* 6 tablespoons table salt, plus more to taste
¾ cup sugar
1 chicken (3 to 3½ pounds), rinsed, patted dry, and cut into 8 pieces (see "Cutting Up a Whole Chicken," page 10)
2 tablespoons butter, softened
Pepper
1 teaspoon vegetable oil
1 cup barbecue sauce

1. If brining the chicken pieces: In a gallon-size sealable plastic bag, dissolve the ¾ cup salt and the sugar in 1 quart of water. Add the chicken, pressing out as much air as possible; seal and refrigerate until fully seasoned, about 1½ hours. Rinse the chicken pieces well and pat dry.

2. Preheat the oven to 425 degrees. With a fork, mash together the butter and salt and pepper to taste (use salt sparingly if the chicken was brined) in a small bowl. Rub the butter mixture under the skin of each chicken piece (see figure, page 38). Place a rack in a large roasting pan and transfer the chicken, skin side up, to the rack. Brush the chicken with oil and lightly season with salt and pepper.

3. Roast for 15 minutes. Add ½ cup of water to the pan to prevent excessive smoking and brush the chicken with the barbecue sauce. Cook the parts until the juices run clear, another 15 to 20 minutes for the legs and wings, 25 to 30 minutes for breasts and thighs. Remove the legs and wings to a plate when cooked through, and cover with foil to keep warm; remove the breasts and thighs when cooked through, and serve.

Roasted Chicken Parts with Shallot and Anchovy Butter

ANCHOVIES MAKE AN ESPECIALLY GOOD COMPOUND BUTTER FOR CHICKEN. ALONG WITH SHALLOTS, THEY LEND THIS CHICKEN A POWERFUL, BUT NOT FISHY, FLAVOR. SERVES 4.

¾ cup kosher salt *or* 6 tablespoons table
    salt, plus more to taste
¾ cup sugar
1 chicken (3 to 3½ pounds), rinsed, patted
    dry, and cut into 8 pieces (see "Cutting
    Up a Whole Chicken," page 10)
2 tablespoons butter, softened
4 flat anchovy fillets, rinsed, dried, and
    finely chopped
1 small shallot, finely chopped
1 teaspoon vegetable oil
Pepper

1. If brining the chicken pieces: In a gallon-size seal-able plastic bag, dissolve the ¾ cup salt and the sugar in 1 quart of water. Add the chicken, pressing out as much air as possible; seal and refrigerate until fully seasoned, about 1½ hours. Rinse the chicken pieces well and pat dry.

2. Preheat the oven to 425 degrees. With a fork, mash together the butter, anchovies, and shallot in a small bowl. Rub the butter mixture under the skin of each chicken piece (see figure, page 38). Place a rack in a large roasting pan and transfer the chicken, skin side up, to the rack. Brush the chicken with oil and lightly season with salt and pepper.

3. Roast for 15 minutes. Add ½ cup of water to the pan to prevent excessive smoking. Cook the parts until the juices run clear, another 15 to 20 minutes for the legs and wings, 25 to 30 minutes for breasts and thighs. Remove the legs and wings to a plate when cooked through, and cover with foil to keep warm; remove the breasts and thighs when cooked through, and serve.

Roasted Chicken Parts with Tarragon and Sun-Dried Tomato Paste

A SIMPLE PARMESAN RISOTTO WOULD PAIR WELL WITH THIS HIGHLY FLAVORED DISH. OTHER FRESH HERBS, ESPECIALLY PARSLEY, BASIL, OR MINT, COULD SUBSTI-TUTE FOR THE TARRAGON. SERVES 4.

¾ cup kosher salt *or* 6 tablespoons table
    salt, plus more to taste
¾ cup sugar
1 chicken (3 to 3½ pounds), rinsed, patted
    dry, and cut into 8 pieces (see "Cutting
    Up a Whole Chicken," page 10)
15 sun-dried tomatoes packed in oil,
    drained (about ⅔ cup)
1 medium shallot, peeled and coarsely
    chopped
2 tablespoons fresh tarragon leaves
2 tablespoons extra-virgin olive oil
Pepper
1 teaspoon vegetable oil

1. If brining the chicken pieces: In a gallon-size seal-able plastic bag, dissolve the ¾ cup salt and the sugar in 1 quart of water. Add the chicken, pressing out as much air as possible; seal and refrigerate until fully seasoned, about 1½ hours. Rinse the chicken pieces well and pat dry.

2. Preheat the oven to 425 degrees. Place the toma-toes, shallot, tarragon, olive oil, and salt and pepper to taste (use salt sparingly if the chicken was brined) in the work bowl of a food processor. Process until well combined, scraping down the sides of the bowl as necessary. Spread some tomato paste under the skin of each chicken piece (see figure, page 38). Place a rack in a large roasting pan and transfer the chicken, skin side up, to the rack. Brush the chicken with oil and lightly season with salt and pepper.

3. Roast for 15 minutes. Add ½ cup of water to the pan to prevent excessive smoking. Cook the parts until

(continued on next page)

the juices run clear, another 15 to 20 minutes for the legs and wings, 25 to 30 minutes for breasts and thighs. Remove the legs and wings to a plate when cooked through, and cover with foil to keep warm; remove the breasts and thighs when cooked through, and serve.

◆

Roasted Chicken Parts with Olive Paste

PUREED OLIVES REPLACE BUTTER UNDERNEATH THE SKIN IN THIS RECIPE. THIS MEDITERRANEAN-FLAVORED DISH GOES WELL WITH A COUSCOUS PILAF AND MAYBE SOME ROASTED EGGPLANT AND PEPPERS. SERVES 4.

> ¾ cup kosher salt *or* 6 tablespoons table salt, plus more to taste
> ¾ cup sugar
> 1 chicken (3 to 3½ pounds), rinsed, patted dry, and cut into 8 pieces (see "Cutting Up a Whole Chicken," page 10)
> ½ cup Kalamata or other large black olives, pitted and coarsely chopped
> ¼ cup tightly packed parsley leaves
> 1 small garlic clove, peeled
> 2 tablespoons olive oil
> 1 teaspoon sherry vinegar
> 1 teaspoon vegetable oil
> Pepper

1. If brining the chicken pieces: In a gallon-size sealable plastic bag, dissolve the ¾ cup salt and the sugar in 1 quart of water. Add the chicken, pressing out as much air as possible; seal and refrigerate until fully seasoned, about 1½ hours. Rinse the chicken pieces well and pat dry.

2. Preheat the oven to 425 degrees. Combine the olives, parsley, garlic, olive oil, and vinegar in the work bowl of a food processor. Process until well combined, scraping down the sides of the bowl as necessary. Spread some olive paste under the skin of each chicken piece (see figure, page 38). Place a rack in a large roasting pan and transfer the chicken, skin side up, to the rack. Brush the chicken with oil and lightly season with salt and pepper.

3. Roast for 15 minutes. Add ½ cup of water to the pan to prevent excessive smoking. Cook the parts until the juices run clear, another 15 to 20 minutes for the legs and wings, 25 to 30 minutes for breasts and thighs. Remove the legs and wings to a plate when cooked through, and cover with foil to keep warm; remove the breasts and thighs when cooked through, and serve.

◆

Ginger-Lime Roasted Chicken Parts with Toasted Sesame Crust

WE ESPECIALLY LIKE THE COMBINATION OF GINGER AND LIME HERE, BUT LEMON OR ORANGE ZEST MAY BE SUBSTITUTED WITH GOOD RESULTS. SERVES 4.

> ¾ cup kosher salt *or* 6 tablespoons table salt, plus more to taste
> ¾ cup sugar
> 1 chicken (3 to 3½ pounds), rinsed, patted dry, and cut into 8 pieces (see "Cutting Up a Whole Chicken," page 10)
> 2 tablespoons butter, softened
> 1 teaspoon minced lime zest
> 1 tablespoon peeled and minced fresh gingerroot
> 1 large garlic clove, minced
> Pepper
> 2 teaspoons soy sauce
> 1 teaspoon Asian sesame oil
> 1 tablespoon sesame seeds

1. If brining the chicken pieces: In a gallon-size sealable plastic bag, dissolve the ¾ cup salt and the sugar in 1 quart of water. Add the chicken, pressing out as much air as possible; seal and refrigerate until fully seasoned, about 1½ hours. Rinse the chicken pieces well and pat dry.

2. Preheat the oven to 425 degrees. With a fork, mash together the butter, zest, ginger, garlic, and salt and pepper to taste (use salt sparingly if the chicken was brined) in a small bowl. Rub the butter mixture under the skin of each chicken piece (see figure, page 38). Place a rack in a large roasting pan and transfer the chicken, skin side up, to the rack. Combine the soy sauce and sesame oil in a small bowl and brush about half of the mixture on the chicken.

3. Roast for 15 minutes. Add ½ cup of water to the pan to prevent excessive smoking and brush the chicken with the remaining soy sauce mixture. Sprinkle with the sesame seeds. Cook the parts until the juices run clear, another 15 to 20 minutes for the legs and wings, 25 to 30 minutes for breasts and thighs. Remove the legs and wings to a plate when cooked through, and cover with foil to keep warm; remove the breasts and thighs when cooked through, and serve.

◆

Roasted Chicken Parts with Herb Crust

WE LIKE HERB-CRUSTED ROASTED CHICKEN (PAGE 26) SO MUCH THAT WE WANTED TO ADAPT IT FOR THIS CHAPTER. IT MAY WORK EVEN BETTER HERE, BECAUSE ROASTED PARTS DON'T NEED TO BE TURNED, SO THERE'S NO DANGER OF LOSING THE CRUST. WE LIKE THE COMBINATION OF TARRAGON, PARSLEY, AND DILL, BUT OTHER FRESH HERBS, ESPECIALLY MINT, SAVORY, OR CILANTRO, WOULD WORK AS WELL. SERVES 4.

> ¾ cup kosher salt *or* 6 tablespoons table
>   salt, plus more to taste
> ¾ cup sugar
> 1 chicken (3 to 3½ pounds), rinsed, patted
>   dry, and cut into 8 pieces (see "Cutting
>   Up a Whole Chicken," page 10)
> 2 tablespoons butter, softened
> Pepper
> 2 cups loosely packed fresh tarragon
>   leaves
> 2 cups loosely packed fresh parsley leaves
> 2 cups loosely packed fresh dill leaves
> 2 egg yolks, lightly beaten
> Oil for rack

1. If brining the chicken pieces: In a gallon-size sealable plastic bag, dissolve the ¾ cup salt and the sugar in 1 quart of water. Add the chicken, pressing out as much air as possible; seal and refrigerate until fully seasoned, about 1½ hours. Rinse the chicken pieces well and pat dry.

2. Preheat the oven to 425 degrees. With a fork, mash the butter and salt and pepper to taste (use salt sparingly if the chicken was brined) in a small bowl. Rub the butter under the skin of each chicken piece (see figure, page 38).

3. Place the herbs in the work bowl of a food processor fitted with a steel blade. Process until finely chopped. Brush the chicken pieces all over with the egg yolks. Sprinkle lightly with salt and pepper. Sprinkle the herb mixture over the chicken and lightly pat the herbs so that the chicken is evenly coated. Oil a rack and place it in a large roasting pan; transfer the chicken, skin side up, to the rack.

4. Roast the parts until the juices run clear, another 30 to 35 minutes for the legs and wings, 40 to 45 minutes for breasts and thighs. Remove the legs and wings to a plate when cooked through, and cover with foil to keep warm; remove the breasts and thighs when cooked through, and serve.

Tandoori Roasted Chicken Parts

ALTHOUGH THE INCREDIBLE BAKED CRUST OF TAN-DOORI CHICKEN, WHICH IS TRADITIONALLY PREPARED IN A VERY HOT CLAY OVEN, CANNOT BE ACHIEVED AT HOME, THE FLAVORS OF THE YOGURT-MARINATED DISH ARE STILL VERY GOOD ON SIMPLE ROASTED CHICKEN PARTS. SINCE THE YOGURT AND SPICE MIXTURE NEEDS TIME TO PENETRATE THE CHICKEN, WE MARINATE RATHER THAN BRINE THE CHICKEN IN THIS RECIPE. ALSO, THE MARINATED CHICKEN GIVES OFF ENOUGH LIQUID DURING COOKING TO MAKE THE ADDITION OF WATER IN THE PAN UNNECESSARY. SERVES 4.

1 small onion, cut into several chunks
2 garlic cloves, coarsely chopped
1 tablespoon lemon juice
½ teaspoon ground coriander
½ teaspoon paprika, plus additional for
    sprinkling on chicken
¼ teaspoon ground ginger
¼ teaspoon cayenne pepper
Pinch ground turmeric
Pinch ground cloves
½ cup plain low-fat yogurt
Salt and pepper
1 chicken (3 to 3½ pounds), rinsed, patted
    dry, and cut into 8 pieces (see "Cutting
    Up a Whole Chicken," page 10)

1. Combine the onion, garlic, lemon juice, spices, yogurt, and salt and pepper to taste in the work bowl of a food processor. Process until smooth.

2. Place the chicken parts in a gallon-size sealable plastic bag; pour the yogurt mixture into the bag, seal, and turn several times to coat the chicken. Refrigerate for 1 hour.

3. Preheat the oven to 425 degrees. Place a rack in a large roasting pan and transfer the chicken, skin side up, to the rack. Remove excess yogurt mixture with a brush. Sprinkle the chicken parts with additional paprika and lightly season with salt and pepper.

4. Roast the parts until the juices run clear, 30 to 35 minutes for the legs and wings, 40 to 45 minutes for breasts and thighs. Remove the legs and wings to a plate when cooked through, and cover with foil to keep warm; remove the breasts and thighs when cooked through, and serve.

SAUTEED CHICKEN CUTLETS

/|\

BONELESS, SKINLESS CHICKEN BREASTS ARE A

WORKHORSE INGREDIENT IN THE CONTEMPORARY

AMERICAN KITCHEN. THE REASONS FOR THEIR POP-

ULARITY ARE OBVIOUS: PREPARATION TIME IS MINI-

MAL SINCE BUTCHERING HAS BEEN DONE IN THE

STORE; COOKING TIME IS MINIMAL; AND THEY WORK

much like pasta as a canvas open to any number of possible interpretations and variations.

Boneless, skinless breasts tend to be a bit bland. Thus, we find that cutlets need boldly flavored sauces. Sautéing also helps since it promotes caramelization and the formation of a nicely browned crust.

In our testing, we found that there are several keys to correctly sautéing boneless chicken breasts, but one is paramount: there must be enough heat. Home cooks often shy away from the smoke and spatters that can accompany high heat. But a thin, delicate food like boneless chicken breast must be cooked through quickly. Sautéing over low or even moderate heat pushes the meat's moisture to the surface before any browning can occur. Once the juices hit the pan, the meat will not brown at all, unless it is cooked for a long, long time. Furthermore, these juices provide the moisture in such a lean piece of meat; expel them, and the result is a tough, leathery piece of meat. Our aim is a tender, juicy cutlet with a crisp crust. Only high heat can accomplish these two goals.

There are several other points to bear in mind. Before the cutlets go into the pan, the excess fat must be trimmed. If the tendon is especially large or prominent, we recommend that you remove it since it may become tough when cooked. It's also a good idea to rinse off the meat (to remove any off flavors) and then to dry the chicken thoroughly with paper towels.

The next step is to salt and pepper the chicken generously; we use a full teaspoon of salt for four cutlets (each whole boneless breast from one chicken yields two cutlets). We then recommend that you flour the cutlets. Flouring the chicken helps reduce spitting and spattering of the fat when the chicken is cooking because the flour absorbs any excess water on the surface of the cutlets; floured cutlets are also less likely to stick. Finally, flouring the cutlets promotes a crisper crust that is so thick and dark it actually resembles skin.

Once the chicken is floured, it's imperative to get the cutlets into the hot pan quickly or the flour coating will become soggy. We recommend a heavy skillet that measures at least 9 inches across the bottom. (For more information, see "Buying a Good Skillet," page 54.) We recommend using both butter (for flavor and browning of the meat) and oil (which will keep smoking and burning under control). Three tablespoons of

PREPARING CUTLETS FOR SAUTEING

1. Lay each cutlet tenderloin side down and smooth the top with your fingers. Any fat will slide to the periphery, where it is easy to see; trim it with a knife.

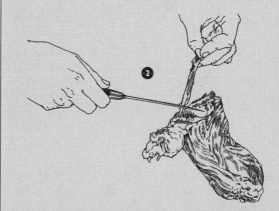

2. To remove the tough, white tendon, turn the cutlet tenderloin side up and peel back the thick half of the tenderloin so it lies top down on the work surface. Use the point of a paring knife to cut around the tip of the tendon to expose it, then scrape the tendon free with the knife.

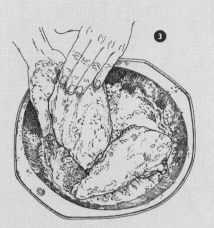

3. When flouring, make sure that the tenderloin is tucked beneath and fused to the main portion of the breast.

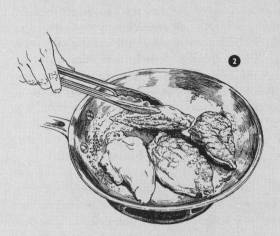

2. Use tongs to turn the cutlets after the bottoms are browned, about 4 minutes. Do not use a fork; it will pierce the meat and cause juices to escape.

SAUTEING CUTLETS

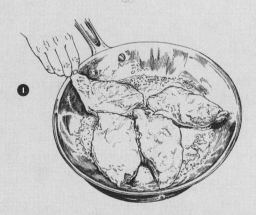

1. To avoid being splashed with hot fat when putting chicken cutlets into the pan, lay them in thick side first, hanging on to the tapered end until the whole cutlet is in the pan. The tapered ends of the cutlets should be at the edges of the pan where the heat is less intense.

SLICING COOKED CUTLETS

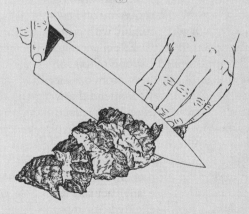

To make an eye-pleasing presentation with a simply sautéed chicken cutlet, use a chef's knife to cut the breast on the bias, cutting all the way through the breast. Arrange the segments in a fan shape, spreading them out on the plate around a central axis.

fat (half butter, half oil) is needed to brown the cutlets uniformly in a skillet that measures 9 inches across. If your skillet is larger, use 4 tablespoons of fat to maintain the same depth (about ⅛ inch) of fat in the pan.

Whatever you do, don't skimp on the fat at this point. You can make a lower-fat pan sauce, but without this much fat for cooking, the meat will steam and not brown properly. That's because the surface of the cutlet is irregular and the fat must be deep enough to ensure that the entire cutlet is cooking in fat. If you want to cook your cutlets using less fat, try other techniques like grilling or baking.

With your fat in the pan, turn the heat all the way to high. The butter will foam, and possibly sputter as the moisture boils out. As soon as the butter becomes fragrant and starts to darken (the color will be pale brown and resemble roasted peanuts), quickly lay the cutlets into the pan, with the thinner tenderloins facing down and the tapered ends of the cutlets at the edges of the pan where the heat is not quite as intense.

Keep the heat at the same level so that it sizzles briskly but does not quite smoke. Expect quite a bit of spattering, so wear a long-sleeved shirt or a large oven mitt. When cutlets are browned on the first side (after about four minutes), use a pair of tongs to turn the meat. (A fork will pierce the cutlets and cause juices to be lost.) When the thickest part of the cutlet feels firm (not squishy) when pressed and clotted juices appear at the crack between the tenderloin and top of the meat, the chicken is cooked through. (You can always cut into the cutlets, but you will lose some juices. Or, slide an instant-read thermometer diagonally into the thickest part of the cutlet; it should register 160 degrees.) Transfer the cooked cutlets to a plate and place them in a warm oven while you make a pan sauce.

Almost any liquid (stock, wine, juice, vinegar) can be used to deglaze the pan. The liquid should loosen the browned bits; use a wooden spoon to help the process along. Other ingredients, anything from garlic to fresh herbs to mustard, can also be added. When the sauce has reduced to a nice thick consistency, we like to swirl in some butter to further enrich it and give it more body. (Swirl in the butter with a wooden spoon off heat so that the butter does not curdle and separate.) Transfer the cutlets to individual plates, spoon a little sauce over each, and serve immediately.

Sautéed Chicken Cutlets

SERVES 4

IGH HEAT IS THE key to proper caramelization of the exterior crust. Be prepared for a fair amount of spattering. After the cutlets are nicely browned on both sides, place them on a plate in a warm oven and use the drippings to make a quick pan sauce. The breasts may be served whole with sauce spooned over them or sliced and fanned over some sauce (see figure on page 51).

> Salt and pepper
> 4 chicken breast cutlets (1½ pounds), trimmed of fat and tendons removed (see figures 1 and 2, page 50); rinsed and thoroughly dried
> ¼ cup all-purpose flour
> 1½ tablespoons unsalted butter
> 1½ tablespoons neutral vegetable oil or olive oil

1. Preheat the oven at the lowest possible temperature. Place a plate in the oven for keeping the cooked cutlets warm while making a sauce.

2. Sprinkle 1 teaspoon salt and ¼ to ½ teaspoon pepper on both sides of the cutlets. Measure the flour onto a plate or pie tin. Working with one cutlet at a time, press both sides into the flour. Make sure the tenderloin is tucked beneath and fused to the main portion of the breast (see figure 3, page 51). Pick up the cutlet from the tapered end; shake gently to remove excess flour.

3. Heat the butter and oil in a heavy-bottomed skillet measuring at least 9 inches across the bottom. Swirl the skillet over high heat until the butter has melted. Continue to heat until the butter stops foaming and has just begun to color. Lay the cutlets in the skillet, tenderloin side down and tapered ends pointing out (see figure 1, page 51).

4. Maintain medium-high heat, so the fat sizzles but does not smoke, and sauté the cutlets until browned on one side, about 4 minutes. Turn the cutlets with tongs (see figure 2, page 51); cook on other side until meat feels firm when pressed and clotted juices begin to emerge around tenderloin, 3 to 4 minutes. Transfer the cutlets to the plate in the oven; keep warm until ready to serve.

◆

Sautéed Chicken Cutlets with Wine and Shallots

WINE AND SHALLOTS ARE A CLASSIC PAN SAUCE COMBINATION. THE PARSLEY AND LEMON JUICE ADD FRESHNESS AND COLOR. SERVES 4.

> Salt and pepper
> 4 chicken breast cutlets (about 1½ pounds), trimmed of fat and tendons removed (see page 50); rinsed and thoroughly dried
> ¼ cup all-purpose flour
> 4½ tablespoons unsalted butter, softened
> 1½ tablespoons olive oil
> 2 medium garlic cloves, minced
> 1 medium shallot, minced
> 1 cup dry white wine
> 3 tablespoons fresh lemon juice
> ¼ cup minced fresh parsley leaves

1. Preheat the oven at the lowest possible temperature. Place a plate in the oven for keeping the cooked cutlets warm while making a sauce.

2. Sprinkle 1 teaspoon salt and ¼ to ½ teaspoon pepper on both sides of the cutlets. Measure the flour onto a plate or pie tin. Working with one cutlet at a time, press both sides into the flour. Make sure the tenderloin is tucked beneath and fused to the main portion of the breast. Pick up the cutlet from the tapered end; shake gently to remove excess flour.

3. Heat 1½ tablespoons butter and the oil in a heavy-bottomed skillet measuring at least 9 inches across the bottom. Swirl the skillet over high heat until the butter has melted. Continue to heat until the butter stops foaming and has just begun to color. Lay the cutlets in the skillet, tenderloin side down and tapered ends pointing out.

4. Maintain medium-high heat, so the fat sizzles but does not smoke, and sauté the cutlets until browned on one side, about 4 minutes. Turn the cutlets with tongs; cook on other side until meat feels firm when pressed and clotted juices begin to emerge around tenderloin, 3 to 4 minutes. Transfer cutlets to the plate in the oven; keep warm until ready to serve.

5. Without discarding the fat, set the skillet over medium heat. Add the garlic and shallot; sauté until softened, about 1 minute. Increase the heat to high, add the wine and lemon juice, and scrape the skillet bottom with a wooden spatula or spoon to loosen the browned bits. Boil until the liquid reduces to about ⅓ cup, about 3 minutes. Add any accumulated chicken juices; reduce the sauce again to ⅓ cup. Add the parsley and season to taste with salt and pepper. Off the heat, swirl in the remaining 3 tablespoons butter until it melts and thickens the sauce. Spoon the sauce over the cutlets; serve immediately.

BUYING A GOOD SKILLET

A GOOD SKILLET IS ESPECIALLY IMPORTANT WHEN SAUTEING OVER HIGH HEAT. WHEN DEVELOPING THE MASTER RECIPE FOR SAUTEED CHICKEN CUTLETS, WE TRIED SEVERAL TYPES OF PANS. ALTHOUGH NONSTICK AND ENAMEL-COATED PANS WORKED FINE, WE FOUND THAT A BARE METAL SURFACE (EITHER STAIN-

less steel or anodized aluminum) created the darkest, crispest crust. Cast-iron is not recommended when making pan sauces since acidic ingredients (like wine, vinegar, or tomatoes) can react with the pan and pick up some metallic flavor.

So how do you buy an all-purpose skillet for sautéing? There are a number of general factors to consider. First is size. For this recipe (and many others), a large pan that measures at least 9 inches across the bottom is needed to comfortably hold enough meat to serve four. Second, pick up the pan. It should not be especially light (a sign of poor construction that will likely lead to hot spots) or overly heavy (many copper and cast-iron pans are difficult to lift when filled, and swirling butter in them is never very easy). We find that a large skillet should weigh about 3 pounds. In any case, avoid lightweight pans that register less than 2 pounds.

The handle is also another matter of concern. Solid metal handles will often heat up quite quickly. Wooden, plastic, or hollowed-out metal handles should do a better job of diffusing heat. We generally prefer the hollowed-out or rolled metal handles since these skillets can still go into the oven or under the broiler.

The final consideration is the material used to construct the pan surface. With the exception of pricey copper, aluminum is the most conductive metal used to make cookware. It is also lightweight and cheap. However, untreated aluminum is quite soft and prone to dents and scratching. Some companies subject aluminum to a process called anodization, which strengthens the metal and eliminates its reactive properties, which otherwise can cause off flavors in acidic sauces. These surfaces are generally quite dark (almost black) and do not provide the ideal surface against which to judge how dark a sauce is becoming. However, this is a fairly minor quibble.

We also like stainless steel skillets. They look good, are usually quite durable, and provide a reflective surface against which to view sauces. However, stainless steel is a poor conductor of heat. Most stainless steel pans have a layer of conductive aluminum on the bottom of the pan. Even better are "clad" pans, where the aluminum layer runs across the bottom and completely up the sides, and is sandwiched between an inner and outer layer of stainless steel. This construction promotes the best heating, reduces hot spots, and makes cleanup easy.

Sautéed Chicken Cutlets with Lemon-Caper Sauce

SMALL CAPERS MAY BE LEFT WHOLE FOR THIS QUICK PAN SAUCE. IF USING LARGER CAPERS, CHOP THEM COARSELY. SERVES 4.

Salt and pepper
4 chicken breast cutlets (about 1 1/2 pounds), trimmed of fat and tendons removed (see page 50); rinsed and thoroughly dried
1/4 cup all-purpose flour
4 1/2 tablespoons unsalted butter, softened
1 1/2 tablespoons olive oil
1 shallot or scallion, white and light green parts only, minced
1 cup chicken stock or low-sodium canned broth
1/4 cup fresh lemon juice
2 tablespoons drained small capers

1. Preheat the oven at the lowest possible temperature. Place a plate in the oven for keeping the cooked cutlets warm while making a sauce.

2. Sprinkle 1 teaspoon salt and 1/4 to 1/2 teaspoon pepper on both sides of the cutlets. Measure the flour onto a plate or pie tin. Working with one cutlet at a time, press both sides into the flour. Make sure the tenderloin is tucked beneath and fused to the main portion of the breast. Pick up the cutlet from the tapered end; shake gently to remove excess flour.

3. Heat 1 1/2 tablespoons butter and the oil in a heavy-bottomed skillet measuring at least 9 inches across the bottom. Swirl the skillet over high heat until the butter has melted. Continue to heat until the butter stops foaming and has just begun to color. Lay the cutlets in the skillet, tenderloin side down and tapered ends pointing out.

4. Maintain medium-high heat, so the fat sizzles but does not smoke, and sauté the cutlets until browned on one side, about 4 minutes. Turn the cutlets with tongs; cook on other side until meat feels firm when pressed and clotted juices begin to emerge around tenderloin, 3 to 4 minutes. Transfer cutlets to the plate in the oven; keep warm until ready to serve.

5. Without discarding the fat, set the skillet over medium heat. Add the shallot; sauté until softened, about 1 minute. Increase the heat to high, add the stock, and scrape the skillet bottom with a wooden spatula or spoon to loosen the browned bits. Add the lemon juice and capers; boil until the liquid reduces to about 1/3 cup, 3 to 4 minutes. Add any accumulated chicken juices; reduce the sauce again to 1/3 cup. Off the heat, swirl in the remaining 3 tablespoons butter until it melts and thickens the sauce. Spoon the sauce over the cutlets; serve immediately.

◆

Sautéed Chicken Cutlets with Mushrooms, Garlic, and Balsamic Vinegar

THE TANGY, SLIGHTLY SWEET FLAVOR OF BALSAMIC VINEGAR ENLIVENS THIS BASIC GARLIC AND MUSH-ROOM PAN SAUCE. CREMINI MUSHROOMS ARE OUR FIRST CHOICE, BUT ANY FRESH MUSHROOMS, INCLUD-ING WHITE BUTTONS, ARE FINE IN THIS DISH. SERVES 4.

Salt and pepper
4 chicken breast cutlets (about 1 1/2 pounds), trimmed of fat and tendons removed (see page 50); rinsed and thoroughly dried
1/4 cup all-purpose flour
4 1/2 tablespoons unsalted butter, softened
1 1/2 tablespoons olive oil
6 medium garlic cloves, peeled and crushed
1/2 pound fresh mushrooms, ends trimmed and sliced thin (about 2 1/2 cups)
1/4 cup balsamic vinegar
3/4 cup chicken stock or low-sodium canned broth
1/2 teaspoon minced fresh thyme leaves or 1/4 teaspoon dried

(continued on next page)

1. Preheat the oven at the lowest possible temperature. Place a plate in the oven for keeping the cooked cutlets warm while making a sauce.

2. Sprinkle 1 teaspoon salt and ¼ to ½ teaspoon pepper on both sides of the cutlets. Measure the flour onto a plate or pie tin. Working with one cutlet at a time, press both sides into the flour. Make sure the tenderloin is tucked beneath and fused to the main portion of the breast. Pick up the cutlet from the tapered end; shake gently to remove excess flour.

3. Heat 1½ tablespoons butter and the oil in a heavy-bottomed skillet measuring at least 9 inches across the bottom. Swirl the skillet over high heat until the butter has melted. Continue to heat until the butter stops foaming and has just begun to color. Lay the cutlets in the skillet, tenderloin side down and tapered ends pointing out.

4. Maintain medium-high heat, so the fat sizzles but does not smoke, and sauté the cutlets until browned on one side, about 4 minutes. Turn the cutlets with tongs; cook on other side until meat feels firm when pressed and clotted juices begin to emerge around tenderloin, 3 to 4 minutes. Transfer cutlets to the plate in the oven; keep warm until ready to serve.

5. Without discarding the fat, set the skillet over medium heat. Add the garlic cloves; sauté until golden, 1 to 2 minutes. Increase the heat to high, add the mushrooms, and cook, stirring frequently, until golden brown, 2 to 3 minutes. Add the vinegar, stock, and dried thyme (if using). Scrape the skillet bottom with a wooden spatula or spoon to loosen the browned bits. Boil until the liquid reduces to ⅓ cup, 3 to 4 minutes. Season to taste with salt and pepper. Off the heat, add the fresh thyme (if using) and swirl in the remaining 3 tablespoons butter until it melts and thickens the sauce. Discard the garlic cloves. Spoon the sauce over the cutlets; serve immediately.

Sautéed Chicken Cutlets with Marsala

LIKE SHERRY, MARSALA IS A FORTIFIED WINE THAT CAN BE SWEET OR DRY. MARSALA ORIGINATED IN ITALY BUT IS NOW MADE IN CALIFORNIA AS WELL. ANY DECENT MARSALA WILL WORK IN THIS RECIPE, BUT TRY TO AVOID THOSE THAT ARE OVERLY SWEET. THE WINE SHOULD GIVE THE SAUCE A DISTINCTIVE (NOT CLOYING) SWEETNESS AND THICK, SYRUPY CONSISTENCY. **SERVES 4.**

> Salt and pepper
> 4 chicken breast cutlets (about 1½ pounds), trimmed of fat and tendons removed (see page 50); rinsed and thoroughly dried
> ¼ cup all-purpose flour
> 4½ tablespoons unsalted butter, softened
> 1½ tablespoons olive oil
> 1 cup Marsala wine

1. Preheat the oven at the lowest possible temperature. Place a plate in the oven for keeping the cooked cutlets warm while making a sauce.

2. Sprinkle 1 teaspoon salt and ¼ to ½ teaspoon pepper on both sides of the cutlets. Measure the flour onto a plate or pie tin. Working with one cutlet at a time, press both sides into the flour. Make sure the tenderloin is tucked beneath and fused to the main portion of the breast. Pick up the cutlet from the tapered end; shake gently to remove excess flour.

3. Heat 1½ tablespoons butter and the oil in a heavy-bottomed skillet measuring at least 9 inches across the bottom. Swirl the skillet over high heat until the butter has melted. Continue to heat until the butter stops foaming and has just begun to color. Lay the cutlets in the skillet, tenderloin side down and tapered ends pointing out.

4. Maintain medium-high heat, so the fat sizzles but does not smoke, and sauté the cutlets until browned on one side, about 4 minutes. Turn the cutlets with tongs; cook on other side until meat feels firm when pressed and clotted juices begin to emerge around tenderloin, 3 to 4 minutes. Transfer cutlets to the plate in the oven; keep warm until ready to serve.

5. Without discarding the fat, set the skillet over high heat. Add the wine and scrape the skillet bottom with a wooden spatula or spoon to loosen the browned bits. Boil until the liquid reduces to about 1/3 cup, 2 to 3 minutes. Off the heat, swirl in the remaining 3 tablespoons butter until it melts and thickens the sauce. Season to taste with salt and pepper. Spoon the sauce over the cutlets; serve immediately.

◆

Sautéed Chicken Cutlets with Oaxacan-Style Sauce

GROUND CINNAMON AND CLOVES GIVE THIS SPICY MEXICAN SAUCE A WARM, EARTHY FLAVOR. CRUSHED PINEAPPLE, GREEN OLIVES, CURRANTS, AND TOMATOES CREATE A COMPLEX MIXTURE OF SWEET, SALTY, AND ACIDIC ELEMENTS. SERVE WITH STEAMED WHITE RICE. SERVES 4.

Salt and pepper
4 chicken breast cutlets (about 1 1/2 pounds), trimmed of fat and tendons removed (see page 50); rinsed and thoroughly dried
1/4 cup all-purpose flour
1 1/2 tablespoons unsalted butter
1 1/2 tablespoons olive oil
1 small onion, minced
2 large or 3 small jalapeño chiles, stemmed, seeded, and minced
2 garlic cloves, minced
1/2 teaspoon ground cinnamon
1/4 teaspoon (scant) ground cloves
1/2 cup chicken stock or low-sodium canned broth
1 tablespoon cider vinegar
1/2 cup unsweetened crushed pineapple, undrained
1/3 cup pimiento-stuffed green olives, sliced thin
1/4 cup currants or chopped raisins
1/4 cup canned crushed tomatoes

1 1/2 tablespoons minced fresh cilantro leaves
3 tablespoons pine nuts, toasted (optional)

1. Preheat the oven at the lowest possible temperature. Place a plate in the oven for keeping the cooked cutlets warm while making a sauce.

2. Sprinkle 1 teaspoon salt and 1/4 to 1/2 teaspoon pepper on both sides of the cutlets. Measure the flour onto a plate or pie tin. Working with one cutlet at a time, press both sides into the flour. Make sure the tenderloin is tucked beneath and fused to the main portion of the breast. Pick up the cutlet from the tapered end; shake gently to remove excess flour.

3. Heat the butter and oil in a heavy-bottomed skillet measuring at least 9 inches across the bottom. Swirl the skillet over high heat until the butter has melted. Continue to heat until the butter stops foaming and has just begun to color. Lay the cutlets in the skillet, tenderloin side down and tapered ends pointing out.

4. Maintain medium-high heat, so the fat sizzles but does not smoke, and sauté the cutlets until browned on one side, about 4 minutes. Turn the cutlets with tongs; cook on other side until meat feels firm when pressed and clotted juices begin to emerge around tenderloin, 3 to 4 minutes. Transfer the cutlets to the plate in the oven; keep warm until ready to serve.

5. Without discarding the fat, set the skillet over medium heat. Add the onion and jalapeños and sauté until softened, about 1 minute. Stir in the garlic, cinnamon, and cloves and cook until the garlic softens, about 30 seconds longer. Add the stock and vinegar and bring the mixture to a boil, scraping the bottom of the skillet with a wooden spoon to incorporate the browned bits. Increase the heat to high, add the pineapple, olives, currants, and tomatoes, and boil the sauce, stirring until thick, about 3 minutes.

6. Return the cutlets to the pan and spoon the sauce over the cutlets. Cover and let the cutlets stand over very low heat to blend the flavors, about 5 minutes. Adjust the seasonings; transfer the cutlets to a plate, spoon the sauce over the cutlets, and sprinkle with the cilantro and optional pine nuts; serve immediately.

Sautéed Chicken Cutlets with Arugula

THE PEPPERY FLAVOR OF ARUGULA IS MELLOWED BY BLANCHING, AND BY THE ADDITION OF CREAM TO THE SAUCE. SERVES 4.

2 bunches arugula, stemmed and washed
Salt and pepper
4 chicken breast cutlets (about 1½ pounds), trimmed of fat and tendons removed (see page 50); rinsed and thoroughly dried
¼ cup all-purpose flour
1½ tablespoons unsalted butter
1½ tablespoons olive oil
1 medium shallot, minced
½ cup dry white wine
½ cup heavy cream

1. Bring several quarts of water to a boil in a medium saucepan. Add the arugula and cook until tender, 2 to 3 minutes. Drain well and squeeze dry with paper towels. Finely chop the arugula and set it aside.

2. Preheat the oven at the lowest possible temperature. Place a plate in the oven for keeping the cooked cutlets warm while making a sauce.

3. Sprinkle 1 teaspoon salt and ¼ to ½ teaspoon pepper on both sides of the cutlets. Measure the flour onto a plate or pie tin. Working with one cutlet at a time, press both sides into the flour. Make sure the tenderloin is tucked beneath and fused to the main portion of the breast. Pick up the cutlet from the tapered end; shake gently to remove excess flour.

4. Heat the butter and oil in a heavy-bottomed skillet measuring at least 9 inches across the bottom. Swirl the skillet over high heat until the butter has melted. Continue to heat until the butter stops foaming and has just begun to color. Lay the cutlets in the skillet, tenderloin side down and tapered ends pointing out.

5. Maintain medium-high heat, so the fat sizzles but does not smoke, and sauté the cutlets until browned on one side, about 4 minutes. Turn the cutlets with tongs; cook on other side until meat feels firm when pressed and clotted juices begin to emerge around tenderloin, 3 to 4 minutes. Transfer the cutlets to the plate in the oven; keep warm until ready to serve.

6. Without discarding the fat, set the skillet over medium heat. Add the shallot; sauté until softened, about 1 minute. Increase the heat to high, add the wine, and scrape the skillet bottom with a wooden spatula or spoon to loosen the browned bits. Add the cream. Boil until the sauce is reduced by about half, 2 to 3 minutes. Stir in the arugula and salt and pepper to taste. Spoon the sauce over the cutlets. Serve immediately.

◆

Sautéed Chicken Cutlets with Citrus Sauce

FRESH-SQUEEZED ORANGE AND LIME JUICES ARE REDUCED TO A SYRUPY SAUCE HERE. A LITTLE DIJON MUSTARD TEMPERS THE SWEETNESS OF THE FRUIT JUICES. SERVES 4.

Salt and pepper
4 chicken breast cutlets (about 1½ pounds), trimmed of fat and tendons removed (see page 50); rinsed and thoroughly dried
¼ cup all-purpose flour
4½ tablespoons unsalted butter
1½ tablespoons olive oil
2 medium garlic cloves, peeled and crushed
½ cup chicken stock or low-sodium canned broth
¼ cup fresh lime juice
1 cup fresh orange juice
1 tablespoon Dijon mustard
1 teaspoon minced fresh thyme leaves or ½ teaspoon dried

1. Preheat the oven at the lowest possible temperature. Place a plate in the oven for keeping the cooked cutlets warm while making a sauce.

2. Sprinkle 1 teaspoon salt and ¼ to ½ teaspoon pepper on both sides of the cutlets. Measure the flour onto a plate or pie tin. Working with one cutlet at a time, press both sides into the flour. Make sure the tenderloin is tucked beneath and fused to the main portion of the breast. Pick up the cutlet from the tapered end; shake gently to remove excess flour.

3. Heat 1½ tablespoons butter and the oil in a heavy-bottomed skillet measuring at least 9 inches across the bottom. Swirl the skillet over high heat until the butter has melted. Continue to heat until the butter stops foaming and has just begun to color. Lay the cutlets in the skillet, tenderloin side down and tapered ends pointing out.

4. Maintain medium-high heat, so the fat sizzles but does not smoke, and sauté the cutlets until browned on one side, about 4 minutes. Turn the cutlets with tongs; cook on other side until meat feels firm when pressed and clotted juices begin to emerge around tenderloin, 3 to 4 minutes. Transfer the cutlets to the plate in the oven; keep warm until ready to serve.

5. Without discarding the fat, set the skillet over medium heat. Add the garlic; sauté until golden, about 1 minute. Increase the heat to high, add the stock, and scrape the skillet bottom with a wooden spatula or spoon to loosen the browned bits. Add the juices, mustard, and dried thyme (if using); boil until the liquid reduces to about ⅓ cup, 4 to 5 minutes. Add any accumulated chicken juices; reduce the sauce again to ⅓ cup. Season to taste with salt and pepper. Off the heat, stir in the fresh thyme (if using) and swirl in the remaining 3 tablespoons butter until it melts and thickens sauce. Discard the garlic. Spoon the sauce over the cutlets. Serve immediately.

Sautéed Chicken Cutlets with Cilantro Sauce

BASIL OR PARSLEY MAY BE SUBSTITUTED FOR A MORE MUTED, BUT STILL DELICIOUS, SAUCE. **SERVES 4.**

> Salt and pepper
> 4 chicken breast cutlets (about 1½ pounds), trimmed of fat and tendons removed (see page 50); rinsed and thoroughly dried
> ¼ cup all-purpose flour
> 4½ tablespoons unsalted butter
> 1½ tablespoons olive oil
> 1 small onion, minced
> ¾ cup chicken stock or low-sodium canned broth
> ½ cup dry white wine
> ⅓ cup minced fresh cilantro leaves

1. Preheat the oven at the lowest possible temperature. Place a plate in the oven for keeping the cooked cutlets warm while making a sauce.

2. Sprinkle 1 teaspoon salt and ¼ to ½ teaspoon pepper on both sides of the cutlets. Measure the flour onto a plate or pie tin. Working with one cutlet at a time, press both sides into the flour. Make sure the tenderloin is tucked beneath and fused to the main portion of the breast. Pick up the cutlet from the tapered end; shake gently to remove excess flour.

3. Heat 1½ tablespoons butter and the oil in a heavy-bottomed skillet measuring at least 9 inches across the bottom. Swirl the skillet over high heat until the butter has melted. Continue to heat until the butter stops foaming and has just begun to color. Lay the cutlets in the skillet, tenderloin side down and tapered ends pointing out.

4. Maintain medium-high heat, so the fat sizzles but does not smoke, and sauté the cutlets until browned on one side, about 4 minutes. Turn the cutlets with tongs; cook on other side until meat feels firm when pressed and clotted juices begin to emerge around

(continued on next page)

tenderloin, 3 to 4 minutes. Transfer the cutlets to the plate in the oven; keep warm until ready to serve.

5. Without discarding the fat, set the skillet over medium heat. Add the onion; sauté until softened, 2 to 3 minutes. Increase the heat to high, add the stock and wine, and scrape the skillet bottom with a wooden spatula or spoon to loosen the browned bits. Boil until the liquid reduces to about ⅓ cup, 3 to 4 minutes. Stir in the cilantro and season to taste with salt and pepper. Off the heat, swirl in the remaining 3 tablespoons of butter. Spoon the sauce over the cutlets; serve immediately.

◆

Sautéed Chicken Cutlets with Rice Wine and Szechwan Peppercorn Sauce

SZECHWAN PEPPERCORNS, AVAILABLE AT ASIAN GROCERY STORES, CAN BE PURCHASED WHOLE, TOASTED FOR SEVERAL MINUTES IN A SKILLET, AND GROUND IN A COFFEE MILL OR SPICE GRINDER. THEY ARE ALSO AVAILABLE ALREADY GROUND IN THE SPICE SECTION OF MANY GOURMET STORES AND SUPERMARKETS. THEY HAVE A FLORAL, LESS SHARP FLAVOR THAN BLACK PEPPERCORNS. LOOK FOR RICE WINE IN ASIAN GROCERY STORES. MANY SUPERMARKETS ALSO STOCK THIS ITEM. SERVES 4.

Salt and pepper
4 chicken breast cutlets (about 1½ pounds), trimmed of fat and tendons removed (see page 50); rinsed and thoroughly dried
¼ cup all-purpose flour
4½ tablespoons unsalted butter
1½ tablespoons peanut oil or vegetable oil
1 tablespoon ground Szechwan peppercorns
2 whole scallions, chopped
½ cup chicken stock or low-sodium canned broth
½ cup rice wine

1. Preheat the oven at the lowest possible temperature. Place a plate in the oven for keeping the cooked cutlets warm while making a sauce.

2. Sprinkle 1 teaspoon salt and ¼ to ½ teaspoon pepper on both sides of the cutlets. Measure the flour onto a plate or pie tin. Working with one cutlet at a time, press both sides into the flour. Make sure the tenderloin is tucked beneath and fused to the main portion of the breast. Pick up the cutlet from the tapered end; shake gently to remove excess flour.

3. Heat 1½ tablespoons butter and the oil in a heavy-bottomed skillet measuring at least 9 inches across the bottom. Swirl the skillet over high heat until the butter has melted. Continue to heat until the butter stops foaming and has just begun to color. Lay the cutlets in the skillet, tenderloin side down and tapered ends pointing out.

4. Maintain medium-high heat, so the fat sizzles but does not smoke, and sauté the cutlets until browned on one side, about 4 minutes. Turn the cutlets with tongs; cook on other side until meat feels firm when pressed and clotted juices begin to emerge around tenderloin, 3 to 4 minutes. Transfer the cutlets to the plate in the oven; keep warm until ready to serve.

5. Without discarding the fat, set the skillet over medium heat. Add the Szechwan pepper and scallions; sauté until the scallions are fragrant, about 1 minute. Increase the heat to high, add the stock, and scrape the skillet bottom with a wooden spatula or spoon to loosen the browned bits. Add the rice wine; boil until the liquid reduces to about ⅓ cup, 3 to 4 minutes. Add any accumulated chicken juices; reduce the sauce again to ⅓ cup. Season to taste with salt. Off the heat, swirl in the remaining 3 tablespoons butter until it melts and thickens sauce. Spoon the sauce over the cutlets and serve immediately.

Sautéed Chicken Cutlets
with Sweet-and-Sour Pan Sauce

THIS CLASSIC ASIAN SWEET-AND-SOUR SAUCE COM-
BINES DARK BROWN SUGAR AND WHITE VINEGAR. A LIT-
TLE HOT RED PEPPER, SOY SAUCE, AND ANCHOVY
PASTE KEEP THE SWEETNESS IN CHECK BY ADDING
SPICY AND SALTY FLAVORS. SERVES 4.

> Salt and pepper
> 4 chicken breast cutlets (about 1 1/2
>   pounds), trimmed of fat and tendons
>   removed (see page 50); rinsed and
>   thoroughly dried
> 1/4 cup all-purpose flour
> 1 1/2 tablespoons unsalted butter
> 1 1/2 tablespoons peanut oil or vegetable oil
> 2 large garlic cloves, minced
> 2 teaspoons minced fresh gingerroot
> 1/4 teaspoon hot red pepper flakes
> 1/4 cup firmly packed dark brown sugar
> 1/4 cup distilled white vinegar
> 2 tablespoons soy sauce
> 1/2 teaspoon anchovy paste or Thai or
>   Vietnamese fish sauce
> 4 whole scallions, sliced thin

1. Preheat the oven at the lowest possible temperature. Place a plate in the oven for keeping the cooked
cutlets warm while making a sauce.

2. Sprinkle 1 teaspoon salt and 1/4 to 1/2 teaspoon
pepper on both sides of the cutlets. Measure the flour
onto a plate or pie tin. Working with one cutlet at a
time, press both sides into the flour. Make sure the
tenderloin is tucked beneath and fused to the main
portion of the breast. Pick up the cutlet from the
tapered end; shake gently to remove excess flour.

3. Heat the butter and oil in a heavy-bottomed skillet
measuring at least 9 inches across the bottom. Swirl
the skillet over high heat until the butter has melted.
Continue to heat until the butter stops foaming and
has just begun to color. Lay the cutlets in the skillet,
tenderloin side down and tapered ends pointing out.

4. Maintain medium-high heat, so the fat sizzles but
does not smoke, and sauté the cutlets until browned
on one side, about 4 minutes. Turn the cutlets with
tongs; cook on other side until meat feels firm when
pressed and clotted juices begin to emerge around
tenderloin, 3 to 4 minutes. Transfer the cutlets to the
plate in the oven; keep warm until ready to serve.

5. While the chicken is cooking, place the garlic, ginger, and hot pepper flakes on a cutting board; mince
them further to pulverize the pepper.

6. Without draining the fat, return the skillet to
medium heat; add the garlic mixture and sauté until
softened, about 1 minute. Increase the heat to high;
add the sugar, vinegar, soy sauce, anchovy paste, and
any accumulated pan juices; boil, stirring to loosen the
browned bits from the pan bottom, until the mixture
thickens to a light syrup, less than 1 minute. Pour the
sauce over the chicken cutlets, scatter the scallions on
top, and serve immediately.

◆

Sautéed Chicken Cutlets
with Fresh Tomatoes and Tarragon

THIS FRESH TOMATO TOPPING REQUIRES LESS BUTTER
THAN A TRADITIONAL PAN SAUCE. AN EQUAL AMOUNT
OF WHITE WINE VINEGAR, ALONG WITH 1 TABLE-
SPOON MINCED FRESH TARRAGON, COULD BE SUBSTI-
TUTED FOR TARRAGON VINEGAR. SERVES 4.

> Salt and pepper
> 4 chicken breast cutlets (about 1 1/2
>   pounds), trimmed of fat and tendons
>   removed (see page 50); rinsed and
>   thoroughly dried
> 1/4 cup all-purpose flour
> 1 1/2 tablespoons unsalted butter
> 1 1/2 tablespoons vegetable oil
> 1 medium shallot, minced
> 2 medium-large tomatoes (about 1 pound),
>   cored, seeded, and chopped (about 2 cups)
> 1/4 cup tarragon vinegar
> 2 tablespoons minced fresh parsley leaves

(continued on next page)

1. Preheat the oven at the lowest possible temperature. Place a plate in the oven for keeping the cooked cutlets warm while making a sauce.

2. Sprinkle 1 teaspoon salt and ¼ to ½ teaspoon pepper on both sides of the cutlets. Measure the flour onto a plate or pie tin. Working with one cutlet at a time, press both sides into the flour. Make sure the tenderloin is tucked beneath and fused to the main portion of the breast. Pick up the cutlet from the tapered end; shake gently to remove excess flour.

3. Heat the butter and oil in a heavy-bottomed skillet measuring at least 9 inches across the bottom. Swirl the skillet over high heat until the butter has melted. Continue to heat until the butter stops foaming and has just begun to color. Lay the cutlets in the skillet, tenderloin side down and tapered ends pointing out.

4. Maintain medium-high heat, so the fat sizzles but does not smoke, and sauté the cutlets until browned on one side, about 4 minutes. Turn the cutlets with tongs; cook on other side until meat feels firm when pressed and clotted juices begin to emerge around tenderloin, 3 to 4 minutes. Transfer the cutlets to the plate in the oven; keep warm until ready to serve.

5. Without discarding the fat, set the skillet over medium heat. Add the shallot and sauté until softened, about 1 minute. Stir in the tomatoes. Increase the heat to high and cook, stirring frequently, until the tomatoes have given up most of their juice, forming a lumpy puree, about 2 minutes. Add the vinegar and any accumulated chicken juices; boil the sauce until thick enough to mound slightly in a spoon, about 1 minute. Stir in the parsley and season to taste with salt and pepper. Spoon the sauce over the cutlets and serve immediately.

Sautéed Chicken Cutlets with Snow Peas and Shiitake Mushrooms

THIS DISH BORROWS THE FLAVORS OF A TRADITIONAL CHINESE STIR-FRY BUT HAS A RICHER FLAVOR, THANKS TO THE ADDED BUTTER AND WINE, AND A MORE ELEGANT PRESENTATION. SERVES 4.

Salt and pepper
4 chicken breast cutlets (about 1½ pounds), trimmed of fat and tendons removed (see page 50); rinsed and thoroughly dried
¼ cup all-purpose flour
4½ tablespoons unsalted butter
1½ tablespoons vegetable oil
2 whole scallions, chopped
1 small garlic clove, minced
1 tablespoon minced fresh gingerroot
1 cup stemmed and sliced shiitake mushrooms
1 cup snow peas
1 tablespoon soy sauce
1 cup chicken stock or low-sodium canned chicken broth
¼ cup dry white wine
2 teaspoons toasted sesame seeds

1. Preheat the oven at the lowest possible temperature. Place a plate in the oven for keeping the cooked cutlets warm while making a sauce.

2. Sprinkle 1 teaspoon salt and ¼ to ½ teaspoon pepper on both sides of the cutlets. Measure the flour onto a plate or pie tin. Working with one cutlet at a time, press both sides into the flour. Make sure the tenderloin is tucked beneath and fused to the main portion of the breast. Pick up the cutlet from the tapered end; shake gently to remove excess flour.

3. Heat 1½ tablespoons butter and the oil in a heavy-bottomed skillet measuring at least 9 inches across the bottom. Swirl the skillet over high heat until the butter has melted. Continue to heat until the butter stops foaming and has just begun to color. Lay the cutlets in the skillet, tenderloin side down and tapered ends pointing out.

4. Maintain medium-high heat, so the fat sizzles but does not smoke, and sauté the cutlets until browned on one side, about 4 minutes. Turn the cutlets with tongs; cook on other side until meat feels firm when pressed and clotted juices begin to emerge around tenderloin, 3 to 4 minutes. Transfer the cutlets to the plate in the oven; keep warm until ready to serve.

5. Without discarding the fat, set the skillet over medium heat. Add the scallions, garlic, and ginger; sauté until fragrant, about 1 minute. Increase heat to high, add the mushrooms, and sauté until soft, 2 to 3 minutes. Add the snow peas and sauté 2 more minutes. Add the soy sauce, stock, and wine; boil until the liquid reduces to about ½ cup, 4 to 5 minutes. Off the heat, swirl in the remaining 3 tablespoons butter until it melts and thickens sauce. Season to taste with salt and pepper. Spoon the sauce over the cutlets, sprinkle with the sesame seeds, and serve immediately.

◆

Sautéed Chicken Cutlets with Tomato-Basil-Caper Sauce

BUTTERED ORZO MAKES AN EXCELLENT SIDE DISH FOR THIS ITALIAN-INSPIRED PAN SAUCE. SERVES 4.

Salt and pepper
4 chicken breast cutlets (about 1½ pounds), trimmed of fat and tendons removed (see page 50); rinsed and thoroughly dried
¼ cup all-purpose flour
1½ tablespoons unsalted butter
1½ tablespoons vegetable oil
2 to 3 shallots or scallions, minced (about ⅓ cup)
3 large garlic cloves, minced
2 medium-large tomatoes (about 1 pound), cored, seeded, and chopped (about 2 cups)
¼ cup dry white wine or 3 tablespoons dry vermouth
2 tablespoons drained small capers
2 tablespoons shredded fresh basil leaves

1. Preheat the oven at the lowest possible temperature. Place a plate in the oven for keeping the cooked cutlets warm while making a sauce.

2. Sprinkle 1 teaspoon salt and ¼ to ½ teaspoon pepper on both sides of the cutlets. Measure the flour onto a plate or pie tin. Working with one cutlet at a time, press both sides into the flour. Make sure the tenderloin is tucked beneath and fused to the main portion of the breast. Pick up the cutlet from the tapered end; shake gently to remove excess flour.

3. Heat the butter and oil in a heavy-bottomed skillet measuring at least 9 inches across the bottom. Swirl the skillet over high heat until the butter has melted. Continue to heat until the butter stops foaming and has just begun to color. Lay the cutlets in the skillet, tenderloin side down and tapered ends pointing out.

4. Maintain medium-high heat, so the fat sizzles but does not smoke, and sauté the cutlets until browned on one side, about 4 minutes. Turn the cutlets with tongs; cook on other side until meat feels firm when pressed and clotted juices begin to emerge around tenderloin, 3 to 4 minutes. Transfer the cutlets to the plate in the oven; keep warm until ready to serve.

5. Without discarding the fat, set the skillet over medium heat. Add the shallots and sauté until softened, about 1 minute. Stir in the garlic and tomatoes. Increase the heat to high and cook, stirring frequently, until the tomatoes have given up most of their juices, forming a lumpy puree, about 2 minutes. Add the wine, capers, and any accumulated chicken juices; boil until thick enough to mound slightly in a spoon, about 2 minutes. Stir in the basil and season with salt and pepper. Spoon the sauce over the cutlets and serve immediately.

Sautéed Chicken Cutlets with Sherry-Cream Mushroom Sauce

WHITE WINE, CHAMPAGNE, PORT, OR MADEIRA CAN BE SUBSTITUTED FOR THE SHERRY IN THIS CLASSIC CHICKEN SAUTÉ. THE MACE CAN BE REPLACED WITH A PINCH OF NUTMEG, IF DESIRED. ANY FRESH MUSHROOMS, INCLUDING WHITE BUTTONS, ARE FINE IN THIS DISH. SERVES 4.

Salt and pepper
4 chicken breast cutlets (about 1½ pounds), trimmed of fat and tendons removed (see page 50); rinsed and thoroughly dried
¼ cup all-purpose flour
1½ tablespoons unsalted butter, softened
1½ tablespoons olive oil
2 shallots or scallions, minced (about ¼ cup)
½ pound fresh mushrooms, stems trimmed and sliced thin (about 2½ cups)
⅓ cup sherry, preferably cream or amontillado
½ cup chicken stock or low-sodium canned broth
1 cup heavy cream
2 tablespoons minced fresh parsley leaves
Pinch ground mace
1 small lemon wedge

1. Preheat the oven at the lowest possible temperature. Place a plate in the oven for keeping the cooked cutlets warm while making a sauce.

2. Sprinkle 1 teaspoon salt and ¼ to ½ teaspoon pepper on both sides of the cutlets. Measure the flour onto a plate or pie tin. Working with one cutlet at a time, press both sides into the flour. Make sure the tenderloin is tucked beneath and fused to the main portion of the breast. Pick up the cutlet from the tapered end; shake gently to remove excess flour.

3. Heat the butter and oil in a heavy-bottomed skillet measuring at least 9 inches across the bottom. Swirl the skillet over high heat until the butter has melted. Continue to heat until the butter stops foaming and has just begun to color. Lay the cutlets in the skillet, tenderloin side down and tapered ends pointing out.

4. Maintain medium-high heat, so the fat sizzles but does not smoke, and sauté the cutlets until browned on one side, about 4 minutes. Turn the cutlets with tongs; cook on other side until meat feels firm when pressed and clotted juices begin to emerge around tenderloin, 3 to 4 minutes. Transfer the cutlets to the plate in the oven; keep warm until ready to serve.

5. Without discarding the fat, set the skillet over medium heat. Add the shallots; sauté until softened, about 1 minute. Increase the heat to high, add the mushrooms and sauté until golden brown, 2 to 3 minutes. Add the sherry; boil until the sherry completely evaporates, about 1 minute. Add the stock and cream; boil, stirring frequently, until the sauce reduces to about ⅔ cup and is thick enough to lightly coat a spoon, 5 to 6 minutes. Add any accumulated chicken juices; reduce the sauce to its previous consistency. Stir in the parsley and mace and season to taste with salt, pepper, and a few drops of lemon juice. Spoon the sauce over the cutlets and serve immediately.

◆

Sautéed Chicken Cutlets with Mustard and Green Peppercorns

GREEN PEPPERCORNS CAN BE PURCHASED FREEZE-DRIED OR PACKED IN BRINE—EITHER TYPE CAN BE USED IN THIS RECIPE. IF YOU USE BRINED PEPPERCORNS, THOUGH, BE SURE TO RINSE THE SALT FROM THEM AND BE CAREFUL NOT TO OVERSALT THE FINISHED SAUCE. SERVES 4.

Salt and pepper
4 chicken breast cutlets (about 1½ pounds), trimmed of fat and tendons removed (see page 50); rinsed and thoroughly dried
¼ cup all-purpose flour
1½ tablespoons unsalted butter, softened
1½ tablespoons olive oil
2 medium garlic cloves, sliced thin

½ cup chicken stock or low-sodium
  canned broth
½ cup dry white wine
¼ cup heavy cream
1 tablespoon grainy mustard
1 tablespoon green peppercorns
1 tablespoon minced fresh parsley leaves

1. Preheat the oven at the lowest possible temperature. Place a plate in the oven for keeping the cooked cutlets warm while making a sauce.

2. Sprinkle 1 teaspoon salt and ¼ to ½ teaspoon pepper on both sides of the cutlets. Measure the flour onto a plate or pie tin. Working with one cutlet at a time, press both sides into the flour. Make sure the tenderloin is tucked beneath and fused to the main portion of the breast. Pick up the cutlet from the tapered end; shake gently to remove excess flour.

3. Heat the butter and oil in a heavy-bottomed skillet measuring at least 9 inches across the bottom. Swirl the skillet over high heat until the butter has melted. Continue to heat until the butter stops foaming and has just begun to color. Lay the cutlets in the skillet, tenderloin side down and tapered ends pointing out.

4. Maintain medium-high heat, so the fat sizzles but does not smoke, and sauté the cutlets until browned on one side, about 4 minutes. Turn the cutlets with tongs; cook on other side until meat feels firm when pressed and clotted juices begin to emerge around tenderloin, 3 to 4 minutes. Transfer the cutlets to the plate in the oven; keep warm until ready to serve.

5. Without discarding the fat, set the skillet over medium heat. Add the garlic; sauté until softened, about 1 minute. Increase the heat to high, add the stock and wine, and scrape the skillet bottom with a wooden spatula or spoon to loosen the browned bits. Add the cream and mustard; boil until the liquid reduces to about ⅓ cup, 3 to 5 minutes. Add any accumulated chicken juices; reduce the sauce again to ⅓ cup. Stir in the green peppercorns and parsley. Season to taste with salt. Spoon the sauce over the cutlets and serve immediately.

Sautéed Chicken Cutlets
with Apples

SAUTEED AND CARAMELIZED APPLES ARE STIRRED INTO THIS PAN SAUCE FLAVORED WITH CIDER VINEGAR. CRUNCHY VARIETIES LIKE GRANNY SMITH SHOULD BE USED BECAUSE THEY WILL NOT FALL APART IN COOKING. SERVES 4.

2½ tablespoons unsalted butter
3 firm apples (Granny Smith or Golden
  Delicious), peeled, cored, and cut into
  ¼-inch-thick slices
1 tablespoon sugar
Salt and pepper
4 chicken breast cutlets (about 1½
  pounds), trimmed of fat and tendons
  removed (see page 50); rinsed and
  thoroughly dried
¼ cup all-purpose flour
1½ tablespoons vegetable oil
1 small onion, finely chopped
¼ cup cider vinegar
¾ cup chicken stock or low-sodium
  canned broth
2 tablespoons heavy cream

1. Melt 1 tablespoon butter in a heavy-bottomed skillet measuring at least 9 inches across bottom. Swirl the skillet over medium heat until the butter has melted. Add the apples and sauté, stirring occasionally, until softened, 5 to 7 minutes. Sprinkle apples with sugar, raise heat to high, and cook until lightly browned, shaking the pan often to make sure the apples don't stick, about 2 minutes. Remove apples with a slotted spoon to a plate and set aside.

2. Preheat the oven at the lowest possible temperature. Place a plate in the oven for keeping the cooked cutlets warm while making a sauce.

3. Sprinkle 1 teaspoon salt and ¼ to ½ teaspoon pepper on both sides of the cutlets. Measure the flour onto a plate or pie tin. Working with one cutlet at a time, press both sides into the flour. Make sure the

(continued on next page)

tenderloin is tucked beneath and fused to the main portion of the breast. Pick up the cutlet from the tapered end; shake gently to remove excess flour.

4. Heat the remaining 1½ tablespoons butter and the oil in empty skillet. Swirl the skillet over high heat until the butter has melted. Continue to heat until the butter stops foaming and has just begun to color. Lay the cutlets in the skillet, tenderloin side down and tapered ends pointing out.

5. Maintain medium-high heat, so the fat sizzles but does not smoke, and sauté the cutlets until browned on one side, about 4 minutes. Turn the cutlets with tongs; cook on other side until meat feels firm when pressed and clotted juices begin to emerge around tenderloin, 3 to 4 minutes. Transfer the cutlets to the plate in the oven; keep warm until ready to serve.

6. Without discarding the fat, set the skillet over medium heat. Add the onion; sauté until softened, about 2 minutes. Increase the heat to high, add the vinegar and stock, and scrape the skillet bottom with a wooden spatula or spoon to loosen the browned bits. Stir in the cream. Boil until the sauce reduces to about ⅔ cup, 3 to 4 minutes. Season with salt. Add the apple slices and cook until thoroughly heated, about 1 minute. Spoon the sauce over the cutlets and serve immediately.

◆

Sautéed Chicken Cutlets with Fresh Corn

ALTHOUGH FROZEN CORN CAN BE SUBSTITUTED, FRESH CORN IS GENERALLY SWEETER AND ADDS MORE TEXTURE AND FLAVOR TO THIS RECIPE. TO SAFELY AND EASILY REMOVE KERNELS FROM AN EAR OF CORN, STAND THE EAR ON END AND SLICE DOWNWARD WITH A CHEF'S KNIFE. CHIVES OR CHERVIL ALSO GO WELL WITH CORN AND CAN REPLACE THE PARSLEY, IF DESIRED. SERVES 4.

REMOVING KERNELS FROM AN EAR OF CORN

Holding an ear of corn in an upright position, slice the corn kernels from the cob.

Salt and pepper

4 chicken breast cutlets (about 1½ pounds), trimmed of fat and tendons removed (see page 50); rinsed and thoroughly dried

¼ cup all-purpose flour

1½ tablespoons unsalted butter, softened

1½ tablespoons olive oil

1 medium shallot, minced

½ cup chicken stock or low-sodium canned broth

½ cup dry white wine

Kernels from 1 large ear of corn (about ½ cup; see figure, above) or ½ cup frozen corn kernels

1 tablespoon Dijon mustard

¼ cup heavy cream

2 tablespoons chopped fresh parsley leaves

1. Preheat the oven at the lowest possible temperature. Place a plate in the oven for keeping the cooked cutlets warm while making a sauce.

2. Sprinkle 1 teaspoon salt and ¼ to ½ teaspoon pepper on both sides of the cutlets. Measure the flour onto a plate or pie tin. Working with one cutlet at a time, press both sides into the flour. Make sure the tenderloin is tucked beneath and fused to the main portion of the breast. Pick up the cutlet from the tapered end; shake gently to remove excess flour.

3. Heat the butter and oil in a heavy-bottomed skillet measuring at least 9 inches across the bottom. Swirl the skillet over high heat until the butter has melted. Continue to heat until the butter stops foaming and has just begun to color. Lay the cutlets in the skillet, tenderloin side down and tapered ends pointing out.

4. Maintain medium-high heat, so the fat sizzles but does not smoke, and sauté the cutlets until browned on one side, about 4 minutes. Turn the cutlets with tongs; cook on other side until meat feels firm when pressed and clotted juices begin to emerge around tenderloin, 3 to 4 minutes. Transfer the cutlets to the plate in the oven; keep warm until ready to serve.

5. Without discarding the fat, set the skillet over medium heat. Add the shallot; sauté until softened, about 1 minute. Increase the heat to high, add the stock, and scrape the skillet bottom with a wooden spatula or spoon to loosen the browned bits. Add the wine. Bring to a boil. Stir in the corn and mustard. Add the cream and boil, stirring frequently, until the sauce thickens and reduces to about ⅔ cup, 3 or 4 minutes. Stir in the parsley and season with salt and pepper to taste. Spoon the sauce over the cutlets and serve immediately.

Sautéed Chicken Cutlets with Peach Salsa

A SIMPLE FRESH PEACH SALSA FLAVORED WITH CUCUMBER, TOMATO, RED ONION, JALAPEÑO CHILE, AND LIME JUICE IS AN EXCELLENT ACCOMPANIMENT TO SAUTEED CHICKEN CUTLETS. THE SALSA MAY BE MADE WELL IN ADVANCE OF SERVING. USE NECTARINES IN PLACE OF THE PEACHES, IF DESIRED. SERVES 4.

2 small peaches, peeled and cut into small dice (about 1 cup)
½ large cucumber, seeded and cut into small dice (about ⅔ cup)
1 plum tomato, cored, seeded, and cut into small dice (about ¼ cup)
2 tablespoons chopped red onion
1 serrano or jalapeño chile, stemmed, seeded, and minced
4 teaspoons fresh lime juice
Salt and pepper
4 chicken breast cutlets (about 1½ pounds), trimmed of fat and tendons removed (see page 50); rinsed and thoroughly dried
¼ cup all-purpose flour
1½ tablespoons unsalted butter, softened
1½ tablespoons vegetable oil
1 cup chicken stock or low-sodium canned broth
2 teaspoons fresh lemon or lime juice

1. Mix the peaches, cucumber, tomato, red onion, chile, and 4 teaspoons lime juice in a medium bowl. (The salsa may be covered and refrigerated up to 24 hours.) Shortly before serving, season the salsa with ¼ teaspoon salt or to taste; set it aside at room temperature.

2. Preheat the oven at the lowest possible temperature. Place a plate in the oven for keeping the cooked cutlets warm while making a sauce.

3. Sprinkle 1 teaspoon salt and ¼ to ½ teaspoon pepper on both sides of the cutlets. Measure the flour

(continued on next page)

onto a plate or pie tin. Working with one cutlet at a time, press both sides into the flour. Make sure the tenderloin is tucked beneath and fused to the main portion of the breast. Pick up the cutlet from the tapered end; shake gently to remove excess flour.

4. Heat the butter and oil in a heavy-bottomed skillet measuring at least 9 inches across the bottom. Swirl the skillet over high heat until the butter has melted. Continue to heat until the butter stops foaming and has just begun to color. Lay the cutlets in the skillet, tenderloin side down and tapered ends pointing out.

5. Maintain medium-high heat, so the fat sizzles but does not smoke, and sauté the cutlets until browned on one side, about 4 minutes. Turn the cutlets with tongs; cook on other side until meat feels firm when pressed and clotted juices begin to emerge around tenderloin, 3 to 4 minutes. Transfer the cutlets to the plate in the oven; keep warm until ready to serve.

6. Pour off any remaining fat, set the skillet over high heat; add the stock and boil until it reduces to ⅓ cup, scraping up the browned bits from the pan bottom. Add any accumulated chicken juices and reduce the sauce to its previous consistency; stir in the lemon juice. Spoon the pan sauce over the chicken. Spoon the salsa alongside the chicken and serve immediately.

Breaded Sautéed Chicken Cutlets

SERVES 4

FOR THIS RECIPE, chicken cutlets pounded to a thickness of ½ inch are floured, dipped in beaten egg, and then coated with bread crumbs. Of course, if you can buy thin cutlets, skip the pounding step. A combination of oil and butter ensures crispness and great flavor. These thin cutlets can be used in sandwiches or sliced and fanned (see figure on page 51) over a salad or bed of cooked greens. Unlike unbreaded cutlets, they can be packed for picnics and served at room temperature.

1 large egg
1 tablespoon water
½ cup dry bread crumbs, preferably homemade

4 chicken breast cutlets (about 1 1/2
  pounds), trimmed of fat and tendons
  removed (see page 50); rinsed and
  thoroughly dried
Salt and pepper
1/4 cup all-purpose flour
1 1/2 tablespoons unsalted butter
1 1/2 tablespoons olive oil

1. Whisk the egg with the water in a small, flat bowl. Measure the bread crumbs onto a plate or pie tin.

2. If necessary, pound the chicken cutlets to a thickness of 1/2 inch (see figure on page 71). Sprinkle 1 teaspoon salt and 1/4 to 1/2 teaspoon pepper on both sides of the cutlets. Measure the flour onto a plate or pie tin. Working with one cutlet at a time, press both sides into the flour. Make sure the tenderloin is tucked beneath and fused to the main portion of the breast. Pick up the cutlet from the tapered end; shake gently to remove excess flour. Dip the cutlet in the egg; then press both sides into the bread crumbs. Place the cutlet on a plate, tenderloin side down, and lightly press it with your fingertips to ensure that the crumbs adhere to the surface of the cutlet.

3. Heat the butter and oil in a heavy-bottomed skillet measuring at least 9 inches across the bottom. Swirl the skillet over medium-high heat until the butter has melted. Continue to heat until the butter stops foaming but has not begun to color. Lay the cutlets in the skillet, tenderloin side down and tapered ends pointing out.

4. Maintain medium-high heat, so the fat sizzles but does not smoke, and sauté the cutlets until golden brown and crispy on one side, about 3 minutes. Check the underside of the cutlets once or twice to make sure they're not coloring too quickly. If they look very brown, lower the heat slightly. Turn the cutlets with tongs; lower heat to medium and cook on other side until meat feels firm when pressed, about 3 minutes. Serve immediately or transfer the cutlets to a plate in a warm oven until ready to serve. (Cutlets may be refrigerated for up to 1 day. Bring to room temperature before serving.)

Lemon and Herb-Crusted Chicken Cutlets

IN THIS SIMPLE VARIATION ON BASIC BREADED CUT-LETS, LEMON JUICE IS ADDED TO THE EGG, AND HERBS TO THE BREAD CRUMBS, FOR EXTRA FLAVOR. LEMON AND HERB CUTLETS, LIKE PLAIN BREADED ONES, ARE GOOD IN SALADS AND SANDWICHES. SERVES 4.

1 large egg
1 tablespoon fresh lemon juice
1/2 cup dry bread crumbs, preferably
  homemade
1 tablespoon chopped fresh herbs (dill,
  tarragon, marjoram, oregano, and/or
  thyme)
4 chicken breast cutlets (about 1 1/2
  pounds), trimmed of fat and tendons
  removed (see page 50); rinsed and
  thoroughly dried
Salt and pepper
1/4 cup all-purpose flour
1 1/2 tablespoons unsalted butter
1 1/2 tablespoons olive oil

1. Whisk the egg with the lemon juice in a small, flat bowl. Measure the bread crumbs onto a plate or pie tin; stir in herbs.

2. If necessary, pound the chicken cutlets to a thickness of 1/2 inch (see figure on page 71). Sprinkle 1 teaspoon salt and 1/4 to 1/2 teaspoon pepper on both sides of the cutlets. Measure the flour onto a plate or pie tin. Working with one cutlet at a time, press both sides into the flour. Make sure the tenderloin is tucked beneath and fused to the main portion of the breast. Pick up the cutlet from the tapered end; shake gently to remove excess flour. Dip the cutlet in the egg and lemon mixture; then press both sides into the herbed bread crumbs. Place the cutlet on a plate, tenderloin side down, and lightly press it with your fingertips to ensure that the crumbs adhere to the surface of the cutlet.

(continued on next page)

3. Heat the butter and oil in a heavy-bottomed skillet measuring at least 9 inches across the bottom. Swirl the skillet over medium-high heat until the butter has melted. Continue to heat until the butter stops foaming but has not begun to color. Lay the cutlets in the skillet, tenderloin side down and tapered ends pointing out.

4. Maintain medium-high heat, so the fat sizzles but does not smoke, and sauté the cutlets until golden brown and crispy on one side, about 3 minutes. Check the underside of the cutlets once or twice to make sure they're not coloring too quickly. If they look very brown, lower the heat slightly. Turn the cutlets with tongs; lower heat to medium, and cook on other side until meat feels firm when pressed, about 3 minutes. Serve immediately or transfer the cutlets to a plate in a warm oven until ready to serve. (Cutlets may be refrigerated for up to 1 day. Bring to room temperature before serving.)

◆

Chicken Milanese

IN THIS VARIATION, GRATED PARMESAN IS ADDED TO THE BREAD CRUMBS FOR A CLASSIC ITALIAN FLAVOR. A SIMPLE SQUEEZE OF LEMON JUICE IS ALL THAT IS NEEDED TO GARNISH THE CUTLETS. **SERVES 4.**

- 1 large egg
- 1 tablespoon water
- ⅓ cup dry bread crumbs, preferably homemade
- ⅓ cup grated Parmesan cheese
- 4 chicken breast cutlets (about 1½ pounds), trimmed of fat and tendons removed (see page 50); rinsed and thoroughly dried
- Salt and pepper
- ¼ cup all-purpose flour
- 1½ tablespoons unsalted butter
- 1½ tablespoons olive oil
- 1 lemon, cut into 8 wedges

1. Whisk the egg with the water in a small, flat bowl. Measure the bread crumbs and cheese onto a plate or pie tin and stir to combine.

2. If necessary, pound the chicken cutlets to a thickness of ½ inch (see figure on page 71). Sprinkle 1 teaspoon salt and ¼ to ½ teaspoon pepper on both sides of the cutlets. Measure the flour onto a plate or pie tin. Working with one cutlet at a time, press both sides into the flour. Make sure the tenderloin is tucked beneath and fused to the main portion of the breast. Pick up the cutlet from the tapered end; shake gently to remove excess flour. Dip the cutlet in the egg; then press both sides into the bread crumb and cheese mixture. Place the cutlet on a plate, tenderloin side down, and lightly press it with your fingertips to ensure that the crumbs adhere to the surface of the cutlet.

3. Heat the butter and oil in a heavy-bottomed skillet measuring at least 9 inches across the bottom. Swirl the skillet over medium-high heat until the butter has melted. Continue to heat until the butter stops foaming but has not begun to color. Lay the cutlets in the skillet, tenderloin side down and tapered ends pointing out.

4. Maintain medium-high heat, so the fat sizzles but does not smoke, and sauté the cutlets until golden brown and crispy on one side, about 3 minutes. Check the underside of the cutlets once or twice to make sure they're not coloring too quickly. If they look very brown, lower the heat slightly. Turn the cutlets with tongs; lower heat to medium, and cook on other side until meat feels firm when pressed, about 3 minutes. Serve immediately with the lemon wedges or transfer the cutlets to a plate in a warm oven until ready to serve. (Cutlets may be refrigerated for up to 1 day. Bring to room temperature before serving.)

BREADING CHICKEN CUTLETS

CHICKEN CUTLETS MAY BE FLOURED, DIPPED IN LIQUID, COATED WITH BREAD CRUMBS (OR OTHER CRUNCHY COATING), AND THEN SAUTEED. MANY OF THE ISSUES ARE THE SAME AS FOR SAUTEING FLOURED CUTLETS (PAN SIZE, FOR INSTANCE), BUT THERE ARE SOME IMPORTANT DIFFERENCES.

Breaded cutlets tend to burn faster than floured cutlets. We found that cooking breaded cutlets according to our Master Recipe for Sautéed Chicken Cutlets resulted in either burnt coatings or raw centers. It is necessary to modify this recipe to keep the coating from burning before the chicken is completely cooked through. First, the cutlets must be pounded to a thickness of ½ inch or less. A meat pounder or the side of a large chef's knife (see figure) will do this quickly. Second, breaded cutlets should be cooked at a slightly lower temperature than plain floured cutlets. Once they are turned, be especially vigilant about the heat and make sure they do not burn. We found it helpful to add the breaded cutlets to the pan as soon as the fat becomes hot and before the butter starts to color.

When developing our Master Recipe for Breaded Sautéed Chicken Cutlets, we tested a number of different coatings. We found that homemade bread crumbs (take stale bread and simply grind it in a food processor into coarse crumbs) are superior to store-bought. Homemade crumbs are larger and more irregular in shape and promote a crisper crust. As for the liquids, we tested egg, milk, and a combination of egg and milk. Lightly beaten egg (thinned with a table-spoon of water) makes the lightest, most crisp coating. We found that flouring the cutlets first, then dipping them in the egg and the bread crumbs helps keep moisture in the cutlets. Cutlets are best cooked as soon as they are breaded.

POUNDING CUTLETS FOR BREADING

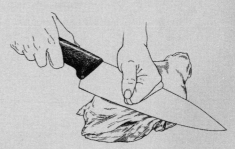

It's possible to pound chicken for breading without a heavy-duty meat pounder or mallet. After trimming fat and removing the tendon, place the breast on a cutting board, tenderloin side down. Lay the side of a large chef's knife on the breast and pound with your fist to flatten the chicken to a thickness of ½ inch. Of course, if you own a meat pounder, use it.

Cornmeal-Crusted Chicken Cutlets

CORNMEAL ADDED TO BREAD CRUMBS GIVES THESE CUTLETS A DOWN-HOME FLAVOR AND CRUNCH. FOR A SPICY COATING, STIR CAYENNE PEPPER TO TASTE IN WITH CORNMEAL AND BREAD CRUMBS. SERVES 4.

- 1 large egg
- 1 tablespoon water
- ¼ cup dry bread crumbs, preferably homemade
- ¼ cup yellow cornmeal
- 4 chicken breast cutlets (about 1½ pounds), trimmed of fat and tendons removed (see page 50); rinsed and thoroughly dried
- Salt and pepper
- ¼ cup all-purpose flour
- 1½ tablespoons unsalted butter
- 1½ tablespoons olive oil

1. Whisk the egg with the water in a small, flat bowl. Measure the bread crumbs and cornmeal onto a plate or pie tin and stir to combine.

2. If necessary, pound the chicken cutlets to a thickness of ½ inch (see figure on page 71). Sprinkle 1 teaspoon salt and ¼ to ½ teaspoon pepper on both sides of the cutlets. Measure the flour onto a plate or pie tin. Working with one cutlet at a time, press both sides into the flour. Make sure the tenderloin is tucked beneath and fused to the main portion of the breast. Pick up the cutlet from the tapered end; shake gently to remove excess flour. Dip the cutlet in the egg; then press both sides into the bread crumb and cornmeal mixture. Place the cutlet on a plate, tenderloin side down, and lightly press it with your fingertips to ensure that the crumbs adhere to the surface of the cutlet.

3. Heat the butter and oil in a heavy-bottomed skillet measuring at least 9 inches across the bottom. Swirl the skillet over medium-high heat until the butter has melted. Continue to heat until the butter stops foaming but has not begun to color. Lay the cutlets in the skillet, tenderloin side down and tapered ends pointing out.

4. Maintain medium-high heat, so the fat sizzles but does not smoke, and sauté the cutlets until golden brown and crispy on one side, about 3 minutes. Check the underside of the cutlets once or twice to make sure they're not coloring too quickly. If they look very brown, lower the heat slightly. Turn the cutlets with tongs (a fork will pierce meat); lower heat to medium and cook on other side until meat feels firm when pressed, about 3 minutes. Serve immediately or transfer the cutlets to a plate in a warm oven until ready to serve. (Cutlets may be refrigerated for up to 1 day. Bring to room temperature before serving.)

BAKED

CHICKEN

CUTLETS

HEALTH CONSIDERATIONS ASIDE, SAUTEING IS OUR

PREFERRED METHOD FOR COOKING A BONELESS,

SKINLESS CHICKEN CUTLET. THE THICK, BROWN

CRUST AND TENDER, JUICY INNER MEAT CANNOT

BE DUPLICATED BY ANY OTHER COOKING METHOD.

Grilling is a good low-fat alternative to sautéing (see chapter 11), but there are no pan juices with which to make a sauce. In many cases, it is the pan sauce that makes bland cutlets worth eating. Of course, these sauces usually add even more fat to the dish.

Since roasting chicken cutlets in the oven is an obvious alternative to grilling, we set out to develop a technique that could be used year-round and that would also give us some precious pan juices. From the start, we knew this would be a tough assignment. Roasting a piece of meat that contains almost no fat has an obvious challenge: how to keep it moist and juicy.

Many traditional recipes for baked chicken cutlets call for lots of butter and cream to keep the meat moist. While this undoubtedly works, the results are generally not as good (the chicken does not brown when it sits in a bath of heavy cream) as similar dishes made on the stove. We think the oven makes sense only when there is a desire to keep the fat content to a minimum.

With that goal in mind, we started testing a number of variables—especially oven temperature and the role of additional ingredients (other than cream) that might keep the chicken moist as it bakes. It was soon apparent that getting the chicken in and out of the oven as quickly as possible is key. The longer the chicken stays in the oven, the drier the meat gets. High oven temperatures (after testing, we settled on a constant 450 degrees) cook the chicken cutlets quickly and prevent dryness. Baking cutlets in a very hot oven also causes some browning to occur, which in turn boosts flavor in what is otherwise a fairly bland piece of meat.

Roasting chicken cutlets at a high temperature is only part of the answer. The meat still tends to dry out a bit, especially where the cutlets are thin or toward the exterior. We needed to give the cutlets enough time to cook through in the center, while protecting the outside layer of meat from becoming too tough and dry. It was clear we needed to add moisture and, yes, a little fat. Brushing the chicken with a little oil (no more than ½ tablespoon per cutlet) helps create the impression of moistness in the outer layer of meat and also promotes better browning. Since cutlets are so bland, we use olive oil to add flavor as well.

Liquids, such as lemon juice, as well as moist vegetables, such as tomatoes and mushrooms, also can help to keep the chicken from becoming tough and dry. Our testing showed that placing the vegetables both underneath and on top of the chicken was the best guarantee of moistness in the end. While the vegetables won't affect the interior of the cutlet, their juices do flavor and moisten the exterior layer, which is so prone to drying out in the oven.

We also found that bold flavorings are essential. Even if the meat is juicy, without seasonings it's not worth eating. Spices, garlic, and herbs all help. With our testing complete, we realized our results had produced an unintended side effect. Roasting chicken with vegetables as a protective measure means that we had created nearly complete meals. With the addition of a leafy salad or a starch, dinner was done.

A related oven-based technique also holds interest for cooks looking for low-fat ways to prepare chicken cutlets. Cooking *en papillote* is a classic French technique for oven-steaming fish, chicken, and vegetables in parchment paper packets. The food cooks in its own juices and stays especially moist. We tested parchment paper and heavy-duty aluminum foil packets and found no difference in the end results. Foil is easier to find and work with, and is our first choice.

Like oven-roasted cutlets, oven-steamed cutlets need a little liquid to keep them juicy. The liquid also becomes an instant sauce when the chicken is cooked. Wine, citrus juices, soy sauces, and moist vegetables like tomatoes are all possible choices. In addition, heavy seasonings and the use of flavorful ingredients (chiles, garlic, and herbs) are necessary to keep oven-steamed chicken from being too bland. No browning or caramelization can occur when chicken is cooked in foil packets, so bold seasonings are a must.

Since the chicken is actually cooking in its own juices (plus a little wine or some other liquid), there is less chance of it drying out than when roasted in an open pan. For this reason, there is no need to obsess about the cooking time. While it is possible to overcook cutlets in foil packets, it's not that easy. Opening up the packets only to find out the chicken is not done releases built-up steam and should be avoided. For this reason, bake the packets for at least twenty minutes (twenty-five minutes if the cutlets are particularly thick). When you bring the packets to the table, you can rest assured that they will be cooked through but still juicy.

Baked Chicken Cutlets

SERVES 4

WITH LEMON, GARLIC, AND rosemary, this dish has the flavors of a classic roast chicken, but cooks in 20 minutes and is very low in fat. Lemon juice provides a little moisture, but be very careful not to overcook these breasts, since they don't have the protection of any vegetables and will dry out if baked too long. These roasted breasts can also be refrigerated for up to 2 days and are best used in salads and sandwiches. As a main course, we prefer the following recipes which combine chicken and vegetables. This recipe, however, outlines the basic technique.

2 tablespoons olive oil
2 tablespoons lemon juice
1 teaspoon chopped fresh rosemary leaves
1 garlic clove, minced very fine
Salt and pepper
4 chicken breast cutlets (1½ pounds), trimmed and tendons removed (see figures 1 and 2, page 50); rinsed and dried

1. Preheat the oven to 450 degrees. Combine the oil, lemon juice, rosemary, garlic, and salt and pepper to taste in a small bowl. Brush the breasts with the mixture and place them in a 13-by-9-inch roasting pan.

2. Roast until the chicken is cooked through, 15 to 20 minutes, turning once and basting with the pan juices. To check for doneness, cut into the thickest part of one of the breasts with a small knife. If there is any hint of pinkness, return the chicken to the oven. Serve immediately or let cool and refrigerate up to 2 days for later use.

◆

Baked Chicken Cutlets with Roasted Onions and Mushrooms

ONIONS AND MUSHROOMS ARE ROASTED FOR 15 MINUTES BEFORE THE CHICKEN IS ADDED TO THE PAN SO THAT THEY BECOME A WELL-CARAMELIZED VEGETABLE ACCOMPANIMENT. **SERVES 4.**

2 medium onions, peeled and sliced thin
10 ounces white button mushrooms, stem ends trimmed and sliced thin
2 tablespoons olive oil
Salt and pepper
2 tablespoons chopped fresh thyme leaves
2 garlic cloves, minced very fine
4 chicken breast cutlets (1½ pounds), trimmed and tendons removed (see page 50); rinsed and dried

1. Preheat the oven to 450 degrees. Combine the onions, mushrooms, olive oil, and salt and pepper to taste in a 13-by-9-inch roasting pan. Roast, stirring once or twice, until the onions begin to brown and the mushrooms give off their juices, about 15 minutes.

2. Combine the thyme, garlic, and salt and pepper to taste in a small bowl. Rub the chicken with the herb mixture.

3. Remove half of the onions and mushrooms from the roasting pan, spread the remaining half across the bottom of the pan, and place the chicken cutlets

(continued on next page)

on top. Cover the chicken with the remaining mushrooms and onions. Roast until the chicken is cooked through, 15 to 20 minutes, basting once or twice with the pan juices. To check for doneness, cut into the thickest part of one of the breasts with a small knife. If there is any hint of pinkness, return the chicken to the oven. Serve immediately.

◆

Baked Chicken Cutlets with Tomatoes and Herbs

TOMATOES UNDERNEATH AND ON TOP OF THE CHICKEN KEEP THIS DISH MOIST BUT LOW IN FAT. CAYENNE PEPPER RUBBED INTO THE BREASTS GIVES THEM SOME HEAT, BUT YOU CAN ELIMINATE IT. FOR AN ASIAN RATHER THAN MEDITERRANEAN FLAVOR, ADD 1 TABLESPOON OF CHOPPED FRESH GINGERROOT TO THE PARSLEY MIXTURE, OMIT THE OREGANO, AND ADD FOUR CHOPPED SCALLIONS TO THE TOMATOES. SERVES 4.

¼ cup chopped fresh parsley leaves
¼ teaspoon cayenne pepper (optional)
2 garlic cloves, minced very fine
Salt and pepper
4 chicken breast cutlets (1½ pounds), trimmed and tendons removed (see page 50); rinsed and dried
2 tablespoons olive oil
½ teaspoon dried oregano
2 cups cored and chopped fresh plum tomatoes (about 6 tomatoes) or drained and chopped canned tomatoes

1. Preheat the oven to 450 degrees. Combine the parsley, cayenne, garlic, and salt and pepper to taste in a small bowl. Rub the chicken all over with the herb mixture.

2. Combine the olive oil, oregano, tomatoes, and salt and pepper to taste in a medium bowl. Spoon half of the tomato mixture into a 13-by-9-inch roasting pan. Place the chicken on top and cover with the remaining tomato mixture. Roast until the chicken is cooked through, 15 to 20 minutes, basting once or twice with the pan juices. To check for doneness, cut into the

thickest part of one of the breasts with a small knife. If there is any hint of pinkness, return the chicken to the oven. Serve immediately.

◆

Baked Chicken Cutlets with Tomatoes and Porcini Mushrooms

DRIED ITALIAN PORCINI MUSHROOMS LEND RICHNESS BUT NOT FAT TO ROASTED CHICKEN BREASTS. A LITTLE OF THEIR SOAKING LIQUID IS ADDED TO THE PAN FOR MOISTURE. ANY OTHER DRIED MUSHROOMS—ESPECIALLY MORELS OR SHIITAKES—MAY BE SUBSTITUTED. SERVES 4.

1 ounce dried porcini mushrooms
¼ cup chopped fresh basil leaves
2 garlic cloves, minced very fine
Salt and pepper
4 chicken breast cutlets (1½ pounds), trimmed and tendons removed (see page 50); rinsed and dried
2 tablespoons olive oil
2 cups cored and chopped fresh plum tomatoes (about 6 tomatoes) or drained and chopped canned tomatoes

1. Place the porcini in a medium bowl and cover with boiling water. Let the mushrooms soak until softened, about 20 minutes. Drain and coarsely chop the mushrooms, reserving the soaking liquid. Strain the soaking liquid through a sieve lined with a paper towel. Reserve ¼ cup strained soaking liquid for this recipe; save the rest for another use.

2. Preheat the oven to 450 degrees. Combine the basil, garlic, and salt and pepper to taste in a small bowl. Rub the chicken all over with the herb mixture.

3. Combine the olive oil, tomatoes, porcini, reserved soaking liquid, and salt and pepper to taste in a medium bowl. Spoon half of the tomato mixture into a 13-by-9-inch roasting pan. Place the chicken on top and cover with the remaining tomato mixture. Roast until the chicken is cooked through, 15 to 20 minutes, basting once or twice with the pan juices. To check for doneness, cut into the thickest part of one of the breasts with a small knife. If there is any hint of pinkness, return the chicken to the oven. Serve immediately.

◆

Baked Chicken Cutlets with Roasted Peppers

IN THIS RECIPE, BELL PEPPERS ARE OVEN-ROASTED FIRST, AND THEN BAKED AGAIN WITH THE CHICKEN. THEY KEEP THE CHICKEN MOIST AND SERVE AS A FLA-VORFUL VEGETABLE ACCOMPANIMENT. **SERVES 4.**

2 red bell peppers, cored, seeded, and cut into ½-inch-thick strips
4 garlic cloves, minced very fine
1 tablespoon olive oil
Salt and pepper
4 chicken breast cutlets (1½ pounds), trimmed and tendons removed (see page 50); rinsed and dried
1 teaspoon chopped fresh thyme leaves or ½ teaspoon dried

1. Preheat the oven to 450 degrees. Combine the bell peppers, garlic, olive oil, and salt and pepper to taste in a 13-by-9-inch roasting pan. Roast, stirring once or twice, until the peppers begin to brown, about 25 minutes.

2. Sprinkle the chicken with the thyme and salt and pepper to taste.

3. Remove half of the peppers from the roasting pan, spread the remaining half across the bottom of the pan, and place the chicken cutlets on top. Cover the chicken with the remaining peppers. Roast until the chicken is cooked through, 15 to 20 minutes, basting once or twice with the pan juices. To check for done-ness, cut into the thickest part of one of the breasts with a small knife. If there is any hint of pinkness, return the chicken to the oven. Serve immediately.

Oven-Fried Chicken Cutlets

UNLIKE OTHER BAKED CUTLETS, THIS RECIPE CALLS FOR NO VEGETABLES OR LIQUID. LIKE REGULAR BONE-IN FRIED CHICKEN, THE CUTLETS ARE DIPPED IN BUTTER-MILK TO GIVE THEM A TANGY FLAVOR AND TO HELP THE CRUST ADHERE. THE BUTTERMILK ALSO HELPS KEEP THE CUTLETS FROM DRYING OUT. WHILE FLOUR MAKES THE BEST COATING WHEN PAN-FRYING OR DEEP-FRYING, OVEN-FRYING REQUIRES SOMETHING CRUNCHIER. WE PREFER SEASONED BREAD CRUMBS. BE SURE TO REFRIG-ERATE THE CHICKEN FOR AT LEAST 30 MINUTES BEFORE BAKING TO ALLOW THE CRUST TO SET. DRIZZLE A LIT-TLE OLIVE OIL ON THE BREASTS RIGHT BEFORE BAKING FOR FLAVOR AND MOISTNESS. **SERVES 4.**

1 cup buttermilk
1 cup plain bread crumbs
¼ teaspoon paprika
¼ teaspoon cayenne pepper
Salt and pepper
Nonstick vegetable oil spray
4 chicken breast cutlets (1½ pounds), trimmed and tendons removed (see page 50); rinsed and dried
1½ tablespoons olive oil

1. Place the buttermilk in a wide soup bowl or pie plate and set it aside. Combine the bread crumbs, paprika, cayenne, and salt and pepper to taste in another wide soup bowl or pie plate. Liberally spray a 13-by-9-inch roasting pan with vegetable oil spray. Dip each cutlet in buttermilk and then dredge in the bread crumb mixture. Place the coated chicken in the roasting pan and refrigerate for at least 30 minutes or up to 2 hours.

2. Preheat the oven to 450 degrees. Drizzle the chicken with the olive oil and roast until the chicken is cooked through and the coating browned, 15 to 20 minutes. To check for doneness, cut into the thickest part of one of the breasts with a small knife. If there is any hint of pinkness, return the chicken to the oven. Serve hot or at room temperature.

Oven-Steamed Chicken Cutlets

SERVES 4

I N THIS AND THE following five recipes, individual portions of chicken and vegetables are wrapped in foil packets and steamed in the oven. Zucchini and green peppercorns are used here, but you can vary the ingredients almost endlessly according to taste and availability. The technique is a variation on the French tradition of cooking *en papillote* (in parchment paper); the steam inside each packet cooks the food, keeps it moist, and mingles the flavors of the ingredients. Although foil is much easier to work with, you can cut out rounds of parchment paper, layer ingredients onto one half of each round, and then fold over the paper and crimp the edges to seal the packets.

2 medium zucchini (about 1/2 pound), sliced into 1/4-inch-thick matchsticks about 2 inches long
4 chicken breast cutlets (1 1/2 pounds), trimmed and tendons removed (see page 50); rinsed and dried
1 teaspoon green peppercorns in brine, rinsed, and crushed with the side of a chef's knife
1 garlic clove, finely chopped
2 tablespoons chopped fresh chives
Salt
1/4 cup white wine
1 teaspoon fresh thyme leaves or 1/2 teaspoon dried

1. Preheat the oven to 450 degrees. Cut 4 pieces of heavy-duty aluminum foil about 12 inches square. Arrange the zucchini on the aluminum foil. Top each portion of zucchini with a chicken cutlet; sprinkle each piece of chicken with some of the peppercorns, garlic, chives, and salt to taste. Spoon 1 tablespoon of wine over each portion and sprinkle with thyme.

2. Bring opposite sides of the foil up to meet over the chicken. Fold the edges together in a 1/4-inch fold, and then fold over 3 more times. Fold the open edges at either end of the packet together in a 1/4-inch fold, and then fold over twice again to seal (see figures 1 through 3).

3. Put the foil packets on a baking sheet and bake for 20 to 25 minutes. Transfer the contents of each packet to a dinner plate and serve.

MAKING FOIL PACKETS

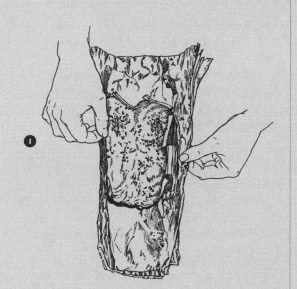

1. Arrange vegetables, seasonings, and chicken cutlets on 4 sheets of heavy-duty aluminum foil, each about 12 inches square. When ready to seal, start by bringing the opposite sides of the foil up to meet over the chicken.

2. Crimp the edges together in a ¼-inch fold, and then fold over 3 more times.

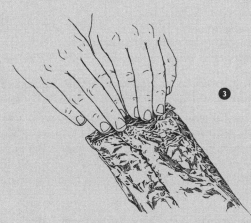

3. Fold the open edges at either end of the packet together in a ¼-inch fold, and then fold over twice again to seal. When opening the packets after baking, take care to keep steam away from your hands and face.

Oven-Steamed Chicken Cutlets with Scallions, Ginger, and Szechwan Peppercorns

IN THIS RECIPE, CHICKEN IS STEAMED OVER A BED OF SCALLIONS. THE DISH IS MADE FRAGRANT BY FRESH GINGER AND WHOLE CRACKED SZECHWAN PEPPERCORNS, AVAILABLE AT ASIAN GROCERIES AND MANY SUPERMARKETS. SERVE WITH WHITE RICE. **SERVES 4**.

24 scallions, washed and tough green parts trimmed
1 (1-inch) piece fresh gingerroot, peeled and sliced thin
4 chicken breast cutlets (1½ pounds), trimmed and tendons removed (see page 50), rinsed and dried
1 teaspoon Szechwan peppercorns, crushed with the side of a chef's knife
1 garlic clove, finely chopped
¼ cup rice wine
2 teaspoons soy sauce
2 tablespoons chopped fresh cilantro leaves

1. Preheat the oven to 450 degrees. Cut 4 pieces of heavy-duty aluminum foil about 12 inches square. Divide the scallions and ginger among the 4 squares. Top each portion of scallions with a chicken cutlet; sprinkle each piece of chicken with some of the peppercorns and garlic. Spoon 1 tablespoon of wine and ½ teaspoon soy sauce over each portion and sprinkle with cilantro.

2. Bring opposite sides of the foil up to meet over the chicken. Fold the edges together in a ¼-inch fold, and then fold over 3 more times. Fold the open edges at either end of the packet together in a ¼-inch fold, and then fold over twice again to seal.

3. Put the foil packets on a baking sheet and bake for 20 to 25 minutes. Transfer the contents of each packet to a dinner plate and serve.

Oven-Steamed Chicken Cutlets with Fennel and Tomatoes

THE FENNEL MUST BE SLICED *VERY* THIN SO THAT IT SOFTENS PROPERLY DURING COOKING. THE TOUCH OF HEAVY CREAM MAKES THE DISH MORE LUXURIOUS, BUT IT CAN BE OMITTED. **SERVES 4**.

1 medium fennel bulb, stems, fronds, and base trimmed; bulb cored and sliced thin (see page 97)
4 plum tomatoes, cored, seeded, and cut into ¼-inch dice (about 1½ cups)
4 chicken breast cutlets (1½ pounds), trimmed and tendons removed (see page 50); rinsed and dried
1 garlic clove, finely chopped
2 tablespoons chopped fresh oregano leaves
Salt and pepper
¼ cup white wine
¼ cup heavy cream (optional)

1. Preheat the oven to 450 degrees. Cut 4 pieces of heavy-duty aluminum foil about 12 inches square. Arrange the fennel and tomatoes on the aluminum foil. Top each portion of vegetables with a chicken cutlet; sprinkle each piece of chicken with some of the garlic, oregano, and salt and pepper to taste. Spoon 1 tablespoon of wine and 1 tablespoon of cream, if using, over each portion.

2. Bring opposite sides of the foil up to meet over the chicken. Fold the edges together in a ¼-inch fold, and then fold over 3 more times. Fold the open edges at either end of the packet together in a ¼-inch fold, and then fold over twice again to seal.

3. Put the foil packets on a baking sheet and bake for 20 to 25 minutes. Transfer the contents of each packet to a dinner plate and serve.

Oven-Steamed Chicken Cutlets with Asparagus and Leeks

STEAMING PRESERVES THE FRESH TASTE AND COLOR OF SPRING VEGETABLES. CHOOSE VERY THIN ASPARAGUS IF YOU CAN. IF ONLY THICK SPEARS ARE AVAILABLE, CUT THEM IN HALF LENGTHWISE BEFORE PACKAGING THEM UP. SERVES 4.

> 24 thin asparagus spears, tough ends snapped off (see figures 1–2, page 263)
> 2 leeks, white parts only, cleaned and cut into 1/8-inch-thick rings
> 4 chicken breast cutlets (1 1/2 pounds), trimmed and tendons removed (see page 50); rinsed and dried
> 1 garlic clove, finely chopped
> 2 tablespoons fresh tarragon leaves
> 1 teaspoon fresh thyme leaves or 1/2 teaspoon dried
> Salt and pepper
> 1/4 cup white wine

1. Preheat the oven to 450 degrees. Cut 4 pieces of aluminum foil about 12 inches square. Arrange the asparagus and leeks on the aluminum foil. Top each portion of vegetables with a chicken cutlet; sprinkle each piece of chicken with some of the garlic, tarragon, thyme, and salt and pepper to taste. Spoon 1 tablespoon of wine over each portion.

2. Bring opposite sides of the foil up to meet over the chicken. Fold the edges together in a 1/4-inch fold, and then fold over 3 more times. Fold the open edges at either end of the packet together in a 1/4-inch fold, and then fold over twice again to seal.

3. Put the foil packets on a baking sheet and bake for 20 to 25 minutes. Transfer the contents of each packet to a dinner plate and serve.

Oven-Steamed Chicken Cutlets with Baby Carrots and Sugar Snap Peas

A BRUSH OF HOISIN SAUCE—A SOY-BASED COMBINATION OF SWEET AND SPICY FLAVORS—IS A QUICK WAY TO ADD FLAVOR TO OVEN-STEAMED CHICKEN. BABY CARROTS ARE JUST THE RIGHT SIZE TO COOK THROUGH ALONG WITH THE CHICKEN CUTLETS. REGULAR CARROTS MAY BE USED IF THEY'RE CUT IN HALF LENGTHWISE AND THEN CUT INTO 2-INCH LENGTHS. SERVES 4.

> 24 baby carrots (about 6 ounces), peeled and trimmed
> 2 cups sugar snap peas (about 8 ounces)
> 1 (1-inch) piece fresh gingerroot, peeled and finely chopped
> 1 garlic clove, finely chopped
> Salt and pepper
> 4 chicken breast cutlets (1 1/2 pounds), trimmed and tendons removed (see page 50); rinsed and dried
> 2 tablespoons hoisin sauce
> 2 tablespoons chopped fresh cilantro leaves

1. Preheat the oven to 450 degrees. Cut 4 pieces of aluminum foil about 12 inches square. Arrange the carrots and peas on the aluminum foil. Sprinkle with the ginger, garlic, and salt and pepper to taste. Brush the chicken on both sides with the hoisin sauce. Top each portion of vegetables with a chicken cutlet. Sprinkle with cilantro.

2. Bring opposite sides of the foil up to meet over the chicken. Fold the edges together in a 1/4-inch fold, and then fold over 3 more times. Fold the open edges at either end of the packet together in a 1/4-inch fold, and then fold over twice again to seal.

3. Put the foil packets on a baking sheet and bake for 20 to 25 minutes. Transfer the contents of each packet to a dinner plate and serve.

Oven-Steamed Chicken Cutlets with Fresh Corn and Chiles

A HIGHLY SPICED MIXTURE OF CORN AND TOMATOES IS A FLAVORFUL BUT LOW-FAT COOKING MEDIUM FOR CHICKEN BREASTS. SWEET, FRESH CORN REMOVED FROM THE COB IS IDEAL, BUT FROZEN MAY BE SUBSTITUTED. SERVES 4.

2 cups fresh (about 4 ears, see figure on
    page 66) or frozen corn kernels
3 plum tomatoes, cored, seeded, and cut
    into ¼-inch dice (about 1⅓ cups)
1 jalapeño or other hot chile, stemmed,
    seeded, and finely chopped
½ teaspoon ground cumin
4 chicken breast cutlets (1½ pounds),
    trimmed and tendons removed (see
    page 50); rinsed and dried
1 garlic clove, finely chopped
2 tablespoons chopped fresh parsley
    leaves
Salt
2 tablespoons fresh lime juice

1. Preheat the oven to 450 degrees. Cut 4 pieces of aluminum foil about 12 inches square. Combine the corn, tomatoes, chile, and cumin in a medium bowl. Spoon the mixture onto the foil. Top each portion of vegetables with a chicken cutlet; sprinkle each piece of chicken with garlic, parsley, and salt to taste. Sprinkle with lime juice.

2. Bring opposite sides of the foil up to meet over the chicken. Fold the edges together in a ¼-inch fold, and then fold over 3 more times. Fold the open edges at either end of the packet together in a ¼-inch fold, and then fold over twice again to seal.

3. Put the foil packets on a baking sheet and bake for 20 to 25 minutes. Transfer the contents of each packet to a dinner plate and serve.

STIR-FRIED
CHICKEN

/|\

TO STIR-FRY PROPERLY YOU NEED PLENTY OF

INTENSE HEAT. THE PAN MUST BE HOT ENOUGH TO

CARAMELIZE SUGARS, DEEPEN FLAVORS, AND EVAPO-

RATE UNNECESSARY JUICES—ALL WITHIN MINUTES.

THE PROBLEM FOR MOST AMERICAN COOKS IS THAT

THE CHINESE WOK AND AMERICAN STOVETOP ARE

A LOUSY MATCH THAT GENERATE MODERATE HEAT AT

BEST. ◆ WOKS ARE CONICAL BECAUSE IN CHINA THEY

traditionally rest in cylindrical pits containing the fire. Food is cut into small pieces to shorten cooking time, thus conserving fuel. Only one vessel is required for many different cooking methods, including sautéing (stir-frying), steaming, boiling, and deep-frying.

Unfortunately, what is practical in China makes no sense in America. A wok was not designed for stovetop cooking, where heat comes only from the bottom. On an American stove, the bottom of the wok gets hot but the sides are warm. We have found that a horizontal heat source requires a horizontal pan. Therefore, for stir-frying at home, we recommend a large skillet, 12 to 14 inches in diameter, with a nonstick coating. Some cookware companies have begun to make flat-bottomed woks with greater horizontal surface area. They are better than traditional round-bottomed woks, but still not as a good as a large flat skillet.

American stoves require still other adjustments. In China, intense flames lick the bottom and sides of a wok, heating the whole surface to extremely high temperatures. Conventional stoves simply don't have enough British Thermal Units (BTUs) to heat any pan (a wok or flat skillet) as well. American cooks must accommodate the lower horsepower on their stoves. Throw everything into the pan at one time and the ingredients will steam and stew, not stir-fry.

One school of thought suggests blanching all vegetables so that they are merely heated through in the pan with the other stir-fry ingredients. We find this precooking to be burdensome and reserve it only for vegetables that require it, such as broccoli and asparagus. We prefer to cut vegetables quite small and then add them in batches to the pan based on their cooking times. By adding a small volume of food at a time, the heat in the pan does not dissipate.

When the vegetables are done, the aromatics (scallions, ginger, and garlic) are briefly cooked and then the seared chicken is added back to the pan along with the sauce. The result is a complete meal perfect for weeknight dinners that takes into account the realities of cooking in an American kitchen.

Plain white rice is our preferred accompaniment to a highly seasoned stir-fry. However, if you like, you may serve any of the stir-fries in this chapter with rice pilaf, pan-seared noodles, or even orzo that has been tossed with a little peanut oil.

Stir-Fried Chicken

SERVES 4

IF YOU CAN FIND boneless, skinless thighs (or want to bone and skin thighs yourself), go ahead and use this tasty dark meat. Thighs should be cut into 1-inch pieces for stir-frying. You may use a regular 12- or 14-inch skillet or a 12-inch Dutch oven in place of the recommended nonstick skillet, but be prepared to use slightly more oil. See figures on pages 86–87 for a step-by-step illustration of the stir-fry technique.

¾ pound boneless, skinless chicken breast cut into ½-inch-wide strips no longer than 1½ to 2 inches (see figures 1–3, page 86)
1 tablespoon soy sauce
1 tablespoon dry sherry
2 to 4 tablespoons peanut or vegetable oil
1½ pounds prepared vegetables, cut into small pieces and divided into several batches based on cooking times
2 tablespoons minced scallions, white parts only
1 tablespoon minced garlic
1 tablespoon minced fresh gingerroot
1 recipe from Ten Sauces for Stir-Fry (pages 92–94)

1. Toss the chicken with the soy sauce and sherry in a medium bowl; set aside for 15 minutes, tossing once or twice (see page 86).

2. Heat a 12- or 14-inch skillet over high heat for 3 to 4 minutes. The pan should be so hot you can hold an outstretched hand 1 inch over the pan for only 3 seconds (see page 86). Add 1 tablespoon oil and swirl it so the oil evenly coats the bottom of the pan. Heat the oil until it just starts to shimmer and smoke. Check the heat with your hand as before.

3. Drain the chicken and add it to the pan (see page 87). Stir-fry until seared and about three-quarters cooked, 2½ to 3 minutes. Scrape the cooked chicken and all of the liquid into a bowl. Cover and keep warm.

4. Let the pan come back up to temperature, 1 to 2 minutes. When it is hot, drizzle in 2 teaspoons oil. When the oil just starts to smoke, add the first batch of long-cooking vegetables (see page 87). Stir-fry until the vegetables are just tender-crisp, 1 to 2 minutes. Leaving the first batch in the pan, repeat with the remaining vegetables (see page 87), adding 1 teaspoon oil for each batch and cooking each set until crisp-tender, or wilted for leafy greens.

5. Clear the center of the pan and add the scallions, garlic, and ginger. Drizzle with ½ teaspoon oil. Mash into the pan with the back of a spatula (see page 87). Cook until fragrant but not colored, about 10 seconds. Remove the pan from heat and stir the scallions, garlic, and ginger into the vegetables for 20 seconds.

6. Return the pan to the heat and add the cooked chicken (see page 87). Stir in the sauce (see page 87) and stir-fry until the ingredients are well coated with sauce and sizzling hot, about 1 minute. Serve immediately with rice.

PEELING AND MINCING GINGER

1. Use a knife to trim away the knotty skin from a knob of fresh ginger. Most gingerroots will trim into a rectangular shape.

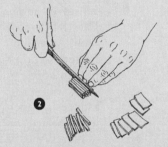

2. Slice peeled ginger into thin rounds, then fan the rounds out and cut them into thin matchsticks.

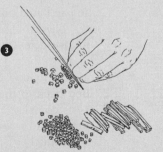

3. Chop matchsticks crosswise into a fine mince. Peeled ginger may also be cut into small cubes and then crushed in a standard garlic press.

PREPARING CHICKEN FOR STIR-FRYING

1. Slightly frozen meat is easier to slice thin than meat at room temperature. Place the chicken in the freezer for 1 hour to firm up its texture or slice frozen chicken that has partially defrosted. To produce uniform pieces of chicken that will cook evenly, start by separating the tenderloins from the partially frozen skinless, boneless breasts.

2. Slice the breasts across the grain into ½-inch-wide strips that are 1½ to 2 inches long. The center pieces need to be cut in half so that they are approximately the same length as the end pieces.

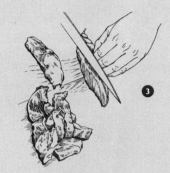

3. Cut the tenderloins on the diagonal to produce pieces about the same size as the other strips.

ANATOMY OF A STIR-FRY

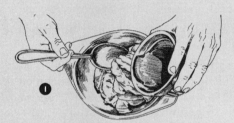

1. Toss the chicken with the soy sauce and sherry in a medium bowl; set aside for 15 minutes, tossing once or twice.

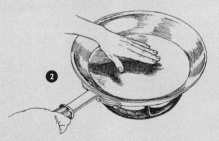

2. When the ingredients are ready, heat a 12- or 14-inch nonstick skillet over high heat for 3 to 4 minutes. Hold a hand 1 inch over the pan. When the pan is so hot you can keep your hand there for only 3 seconds, add oil and swirl it so the oil evenly coats the bottom of the pan. Heat until it just starts to shimmer and smoke.

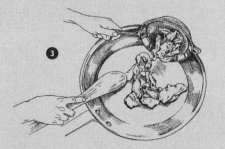

3. Drain the chicken and add it to the hot pan. Cook until it is seared and three-quarters done and then transfer the chicken and all the liquid in the pan to a bowl. Cover and keep warm.

4. When the pan comes back up to heat, after 1 to 2 minutes, add 2 teaspoons oil. Heat briefly, then add the first batch of long-cooking vegetables.

5. Leaving the first batch of vegetables in the pan, add the additional oil and remaining vegetables in 2 more batches.

6. When all the vegetables are crisp-tender, clear the center of the pan, add the scallions, garlic, and ginger, and drizzle with ½ teaspoon oil. Mash the scallions, garlic, and ginger into the pan with the back of a spatula. Cook 10 seconds; remove the pan from the heat and stir the scallion mixture into the vegetables.

7. Return the pan to the heat and add the cooked chicken along with the juices in the bowl.

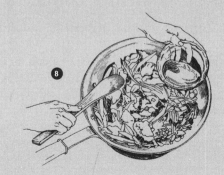

8. Stir in the sauce and stir-fry for a minute or so to coat all ingredients and make sure they are sizzling hot.

POINTERS FOR SUCCESS

/I\

WE UNCOVERED A NUMBER OF HELPFUL TIPS AND DIS-
COVERIES IN OUR STIR-FRY TESTING. KEEP THESE
POINTS IN MIND AS YOU WORK THROUGH THE
RECIPES IN THIS CHAPTER AND BE SURE OF SUCCESS.

◆ **MARINATE THE CHICKEN.** We marinate sliced chicken in a mixture of soy sauce and dry sherry. Just make sure to drain the chicken before stir-frying. If you add the liquid, the meat will stew rather than sear.

◆ **MAINTAIN THE PROPER RATIO OF PRO-TEIN TO VEGETABLES.** A good stir-fry for four people needs ¾ pound of chicken to 1½ pounds of prepared vegetables. This ratio keeps the stir-fry from becoming too heavy and is more authentic since meat is a luxury used sparingly in China. Serve with plenty of rice (see recipe on page 100).

◆ **COOK IN BATCHES.** We sear the chicken first and then remove it from the pan before cooking the vegetables. Vegetables must be batched so that no more than ½ pound is added to the pan at one time. We start long-cooking vegetables, such as onions and carrots, first. With them still in the pan, we add medium-cooking vegetables, such as bell peppers and mushrooms, and then finally add fast-cooking leafy greens and fresh herbs. Note that cooking times will be affected by how the vegetables are prepared. For instance, sliced mushrooms will cook more quickly than whole mushrooms. Keep this in

Stir-Fried Chicken and Vegetables in Spicy Tomato Sauce

FOR THIS RECIPE, CUT THE VEGETABLES INTO VERY THIN STRIPS THAT RESEMBLE MATCHSTICKS OR CON-FETTI. START BY SLICING THE CARROTS, ZUCCHINI, AND SQUASH INTO THIN OVALS ON THE BIAS. FAN OUT THE VEGETABLE ROUNDS AND THEN CUT THEM INTO STRIPS THAT MEASURE ABOUT 2 INCHES LONG AND ¼ INCH THICK. SERVES 4.

> ¾ pound boneless, skinless chicken
> breast, cut into uniform pieces (see
> page 86)
> 1 tablespoon soy sauce

> 1 tablespoon dry sherry
> 3 to 4 tablespoons peanut or vegetable oil
> 2 medium carrots, peeled and julienned
> 1 medium zucchini, julienned
> 1 medium yellow summer squash,
> julienned
> ½ medium napa cabbage (about
> ½ pound), shredded
> 2 tablespoons minced scallions, white
> parts only
> 1 tablespoon minced garlic
> 2 tablespoons minced fresh gingerroot
> 1 recipe Spicy Tomato Stir-Fry Sauce
> (page 93)

mind when deciding in what order to add vegetables to your own stir-fries.

◆ **PRECOOK THE VEGETABLES ONLY AS NEEDED.** Blanching often adds an unnecessary step, so we prefer not to precook vegetables. We would rather cut vegetables quite small (no larger than a quarter). However, some vegetables, such as broccoli and cauliflower florets, are hard to cut this small without causing them to fall apart. Other vegetables, such as asparagus and green beans, may burn on the exterior before cooking through if added raw to a stir-fry. Therefore, we find it is necessary to blanch broccoli and cauliflower florets as well as asparagus and green beans.

◆ **ADD THE AROMATICS AT THE END.** Many stir-fry recipes add the aromatics (scallions, garlic, and ginger) too early and they burn. After the vegetables have been cooked, we push them to the sides of the pan, add a little oil and the aromatics to the center of the pan, and cook briefly until fragrant but not colored, about 10 seconds. To keep the aromatics from burning and becoming harsh-tasting, we then remove the pan from the heat and stir them into the vegetables for 20 seconds.

◆ **VARY THE AROMATICS AS DESIRED.** We find that 2 tablespoons of chopped scallion whites, 1 tablespoon of minced garlic, and 1 tablespoon of minced ginger work well in a basic stir-fry for four. But feel free to adjust these amounts based on personal tastes and other ingredients in the stir-fry. To lend heat to any stir-fry, add hot red pepper flakes or minced fresh chiles with the aromatics.

◆ **NO CORNSTARCH IN SAUCES.** Once the aromatics have been cooked, it's time to add the cooked protein and the sauce. We find that cornstarch often makes sauces gloppy and thick and prefer to omit this ingredient. Our sauces are cleaner tasting and brighter. Without cornstarch, it is necessary to keep the amount of sauce to a reasonable amount (about ½ cup) that will thicken up slightly with a minute or so of cooking.

◆ **USE SUGAR SPARINGLY.** Even sweet sauces, like sweet-and-sour, should contain a minimum of sugar. Too much Chinese food prepared in this country is overly sweet. A little sugar is authentic (and delicious) in many recipes; a lot of sugar is not.

1. Toss the chicken with the soy sauce and sherry in a medium bowl; set aside for 15 minutes, tossing once or twice.

2. Heat a 12- or 14-inch skillet over high heat for 3 to 4 minutes. (The pan should be so hot you can hold an outstretched hand 1 inch over the pan for only 3 seconds.) Add 1 tablespoon oil and swirl it so the oil evenly coats the bottom of the pan. Heat the oil until it just starts to shimmer and smoke. Check the heat with your hand as before.

3. Drain the chicken and add it to the pan. Stir-fry until seared and about three-quarters cooked, 2½ to 3 minutes. Scrape the cooked chicken and all of the liquid into a bowl. Cover and keep warm.

4. Let the pan come back up to temperature, 1 to 2 minutes. When it is hot, drizzle in 2 teaspoons oil. When the oil just starts to smoke, add the carrots and cook 1 minute. Add the zucchini and squash and cook 15 seconds. Add the cabbage and cook 15 seconds.

5. Clear the center of the pan and add the scallions, garlic, and ginger. Drizzle with ½ teaspoon oil. Mash into the pan with the back of a spatula. Cook until fragrant but not colored, about 10 seconds. Remove the pan from heat and stir the scallions, garlic, and ginger into the vegetables for 20 seconds.

6. Return the pan to the heat and add the cooked chicken. Stir in the sauce and stir-fry until the ingredients are well coated with sauce and sizzling hot, about 1 minute. Serve immediately with rice.

Stir-Fried Chicken, Pineapple, and Red Onion in Sweet-and-Sour Sauce

FOR THIS RECIPE, CUT FRESH OR CANNED PINEAPPLE RINGS INTO ½-INCH-THICK TRIANGLES THAT MEASURE ABOUT 1 INCH LONG PER SIDE. **SERVES 4.**

- ¾ pound boneless, skinless chicken breast, cut into uniform pieces (see page 86)
- 1 tablespoon soy sauce
- 1 tablespoon dry sherry
- 2 to 3 tablespoons peanut or vegetable oil
- 2 small red onions, peeled and cut into thin wedges
- 1 20-ounce can pineapple rings in juice, drained, or 2 cups fresh pineapple cut into wedges
- 3 medium scallions, green parts cut into ¼-inch lengths and white parts minced
- 1 tablespoon minced garlic
- 1 tablespoon minced fresh gingerroot
- 1 recipe Sweet-and-Sour Stir-Fry Sauce (page 93)

1. Toss the chicken with the soy sauce and sherry in a medium bowl; set aside for 15 minutes, tossing once or twice.

2. Heat a 12- or 14-inch skillet over high heat for 3 to 4 minutes. (The pan should be so hot you can hold an outstretched hand 1 inch over the pan for only 3 seconds.) Add 1 tablespoon oil and swirl it so the oil evenly coats the bottom of the pan. Heat the oil until it just starts to shimmer and smoke. Check the heat with your hand as before.

3. Drain the chicken and add it to the pan. Stir-fry until seared and about three-quarters cooked, 2½ to 3 minutes. Scrape the cooked chicken and all of the liquid into a bowl. Cover and keep warm.

4. Let the pan come back up to temperature, 1 to 2 minutes. When it is hot, drizzle in 2 teaspoons oil. When the oil just starts to smoke, add the onions and stir-fry until just tender-crisp, 1 to 2 minutes. Add the pineapple and cook 1 minute. Add the scallion greens and cook 15 to 30 seconds.

5. Clear the center of the pan and add the white parts of the scallions, garlic, and ginger. Drizzle with ½ teaspoon oil. Mash into the pan with the back of a spatula. Cook until fragrant but not colored, about 10 seconds. Remove the pan from heat and stir the scallions, garlic, and ginger into the vegetables for 20 seconds.

6. Return the pan to the heat and add the cooked chicken. Stir in the sauce and stir-fry until the ingredients are well coated with sauce and sizzling hot, about 1 minute. Serve immediately with rice.

◆

Stir-Fried Chicken and Bok Choy in Ginger Sauce

THE WHITE BOK CHOY STALKS REQUIRE MORE COOKING TIME THAN THE GREENS, SO SEPARATE THE STALKS AND LEAVES BEFORE SLICING THEM. **SERVES 4.**

- ¾ pound boneless, skinless chicken breast, cut into uniform pieces (see page 86)
- 1 tablespoon soy sauce
- 1 tablespoon dry sherry
- 3 tablespoons peanut or vegetable oil
- 1 pound bok choy, stalks and greens separated and shredded (see opposite)
- 1 red bell pepper, stemmed, seeded, and cut into 3-by-½-inch strips
- 2 tablespoons minced scallions, white parts only
- 1 tablespoon minced garlic
- 1 tablespoon minced fresh gingerroot
- 1 recipe Ginger Stir-Fry Sauce (page 93)

1. Toss the chicken with the soy sauce and sherry in a medium bowl; set aside for 15 minutes, tossing once or twice.

2. Heat a 12- or 14-inch skillet over high heat for 3 to 4 minutes. (The pan should be so hot you can hold an outstretched hand 1 inch over the pan for only 3 seconds.) Add 1 tablespoon oil and swirl it so the oil evenly coats the bottom of the pan. Heat the oil until it just starts to shimmer and smoke. Check the heat with your hand as before.

3. Drain the chicken and add it to the pan. Stir-fry until seared and about three-quarters cooked, 2½ to 3 minutes. Scrape the cooked chicken and all of the liquid into a bowl. Cover and keep warm.

4. Let the pan come back up to temperature, 1 to 2 minutes. When it is hot, drizzle in 2 teaspoons oil. When the oil just starts to smoke, add the bok choy stalks and cook 1 to 2 minutes. Add the bell pepper and cook 30 to 60 seconds. Add the bok choy greens and cook 15 to 30 seconds.

5. Clear the center of the pan and add the scallions, garlic, and ginger. Drizzle with ½ teaspoon oil. Mash into the pan with the back of a spatula. Cook until fragrant but not colored, about 10 seconds. Remove the pan from heat and stir the scallions, garlic, and ginger into the vegetables for 20 seconds.

6. Return the pan to the heat and add the cooked chicken. Stir in the sauce and stir-fry until the ingredients are well coated with sauce and sizzling hot, about 1 minute. Serve immediately with rice.

SHREDDING BOK CHOY

1. The green and white portions of a bok choy leaf will cook at different rates and must be separated. Start by cutting the leafy green portions of the bok choy away from the white stalks.

2. Cut each white stalk in half lengthwise and then crosswise into thin strips.

3. Stack the greens and then slice them crosswise into strips. Keep the sliced stalks and leaves separate.

TEN SAUCES FOR STIR-FRY

S TRONGLY FLAVORED SAUCES ARE THE KEY TO VIBRANT STIR-FRIES. IN OUR TESTING, WE FOUND THAT CORNSTARCH SIMPLY MUDDIES THE FLAVOR AND TEXTURE OF SAUCES. WE PREFER THE CLEANER FLAVOR AND TEXTURE OF SAUCES MADE WITHOUT ANY THICKENER. A HALF-CUP OF SAUCE (ALL OF THE FOLLOWING

recipes yield about this amount) will nicely coat the ingredients in our standard stir-fry without being too liquid. We have made a specific sauce suggestion for each stir-fry, but feel free to create your own combinations of sauce, vegetables, and chicken.

◆

Hot-and-Sour Stir-Fry Sauce

FOR A SPICIER SAUCE, INCREASE THE CHILE TO 2 TABLESPOONS OR MORE, IF DESIRED. MAKES ABOUT 1/2 CUP.

- 3 tablespoons cider vinegar
- 2 tablespoons chicken stock
- 1 tablespoon soy sauce
- 2 teaspoons sugar
- 1 1/2 tablespoons minced jalapeño or other fresh chile

1. Combine all the ingredients except for the jalapeño in a small bowl and set the sauce aside.

2. Add the jalapeño to the stir-fry along with the scallions, garlic, and ginger (see Master Recipe, page 84).

Garlic Stir-Fry Sauce

THIS SAUCE ADDS A RICH GARLIC AROMA TO CHICKEN BUT DOES NOT OVERPOWER OTHER INGREDIENTS. ADJUST THE HEAT AS DESIRED. BECAUSE SO MUCH SOY SAUCE IS USED HERE, WE RECOMMEND A COMBINATION OF LIGHT SOY (REDUCED-SODIUM) AND REGULAR SOY SAUCE. MAKES ABOUT 1/2 CUP.

- 3 tablespoons light soy sauce
- 4 teaspoons dry sherry
- 1 tablespoon chicken stock
- 2 teaspoons soy sauce
- 1/2 teaspoon Asian sesame oil
- 1 tablespoon very finely minced garlic
- 1/2 teaspoon sugar
- 1/4 teaspoon hot red pepper flakes

1. Combine all the ingredients except for the red pepper flakes in a small bowl and set the sauce aside.

2. Add the red pepper flakes to the stir-fry along with the scallions, garlic, and ginger (see Master Recipe, page 84).

Spicy Tomato Stir-Fry Sauce

THIS SAUCE GETS MUCH OF ITS HEAT FROM CHILE PASTE, ALSO CALLED CHILI SAUCE. THIS SPICY SEASONING IS MADE WITH CRUSHED CHILES, VINEGAR, AND USUALLY GARLIC. THE TEXTURE IS THICK AND SMOOTH AND THE COLOR IS BRIGHT RED. BRANDS VARY FROM MILD TO INCENDIARY, SO TASTE BEFORE USING AND ADJUST AS NEEDED. LIKE KETCHUP, OPENED BOTTLES OF CHILI PASTE WILL KEEP INDEFINITELY IN THE REFRIGERATOR. MAKES ABOUT ½ CUP.

- 3 tablespoons tomato paste
- 2 tablespoons soy sauce
- 1 tablespoon chicken stock
- 1 tablespoon dry sherry
- 2 tablespoons chile paste
- ½ teaspoon Asian sesame oil
- ½ teaspoon toasted and ground Szechwan peppercorns
- ½ teaspoon sugar
- ½ teaspoon hot red pepper flakes

1. Combine all the ingredients except for the red pepper flakes in a small bowl and set the sauce aside.

2. Add the red pepper flakes to the stir-fry along with the scallions, garlic, and ginger (see Master Recipe, page 84).

◆

Sweet-and-Sour Stir-Fry Sauce

PINEAPPLE JUICE CAN BE USED IN THIS RECIPE INSTEAD OF ORANGE JUICE, IF DESIRED. IT'S ESPECIALLY APPROPRIATE WHEN USING PINEAPPLE IN THE STIR-FRY. MAKES ABOUT ½ CUP.

- 3 tablespoons red wine vinegar
- 3 tablespoons sugar
- 1 ½ tablespoons tomato sauce
- 1 ½ tablespoons orange juice
- ¼ teaspoon salt

Combine all the ingredients in a small bowl and set the sauce aside.

◆

Ginger Stir-Fry Sauce

FOR HINTS ON PEELING AND MINCING GINGER, SEE FIGURES 1 THROUGH 3 ON PAGE 85. MAKES ABOUT ½ CUP.

- 3 tablespoons light soy sauce
- 2 tablespoons chicken stock
- 1 tablespoon dry sherry
- 3 tablespoons very finely minced fresh gingerroot
- ½ teaspoon sugar

Combine all the ingredients in a small bowl and set the sauce aside.

◆

Black Bean Stir-Fry Sauce

CHINESE FERMENTED BLACK BEANS ARE AVAILABLE IN ASIAN FOOD SHOPS. THEY SHOULD BE MOIST AND SOFT TO THE TOUCH. DON'T BUY BEANS THAT ARE DRIED OUT OR SHRIVELED. MAKES ABOUT ½ CUP.

- 3 tablespoons dry sherry
- 2 tablespoons chicken stock
- 1 tablespoon soy sauce
- 1 tablespoon Asian sesame oil
- ½ teaspoon sugar
- ¼ teaspoon pepper
- 1 tablespoon Chinese fermented black beans, chopped

(continued on next page)

1. Combine all the ingredients except for the beans in a small bowl and set the sauce aside.

2. Add the beans to the stir-fry along with the scallions, garlic, and ginger (see Master Recipe, page 84).

◆

Coconut Curry Stir-Fry Sauce

USE CANNED UNSWEETENED COCONUT MILK IN THIS RECIPE, NOT SWEETENED COCONUT CREAM. THIS VELVETY SAUCE COATS FOOD ESPECIALLY WELL. MAKES ABOUT ½ CUP.

> ¼ cup unsweetened coconut milk
> 1 tablespoon dry sherry
> 1 tablespoon chicken stock
> 1½ teaspoons soy sauce
> 1½ teaspoons curry powder
> ¼ teaspoon sugar
> ¼ teaspoon salt

Combine all the ingredients in a small bowl and set the sauce aside.

◆

Szechwan Chile Stir-Fry Sauce

THIS SAUCE GETS ITS HEAT FROM CHILE PASTE. SZECHWAN PEPPERCORNS ADD AN AROMATIC, HERBACEOUS FLAVOR. MAKES ABOUT ½ CUP.

> 3 tablespoons dry sherry
> 1 tablespoon soy sauce
> 1 tablespoon Asian sesame oil
> 2 tablespoons chile paste
> ¼ teaspoon toasted and ground
>   Szechwan peppercorns
> ¼ teaspoon sugar

Combine all the ingredients in a small bowl and set the sauce aside.

Spicy Tangerine Stir-Fry Sauce

THREE TANGERINES WILL PROVIDE ENOUGH ZEST FOR THIS RECIPE. AN ORANGE MAY BE USED INSTEAD, IF DESIRED. WEAR RUBBER GLOVES WHEN MINCING THE FRESH CHILE AND USE THE SEEDS TO MAXIMIZE THE HEAT. MAKES ABOUT ½ CUP.

> 3 tablespoons dry sherry
> 1 tablespoon soy sauce
> 1 tablespoon Asian sesame oil
> 2 teaspoons red wine vinegar
> ½ teaspoon toasted and ground
>   Szechwan peppercorns
> ¼ teaspoon sugar
> ¼ teaspoon salt
> 1 tablespoon minced jalapeño or
>   other fresh chile
> 1 tablespoon grated tangerine zest

1. Combine all the ingredients except for the jalapeño and tangerine zest in a small bowl and set the sauce aside.

2. Add the jalapeño and tangerine zest to the stir-fry along with the scallions, garlic, and ginger (see Master Recipe, page 84).

◆

Lemon Stir-Fry Sauce

ONE MEDIUM LEMON WILL YIELD ENOUGH JUICE AND ZEST FOR THIS RECIPE. MAKES ABOUT ½ CUP.

> 3 tablespoons lemon juice
> ½ teaspoon minced lemon zest
> 3 tablespoons chicken stock
> 1 tablespoon soy sauce
> 2 teaspoons sugar

Combine all the ingredients in a small bowl and set the sauce aside.

Stir-Fried Chicken, Celery, and Peanuts in Szechwan Chile Sauce

SALTED OR NATURAL PEANUTS MAY BE USED IN THIS RECIPE. TO CUT LONG, THIN VEGETABLES SUCH AS CELERY ON THE BIAS, HOLD THE KNIFE AT A 45-DEGREE ANGLE TO THE VEGETABLE AS YOU SLICE. SERVES 4.

- ¾ pound boneless, skinless chicken breast, cut into uniform pieces (see page 86)
- 1 tablespoon soy sauce
- 1 tablespoon dry sherry
- 2 to 3 tablespoons peanut or vegetable oil
- 8 celery stalks, sliced on the bias into ¼-inch-thick pieces
- 2 tablespoons minced scallions, white parts only
- 1 tablespoon minced garlic
- 1 tablespoon minced fresh gingerroot
- ½ cup peanuts
- 1 recipe Szechwan Chile Stir-Fry Sauce (opposite page)

1. Toss the chicken with the soy sauce and sherry in a medium bowl; set aside for 15 minutes, tossing once or twice.

2. Heat a 12- or 14-inch skillet over high heat for 3 to 4 minutes. (The pan should be so hot you can hold an outstretched hand 1 inch over the pan for only 3 seconds.) Add 1 tablespoon oil and swirl it so the oil evenly coats the bottom of the pan. Heat the oil until it just starts to shimmer and smoke. Check the heat with your hand as before.

3. Drain the chicken and add it to the pan. Stir-fry until seared and about three-quarters cooked, 2½ to 3 minutes. Scrape the cooked chicken and all of the liquid into a bowl. Cover and keep warm.

4. Let the pan come back up to temperature, 1 to 2 minutes. When it is hot, drizzle in 2 teaspoons oil. When the oil just starts to smoke, add half the celery. Stir-fry until the celery is just tender-crisp, 1 to 2 minutes. Scrape the cooked celery into a bowl; add 1 tea-spoon oil to the pan and stir-fry the remaining celery 1 to 2 minutes.

5. Return the first batch of celery to the pan. Clear the center of the pan and add the scallions, garlic, and ginger. Drizzle with ½ teaspoon oil. Mash into the pan with the back of a spatula. Cook until fragrant but not colored, about 10 seconds. Remove the pan from heat and stir the scallions, garlic, and ginger into the celery for 20 seconds.

6. Return the pan to the heat and add the cooked chicken and the peanuts. Stir in the sauce and stir-fry until the ingredients are well coated with sauce and sizzling hot, about 1 minute. Serve immediately with rice.

◆

Stir-Fried Chicken, Scallions, and Peppers in Garlic Sauce

SCALLIONS ARE USED AS A VEGETABLE IN THIS RECIPE. YOU WILL NEED FOUR OR FIVE BUNCHES, ABOUT ¾ POUND. SERVES 4.

- ¾ pound boneless, skinless chicken breast, cut into uniform pieces (see page 86)
- 1 tablespoon soy sauce
- 1 tablespoon dry sherry
- 2 to 3 tablespoons peanut or vegetable oil
- 1 cup scallion whites sliced on the bias into 1-inch pieces
- 2 medium red bell peppers, stemmed, seeded, and cut into 1-inch cubes
- 1½ cups scallion greens sliced on the bias into ½-inch pieces
- 2 tablespoons minced scallions, white parts only
- 1 tablespoon minced garlic
- 1 tablespoon minced fresh gingerroot
- 1 recipe Garlic Stir-Fry Sauce (page 92)

1. Toss the chicken with the soy sauce and sherry in a medium bowl; set aside for 15 minutes, tossing once or twice.

(continued on next page)

2. Heat a 12- or 14-inch skillet over high heat for 3 to 4 minutes. (The pan should be so hot you can hold an outstretched hand 1 inch over the pan for only 3 seconds.) Add 1 tablespoon oil and swirl it so the oil evenly coats the bottom of the pan. Heat the oil until it just starts to shimmer and smoke. Check the heat with your hand as before.

3. Drain the chicken and add it to the pan. Stir-fry until seared and about three-quarters cooked, 2½ to 3 minutes. Scrape the cooked chicken and all of the liquid into a bowl. Cover and keep warm.

4. Let the pan come back up to temperature, 1 to 2 minutes. When it is hot, drizzle in 2 teaspoons oil. When the oil just starts to smoke, add the sliced scallion whites and cook 1 to 2 minutes. Add the bell peppers and cook 1 minute. Add the scallion greens and cook 30 seconds.

5. Clear the center of the pan and add the minced scallions, garlic, and ginger. Drizzle with ½ teaspoon oil. Mash into the pan with the back of a spatula. Cook until fragrant but not colored, about 10 seconds. Remove the pan from heat and stir the scallions, garlic, and ginger into the vegetables for 20 seconds.

6. Return the pan to the heat and add the cooked chicken. Stir in the sauce and stir-fry until the ingredients are well coated with sauce and sizzling hot, about 1 minute. Serve immediately with rice.

◆

Stir-Fried Chicken and Fennel in Spicy Tangerine Sauce

FENNEL IS NOT TRADITIONAL IN CHINESE STIR-FRIES BUT IT SOFTENS NICELY AND COMPLEMENTS THE SWEETNESS IN THE SHRIMP. SERVES 4.

    ¾ pound boneless, skinless chicken
      breast, cut into uniform pieces (see
      page 86)
    1 tablespoon soy sauce
    1 tablespoon dry sherry

    2 to 3 tablespoons peanut or vegetable oil
    2 medium fennel bulbs, trimmed and
      sliced thin (see opposite)
    1 red bell pepper, stemmed, seeded, and
      cut into ½-inch cubes
    3 medium scallions, green parts cut into
      ¼-inch lengths and white parts minced
    ¾ cup tightly packed fresh basil leaves
    1 tablespoon minced garlic
    1 tablespoon minced fresh gingerroot
    1 recipe Spicy Tangerine Stir-Fry Sauce
      (page 94)

1. Toss the chicken with the soy sauce and sherry in a medium bowl; set aside for 15 minutes, tossing once or twice.

2. Heat a 12- or 14-inch skillet over high heat for 3 to 4 minutes. (The pan should be so hot you can hold an outstretched hand 1 inch over the pan for only 3 seconds.) Add 1 tablespoon oil and swirl it so the oil evenly coats the bottom of the pan. Heat the oil until it just starts to shimmer and smoke. Check the heat with your hand as before.

3. Drain the chicken and add it to the pan. Stir-fry until seared and about three-quarters cooked, 2½ to 3 minutes. Scrape the cooked chicken and all of the liquid into a bowl. Cover and keep warm.

4. Let the pan come back up to temperature, 1 to 2 minutes. When it is hot, drizzle in 2 teaspoons oil. When the oil just starts to smoke, add the fennel and cook 1½ minutes. Add the bell pepper and cook 30 seconds. Add the scallion greens and basil and cook 15 seconds.

5. Clear the center of the pan and add the scallion whites, garlic, and ginger. Drizzle with ½ teaspoon oil. Mash into the pan with the back of a spatula. Cook until fragrant but not colored, about 10 seconds. Remove the pan from heat and stir the scallion whites, garlic, and ginger into the vegetables for 20 seconds.

6. Return the pan to the heat and add the cooked chicken. Stir in the sauce and stir-fry until the ingredients are well coated with sauce and sizzling hot, about 1 minute. Serve immediately with rice.

TRIMMING AND SLICING FENNEL

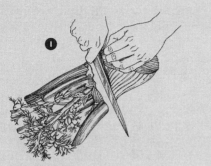

1. Trim and discard the fronds and stems. Trim a very thin slice from the base of the bulb and remove any tough or blemished outer layers from the bulb.

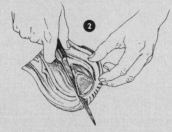

2. Cut the bulb in half through the base. Use a small, sharp knife to remove the pyramid-shaped piece of the core in the bottom of each half.

3. Cut the cored fennel half into 3 or 4 thick slices.

4. Cut the fennel pieces into ¼-inch-thick strips. They are now small enough to stir-fry.

Stir-Fried Chicken and Asparagus in Lemon Sauce

ASPARAGUS BLANCHED FOR FOUR MINUTES WILL COOK EVENLY IN A SINGLE BATCH IN THIS DISH. SERVES 4.

¾ pound boneless, skinless chicken
    breast, cut into uniform pieces (see
    page 86)
1 tablespoon soy sauce
1 tablespoon dry sherry
2 pounds asparagus, ends snapped off and
    sliced on the bias into 2-inch pieces (see
    figures 1 and 2, page 263)
3 to 4 tablespoons peanut or vegetable oil
2 tablespoons minced scallions, white
    parts only
1 tablespoon minced garlic
1 tablespoon minced fresh gingerroot
1 recipe Lemon Stir-Fry Sauce (page 94)
¼ cup chopped fresh parsley leaves
Salt and pepper

1. Toss the chicken with the soy sauce and sherry in a medium bowl; set aside for 15 minutes, tossing once or twice.

2. Meanwhile, bring several quarts of water to a boil in a medium saucepan. Add the asparagus and cook until crisp-tender, about 4 minutes. Drain and set aside.

3. Heat a 12- or 14-inch skillet over high heat for 3 to 4 minutes. (The pan should be so hot you can hold an outstretched hand 1 inch over the pan for only 3 seconds.) Add 1 tablespoon oil and swirl it so the oil evenly coats the bottom of the pan. Heat the oil until it just starts to shimmer and smoke. Check the heat with your hand as before.

4. Drain the chicken and add it to the pan. Stir-fry until seared and about three-quarters cooked, 2½ to 3 minutes. Scrape the cooked chicken and all of the liquid into a bowl. Cover and keep warm.

5. Let the pan come back up to temperature, 1 to 2 minutes. When it is hot, drizzle in 2 teaspoons oil. When the oil just starts to smoke, add the asparagus and cook 1½ minutes.

6. Clear the center of the pan and add the scallions, garlic, and ginger. Drizzle with ½ teaspoon oil. Mash into the pan with the back of a spatula. Cook until fragrant but not colored, about 10 seconds. Remove the pan from heat and stir the scallions, garlic, and ginger into the asparagus for 20 seconds.

7. Return the pan to the heat and add the cooked chicken. Stir in the sauce and parsley and stir-fry until the ingredients are well coated with sauce and sizzling hot, about 1 minute. Season with salt and pepper. Serve immediately with rice.

◆

Stir-Fried Chicken and Broccoli in Coconut Curry Sauce

UNLIKE MOST VEGETABLES, BROCCOLI MUST BE BLANCHED BEFORE BEING ADDED TO A STIR-FRY. BOTH THE FLORETS AND STALKS (WHICH ARE PEELED AND DICED) ARE USED IN THIS RECIPE. SERVES 4.

¾ pound boneless, skinless chicken
    breast, cut into uniform pieces (see
    page 86)
1 tablespoon soy sauce
1 tablespoon dry sherry
1½ pounds broccoli, florets broken into
    bite-size pieces; stems trimmed, peeled,
    and cut into ¼-inch dice
2 to 3 tablespoons peanut or vegetable oil
1 small onion, cut into 1-inch cubes
1 yellow bell pepper, stemmed, seeded,
    and cut into 3-by-½-inch strips
2 tablespoons minced scallions, white parts only
½ tablespoon minced garlic
1 tablespoon minced fresh gingerroot
1 recipe Coconut Curry Stir-Fry Sauce
    (page 94)

1. Toss the chicken with the soy sauce and sherry in a medium bowl; set aside for 15 minutes, tossing once or twice.

2. Meanwhile, bring several quarts of water to a boil in a medium saucepan. Add the broccoli and cook until crisp-tender, about 2 minutes. Drain and set aside.

3. Heat a 12- or 14-inch skillet over high heat for 3 to 4 minutes. (The pan should be so hot you can hold an outstretched hand 1 inch over the pan for only 3 seconds.) Add 1 tablespoon oil and swirl it so the oil evenly coats the bottom of the pan. Heat the oil until it just starts to shimmer and smoke. Check the heat with your hand as before.

4. Drain the chicken and add it to the pan. Stir-fry until seared and about three-quarters cooked, 2½ to 3 minutes. Scrape the cooked chicken and all of the liquid into a bowl. Cover and keep warm.

5. Let the pan come back up to temperature, 1 to 2 minutes. When it is hot, drizzle in 2 teaspoons oil. When the oil just starts to smoke, add the onion and cook 2 minutes. Add the broccoli and cook 1 minute. Add the bell pepper and cook 1 minute.

6. Clear the center of the pan and add the scallions, garlic, and ginger. Drizzle with ½ teaspoon oil. Mash into the pan with the back of a spatula. Cook until fragrant but not colored, about 10 seconds. Remove the pan from heat and stir the scallions, garlic, and ginger into the vegetables for 20 seconds.

7. Return the pan to the heat and add the cooked chicken. Stir in the sauce and stir-fry until the ingredients are well coated with sauce and sizzling hot, about 1 minute. Serve immediately with rice.

◆

Stir-Fried Chicken in Black Bean Sauce

CELERY, SHIITAKE MUSHROOMS, SUMMER SQUASH, AND SUGAR SNAP PEAS ENLIVEN THIS CLASSIC STIR-FRY WITH CHINESE FERMENTED BLACK BEANS. SERVES 4.

- ¾ **pound boneless, skinless chicken breast, cut into uniform pieces (see page 86)**
- 1 tablespoon soy sauce
- 1 tablespoon dry sherry
- 3 to 4 tablespoons peanut or vegetable oil
- 2 celery stalks, halved lengthwise and sliced on the bias into ¼-inch-thick pieces
- ¼ pound shiitake mushrooms, stemmed and left whole
- 1 medium yellow summer squash, quartered lengthwise and cut crosswise into ½-inch-thick triangles
- ½ pound sugar snap peas, stringed (about 3 cups)
- 2 tablespoons minced scallions, white parts only
- 1 tablespoon minced garlic
- 1 tablespoon minced fresh gingerroot
- 1 recipe Black Bean Stir-Fry Sauce (page 93)

1. Toss the chicken with the soy sauce and sherry in a medium bowl; set aside for 15 minutes, tossing once or twice.

2. Heat a 12- or 14-inch skillet over high heat for 3 to 4 minutes. (The pan should be so hot you can hold an outstretched hand 1 inch over the pan for only 3 seconds.) Add 1 tablespoon oil and swirl it so the oil evenly coats the bottom of the pan. Heat the oil until it just starts to shimmer and smoke. Check the heat with your hand as before.

3. Drain the chicken and add it to the pan. Stir-fry until seared and about three-quarters cooked, 2½ to 3 minutes. Scrape the cooked chicken and all of the liquid into a bowl. Cover and keep warm.

4. Let the pan come back up to temperature, 1 to 2 minutes. When it is hot, drizzle in 2 teaspoons oil. When the oil just starts to smoke, add the celery and cook 1½ minutes. Add the mushrooms and cook 1 minute. Add the squash and cook 1 minute. Add the peas and cook 30 to 60 seconds.

5. Clear the center of the pan and add the scallions, garlic, and ginger. Drizzle with ½ teaspoon oil. Mash into the pan with the back of a spatula. Cook until fragrant but not colored, about 10 seconds. Remove the pan from heat and stir the scallions, garlic, and ginger into the vegetables for 20 seconds.

6. Return the pan to the heat and add the cooked chicken. Stir in the sauce and stir-fry until the ingredients are well coated with sauce and sizzling hot, about 1 minute. Serve immediately with rice.

Stir-Fried Chicken and Water Chestnuts in Hot-and-Sour Sauce

CELERY AND WATER CHESTNUTS ADD CRUNCH TO THIS STIR-FRY. USE EITHER SALTED OR NATURAL CASHEWS. SERVES 4.

¾ pound boneless, skinless chicken breast, cut into uniform pieces (see page 86)
1 tablespoon soy sauce
1 tablespoon dry sherry
2 to 3 tablespoons peanut or vegetable oil
3 celery stalks, sliced on the bias into ¼-inch-thick pieces
2 8-ounce cans whole water chestnuts, drained and halved crosswise
2 tablespoons minced scallions, white parts only
1 tablespoon minced garlic
1 tablespoon minced fresh gingerroot
½ cup cashews
1 recipe Hot-and-Sour Stir-Fry Sauce (page 92)

1. Toss the chicken with the soy sauce and sherry in a medium bowl; set aside for 15 minutes, tossing once or twice.

2. Heat a 12- or 14-inch skillet over high heat for 3 to 4 minutes. (The pan should be so hot you can hold an outstretched hand 1 inch over the pan for only 3 seconds.) Add 1 tablespoon oil and swirl it so the oil evenly coats the bottom of the pan. Heat the oil until it just starts to shimmer and smoke. Check the heat with your hand as before.

3. Drain the chicken and add it to the pan. Stir-fry until seared and about three-quarters cooked, 2½ to 3 minutes. Scrape the cooked chicken and all of the liquid into a bowl. Cover and keep warm.

4. Let the pan come back up to temperature, 1 to 2 minutes. When it is hot, drizzle in 2 teaspoons oil. When the oil just starts to smoke, add the celery and cook 1 minute. Add the water chestnuts and cook 1 minute.

Sticky White Rice

THIS TRADITIONAL CHINESE COOKING METHOD YIELDS STICKY RICE THAT WORKS WELL AS AN ACCOMPANIMENT TO A STIR-FRY, ESPECIALLY IF EATING WITH CHOPSTICKS. THIS RECIPE YIELDS 6 CUPS, A GENEROUS AMOUNT FOR FOUR PEOPLE THAT FOLLOWS THE CHINESE CUSTOM OF "STRETCHING" A STIR-FRY BY SERVING IT WITH PLENTY OF RICE. SERVES 4.

2 cups long-grain white rice
3 cups water
½ teaspoon salt

1. Place the rice, water, and salt in a medium saucepan and set over medium-high heat. Bring the water to a boil. Cook, uncovered, until the water level drops below the top surface of the rice and small holes form in the rice, about 10 minutes.

2. Reduce the heat to very low, cover, and cook until the rice is tender, about 15 minutes longer. Spoon the rice into a large bowl and serve immediately.

5. Clear the center of the pan and add the scallions, garlic, and ginger. Drizzle with ½ teaspoon oil. Mash into the pan with the back of a spatula. Cook until fragrant but not colored, about 10 seconds. Remove the pan from heat and stir the scallions, garlic, and ginger into the vegetables for 20 seconds.

6. Return the pan to the heat and add the cooked chicken and cashews. Stir in the sauce and stir-fry until the ingredients are well coated with sauce and sizzling hot, about 1 minute. Serve immediately with rice.

BRAISED CHICKEN

BRAISING—COOKING FOOD IN A COVERED POT IN

SIMMERING LIQUID—HAS MANY ADVANTAGES, ESPE-

CIALLY WHEN APPLIED TO CHICKEN. BECAUSE THE

MEAT IS COOKED IN LIQUID, IT REMAINS MOIST AND

JUICY. ALSO, CARROTS, ONIONS, AND MUSHROOMS

MAY BE SIMMERED WITH THE CHICKEN—AS WELL AS

OTHER VEGETABLES—FOR A ONE-DISH MEAL. FINALLY,

THE COOKING LIQUID BECOMES A SAUCE THAT CAN

moisten the chicken, as well as a starch like rice, potatoes, or noodles, at the table.

Say "braised chicken" to most American cooks and they won't know exactly what you are talking about. Chicken in a pot gets them closer, but this term is not really correct. The classic French recipe for chicken in a pot calls for poaching a mature stewing hen stuffed with forcemeat in stock for hours. Chicken in a pot as Herbert Hoover and most Americans know it is something different, a cross between sautéed chicken and stewed chicken, featuring a chicken cut into pieces and cooked in some liquid, usually with vegetables.

Southerners probably call this dish a fricassee. In classic French cooking, a fricassee has an egg-thickened cream sauce. In this country, a fricassee is generally cooked with more liquid than a braise, but there is no definite dividing point between the two dishes. We often call slightly "saucier" braises made with tomatoes a fricassee, but this is more out of custom than any hard-and-fast rule.

Whatever this dish is called, chicken parts and vegetables are cooked until the chicken and vegetables are tender and a flavorful sauce has formed. Braised chicken is a meal-in-one, done in about forty-five minutes, and using only one pan. Because chicken's mild flesh matches well with delicate seasonings and vegetables, and also stands up well to bold spices and hearty ingredients, you can vary the recipe in almost endless ways.

Although infinitely variable, braised chicken raises a number of important questions. What size bird should be used? Should the skin be removed before cooking? Should the chicken be browned? How should the vegetables be added to the pot and how much liquid is enough?

We started out by testing chickens of various sizes. Very small birds (under 3 pounds) yield small parts that can brown in a single batch but often cook through before the vegetables and other flavorings have had a chance to meld. Even if you can find a very small chicken, we suggest roasting it rather than braising.

We also tried using a large roaster, but didn't like the results. The meat took a very long time to cook, so the white portions were too dry and the vegetables were mush by the time the dark meat cooked through

completely. Large roaster parts are also much harder to stir and maneuver in the pot.

A "mid-sized" chicken, weighing about 3½ pounds, is the best choice for braising. Even though it may be necessary to brown the pieces in batches (if you use a 12-inch sauté pan, as we recommend in the recipes that follow, you can fit the chicken in one batch), we found that the meat was juicier and that the vegetables, seasonings, and fluids had enough time to lend flavors to each other, giving the dish a rich, harmonious taste. This size bird is sold cut up in most supermarkets, but we recommend that you can cut up your own chicken (see "Cutting Up a Whole Chicken," page 10).

Although we like using a whole cut-up chicken with its mix of parts, we know there are families with no dark-meat eaters. Our Master Recipe works fine with only breasts and wings, without any change in time, temperature, or method. All dark-meat pieces can also be cooked according to the Master Recipe, but there will be more fat in the pan after browning the pieces. No matter—you spill off all but a film of fat before you add the vegetables anyway. If you choose to follow the recipe with just one kind of parts, remember you will need about 3½ pounds' worth.

We are very particular in our pot recommendations. We found that by using a deep, straight-sided, 12-inch sauté pan or a Dutch oven, there was less spatter on the stovetop than with a shallow skillet (but the latter will work in a pinch). We preferred the results from anodized aluminum, stainless steel, and pressure-cast aluminum pans; the chicken browned beautifully in all three. Nonstick cookware does not brown as well. We do not use cast-iron (enameled cast-iron is fine though) or regular aluminum cookware for this recipe because those metals react with wine or other acids, causing an off-taste in the food. Given the long cooking time, choose a sturdy pan with some heft to it. A tight-fitting lid is also essential.

With our chicken size and pot requirements tested, we started to focus on the actual cooking process. Up until this point, we had been testing recipes with the skin on. Although the skin becomes nice and crisp after browning, once the liquid is added to the pot it turns soft and not terribly appealing. We tried removing the skin before browning, but found the meat was a bit dry after braising. The skin protects the meat, especially delicate white meat, during the long cooking process. The skin can always be removed just before serving if you like.

We were pretty sure that browning was essential. To test this hunch, we tried skipping the initial browning of the chicken but the sauce was bland. Browning adds flavor to the dish and is worth the extra ten or fifteen minutes of work.

As with sautéing, we found that a combination of butter for flavor and vegetable oil to prevent smoking is the best medium for browning the chicken. Many sautéed and braised chicken recipes call for flouring the chicken before browning it, so we tried that to see what additional benefits it might provide. The results were disappointing. The only asset of the process was an attractive color for the pan gravy. Flouring caused the chicken to absorb more fat (none remained to spill off before adding the vegetables to the pan) and gave the finished chicken a gritty surface. In deciding to eliminate flouring, we found it essential to dry the chicken thoroughly before adding it to the pan—more moisture meant excess spattering.

We found that if you don't wait for the pan to heat adequately, two things happen. First, the chicken absorbs too much fat. Second, it doesn't brown properly because heat rising in the flesh causes a "steam" effect. To brown chicken well, you have to keep the heat moderately high, enough to hear a sizzle. When the butter has melted and begins to look foamy, the pan is hot enough to receive the chicken.

After browning the chicken and spilling off most of the fat, it is time to add the vegetables. The pan is quite hot so we found it is imperative to watch the ingredients carefully and stir them often to prevent scorching. We tried putting the vegetables under and over the chicken pieces and found that they do better on top. When placed below the chicken parts, the vegetables are crushed by the weight of the meat and fall apart.

We experimented quite a bit with the amount of liquid to add. We were looking for just enough to bathe and baste the meat and vegetables for about a half-hour, yet little enough so that it would have an intense, concentrated flavor. We started by using 1 cup of liquid but found the resulting pan gravy too thin and lacking in flavor. Half a cup turned out to be perfect. Of course, you will need to change the amount if you vary the vegetables in the recipe. For example, more watery vegetables such as mushrooms, tomatoes, zucchini, and yellow squash render more liquid so you may need less fluid to begin with. On the other hand, ingredients such as potatoes, beans, dried fruit, and dried mushrooms absorb liquid during cooking, so you will need to increase the amount of fluid with which you start.

The type of liquid is a matter of taste. We used white wine in the Master Recipe because we found it tastier than stock. However, red wine, cider, brandy, tomatoes, or even stock (if other flavorful ingredients are used) will work fine. You need not bother preheating the liquid; there is so little that its temperature is irrelevant.

After adding the liquid, it's time to lower the heat. To assure the meat will soften properly without drying out, the ingredients must cook at a bare simmer—just the occasional bubble rising to the surface. Too high a flame (the entire surface should not be covered with bubbles) and the chicken will contract like a rubber band; too low and the vegetables will turn to mush before the chicken is done.

It is also a good idea to baste the ingredients three to four times during cooking. When we didn't do this, the flavors didn't seem as well blended. For this reason, it is more convenient to complete the cooking on top of the stove. However, if you're short on stovetop space, you can finish the dish in a preheated 300-degree oven. In that case, you'll need a pan with a heatproof handle. Either way, the chicken will cook through in about twenty-five minutes.

When the dish is done, you've got an unpretentious, savory meal of tender meat, flavor-rich vegetables, and ¾ to 1 cup of fragrant juices you can serve over cooked rice, polenta, egg noodles, couscous, or any other starch you choose. There's no need to reduce the liquids unless you prefer to glaze the chicken and vegetables instead of using the pan juices as a sauce. In that case, remove the chicken and the vegetables to a serving platter and keep them warm while you boil the pan fluids until they look syrupy. This takes a minute or two.

Braised Chicken

SERVES 4

CARROTS, MUSHROOMS, AND onions are used in this basic braise. If you like, you can substitute two medium leeks for the onion in this recipe. To prepare the leeks, trim the dark green leaves and root ends, keeping the bases intact. Quarter each leek lengthwise and rinse thoroughly (see opposite). You can make this dish in a smaller sauté pan, but you will then need to brown the chicken in batches. Rice pilaf makes a nice accompaniment.

1 chicken (3 to 4 pounds), rinsed, patted dry, and cut into 8 pieces (see "Cutting Up a Whole Chicken," page 10)
½ teaspoon salt
¼ teaspoon pepper
1 tablespoon butter
1 tablespoon vegetable oil
1 large onion, sliced
4 medium carrots, peeled, halved crosswise, then halved or quartered lengthwise depending on thickness

8 ounces white button mushrooms, cleaned and halved if large
3 large fresh thyme sprigs or ½ teaspoon dried thyme
½ cup dry white wine

1. Sprinkle the chicken with salt and pepper. Heat the butter and oil in a 12-inch sauté pan or small Dutch oven over medium-high heat. When butter foaming subsides, add the chicken; sauté until browned on both sides, moving around to brown evenly, 10 to 15 minutes. Remove the chicken pieces from the pan and set aside.

2. Discard all but a thin film of fat from the pan. Add the onion, carrots, and mushrooms; sauté, stirring frequently to prevent scorching, until the pan juices evaporate, 4 to 5 minutes.

3. Return the chicken and accumulated juices to the pan, moving the vegetables to the top. Add the thyme sprigs and wine; bring to a boil. Lower the heat, cover, and barely simmer until the chicken is cooked through, basting 3 or 4 times, about 25 minutes. Taste for salt and pepper.

4. Place a portion of chicken on each plate; top with the vegetables. Ladle the juices over both chicken and vegetables and/or the accompanying starch and serve immediately.

◆

Braised Chicken with Potatoes and Indian Spices

THE POTATOES MAKE THIS DISH FAIRLY HEARTY, BUT YOU CAN STILL SERVE THE CHICKEN WITH WHITE RICE, PREFERABLY BASMATI RICE. SERVES 4.

1 chicken (3 to 4 pounds), rinsed, patted dry, and cut into 8 pieces (see "Cutting Up a Whole Chicken," page 10)
¾ teaspoon salt
¼ teaspoon pepper
1 tablespoon butter
1 tablespoon vegetable oil
1 large onion, sliced

4 medium carrots, peeled, halved crosswise, then halved or quartered lengthwise depending on thickness

3 medium potatoes, peeled and cut into 1-inch chunks

2 garlic cloves, minced

1 tablespoon minced fresh gingerroot

½ cup plain yogurt

⅓ cup chicken stock

1 teaspoon ground cumin

½ teaspoon ground turmeric

½ teaspoon ground coriander

⅛ teaspoon cayenne pepper

Pinch ground cinnamon

1 cup frozen peas

1. Sprinkle the chicken with ½ teaspoon salt and the pepper. Heat the butter and oil in a 12-inch sauté pan or small Dutch oven over medium-high heat. When butter foaming subsides, add the chicken; sauté until browned on both sides, moving around to brown evenly, 10 to 15 minutes. Remove the chicken pieces from the pan and set aside.

2. Discard all but a thin film of fat from the pan. Add the onion, carrots, and potatoes; sauté, stirring frequently to prevent scorching, until the pan juices evaporate, 4 to 5 minutes. Stir in the garlic and ginger.

3. Return the chicken and accumulated juices to the pan, moving the vegetables to the top. Combine the yogurt and stock in a small bowl. Add the mixture to the pan along with the cumin, turmeric, coriander, cayenne, cinnamon, and remaining ¼ teaspoon salt; bring to a bare simmer, cover, and continue barely simmering until the chicken is cooked through, basting 3 or 4 times, about 25 minutes. Taste for salt and pepper. Add the peas during the last 3 minutes of cooking.

4. Place a portion of chicken on each plate; top with the vegetables. Ladle the juices over both chicken and vegetables and/or the accompanying starch and serve immediately.

TRIMMING AND QUARTERING A LEEK

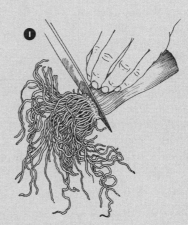

1. To prepare leeks for a braise, trim the dark green leaves and root ends, keeping the bases intact.

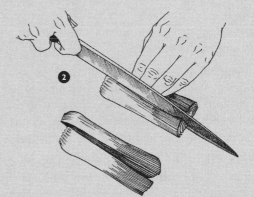

2. Quarter each leek lengthwise and rinse thoroughly. Quartered leeks can be added to a braise without further slicing.

Braised Chicken with Red Cabbage

CABBAGE BECOMES A RICH, RED SAUCE WHEN SLOW-COOKED ALONG WITH THE CHICKEN IN THIS SIMPLE BRAISE. SERVE WITH BUTTERED NOODLES. SERVES 4.

1 chicken (3 to 4 pounds), rinsed, patted dry, and cut into 8 pieces (see "Cutting Up a Whole Chicken," page 10)
1/2 teaspoon salt
1/4 teaspoon pepper
1 tablespoon butter
1 tablespoon vegetable oil
1 large onion, sliced
3 garlic cloves, peeled and crushed
1 small red cabbage, cored and shredded (about 4 cups)
3 large fresh thyme sprigs or 1/2 teaspoon dried thyme
1/2 cup dry white wine

1. Sprinkle the chicken with salt and pepper. Heat the butter and oil in a 12-inch sauté pan or small Dutch oven over medium-high heat. When butter foaming subsides, add the chicken; sauté until browned on both sides, moving around to brown evenly, 10 to 15 minutes. Remove the chicken pieces from the pan and set aside.

2. Discard all but a thin film of fat from the pan. Add the onion; sauté, stirring frequently to prevent scorching, until golden, 3 to 4 minutes; add the garlic and sauté another minute. Add the cabbage and cook, stirring several times, an additional 6 to 7 minutes.

3. Return the chicken and accumulated juices to the pan, moving the cabbage to the top. Add the thyme and wine; bring to a boil. Lower the heat, cover, and barely simmer until the chicken is cooked through, basting 3 or 4 times, about 25 minutes. Taste for salt and pepper.

4. Place a portion of chicken on each plate; top with cabbage. Ladle the juices over both chicken and cabbage and/or the accompanying starch and serve immediately.

Braised Chicken with Turnips and North African Spices

PLAIN COUSCOUS WOULD BE A GOOD ACCOMPANIMENT TO THIS FLAVORFUL DISH. POTATOES MIGHT BE USED IN PLACE OF TURNIPS, IF DESIRED. SERVES 4.

1 chicken (3 to 4 pounds), rinsed, patted dry, and cut into 8 pieces (see "Cutting Up a Whole Chicken," page 10)
1/2 teaspoon salt
1/4 teaspoon pepper
1 tablespoon butter
1 tablespoon vegetable oil
1 large onion, sliced
4 medium carrots, peeled, halved crosswise, then halved or quartered lengthwise depending on thickness
2 turnips (about 1 pound), peeled, sliced 1/4 inch thick, and then cut into 1/2-inch strips
1 garlic clove, minced
1/4 teaspoon cayenne pepper
1/4 teaspoon ground cumin
1/4 teaspoon ground cinnamon
1/8 teaspoon ground coriander
1 cup cooked or canned chickpeas, drained
1/2 cup cooking liquid from chickpeas, or 1/2 cup water

1. Sprinkle the chicken with salt and pepper. Heat the butter and oil in a 12-inch sauté pan or small Dutch oven over medium-high heat. When butter foaming subsides, add the chicken; sauté until browned on both sides, moving around to brown evenly, 10 to 15 minutes. Remove the chicken pieces from the pan and set aside.

2. Discard all but a thin film of fat from the pan. Add the onion, carrots, and turnips; sauté, stirring frequently to prevent scorching, until the pan juices evaporate, 4 to 5 minutes. Stir in the garlic.

3. Return the chicken and accumulated juices to the pan, moving the vegetables to the top. Add the cayenne, cumin, cinnamon, coriander, chickpeas, and liquid; bring to a boil. Lower the heat, cover, and barely simmer until the chicken is cooked through, basting 3 or 4 times, about 25 minutes. Taste for salt and pepper.

4. Place a portion of chicken on each plate; top with the vegetables. Ladle the juices over both chicken and vegetables and/or the accompanying starch and serve immediately.

◆

Braised Chicken with Tomatoes, Black Olives, and Capers

THIS ITALIAN-INSPIRED BRAISE GOES WELL WITH POLENTA OR PASTA. SERVES 4.

- 1 chicken (3 to 4 pounds), rinsed, patted dry, and cut into 8 pieces (see "Cutting Up a Whole Chicken," page 10)
- ¹/₂ teaspoon salt
- ¹/₄ teaspoon pepper
- 1 tablespoon butter
- 1 tablespoon vegetable oil
- 1 large onion, sliced
- 8 ounces white button mushrooms, cleaned and halved if large
- 1 garlic clove, minced
- 1 28-ounce can whole tomatoes, drained, seeded, and coarsely chopped (see figure, right)
- 3 tablespoons chopped fresh parsley leaves
- 3 tablespoons chopped fresh basil leaves
- ¹/₂ cup black olives, pitted and coarsely chopped
- 2 teaspoons drained capers
- 3 large fresh thyme sprigs or ¹/₂ teaspoon dried thyme
- ¹/₄ cup hearty red wine

1. Sprinkle the chicken with salt and pepper. Heat the butter and oil in a 12-inch sauté pan or small Dutch oven over medium-high heat. When butter foaming subsides, add the chicken; sauté until browned on both sides, moving around to brown evenly, 10 to 15 minutes. Remove the chicken pieces from the pan and set aside.

2. Discard all but a thin film of fat from the pan. Add the onion and mushrooms; sauté, stirring frequently to prevent scorching, until the pan juices evaporate, 4 to 5 minutes. Stir in the garlic.

3. Return the chicken and accumulated juices to the pan, moving the vegetables to the top. Add the tomatoes, parsley, basil, olives, capers, thyme sprigs, and wine; bring to a boil. Lower the heat, cover, and barely simmer until the chicken is cooked through, basting 3 or 4 times, about 25 minutes. Taste for salt and pepper.

4. Place a portion of chicken on each plate; top with vegetables. Ladle the juices over both chicken and vegetables and/or the accompanying starch and serve immediately.

STEP-BY-STEP

SEEDING A CANNED TOMATO

As is, canned tomatoes can be too watery for use in a braise. To remove the seeds and surrounding liquid, open each drained tomato with your fingers and push the seeds and surrounding liquid down into a bowl.

Smothered Chicken with Onions

IN THIS DISH, ABUNDANT ONIONS ARE SLOW-COOKED, BRINGING OUT THEIR NATURAL CREAMINESS. BUTTERED PASTA OR PLAIN WHITE RICE MAKES A GOOD ACCOMPANIMENT TO THIS BRAISE. SERVES 4.

- 1 chicken (3 to 4 pounds), rinsed, patted dry, and cut into 8 pieces (see "Cutting Up a Whole Chicken," page 10)
- 1/2 teaspoon salt
- 1/4 teaspoon pepper
- 1 tablespoon butter
- 1 tablespoon vegetable oil
- 4 medium onions, sliced thin (about 6 cups)
- 3 large fresh thyme sprigs or 1/2 teaspoon dried thyme
- 1/4 cup cognac or brandy
- 1/4 cup water

1. Sprinkle the chicken with salt and pepper. Heat the butter and oil in a 12-inch sauté pan or small Dutch oven over medium-high heat. When butter foaming subsides, add the chicken; sauté until browned on both sides, moving around to brown evenly, 10 to 15 minutes. Remove the chicken pieces from the pan, cover, and keep warm.

2. Discard all but a thin film of fat from the pan. Turn the heat to medium-low. Add the onions, cover, and cook, stirring occasionally, until very soft, about 30 minutes. Uncover the pan; turn the heat to medium-high and sauté until the onions turn golden brown, about 5 minutes.

3. Return the chicken and accumulated juices to the pan, moving the onions to the top. Add the thyme, cognac, and water; bring to a boil. Lower the heat, cover, and barely simmer until the chicken is cooked through, basting 3 or 4 times, about 25 minutes. Taste for salt and pepper.

4. Place a portion of chicken on each plate; top with the onions. Ladle the juices over both chicken and onions and/or the accompanying starch and serve immediately.

Braised Chicken with Okra

OKRA IS A POPULAR VEGETABLE NOT ONLY IN THE AMERICAN SOUTH BUT ALSO IN INDIA, THE MIDDLE EAST, AND EASTERN EUROPE. THIS RECIPE IS AN ADAPTATION OF AN ARMENIAN STEW. SERVE WITH BULGUR PILAF OR STEAMED BROWN RICE. SERVES 4.

- 1 chicken (3 to 4 pounds), rinsed, patted dry, and cut into 8 pieces (see "Cutting Up a Whole Chicken," page 10)
- 1/2 teaspoon salt
- 1/4 teaspoon pepper
- 1 tablespoon butter
- 1 tablespoon vegetable oil
- 1 large onion, sliced
- 2 garlic cloves, finely chopped
- 1 16-ounce can whole tomatoes, drained, seeded, and coarsely chopped (see figure on page 107)
- 2 tablespoons lemon juice
- 1/2 cup dry white wine
- 3/4 pound fresh or frozen, thawed okra, stems trimmed
- 1/4 cup chopped fresh parsley leaves

1. Sprinkle the chicken with salt and pepper. Heat the butter and oil in a 12-inch sauté pan or small Dutch oven over medium-high heat. When butter foaming subsides, add the chicken; sauté until browned on both sides, moving around to brown evenly, 10 to 15 minutes. Remove the chicken pieces from the pan and set aside.

2. Discard all but a thin film of fat from the pan. Add the onion and sauté 2 minutes; add the garlic and sauté another minute.

3. Return the chicken and accumulated juices to the pan. Add the tomatoes, lemon juice, and wine; bring to a boil. Lower the heat, cover, and barely simmer. After 15 minutes, baste the chicken with the sauce and add the okra to the pot. Continue simmering until the chicken is cooked through, about 10 more minutes. Taste for salt and pepper. Stir in parsley.

4. Place a portion of chicken on each plate; top with okra. Ladle the juices over both chicken and okra and/or the accompanying starch and serve immediately.

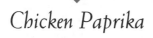

Chicken Paprika

CHICKEN PAPRIKA IS A HUNGARIAN CLASSIC THAT'S BECOME A CLASSIC HERE AS WELL. THE PAPRIKA AND BELL PEPPER SAUCE IS ENRICHED WITH SOUR CREAM AND HEAVY CREAM, MAKING IT A SATISFYING WINTER DISH. SERVE WITH BUTTERED EGG NOODLES. **SERVES 4.**

1 chicken (3 to 4 pounds), rinsed, patted
  dry, and cut into 8 pieces (see "Cutting
  Up a Whole Chicken," page 10)
½ teaspoon salt
¼ teaspoon pepper
1 tablespoon butter
1 tablespoon vegetable oil
1 large onion, sliced
3 tablespoons sweet paprika
1 16-ounce can whole tomatoes, drained,
  seeded, and coarsely chopped (see
  figure on page 107)
1 green bell pepper, stemmed, seeded,
  and cut into strips
1 red bell pepper, stemmed, seeded, and
  cut into strips
1 fresh marjoram sprig or ¼ teaspoon
  dried marjoram
½ cup dry white wine
2 tablespoons sour cream
2 tablespoons heavy cream
2 tablespoons chopped fresh parsley
  leaves, for garnish (optional)

1. Sprinkle the chicken with salt and pepper. Heat the butter and oil in a 12-inch sauté pan or small Dutch oven over medium-high heat. When butter foaming subsides, add the chicken; sauté until browned on both sides, moving around to brown evenly, 10 to 15 minutes. Remove the chicken pieces from the pan and set aside.

2. Discard all but a thin film of fat from the pan. Add the onion; sauté, stirring frequently to prevent scorching, until soft, 4 to 5 minutes. Stir in the paprika.

3. Return the chicken and accumulated juices to the pan, moving the onion to the top. Add the tomatoes, bell peppers, marjoram, and wine; bring to a boil. Lower the heat, cover, and barely simmer until the chicken is cooked through, basting 3 or 4 times, about 25 minutes. Taste for salt and pepper.

4. Whisk together the sour cream and heavy cream in a small bowl. Lift the chicken from the pan and place a portion on each plate. Stir a few tablespoons of the hot sauce into the cream mixture and then stir the mixture back into the remaining peppers and sauce. Ladle the peppers and enriched sauce over the chicken and/or the accompanying starch, sprinkle with parsley if using, and serve immediately.

Chicken Cacciatore

IN THIS CLASSIC ITALIAN FRICASSEE, WE BELIEVE THAT SIMPLER IS BETTER. WE HAVEN'T ADDED THE WHOLE VEGETABLE GARDEN—JUST SOME GREEN BELL PEPPER TO BRIGHTEN THE SIMPLE TOMATO SAUCE. ROSEMARY GIVES IT A WOODSY FLAVOR. SERVE PASTA OR POLENTA ON THE SIDE. **SERVES 4.**

1 chicken (3 to 4 pounds), rinsed, patted
  dry, and cut into 8 pieces (see "Cutting
  Up a Whole Chicken," page 10)
½ teaspoon salt
¼ teaspoon pepper
1 tablespoon butter
1 tablespoon vegetable oil
1 large onion, sliced
1 medium carrot, peeled and coarsely
  chopped
½ celery stalk, coarsely chopped
1 green bell pepper, stemmed, seeded,
  and cut into thin strips
1 garlic clove, finely chopped
1 fresh rosemary sprig or ½ teaspoon
  dried rosemary
1 cup canned whole tomatoes, coarsely
  chopped, with their juice
½ cup dry white wine

(continued on next page)

1. Sprinkle the chicken with salt and pepper. Heat the butter and oil in a 12-inch sauté pan or small Dutch oven over medium-high heat. When butter foaming subsides, add the chicken; sauté until browned on both sides, moving around to brown evenly, 10 to 15 minutes. Remove the chicken pieces from the pan and set aside.

2. Discard all but a thin film of fat from the pan. Add the onion, carrot, celery, and bell pepper; sauté, stirring frequently to prevent scorching, until the pan juices evaporate, 4 to 5 minutes. Stir in the garlic.

3. Return the chicken and accumulated juices to the pan, moving the vegetables to the top. Add the rosemary, tomatoes, and wine; bring to a boil. Lower the heat, cover, and barely simmer until the chicken is cooked through, basting 3 or 4 times, about 25 minutes. Taste for salt and pepper.

4. Place a portion of chicken on each plate; top with the vegetables. Ladle the juices over both chicken and onions and/or the accompanying starch and serve immediately.

Chicken Tagine
with Chickpeas

A TAGINE IS A MOROCCAN STEW. IN THIS SIMPLE VER-SION, THE CHICKEN IS EMBELLISHED WITH CHICKPEAS RATHER THAN THE HEAVIER AND MORE ELABORATE TRA-DITIONAL PREPARATION OF BEATEN EGGS AND CHEESE. SERVE WITH COUSCOUS OR STEAMED POTATOES. COOK YOUR OWN CHICKPEAS FOR THIS RECIPE OR USE TWO 15-OUNCE CANS. SERVES 4.

  1 chicken (3 to 4 pounds), rinsed, patted
    dry, and cut into 8 pieces (see "Cutting
    Up a Whole Chicken," page 10)
  ½ teaspoon salt
  ¼ teaspoon pepper
  1 tablespoon butter
  1 tablespoon vegetable oil
  1 large onion, sliced
  1 garlic clove, finely chopped
  ½ teaspoon ground cinnamon

  ¼ teaspoon cayenne pepper
  4 cups cooked or canned chickpeas,
    drained
  ½ cup dry white wine

1. Sprinkle the chicken with salt and pepper. Heat the butter and oil in a 12-inch sauté pan or small Dutch oven over medium-high heat. When butter foaming subsides, add the chicken; sauté until browned on both sides, moving around to brown evenly, 10 to 15 minutes. Remove the chicken pieces from the pan and set aside.

2. Discard all but a thin film of fat from the pan. Add the onion and sauté, stirring frequently to prevent scorching, until the onion is softened, 3 to 4 minutes. Add the garlic, cinnamon, and cayenne and sauté another minute.

3. Return the chicken and accumulated juices to the pan, moving the onion to the top. Add the chickpeas and wine; bring to a boil. Lower the heat, cover, and barely simmer until the chicken is cooked through, basting 3 or 4 times, about 25 minutes. Taste for salt and pepper.

4. Place a portion of chicken on each plate; top with the chickpeas. Ladle the juices over both chicken and chickpeas and/or the accompanying starch and serve immediately.

Spanish Braised Chicken
with Sherry and Peppers

THE FLAVORS OF SHERRY, PEPPERS, AND ORANGE JUICE EVOKE THE COAST OF SPAIN IN THIS SIMPLE BRAISE. SERVE WITH RICE, PERHAPS PERFUMED WITH A LITTLE SAFFRON FOR COLOR AND FLAVOR. SERVES 4.

  1 chicken (3 to 4 pounds), rinsed, patted
    dry, and cut into 8 pieces (see "Cutting
    Up a Whole Chicken," page 10)
  ½ teaspoon salt
  ¼ teaspoon pepper
  1 tablespoon butter
  1 tablespoon vegetable oil
  1 large onion, sliced

2 garlic cloves, finely chopped
4 red, green, and yellow bell peppers, stemmed, seeded, and cut into thin strips
3 large fresh thyme sprigs or ½ teaspoon dried thyme
12 green olives, pitted and coarsely chopped
½ cup dry sherry
2 tablespoons orange juice

1. Sprinkle the chicken with salt and pepper. Heat the butter and oil in a 12-inch sauté pan or small Dutch oven over medium-high heat. When butter foaming subsides, add the chicken; sauté until browned on both sides, moving around to brown evenly, 10 to 15 minutes. Remove the chicken pieces from the pan and set aside.

2. Discard all but a thin film of fat from the pan. Add the onion and sauté, stirring frequently to prevent scorching, until softened, 3 to 4 minutes. Add the garlic and sauté another minute. Add the bell peppers and thyme and continue cooking until the peppers are soft, about 10 minutes. Stir in the olives.

3. Return the chicken and accumulated juices to the pan, moving the vegetables to the top. Add the sherry and juice; bring to a boil. Lower the heat, cover, and barely simmer until the chicken is cooked through, basting 3 or 4 times, about 25 minutes. Taste for salt and pepper.

4. Place a portion of chicken on each plate; top with the peppers. Ladle the juices over both chicken and peppers and/or the accompanying starch and serve immediately.

Chicken Smothered in Mushrooms

A STAPLE OF FRENCH COUNTRY COOKING, CHICKEN WITH MUSHROOMS IS SIMPLE BUT SATISFYING WHEN SERVED OVER BUTTERED EGG NOODLES OR ALONGSIDE ROASTED POTATOES. SERVES 4.

1 chicken (3 to 4 pounds), rinsed, patted dry, and cut into 8 pieces (see "Cutting Up a Whole Chicken," page 10)
½ teaspoon salt
¼ teaspoon pepper
1 tablespoon butter
1 tablespoon vegetable oil
2 garlic cloves, finely chopped
1 pound white button mushrooms, stemmed and sliced
1 16-ounce can whole tomatoes, drained, seeded, and coarsely chopped (see figure on page 107)
½ cup dry white wine
2 tablespoons chopped fresh parsley leaves, for garnish

1. Sprinkle the chicken with salt and pepper. Heat the butter and oil in a 12-inch sauté pan or small Dutch oven over medium-high heat. When butter foaming subsides, add the chicken; sauté until browned on both sides, moving around to brown evenly, 10 to 15 minutes. Remove the chicken pieces from the pan and set aside.

2. Discard all but a thin film of fat from the pan. Add the garlic and cook, stirring, 1 minute. Add the mushrooms; sauté, stirring frequently to prevent scorching, until the pan juices evaporate, 4 to 5 minutes.

3. Return the chicken and accumulated juices to the pan, moving the mushrooms to the top. Add the tomatoes and wine; bring to a boil. Lower the heat, cover, and barely simmer until the chicken is cooked through, basting 3 or 4 times, about 25 minutes. Taste for salt and pepper.

4. Place a portion of chicken on each plate; top with the mushrooms. Ladle the juices over both chicken and vegetables and/or the accompanying starch, garnish with the parsley, and serve immediately.

Chicken with Forty Cloves of Garlic

THIS DISH IS A COMMON ITEM ON FRENCH BISTRO MENUS. THE GARLIC SOFTENS AND MELLOWS WHEN COOKED WITH THE CHICKEN AND BECOMES A CREAMY VEGETABLE TOPPING. SERVE WITH MASHED POTATOES OR TOASTED BAGUETTE SLICES THAT CAN ALSO BE SPREAD WITH THE SOFTENED GARLIC. SERVES 4.

1 chicken (3 to 4 pounds), rinsed, patted dry, and cut into 8 pieces (see "Cutting Up a Whole Chicken," page 10)
1/2 teaspoon salt
1/4 teaspoon pepper
1 tablespoon butter
1 tablespoon vegetable oil
40 large garlic cloves, peeled (see below)
3 large fresh thyme sprigs or 1/2 teaspoon dried thyme
1/2 cup dry white wine

STEP-BY-STEP

PEELING A WHOLE HEAD OF GARLIC AT ONCE

1. Peeling a lot of garlic cloves, one by one, can be time-consuming. We prefer this method. Start by pressing down on a head of garlic with the heel of your hand to loosen the cloves.

2. Remove as much of the papery skin as possible.

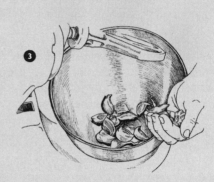

3. Lightly oil the bowl of a standing mixer and fit the mixer with the paddle attachment. Add the garlic cloves.

4. Mix on very low speed until the peels have fallen off, about 1 minute.

1. Sprinkle the chicken with salt and pepper. Heat the butter and oil in a 12-inch sauté pan or small Dutch oven over medium-high heat. When butter foaming subsides, add the chicken; sauté until browned on both sides, moving around to brown evenly, 10 to 15 minutes. Remove the chicken pieces from the pan and set aside.

2. Discard all but a thin film of fat from the pan. Reduce the heat to medium. Add the garlic cloves; sauté, stirring frequently to prevent scorching, until golden and softened, 10 to 12 minutes. (Be careful not to burn or the garlic will become bitter.)

3. Return the chicken and accumulated juices to the pan, moving the garlic to the top. Add the thyme and wine; bring to a boil. Lower the heat, cover, and barely simmer until the chicken is cooked through, basting 3 or 4 times, about 25 minutes. Taste for salt and pepper.

4. Place a portion of chicken on each plate; top with the garlic. Ladle the juices over both chicken and garlic and/or the accompanying starch and serve immediately.

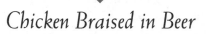

Chicken Braised in Beer

IN THIS BELGIAN RECIPE, THE CHICKEN AND VEGETA-
BLES ARE SIMMERED IN A BOTTLE OF FULL-BODIED BEER
INSTEAD OF WINE. A LITTLE BIT OF FLOUR AND HEAVY
CREAM THICKEN THE DISTINCTIVELY FLAVORED SAUCE.
SERVE WITH EGG NOODLES OR POTATO PANCAKES.
SERVES 4.

 1 chicken (3 to 4 pounds), rinsed, patted
   dry, and cut into 8 pieces (see "Cutting
   Up a Whole Chicken," page 10)
 ½ teaspoon salt
 ¼ teaspoon pepper
 1 tablespoon butter
 1 tablespoon vegetable oil
 6 shallots, peeled and halved
 4 medium carrots, peeled, halved
   crosswise, then halved or quartered
   lengthwise depending on thickness

 8 ounces white button mushrooms,
   cleaned and halved if large
 2 tablespoons flour
 1 bottle (12 ounces) beer, preferably full-
   flavored ale or dark beer
 2 bay leaves
 4 fresh thyme sprigs
 4 fresh parsley sprigs
 ¼ cup heavy cream

1. Sprinkle the chicken with salt and pepper. Heat the butter and oil in a 12-inch sauté pan or small Dutch oven over medium-high heat. When butter foaming subsides, add the chicken; sauté until browned on both sides, moving around to brown evenly, 10 to 15 minutes. Remove the chicken pieces from the pan and set aside.

2. Discard all but a thin film of fat from the pan. Add the shallots, carrots, and mushrooms; sauté, stirring frequently to prevent scorching, until the pan juices evaporate, 4 to 5 minutes. Sprinkle the flour over the vegetables and stir to distribute evenly. Add the beer and bring to a simmer, scraping any browned bits from the bottom of the pan with a wooden spoon.

3. Return the chicken and accumulated juices to the pan, moving the vegetables to the top. Add the bay leaves, thyme, and parsley. Bring to a boil. Lower the heat, cover, and barely simmer until the chicken is cooked through, basting 3 or 4 times, about 25 minutes. Discard the herbs.

4. Remove the chicken to a platter and cover with foil to keep warm. Bring the sauce and vegetables to a boil and reduce by one-third, 3 to 4 minutes. Stir in the cream and reduce further until sauce is thickened, 2 to 3 minutes. Taste for salt and pepper.

5. Place a portion of chicken on each plate; top with the vegetables and some sauce. Ladle the remaining sauce over both the chicken and vegetables and/or the accompanying starch and serve immediately.

Chicken Braised in Wine Vinegar

USE THE BEST QUALITY VINEGAR HERE, SINCE IT IS THE KEY INGREDIENT IN THE SAUCE. IT SHOULD BE POURED INTO THE PAN VERY SLOWLY; OTHERWISE, YOU WILL BE OVERWHELMED BY THE FUMES. SERVE WITH MASHED POTATOES OR PASTA. SINCE THERE ARE NO VEGETABLES (OTHER THAN THE TOMATOES), ADD A SIDE DISH AS WELL. SERVES 4.

- 1 chicken (3 to 4 pounds), rinsed, patted dry, and cut into 8 pieces (see "Cutting Up a Whole Chicken," page 10)
- ½ teaspoon salt
- ¼ teaspoon pepper
- 3 tablespoons butter
- 1 tablespoon vegetable oil
- 1 cup red wine vinegar
- 3 canned whole tomatoes, drained, seeded, and coarsely chopped (see figure on page 107)
- ½ cup water
- 2 tablespoons chopped fresh parsley leaves, for garnish

1. Sprinkle the chicken with salt and pepper. Heat 1 tablespoon butter and the oil in a 12-inch sauté pan or small Dutch oven over medium-high heat. When butter foaming subsides, add the chicken; sauté until browned on both sides, moving around to brown evenly, 10 to 15 minutes. Remove the chicken pieces from the pan and set aside.

2. Discard all but a thin film of fat from the pan. Return the chicken and accumulated juices to the pan. Add the vinegar. Bring to a high simmer and reduce the vinegar by half, turning the chicken occasionally, about 5 minutes. Add the tomatoes and water, lower the heat, cover, and barely simmer until the chicken is cooked through, basting 3 or 4 times, about 20 minutes. Taste for salt and pepper.

3. Remove the pan from the heat. Place a portion of chicken on each plate; stir the remaining 2 tablespoons of butter into the sauce. Pour the sauce over the chicken and the accompanying starch, sprinkle with parsley, and serve immediately.

Braised Chicken with Ham and Peppers

SMOKY HAM AND HOT RED PEPPER FLAKES SEASON THIS STANDARD FROM SOUTHWEST FRANCE. RICE OR PASTA CAN BE SERVED WITH THIS CHICKEN DISH. SERVES 4.

- 1 chicken (3 to 4 pounds), rinsed, patted dry, and cut into 8 pieces (see "Cutting Up a Whole Chicken," page 10)
- ½ teaspoon salt
- ¼ teaspoon pepper
- 1 tablespoon butter
- 1 tablespoon vegetable oil
- 2 large onions, sliced
- 6 garlic cloves, peeled and sliced
- 4 red bell peppers, stemmed, seeded, and sliced thick
- ½ pound thickly sliced prosciutto or country ham, cut into ¼-inch dice
- ½ teaspoon hot red pepper flakes, or to taste
- 1 16-ounce can whole tomatoes, drained, seeded, and coarsely chopped (see figure on page 107)

1. Sprinkle the chicken with salt and pepper. Heat the butter and oil in a 12-inch sauté pan or small Dutch oven over medium-high heat. When butter foaming subsides, add the chicken; sauté until browned on both sides, moving around to brown evenly, 10 to 15 minutes. Remove the chicken pieces from the pan, cover, and keep warm.

2. Discard all but a thin film of fat from the pan. Add the onions; sauté, stirring frequently to prevent scorching, until softened, 3 to 4 minutes; add the garlic and sauté another minute. Turn the heat to medium, add the bell peppers, prosciutto, and red pepper flakes, and cook until soft, about 15 minutes.

3. Return the chicken and accumulated juices to the pan, moving the vegetables to the top. Add the tomatoes; bring to a boil. Lower the heat, cover, and barely simmer until the chicken is cooked through, basting 3 or 4 times, about 25 minutes. Taste for salt and pepper.

4. Place a portion of chicken on each plate; top with the vegetables. Ladle the juices over both chicken and vegetables and/or the accompanying starch and serve immediately.

◆

Chicken and Grapes Braised in White Wine

PEELING THE GRAPES MIGHT SOUND SILLY, BUT THE RESULT—A SILKY SMOOTH FRUIT SAUCE—IS WELL WORTH THE SMALL EFFORT. THIS DISH IS EXCELLENT WITH COUSCOUS OR BUTTERED ORZO. SERVES 4.

> 1 chicken (3 to 4 pounds), rinsed, patted dry, and cut into 8 pieces (see "Cutting Up a Whole Chicken," page 10)
> 1/2 teaspoon salt
> 1/4 teaspoon pepper
> 1 tablespoon butter
> 1 tablespoon vegetable oil
> 3 medium shallots, finely chopped
> 2 tablespoons sugar
> 1/2 cup chicken stock or low-salt canned broth
> 1/2 cup fruity white wine, such as Riesling
> 1/4 cup heavy cream
> 1/2 pound seedless green grapes, peeled and halved

1. Sprinkle the chicken with salt and pepper. Heat the butter and oil in a 12-inch sauté pan or small Dutch oven over medium-high heat. When butter foaming subsides, add the chicken; sauté until browned on both sides, moving around to brown evenly, 10 to 15 minutes. Remove the chicken pieces from the pan and set aside.

2. Discard all but a thin film of fat from the pan. Add the shallots; sauté, stirring frequently to prevent scorching, until softened, 3 to 4 minutes.

3. Add the sugar, stock, and wine. Stir to dissolve the sugar. Return the chicken and accumulated juices to the pan. Bring to a boil. Lower the heat, cover, and barely simmer until the chicken is cooked through, basting 3 or 4 times, about 25 minutes.

4. Remove the chicken to a platter and cover with foil to keep warm. Bring the sauce to a boil and simmer until it has reduced by one-third, 2 to 3 minutes. Stir in the cream and reduce further until sauce is thickened, 3 to 4 minutes. Taste for salt and pepper. Stir in the grapes and heat through, 1 to 2 minutes.

5. Place a portion of chicken on each plate; top with some sauce and the grapes. Ladle the remaining sauce over both the chicken and grapes and/or the accompanying starch and serve immediately.

◆

Braised Chicken with Eggplant and Zucchini

BRAISED EGGPLANT, ZUCCHINI, AND ONIONS BECOME A RICH BUT LOW-FAT VEGETABLE JAM THAT MOISTENS THE CHICKEN IN THIS DISH. CHOP THE MINT AT THE LAST MINUTE TO MAINTAIN MAXIMUM FLAVOR. SERVE WITH COUSCOUS OR PASTA. SERVES 4.

> 1 chicken (3 to 4 pounds), rinsed, patted dry, and cut into 8 pieces (see "Cutting Up a Whole Chicken," page 10)
> 1/2 teaspoon salt
> 1/4 teaspoon pepper
> 1 tablespoon butter
> 1 tablespoon vegetable oil
> 1 large onion, sliced
> 2 garlic cloves, finely chopped
> 1 medium eggplant (about 1 pound), peeled and cut into 1-inch cubes
> 3 small zucchini (about 1 pound), cut into 1/2-inch rounds
> 1 teaspoon fresh thyme leaves
> 1/2 cup chicken stock or low-salt canned broth
> 1/2 cup dry white wine
> 1/4 cup chopped fresh mint leaves

1. Sprinkle the chicken with salt and pepper. Heat the butter and oil in a 12-inch sauté pan or small Dutch oven over medium-high heat. When butter foaming subsides, add the chicken; sauté until browned

(continued on next page)

on both sides, moving around to brown evenly, 10 to 15 minutes. Remove the chicken pieces from the pan, cover, and keep warm.

2. Discard all but a thin film of fat from the pan. Add the onion; sauté, stirring frequently to prevent scorching, until softened, 3 to 4 minutes. Add the garlic, eggplant, and zucchini. Sauté until the eggplant begins to soften, about 5 minutes.

3. Return the chicken and accumulated juices to the pan, moving the vegetables to the top. Add the thyme, stock, and wine; bring to a boil. Lower the heat, cover, and barely simmer until the chicken is cooked through, basting 3 or 4 times, about 25 minutes. Stir in the mint. Taste for salt and pepper.

4. Place a portion of chicken on each plate; top with the vegetables. Ladle the juices over both chicken and vegetables and/or the accompanying starch and serve immediately.

◆

Braised Chicken with New Mexico Chiles and White Beans

DRIED NEW MEXICO CHILES (ALSO KNOWN AS ANAHEIM CHILES) MAKE A MILD BUT FLAVORFUL SOUTHWESTERN-STYLE SAUCE FOR BRAISED CHICKEN AND WHITE BEANS. KIDNEY BEANS MAY BE SUBSTITUTED. SERVE AS IS OR WITH WHITE RICE. YOU WILL NEED TWO 15-OUNCE CANS OF BEANS FOR THIS RECIPE. SERVES 4.

4 dried New Mexico chiles
1 chicken (3 to 4 pounds), rinsed, patted dry, and cut into 8 pieces (see "Cutting Up a Whole Chicken," page 10)
½ teaspoon salt
¼ teaspoon pepper
1 tablespoon butter
1 tablespoon vegetable oil
1 large onion, sliced
2 garlic cloves, finely chopped
1 bay leaf

½ teaspoon ground allspice
1 tablespoon sugar
4 cups cooked or canned white beans, drained
½ cup chicken stock or low-salt canned broth
¼ cup red wine vinegar

1. Place the chiles in a small bowl and cover with boiling water. Soak until soft, about 15 minutes. Drain the chiles and discard the soaking liquid. Stem and seed the chiles; coarsely chop them and set aside.

2. Sprinkle the chicken with salt and pepper. Heat the butter and oil in a 12-inch sauté pan or small Dutch oven over medium-high heat. When butter foaming subsides, add the chicken; sauté until browned on both sides, moving around to brown evenly, 10 to 15 minutes. Remove the chicken pieces from the pan and set aside.

3. Discard all but a thin film of fat from the pan. Add the onion; sauté, stirring frequently to prevent scorching, until softened, 3 to 4 minutes. Add the garlic and sauté another minute. Add the chiles, bay leaf, allspice, sugar, beans, stock, and vinegar.

4. Return the chicken and accumulated juices to the pan, moving onion and beans to the top; bring to a boil. Lower the heat, cover, and barely simmer until the chicken is cooked through, basting 3 or 4 times, about 25 minutes. Taste for salt and pepper.

5. Place a portion of chicken on each plate; top with the beans. Ladle the juices over both chicken and/or the accompanying starch and serve immediately.

Cuban-Style Chicken Fricassee

THIS HEARTY CARIBBEAN STEW IS STUDDED WITH OLIVES, CAPERS, AND RAISINS. DICED POTATOES MAKE IT A ONE-DISH MEAL. SERVES 4.

> 1 chicken (3 to 4 pounds), rinsed, patted dry, and cut into 8 pieces (see "Cutting Up a Whole Chicken," page 10)
> 1/2 teaspoon salt
> 1/4 teaspoon pepper
> 1 tablespoon butter
> 1 tablespoon vegetable oil
> 2 large onions, sliced
> 2 garlic cloves, finely chopped
> 3 medium potatoes (about 1 1/2 pounds), peeled and cut into 1-inch chunks
> 1 green bell pepper, stemmed, seeded, and cut into 1/4-inch dice
> 2 tablespoons drained capers, rinsed
> 1/2 cup whole green olives stuffed with pimientos
> 1/2 cup raisins
> 1 cup canned whole tomatoes, drained, seeded, and coarsely chopped (see figure on page 107)
> 1/2 cup red wine vinegar

1. Sprinkle the chicken with salt and pepper. Heat the butter and oil in a 12-inch sauté pan or small Dutch oven over medium-high heat. When butter foaming subsides, add the chicken; sauté until browned on both sides, moving around to brown evenly, 10 to 15 minutes. Remove the chicken pieces from the pan and set aside.

2. Discard all but a thin film of fat from the pan. Add the onions; sauté, stirring frequently to prevent scorching, until softened, 3 to 4 minutes. Add the garlic and sauté another minute. Add the potatoes and bell pepper and sauté, stirring frequently, until the pan juices evaporate, 4 to 5 minutes.

3. Return the chicken and accumulated juices to the pan, moving the vegetables to the top. Add the capers, olives, raisins, tomatoes, and vinegar; bring to a boil. Lower the heat, cover, and barely simmer until

the chicken is cooked through, basting 3 or 4 times, about 25 minutes. Taste for salt and pepper.

4. Place a portion of chicken on each plate; top with the vegetables. Ladle the juices over both chicken and vegetables and/or the accompanying starch and serve immediately.

◆

Braised Chicken with Tarragon Vinegar

FRESH TARRAGON STIRRED INTO THE FINISHED DISH ENHANCES THE FLAVOR OF THE TARRAGON VINEGAR AND TOMATOES IN THIS LIGHT BRAISE. SERVE WITH PASTA OR RICE. SERVES 4.

> 1 chicken (3 to 4 pounds), rinsed, patted dry, and cut into 8 pieces (see "Cutting Up a Whole Chicken," page 10)
> 1/2 teaspoon salt
> 1/4 teaspoon pepper
> 1 tablespoon butter
> 1 tablespoon vegetable oil
> 3 medium shallots, finely chopped
> 4 fresh or canned plum tomatoes, peeled, cored, seeded, and chopped (see figure on page 107)
> 1/2 cup tarragon vinegar
> 1/2 cup dry white wine
> 1/4 cup chopped fresh tarragon leaves

1. Sprinkle the chicken with salt and pepper. Heat the butter and oil in a 12-inch sauté pan or small Dutch oven over medium-high heat. When butter foaming subsides, add the chicken; sauté until browned on both sides, moving around to brown evenly, 10 to 15 minutes. Remove the chicken pieces from the pan and set aside.

2. Discard all but a thin film of fat from pan. Add the shallots and sauté, stirring frequently to prevent scorching, until softened, 2 to 3 minutes. Add the tomatoes and cook until they start to break down, 3 to 4 minutes.

(continued on next page)

3. Return the chicken and accumulated juices to the pan. Add the vinegar and wine; bring to a boil. Lower the heat, cover, and barely simmer until the chicken is cooked through, basting 3 or 4 times, about 25 minutes. Stir in the tarragon. Taste for salt and pepper.

4. Place a portion of chicken on each plate; top with the sauce. Ladle the remaining sauce over the accompanying starch and serve immediately.

◆

Braised Chicken with Lentils and Yogurt

EXOTICALLY SPICED LENTILS AND YOGURT MAKE A SAUCE HERE. GARAM MASALA, AVAILABLE IN MANY SUPERMARKETS AND GOURMET SHOPS, IS AN INDIAN BLEND OF CUMIN, PEPPER, CINNAMON, CLOVES, CORIANDER, AND CARDAMOM. THE LENTILS MIGHT TAKE A HALF HOUR OR MORE TO SOFTEN, THUS THE SLIGHTLY LONGER BRAISING TIME IN THIS RECIPE. SERVE STEAMED WHITE, BROWN, OR BASMATI RICE ON THE SIDE. SERVES 4.

> 1 chicken (3 to 4 pounds), rinsed, patted dry, and cut into 8 pieces (see "Cutting Up a Whole Chicken," page 10)
> ¾ teaspoon salt
> ¼ teaspoon pepper
> 1 tablespoon butter
> 1 tablespoon vegetable oil
> 6 whole scallions, chopped
> 2 garlic cloves, finely chopped
> ½ cup plain yogurt
> 1½ cups chicken stock or low-salt canned broth
> 3 fresh or canned plum tomatoes, peeled, cored, seeded, and chopped (see figure on page 107)
> ½ cup lentils
> 3 teaspoons garam masala
> ¼ cup chopped fresh cilantro leaves

1. Sprinkle the chicken with ½ teaspoon salt and the pepper. Heat the butter and oil in a 12-inch sauté pan or small Dutch oven over medium-high heat. When butter foaming subsides, add the chicken; sauté until browned on both sides, moving around to brown evenly, 10 to 15 minutes. Remove the chicken pieces from the pan and set aside.

2. Discard all but a thin film of fat from the pan. Add the scallions; sauté, stirring frequently to prevent scorching, until softened, 3 to 4 minutes. Add the garlic and sauté another minute.

3. Return the chicken and accumulated juices to the pan, moving the vegetables to the top. Combine the yogurt and stock in a small bowl. Add the mixture to the pan along with the tomatoes, lentils, and garam masala. Bring to a bare simmer, cover, and barely simmer until the chicken is cooked through and lentils are tender, 30 to 35 minutes. Stir in the cilantro. Taste for salt and pepper.

4. Place a portion of chicken on each plate; top with the lentils. Ladle the juices over both chicken and vegetables and/or the accompanying starch and serve immediately.

◆

Braised Chicken with Morels and Cream

MAKE THIS LUXURIOUS DISH IN THE SPRING, WHEN FRESH MORELS ARE AVAILABLE. IT IS ESPECIALLY GOOD SERVED OVER BUTTERED EGG NOODLES. SERVES 4.

> 1 chicken (3 to 4 pounds), rinsed, patted dry, and cut into 8 pieces (see "Cutting Up a Whole Chicken," page 10)
> ½ teaspoon salt
> ¼ teaspoon pepper
> 1 tablespoon butter
> 1 tablespoon vegetable oil
> 2 medium shallots, finely chopped
> ½ pound morel mushrooms, halved if large
> ½ cup dry white wine
> 2 tablespoons minced fresh chives
> ½ cup heavy cream

1. Sprinkle the chicken with salt and pepper. Heat the butter and oil in a 12-inch sauté pan or small Dutch oven over medium-high heat. When butter foaming subsides, add the chicken; sauté until browned on both sides, moving around to brown evenly, 10 to 15 minutes. Remove the chicken pieces from the pan and set aside.

2. Discard all but a thin film of fat from the pan. Add the shallots and sauté, stirring frequently, until softened but not browned, 2 to 3 minutes. Add the morels; sauté, stirring frequently to prevent scorching, until the pan juices evaporate, 4 to 5 minutes.

3. Return the chicken and accumulated juices to the pan, moving the morels to the top. Add the wine; bring to a boil. Lower the heat, cover, and barely simmer until the chicken is cooked through, basting 3 or 4 times, about 25 minutes. Stir in the chives.

4. Lift the chicken from the pan and place a portion on each plate; stir the heavy cream into the mushroom sauce, bring to a boil, and simmer until slightly thickened, 3 to 4 minutes. Taste for salt and pepper. Top the chicken with the mushrooms. Ladle the remaining sauce over both chicken and mushrooms and/or the accompanying starch, and serve immediately.

◆

Braised Chicken with Leeks, Potatoes, and Saffron

THE CHICKEN CAN BE SERVED OVER THE SLICED POTATOES HERE SO THERE IS NO NEED FOR ANOTHER STARCH. ALLOW AT LEAST A HALF HOUR OF BRAISING TIME FOR THE POTATOES TO SOFTEN PROPERLY. **SERVES 4.**

  1 chicken (3 to 4 pounds), rinsed, patted
    dry, and cut into 8 pieces (see "Cutting
    Up a Whole Chicken," page 10)
  ½ teaspoon salt
  ¼ teaspoon pepper
  1 tablespoon butter
  1 tablespoon vegetable oil

  4 large leeks, light green and white parts,
    trimmed, washed, and quartered
    lengthwise (see figures 1 and 2,
    page 105)
  3 medium potatoes (about 1½ pounds),
    peeled and cut into ¼-inch-thick slices
  Pinch saffron threads, crushed
  1 teaspoon sweet paprika
  1 cup canned whole tomatoes, drained,
    seeded, and coarsely chopped (see
    figure on page 107)
  ½ cup chicken stock or low-salt canned
    broth

1. Sprinkle the chicken with salt and pepper. Heat the butter and oil in a 12-inch sauté pan or small Dutch oven over medium-high heat. When butter foaming subsides, add the chicken; sauté until browned on both sides, moving around to brown evenly, 10 to 15 minutes. Remove the chicken pieces from the pan and set aside.

2. Discard all but a thin film of fat from the pan. Add the leeks and potatoes; sauté, stirring frequently to prevent scorching, until softened, 5 to 7 minutes.

3. Return the chicken and accumulated juices to the pan, moving the vegetables to the top. Add the saffron, paprika, tomatoes, and stock; bring to a boil. Lower the heat, cover, and barely simmer until the chicken and potatoes are cooked through, basting 3 or 4 times, 30 to 35 minutes. Taste for salt and pepper.

4. Place some potatoes on each plate and top with a portion of chicken and leeks. Ladle the juices over the chicken and serve immediately.

Coq au Vin

COQ AU VIN, OR CHICKEN SIMMERED IN RED WINE ENRICHED WITH BUTTER JUST BEFORE SERVING AND USED AS A SAUCE, IS FRANCE'S MOST FAMOUS BRAISE. OFTEN THIS RECIPE CONTAINS BITS OF BACON. WE PREFER TO COOK THE CHICKEN IN BACON FAT BUT THEN DISCARD THE BACON STRIPS, WHICH BECOME RUBBERY IF LEFT IN THE BRAISE. TRADITIONALLY, THE BACON IS BLANCHED TO TEMPER ITS SALTINESS AND SMOKY FLAVOR. TO BLANCH BACON, PLACE IT IN A SMALL SAUCEPAN AND COVER WITH WATER. BRING TO A BOIL AND SIMMER FOR 5 MINUTES. DRAIN THE BACON AND PAT DRY WITH PAPER TOWELS. USE A GOOD-QUALITY RED WINE HERE. WE LIKE COQ AU VIN WITH MASHED POTATOES OR BUTTERED NOODLES. SERVES 4.

> ¼ pound bacon, blanched
> 1 chicken (3 to 4 pounds), rinsed, patted dry, and cut into 8 pieces (see "Cutting Up a Whole Chicken," page 10)
> ½ teaspoon salt
> ¼ teaspoon pepper
> 12 pearl onions, peeled
> 2 garlic cloves, finely chopped
> 8 ounces white button mushrooms, cleaned and halved if large
> 2 tablespoons flour
> 3 large fresh thyme sprigs or ½ teaspoon dried thyme
> 1 bay leaf
> 1 cup canned whole tomatoes, drained, seeded, and coarsely chopped (see figure on page 107)
> 2 cups red wine
> 2 tablespoons butter

1. Cook the bacon in a 12-inch sauté pan or small Dutch oven over medium-high heat. When it is browned, remove and discard, leaving the bacon fat in the pan. Sprinkle the chicken with salt and pepper. Add the chicken; sauté until browned on both sides, moving around to brown evenly, 10 to 15 minutes. Remove the chicken pieces from the pan and set aside.

2. Discard all but a thin film of fat from pan. Add the onions, garlic, and mushrooms; sauté, stirring frequently to prevent scorching, until the pan juices evaporate, 4 to 5 minutes. Add the flour and stir to distribute evenly.

3. Return the chicken and accumulated juices to the pan, moving the vegetables to the top. Add the thyme, bay leaf, tomatoes, and wine; bring to a boil. Lower the heat, cover, and barely simmer until the chicken is cooked through, basting 3 or 4 times, about 25 minutes.

4. Remove the chicken, onions, and mushrooms to a platter and cover with foil to keep warm. Bring the sauce to a boil and reduce by one-third. Pour the sauce through a medium-fine strainer, pressing to extract all the juices. Return the strained sauce to the pan, taste for salt and pepper, and whisk in the butter.

5. Place a portion of chicken on each plate; top with the vegetables. Ladle the sauce over both chicken and vegetables and/or the accompanying starch and serve immediately.

◆

Country Captain Chicken

A SIMPLIFIED VERSION OF A SOUTHERN FAVORITE. WE LIKE THIS CURRIED CHICKEN DISH WITH FRESH MANGO RATHER THAN THE USUAL MANGO CHUTNEY. SERVE WITH RICE. SERVES 4.

> 1 chicken (3 to 4 pounds), rinsed, patted dry, and cut into 8 pieces (see "Cutting Up a Whole Chicken," page 10)
> ½ teaspoon salt
> ¼ teaspoon pepper
> 1 tablespoon butter
> 1 tablespoon vegetable oil
> 2 large onions, coarsely chopped
> 3 garlic cloves, finely chopped
> ¼ teaspoon cayenne pepper
> 1 tablespoon curry powder
> 1½ tablespoons paprika
> ½ cup raisins
> 1 ripe mango, peeled, pitted, and cut into ¼-inch dice (see figures, opposite)

PEELING AND PITTING A MANGO

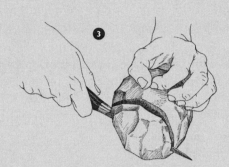

1. Remove a thin piece from one end of the mango so that it sits flat on a work surface.

2. Hold the mango, cut side down, and remove the skin in thin strips with a paring knife, working from top to bottom.

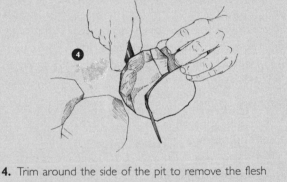

3. Once the peel has been removed, cut down along the side of the flat pit to remove the flesh from one side of the mango. Do the same thing on the other side of the pit.

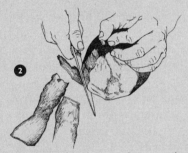

4. Trim around the side of the pit to remove the flesh still clinging to it. Slice the flesh as needed.

---

1 16-ounce can whole tomatoes, drained,
    seeded, and coarsely chopped (see
    figure on page 107)
½ cup dry red wine

1. Sprinkle the chicken with salt and pepper. Heat the butter and oil in a 12-inch sauté pan or small Dutch oven over medium-high heat. When butter foaming subsides, add the chicken; sauté until browned on both sides, moving around to brown evenly, 10 to 15 minutes. Remove the chicken pieces from the pan and set aside.

2. Discard all but a thin film of fat from the pan. Add the onions; sauté, stirring frequently to prevent scorching, until softened, 3 to 4 minutes. Add the garlic and sauté another minute.

3. Return the chicken and accumulated juices to the pan, moving the onions to the top. Add the cayenne, curry powder, paprika, raisins, mango, tomatoes, and wine; bring to a boil. Lower the heat, cover, and barely simmer until the chicken is cooked through, basting 3 or 4 times, about 25 minutes. Taste for salt and pepper.

4. Place a portion of chicken on each plate; top with the mango. Ladle the juices over both chicken and mango and/or the accompanying starch and serve immediately.

Chicken Mole

ENTIRE BOOKS HAVE BEEN WRITTEN ON MAKING MEXI-
CAN MOLE SAUCES, OF WHICH THERE ARE COUNTLESS
VARIATIONS. THIS IS OUR VERSION, WITH PUMPKIN
SEEDS AND COCOA POWDER. IT IS A LITTLE MORE TIME-
CONSUMING THAN MOST OTHER CHICKEN BRAISES,
BUT NOT A DIFFICULT INTRODUCTION TO THE GREAT
TRADITION OF MEXICAN SAUCES. SERVE WITH WHITE
RICE, POLENTA, OR CORN TORTILLAS. SERVES 4.

1 dried ancho chile
¾ cup boiling water
¾ cup canned crushed tomatoes
2 jalapeño chiles, stemmed, seeded, and
   coarsely chopped
¼ cup raisins
1½ tablespoons unsweetened cocoa
   powder
¼ teaspoon ground cloves
½ cup hulled pumpkin seeds
½ teaspoon coriander seeds
½ teaspoon anise seeds
½ teaspoon cumin seeds
1 chicken (3 to 4 pounds), rinsed, patted
   dry, and cut into 8 pieces (see "Cutting
   Up a Whole Chicken," page 10)
½ teaspoon salt
¼ teaspoon pepper
1 tablespoon butter
1 tablespoon vegetable oil
1 large onion, sliced
3 garlic cloves, finely chopped
1½ cups chicken stock or low-salt canned
   broth, or more as needed
2 cinnamon sticks, each about 5 inches long
2 tablespoons sugar

1. Soak the ancho chile in the boiling water until soft, about 30 minutes. Drain, reserving the soaking liquid. Stem, seed, and coarsely chop the chile. Combine the ancho chile, tomatoes, and jalapeños in the work bowl of a food processor. Process until smooth, scraping down the sides of the bowl as necessary. Scrape the puree into a medium bowl and stir in the raisins, cocoa, and cloves.

2. Toast the pumpkin seeds over medium heat in a small skillet until golden, 5 to 7 minutes. Combine the toasted pumpkin seeds, coriander, anise, and cumin seeds in the work bowl of the food processor and puree, adding a little of the soaking liquid to form a thick, smooth paste. Stir the seed mixture into the tomato mixture. Set aside.

3. Sprinkle the chicken with salt and pepper. Heat the butter and oil in a 12-inch sauté pan or small Dutch oven over medium-high heat. When butter foaming subsides, add the chicken; sauté until browned on both sides, moving around to brown evenly, 10 to 15 minutes. Remove the chicken pieces from the pan, cover, and keep warm.

4. Discard all but a thin film of fat from the pan. Add the onion; sauté, stirring frequently to prevent scorching, until softened, 3 to 4 minutes. Add the garlic and sauté another minute. Scrape the garlic and onion into the work bowl of the food processor. Process until finely chopped. Add the sauce and process until smooth. Return the sauce to the pan, add 1½ cups stock, the cinnamon sticks, sugar, and salt to taste; simmer, uncovered, until the sauce is the consistency of tomato puree, about 30 minutes. If the sauce becomes too thick, stir in more stock as needed.

5. Return the chicken and accumulated juices to the pan; bring to a boil. Lower the heat, cover, and barely simmer until the chicken is cooked through, basting 3 or 4 times, about 25 minutes. Taste for salt and pepper.

6. Place a portion of chicken on each plate; top with the sauce. Ladle any remaining sauce over the accompanying starch and serve immediately.

Braised Chicken with Brandy, Sausages, and Prunes

CHICKEN TOPPED WITH SAUSAGES, PRUNES, AND BRANDY MAKES A SATISFYING WINTER MEAL. SERVE WITH FETTUCCINE OR OTHER WIDE NOODLES THAT WILL HOLD THE SAUCE. SERVES 4.

- 1 pound sweet Italian sausage, cut into 1/2-inch-thick slices
- 1 chicken (3 to 4 pounds), rinsed, patted dry, and cut into 8 pieces (see "Cutting Up a Whole Chicken," page 10)
- 1/2 teaspoon salt
- 1/4 teaspoon pepper
- 1 large onion, sliced
- 3 garlic cloves, finely chopped
- 1 cup pitted prunes, halved
- 3 large fresh thyme sprigs or 1/2 teaspoon dried thyme
- 1 bay leaf
- 1/4 cup chicken stock or low-salt canned broth
- 1/4 cup brandy
- 1/4 cup chopped fresh parsley leaves

1. Brown the sausage over medium-high heat in a 12-inch sauté pan or small Dutch oven. Remove the sausage pieces with a slotted spoon and drain over paper towels. Drain all but 2 tablespoons of fat from the pan.

2. Sprinkle the chicken with salt and pepper. Add the chicken to the pan; sauté until browned on both sides, moving around to brown evenly, 10 to 15 minutes. Remove the chicken pieces from the pan and set aside.

3. Discard all but a thin film of fat from the pan. Add the onion; sauté, stirring frequently to prevent scorching, until softened. Add the garlic and sauté another minute.

4. Return the chicken and accumulated juices to the pan, moving the onion to the top. Add the sausage, prunes, thyme, bay leaf, stock, and brandy; bring to a boil. Lower the heat, cover, and barely simmer until

the chicken is cooked through, basting 3 or 4 times, about 25 minutes. Discard the thyme sprigs and bay leaf. Stir in the parsley. Taste for salt and pepper.

5. Place a portion of chicken on each plate; top with the sausage and prunes. Ladle the juices over both chicken and/or the accompanying starch and serve immediately.

◆

Braised Chicken with Onions, Fennel, and Raisins

SLICED FENNEL, ONIONS, AND RAISINS, A TYPICAL SOUTHERN ITALIAN COMBINATION, MAKE A GREAT VEGETABLE TOPPING FOR CHICKEN. SERVE WITH COUSCOUS OR PASTA. SERVES 4.

- 1 chicken (3 to 4 pounds), rinsed, patted dry, and cut into 8 pieces (see "Cutting Up a Whole Chicken," page 10)
- 1/2 teaspoon salt
- 1/4 teaspoon pepper
- 1 tablespoon butter
- 1 tablespoon vegetable oil
- 2 large onions, sliced
- 2 garlic cloves, finely chopped
- 2 medium fennel bulbs, stems, fronds, and base trimmed; bulb halved, cored, and sliced (see page 97)
- 1/2 cup raisins
- 1 16-ounce can whole tomatoes, drained, seeded, and coarsely chopped (see page 107)
- 3 large fresh thyme sprigs or 1/2 teaspoon dried thyme
- 1/2 cup dry white wine

1. Sprinkle the chicken with salt and pepper. Heat the butter and oil in a 12-inch sauté pan or small Dutch oven over medium-high heat. When butter foaming subsides, add the chicken; sauté until browned on both sides, moving around to brown evenly, 10 to 15 minutes. Remove the chicken pieces from the pan and set aside.

(continued on next page)

2. Discard all but a thin film of fat from the pan. Add the onions, garlic, and fennel; sauté, stirring frequently to prevent scorching, until the pan juices evaporate, 4 to 5 minutes.

3. Return the chicken and accumulated juices to the pan, moving the vegetables to the top. Add the raisins, tomatoes, thyme, and wine; bring to a boil. Lower the heat, cover, and barely simmer until the chicken is cooked through, basting 3 or 4 times, about 25 minutes. Taste for salt and pepper.

4. Place a portion of chicken on each plate; top with the vegetables. Ladle the juices over both chicken and vegetables and/or the accompanying starch and serve immediately.

◆

Braised Chicken with Apples and Brandy

CIDER IS ADDED ALONG WITH THE BRANDY TO GIVE THE SAUCE A PLEASANT SWEETNESS. A LITTLE CREAM GIVES THE SAUCE BODY. SERVE WITH POTATO PANCAKES OR ROASTED POTATOES. **SERVES 4.**

    1 chicken (3 to 4 pounds), rinsed, patted dry, and cut into 8 pieces (see "Cutting Up a Whole Chicken," page 10)
    1/2 teaspoon salt
    1/4 teaspoon pepper
    1 tablespoon butter
    1 tablespoon vegetable oil
    1 large onion, finely chopped
    3 tart apples (such as Granny Smith, Cortland, Rome, or Gravenstein), cored, peeled, and cut into 1/2-inch dice
    1 cup apple cider
    1/2 cup brandy
    3 large fresh thyme sprigs or 1/2 teaspoon dried thyme
    1 tablespoon sugar
    1/4 cup heavy cream
    2 tablespoons minced fresh parsley leaves

1. Sprinkle the chicken with salt and pepper. Heat the butter and oil in a 12-inch sauté pan or small Dutch oven over medium-high heat. When butter foaming subsides, add the chicken; sauté until browned on both sides, moving around to brown evenly, 10 to 15 minutes. Remove the chicken pieces from the pan and set aside.

2. Discard all but a thin film of fat from the pan. Add the onion and apples; sauté, stirring frequently to prevent scorching, until the pan juices evaporate, 4 to 5 minutes.

3. Return the chicken and accumulated juices to the pan, moving the vegetables to the top. Add the cider, brandy, thyme, and sugar; bring to a boil. Lower the heat, cover, and barely simmer until the chicken is cooked through, basting 3 or 4 times, about 25 minutes.

4. Remove the chicken to a platter and cover with foil to keep warm. Add the cream and parsley to the pan, bring to a boil, and reduce the sauce by one-third. Taste for salt and pepper. Place a portion of chicken on each plate; top with the apples. Ladle the sauce over both chicken and vegetables and/or the accompanying starch and serve immediately.

CHICKEN
CURRY

/|\

MAKING CURRY IS A CHALLENGE FOR ANY COOK

ACCUSTOMED TO WESTERN RECIPES AND TECH-

NIQUES. THE TERM *CURRY* REFERS TO ALMOST INDIAN

STEW, BUT THIS "STEW" IS NOT PREPARED IN THE MAN-

NER AMERICAN COOKS ARE MOST FAMILIAR WITH. A

STANDARD STEW RECIPE BEGINS BY BROWNING THE

MEAT TO DEVELOP FLAVOR. THE PAN IS USUALLY

DEGLAZED WITH LIQUID (WINE, TOMATOES, STOCK)

to pick up flavorful browned bits stuck to the bottom of the pan. The liquid is reduced and thickened into a sauce that surrounds the meat. Vegetables are added but usually remain distinct elements.

For curry, the whole process changes. There is no browning of the meat. Vegetables are often cooked much longer so that they begin to lose their shape. Most important, spices are handled quite differently. Releasing the full flavor of the spices is the key to good curry, not properly browning the meat, as with Western stews.

The first step when making curry is to fry whole spices (a cinnamon stick, cloves, green cardamom pods, peppercorns, and a bay leaf) in hot oil. Although this step may be omitted for a milder spice flavor, the whole spices release their flavor into the oil, thus perfuming everything else that comes into contact with the oil. (The whole spices are optional in the Master Recipe and have been recommended in variations where we think their flavor is essential.)

Next, a sliced onion is added and cooked until translucent. For a richer flavor (and one we like with yogurt and nut sauces), the onion can be browned. At this point, the garlic and ginger go into the pot, along with the chicken, ground spices, salt, and a moistening agent. Traditionally, the garlic and ginger are ground in a mortar and pestle. We found it more convenient to puree the garlic and ginger with a little water in a mini-chopper. With no surfaces to burn, the garlic and ginger cook more evenly than a mince and melt into the sauce for a smooth finish. Also, the moisture in the puree provides a cushion against burning.

The moistening agent (canned tomatoes or yogurt) cools down the pot so that the spices do not burn. Once the moisture in the pot evaporates, the oil will separate out and pool around pieces of chicken, onion, and spice paste. This is the secret to a well-made curry. To release and develop their flavors, the ground spices must fry in this hot oil, uninhibited by liquid.

The science behind this phenomenon can be easily explained by heat. When the spices are simmering in liquid, the temperature never goes above 212 degrees. However, once the liquid evaporates, the spices can cook right in the oil, where the temperature can rise well above 212 degrees. This intense heat causes volatile compounds in the spices to break down and reform into new compounds with different tastes and aromas. Thirty seconds of frying is enough (we tested longer periods and could not taste any difference). However, if this step is omitted, the flavors in the curry will be muddy and heavy.

Once the spices have fried in the oil, it's time to add the water and some fresh chiles for heat (of course, the chiles can be increased or omitted altogether) and simmer the curry until the chicken is tender. Vegetables (diced potatoes, diced zucchini, peas, or split peas) can be added at this point and are cooked until tender. A final flavoring of fresh cilantro and the curry is ready to be served.

The Master Recipe works with boneless leg of lamb, top sirloin, and shrimp, as well as chicken. We tried several times to use white meat (boneless, skinless breasts, both whole and cut into chunks, as well as whole bone-in breasts). Each time the meat was tough and stringy, no doubt because of the long cooking time needed for the flavors in curry to meld. The extra fat in the thigh meat is essential; it's hard to overcook them. Look for large boneless, skinless thighs from a large roasting chicken.

We tested a variety of pots when developing recipes for this chapter. A deep 12-inch sauté pan is our favorite choice. A 5- or 6-quart Dutch oven or a small soup kettle also will work fine. There is a fair amount of splattering so avoid shallow sauté pans or skillets.

CURRY, STEP-BY-STEP

1. Cook the whole spices in the hot oil until the cinnamon stick unfurls and the cloves pop, about 5 seconds.

2. Add the onion to the oil and sauté it until it is soft and translucent or browned, depending on the individual curry. The more the onion is cooked, the more flavor and richness it will contribute to the sauce.

3. Once the onion is cooked, add the pureed garlic and ginger, chicken, ground spices, salt, and tomatoes or yogurt.

4. Watch carefully to see when the oil separates and turns orange, 5 to 7 minutes. At this point the spices will begin to fry (the sound emanating from the pan will change from a gentle simmer to loud, staccato frying) and should smell fragrant. Allow the spices to fry for at least 30 seconds.

5. Add the water and halved jalapeño chile and cook until the chicken is tender, about 20 to 30 minutes.

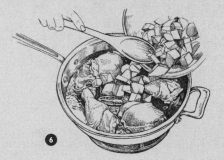

6. Add the vegetables and cook until both the chicken and vegetables are fully tender, about 15 minutes longer.

Chicken Curry

SERVES 4 TO 6

GATHER AND PREPARE all of your ingredients before you begin. Garlic and ginger may be pureed by hand or in a mini-chop food processor. (See opposite for information on hand-pureeing.) If using the mini-chopper, process the garlic and ginger with 1 or 2 tablespoons of water until pureed. You may substitute a scant ½ teaspoon of cayenne pepper for the jalapeño, adding it to the skillet with the other ground spices. Serve the curry with basmati rice (see "Curry Accompaniments," pages 132–133).

WHOLE SPICE BLEND (OPTIONAL)
1 cinnamon stick, about 4 inches long
4 whole cloves
4 green cardamom pods
8 peppercorns
1 bay leaf

BASIC CHICKEN CURRY
¼ cup flavorless oil (vegetable or canola)
1 medium onion, halved and sliced thin
4 large garlic cloves, pureed
1 chunk (1 ½ inches) fresh gingerroot, peeled and pureed

6 boneless, skinless chicken thighs (about 2 pounds)
2 teaspoons ground cumin
2 teaspoons ground coriander
1 teaspoon ground turmeric
½ teaspoon salt, or more as needed
3 canned whole tomatoes, chopped, plus 1 tablespoon juice, or ⅔ cup canned crushed tomatoes, or ½ cup plain low-fat yogurt
1 jalapeño chile, stemmed and cut in half through the stem end
3 to 4 cups vegetables, such as diced potatoes, diced zucchini, or whole thawed frozen peas (use one vegetable or a combination)
2 to 4 tablespoons chopped fresh cilantro

1. If using, mix the whole spices in a small bowl. Heat the oil in a large deep sauté pan over medium-high heat until hot, but not smoking. Add the whole spices to the oil and cook, stirring with a wooden spoon until the cinnamon stick unfurls and the cloves pop, about 5 seconds (see figure 1, page 127). (If not using whole spices, simply heat the oil and proceed to step 2.)

2. Add the onion to the skillet; sauté until softened, 3 to 4 minutes, or browned, 5 to 7 minutes (see figure 2, page 127), depending on the flavor desired.

3. Stir in the garlic, ginger, chicken, ground spices, ½ teaspoon salt, and tomatoes or yogurt (see figure 3, page 127); cook, stirring almost constantly, until the liquid evaporates, the oil separates and turns orange, and the spices begin to fry, 5 to 7 minutes (see figure 4, page 127). Continue to cook, stirring constantly, until the spices smell cooked, about 30 seconds longer.

4. Add 2 cups water and the jalapeño and taste for salt (see figure 5, page 127); bring to a simmer. Reduce the heat; cover and simmer until the chicken is tender, 20 to 30 minutes.

5. Add the selected vegetables, except for green peas (see figure 6, page 127); cook until tender, about 15 minutes. Stir in the cilantro. Add the peas, if using. Simmer 3 minutes longer. Remove and discard the whole spices and the jalapeño. Serve.

PUREEING GARLIC AND GINGER BY HAND

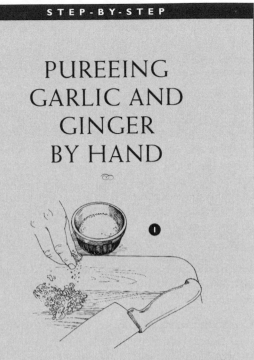

1. Although we recommend that you puree garlic and ginger in a mini-chopper, you can puree them by hand. Roughly chop as many garlic cloves and as much peeled gingerroot as you'll need. Sprinkle the chopped garlic and ginger with a generous pinch of salt (table salt will work, but the larger crystals of kosher salt work better).

2. Gently lay the flat side of your chef's knife on the salted garlic and ginger and pull it across the garlic and ginger while applying light pressure. Repeat this process 7 or 8 times (or more) until the garlic and ginger are smooth and partially liquefied.

Chicken Curry with Whole Spices and Potatoes

THE CLEAR, BRIGHT FLAVORS OF WHOLE CINNAMON, CLOVES, AND CARDAMOM ARE PICKED UP BY THE CHICKEN AND POTATOES IN THIS BASIC CURRY. SERVES 4 TO 6.

WHOLE SPICE BLEND
1 cinnamon stick, about 4 inches long
4 whole cloves
4 green cardamom pods
8 peppercorns
1 bay leaf

¼ cup flavorless oil (vegetable or canola)
1 medium onion, sliced thin
4 large garlic cloves, pureed
1 chunk (1½ inches) fresh gingerroot, peeled and pureed
6 boneless, skinless chicken thighs (about 2 pounds)
2 teaspoons ground cumin
2 teaspoons ground coriander
1 teaspoon ground turmeric
½ teaspoon salt, or more as needed
3 canned whole tomatoes, chopped, plus 1 tablespoon juice, *or* ⅔ cup canned crushed tomatoes
1 jalapeño chile, stemmed and cut in half through the stem end
4 medium boiling potatoes, peeled and cut into ¾-inch cubes
4 tablespoons chopped fresh cilantro leaves

1. Place the whole spices in a small bowl. Heat the oil in a large, deep sauté pan over medium-high heat until hot, but not smoking. Add the whole spices and cook, stirring with a wooden spoon until the cinnamon stick unfurls and the cloves pop, about 5 seconds. Add the onion to the skillet; sauté until softened, 3 to 4 minutes.

2. Stir in the garlic, ginger, chicken, ground spices, ½ teaspoon salt, and tomatoes; cook, stirring almost constantly, until the liquid evaporates, the oil sepa-

(continued on next page)

rates and turns orange, and the spices begin to fry, 5 to 7 minutes. Continue to cook, stirring constantly, until the spices smell cooked, about 30 seconds longer.

3. Add 2 cups water and the jalapeño and taste for salt; bring to a simmer. Reduce the heat; cover and simmer until the chicken is tender and the sauce is slightly reduced, 20 to 30 minutes.

4. Add the potatoes and cook until tender, about 20 minutes. Stir in the cilantro. Remove and discard the whole spices and the jalapeño. Serve.

◆

Chicken Curry with Yogurt, Cilantro, and Zucchini

BROWNED ONIONS AND THE WHOLE SPICE BLEND ADD DEPTH TO THIS DISH. SERVES 4 TO 6.

WHOLE SPICE BLEND
1 cinnamon stick, about 4 inches long
4 whole cloves
4 green cardamom pods
8 peppercorns
1 bay leaf

¼ cup flavorless oil (vegetable or canola)
1 medium onion, sliced thin
4 large garlic cloves, pureed
1 chunk (1½ inches) fresh gingerroot, peeled and pureed
6 boneless, skinless chicken thighs (about 2 pounds)
2 teaspoons ground cumin
2 teaspoons ground coriander
1 teaspoon ground turmeric
½ teaspoon salt, or more as needed
½ cup plain low-fat yogurt
1 cup plus 2 tablespoons chopped fresh cilantro leaves
1 jalapeño chile, stemmed and cut in half through the stem end
4 medium zucchini, cut into ½-inch cubes

1. Place the whole spices in a small bowl. Heat the oil in a large, deep sauté pan over medium-high heat until hot, but not smoking. Add the whole spices to the oil and cook, stirring with a wooden spoon until the cinnamon stick unfurls and the cloves pop, about 5 seconds. Add the onion to the skillet; sauté until browned, 5 to 7 minutes.

2. Stir in the garlic, ginger, chicken, ground spices, ½ teaspoon salt, and yogurt; cook, stirring almost constantly, until the liquid evaporates, the oil separates and turns orange, and the spices begin to fry, 5 to 7 minutes. Continue to cook, stirring constantly, until the spices smell cooked, about 30 seconds longer.

3. Stir in 1 cup chopped cilantro. Add 2 cups water and the jalapeño and taste for salt; bring to a simmer. Reduce the heat; cover and simmer until the sauce is slightly thickened and the chicken is tender, 20 to 30 minutes.

4. Add the zucchini; cook until tender, about 15 minutes. Stir in the remaining 2 tablespoons cilantro. Remove and discard the whole spices and the jalapeño. Serve.

◆

Chicken Curry with Channa Dal

CHANNA DAL IS A KIND OF INDIAN SPLIT PEAS, AVAILABLE AT INDIAN SPECIALTY FOOD SHOPS. POTATOES OR REGULAR GREEN OR YELLOW SPLIT PEAS MAY BE SUBSTITUTED FOR THE CHANNA DAL. IF DESIRED, CRUSH CUMIN AND CORIANDER SEEDS IN A MORTAR AND PESTLE AND USE THEM IN PLACE OF THE GROUND VERSIONS. SERVES 4 TO 6.

¼ cup flavorless oil (vegetable or canola)
1 medium onion, sliced thin
4 large garlic cloves, pureed
1 chunk (1½ inches) fresh gingerroot, peeled and pureed
6 boneless, skinless chicken thighs (about 2 pounds)
2 teaspoons ground cumin
2 teaspoons ground coriander
1 teaspoon ground turmeric

½ teaspoon salt, or more as needed

3 canned whole tomatoes, chopped, plus
1 tablespoon juice, *or* ⅔ cup canned
crushed tomatoes

1 jalapeño chile, stemmed and cut in half
through the stem end

½ cup Indian yellow split peas (channa dal)

4 tablespoons chopped fresh cilantro
leaves

1. Heat the oil in a large, deep sauté pan over medium-high heat until hot, but not smoking. Add the onion to the skillet; sauté until softened, 3 to 4 minutes.

2. Stir in the garlic, ginger, chicken, ground spices, ½ teaspoon salt, and tomatoes; cook, stirring almost constantly, until the liquid evaporates, the oil separates and turns orange, and the spices begin to fry, 5 to 7 minutes. Continue to cook, stirring constantly, until the spices smell cooked, about 30 seconds longer.

3. Add 2 cups water and the jalapeño and taste for salt; bring to a simmer. Reduce the heat; cover and simmer until the meat is tender, 20 to 30 minutes.

4. Add the channa dal and simmer, covered, until soft, about 20 minutes. Stir in the cilantro. Remove and discard the jalapeño. Serve.

◆

Chicken Curry with Yogurt and Peas

THIS IS A MILDER CURRY, WITHOUT THE ASSERTIVE OVERTONES OF THE WHOLE SPICE BLEND. THE ONIONS ARE BROWNED IN THIS RECIPE TO GIVE THE YOGURT SAUCE A RICHER FLAVOR. FEEL FREE TO INCREASE THE GARLIC, GINGER, AND/OR GROUND SPICES TO TASTE. SERVES 4 TO 6.

¼ cup flavorless oil (vegetable or canola)

1 medium onion, sliced thin

4 large garlic cloves, pureed

1 chunk (1½ inches) fresh gingerroot,
peeled and pureed

6 boneless, skinless chicken thighs (about
2 pounds)

2 teaspoons ground cumin

2 teaspoons ground coriander

1 teaspoon ground turmeric

½ teaspoon salt, or more as needed

½ cup plain low-fat yogurt

1 cup plus 2 tablespoons chopped fresh
cilantro leaves

1 jalapeño chile, stemmed and cut in half
through the stem end

1 cup thawed frozen green peas

1. Heat the oil in a large, deep sauté pan over medium-high heat until hot, but not smoking. Add the onion to the skillet; sauté until browned, 5 to 7 minutes.

2. Stir in the garlic, ginger, chicken, ground spices, ½ teaspoon salt, and yogurt; cook, stirring almost constantly, until the liquid evaporates, the oil separates and turns orange, and the spices begin to fry, 5 to 7 minutes. Continue to cook, stirring constantly, until the spices smell cooked, about 30 seconds longer.

3. Stir in 1 cup chopped cilantro. Add 2 cups water and the jalapeño and taste for salt; bring to a simmer. Reduce the heat; cover and simmer until the chicken is just cooked and the sauce is thickened, about 20 minutes.

4. Stir in the remaining 2 tablespoons cilantro and the peas. Simmer 3 minutes longer. Remove and discard the jalapeño. Serve.

CURRY ACCOMPANIMENTS

⚊

IN INDIA, CURRY WITHOUT RICE IS LIKE PASTA SAUCE WITHOUT THE PASTA. THE RICE STRETCHES A SMALL AMOUNT OF CURRY TO SERVE MORE PEOPLE AND MELLOWS SOME OF THE HEAT. AROMATIC BASMATI RICE IS THE STANDARD IN INDIA AND WE RECOMMEND THAT YOU SERVE IT WITH THESE CURRY RECIPES. AS IT COOKS,

basmati rice perfumes your kitchen with an intoxicating aroma akin to popcorn.

Traditional basmati recipes call for soaking or rinsing the grains before cooking. We tested soaking the rice for 20 minutes, rinsing the rice, and just adding the rice as is to the pot. In this case, the simplest method delivers the best results. Soaked rice tends to overcook and can become a bit mushy. Although the grains do elongate nicely, the extra millimeter or two hardly seems worth the tradeoff in texture. Rinsing the rice can also make it a bit sticky. We prefer to just add the rice as is. It will cook up firm and flavorful.

We also tested three cooking methods: boiling basmati rice like pasta and draining it when tender; adding rice and water to the pot, bringing to a boil, covering, and simmering (most Americans prepare rice this way); and pilaf style, where the rice is sautéed in oil, covered with water, and simmered in a covered pot until the water has been absorbed. We found that the pilaf method gives the rice a stronger flavor (sautéing the rice really brings out its nutty flavor) and produces grains that are more separate than the other methods.

Traditionally, Indians mash the rice and curry together with their fingers into small balls to pop into their mouth. This releases more fragrance

from both the spices in the curry and the rice. A fork can also be used to mash them together.

In addition to rice, Indians often serve chutney or sauces to complement the flavors in the curry. We particularly like to serve curry with raita, a cooling cucumber and yogurt salad. Salting and weighting the cucumbers for at least 1 hour makes them especially crisp and crunchy.

◆

Basmati Rice, Pilaf Style

BASMATI IS AN AROMATIC VARIETY OF RICE GROWN IN INDIA AND PAKISTAN. IT HAS A NUTTY FLAVOR AND FLUFFY BUT FIRM TEXTURE. AMERICAN VERSIONS ARE TEXMATI, DELLA, AND KASMATI. IN OUR TESTS, WE FOUND THAT TEXMATI AND DELLA DO NOT ELONGATE AS MUCH AS BASMATI AND THE FLAVOR IS NOT QUITE AS INTENSE. KASMATI IS NOT AS FLUFFY AS BASMATI AND THE GRAINS CAN BE SOMEWHAT STICKY, BUT THE FLAVOR HOLDS ITS OWN AGAINST IMPORTED BASMATI. LOOK FOR BASMATI RICE IN WELL-STOCKED SUPERMARKETS, NATURAL FOODS STORES, AND INDIAN MARKETS, WHERE THE PRICE IS USUALLY LOWER. IT CAN BE SERVED WITH ANY OF THE CURRY RECIPES. SERVES 4 AS AN ACCOMPANIMENT TO CURRY.

1 tablespoon flavorless oil (vegetable
  or canola)
1 5-inch-long cinnamon stick, broken
  in half
2 green cardamom pods
2 whole cloves
¼ cup thinly sliced onion
1 cup basmati rice
1 teaspoon salt

1. Heat the oil in a medium saucepan set over high heat until almost smoking. Add the whole spices and cook, stirring with a wooden spoon until the cinnamon stick unfurls and the cloves pop, about 5 seconds. Add the onion and cook, stirring until translucent, about 2 minutes. Add the rice and cook, stirring constantly, until fragrant, about 1 minute.

2. Add 1½ cups water and the salt; bring to a boil. Reduce the heat, cover tightly, and simmer until all the water has been absorbed, about 17 minutes. Let stand, covered, at least 10 minutes. Remove and discard whole spices, fluff with a fork, and serve.

◆

Yellow Rice

THIS TRADITIONAL RECIPE IS A COLORFUL ALTERNATIVE TO PLAIN RICE. TURMERIC ADDS COLOR BUT NOT FLAVOR, SO THE RICE REMAINS A QUIET BACKGROUND FOR SPICIER CURRIES. SERVES 4 AS AN ACCOMPANIMENT TO CURRY.

1 tablespoon flavorless oil (vegetable
  or canola)
1 cup basmati rice
Pinch ground turmeric
1 teaspoon salt

1. Heat the oil in a medium saucepan over high heat until almost smoking. Add the rice and

turmeric and cook, stirring constantly, until fragrant, about 1 minute.

2. Add 1½ cups of water and the salt; bring to a boil. Reduce the heat, cover tightly, and simmer until all the water has been absorbed, about 17 minutes. Let stand, covered, at least 10 minutes, fluff with a fork, and serve.

◆

Cucumber Raita

THIS COOLING CUCUMBER AND YOGURT SALAD IS TRADITIONALLY SERVED ON THE SIDE WITH MANY CURRIES. THE CUCUMBERS ARE SALTED, WEIGHTED DOWN WITH A SEALABLE BAG FULL OF WATER, AND DRAINED SO THAT THEY REMAIN CRISP AND CRUNCHY. SERVES 4 AS AN ACCOMPANIMENT TO CURRY.

1 cucumber
1 teaspoon salt
1 cup plain low-fat yogurt
1 small garlic clove, finely chopped
⅛ teaspoon ground cumin
1 tablespoon chopped fresh cilantro
  leaves

1. Peel and halve the cucumber lengthwise. Use a small spoon to scoop out and discard the seeds. Place the cucumber halves flat side down; slice diagonally into ¼-inch-thick pieces.

2. Toss the cucumber with the salt in a colander set over a bowl. Fill a 1-gallon sealable plastic bag with water and seal tight. Place filled bag over cucumbers as weight. Drain for at least 1 hour and up to 3 hours.

3. Whisk the yogurt in a medium bowl until smooth. Add the cucumber, garlic, cumin, and cilantro and stir to combine. Refrigerate, up to several hours, until serving.

Chicken Curry with Spinach, Potatoes, and Fenugreek

IN INDIA, FENUGREEK, A PLANT IN THE PEA FAMILY, IS PRIZED FOR ITS LEAVES AS WELL AS ITS SEEDS. GROUND FENUGREEK SEEDS IMPART A BITTERSWEET FLAVOR TO THIS CURRY THICKENED WITH SPINACH. TO PERMIT THE SPINACH TO COOK DOWN INTO A SAUCE, REMOVE THE CHICKEN FROM THE POT WHEN IT IS TENDER. ADD THE COOKED CHICKEN JUST BEFORE SERVING. SERVES 4 TO 6.

- ¼ cup flavorless oil (vegetable or canola)
- 1 medium onion, sliced thin
- 4 large garlic cloves, pureed
- 1 chunk (1½ inches) fresh gingerroot, peeled and pureed
- 6 boneless, skinless chicken thighs (about 2 pounds)
- 2 teaspoons ground cumin
- 2 teaspoons ground coriander
- ½ teaspoon ground fenugreek
- 1 teaspoon ground turmeric
- ½ teaspoon salt, or more as needed
- 3 canned whole tomatoes, chopped, plus 1 tablespoon juice, *or* ⅔ cup canned crushed tomatoes
- 2 bunches spinach (about 1½ pounds), stemmed, thoroughly washed, and chopped coarse
- 1 jalapeño chile, stemmed and cut in half through the stem end
- 4 medium boiling potatoes, peeled and cut into ¾-inch cubes
- 4 tablespoons chopped fresh cilantro leaves

1. Heat the oil in a large, deep sauté pan over medium-high heat until hot, but not smoking. Add the onion to the skillet; sauté until softened, 3 to 4 minutes.

2. Stir in the garlic, ginger, chicken, ground spices, ½ teaspoon salt, and tomatoes; cook, stirring almost constantly, until the liquid evaporates, the oil separates and turns orange, and the spices begin to fry, 5 to 7 minutes. Continue to cook, stirring constantly, until the spices smell cooked, about 30 seconds longer.

3. Stir in the spinach. Add 2 cups water and the jalapeño and taste for salt; bring to a simmer. Reduce the heat; cover and simmer until the meat is tender, 20 to 30 minutes. Remove the chicken and keep warm.

4. Add the potatoes; cook until tender, about 15 minutes. Increase the heat to high and cook until the sauce thickens, about 10 minutes (the spinach becomes the sauce). Stir in the cilantro. Return the cooked chicken to the pan and heat through for several minutes. Remove and discard the jalapeño. Serve.

◆

Chicken Curry with Apricots

DRIED APRICOTS, PLUMPED WITH WARM WATER, LEND A RICH SWEETNESS TO THIS DISH. INSTEAD OF A WHOLE SPICE BLEND AT THE BEGINNING OF COOKING, THE RECIPE CALLS FOR A SPRINKLING OF GARAM MASALA—A MIXTURE OF CINNAMON, CLOVES, AND CARDAMOM—TO BE ADDED PARTWAY THROUGH THE COOKING PROCESS WITH THE OTHER GROUND SPICES; IT LENDS A STRONGER SPICE FLAVOR THIS WAY. SERVES 4 TO 6.

- 1 cup (6 ounces) dried apricots
- ¼ cup flavorless oil (vegetable or canola)
- 1 medium onion, sliced thin
- 4 large garlic cloves, pureed
- 1 chunk (1½ inches) fresh gingerroot, peeled and pureed
- 6 boneless, skinless chicken thighs (about 2 pounds)
- 2 teaspoons ground cumin
- 2 teaspoons ground coriander
- 1 teaspoon ground turmeric
- ¾ teaspoon garam masala
- ½ teaspoon salt, or more as needed
- 3 canned whole tomatoes, chopped, plus 1 tablespoon juice, *or* ⅔ cup canned crushed tomatoes
- 1 jalapeño chile, stemmed and cut in half through the stem end
- 4 tablespoons chopped fresh cilantro leaves

1. Soak the apricots in ½ cup warm water for 2 hours. Drain and halve.

2. Heat the oil in a large, deep sauté pan over medium-high heat until hot, but not smoking. Add the onion to the skillet; sauté until browned, 5 to 7 minutes.

3. Stir in the garlic, ginger, chicken, ground spices, garam masala, ½ teaspoon salt, and tomatoes; cook, stirring almost constantly, until the liquid evaporates, the oil separates and turns orange, and the spices begin to fry, 5 to 7 minutes. Continue to cook, stirring constantly, until the spices smell cooked, about 30 seconds longer.

4. Add 2 cups water and the jalapeño and taste for salt; bring to a simmer. Reduce the heat; cover and simmer until the chicken is tender, 20 to 30 minutes.

5. Add the apricots; simmer 15 minutes. Stir in the cilantro. Remove and discard the jalapeño. Serve.

◆

Chicken Curry with Pistachios

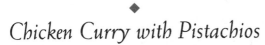

GROUND NUTS ARE OFTEN USED IN CURRIES AS THICKENERS AND FOR FLAVOR. THIS DISH TAKES ON THE LOVELY PALE GREEN COLOR OF THE GROUND PISTACHIOS. TO REMOVE THE SKINS FROM THE NUTS, SIMMER THEM IN BOILING WATER FOR 5 MINUTES, DRAIN, COOL, AND RUB THE SKINS OFF WITH YOUR FINGERS. THE CHILES ARE PUREED ALONG WITH THE NUTS TO CREATE A THICK, MOIST PASTE. YOGURT FORMS THE BACKBONE OF THE SAUCE FOR THIS CURRY, ALTHOUGH A LITTLE FRESH TOMATO IS ADDED JUST BEFORE SERVING AS A GARNISH. SERVES 4 TO 6.

WHOLE SPICE BLEND
1 cinnamon stick, about 4 inches long
4 whole cloves
4 green cardamom pods
8 peppercorns
1 bay leaf

⅔ cup (about 3 ounces) shelled, skinned, unsalted pistachio nuts
1 or 2 jalapeño chiles, stemmed
¼ cup flavorless oil (vegetable or canola)
1 medium onion, sliced thin
4 large garlic cloves, pureed
1 chunk (1½ inches) fresh gingerroot, peeled and pureed
6 boneless, skinless chicken thighs (about 2 pounds)
2 teaspoons ground cumin
2 teaspoons ground coriander
1 teaspoon ground turmeric
½ teaspoon salt, or more as needed
½ cup plain low-fat yogurt
1 cup plus 2 tablespoons chopped fresh cilantro leaves
1 plum tomato, cored and chopped

1. Place the whole spices in a small bowl and set them aside. Combine the pistachios and the jalapeños in the work bowl of a food processor. Process until a thick paste forms. Scrape the mixture into another small bowl and set aside.

2. Heat the oil in a large, deep sauté pan over medium-high heat until hot, but not smoking. Add the whole spices and cook, stirring with a wooden spoon until the cinnamon stick unfurls and the cloves pop, about 5 seconds. Add the onion to the skillet; sauté until softened, 3 to 4 minutes. Add the pistachio mixture and fry for an additional 2 minutes.

3. Stir in the garlic, ginger, chicken, ground spices, ½ teaspoon salt, and yogurt. Cook, stirring almost constantly, until the liquid evaporates, the oil separates and turns orange, and the spices begin to fry, 5 to 7 minutes. Continue to cook, stirring constantly, until the spices smell cooked, about 30 seconds longer.

4. Stir in 1 cup chopped cilantro. Add 2 cups water and taste for salt; bring to a simmer. Reduce the heat; cover and simmer until the meat is tender, 20 to 30 minutes. Stir in the tomato and the remaining 2 tablespoons cilantro. Simmer 3 minutes longer. Remove and discard the whole spices. Serve.

Chicken Curry with Cashews and Coconut

BE SURE TO GRIND THE CASHEWS INTO A VERY SMOOTH, FINE PASTE. OTHERWISE, THE FINISHED DISH MIGHT LOOK LUMPY AND CURDLED. UNSWEETENED GRATED COCONUT IS SOLD AT MOST NATURAL FOODS STORES. SERVES 4 TO 6.

WHOLE SPICE BLEND
1 cinnamon stick, about 4 inches long
4 whole cloves
4 green cardamom pods
8 peppercorns
1 bay leaf

2/3 cup (6 ounces) whole unsalted cashews
1/4 cup flavorless oil (vegetable or canola)
1 medium onion, sliced thin
4 large garlic cloves, pureed
1 chunk (1 1/2 inches) fresh gingerroot, peeled and pureed
6 boneless, skinless chicken thighs (about 2 pounds)
2 teaspoons ground cumin
2 teaspoons ground coriander
1 teaspoon ground turmeric
1/2 teaspoon salt, or more as needed
3 canned whole tomatoes, chopped, plus 1 tablespoon juice, or 2/3 cup canned crushed tomatoes
1 cup (4 ounces) dried unsweetened grated coconut
1 jalapeño chile, stemmed and cut in half through the stem end
4 tablespoons chopped fresh cilantro leaves

1. Gather the whole spices in a small bowl and set them aside. Place 1/2 cup cashews in the work bowl of a food processor. Process until a smooth paste forms. Scrape the cashew paste into a small bowl and set aside. Toast the remaining cashews in a small skillet set over medium heat until golden and fragrant, 4 to 5 minutes. Set aside.

2. Heat the oil in a large, deep sauté pan over medium-high heat until hot, but not smoking. Add the whole spices and cook, stirring with a wooden spoon until the cinnamon stick unfurls and the cloves pop, about 5 seconds. Add the onion to the skillet; sauté until softened, 3 to 4 minutes.

3. Stir in the garlic, ginger, chicken, ground spices, 1/2 teaspoon salt, tomatoes, and coconut; cook, stirring almost constantly, until the liquid evaporates, the oil separates and turns orange, and the spices begin to fry, 5 to 7 minutes. Continue to cook, stirring constantly, until the spices smell cooked, about 30 seconds longer.

4. Stir in the ground cashews. Add 2 cups water and the jalapeño and taste for salt; bring to a simmer. Reduce the heat; cover and simmer until the meat is tender, 20 to 30 minutes.

5. Add the whole toasted cashews. Stir in the cilantro. Simmer 3 minutes longer. Remove and discard the whole spices and the jalapeño. Serve.

CHAPTER 10

FRIED
CHICKEN

/Ι\

THANKS MAINLY TO THE FAST-FOOD INDUSTRY, MOST

AMERICANS ASSUME ALL FRIED CHICKEN IS DEEP-FRIED.

THERE ARE ACTUALLY TWO KINDS OF FRIED CHICKEN.

DEEP-FRIED CHICKEN, SIMULTANEOUSLY ATTACKED ON

ALL SIDES BY HOT OIL, QUICKLY DEVELOPS A BRITTLE,

PROTECTIVE SHELL RIGHT DOWN TO THE MEAT.

WHILE THIS WORKS WELL IN STRIPS OF BONELESS,

skinless breast or thigh (see "Deep-Frying Boneless Chicken Pieces," page 143), we don't like the results when the cooking times are increased for bone-in parts.

In our opinion, pan-fried chicken parts are more complex and superior. In older cookbooks, the recipe usually starts with a cast-iron skillet and a lid. More often than not, the chicken was cut into ten pieces—two legs, two thighs, two wings, and two breast halves each cut crosswise in half to yield four small pieces. The parts have the same crunchy exterior as deep-fried chicken, but when the pan is covered, the half of the meat not submerged in oil is exposed to a sort of steaming process. This creates a moist sublayer that offers a nice contrast to the crisp exterior.

Our goal was to re-create this old-fashioned cooking method and flavor. Although we were pretty sure that a cast-iron pan, with its ability to hold in heat for long cooking times, would be essential, we knew there were other issues to consider. What size chicken is best? Should the chicken parts be soaked before frying and, if so, in what? Is all-purpose flour the best coating, or could cornstarch or even self-rising flour produce a better crust? Is it best to dredge the chicken parts in a pan of flour to coat the chicken, or is a paper bag better? Should the cook season the chicken, the flour, or both? Some recipes recommend air-drying the chicken before frying for an extra-crispy effect. Is this worth the time? What size pan, and what fat or combination of fats is best for frying chicken? During frying, should the pan be covered or partially covered? Covered part of the time or not at all? How should the fried chicken be drained?

We've always thought that frying chicken was a time-consuming project, mainly because it had to be cooked in two batches. We discovered, though, that if the bird is small enough and the pan big enough, you can fry a whole chicken at one time. Birds weighing 2½ to 3 pounds work best. Of course, a larger bird will work fine, but then you must be prepared to fry in batches.

We wanted to like the 13 ⅜-inch cast-iron skillet we had specially purchased for this fried chicken, because it was large enough to hold all ten pieces of chicken. But we soon found that its size was a handicap because the perimeter of the pan sat off the burner. Getting the fat temperature right for frying

chicken around the edge of the pan meant scorching the chicken in the center, while properly cooking the chicken in the center of the pan meant blond-skinned, greasy chicken around the edges. The skillet we came to prefer was a standard 12-inch cast-iron skillet (a modest $15 investment if you don't own one), though any heavy-bottomed 12-inch skillet will work. The ten pieces will snugly fit into this pan. If you need to use a smaller pan, plan on frying in batches.

Of all the stages—buying, butchering, seasoning, coating, and frying—we found the greatest recipe diversity in the soaking period. After testing thirteen different soaking methods, we discovered that dairy-soaked chicken displayed the most beautifully textured and richly colored skin.

This is not surprising. Since milk is thicker than water, these dairy-based soaking liquids tend to cling better to the slippery, raw chicken parts, which, in turn, attract more flour during dredging. The end result is a thick, even coating. Lactose, the sugar found in milk, caused the chicken to develop a deep mahogany color during frying. Heavy cream also coated the chicken beautifully, but the resulting fried chicken was too rich. The milk and lemon juice combination gave the chicken a clean, heightened flavor, but since it was thinner it didn't adhere as well and offered a less impressive coat. The buttermilk, on the other hand, was as viscous as cream and as tangy as the milk with lemon juice, with none of the liabilities. This became our favorite soaking medium.

With the soaking issue resolved, we moved on to coatings. We were particularly intrigued by two coatings that we found in our research—self-rising flour and a combination of cornstarch and all-purpose flour. After putting these and other coatings to the test, we found that none surpassed all-purpose flour; in fact, most alternatives were inferior.

The self-rising flour produced a coating that ballooned, then deflated during frying. Once cooked, this chicken shed its crumbly coat. A cornstarch coating produced disastrous-looking and -tasting chicken. It fried to an unpleasant white with scattered hard spots, and tasted pasty, like uncooked starch. We cut the cornstarch with flour, which proved more successful but did not surpass the plain flour. We then tried various other combinations with all-purpose flour—corn-

IT ALL COMES BACK

⋏⋏

REMEMBER THE OLD CRISCO COMMERCIALS, "IT ALL COMES BACK BUT ONE TABLESPOON"? WE PUT THIS CLAIM TO THE TEST AND FOUND IT TO BE ABSOLUTELY TRUE. WE HEATED 3 CUPS OF SOLID FAT TO 350 DEGREES IN A 12-INCH SKILLET, PAN-FRIED A WHOLE CHICKEN, AND POURED BACK ALMOST

exactly 3 cups of fat after frying. We conducted the test a number of times to confirm our findings, and each time we ended up with virtually the same amount of fat before and after.

It seems that if the water in the food you are frying is kept above the boiling point (212 degrees), the outward pressure of the escaping water vapor keeps oil from soaking into the food. On the other hand, if the frying oil is not hot enough it will seep into the food, making it greasy. The key is to start the oil hot enough (we found 350 degrees worked well) so that you maintain a temperature (between 250 and 300 degrees), which keeps the moisture in the food, in essence, boiling. You cannot fry chicken parts at a higher temperature (most thinner foods are cooked at temperatures between 335 and 360 degrees) or the crust will burn before the inside cooks through.

meal, whole wheat flour, cornstarch, and bread crumbs. The cornmeal coating was pleasant, but didn't bind as well as straight flour. The whole wheat coating displayed flecks of unabsorbed grain on the skin's surface. Both the cornmeal and the whole wheat coatings had a coarse, raw taste to them. And although the cornstarch sounded like a good idea, it was barely discernible on the fried chicken. Bread crumbs mixed with flour delivered a respectable crust—nice dark brown, fairly crispy—but we wouldn't recommend it over plain flour.

Several recipes recommended drying the chicken on a rack for a couple of hours to allow the flour to adhere. We found that this extra step produced a brittle, thin, shell-like crust—not unpleasant but certainly not worth the wait. On the other hand, if you want to coat your chicken and let it sit for a couple of hours before frying, it certainly won't hurt it.

We were also intent on finding the best way to get the coating on the chicken. We compared dredging the chicken parts in a flour-filled pie tin to shaking the chicken and flour in a brown paper bag. After only one try with each, we quickly declared the bag method the winner in both consistency of coating and easy cleanup. We have to add, however, that after shaking a thin dusting of flour over the kitchen floor and watching as heavy chicken parts threatened to break through the bag, we quickly switched to a double brown bag.

We also wanted to determine at what point the chicken should be seasoned. After a number of experiments, we decided that seasoning only the flour or the soaking liquid wasn't enough—the sound culinary principle of seasoning all along the way produced the best fried chicken. We started off with small amounts of salt, but discovered that the soaking liquid must be generously seasoned for the chicken to absorb the salt. And since only a portion of seasoned flour clings to the chicken parts, it's important that it is heavily seasoned as well.

We tested every conceivable fat and combination of fats for frying, and found less dramatic results in this area. Lard produced gorgeous, deeply tanned chicken, but we disliked the heavy, porky smell it produced during frying. Also, while this fat seemed to enforce and enhance the chicken's meatiness, it overpowered the skin and crust. We appreciated its rich, heavy taste, but tired of it after only a few bites. Even when we cut the lard with shortening, the crust was still tainted with a distinctive lard flavor.

Chicken fried in a combination of butter and vegetable oil was sweet and mild, but too rich. It was also lighter in color than any of the other chickens we fried, and the fat foamed nonstop during frying. The butter and vegetable oil combination is also more perishable, making it difficult to store and use again like other fats. Plain vegetable oil worked only relatively well; the resulting chicken, although pleasant and fast-food-like, was a bit splotchy.

Our overall preference turned out to be straight shortening. Chicken fried in this medium had a consistent mahogany color, and because it is so highly refined, shortening also turned out to be the most odor-free of all the fats. A few recipes called for flavoring the shortening with bacon drippings. We tried this, but were unimpressed. Although we could distinctly smell bacon as the chicken was frying, we could barely identify it during tasting.

We then moved on to the next frying question: Should the chicken be covered during frying and, if so, when? The point of covering the pan during frying is to trap moisture; the chicken we left uncovered during the entire frying time did not develop the soft undercoating we came to like. Yet we found that covering the chicken during the entire process created too much steam, leaving the coating too soft. In some cases the oversteaming caused the skin to separate from the meat and fall into the hot oil. Covering the chicken during the first half of the cooking time allows the chicken to steam and fry; leaving it uncovered for the second half keeps the already browned side from getting soggy.

Chicken drained on paper towels gets soggy faster than chicken drained on brown paper, but both were inferior to a wire rack set over a jelly-roll pan. The pan and wire rack mimic the draining system used by so many fast-food restaurants. In the prefrying stage, the rack offers the ideal resting place for the coated chicken. After frying (make sure to wash the rack and pan with hot soapy water and then dry it), it keeps the chicken grease-free and crisp. The pan and rack sit safely on a stovetop as well as in a warm oven—not true for either paper towels or bags.

Buttermilk Fried Chicken

SERVES 4

T HE KEY TO GREASELESS, crisp fried chicken is high temperature. Don't begin frying until the shortening has reached 350 degrees, and make sure that the temperature of the shortening stays between 250 and 300 degrees during the course of cooking. (Stick a candy or deep-frying thermometer into the oil periodically to measure the temperature.) In order to keep the breast pieces to a manageable size, cut each breast in half crosswise to yield a total of four breast pieces.

1 whole small chicken (2½ to 3 pounds),
    rinsed, patted dry, and cut into 8 pieces
    (see "Cutting Up a Whole Chicken,"
    page 10); breast pieces halved crosswise
1½ cups buttermilk
Salt and pepper
2 cups all-purpose flour
3 to 4 cups vegetable shortening, for frying

1. Place the chicken pieces in a gallon-size sealable plastic bag. Mix the buttermilk with 1 teaspoon salt and ½ teaspoon pepper in a measuring cup. Pour the mixture over the chicken; seal the bag, then refrigerate for at least 2 hours and up to 24 hours.

2. Measure the flour, 2 teaspoons salt, and ½ teaspoon pepper into a large double brown paper or plastic bag; shake to combine. Lift half of the chicken pieces from the buttermilk and drop them into the flour mixture. Shake thoroughly to completely coat the chicken with the flour. Remove the chicken from the bag, shaking the excess flour from each piece. Place the coated chicken pieces on a large wire rack set over a jelly-roll pan until ready to fry. Coat the remaining chicken pieces and set them on the rack.

3. Meanwhile, spoon enough shortening to measure ½ inch deep into a 12-inch skillet set over high heat; heat to 350 degrees. Place the chicken pieces, skin side down, into the hot oil; cover with a lid or cookie sheet and cook for 5 minutes. Lift the chicken pieces with tongs to make sure the chicken is frying evenly; rearrange if some of the pieces are browning faster than others. Cover again and continue cooking until the chicken pieces are evenly browned, about 5 minutes longer. (Be sure that the oil continues to bubble; oil temperature at this point should be between 250 and 300 degrees, and should be maintained at this level until the chicken is done.) Turn the chicken over with tongs and cook, uncovered, until the chicken is browned all over, 10 to 12 minutes longer. Remove the chicken from the skillet with tongs and return it to a clean wire rack set over a clean jelly-roll pan.

Buttermilk Fried Chicken with Herb Crust

ABUNDANT FRESH HERBS MIXED IN WITH BOTH THE BUTTERMILK AND THE FLOUR MAKE FOR A PARTICU-LARLY TASTY, AROMATIC FRIED CHICKEN. **SERVES 4.**

Follow the Buttermilk Fried Chicken recipe (page 141), adding ¼ cup chopped fresh parsley, thyme, chives, tarragon, and/or oregano leaves to the butter-milk soaking mixture and another ¼ cup chopped fresh parsley, thyme, chives, tarragon, and/or oregano leaves to the flour mixture.

Spicy Buttermilk Fried Chicken

SPICES SHOULD BE APPLIED IN LAYERS TO CHICKEN PIECES THAT ARE TO BE PAN-FRIED. WE POUR SOME TABASCO SAUCE INTO THE BUTTERMILK AND SPRINKLE THE FLOUR MIXTURE WITH CAYENNE PEPPER TO GIVE THE CRUST SOME HEAT. **SERVES 4.**

Follow the Buttermilk Fried Chicken recipe (page 141), adding 1½ tablespoons Tabasco or other hot sauce to the buttermilk soaking mixture and ½ tea-spoon cayenne pepper to the flour mixture.

SKINLESS BUTTERMILK FRIED CHICKEN

FOR THOSE WHO MIGHT FEEL BETTER ABOUT EATING FRIED CHICKEN IF THEY COULD JUST LOSE THE SKIN, READ ON. WE FRIED THREE SKINLESS CHICKENS—ONE SIMPLY DUSTED WITH SEASONED FLOUR; ONE DIPPED IN FLOUR, THEN BUTTER-MILK, THEN BACK IN FLOUR; AND FINALLY ONE SIMPLY SOAKED IN buttermilk, then dipped in flour, as in the recipe for Buttermilk Fried Chicken. The meat of the simple flour-coated chicken fried up leathery; there just wasn't enough coating to protect the meat from the boiling oil. The flour-buttermilk-flour treatment formed a tough, leathery protec-tive coating. Although it adhered to the chicken, it ballooned during frying and separated from the meat. We determined that simply coating the buttermilk-soaked chicken with flour provided just the right coating and protection for the skinned meat.

Many of those participating in our taste tests did not detect the missing skin, and those who noticed didn't really miss it. To make the skinless fried chicken, follow the Master Recipe for But-termilk Fried Chicken, removing the skin from each piece before soaking it in the buttermilk.

Deep-Frying Boneless Chicken Pieces

IN SOME WAYS, deep-frying boneless, skinless pieces of breast or thigh meat is the same as pan-frying bone-in parts. Buttermilk is still the best soaking medium and the goal is the same—a crisp coating with tender, juicy meat. But in our testing, we found that there are plenty of differences.

While flour is the only coating we recommend for pan-fried parts, a variety of coatings can be used for deep-fried pieces. The reason is simple. Many coatings burn during the twenty minutes it takes to pan-fry bone-in parts. Boneless pieces deep-fry in just four minutes, so this is not an issue. We like seasoned flour, spiced flour, flour mixed with a little cornmeal (this makes an especially crisp coating), as well as a beer batter that balloons into a soft, puffy coating somewhat like tempura.

While we found that it was best to shake chicken parts in a paper bag with the flour for even coating, it's easy enough to dredge small chicken strips in a bowl of seasoned flour. Also, there is no need to break out a rack for draining the chicken. There aren't as many crevices to trap grease on boneless pieces, so they are less likely to have excess grease in the first place. A quick roll in paper towels absorbs any that remains.

Of course, the biggest difference between pan-frying and deep-frying is the actual frying. Pan-frying requires a wide skillet, but deep-frying is best accomplished in an electric fryer or deep, heavy pot. While we found that shortening is best when pan-frying, the difference between shortening and oil in deep-frying was hard to detect, most likely owing to the much shorter cooking time. Since more cooks are likely to have oil on hand, we have called for oil in the recipes that follow. (Of course, shortening can also be used if desired.) Smoke points for most oils, including safflower, soybean, corn, pure olive, canola, peanut, and sunflower, are well above the temperatures required for deep-frying at home, so this is not a consideration when choosing an oil for deep-frying. Flavor differences among oils are quite subtle. In the end, cost and whatever is in your pantry should be the determining factors when choosing an oil.

While most pan-frying occurs between 250 and 300 degrees (prolonged pan-frying at a higher temperature would cause the coating to burn before the meat was cooked through), deep-frying should happen as quickly as possible. We found that heating the oil to 360 degrees was best. (The oil can be heated higher, to 375 degrees, but we found no added benefit.) At this temperature, the chicken will cook through quickly (in about four minutes) and the temperature of the oil will stay above 325 degrees throughout the frying process.

If using a large pot, you will want to wear long sleeves and use a slotted spoon or Chinese mesh skimmer to move pieces of chicken in and out of the oil. While this method will certainly work, we much prefer to use an electric deep-fryer for this recipe. There is less chance that oil will splatter on you or your clothes, there is less mess, and a good deep-fryer regulates the heat evenly. Electric deep-fryers are also much safer to use since they separate bubbling hot oil from pilot lights and open flames. Grease fires are all but impossible in these fryers.

If you want to reuse the oil, let it cool completely, then strain it through a coffee filter to remove food particles that can cause the oil to degrade. We found that as long as the oil is strained after each use, it can survive four or five fryings without any noticeable drop in quality. If at any point the oil becomes overheated and smokes, it is a sign that the oil has degraded and should be discarded once it has cooled. Also, frying strongly flavored foods, such as seafood, will impart off flavors to the oil and subsequently fried foods.

ELECTRIC DEEP-FRYERS

∧

IF YOU DON'T OWN AN ELECTRIC DEEP-FRYER AND WANT TO BUY ONE (THEY ALSO MAKE WONDERFUL FRENCH FRIES AND FRIED SEAFOOD), HERE'S WHAT YOU SHOULD LOOK FOR. MOST MODELS CONSIST OF A LARGE CIRCULAR VAT THAT HEATS AND HOLDS THE OIL, AS WELL AS A WIRE BASKET THAT HOLDS THE FOOD. A KNOB

controls the basket, allowing the cook to raise and lower the food into the oil when the lid is closed.

Look for a model that will comfortably hold 1 pound of food at a time. We found baskets that rotate during cooking promote even browning and allow less oil to be used. Food is not any less greasy, but it costs less to cook in these models which use 4 or 5 cups of oil to fry a batch of food, not 8 or 10. Most electric fryers come with a clear plastic viewing window so that you can judge how the food is progressing without opening the lid and causing the temperature to drop. The viewing window should come with a wiping mechanism or it will be useless—steam will quickly cloud it over. Finally, look for a model with a button on the side to release the lid. The lids on some models must be opened manually, often putting the cook's hand right in the path of escaping steam.

In our testing, models from DeLonghi and Tefal both performed well, although the DeLonghi fryers were our favorites. With both models (as well as most stovetop setups), you should fry the chicken in two batches to avoid overcrowding. If you like, you can reuse oil for frying. Eventually the fat in the oil will start to break down, though. As boiling oil comes into contact with oxygen in the air, decomposition of the fat begins. This process, known as oxidation, can be slowed by using a tall, narrow pot that minimizes the amount of oil in direct contact with the air. Covered electric fryers also reduce oxidation.

Buttermilk Deep-Fried Boneless Chicken Pieces

SERVES 4 TO 6

ONELESS THIGHS may be substituted for breasts if you prefer dark meat. Serve as is, with lemon or lime wedges, or with any of the dipping sauces that follow.

2 pounds boneless, skinless chicken
    breasts, tendons and excess fat removed
    (see figures 1 and 2, page 50); rinsed,
    dried, and cut into 2-inch-wide strips
1 cup buttermilk
Salt and pepper
Vegetable oil, for deep-frying
1 cup all-purpose flour

1. Place the chicken pieces in a large sealable plastic bag. Mix the buttermilk with ½ teaspoon salt and ¼ teaspoon pepper in a measuring cup. Pour the mixture over the chicken; seal the bag, then refrigerate for at least 2 hours and up to 24 hours.

2. Pour 2 inches of oil into an electric fryer or large kettle set over high heat; heat to 360 degrees. Mix the flour, 2 teaspoons salt, and ½ teaspoon pepper in a small bowl or pie plate. Lift the chicken pieces from the buttermilk and dredge them in the seasoned flour. Fry the chicken, in batches if necessary, until golden,

about 4 minutes. If you like, keep the chicken warm in a 200-degree oven until serving.

◆

Beer Batter Deep-Fried Chicken Pieces

BEER BATTER MAKES A FLUFFY, RATHER THAN CRISP AND CRUNCHY, COATING. IF USING A DEEP-FAT FRYER WITH A BASKET, BE SURE TO HEAT THE BASKET IN THE HOT OIL BEFORE PLACING THE CHICKEN PIECES IN IT. THIS WILL PREVENT THE BATTER FROM STICKING TO THE BASKET. TRY THIS CHICKEN WITH MAPLE MUSTARD DIPPING SAUCE (PAGE 148). **SERVES 4 TO 6.**

3 eggs, separated
4 tablespoons unsalted butter, melted and
    cooled
¾ cup flat beer
1 cup all-purpose flour
2 teaspoons salt
Pepper
1 quart vegetable oil, for deep-frying
2 pounds boneless, skinless chicken
    breasts, tendons and excess fat removed
    (see page 50); rinsed, dried, and cut
    into 2-inch-wide strips

1. Mix the yolks, butter, and beer in a medium bowl. Whisk in the flour, salt, and pepper to taste, stirring until smooth. Cover and refrigerate the batter for at least 3 hours or up to overnight.

2. Beat the egg whites until they hold soft peaks. Fold the whites into the batter.

3. Pour 2 inches of oil into an electric fryer or large kettle set over high heat; heat to 360 degrees. Pat the chicken pieces dry. Dip the chicken pieces in the batter and fry, in batches if necessary, until golden, about 4 minutes. If you like, keep the chicken warm in a 200-degree oven until serving.

MAKING IT A MEAL

／l＼

FRIED CHICKEN IS WONDERFUL ON ITS OWN, BUT THE ACCOM-
PANIMENTS RIGHTLY MERIT JUST AS MUCH ATTENTION. BIS-
CUITS, MASHED POTATOES, AND A CREAM GRAVY ARE
TRADITIONAL PARTNERS FOR FRIED CHICKEN IN THE SOUTH. THIS
COMBINATION CANNOT BE IMPROVED UPON. FOR INFORMATION ON

biscuits (including a recipe), see page 267. For
mashed potatoes, choose high-starch potatoes,
which create a delightfully fluffy texture when
mashed and are dry enough to absorb milk and

butter without becoming gummy. The pale-
colored cream gravy is a traditional but optional
accompaniment.

Spicy Deep-Fried Chicken Pieces

HOT SAUCE AND CAYENNE PEPPER GIVE THIS CHICKEN
GREAT FLAVOR. NO DIPPING SAUCE IS NECESSARY, BUT
IF YOU LIKE YOUR CHICKEN EXTRA-SPICY, CREAMY
CHIPOTLE DIPPING SAUCE (PAGE 149) WOULD BE THE
WAY TO GO. SERVES 4 TO 6.

Follow the Buttermilk Deep-Fried Boneless Chicken
Pieces recipe (page 145), adding 1 tablespoon
Tabasco or other hot sauce to the buttermilk soaking
mixture and ½ teaspoon cayenne pepper to the flour
mixture.

Cornmeal Deep-Fried Chicken Pieces

CORNMEAL ADDED TO THE FLOUR GIVES CHICKEN
PIECES A FLAVORFUL, ESPECIALLY CRUNCHY CRUST.
SERVES 4 TO 6.

Follow the Buttermilk Deep-Fried Boneless Chicken
Pieces recipe (page 145), replacing ¼ cup of flour
with equal amount of cornmeal and adding 1 teaspoon
dried thyme or oregano to the flour-cornmeal mixture.

Perfect Mashed Potatoes

IF YOU'RE SERVING MASHED POTATOES WITH GRAVY, THIS IS THE RECIPE YOU WANT. IT DELIVERS SPECTACULARLY SMOOTH, FLUFFY POTATOES, NOT TOO RICH OR ASSERTIVELY FLAVORED. A RICER ENSURES PERFECTLY SMOOTH MASHED POTATOES; A MASHER CAN DELIVER THE SAME RESULTS OR LEAVE BEHIND LUMPS DEPENDING ON THE SKILL AND INTENT OF THE COOK. MAKES ABOUT 4 CUPS.

> 2 pounds russet or Yukon Gold
>   potatoes, peeled, eyes and
>   blemishes removed, and cut into 2-
>   inch chunks
> ¾ teaspoon salt
> 6 tablespoons butter, softened
> 1 cup whole milk or half-and-half, warmed
> Pepper

1. Put the potatoes in a large saucepan; add cold water to cover and ½ teaspoon salt. Bring to a boil and continue to cook over medium heat until the potatoes are tender when pierced with a knife, 15 to 20 minutes.

2. Drain the potatoes well and return the pan to low heat. Rice the potatoes into the pan. With a whisk or a wooden spoon, blend in the butter, then the warm milk. Or, return the potatoes to the saucepan; mash over low heat with a potato masher, adding the butter as you mash. Stir in the warm milk. Season with the remaining ¼ teaspoon salt and a pinch of black pepper, or to taste. Serve immediately with Cream Gravy.

Cream Gravy

CREAM GRAVY IS TRADITIONALLY SERVED WITH MASHED POTATOES, ALONGSIDE FRIED CHICKEN. IT'S POURED OVER THE POTATOES, NOT THE CHICKEN, SO AS NOT TO SOFTEN THE CHICKEN'S CRISP CRUST. WHILE MANY COOKS MAKE GRAVY FROM THE DRIPPINGS LEFT IN THE FRYING PAN, WE PREFER A LESS GREASY GRAVY THAT HAS JUST AS MUCH CHICKEN FLAVOR. HERE, WE MAKE A QUICK STOCK FROM THE UNUSED PARTS OF THE CHICKEN WE ARE FRYING, AND THEN USE THE STOCK TO MAKE A RICH GRAVY. IF YOU'RE USING CUT-UP CHICKEN PARTS AND DON'T HAVE ANY HOMEMADE STOCK ON HAND, SUBSTITUTE 1 CUP CANNED BROTH. MAKES ABOUT 1 CUP.

> Neck, wing tips, and back from 1
>   frying chicken
> ½ onion, coarsely chopped
> 2 tablespoons cornstarch
> ¼ cup heavy cream
> Salt and pepper

1. Combine the chicken parts, onion, and 2 cups water in a small saucepan. Bring to a boil, reduce heat to low, and skim any foam that rises to the surface. Simmer for 1½ hours, strain, and skim fat. Pour the stock into a measuring cup and measure out 1 cup. (If necessary, add water to make 1 cup.)

2. Return the stock to a clean saucepan and bring to a simmer. Combine the cornstarch and cream in a small bowl. Whisk the mixture into the simmering stock and continue to whisk until the gravy returns to a simmer and begins to thicken. Season with salt and pepper to taste. Serve immediately; keep warm over a double boiler, or reheat in a microwave.

DIPPING SAUCES

/I\

STRIPS OF BONELESS FRIED CHICKEN CALL OUT FOR SOME SORT OF DIPPING SAUCE. THE FOLLOWING ARE OUR FAVORITES, AND ALL ARE QUICK AND SIMPLE.

Maple Mustard Dipping Sauce

GROUND MUSTARD MAKES A VERY PUNGENT SAUCE. LET THE SAUCE SIT FOR AT LEAST 10 MINUTES BEFORE SERVING TO ALLOW THE MUSTARD FLAVOR TO DEVELOP. MAKES ABOUT 1/2 CUP.

- 1/4 cup dry mustard
- 2 tablespoons maple syrup
- 1 teaspoon brown sugar
- 1 teaspoon chopped fresh thyme leaves
- 1 teaspoon cider vinegar
- 1/2 teaspoon salt

Combine all the ingredients in a small bowl. Stir until smooth. Let stand for 10 minutes before serving. Extra sauce can be refrigerated for several days.

◆

Classic Red Salsa

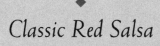

THIS SPICY TOMATO SALSA GOES PARTICULARLY WELL WITH CORNMEAL DEEP-FRIED CHICKEN PIECES (PAGE 146). SERVE ADDITIONAL SALSA ON THE SIDE WITH FRENCH FRIES. MAKES ABOUT 5 CUPS.

- 3 large, very ripe tomatoes (about 2 pounds), cored and diced small
- 1/2 cup tomato juice
- 1 jalapeño or other fresh chile, stemmed, seeded, and finely chopped
- 1 medium red onion, diced small
- 1 medium garlic clove, finely chopped
- 1/2 cup chopped fresh cilantro leaves
- 1/2 cup fresh lime juice
- Salt

Mix all the ingredients, including salt to taste, in a medium bowl. Cover and refrigerate to blend flavors, at least 1 hour or up to 2 days.

◆

Hoisin-Sesame Dipping Sauce

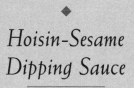

THIS IS A DENSE, RICH SAUCE, PERFECT WITH GOLDEN FRIED CHICKEN PIECES. YOU CAN SPRINKLE THINLY SLICED SCALLIONS AND TOASTED SESAME SEEDS OVER THE SAUCE JUST BEFORE SERVING. MAKES ABOUT 1/2 CUP.

- 2 tablespoons Asian sesame oil
- 1/4 teaspoon hot red pepper flakes
- 1 tablespoon minced fresh gingerroot
- 1 garlic clove, finely chopped

¼ cup hoisin sauce
2 tablespoons balsamic vinegar
2 tablespoons soy sauce
2 tablespoons fresh orange juice
1 teaspoon ground coriander
½ teaspoon Chinese five-spice
  powder

Heat the oil and pepper flakes in a small skillet over medium heat. Add the ginger and garlic; sauté until softened, 1 to 2 minutes. Pour this flavored oil into a small bowl; stir in the remaining ingredients. Serve warm or at room temperature. Extra sauce can be refrigerated for several days.

◆

Creamy Chipotle Dipping Sauce

SERVE THIS SMOKY-HOT SAUCE WITH THE BASIC RECIPE, OR ADD ANOTHER LAYER OF HEAT BY SERVING IT WITH SPICY DEEP-FRIED CHICKEN PIECES (PAGE 146). CANNED CHIPOTLE CHILES ARE AVAILABLE AT LATINO MARKETS AND MANY SUPERMARKETS. MAKES ABOUT ½ CUP.

¼ cup mayonnaise
¼ cup sour cream
2 teaspoons finely chopped chipotle
  chiles in adobo
1 small garlic clove, finely chopped
2 teaspoons chopped fresh cilantro
  leaves
1 teaspoon fresh lime juice

Mix all the ingredients in a small bowl. Cover and refrigerate until the flavors blend, about 30 minutes. Extra sauce can be refrigerated for 1 day.

Spicy Peanut Dipping Sauce

A LITTLE CHICKEN STOCK THINS THE PEANUT BUTTER IN THIS QUICK SAUCE, LENDING A RICH FLAVOR PERFECT FOR FRIED CHICKEN PIECES. MAKES ABOUT 1 CUP.

6 tablespoons smooth peanut butter
½ teaspoon hot red pepper flakes, or
  to taste
2 teaspoons sugar
1 tablespoon lemon juice
2 teaspoons soy sauce
1 teaspoon Asian sesame oil
1 small garlic clove, finely chopped
1 teaspoon finely chopped fresh
  gingerroot
½ cup chicken stock or low-salt
  canned broth

Combine all the ingredients except the chicken stock in a small saucepan. Heat over low until the peanut butter begins to soften and the ingredients can be whisked together. Slowly whisk in the stock. Stir often, until the sauce is smooth, being careful not to let it boil. Cool to room temperature. Extra sauce can be refrigerated for several days.

GRILLED CHICKEN PARTS

/I\

GRILLING IS ABOUT AS STRAIGHTFORWARD A COOKING

METHOD AS THERE IS: YOU BUILD THE FIRE, YOU PUT

THE FOOD OVER THE FIRE, AND YOU COOK IT UNTIL

IT'S DONE. BUT THAT DOESN'T MEAN THAT THERE IS

NO TECHNIQUE INVOLVED. IN FACT, THE PLEASING

simplicity of grilling is nicely balanced by the fact that, when using what is essentially a quick, high-heat cooking method, the griller has to mesh the desire for a good, strong surface sear—the part that gives food that ineffable grilled flavor—with the need to cook the food all the way through before the outside gets incinerated.

So we set out to find the best method for cooking chicken pieces on the grill. Like everybody else who lights the grilling fire, we were looking for a juicy, tender, evenly cooked interior, a nicely seared exterior, and robust grilled flavor. Over the years we'd heard all the tales and backyard improvisations and figured we'd check them all out to see if any of them held particular promise for the griller.

We soon realized we would have to develop separate methods for dark and white meat parts. The higher fat content in thighs and legs makes flare-ups a greater problem, while the breasts have a tendency to dry out and need special handling. We started with dark meat since we feel it has more inherent flavor and its extra fat makes it better suited to grilling. We are also partial to grilling over coals and decided to conduct all our tests on a kettle-style covered grill. (We did adapt our final technique to a gas grill; for more information, see opposite page.)

We divided the tests into three sets. The first set involved partial cooking off the grill; the second involved particular ways of moving the chicken around on the grill surface, as well as using the grill cover for part of the cooking time; and the third involved various ways of treating the chicken before it cooked, both to add flavor and to improve texture.

We had thought that some of the methods of partially cooking the chicken off the grill would work pretty well, but we were wrong. Poaching the chicken before grilling resulted in dry chicken with a cottony texture. Microwaving prior to grilling was even worse: the chicken ended up not only dry but also rubbery, and the skin failed to crisp.

Our next approach was to sear the thighs and legs on the grill first, then finish the cooking off the grill. Using the microwave to finish cooking after a two-minute sear on the grill wasn't bad and would be acceptable for those times when you're in a hurry to get food on the table. Unlike the chicken that was microwaved before grilling, these pieces had crispy skin, and the meat was evenly cooked throughout. But this chicken, too, was slightly less juicy than those that were cooked only on the grill.

Our final attempt at combined cooking methods came even closer to the goal. Again, we seared the thighs and legs on the grill but this time finished cooking them in a 350-degree oven. The meat was evenly cooked and remained juicy, with none of the toughness experienced with other combined cooking methods; the skin, which had crisped up nicely during its time on the grill, remained quite crisp after its sojourn in the oven.

The differences between this method and our final favorite were differences of degree: the meat was just slightly less tender, the skin a bit less crispy. More important, this oven method used two different appliances and required you to do part of the cooking outside on the grill and the rest in the kitchen. Not only was this needlessly cumbersome, but it was also less fun, given that part of the appeal of grilling is standing around the fire sipping your favorite beverage and passing the time of day as you cook. So we consigned this method to the reject pile along with the other less successful combination cooking techniques.

We next moved on to test methods that involved cooking on the grill alone. Each method involved some variation on the two-level fire—that is, a fire with one area hotter than the other. The idea was to get the sear from the hotter fire and cook the chicken all the way through over the cooler fire.

The first of these methods seemed particularly contrary, but a friend had insisted that it worked, so we had to give it a test run. In this method, the chicken was to be cooked on a low fire first, then finished up on a hot fire. Like microwaving, however, this backwards approach resulted in dry meat.

Next we tried the method recommended by the manufacturers of many covered grills and sworn to by legions of backyard cooks across the country: searing chicken over a hot fire, then moving it to a medium fire, putting the cover on, and cooking until done. We found that with this method the chicken indeed cooked through without burning on the outside, stayed relatively moist, and cooked a couple of minutes faster than with other grill-only methods. There

USING A GAS GRILL

/|\

Although purists insist on grilling over a live fire, more and more Americans are using gas grills for obvious reasons—they are a breeze to light, quicker to heat up, and easier to clean. Cooking over a gas grill does present some challenges. In general, gas grills do not get as

hot as charcoal fires. In our testing, it soon became apparent that we would need the cover to build up enough heat to cook the chicken parts quickly enough. Luckily, gas burns more cleanly than charcoal and there is no problem with off flavors contaminating foods when the cover is down.

With gas grills, there was no need to construct a two-level fire. We simply seared the parts over high heat and then turned the heat down to medium-low for thighs and legs and low for breasts, the same temperatures used to cook these parts over charcoal.

was just one problem: it didn't taste that great. The chicken had a faint but definitely noticeable off taste, which we can best describe as resembling the odor of stale smoke. We later found that, with larger or tougher cuts of meat that stay on the grill longer—in other words, when "smoke-roasting"—the flavor of the smoke from the coals overpowers this off taste. But with foods that are not on the grill long, putting the cover on seems to cause the food to absorb the taste of the inside of the cover.

Next we tried the method that intuitively seemed most likely to succeed: searing the chicken over a medium-hot fire and then moving it to a medium-low fire to finish cooking. This approach proved the winner. While the chicken took a couple of minutes longer to cook this way than with covered cooking, it ended up just as we liked it: the interior evenly cooked, moist, and tender, and the skin dark and crisp. We found that we could cook whole legs with thighs attached or just the thighs by this method with only

one difference—timing. Thighs alone take four to eight minutes less than whole legs.

It was now time to consider ways of adding flavor to the chicken. Options included marinating, spice rubs and pastes, barbecue sauces, salsas, and brining.

Marinating the chicken was disappointing. Even several hours in a classic oil-and-acid marinade added only a small amount of flavor to the finished chicken, and oil dripping off the marinated chicken caused constant flare-ups during the initial searing period.

Rubbing the chicken with a spice rub prior to grilling proved far more satisfactory. Because the rubs and pastes are composed almost entirely of spices, they have enough flavor intensity to stand up to the smoky grilled flavor and as a result come through much more clearly. Wet pastes and barbecue sauces often contain some sweetener and can burn if brushed on the chicken before cooking. We found it best to brush them on when cooking was almost done, serving extra sauce at the table if desired. You can skip flavoring the

CHOOSING THE BEST CHARCOAL

/\

O VER THE YEARS, WE HAVE FOUND THAT LUMP HARD-

WOOD CHARCOAL BURNS CLEANER AND HOTTER THAN

REGULAR BRIQUETTES. REGULAR BRIQUETTES ARE MADE

WITH SAWDUST AND OTHER FILLER MATERIAL. AS THE NAME SUG-

GESTS, LUMP CHARCOAL IS FROM HARDWOOD. LOOK FOR THIS

product in hardware stores and other places where grilling equipment is sold.

Lump charcoal is also quite easy to light. We find that chemical starters can impart an off flavor to foods, especially to something as mild tasting as chicken. We prefer to use a chimney starter (see page 156), which requires only a piece of newspaper and a match to light a mound of charcoal.

We find that wood chips and chunks don't add much when the grilling time is relatively short, as is the case with the recipes in this chapter. A spice rub, paste, or sauce is a much more effective way to boost the flavor of grilled chicken parts.

---

chicken altogether (do season with salt and pepper, though) and serve it with a salsa or chutney instead.

As a final test, we tried brining the chicken before grilling it. Admittedly, we didn't approach this test with a lot of enthusiasm—it seemed like too much bother for what should be a simple cooking process. This just goes to show how preconceptions can be faulty, though, because it turned out to be an excellent idea.

We tried brining for various amounts of time and found that by using a brine with a high concentration of salt and sugar, we could achieve the result we wanted in only about 1½ hours. The brine penetrated the chicken, seasoning it and slightly firming up its texture before grilling. On a molecular level, what actually happened was that the salt caused the strands of protein in the chicken meat to unwind, get tangled up with each other, and trap water in the resulting matrix. When the chicken was grilled, this matrix formed a sort of barrier that kept water from leaking out of the bird. As a result, the finished chicken was juicier and more tender.

The sugar in the brine had one very good effect and one minor negative aspect. The traces of sugar left on the exterior of the chicken, while not enough to affect the taste in itself, did cause the chicken to brown more quickly and thoroughly. Since browning adds rich, deep flavor to any food, this was a decided advantage. However, the browning also took place more quickly than with nonbrined chicken, so on our first try we managed to burn the skin of some pieces. Thus, we learned, when grilling brined chicken, be sure to watch it very carefully during the initial browning period.

If you don't have time to brine your chicken, you can still get excellent results with the two-level fire method and by adding deep flavor with a spice rub or paste. If you choose not to brine, sprinkle the chicken with salt and freshly cracked black pepper before heading to the grill.

Breasts proved even more challenging. A chicken breast is thick, it's got a bone to contend with, and it needs to be thoroughly cooked without the skin burning. By comparison, grilling thighs, legs, or boneless breasts is much easier. But when properly grilled, bone-in, skin-on breasts can be particularly tasty. As with dark meat parts, we found that partially cooking the breasts before grilling (by poaching, roasting, or microwaving) was unsatisfactory. Likewise, starting the chicken on the grill and finishing indoors was ruled out. We wanted to figure out how to cook the parts completely on the grill.

Breasts, too, are best started over a medium-hot fire and then moved to a cooler part of the grill. Because breasts are thicker than thighs or legs, we found that cooking times were significantly longer. The breasts refused to cooked through to the bone in less than half an hour. By this time the skin was burning and the outer layers of meat were dry. We tried using the grill cover, but again detected some off flavors from the burned-on ashes on the inside of the cover.

We did notice that cooking with the cover cut the grilling time back to twenty minutes, about the same time we used for legs and thighs. Less time over the flames meant the skin was not black and the meat was still juicy. We decided to improvise a cover, using an old restaurant trick—a disposable aluminum roasting pan—to build up heat around the breasts and help speed along the cooking. After searing for five minutes, we moved the breasts to a cooler part of the fire, covered them with a disposable pan, and continued grilling for another fifteen minutes or so. This allowed the breasts to cook through without burning.

Like legs and thighs, breasts respond well to brining before grilling. The same collection of rubs, pastes, sauces, and salsas will work with either parts. You can grill dark and white meat parts together, if you like. Set up a three-level fire with most of the coals on one side of the grill, some coals in the middle, and no coals on the opposite side. Sear all the chicken parts over the hottest part of the fire, finish cooking the legs and thighs over the medium-low heat in the middle, and move the seared breasts to the coolest part of the grill and cover with a disposable pan. Sounds complicated, but it makes perfect sense once you try it and taste the results.

GRILLING CHICKEN

1. There is a fair amount of fat that hangs off many thighs and legs. Trim this fat before grilling to prevent flare-ups.

2. Covering the chicken breasts with a disposable roasting pan creates an ovenlike effect that speeds up cooking but still allows air to circulate. Do not use the grill cover; it can impart an off flavor to the chicken.

LIGHTING AND REGULATING A CHARCOAL FIRE

1. Our favorite way to start a charcoal fire is to use a chimney starter, also known as a flue starter. (We don't recommend lighter fluid, which can give foods, especially chicken, an unpleasant flavor.) To use this simple device, fill the bottom section with crumpled newspaper, set the flue on the grill grate, and fill the top of the starter with lump hardwood charcoal. When you light the newspaper, flames will shoot up through the charcoal, igniting it. When the flames have died down and all the coals are covered with a layer of fine gray ash, dump them out onto the grate and add more charcoal, if desired.

2. To build a two-level fire for thighs and legs, stack half of the hot coals on one side of the grill to within 3 inches or so of grill rack for a medium-hot fire. Arrange the remaining coals in a single layer on the other side of the grill for a medium-low fire.

3. To build a two-level fire for bone-in breasts, spread the coals out over half of the grill bottom, leaving the other half with no coals.

4. To check the fire temperature, hold your hand about 5 inches above the cooking grate. If you can hold it there for 2 to 3 seconds, you have a medium-hot fire; if for 4 to 5 seconds, you have a medium-low fire.

Charcoal-Grilled Chicken Thighs or Legs

SERVES 4

BRINING IMPROVES the chicken's flavor, but if you're short on time, you can skip step 1. Flavor the chicken with one of the spice rubs, pastes, or sauces from the recipes later in this chapter. Because no two live fires are exactly the same, the cooking time remains an estimate. To check the fire temperature for this recipe, hold your hand about 5 inches above the grill grid (see figure 4, opposite page). If you can hold it there for 2 to 3 seconds, you have a medium-hot fire; if for 4 to 5 seconds, you have a medium-low fire.

8 chicken thighs or 4 whole legs
¾ cup kosher salt *or* 6 tablespoons
  table salt
¾ cup sugar
Pepper

1. To prevent burning, trim all overhanging fat and skin from the chicken pieces (see figure 1, page 155). If brining the pieces: In a gallon-size sealable plastic bag, dissolve the salt and sugar in 1 quart of water. Add the chicken, pressing out as much air as possible; seal and refrigerate until fully seasoned, about 1½ hours.

2. Light 5 quarts of charcoal (1 chimney starter heaped full) and allow to burn until the flames have died down and all the charcoal is covered with a layer of fine gray ash (see figure 1, opposite). Build a 2-level fire by stacking half of the hot coals on one side of the grill to within 3 inches or so of grill rack for a medium-hot fire. Arrange the remaining coals in single layer on the other side of the grill for a medium-low fire (see figure 2, opposite). Return the grill rack to position; cover the grill and let the rack heat 5 minutes.

3. Meanwhile, remove the chicken from the brine, rinse well, dry thoroughly with paper towels, and season with pepper to taste. If you haven't brined the parts, season them generously with salt and pepper.

4. Cook the chicken, uncovered, over medium-hot fire, extinguishing any flames with a squirt bottle, until seared, about 1 to 2 minutes on each side. Move the chicken to the medium-low fire; continue to grill uncovered, turning occasionally, until the chicken is dark and fully cooked, 12 to 16 minutes for thighs, 16 to 20 minutes for whole legs. To test for doneness, either peek into the thickest part of the chicken with the tip of a small knife (you should see no redness near the bone) or check the internal temperature at the thickest part with an instant-read thermometer, which should register 165 degrees. Transfer to a serving platter. Serve warm or at room temperature.

Charcoal-Grilled Bone-In Chicken Breasts

SERVES 4

FLAVORINGS CAN BE added to these chicken breasts before or during cooking. Rub them with a spice rub before they go on the grill or brush them with a spice paste or barbecue sauce during the final 2 minutes of cooking. Although they won't be quite as plump or deeply flavored, the breasts can also be grilled without brining them first. Also, if the fire flares because of dripping fat or a gust of wind, move the chicken to the area without coals until the flames die down.

¾ cup kosher salt *or* 6 tablespoons
    table salt
¾ cup sugar
4 split chicken breasts (bone in, skin on),
    10 to 12 ounces each
Pepper

1. If brining the pieces: In a gallon-size sealable plastic bag, dissolve the salt and sugar in 1 quart of water. Add the chicken, then seal the bag, pressing out as much air as possible; refrigerate until fully seasoned, about 1½ hours.

2. Light 5 quarts of charcoal (1 chimney starter heaped full) and allow to burn until the flames have died down and all the charcoal is covered with a layer of fine gray ash. When coals are medium-hot (you can hold your hand 5 inches above the grill surface for 2 or 3 seconds), spread coals out over half of grill bottom, leaving the other half with no coals (see figure 3, page 156).

3. Meanwhile, remove the chicken from the brine, rinse well, dry thoroughly with paper towels, and season with pepper to taste. If you haven't brined the chicken, season them generously with salt and pepper.

4. Place the chicken, skin side down, on a rack directly over the coals; grill until well browned, 2 to 3 minutes per side. Move the chicken to the area with no fire and cover with a disposable aluminum roasting pan; continue to cook, skin side up, 10 minutes (see figure 2, page 155). Turn and cook 5 minutes more. To test for doneness, either peek into the thickest part of the chicken with the tip of a small knife (you should see no redness near the bone) or check the internal temperature at the thickest part with an instant-read thermometer, which should register 160 degrees. Transfer to a serving platter. Serve warm or at room temperature.

Gas-Grilled Chicken Thighs or Legs

SERVES 4

OST GRILLING EXPERTS agree that gas-grilled chicken lacks the superior, smoky flavor that a charcoal grill imparts. However, juicy, crispy-skinned parts can be cooked on a gas grill using the following method. Initial high heat is important for a crispy skin. The heat is turned to medium-low to allow the chicken to cook through but remain moist and tender. Because the gas grill generally produces less heat than the charcoal grill, it is necessary to cook the chicken parts covered during both high-heat and low-heat phases.

8 chicken thighs or 4 whole legs
¾ cup kosher salt *or* 6 tablespoons table salt
¾ cup sugar
Pepper

1. To prevent burning, trim all overhanging fat and skin from the chicken pieces (see figure 1, page 155). If brining the pieces: In a gallon-size sealable plastic bag, dissolve the salt and sugar in 1 quart of water. Add the chicken, pressing out as much air as possible; seal and refrigerate until fully seasoned, about 1½ hours.

2. Light the gas grill, set at high heat, and cover. Heat for 10 to 15 minutes.

3. Meanwhile, remove the chicken from the brine, rinse well, dry thoroughly with paper towels, and season with pepper to taste. If you haven't brined the pieces, season them generously with salt and pepper.

4. Cook the chicken, covered, over high, extinguishing any flames with a squirt bottle, until seared, about 1 to 2 minutes on each side. Turn the heat down to medium-low; continue to grill covered, turning 2 or 3 times, until the chicken is dark and fully cooked, 10 to 15 minutes for thighs, 15 to 20 minutes for whole legs. To test for doneness, either peek into the thickest part of the chicken with the tip of a small knife (you should see no redness near the bone) or check the internal temperature at the thickest part with an instant-read thermometer, which should register 165 degrees. Transfer to a serving platter. Serve warm or at room temperature.

Gas-Grilled Chicken Breasts

SERVES 4

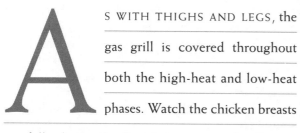

A S WITH THIGHS AND LEGS, the gas grill is covered throughout both the high-heat and low-heat phases. Watch the chicken breasts carefully during the first few minutes of grilling—brining them makes them more likely to burn.

¾ cup kosher salt *or* 6 tablespoons
    table salt
¾ cup sugar
4 split chicken breasts (bone in, skin on),
    10 to 12 ounces each
Pepper

1. If brining the pieces: In a gallon-size sealable plastic bag, dissolve the salt and sugar in 1 quart of water. Add the chicken, then seal the bag, pressing out as much air as possible; refrigerate until fully seasoned, about 1½ hours.

2. Light the gas grill, set at high heat, and cover. Heat for 10 to 15 minutes.

3. Meanwhile, remove the chicken from the brine, rinse well, dry thoroughly with paper towels, and season with pepper to taste. If you have not brined the pieces, season them generously with salt and pepper.

4. Place the chicken, skin side down, on the grill; cook the chicken, covered, over high, until well browned, 2 minutes per side. Keep a close eye on the chicken to make sure it's not burning, and shift it around on the grill if you think that it is. Turn the heat down to low; continue to cook covered, skin side up, for 10 minutes. Turn and cook covered for 5 minutes more. To test for doneness, either peek into the thickest part of the chicken with the tip of a small knife (you should see no redness near the bone) or check the internal temperature at the thickest part with an instant-read thermometer, which should register 160 degrees. Transfer to a serving platter. Serve warm or at room temperature.

◆

Simple Spice Rub for Grilled Chicken Parts

A SPICE RUB IS THE QUICKEST AND EASIEST WAY TO ADD FLAVOR TO GRILLED CHICKEN. IT ALSO PRODUCES A CRISPIER SKIN THAN PASTES OR BARBECUE SAUCES, WHICH ARE BRUSHED ON AT THE END OF GRILLING. THE FOLLOWING IS JUST ONE POSSIBLE COMBINATION. TRY OTHER SPICE COMBINATIONS ACCORDING TO YOUR OWN TASTE. **MAKES ABOUT** ¹/₂ **CUP.**

2 tablespoons ground cumin
2 tablespoons curry powder
2 tablespoons chili powder
1 tablespoon ground allspice
1 tablespoon pepper
1 teaspoon ground cinnamon
¹/₂ teaspoon salt

1. Mix all the ingredients in a small bowl.

2. Proceed with one of the Master Recipes on pages 157–160, rubbing the spice rub on the chicken parts after removing them from the brining mixture and rinsing and drying them.

BONELESS, SKINLESS
BREASTS ON THE GRILL

/\

W E FIND THAT BONE-IN PARTS, WHETHER THIGHS OR BREASTS, HAVE MORE FLAVOR THAN BONELESS PARTS. WE ALSO FIND THAT THE SKIN HELPS KEEP IN MOISTURE AND CAN PREVENT DRYING OUT DURING COOK-ING. HOWEVER, THERE ARE TIMES WHEN BONELESS, SKINLESS

breasts make sense on the grill. They are ideal for sandwiches or salads since they can be used as is, without skinning or boning. Also, much of the flavor of a rub, paste, or sauce will be lost when you discard the skin after cooking. You may as well start with boneless, skinless parts and apply the flavor where you can enjoy it.

Of course, boneless, skinless breasts have almost no fat and can dry out easily with any cooking method. In our tests, it was clear that we needed to get them on and off the grill as quickly as possible. Cooking them over high heat and turning them just once was the best method we tested. Cooking time can range from 10 minutes or less over a very hot charcoal fire to perhaps 15 minutes on a less powerful gas grill. In any case, you should keep a squirt bottle handy to douse any flames and move any pieces that seem to be burning on the exterior to a slightly cooler part of the grill.

To check for doneness, insert a knife into the thickest part of the breast; there should be no pinkness or blood. You could also try to use an instant-read thermometer (an internal temperature of 160 degrees is just right), but this can be tricky on such thin cuts. If you do use a thermometer, slide it on an angle into the thickest part of the breast and make sure that it does not go entirely through and out the bottom of the breast or the reading will be off.

Finally, brining boneless, skinless breasts improves their flavor and texture. Use four chicken breast cutlets (about 1½ pounds total) in a full recipe of the brine solution from the Master Recipe on page 158, but cut the brining time to just 45 minutes. This amount of chicken cutlets works for the recipes for rubs, pastes, sauces, and salsas that follow throughout this chapter and will feed four.

Garam Masala Spice Rub

GARAM MASALA IS A BLEND OF SPICES USED IN INDIAN COOKING. HERE, WHOLE SPICES ARE TOASTED AND THEN FRESHLY GROUND FOR MAXIMUM FLAVOR. THE AMOUNTS BELOW CAN BE VARIED TO TASTE, AND OTHER WHOLE SPICES, SUCH AS CUMIN OR CORIANDER SEEDS, MAY ALSO BE SUBSTITUTED OR ADDED. THE SPICE RUB WILL KEEP IN AN AIRTIGHT CONTAINER FOR SEVERAL WEEKS, BUT IS BEST USED IMMEDIATELY. MAKES ABOUT ½ CUP.

- 2 tablespoons fennel seeds
- 2 tablespoons anise seeds
- 2 tablespoons cardamom pods
- 2 tablespoons black peppercorns
- 1 teaspoon whole cloves
- 1 4-inch-long cinnamon stick, broken into several pieces
- ½ teaspoon salt

1. Combine all the ingredients except for the salt in a medium skillet. Toast over medium heat, shaking constantly, until the spices become fragrant, but do not burn, 2 to 3 minutes.

2. Remove the pan from the heat and grind the spices with a mortar and pestle, electric spice grinder, or clean electric coffee grinder. Stir in the salt.

3. Proceed with one of the Master Recipes on pages 157–160, rubbing the spice rub on the chicken parts after removing them from the brining mixture and rinsing and drying them.

◆

Sweet-and-Sour Curry Spice Paste

THIS WET PASTE IS BRUSHED ON THE CHICKEN DURING THE LAST FEW MINUTES OF COOKING TO GIVE THE CHICKEN A SWEET-AND-SOUR CRUST. MAKES ABOUT ¾ CUP.

- 1 tablespoon ground cumin
- 1 tablespoon curry powder
- 1 tablespoon ground coriander
- 1 tablespoon paprika
- 1 tablespoon brown sugar

- 2 medium garlic cloves, finely chopped
- ¼ cup red wine vinegar
- ¼ cup distilled white vinegar
- ¼ cup peanut oil
- ½ teaspoon salt

1. Mix all the ingredients in a small bowl.

2. Grill the chicken following the instructions in the appropriate Master Recipe (pages 157–160). When the chicken is almost fully cooked, brush some of the mixture on both sides of each piece. Continue to grill the chicken, brushing with the remaining paste, until fully cooked.

◆

Mediterranean Spice Paste

CHICKEN RUBBED WITH THIS MEDITERRANEAN-FLAVORED PASTE MIGHT BE SERVED WITH GRILLED ITALIAN VEGETABLES—BELL PEPPERS, EGGPLANT, ZUCCHINI—AND GRILLED BREAD. MAKES ABOUT ½ CUP.

- 4 medium garlic cloves, peeled
- 2 tablespoons finely grated lemon zest
- ¼ cup fresh parsley leaves
- ¼ cup olive oil
- 1 tablespoon fresh thyme leaves
- 1 tablespoon fresh rosemary leaves
- 1 tablespoon fresh sage leaves
- ½ teaspoon salt

1. Puree all the ingredients in a food processor or blender.

2. Grill the chicken following the instructions in the appropriate Master Recipe (pages 157–160). When the chicken is almost fully cooked, brush some of the mixture on both sides of each piece. Continue to grill the chicken, brushing with the remaining paste, until fully cooked.

Chile Spice Paste with Citrus and Cilantro

ALTHOUGH WE LIKE THE COMBINATION OF ORANGE, PINEAPPLE, AND LIME JUICES, YOU MAY OMIT THE PINEAPPLE OR ORANGE JUICE, ADDING AN EXTRA TABLESPOON OF THE JUICE STILL BEING USED. MAKES ABOUT 1/3 CUP.

- 1 teaspoon ground cumin
- 1 teaspoon chili powder
- 1 teaspoon paprika
- 1 teaspoon ground coriander
- 2 tablespoons fresh cilantro leaves
- 1 small garlic clove
- 1 tablespoon fresh orange juice
- 1 tablespoon pineapple juice
- 1 tablespoon fresh lime juice
- 1 tablespoon olive oil
- 2 dashes Tabasco sauce
- 1/2 teaspoon salt

1. Puree all the ingredients in a food processor or blender.

2. Grill the chicken following the instructions in the appropriate Master Recipe (pages 157–160). When the chicken is almost fully cooked, brush some of the mixture on both sides of each piece. Continue to grill the chicken, brushing with the remaining paste, until fully cooked.

Asian Spice Paste

GINGER, GARLIC, CILANTRO, AND SOY SAUCE GIVE THIS PASTE AN ASIAN FLAVOR. MAKES ABOUT 1/2 CUP.

- 2 tablespoons fresh cilantro leaves
- 1 tablespoon minced fresh chile of your choice
- 2 medium garlic cloves
- 1 tablespoon coarsely chopped fresh gingerroot
- 2 tablespoons soy sauce
- 2 tablespoons peanut oil

1. Puree all the ingredients in a food processor or blender.

2. Grill the chicken following the instructions in the appropriate Master Recipe (pages 157–160). When the chicken is almost fully cooked, brush some of the mixture on both sides of each piece. Continue to grill the chicken, brushing with the remaining paste, until fully cooked.

Chipotle-Orange Paste

CANNED CHIPOTLE CHILES, AVAILABLE AT MOST SUPERMARKETS AND LATIN GROCERIES, VARY IN HEAT, SO YOU'LL WANT TO TASTE AND ADD MORE CHILES ACCORDINGLY AS YOU PUT TOGETHER THE FOLLOWING CITRUS-SPIKED PASTE. MAKES ABOUT 1/3 CUP.

- 2 medium garlic cloves, peeled
- 2 tablespoons finely grated orange zest
- 1/4 cup tightly packed fresh cilantro leaves
- 2 tablespoons olive oil
- 3 tablespoons coarsely chopped chipotle chiles in adobo, or to taste
- 1 tablespoon adobo sauce from canned chipotles
- 1/2 teaspoon salt

1. Puree all the ingredients in a food processor or blender.

2. Grill the chicken following the instructions in the appropriate Master Recipe (pages 157–160). When the chicken is almost fully cooked, brush some of the mixture on both sides of each piece. Continue to grill the chicken, brushing with the remaining paste, until fully cooked.

Roasted Garlic Paste

GARLIC MELLOWS AND BECOMES ALMOST SWEET WHEN IT'S ROASTED. PUREED WITH A LITTLE OIL AND VINEGAR, ROASTED GARLIC IS PERFECT FOR MOISTENING AND FLAVORING GRILLED CHICKEN. MAKES ⅔ CUP.

> 3 large garlic heads, separated into cloves
>   and peeled (see figures 1–4, page 112)
> ¼ cup olive oil
> 1 tablespoon balsamic vinegar
> ½ teaspoon salt
> Pepper

1. Preheat the oven to 350 degrees. Place the garlic cloves on a sheet of aluminum foil, drizzle with 1 tablespoon olive oil, and wrap tightly. Place the foil packet on a baking sheet and bake until the garlic cloves are soft, about 30 minutes. Unwrap and let cool.

2. Puree all the ingredients in a food processor or blender.

3. Grill the chicken following the instructions in the appropriate Master Recipe (pages 157–160). When the chicken is almost fully cooked, brush some of the mixture on both sides of each piece. Continue to grill the chicken, brushing with the remaining paste, until fully cooked.

◆

Yogurt-Tahini Paste

THE FOLLOWING MIDDLE EASTERN PASTE GIVES GRILLED CHICKEN A WONDERFULLY CARAMELIZED CRUST AND SESAME FLAVOR. TAHINI IS AVAILABLE AT NATURAL FOODS STORES AS WELL AS MOST SUPERMARKETS. MAKES ABOUT ⅔ CUP.

> ¼ cup plain low-fat yogurt
> ¼ cup tahini
> 1 tablespoon lemon juice
> ¼ cup tightly packed fresh mint leaves
> 2 garlic cloves, peeled and coarsely chopped
> 1 teaspoon ground cumin
> 1 teaspoon ground coriander
> ½ teaspoon salt

1. Puree all the ingredients in a food processor or blender.

2. Grill the chicken following the instructions in the appropriate Master Recipe (pages 157–160). When the chicken is almost fully cooked, brush some of the mixture on both sides of each piece. Continue to grill the chicken, brushing with the remaining paste, until fully cooked.

◆

Basic Barbecue Sauce

LIKE SPICE PASTES, BARBECUE SAUCES SHOULD BE APPLIED ONLY IN THE LAST FEW MINUTES OF GRILLING, OTHERWISE THE SWEETENERS IN MOST SAUCES WILL CAUSE THE SKIN TO BURN. SERVE ADDITIONAL SAUCE ON THE SIDE AS AN ACCOMPANIMENT TO THE COOKED CHICKEN. REFRIGERATE OR FREEZE EXTRA SAUCE. MAKES 3 CUPS.

> 2 tablespoons vegetable oil
> 1 medium onion, minced
> 1 can (8 ounces) tomato sauce
> 1 can (28 ounces) whole tomatoes with
>   juice
> ¾ cup distilled white vinegar
> ¼ cup firmly packed dark brown sugar
> 2 tablespoons molasses
> 1 tablespoon sweet paprika
> 1 tablespoon chili powder
> 2 teaspoons Liquid Smoke (optional)
> 1 teaspoon salt
> 2 teaspoons pepper
> ¼ cup fresh orange juice

1. Heat the oil in a large, heavy-bottomed saucepan over medium heat until hot and shimmering (but not smoking). Add the onion; sauté until golden brown, 7 to 10 minutes, stirring frequently. Add the remaining ingredients. Bring to a boil, then reduce the heat to the lowest possible setting and simmer, uncovered, until thickened, 2 to 2½ hours.

2. Puree the sauce, in batches if necessary, in a blender or the work bowl of a food processor. Transfer to a bowl and use immediately or cover in an airtight container. (The sauce can be refrigerated for up to 2 weeks or frozen for several months.)

3. To use the barbecue sauce, grill the chicken following the instructions in the appropriate Master Recipe (pages 157–160). During the last 2 minutes of cooking, brush with some of the sauce, cook about 1 minute, turn over, brush again, and cook 1 minute more. Transfer the chicken to a serving platter, brush with additional sauce to taste, and serve.

◆

Barbecue Sauce with Mexican Flavors

A FEW INGREDIENTS ADDED TO BASIC BARBECUE SAUCE GIVE THIS RECIPE A SOUTH-OF-THE-BORDER FLAVOR. MAKES 3 CUPS.

> 2 tablespoons vegetable oil
> 1 medium onion, minced
> 1 can (8 ounces) tomato sauce
> 1 can (28 ounces) whole tomatoes with juice
> ¾ cup distilled white vinegar
> ¼ cup firmly packed dark brown sugar
> 2 tablespoon molasses
> 1 tablespoon sweet paprika
> 2 teaspoons Liquid Smoke (optional)
> 1 teaspoon salt
> 2 teaspoons pepper
> ¼ cup fresh orange juice
> 1½ tablespoons chili powder
> 1½ teaspoons ground cumin
> 6 tablespoons fresh lime juice
> 3 tablespoons chopped fresh cilantro leaves

1. Heat the oil in a large, heavy-bottomed saucepan over medium heat until hot and shimmering (but not smoking). Add the onion; sauté until golden brown, 7 to 10 minutes, stirring frequently. Add the tomato sauce, whole tomatoes and their juice, vinegar, brown sugar, molasses, paprika, Liquid Smoke if using, salt, pepper, orange juice, and 1 tablespoon chili powder. Bring to a boil, then reduce the heat to the lowest possible setting and simmer, uncovered, until thickened, 2 to 2½ hours.

2. Puree the sauce, in batches if necessary, in a blender or the work bowl of a food processor. Transfer to a bowl and stir in the remaining chili powder, cumin, lime juice, and cilantro leaves. Use immediately or cover in an airtight container. (The sauce can be refrigerated for up to 2 weeks or frozen for several months.)

3. To use the barbecue sauce, grill the chicken following the instructions in the appropriate Master Recipe (pages 157–160). During the last 2 minutes of cooking, brush with some of the sauce, cook about 1 minute, turn over, brush again, and cook 1 minute more. Transfer the chicken to a serving platter, brush with additional sauce to taste, and serve.

◆

Barbecue Sauce with Asian Flavors

THIS SAUCE IS ALSO DELICIOUS BRUSHED ON GRILLED PORK CHOPS OR RIBS. MAKES 3 CUPS.

> 2 tablespoons vegetable oil
> 1 medium onion, minced
> 1 can (8 ounces) tomato sauce
> 1 can (28 ounces) whole tomatoes with juice
> ¾ cup distilled white vinegar
> ¼ cup firmly packed dark brown sugar
> 2 tablespoon molasses
> 1 tablespoon sweet paprika
> 1 tablespoon chili powder
> 2 teaspoons Liquid Smoke (optional)
> 1 teaspoon salt
> 2 teaspoons pepper
> ¼ cup fresh orange juice
> 3 teaspoons minced fresh gingerroot
> 6 tablespoons soy sauce
> 6 tablespoons rice wine vinegar
> 3 tablespoons sugar
> 1½ tablespoons Asian sesame oil

1. Heat the oil in a large, heavy-bottomed saucepan over medium heat until hot and shimmering (but not smoking). Add the onion; sauté until golden brown,

(continued on next page)

7 to 10 minutes, stirring frequently. Add the tomato sauce, whole tomatoes and their juice, white vinegar, brown sugar, molasses, paprika, chili powder, Liquid Smoke if using, salt, pepper, and orange juice. Bring it to a boil, then reduce the heat to the lowest possible setting and simmer, uncovered, until thickened, 2 to 2½ hours.

2. Puree the sauce, in batches if necessary, in a blender or the work bowl of a food processor. Transfer to a bowl and stir in the ginger, soy sauce, rice vinegar, sugar, and sesame oil. Use immediately or cover in an airtight container. (The sauce can be refrigerated for up to 2 weeks or frozen for several months.)

3. To use the barbecue sauce, grill the chicken following the instructions in the appropriate Master Recipe (pages 157–160). During the last 2 minutes of cooking, brush with some of the sauce, cook about 1 minute, turn over, brush again, and cook 1 minute more. Transfer the chicken to a serving platter, brush with additional sauce to taste, and serve.

◆

Barbecue Sauce with Caribbean Flavors

SERVE BLACK BEAN–MANGO SALSA (PAGE 169) ON THE SIDE WHEN YOU'RE SERVING CHICKEN BRUSHED WITH THIS SAUCE. **MAKES 3 CUPS.**

> 2 tablespoons vegetable oil
> 1 medium onion, minced
> 1 can (8 ounces) tomato sauce
> 1 can (28 ounces) whole tomatoes with juice
> ¾ cup distilled white vinegar
> ¼ cup firmly packed dark brown sugar
> 2 tablespoon molasses
> 1 tablespoon sweet paprika
> 1 tablespoon chili powder
> 2 teaspoons Liquid Smoke (optional)
> 1 teaspoon salt
> 2 teaspoons pepper
> ¼ cup fresh orange juice
> 2 teaspoons sugar
> 2 tablespoons pineapple juice

> 2 tablespoons dark rum
> 1 tablespoon Caribbean hot sauce
> Pinch ground allspice

1. Heat the oil in a large, heavy-bottomed saucepan over medium heat until hot and shimmering (but not smoking). Add the onion; sauté until golden brown, 7 to 10 minutes, stirring frequently. Add the tomato sauce, whole tomatoes and their juice, white vinegar, brown sugar, molasses, paprika, chili powder, Liquid Smoke if using, salt, pepper, and orange juice. Bring it to a boil, then reduce the heat to the lowest possible setting and simmer, uncovered, until thickened, 2 to 2½ hours.

2. Puree the sauce, in batches if necessary, in a blender or the work bowl of a food processor. Transfer to a bowl and stir in the sugar, pineapple juice, rum, hot sauce, and allspice. Use immediately or cover in an airtight container. (The sauce can be refrigerated for up to 2 weeks or frozen for several months.)

3. To use the barbecue sauce, grill the chicken following the instructions in the appropriate Master Recipe (pages 157–160). During the last 2 minutes of cooking, brush with some of the sauce, cook about 1 minute, turn over, brush again, and cook 1 minute more. Transfer the chicken to a serving platter, brush with additional sauce to taste, and serve.

◆

Maple-Mustard Glaze

WHEN YOU DON'T HAVE ANY BARBECUE SAUCE ON HAND, THIS IS A QUICK ALTERNATIVE FOR BRUSHING ON ALMOST-COOKED CHICKEN. WE LIKE COARSE-GRAIN MUSTARD, BUT ANY MUSTARD MAY BE USED. OF COURSE, USE REAL MAPLE SYRUP FOR THE BEST FLAVOR. **MAKES ABOUT 1 CUP.**

> ½ cup maple syrup
> ½ cup coarse-grain mustard
> 1 teaspoon soy sauce
> 1 tablespoon dark brown sugar
> Salt and pepper

1. Mix all the ingredients, including salt and pepper to taste, in a medium bowl.

2. Grill the chicken following the instructions in the appropriate Master Recipe (pages 157–160). During the last 2 minutes of cooking, brush with some of the glaze, cook about 1 minute, turn over, brush again, and cook 1 minute more. Transfer the chicken to a serving platter, brush with additional glaze to taste, and serve.

◆

Plum Sauce with Sesame Oil and Ginger

THIS ASIAN-FLAVORED SAUCE MAKES A NICE ALTERNATIVE TO TOMATO-BASED BARBECUE SAUCES. IF YOU HAVE A LOW TOLERANCE FOR HOT DISHES, REDUCE THE AMOUNT OF RED PEPPER FLAKES. **MAKES ABOUT 2 CUPS.**

2 tablespoons Asian sesame oil
1 ½ tablespoons minced fresh gingerroot
2 medium garlic cloves, minced
1 pound plums, pitted and halved
¼ cup rice wine vinegar
2 tablespoons fresh lime juice
¼ cup water
1 teaspoon hot red pepper flakes
Salt

1. Heat the oil in a medium saucepan over medium-high heat; add the ginger and garlic and sauté, stirring constantly, until golden, about 1 minute. Add the remaining ingredients, including salt to taste; simmer, stirring frequently, until the plums just begin to break down, 10 to 12 minutes.

2. Cool for 10 minutes, then puree in a food processor or blender. Taste for salt. (The sauce can be stored in an airtight container and refrigerated for up to 3 days; return to room temperature before serving.)

3. To use the plum sauce, grill the chicken following the instructions in the appropriate Master Recipe (pages 157–160). During the last 2 minutes of cooking, brush with some of the sauce, cook about 1 minute, turn over, brush again, and cook 1 minute more. Transfer the chicken to a serving platter, brush with additional sauce to taste, and serve.

Avocado-Corn Salsa

INSTEAD OF FLAVORING THE CHICKEN WITH A SPICE RUB, SPICE PASTE, OR BARBECUE SAUCE, IT CAN BE SEASONED WITH JUST SALT AND PEPPER AND THEN SERVED WITH A SALSA. THIS SALSA GOES WELL WITH ANY GRILLED POULTRY. THE RECIPE YIELDS A PLENTIFUL AMOUNT, SO THAT THE SALSA CAN SERVE AS A SIDE-DISH SALAD AS WELL AS A CONDIMENT. **MAKES ABOUT 5 CUPS.**

3 ears corn, husked
3 ripe but firm avocados, peeled, pitted, and diced large
1 medium red onion, diced small
1 red bell pepper, cored, seeded, and diced small
⅓ cup olive oil
¼ cup red wine vinegar
3 medium garlic cloves, minced
4 dashes hot red pepper sauce, or to taste
1 tablespoon ground cumin
1 teaspoon chili powder
¼ cup chopped fresh oregano leaves
½ cup fresh lime
Salt and pepper

1. Bring a large pot of water to boil; add the corn and boil until just cooked, 3 to 5 minutes. Drain and immediately cool the ears of corn under cold, running water, then cut the kernels from each cob (see figure on page 66).

2. Mix the corn with the remaining ingredients, including salt and pepper to taste, in a medium bowl. Cover and refrigerate to blend the flavors, at least 1 hour or up to 2 days. Serve on the side with grilled chicken.

PREPARING JICAMA

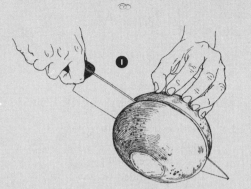

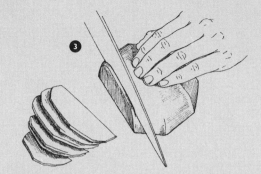

3. Slice the crisp flesh into half-circles.

1. With its rough, uneven skin, jicama can look intimidating to peel and slice. Start by slicing a thin piece off either end of the jicama. Cut the jicama in half across its equator.

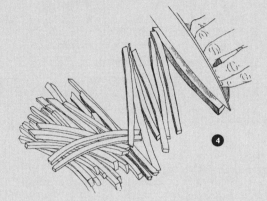

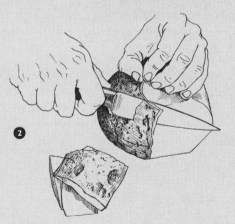

4. Stack the half-circles and slice them lengthwise into matchsticks.

2. Lay the jicama half flat on a work surface. Starting at the exposed edge on top, use a paring knife to peel the brown outer skin from the jicama.

Apricot-Jicama Salsa

CRUNCHY JICAMA IS A GOOD FOIL FOR TENDER APRI-
COTS. PEACHES OR NECTARINES MAY BE USED IN PLACE
OF THE APRICOTS, IF DESIRED. MAKES ABOUT 4 CUPS.

½ pound jicama, peeled, sliced thin, then
   cut into ¼-inch strips (see figures
   opposite)
4 apricots, pitted and cut into ½-inch
   slices
2 tablespoons minced fresh cilantro leaves
½ small red onion, sliced thin
½ small red bell pepper, cored, seeded,
   and sliced thin
1 tablespoon minced chipotle chiles in
   adobo sauce
2 tablespoons fresh lime juice
1 tablespoon olive oil
Salt and pepper

Mix all the ingredients, including salt and pepper to
taste, in a large bowl; toss lightly. Cover and refrigerate to blend the flavors, at least 1 hour or up to 2 days.
Serve on the side with grilled chicken.

◆

Simple Peach Salsa

IF YOU DON'T HAVE PEACHES, SUBSTITUTE ANY
YELLOW-ORANGE FRUIT, INCLUDING MANGOES, PINEAP-
PLES, OR PAPAYA. MAKES ABOUT 3 CUPS.

2 ripe but not mushy peaches, pitted and
   coarsely chopped
1 small red bell pepper, cored, seeded,
   and sliced thin
1 small red onion, sliced into long, thin
   slices
¼ cup chopped fresh parsley leaves
1 medium garlic clove, finely chopped
¼ cup pineapple juice
6 tablespoons fresh lime juice
1 jalapeño or other fresh chile, seeded and
   minced
Salt and pepper

Mix all the ingredients, including salt and pepper to
taste, in a medium bowl. Cover and refrigerate to
blend the flavors, at least 1 hour or up to 2 days. Serve
on the side with grilled chicken.

◆

Black Bean–Mango Salsa

THIS CARIBBEAN-INSPIRED MIXTURE IS GREAT WITH
GRILLED CHICKEN, BUT ALSO AS A SUMMER SALAD.
MAKES ABOUT 5 CUPS.

1 cup cooked black beans
2 mangoes, peeled, pitted, and diced
   small (see figures 1–4, page 121)
½ medium green bell pepper, cored,
   seeded, and diced small
½ medium red onion, diced small
¾ cup pineapple juice
½ cup fresh lime juice
½ cup chopped fresh cilantro leaves
2 tablespoons ground cumin
1 small jalapeño or chile pepper, seeded
   and minced
Salt and pepper

Mix all the ingredients, including salt and pepper to
taste, in a medium bowl. Cover and refrigerate to
blend the flavors, at least 1 hour or up to 2 days. Serve
on the side with grilled chicken.

GRILLED LEMON CHICKEN

/I\

LEMONY CHICKEN IS ONE OF OUR FAVORITE DISHES FROM THE GRILL. THE FLAVOR OF THE LEMON MUST BE INTENSE, SUPPORTED BY SOME GARLIC AND FRESH HERBS. WE KNOW FROM PAST EXPERIENCE THAT THE CHICKEN CAN BE BURSTING WITH LEMON FLAVOR. HOWEVER, JUST AS OFTEN, THE LEMON FLAVOR

is too weak. We set out to ensure the chicken would taste lemony every time.

We grilled three chickens—one that was marinated in lemon juice, garlic, and olive oil for two hours; a second that was basted with the same mixture throughout grilling; and a third that was grilled, rolled around in the lemon mixture, returned to the grill, and basted with the sauce for a few minutes longer.

The marinated and basted chickens were just fine, but the chicken flavored at the end stole the show. Not only was the lemon flavor fresher, but the chicken's juices mingled with the lemon, garlic, and oil to make a wonderful sauce. Unlike chicken number one, whose marinade had to be cooked if used as a dipping sauce, the sauce applied to the fully cooked chicken was salmonella-safe.

We did need to make some refinements. Since the chicken was on the grill for such a relatively short time once the sauce was applied, the garlic tasted raw. Mincing the garlic to almost a paste (a garlic press is helpful) and warming it in a small saucepan with the oil until it just began to sizzle improved the garlic flavor immensely.

Since the lemon flavor was so much cleaner and brighter when applied at the end of cooking, we thought other acids might work equally well. Lime, certainly, was good, but low-acid vinegar sauces, such as rice wine and balsamic vinegars, were less impressive, primarily, we think, because there wasn't a fresh flavor to preserve.

In sum, for lemon (or lime) chicken that tastes fresh and citrusy, grill it before rolling it around in the sauce.

Curried Fruit Chutney with Lime and Ginger

LIKE A SALSA, THIS CHUTNEY IS SERVED ON THE SIDE WITH SIMPLY GRILLED CHICKEN. MAKE IT IN THE SUMMER WHEN PEACHES, PLUMS, APRICOTS, AND MANGOES ARE PLENTIFUL. MAKES ABOUT 4 CUPS.

    1 tablespoon olive oil
    1 small onion, halved and sliced very thin
    1 tablespoon minced fresh gingerroot
    1 large garlic clove, finely chopped
    1½ teaspoons ground coriander
    ½ teaspoon ground cinnamon
    1 teaspoon curry powder
    ½ teaspoon hot red pepper flakes
    ½ ripe mango, peeled, pitted, and cut
        into ¼-inch dice (see figures 1–4,
        page 121)
    1 peach, pitted and cut into 8 pieces
    1 plum, pitted and quartered
    1 apricot, pitted and quartered
    1 nectarine, pitted and cut into 8 pieces
    1 tablespoon fresh orange juice
    2 tablespoons fresh lime juice
    Salt and pepper

Heat the oil in a large saucepan over medium-high heat. Add the onion; sauté, stirring frequently until the onion browns, 4 to 5 minutes. Add the ginger and garlic; sauté until fragrant, about 1 minute longer. Lower heat to medium; add the remaining ingredients; cook until the fruit starts to soften, but not fall apart, about 5 minutes longer. Adjust the seasonings. (The chutney can be set aside at room temperature for several hours; heat before serving.) Serve on the side with grilled chicken.

Grilled Lemon Chicken

THIS RECIPE IS WRITTEN FOR DARK MEAT PARTS BUT IT CAN BE MADE WITH BREASTS IF YOU PREFER; JUST FOLLOW THE COOKING INSTRUCTIONS IN MASTER RECIPE FOR CHARCOAL-GRILLED BONE-IN CHICKEN BREASTS (PAGE 158). A WHOLE CHICKEN ALSO CAN BE GRILLED; SIMPLY REMOVE THE BACK OF THE CHICKEN AND BUTTERFLY IT BEFORE BRINING (SEE FIGURES 1–5, PAGE 208). FOR THOSE WHO DON'T HAVE TIME, BRINING MAY BE OMITTED. THE QUICK SALTWATER SOAK, HOWEVER, IS WELL WORTH THE EFFORT. AFTER COOKING BATCH AFTER BATCH OF CHICKEN, WE FOUND THAT FLARE-UPS USUALLY OCCURRED DURING THE FIRST 2 TO 3 MINUTES ON THE GRILL. SINCE THE CHICKEN SKIN IS PRETTY STURDY AND CAN USUALLY WITHSTAND THE INITIAL HIGH HEAT OF THESE FLARE-UPS, DON'T BE TOO CONCERNED. BUT IF THE CHICKEN BEGINS TO CHAR, TEMPORARILY MOVE IT OVER TO THE COOLER SIDE OF THE GRILL. YOU WILL NEED FIVE GOOD-SIZED LEMONS FOR THIS RECIPE. SERVES 4.

    8 chicken thighs or 4 whole legs
    ¾ cup kosher salt or 6 tablespoons
        table salt
    2 tablespoons olive oil
    2 large garlic cloves, minced very fine
    ½ cup fresh lemon juice
    Pepper
    1½ teaspoons minced fresh oregano or
        thyme leaves

1. To prevent burning, trim all overhanging fat from the chicken pieces (see figure 1, page 155). If brining the pieces: In gallon-size sealable plastic bag, dissolve salt in 1 quart of water. Add the chicken, pressing out as much air as possible; seal and refrigerate until fully seasoned, about 1½ hours.

2. Light 5 quarts of charcoal (1 chimney starter heaped full) and allow to burn until the flames have died down and all the charcoal is covered with a layer of fine gray ash. Build a 2-level fire by stacking half of the hot coals on one side of the grill to within 3 inches or so of grill rack for a medium-hot fire. Arrange the remaining coals in single layer on the

(continued on next page)

other side of the grill for a medium-low fire. Return the grill rack to position; cover the grill and let the rack heat 5 minutes.

3. Meanwhile, place the olive oil and garlic in a small saucepan over low heat. When the garlic just starts to sizzle, remove the pan from the heat. Mix with the lemon juice in a large, shallow nonreactive pan, such as a 13-by-9-inch baking dish; set aside.

4. Remove the chicken from the brine, rinse well, dry thoroughly with paper towels, and season with pepper to taste. If you haven't brined the parts, season them generously with salt and pepper.

5. Cook the chicken, uncovered, over medium-hot fire, extinguishing any flames with a squirt bottle, until seared, about 1 to 2 minutes on each side. Move the chicken to the medium-low fire; continue to grill uncovered, turning occasionally, until the chicken is dark and fully cooked, 12 to 16 minutes for thighs, 16 to 20 minutes for whole legs. To test for doneness, either peek into the thickest part of the chicken with the tip of a small knife (you should see no redness near the bone) or check the internal temperature at the thickest part with an instant-read thermometer, which should register 165 degrees.

6. Add the oregano to the lemon sauce. As the chicken parts are nicely colored, place them in the lemon sauce, rolling them around completely with sauce to coat. Return the parts to the coolest part of the grill; cook over low heat so that the lemon sauce flavors meat, about 5 minutes longer, turning each piece and brushing it with sauce once or twice more. Return the chicken to the pan, and roll in the lemon sauce; serve warm or at room temperature.

Grilled Lime Chicken with Coriander and Chiles

AN EQUAL AMOUNT OF TOASTED AND CRUSHED CUMIN SEEDS MAY SUBSTITUTED FOR THE CORIANDER SEEDS. JALAPEÑOS OR OTHER MEDIUM-HOT FRESH CHILES ARE BEST IN THIS DISH. SERVES 4.

Follow the recipe for Grilled Lemon Chicken (page 171), sautéing 1 teaspoon minced fresh jalapeños along with the minced garlic; substituting lime juice for the lemon juice; substituting 1 tablespoon minced fresh cilantro leaves for the oregano; and adding 1 teaspoon toasted and crushed coriander seeds, along with the cilantro, to the sauce.

◆

Grilled Lemon Chicken with Rosemary

THIS ITALIAN CLASSIC MATCHES RESINOUS ROSEMARY WITH THE FLAVORS OF LEMON, GARLIC, AND OLIVE OIL. SERVES 4.

Follow the recipe for Grilled Lemon Chicken (page 171), replacing the oregano with an equal amount of minced fresh rosemary.

GRILL-ROASTED

WHOLE

CHICKEN

/|\

FOR THE MOST PART, AMERICANS ARE ACCUSTOMED

TO GRILLING OVER DIRECT HEAT. STEAK, CHOPS,

CHICKEN PARTS, OR FISH STEAKS ARE THROWN OVER

THE HOTTEST PART OF THE FIRE AND COOKED AS

QUICKLY AS POSSIBLE. BUT WHAT ABOUT LARGER

CUTS? BY USING INDIRECT HEAT AND THE COVER,

it's possible to cook a whole chicken, even a whole turkey, on the grill. The results are impressive, especially the beautifully tanned, crackling crisp skin, the likes of which are rarely seen outside of a restaurant. Adding wood chips to the fire imparts a mild smoky flavor, which is certainly not possible when oven-roasting a chicken.

The technique, which in effect turns a covered grill into an oven, is remarkably simple. Build a fire, place the hot coals on either side of a kettle grill, throw soaked chips on top of the coals, stick a whole, untrussed bird in the middle of the grill where there is no charcoal, and walk away. Glance at the grill occasionally to make sure there are no flare-ups, but other-

wise don't open the lid (except once to add more chips) until the chicken is done in about an hour. While this technique has been around for a long time, we wanted to perfect it and also come up with an adaptation for modern gas grills.

In order to maintain a fairly constant temperature of 350 to 400 degrees, it's important to start with a strong fire. We found adding more charcoal to the fire to be a hassle, so start with about 5 quarts, enough to fill a chimney starter all the way to the top. Light the charcoal and wait about half an hour, until the top of the heap is coated with a thin layer of white ash. Pile the charcoal up on the sides of the grill and open the bottom and lid vents halfway to draw air through the ket-

SETTING UP A GAS GRILL FOR INDIRECT COOKING

/\

Turn both burners to high and heat the grill to about 400 degrees; this will take about 15 minutes. Turn off the heat on one side. Use tongs to lift up the grate over the extinguished burner and slide a disposable aluminum pan or piece of heavy-duty aluminum foil,

with sides turned up to form a shallow lip, under the grill rack. Use tongs to lift up the grate on the other side and toss a large handful of soaked chips on the side opposite the drip pan. Put the chicken on the grill rack over the drip pan. Close the lid and roast the chicken for about 30 minutes. Add a second batch of soaked chips and continue grill-roasting until the chicken is done, about another

30 minutes. You may start off with a 400-degree temperature, but with only one burner going, the temperature will eventually fall to about 300 degrees.

For further information on setting up the grill, refer to the illustrations on pages 346–347 in chapter 26.

tle grill and maintain a steady, constant level of heat.

We found that topping the coals with soaked wood chips (hickory and mesquite are especially good) gives the chicken a light smoky flavor. (For more smoke flavor, you could use wood chunks, but the idea is to roast, not smoke a chicken with this method. For more information on smoking, which occurs at much lower temperatures so that food cooks slowly enough to absorb a lot of smoke flavor, see chapter 38.) Since chips will be spent in a few minutes, they should be added just as the chicken goes on the grill and then halfway (about thirty minutes) through the cooking time. Although you can skip this second batch of chips, we prefer the stronger (but not overpowering) flavor of a chicken grill-roasted with two batches of chips.

We found one final refinement—a drip pan—to be important. If possible, use a disposable aluminum pan that measures 13 by 9 inches. Just place the pan under the grill rack where there are no coals and then grill-roast the chicken right over the pan. The pan catches fat and helps prevents flare-ups that might otherwise char the skin. If you like, improvise a drip pan by taking a sheet of heavy-duty aluminum foil (cheap, thin foil does not offer enough protection) and turning up the edges to form a lip. Although this does not work quite as well as a disposable pan, it's fine in a pinch.

The construction of gas grills varies from one to the next, but most have two adjustable burners, either on the left and right or front and back of the grill rack. The burners make it possible to adjust the temperature so that half of the grill is hot and the other half is warm. When using a gas grill, we found it best to heat the grill with both burners on high. When the covered grill was hot, we turned off one burner, lifted the grate over the extinguished burner, put our pan underneath, and then placed the chicken over the pan. Soaked wood chips can be scattered on the other side of the grill. As with charcoal grilling, keep the lid shut to retain heat, opening only once to add more soaked chips.

Grill-Roasted Chicken

SERVES 4

GRILL-ROASTING GIVES chicken a bronzed skin the likes of which you will not see outside of a restaurant. Soaked hickory or mesquite chips give the bird a good smoky flavor.

- 1 whole chicken (about 3½ pounds), giblets removed and reserved for another use, chicken rinsed and patted dry with paper towels
- 1 tablespoon olive oil
- Salt and pepper
- 3 cups hickory or mesquite wood chips, soaked in cold water to cover for 30 minutes and drained

1. Set up a charcoal or gas grill using the indirect cooking method (see page 174 or 176).

2. Brush the chicken, including the cavity, with oil and sprinkle with salt and pepper to taste.

3. Add half the chips to the fire. Grill-roast the chicken for 30 minutes. Add the second batch of chips and continue to grill-roast until an instant-read thermometer inserted into the thigh registers between 165 and 170 degrees, about 30 minutes longer, depending on the grill temperature. Remove from the grill, let rest for 10 minutes, carve, and serve.

SETTING UP A CHARCOAL GRILL FOR INDIRECT COOKING

/∖

LIGHT 5 QUARTS OF CHARCOAL (1 CHIMNEY STARTER HEAPED FULL) AND ALLOW TO BURN UNTIL THE FLAMES HAVE DIED AND EVEN THOSE COALS AT THE TOP ARE COVERED WITH A THIN LAYER OF WHITE ASH. REMOVE THE GRILL RACK. PLACE A DISPOSABLE ALUMINUM PAN OR A PIECE OF HEAVY-DUTY ALUMINUM

foil, with sides turned up to form a shallow lip, in the center of the grill to act as a drip pan. Pour the hot coals into two piles on opposite sides of the grill and use long-handled tongs to move any stray coals into place.

If you heat the coals in the grill (rather than in the chimney starter), use long-handled tongs to separate the coals into two piles, on opposite sides of the grill, once they have heated. Next, carefully place the disposable drip pan or shaped foil in the grill between the coals.

Replace the grill rack and the lid. Open the bottom and lid vents halfway and heat the grill to about 400 degrees. To measure the temperature accurately, stick a grill thermometer into the open vent on the lid. In about 5 minutes, the grill should be up to temperature.

Remove the grill lid. Use tongs to pull the rack halfway off the grill and toss a handful of soaked chips onto each pile of coals. Return the rack and place the chicken on the rack over the drip pan. Cover and roast the chicken for about 30 minutes. Add a second batch of soaked chips (remove the chicken and use tongs to pull the rack halfway off the grill) and continue grill-roasting until the chicken is done, about another 30 minutes.

For further information on setting up the grill, refer to the information on page 348.

Grill-Roasted Tandoori Chicken

THE FLAVORS IN THIS YOGURT-BASED MARINADE ARE BORROWED FROM THE CLASSIC INDIAN RECIPE FOR ROASTING MARINATED CHICKEN IN A VERY HOT CLAY OVEN. SERVES 4.

1 small onion, cut into several chunks
2 garlic cloves, coarsely chopped
2 tablespoons fresh lemon juice
1 teaspoon ground coriander
1 teaspoon sweet paprika, plus additional
   for sprinkling
1/2 teaspoon ground ginger
1/4 teaspoon cayenne pepper
1/4 teaspoon ground turmeric
1/4 teaspoon ground cloves
1/4 teaspoon ground cardamom
1 teaspoon salt
Pepper
1 cup plain low-fat yogurt
1 whole chicken (about 3 1/2 pounds),
   giblets removed and reserved for
   another use, chicken rinsed and patted
   dry with paper towels
3 cups hickory or mesquite wood chips,
   soaked in cold water to cover for 30
   minutes and drained

1. Place the onion, garlic, and lemon juice in the work bowl of a food processor or blender and puree. Add the coriander, paprika, ginger, cayenne, turmeric, cloves, cardamom, salt, pepper to taste, and yogurt. Process until smooth.

2. Place the chicken in a nonreactive dish and pour the yogurt mixture over it. Cover and refrigerate, turning the chicken occasionally, at least 2 hours or overnight.

3. Set up a charcoal or gas grill using the indirect cooking method (see page 174 or 176).

4. Remove any excess yogurt mixture with a pastry brush. Add half the chips to the fire. Grill-roast the chicken for 30 minutes. Add the second batch of chips and continue to grill-roast until an instant-read thermometer inserted into the thigh registers between 165 and 170 degrees, about 30 minutes longer, depending on the grill temperature. Remove from the grill, let rest for 10 minutes, carve, and serve.

◆

Grill-Roasted Chicken with Barbecue Sauce

BECAUSE GRILLED CHICKEN PIECES ARE COOKED OVER DIRECT HEAT, THEY SHOULD ONLY BE BRUSHED WITH BARBECUE SAUCE TOWARD THE END OF COOKING, WHEN THEY'VE DEVELOPED A CRISPY SKIN AND THERE'S NO DANGER OF THE BARBECUE SAUCE FLAMING AND BURNING. BUT A WHOLE GRILL-ROASTED CHICKEN COOKED OVER COOLER INDIRECT HEAT BENEFITS FROM A BRUSH OF BARBECUE SAUCE WHEN IT FIRST GOES ON THE GRILL AND THERE IS NO DANGER OF FLARE-UPS. THE SAUCE FLAVORS THE MEAT DURING COOKING AND DEVELOPS INTO A TOOTHSOME, BUT NOT BURNT, COATING. USE ONE OF THE SAUCES FROM CHAPTER 11 OR ONE OF YOUR OWN CHOOSING. SERVES 4.

1 whole chicken (about 3 1/2 pounds),
   giblets removed and reserved for
   another use, chicken rinsed and patted
   dry with paper towels
3/4 cup barbecue sauce
3 cups hickory or mesquite wood chips,
   soaked in cold water to cover for 30
   minutes and drained

1. Set up a charcoal or gas grill using the indirect cooking method (see page 174 or 176).

2. Generously brush the chicken, including the cavity, with the sauce.

3. Add half the chips to the fire. Grill-roast the chicken for 30 minutes. Add the second batch of chips and continue to grill-roast until an instant-read thermometer inserted into the thigh registers between 165 and 170 degrees, about 30 minutes longer, depending on the grill temperature. Remove from the grill, let rest for 10 minutes, carve, and serve.

Grill-Roasted Chicken with Rosemary and Garlic

GARLIC AND HERBS SANDWICHED BETWEEN SKIN AND BREAST GIVE THE CHICKEN MEAT A MEDITERRANEAN FLAVOR. SERVES 4.

- 1 whole chicken (about 3½ pounds), giblets removed and reserved for another use, chicken rinsed and patted dry with paper towels
- 2 tablespoons chopped fresh rosemary leaves
- 4 garlic cloves, finely chopped
- 1 tablespoon olive oil
- Salt and pepper
- 3 cups hickory or mesquite wood chips, soaked in cold water to cover for 30 minutes and drained

1. Set up a charcoal or gas grill using the indirect cooking method (see page 174 or 176).

2. Gently loosen the skin from the breast and slip the rosemary and garlic in over the meat. Brush the chicken, including the cavity, with oil and sprinkle with salt and pepper to taste.

3. Add half the chips to the fire. Grill-roast the chicken for 30 minutes. Add the second batch of chips and continue to grill-roast until an instant-read thermometer inserted into the thigh registers between 165 and 170 degrees, about 30 minutes longer, depending on the grill temperature. Remove from the grill, let rest for 10 minutes, carve, and serve.

◆

Five-Spice Grill-Roasted Chicken

HERE A WET RUB SPICED WITH BLACK PEPPER AND FIVE-SPICE POWDER GIVES GRILL-ROASTED CHICKEN GREAT HEAT AND AROMA. SERVES 4.

- ½ cup soy sauce
- ½ cup distilled white vinegar
- ¼ cup packed light brown sugar
- 2 tablespoons coarsely ground black pepper

- 2 tablespoons five-spice powder
- 1 whole chicken (about 3½ pounds), giblets removed and reserved for another use, chicken rinsed and patted dry with paper towels
- 3 cups hickory or mesquite wood chips, soaked in cold water to cover for 30 minutes and drained

1. Combine the soy sauce, vinegar, brown sugar, pepper, and five-spice powder in a small bowl. Place the chicken in a nonreactive dish and pour the marinade over it. Cover and refrigerate for 1 hour, turning occasionally.

2. Set up a charcoal or gas grill using the indirect cooking method (see page 174 or 176).

3. Generously brush the chicken, including the cavity, with the marinade. Add half the chips to the fire. Grill-roast the chicken for 30 minutes. Add the second batch of chips and continue to grill-roast until an instant-read thermometer inserted into the thigh registers between 165 and 170 degrees, about 30 minutes longer, depending on the grill temperature. Remove from the grill, let rest for 10 minutes, carve, and serve.

◆

Grill-Roasted Chicken with Cumin and Horseradish Crust

A RUB OF BOTTLED HORSERADISH AND GROUND CUMIN METAMORPHOSES INTO A HIGHLY FLAVORED CRUNCHY CRUST DURING THE GRILL-ROASTING. SERVES 4.

- ½ cup prepared horseradish
- 1 tablespoon ground cumin
- 4 garlic cloves, finely chopped
- 2 tablespoons olive oil
- 1 teaspoon salt
- Pepper
- 1 whole chicken (about 3½ pounds), giblets removed and reserved for another use, chicken rinsed and dried
- 3 cups hickory or mesquite wood chips, soaked in cold water to cover for 30 minutes and drained

1. Set up a charcoal or gas grill using the indirect cooking method (see page 174 or 176).

2. Combine the horseradish, cumin, garlic, oil, salt, and pepper to taste in a small bowl. Generously brush the chicken, including the cavity, with the horseradish mixture.

3. Add half the chips to the fire. Grill-roast the chicken for 30 minutes. Add the second batch of chips and continue to grill-roast until an instant-read thermometer inserted into the thigh registers between 165 and 170 degrees, about 30 minutes longer, depending on the grill temperature. Remove from the grill, let rest for 10 minutes, carve, and serve.

◆

Grill-Roasted Chicken with Herbes de Provence

HERBES DE PROVENCE—A MIXTURE OF ROSEMARY, BASIL, SAVORY, MARJORAM, FENNEL SEED, AND LAVENDER—IS A QUICK WAY TO SEASON A GRILL-ROASTED CHICKEN. OTHER COMBINATIONS OF DRIED HERBS OF YOUR CHOICE MIGHT BE SUBSTITUTED. SERVES 4.

 2 tablespoons olive oil
 4 garlic cloves, finely chopped
 1 tablespoon *herbes de Provence*
 1 whole chicken (about 3 1/2 pounds), giblets removed and reserved for another use, chicken rinsed and patted dry with paper towels
 Salt and pepper
 3 cups hickory or mesquite wood chips, soaked in cold water to cover for 30 minutes and drained

1. Set up a charcoal or gas grill using the indirect cooking method (see page 174 or 176).

2. Combine the oil, garlic, and *herbes de Provence* in a small bowl. Brush the chicken, including the cavity, with the mixture and sprinkle with salt and pepper to taste.

3. Add half the chips to the fire. Grill-roast the chicken for 30 minutes. Add the second batch of chips and continue to grill-roast until an instant-read thermometer inserted into the thigh registers between 165 and 170 degrees, about 30 minutes longer, depending on the grill temperature. Remove from the grill, let rest for 10 minutes, carve, and serve.

◆

Grill-Roasted Chicken with Apricot-Mustard Glaze

A SIMPLE COMBINATION OF APRICOT JAM AND GRAINY MUSTARD GIVES GRILL-ROASTED CHICKEN A SPICY-SWEET GLAZE. SERVES 4.

 1/2 cup apricot jam
 1/4 cup grainy mustard
 1 teaspoon dark brown sugar
 1 teaspoon lemon juice
 1/2 teaspoon salt
 1 whole chicken (about 3 1/2 pounds), giblets removed and reserved for another use, chicken rinsed and patted dry with paper towels
 3 cups hickory or mesquite wood chips, soaked in cold water to cover for 30 minutes and drained

1. Set up a charcoal or gas grill using the indirect cooking method (see page 174 or 176).

2. Combine the jam, mustard, brown sugar, lemon juice, and salt in a small saucepan. Cook over medium-low heat, stirring frequently, until smooth. Cool slightly (if you let the glaze get too cool it will be hard to spread). Generously brush the chicken, including the cavity, with the mixture.

3. Add half the chips to the fire. Grill-roast the chicken for 30 minutes. Add the second batch of chips and continue to grill-roast until an instant-read thermometer inserted into the thigh registers between 165 and 170 degrees, about 30 minutes longer, depending on the grill temperature. Remove from the grill, let rest for 10 minutes, carve, and serve.

Grill-Roasted Chicken with Chili-Lime Glaze

THE QUANTITY OF CHILI POWDER HERE CAN BE INCREASED UP TO ¼ CUP, IF YOU LIKE YOUR CHICKEN ON THE HOT SIDE. SERVES 4.

2 tablespoons chili powder, or to taste
¼ cup fresh lime juice
1 tablespoon molasses
3 garlic cloves, coarsely chopped
½ teaspoon salt
1 whole chicken (about 3½ pounds), giblets removed and reserved for another use, chicken rinsed and patted dry with paper towels
3 cups hickory or mesquite wood chips, soaked in cold water to cover for 30 minutes and drained

1. Set up a charcoal or gas grill using the indirect cooking method (see page 174 or 176).

2. Combine the chili powder, lime juice, molasses, garlic, and salt in the work bowl of a food processor or blender. Process until smooth. Brush the chicken, including the cavity, with the chili paste.

3. Add half the chips to the fire. Grill-roast the chicken for 30 minutes. Add the second batch of chips and continue to grill-roast until an instant-read thermometer inserted into the thigh registers between 165 and 170 degrees, about 30 minutes longer, depending on the grill temperature. Remove from the grill, let rest for 10 minutes, carve, and serve.

Grill-Roasted Chicken Adobo

ADOBO IS THE TERM FOR MARINADE IN MEXICO AND MANY LATIN AMERICAN AND CARIBBEAN COUNTRIES. OUR VERSION, CONTAINING OREGANO AND CUMIN, IS ADAPTED FROM A PUERTO RICAN RECIPE. SERVES 4.

½ cup fresh orange juice
6 garlic cloves, coarsely chopped
1 teaspoon ground cumin
1 teaspoon dried oregano
1 teaspoon salt
1 whole chicken (about 3½ pounds), giblets removed and reserved for another use, chicken rinsed and patted dry with paper towels
3 cups hickory or mesquite wood chips, soaked in cold water to cover for 30 minutes and drained

1. Combine the orange juice, garlic, cumin, oregano, and salt in the work bowl of a food processor or blender. Process until smooth. Place the chicken in a nonreactive dish and pour the marinade over it. Cover and refrigerate for 1 hour, turning occasionally.

2. Set up a charcoal or gas grill using the indirect cooking method (see page 174 or 176).

3. Generously brush the chicken, including the cavity, with the marinade. Add half the chips to the fire. Grill-roast the chicken for 30 minutes. Add the second batch of chips and continue to grill-roast until an instant-read thermometer inserted into the thigh registers between 165 and 170 degrees, about 30 minutes longer, depending on the grill temperature. Remove from the grill, let rest for 10 minutes, carve, and serve.

GRILLED CHICKEN KEBABS

CHICKEN AND FRESH VEGETABLE KEBABS GRILLED TO

JUICY PERFECTION MAKE GREAT SUMMER FARE, EITHER

AS APPETIZERS EATEN RIGHT OFF THE SKEWERS OR AS

THE MAIN COURSE. THEY'RE SIMPLE AND PRACTICAL—NO

NEED FOR SEPARATE MEAT AND VEGETABLE PREPARATIONS.

The best grilled chicken kebabs are succulent, well seasoned, and really taste like they've been cooked over an open fire. They are complemented by fruits and vegetables that are equally satisfying—grill-marked but juicy, cooked all the way through but not shrunken or incinerated. When we started our testing, we figured it would be simple. After all, skewered chicken is simple food, a standby of every street-corner grill cook from here to China.

But after some early attempts, we found that a few difficulties in cooking and flavoring kebabs often make them more fun to look at than to eat. When we simply threaded the chicken and veggies on skewers, brushed them with a little oil, and sprinkled with salt and pepper, we were always disappointed. Sometimes the components cooked at different rates, resulting in dry meat and undercooked vegetables. Even when nicely grilled, quick-cooking kebabs didn't absorb much flavor from the fire and were bland. White meat seemed to lose moisture as it cooked, so that by the time it was safe to eat, it was also too dry to enjoy. With its extra fat, dark meat was invariably juicier than white meat, but still needed a considerable flavor boost before it could be called perfect. Sticking with dark meat, we decided to attack the flavor problem first, reasoning that once we could produce well-seasoned, juicy chicken chunks, we'd work out the kinks of cooking fruits and vegetables at the same time.

Simpler always being better, we thought we'd start with the simplest solution, a spice rub. We had success with rubs on grilled chicken parts, and we saw no reason why rubs wouldn't lend flavor to kebabs also. Intrigued by a suggestion in a recent cookbook that the rub might be sprinkled on the cooked meat immediately after grilling rather than worked into it beforehand, we decided to try this also. The spice rub was disappointing both ways. The chicken pieces looked and tasted dry. Because chicken chunks are mostly surface, the flavors of the rub are much more prominent than with grilled parts, obscuring any grilled flavor. Furthermore, because the chunks are skinless, there was no fat to dissolve the spices and help form a crispy crust. The surface of the chunks looked and tasted dry and the spices were a little powdery and raw-tasting, especially when sprinkled on afterwards.

Wanting to add a little moisture, we turned to "wet" preparations, or marinades. We mixed a simple marinade of lemon juice, olive oil, garlic, and herbs and soaked the chicken in it for 3 hours, the recommended time for skin-on chicken parts. We liked the glossy, slightly moist grilled crust that the marinade produced, and the way the garlic and herb flavors had penetrated the meat. But we found the flavor of the lemon juice to be overpowering on these small chunks. More of a problem, however, was the way the acid-based marinade "tenderized" the chicken. When chicken parts are bathed in this solution, the skin protects the meat, which grills up juicy and firm. Even with shorter marinating times (we tried one hour and half an hour), the skinless chunks were mushy after cooking.

Was there a way to season the chicken all the way through and keep it moist on the grill without the acid? We ruled out brining because it would make the small skinless chicken chunks much too salty. But we wanted to get the juiciness and flavor that brining imparts. Figuring that soaking the chicken in a lightly salted marinade (rather than the large quantities of water and salt called for in brining) might work, we prepared two batches of acid-free olive oil marinade, one with salt and one without. We let the chunks sit in the marinade for three hours before grilling. The results were what we hoped for. The salted marinade produced plump, well-seasoned kebabs. The chicken marinated without salt was drier and seemed to absorb less flavor from the garlic and herbs.

One small problem remained. What if we wanted a little bit of lemon flavor on our chicken without sacrificing texture? We made up a batch of our marinade and added just a teaspoon of lemon juice to see what would happen. After just half an hour with such a small amount of juice, the chicken chunks had turned white, indicating that they had been partially cooked by the acid. When cooked, they exhibited the same softening as chicken marinated for a longer time in a much more acidic solution. Our suggestion for people who like their chicken kebabs lemony is to squirt the kebabs with a wedge of lemon after they come off the grill instead of adding lemon juice to the marinade.

After fine-tuning the method, we settled on 1 teaspoon salt (this quantity seasons the chicken without making it overly salty) for 1½ pounds of chicken and a marinating time of at least three hours (during testing, chicken marinated for less time than this did not absorb enough of the marinade flavorings). Because there is no acid in the marinade and thus no danger of it breaking down the texture of the meat, it can be combined with the chicken up to 24 hours before cooking.

It was clear early on that cooking chicken and vegetables together enhances the flavor of both. Therefore, we needed to figure out how to prepare the vegetables so that they would cook at the same rate as the chicken. Precooking seemed like a hassle, so we eliminated items like potatoes and yams, which were always going to take longer to cook on the grill than chicken. Because the chicken was so highly flavored from the marinade, and because we did not like the way some vegetables and fruits began to lose their characteristic flavor after just a short dip, we decided against marinating them. We found that simply tossing the fruits and vegetables with a little olive oil, salt, and pepper produced the best-textured and flavored chunks.

In general, resilient (but not rock-hard) vegetables fared well. When cut in proper sizes, zucchini, eggplant, mushrooms, and bell peppers cook thoroughly but stay moist and lend good flavor and crunch to chicken skewers. Cherry tomatoes, on the other hand, cook too quickly and tend to disintegrate by the time the chicken is done. Firm-textured fruits like apples, pears, and pineapples grill beautifully, holding their shape while cooking all the way through. Fruits that tend toward softness when overripe, like peaches or nectarines, will work fine if still firm. Softer fruits like mangoes or grapes turn to mush after ten minutes over the fire, no matter what size you cut them. See the chart on page 190 for information on preparing individual fruits and vegetables for chicken skewers.

Certain fruits and vegetables are obvious matches for certain marinades. With curry-marinated chicken, we like pineapple cubes and slices of onion. With Middle Eastern flavors, zucchini and eggplant are good choices.

As for the fire, medium-low is best (you should be able to keep your hand 5 inches above the fire for three to four seconds). A hotter fire chars the outside before the inside is done; a cooler fire won't give you

THREADING CHICKEN ON DOUBLE SKEWERS

Thread the chicken pieces and vegetables onto 2 skewers to ensure that the chunks don't spin around when you try to flip the skewers.

those appetizing grill marks and may dry out the chicken as it cooks it. For the juiciest chicken with the strongest grilled flavor, skewers should be cooked uncovered for eight to ten minutes (dark meat will take a minute or two longer than white). Cooking the chicken uncovered is a good idea for a couple of reasons. Chicken chunks can absorb the off flavors of the inside of the grill cover quickly, but since they are so small there's no time to allow those off flavors to cook off. With the cover on, there is also the risk of overcooking and even incineration if your fire is hotter than you think or your chicken fatty enough to cause a flare-up. Check for doneness by cutting into one of the pieces with a small knife as soon as the chicken looks opaque on all sides. Remove it from the grill as soon as there is no sign of pink at the center.

After experimenting with various sizes and shapes, we chose 1½-inch chunks, small enough for easy eating but big enough to get some good grilled flavor before they have to come off the grill. With smaller chunks and thin strips, there's no margin for error; a few seconds too long on the grill and you'll wind up with a dry-as-dust dinner.

A final note on skewering itself. Chicken and vegetables simply skewered through the center may spin around when you lift them from the grill, inhibiting even cooking. We tried out some heavy-gauge twisted metal skewers designed to prevent this problem, but in the end found that threading the ingredients through two thinner skewers at once (see figure on page 183) was more effective. We prefer thin but sturdy metal skewers that can fit two at a time through the kebabs but won't bend under the weight of the food.

MASTER RECIPE

Grilled Chicken and Vegetable Kebabs

SERVES 4

ALTHOUGH WHITE MEAT can be substituted, we much prefer juicier, more flavorful dark meat for this and the following recipes.

1 recipe marinade of choice
   (see page 186)
1½ pounds boneless, skinless chicken
   thighs, cut into 1½-inch chunks
3 cups vegetables and/or fruit, prepared
   according to chart directions (page
   190)
2 tablespoons olive oil
Salt and pepper

1. Combine the marinade and chicken in a sealable plastic bag. Turn several times to coat the chicken pieces, and refrigerate at least 3 hours and up to 24 hours, turning once or twice.

2. Prepare the fire for grilling (see figures 1–4, page 156). Combine the vegetables and/or fruit and oil in a medium bowl. Sprinkle with salt and pepper to taste and toss until coated.

3. Thread the chicken chunks and vegetables onto double skewers for easy turning (see figure on page 183). Grill over medium-low fire (you should be able to keep your hand 5 inches above the fire for 3 to 4 seconds), turning once, for 8 to 10 minutes. When chicken looks opaque on all sides, check for doneness by cutting into one of the pieces with a small knife. Serve immediately.

Broiled Chicken and Vegetable Skewers

SERVES 4

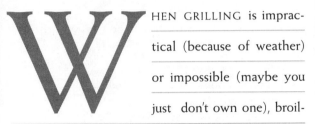

WHEN GRILLING is impractical (because of weather) or impossible (maybe you just don't own one), broiling is an acceptable substitute. You won't get the same char-grilled, outdoorsy flavor, but you will get juicy, boneless chunks of chicken that can be paired with vegetables of your choice and dipped in a variety of sauces. Unlike parts (which we position far from the broiler to ensure even cooking down to the bone without any grease fires), lean boneless chunks should be cooked as quickly as possible under the broiler. Therefore, set the rack to the highest setting that will still accommodate the broiler pan and kebabs safely under the heating element.

1 recipe marinade of choice (see page 186)
1 ½ pounds boneless, skinless chicken
    thighs, cut into 1 ½-inch chunks
3 cups vegetables and/or fruit, prepared
    according to chart directions
    (see page 190)
2 tablespoons olive oil
Salt and pepper

1. Combine the marinade and chicken in a sealable plastic bag. Turn several times to coat chicken pieces, and refrigerate at least 3 hours and up to 24 hours, turning once or twice.

2. Position an oven rack as close to the heat source as possible and preheat the broiler. Combine the vegetables and/or fruit and oil in a medium bowl. Sprinkle with salt and pepper to taste and toss until coated.

3. Thread the chicken chunks and vegetables onto double skewers for easy turning (see figure on page 183). Place the skewers on a broiler pan and broil, turning once, for 10 to 12 minutes. When chicken looks opaque on all sides, check for doneness by cutting into one of the pieces with a small knife. Serve immediately.

Garlic and Herb Marinade

MAKES SCANT ¾ CUP, ENOUGH TO COAT
1½ POUNDS CHICKEN CHUNKS

½ cup olive oil
2 tablespoons minced garlic
¼ cup minced fresh basil, parsley,
 tarragon, oregano, mint, or snipped
 chives *or* 2 tablespoons minced fresh
 thyme or rosemary
1 teaspoon salt
Pepper

Whisk the ingredients, including pepper to taste, together in a small bowl.

◆

Middle Eastern Marinade

Follow Master Recipe. Use mint and/or parsley; add ½ teaspoon ground cinnamon, ½ teaspoon ground allspice, and ¼ teaspoon cayenne.

◆

Southwestern Marinade

Follow Master Recipe. Use cilantro; add 1 teaspoon ground cumin, 1 teaspoon chili powder, 1 teaspoon ground turmeric, and 1 seeded and minced small fresh chile.

Curry Marinade

Follow Master Recipe. Use mint or cilantro; add 1 teaspoon curry powder.

◆

Jerk Marinade

Follow Master Recipe. Use parsley; add 1 teaspoon ground cumin, 1 teaspoon chili powder, ½ teaspoon ground allspice, ¼ teaspoon ground cinnamon and ½ teaspoon pepper.

◆

Asian Marinade

SOY SAUCE REPLACES THE SALT IN THIS MARINADE. MAKES ¾ CUP, ENOUGH TO COAT 1½ POUNDS CHICKEN CHUNKS.

6 tablespoons vegetable oil
2 tablespoons Asian sesame oil
¼ cup soy sauce
2 tablespoons minced garlic
1 tablespoon minced fresh gingerroot
¼ cup minced fresh cilantro leaves
2 scallions, white and green parts, thinly sliced
Pepper

Whisk the ingredients, including pepper to taste, together in a small bowl.

◆

Chicken Satays
with Quick Peanut Sauce

SATAYS ARE USUALLY SERVED AS HORS D'OEUVRES OR APPETIZERS, BUT THERE'S NO REASON WHY THESE CHICKEN BROCHETTES WITH ACCOMPANYING PEANUT SAUCE CAN'T BE SERVED AS A MAIN COURSE. FISH SAUCE, A POPULAR ASIAN CONDIMENT SOLD IN MANY SUPERMARKETS AND GOURMET STORES, GIVES THIS DISH AN AUTHENTIC SOUTHEAST ASIAN FLAVOR. SOY SAUCE MAY BE USED IN ITS PLACE. **SERVES 4 AS A MAIN COURSE, 8 AS AN APPETIZER.**

1 recipe Asian Marinade (page 186)
1 ½ pounds boneless, skinless chicken
   thighs, cut into 1 ½-inch chunks
⅓ cup smooth peanut butter
⅓ cup unsweetened coconut milk
2 tablespoons fresh lemon juice
1 tablespoon sugar
2 teaspoons fish sauce or soy sauce
1 small garlic clove, coarsely chopped
½ jalapeño chile, seeded and finely
   chopped
2 medium onions, peeled and cut into
   ½-inch-thick slices
2 tablespoons olive oil
Salt and pepper

1. Combine the marinade and chicken in a sealable plastic bag. Turn several times to coat chicken pieces, and refrigerate at least 3 hours and up to 24 hours, turning once or twice.

2. Prepare a charcoal fire (see figures 1–4, page 156) or preheat a gas grill or broiler.

3. Combine the peanut butter, coconut milk, lemon juice, sugar, fish sauce, garlic, and chile in the work bowl of a food processor; process until smooth. Scrape the peanut sauce into a small bowl, cover with plastic wrap, and set aside.

4. Combine the onions and oil in a medium bowl. Sprinkle with salt and pepper to taste and toss until coated. Thread the chicken and onions on doubled skewers.

5. Cook according to the appropriate Master Recipe. When the chicken looks opaque on all sides, check for doneness by cutting into one of the pieces with a small knife. Serve immediately with the peanut sauce on the side.

Grilled Mediterranean Chicken Skewers with Grilled Garlic Bread

SLICES OF BAGUETTE, RUBBED WITH GARLIC AND DRIZZLED WITH OLIVE OIL, COME OFF THE GRILL TOASTED AND GOLDEN WHEN GRILLED ALONG WITH THESE MARINATED CHICKEN CHUNKS. SERVE WITH A SALAD AND SOME GRILLED VEGETABLES FOR A COMPLETE MEAL. **SERVES 4.**

1 recipe Garlic and Herb Marinade (page
   186)
1 ½ pounds boneless, skinless chicken
   thighs, cut into 1 ½-inch chunks
18 mushrooms, stems removed
6 tablespoons olive oil
Salt and pepper
12 1-inch-thick slices French or Italian
   bread
1 garlic clove, peeled and halved

1. Combine the marinade and chicken in a sealable plastic bag. Turn several times to coat chicken pieces, and refrigerate at least 3 hours and up to 24 hours, turning once or twice.

2. Prepare a charcoal fire (see figures 1–4, page 156) or preheat a gas grill or broiler. Combine the mushrooms and 2 tablespoons oil in a medium bowl. Sprinkle with salt and pepper to taste and toss until coated. Rub each side of each piece of bread with the cut side of a garlic half and brush with the remaining 4 tablespoons oil. Thread the chicken, mushrooms, and bread (through crumb so that crust is exposed) on doubled skewers.

3. Cook according to the appropriate Master Recipe. When the chicken looks opaque on all sides and the bread slices are golden brown, check for doneness by cutting into one of the pieces with a small knife. Serve immediately.

Southwestern Chicken Skewers with Grilled Corn and Tomato Salsa

CORN AND TOMATOES ARE DIFFICULT TO GRILL ON THE SAME SKEWERS WITH CHICKEN, SO WE GRILL THEM FIRST AND MAKE A SALSA TO ACCOMPANY THE CHICKEN. THIS SALSA IS SUBSTANTIAL ENOUGH TO SERVE AS A SIDE DISH AS WELL AS A CONDIMENT TO THE GRILLED CHICKEN. SERVES 4.

  1 recipe Southwestern Marinade (page 186)
  1½ pounds boneless, skinless chicken thighs, cut into 1½-inch chunks
  4 ripe tomatoes, cored and quartered
  4 ears of corn, husked
  3 tablespoons olive oil
  Salt and pepper
  1 jalapeño chile, seeded and finely chopped
  ¼ cup fresh lime juice
  2 teaspoons minced fresh oregano leaves
  2 medium onions, peeled and cut into ½-inch-thick slices

1. Combine the marinade and chicken in a sealable plastic bag. Turn several times to coat chicken pieces, and refrigerate at least 3 hours and up to 24 hours, turning once or twice.

2. Prepare a charcoal fire (see figures 1–4, page 156) or preheat a gas grill or broiler.

3. Brush the tomatoes and corn with 1 tablespoon oil and sprinkle with salt and pepper. Sear the tomato quarters, turning frequently, 3 to 4 minutes. Remove from the grill and set aside to cool. Grill the corn, turning frequently, until cooked through and lightly charred, 8 to 10 minutes. Remove from the grill and set aside to cool. Chop the tomatoes and remove the corn from the cobs (see figure on page 66). Combine the tomatoes, corn, chile, lime juice, oregano, and salt to taste in a medium bowl. Set aside.

4. Combine the onions and remaining 2 tablespoons oil in a medium bowl. Sprinkle with salt and pepper to taste and toss until coated. Thread the chicken and onions on doubled skewers.

5. Cook according to the appropriate Master Recipe. When the chicken looks opaque on all sides, check for doneness by cutting into one of the pieces with a small knife. Serve immediately with the salsa on the side.

◆

Indian Chicken Skewers with Mango-Raisin Chutney

TANGY, YOGURT-MARINATED CHICKEN PAIRS WELL WITH A SIMPLE CHUTNEY OF MANGO AND RAISINS. ADD MORE OR LESS JALAPEÑO ACCORDING TO TASTE. SERVES 4.

  1 recipe Curry Marinade (page 186)
  1½ pounds boneless, skinless chicken thighs, cut into 1½-inch chunks
  1 tablespoon vegetable oil
  1 small red onion, peeled and finely chopped
  1 tablespoon peeled and finely chopped fresh gingerroot
  1 jalapeño chile, seeded and finely chopped
  2 ripe mangoes, peeled, pitted, and cut into ¼-inch dice (see figures 1–4, page 121)
  ½ cup raisins
  6 tablespoons distilled white vinegar
  ¼ cup sugar
  Salt
  1 red bell pepper, cored, seeded, and cut into 1-inch-wide wedges
  1 red onion, peeled and cut into ½-inch-thick slices
  2 tablespoons olive oil
  Pepper

1. Combine the marinade and chicken in a sealable plastic bag. Turn several times to coat chicken pieces, and refrigerate at least 3 hours and up to 24 hours, turning once or twice.

2. Prepare a charcoal fire (see figures 1–4, page 156) or preheat a gas grill or broiler.

3. Heat the vegetable oil in a medium saucepan over medium heat. Add the chopped onion and sauté, stirring frequently, until softened, 4 to 5 minutes. Add the ginger and chile and sauté for another minute. Turn the heat to low; add the mangoes, raisins, vinegar, and sugar, and cook, stirring occasionally, until the mixture thickens, 10 to 12 minutes. Remove from heat, season with salt to taste, and set aside.

4. Combine the bell pepper, onion slices, and olive oil in a medium bowl. Sprinkle with salt and pepper to taste and toss until coated. Thread the chicken and vegetables on doubled skewers.

5. Cook according to the appropriate Master Recipe. When the chicken looks opaque on all sides, check for doneness by cutting into one of the pieces with a small knife. Serve immediately with the chutney on the side.

◆

Skewered Chicken and Peaches

RIPE BUT FIRM PEACHES ARE ESSENTIAL IN THIS RECIPE. SOFT PEACHES WILL FALL APART ON THE GRILL. FIRM NECTARINES MAY BE SUBSTITUTED, IF DESIRED. **SERVES 4.**

> 1 recipe Garlic and Herb Marinade (page 186) made with rosemary
> 1 1/2 pounds boneless, skinless chicken thighs, cut into 1 1/2-inch chunks
> 4 peaches, halved, pitted, and each half cut into thirds
> 2 small red onions, peeled and cut into 1/2-inch-thick slices
> 2 tablespoons olive oil
> Salt and pepper

1. Combine the marinade and chicken in a sealable plastic bag. Turn several times to coat chicken pieces, and refrigerate at least 3 hours and up to 24 hours, turning once or twice.

2. Prepare a charcoal fire (see figures 1–4, page 156) or preheat a gas grill or broiler.

3. Combine the peaches, onions, and oil in a medium bowl. Sprinkle with salt and pepper to taste and toss until coated. Thread the chicken, peaches, and onions on doubled skewers.

4. Cook according to the appropriate Master Recipe. When the chicken looks opaque on all sides, check for doneness by cutting into one of the pieces with a small knife. Serve immediately.

◆

Chicken Skewers with Zucchini and Eggplant

THIS COMBINATION OF CHICKEN, ZUCCHINI, AND EGGPLANT TASTES GREAT WITH EITHER THE GARLIC AND HERB OR THE ASIAN MARINADE. **SERVES 4.**

> 1 recipe Garlic and Herb *or* Asian Marinade (page 186)
> 1 1/2 pounds boneless, skinless chicken thighs, cut into 1 1/2-inch chunks
> 1 medium eggplant, peeled and cut into 1/2-inch cubes
> 1 medium zucchini, ends trimmed and cut into 1/2-inch-thick rounds
> 2 tablespoons olive oil
> Salt and pepper

1. Combine the marinade and chicken in a sealable plastic bag. Turn several times to coat chicken pieces, and refrigerate at least 3 hours and up to 24 hours, turning once or twice.

2. Prepare a charcoal fire (see figures 1–4, page 156) or preheat a gas grill or broiler.

3. Combine the eggplant, zucchini, and oil in a medium bowl. Sprinkle with salt and pepper to taste and toss until coated. Thread the chicken and vegetables on doubled skewers.

4. Cook according to the appropriate Master Recipe. When the chicken looks opaque on all sides, check for doneness by cutting into one of the pieces with a small knife. Serve immediately.

PREPARING VEGETABLES
AND FRUITS FOR SKEWERING

/I\

IF PREPARED according to the directions, these vegetables and fruits will cook through at the same rate as the chicken chunks. Use ripe fruit that is still fairly firm. Mushy fruit will fall apart on the grill. We suggested marinades for the chicken (see page 186) that will work well with each vegetable, keeping in mind cultural traditions as well as the flavor and texture of the vegetable.

VEGETABLE OR FRUIT	PREPARATION	MARINADE FOR CHICKEN
EGGPLANT	Peel and cut into ½-inch cubes	Garlic and Herb, Middle Eastern, Asian, Curry
MUSHROOMS, BUTTON	Slice off stems and wipe clean	Garlic and Herb, Southwestern, Asian
MUSHROOMS, PORTOBELLO	Slice off stems, wipe caps clean, and cut into 1-inch chunks	Any marinade
ONIONS	Peel and cut into ½-inch-thick slices	Any marinade
PEPPERS, BELL	Core, seed, and cut into 1-inch-wide wedges	Any marinade
SHALLOTS	Peel and skewer whole	Any marinade
ZUCCHINI	Remove ends; slice into ½-inch-thick rounds	Garlic and Herb, Middle Eastern, Curry, Asian
APPLES	Core and cut into 1-inch cubes	Garlic and Herb, Middle Eastern, Curry, Asian
PEACHES	Halve, pit, and cut each half in thirds	Garlic and Herb, Southwestern, Curry, Jerk
PEARS	Core and cut into 1-inch cubes	Garlic and Herb, Middle Eastern, Curry, Asian
PINEAPPLES	Peel, core, and cut into 1-inch cubes	Southwestern, Curry, Jerk

BROILED CHICKEN PARTS

WHEN THE GRILL IS NOT AN OPTION, BROILING CAN

BE AN EXCELLENT WAY TO COOK CHICKEN PARTS. OUR

GOALW FOR THIS TESTING WERE SIMPLE: RICHLY FLA-

VORED, JUICY MEAT AND CRISP (NOT BURNED) SKIN.

THE CHALLENGE WITH THIS COOKING METHOD IS

that the broiling element in most home ovens does not produce all that much heat, especially compared to a hot charcoal or gas grill fire.

There are two schools of thought about how to deal with the lower BTU output from home broilers. Many cookbooks recommend placing the chicken fairly close to the heating element (3 or 4 inches), in order to maximize its effect on the chicken. Other sources recommend keeping the chicken farther way (often 6 inches) and increasing the cooking time.

In addition to the positioning issue, we were concerned about grease fires, a constant threat when broiling. Once the pan drippings catch fire, extinguishing the fire becomes the priority—little can be done to save dinner.

With all this in mind, we started our testing with whole small (about 3½ pounds) chickens cut into eight parts. We quickly found that placing the chicken 3 or 4 inches from the heating element is a recipe for disaster. At this distance, the skin burns long before the meat, especially in the thicker breast, is cooked through.

We moved our rack down so that the top of the chicken was about 6 inches from the heat source. While this was an improvement, the meat was still a little bloody at the bone when the skin started to blacken. Finally, we moved the rack down to the center-lower position in our broiler, about 12 inches below the heat source. Since the chicken was on a broiler pan, the top of the chicken was now about 8 inches from the broiler. At this distance, the cooking time was much longer (more than twenty minutes for the thicker pieces) but the results were far better. The meat was cooked through and still juicy while the skin was nicely crisped and not at all singed. Clearly, keeping the chicken far from the broiler is one piece of the puzzle.

We tried various turning regimens and found it was best to start chicken parts with the skin side facing up. Once the skin was golden brown, we flipped each piece and continued cooking until the meat was done. This method was slightly better than the opposite (skin down, then up) at keeping the chicken from burning since the fatty skin was face down during the crucial last minutes of cooking.

During our testing, we had noticed that the smaller,

thinner wing and leg pieces were cooking faster than the thicker thighs and breasts. Even though the wing and leg have more fat than the breast (which helps to keep the meat moist), it was clear that they did not need to be in the broiler as long as a breast that was several inches thick. Our solution was twofold. We placed the wings and legs around the perimeter of the broiling pan where the heat is less intense and then took them out of the broiler a few minutes ahead of the thigh and breast pieces. (Even though the breast is thicker than the thigh, we found that the extra fat in the dark meat allowed the two parts to cook at the same rate.)

At this point, our chicken was good, not great. We had been broiling pieces with no seasonings other than salt and pepper. It was time to try boosting the flavor of the chicken. As with grilled parts, we found that marinating was not terribly effective. The marinade flavored the skin but not the meat. We found that spice rubs and herbs pastes added much more flavor to the meat and were quicker and easier to use. We found it best to rub spice mixtures right into the skin; for herb pastes (and pestos), it's better to tuck the wet mixture under the skin and then lightly brush the skin with a tiny bit of oil to promote optimum browning.

In addition to rubs and pastes, we found that broiled chicken takes well to glazes and crisp coatings made from bread crumbs or finely chopped nuts. To prevent glazes and coatings from burning, it is essential to add them when the chicken is basically done. We found it best to turn the breast and thigh back so the skin side is facing the heat source, add the cooked wing and leg pieces back to the pan, brush everything with a little glaze, and then broil for just a few minutes until the glaze is bubbling. For coatings, we did the same thing, brushing the skin with a little of the pan juices to help the crumbs or nuts to adhere. Since coatings are by nature dry, we like to add them to chicken that has been cooked with an herb paste under the skin for maximum moistness, flavor, and crunch.

We also tested brining, a technique which we had found improved the flavor in parts destined for the grill. The results were much the same here. The salt penetrated deep into the meat, seasoning it evenly, while the sugar added a faint hint of sweetness. In addition to making the chicken taste better, brining firms up the meat and helps it to retain more moisture when it cooks. Although optional, brining takes only 1½ hours and is well worth the minimal effort. If you decide to omit this step, be certain to season the chicken parts very generously with salt and make sure that herb and spice bastes also contain a good amount of salt. Brined parts should be sprinkled very lightly with additional salt just before cooking; herb and salt pastes destined for use with brined chicken should not to be too salty, either.

As a last test, we wondered if the broiler pan that came with our oven was really essential for this recipe. We broiled chicken in a shallow roasting pan and the results were disastrous. Because the parts cooked in their own fat, the skin never crisped up and the meat tasted greasy. Elevating the chicken on a rack solved these problems, but we noticed that the fat in the pan was smoking much more heavily than in tests done with a traditional broiler pan. In fact, in one test, we were unable to avoid the dreaded grease fire. With its coverlike rack, a broiler pan allows fat to drip down but then shields it from direct heat, thus making a grease fire almost impossible as long as the chicken itself is kept a good distance from the broiling element. When the fat rests in an open roasting pan under a regular rack it becomes much hotter, eventually smoking and sometimes igniting. Most ovens come with a broiler pan; look for it in the drawer under the cooking chamber.

One note about the recipes in this chapter. They are designed for ovens with a broiler element at the top of the main cooking chamber. Ovens with separate broilers, often positioned under the main cooking chamber, do not provide enough space to broil chicken parts. In a friend's small apartment range with a pull-out broiler underneath the oven, the chicken was just 2 inches from the broiler.

While the recipes in this chapter were developed with a single cut-up chicken in mind, we also tested them with individual parts. If you would rather cook eight thighs or breasts, follow any of the recipes in this chapter, adjusting the cooking times slightly as needed. The rubs, pastes, glazes, and coatings will be sufficient for eight pieces of chicken, whether they are all the same or from a single chicken.

TWO TIPS FOR BROILING CHICKEN

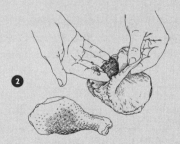

1. Small wings and legs will cook more quickly than thicker breasts and thighs. To help compensate for the different cooking times, arrange the pieces on a broiler pan, skin side up, with the wings and legs around the perimeter and the breasts and thighs in the center, right under the broiler element. Even with this arrangement, you will need to take the wings and legs out of the oven 3 to 5 minutes before the breasts and thighs.

2. To season pieces well, we like to rub dry spice mixtures right into the skin. Wet pastes, compound butters, and pestos should go under the skin. Carefully lift the skin on each piece and rub a little paste into the meat with your fingers.

Broiled Chicken with Spice Rub

SERVES 4

BRINING IMPROVES THE chicken's flavor, but if you're short on time, you can skip step 1 and make sure that the spice rub is well seasoned with salt, at least ½ teaspoon. Dry spice rubs, often used on grilled foods, work well on broiled chicken parts as well, producing a crisp, flavorful skin.

> ¾ cup kosher salt *or* 6 tablespoons table salt, plus more to taste
> ¾ cup sugar
> 1 chicken (3 to 3½ pounds), rinsed, patted dry, and cut into 8 pieces (see "Cutting Up a Whole Chicken," page 10)
> 1 recipe spice rub (recipes follow)

1. If brining the chicken pieces: In a gallon-size sealable plastic bag, dissolve the ¾ cup salt and sugar in 1 quart of water. Add the chicken, pressing out as much air as possible; seal and refrigerate until fully seasoned, about 1½ hours.

2. Rinse the chicken pieces well and pat dry. Rub the chicken pieces generously with the spice mixture.

3. Arrange the chicken pieces on a broiler pan, skin side up, so that the wings and legs are around the perimeter of the pan and the thicker breasts and thighs are in the center (see figure 1, page 193). Adjust the oven rack so that the chicken will be no closer than 8 inches from the heating element and preheat the broiler.

4. Broil the chicken until the skin is a rich brown color, about 12 minutes. Turn the chicken over; continue to broil until the juices run clear. The wings and legs should be done in about 7 minutes; remove them to a plate, cover with foil, and continue to broil the thighs and breasts for an additional 3 to 5 minutes. Remove the remaining chicken from the oven and serve.

◆

All-Purpose Spice Rub

THIS IS ONE OF OUR FAVORITE, SIMPLE RUBS FOR POULTRY. THE ADDITION OF ALLSPICE GIVES CHICKEN A JAMAICAN JERK FLAVOR. ENOUGH TO FLAVOR 8 PIECES OF CHICKEN.

> 1 tablespoon ground cumin
> 1 tablespoon curry powder
> 1 tablespoon chili powder
> 1 teaspoon ground allspice
> 1 teaspoon pepper
> Salt

Combine the cumin, curry powder, chili powder, allspice, pepper, and salt to taste (use sparingly if chicken was brined) in a small bowl. Use in step 2 of the Master Recipe for Broiled Chicken with Spice Rub.

Garam Masala Spice Rub

HERE IS OUR OWN GARAM MASALA—THE INDIAN
BLEND OF SPICES OFTEN USED IN CURRIES—TO RUB
ON CHICKEN PIECES FOR AN EXOTIC-TASTING BROIL.
SPICES MAY BE VARIED ACCORDING TO TASTE AND
WHAT YOU HAVE ON HAND. ENOUGH TO FLAVOR 8
PIECES OF CHICKEN.

    1 tablespoon ground fennel seed
    1 tablespoon ground anise seed
    1 tablespoon ground cardamom
    1 teaspoon pepper
    ¼ teaspoon ground cloves
    ¼ teaspoon ground cinnamon
    Salt

Combine the fennel, anise, cardamom, pepper, cloves,
cinnamon, and salt to taste (use sparingly if chicken
was brined) in a small bowl. Use in step 2 of the Master Recipe for Broiled Chicken with Spice Rub.

◆

Chili Spice Rub

FOR THIS RECIPE, MINCED CILANTRO AND GARLIC ARE
RUBBED UNDERNEATH THE SKIN OF THE CHICKEN TO
COMPLEMENT THIS SOUTHWESTERN SPICE RUB OF
CUMIN, CHILI POWDER, AND PAPRIKA. MAKES ENOUGH
TO FLAVOR 8 PIECES OF CHICKEN.

    2 tablespoons minced fresh cilantro leaves
    1 small garlic clove, minced
    Salt
    1 tablespoon ground cumin
    1 tablespoon chili powder
    1 tablespoon sweet paprika

1. Combine the cilantro, garlic, and salt to taste (use
sparingly if chicken was brined) in a small bowl. Rub
this paste under the skin of each rinsed and dried
chicken piece (see figure 2, page 193).

2. Combine the cumin, chili powder, and paprika in a
small bowl. Use in step 2 of the Master Recipe for
Broiled Chicken with Spice Rub.

Broiled Chicken with Moist Herb Paste

SERVES 4

MOIST MIXTURES SUCH as
herb pastes, compound butters, and pesto are best rubbed
underneath the skin of the
chicken pieces, keeping them moist and flavoring the
meat. When stuffing an herb paste under the skin, we
found it helpful to brush the skin itself with a tiny bit
of vegetable oil to promote browning. When the skin
is coated with a spice rub, this is not necessary.

    ¾ cup kosher salt *or* 6 tablespoons table
       salt, plus more to taste
    ¾ cup sugar
    1 chicken (3 to 3½ pounds), rinsed, patted
       dry, and cut into 8 pieces (see "Cutting
       Up a Whole Chicken," page 10)
    1 recipe herb paste (recipes follow)
    1 teaspoon vegetable oil
    Pepper

(continued on next page)

1. If brining the chicken pieces: In a gallon-size sealable plastic bag, dissolve the ¾ cup salt and sugar in 1 quart of water. Add the chicken, pressing out as much air as possible; seal and refrigerate until fully seasoned, about 1½ hours.

2. Rinse the chicken pieces well and pat dry. Rub the herb paste under the skin of each chicken piece (see figure 2, page 193).

3. Arrange the chicken pieces on a broiler pan, skin side up, so that the wings and legs are around the perimeter of the pan and the thicker breasts and thighs are in the center. Brush the chicken with the vegetable oil and lightly season with salt and pepper (be generous with salt if you have not brined the chicken). Adjust the oven rack so that the chicken will be no closer than 8 inches from the heating element and preheat the broiler.

4. Broil the chicken until the skin is a rich brown color, about 12 minutes. Turn the chicken over; continue to broil until the juices run clear. The wings and legs should be done in about 7 minutes; remove them to a plate, cover with foil, and continue to broil the thighs and breasts for an additional 3 to 5 minutes. Remove the remaining chicken from the oven and serve.

◆

Sage Butter

COMPOUND BUTTER IS A GREAT WAY TO ADD FLAVOR TO BROILED CHICKEN PARTS. IT KEEPS THE CHICKEN JUICY AND MAKES THE SKIN EXTRA CRISPY. ANY CHOPPED FRESH HERB CAN BE SUBSTITUTED FOR SAGE HERE. GARLIC, GINGER, SCALLIONS, AND ANCHOVIES CAN ALSO BE MIXED WITH BUTTER. MAKES ENOUGH TO FLAVOR 8 PIECES OF CHICKEN.

> 2 tablespoons butter, softened
> 10 fresh sage leaves, minced
> Salt and pepper

Combine the butter, sage, and salt and pepper to taste (use salt sparingly if chicken was brined) in a small bowl. Use in step 2 of the Master Recipe for Broiled Chicken with Moist Herb Paste.

Mediterranean Herb Paste

FRESH HERBS AND GARLIC ARE COMBINED HERE TO MAKE A THICK PASTE. OTHER COMBINATIONS OF HERBS (TRY PARSLEY, BASIL, AND MINT) MAY BE SUBSTITUTED ACCORDING TO TASTE AND WHAT YOU HAVE ON HAND. MAKES ENOUGH TO FLAVOR 8 PIECES OF CHICKEN.

> 2 medium garlic cloves, peeled
> ¼ cup fresh parsley leaves
> 2 tablespoons olive oil
> ½ tablespoon fresh thyme leaves
> ½ tablespoon fresh rosemary leaves
> ½ tablespoon sage leaves
> Salt and pepper

Combine the garlic, parsley, oil, thyme, rosemary, and sage in the work bowl of a food processor; process until smooth, scraping down the sides of the bowl as necessary. Transfer the mixture to a small bowl; stir in salt and pepper to taste (use salt sparingly if chicken was brined). Use in step 2 of the Master Recipe for Broiled Chicken with Moist Herb Paste.

◆

Classic Basil Pesto

PESTO, WITH ITS STRONG FLAVORS, IS A GREAT WAY TO DRESS UP BROILED CHICKEN. SPREAD UNDERNEATH THE SKIN, IT ALSO KEEPS THE MEAT MOIST AND MAKES IT ESPECIALLY FLAVORFUL. PINE NUTS ARE TRADITIONAL IN PESTO, BUT ALMONDS OR WALNUTS MAY BE SUBSTITUTED IF THAT'S WHAT YOU HAVE IN YOUR PANTRY. THE OPTIONAL PARSLEY LEAVES WILL HELP KEEP THE PESTO BRIGHT GREEN. MAKES ENOUGH TO FLAVOR 8 CHICKEN PIECES.

> 2 tablespoons pine nuts, toasted (or
>   substitute almonds or walnuts)
> 1 garlic clove, coarsely chopped
> 1 cup packed fresh basil leaves
> 1 tablespoon fresh parsley leaves
>   (optional)
> 3½ tablespoons extra-virgin olive oil
> 2 tablespoons finely grated Parmesan
>   cheese
> Salt and pepper

Place the nuts, garlic, basil, parsley, and olive oil in the work bowl of a food processor fitted with a metal blade; process until smooth, scraping down the sides of the bowl as necessary. Transfer the mixture to a small bowl; stir in the cheese and salt and pepper to taste (use salt sparingly if chicken was brined). Use in step 2 of the Master Recipe for Broiled Chicken with Moist Herb Paste.

◆

Asian "Pesto"

IN THIS PUREED SAUCE WITH ASIAN FLAVORS, CASHEWS SUBSTITUTE FOR PINE NUTS AND CILANTRO FOR BASIL IN A TRADITIONAL PESTO. THE RESULT IS AN EAST-WEST CHICKEN DISH THAT'S GREAT WITH STEAMED VEGETABLES AND WHITE OR BROWN RICE. MAKES ENOUGH TO FLAVOR 8 PIECES OF CHICKEN.

2 tablespoons unsalted cashews
1 garlic clove, coarsely chopped
1 1-inch piece fresh gingerroot, peeled and coarsely chopped
1 cup packed fresh cilantro leaves
1 tablespoon Asian sesame oil
2 tablespoons vegetable oil
1 teaspoon soy sauce
Salt and pepper

Place the nuts, garlic, ginger, cilantro, oils, and soy sauce in the work bowl of a food processor fitted with a metal blade; process until smooth, scraping down the sides of the bowl as necessary. Transfer the mixture to a small bowl; add salt and pepper to taste (use salt sparingly if chicken was brined). Use in step 2 of the Master Recipe for Broiled Chicken with Moist Herb Paste.

◆

Salsa Verde

SALSA VERDE IS AN ITALIAN CONDIMENT USED ON ALL KINDS OF ROASTED AND GRILLED MEATS. THE SECRET INGREDIENT IS ANCHOVIES, WHICH GIVE THE SAUCE ITS BRIGHT, BRINY FLAVOR. MAKES ENOUGH TO FLAVOR 8 PIECES OF CHICKEN.

1 garlic clove, peeled
2 flat anchovy fillets, rinsed
1 tablespoon drained capers, rinsed
1 cup packed fresh parsley leaves
3 tablespoons extra-virgin olive oil
1 tablespoon lemon juice
Salt and pepper

Place the garlic, anchovies, capers, parsley, oil, and lemon juice in the work bowl of a food processor fitted with a metal blade; process until smooth, scraping down the sides of the bowl as necessary. Transfer the mixture to a small bowl; add salt and pepper to taste (use salt sparingly if chicken was brined). Use in step 2 of the Master Recipe for Broiled Chicken with Moist Herb Paste.

◆

Black Olive and Sun-Dried Tomato Pesto

THIS PUNGENT PESTO COMBINES THE SALTY FLAVOR OF BLACK OLIVES WITH THE INTENSE SWEETNESS OF SUN-DRIED TOMATOES. LOOK FOR SUN-DRIED TOMATOES PACKED IN OLIVE OIL. IF THEY'VE BEEN REFRIGERATED, BRING THEM TO ROOM TEMPERATURE BEFORE USING. MAKES ENOUGH TO FLAVOR 8 PIECES OF CHICKEN.

15 sun-dried tomatoes packed in oil, drained (about ⅔ cup)
8 large black olives, pitted
1 medium garlic clove, peeled
2 tablespoons fresh parsley leaves
2 tablespoons extra-virgin olive oil
Salt and pepper

Place the tomatoes, olives, garlic, parsley, and olive oil in the work bowl of a food processor fitted with a metal blade; process until smooth, scraping down the sides of the bowl as necessary. Transfer the mixture to a small bowl; add salt and pepper to taste (use salt sparingly if chicken was brined). Use in step 2 of the Master Recipe for Broiled Chicken with Moist Herb Paste.

Glazed Broiled Chicken

SERVES 4

G LAZES, LIKE BARBECUE sauces, are a quick way to add flavor to broiled chicken. Like barbecue sauces, they should be brushed on in the last minutes of cooking so that they caramelize, but don't burn. For optimum browning, brush parts very lightly with vegetable oil before broiling.

> ¾ cup kosher salt *or* 6 tablespoons table
> salt, plus more to taste
> ¾ cup sugar
> 1 chicken (3 to 3½ pounds), rinsed,
> patted dry, and cut into 8 pieces
> (see "Cutting Up a Whole Chicken,"
> page 10)
> 1 teaspoon vegetable oil
> Pepper
> 1 recipe glaze (recipes follow)

1. If brining the chicken pieces: In a gallon-size sealable plastic bag, dissolve the ¾ cup salt and sugar in 1 quart of water. Add the chicken, pressing out as much air as possible; seal and refrigerate until fully seasoned, about 1½ hours.

2. Rinse the chicken pieces well and pat dry. Arrange the chicken pieces on a broiler pan, skin side up, so that the wings and legs are around the perimeter of the pan and the thicker breasts and thighs are in the center. Brush the chicken with oil and lightly season with salt and pepper (be generous with salt if you have not brined the chicken). Adjust the oven rack so that the chicken will be no closer than 8 inches from the heating element and preheat the broiler.

3. Broil the chicken until the skin is a rich brown color, about 12 minutes. Turn the chicken over; continue to broil until the juices run clear. The wings and legs should be done in about 7 minutes; remove them to a plate, cover with foil, and continue to broil the thighs and breasts for an additional 3 to 5 minutes.

4. When the remaining pieces are cooked, remove the broiler pan from the oven, turn the thighs and breasts skin side up, return the wings and legs to the pan skin side up, and brush each piece with a little of the glaze. Return the chicken to the oven; broil until the glaze begins to brown and bubble, 2 to 3 minutes. Serve.

◆

Chipotle-Orange Glaze

THIS RECIPE COMBINES THE SWEET-TART FLAVOR OF ORANGES WITH THE SMOKY HEAT OF CHIPOTLE CHILES IN ADOBO. CHIPOTLE CHILES ARE AVAILABLE IN MANY SUPERMARKETS AND LATIN GROCERIES. MAKES ENOUGH TO COAT 8 PIECES OF CHICKEN.

> 1 cup fresh orange juice
> ¼ cup fresh lemon juice
> 1 canned chipotle chile in adobo, finely
> chopped
> Salt and ground black pepper

Bring the orange and lemon juices to a boil in a small saucepan and reduce to ⅓ cup, 5 to 7 minutes. Stir in the chile and salt and pepper to taste (use salt sparingly if chicken was brined). Cool to room temperature. Use in step 4 of the Master Recipe for Glazed Broiled Chicken.

Honey-Pecan Glaze

A FEW SIMPLE PANTRY STAPLES BECOME A QUICK GLAZE
FOR BROILED CHICKEN. MAPLE SYRUP MAY SUBSTITUTE
FOR HONEY, AND WALNUTS OR ALMONDS MAY BE USED IN
PLACE OF PECANS, DEPENDING ON WHAT YOU HAVE ON
HAND. **MAKES ENOUGH TO COAT 8 PIECES OF CHICKEN.**

> 2 tablespoons honey
> 4 tablespoons Dijon mustard
> 1/2 cup pecan pieces, finely chopped
> Salt and pepper

Combine the honey, mustard, nuts, and salt and pepper to taste (use salt sparingly if chicken was brined)
in a small bowl. Use in step 4 of the Master Recipe for
Glazed Broiled Chicken.

◆

Curried Apricot Glaze

THE INTENSITY OF THIS HOT-SWEET GLAZE CAN BE
ADJUSTED BY INCREASING OR DECREASING THE QUANTI-
TIES OF CURRY POWDER AND HOT RED PEPPER FLAKES.
MAKES ENOUGH TO COAT 8 PIECES OF CHICKEN.

> 1/2 cup apricot nectar
> 1/4 cup fresh lemon juice
> 1/4 cup apricot preserves
> 1 tablespoon curry powder
> 1/2 teaspoon hot red pepper flakes
>   (optional)
> Salt and pepper

Bring the apricot nectar, lemon juice, and apricot preserves to a simmer in a small saucepan, and reduce to
about 1/2 cup, 5 to 7 minutes. Stir in the curry powder,
red pepper flakes, and salt and pepper to taste (use salt
sparingly if chicken was brined). Cool to room temperature. Use in step 4 of the Master Recipe for
Glazed Broiled Chicken.

Chicken Parts with Parsley and Parmesan Coating

SERVES 4

LEMON AND PARSLEY (or other combinations) under the skin keep the
chicken moist and give it great flavor.
Bread crumbs and cheese sprinkled
on top at the last minute give it a crisp coating. Watch
carefully when you're broiling the crumbed chicken
—a few seconds too long and the coating will burn.

> 3/4 cup kosher salt *or* 6 tablespoons table
>   salt, plus more to taste
> 3/4 cup sugar
> 1 chicken (3 to 3 1/2 pounds), rinsed, patted
>   dry, and cut into 8 pieces (see "Cutting
>   Up a Whole Chicken," page 10)
> 2 tablespoons chopped fresh parsley leaves
> 2 teaspoons grated lemon zest
> 2 large garlic cloves, minced
> 1 teaspoon vegetable oil
> Pepper
> 4 tablespoons grated Parmesan cheese
> 2 tablespoons plain bread crumbs

(continued on next page)

1. If brining the chicken pieces: In a gallon-size sealable plastic bag, dissolve the ¾ cup salt and sugar in 1 quart of water. Add the chicken, pressing out as much air as possible; seal and refrigerate until fully seasoned, about 1½ hours.

2. Rinse the chicken pieces well and pat dry. Mix the parsley, lemon zest, garlic, and salt to taste (use sparingly if chicken was brined) in a small bowl. Rub this paste under the skin of each chicken piece.

3. Arrange the chicken pieces on a broiler pan, skin side up, so that the wings and legs are around the perimeter of the pan and the thicker breasts and thighs are in the center. Brush the chicken with oil and lightly season with salt and pepper (be generous with salt if you have not brined the chicken). Adjust the oven rack so that the chicken will be no closer than 8 inches from the heating element and preheat the broiler. Mix the cheese and bread crumbs in a small bowl; set aside.

4. Broil the chicken until the skin is a rich brown color, about 12 minutes. Turn the chicken over; continue to broil until the juices run clear. The wings and legs should be done in about 7 minutes; remove them to a plate, cover with foil, and continue to broil the thighs and breasts for an additional 3 to 5 minutes.

5. When the remaining pieces are cooked, remove the broiler pan from the oven, turn the thighs and breasts skin side up, return the wings and legs to the pan skin side up. Wearing an oven mitt, carefully lift up the top of the broiler pan and brush each piece of chicken with a little of the pan drippings. Sprinkle the chicken with the cheese mixture. Return the chicken to the oven; broil until the topping turns golden brown, about 1 minute. Serve.

Broiled Tarragon Chicken Parts with Mustard Bread Crumbs

MUSTARD-FLAVORED BREAD CRUMBS ARE PAIRED WITH TARRAGON AND GARLIC UNDERNEATH THE SKIN OF THIS WELL-SEASONED CHICKEN. OTHER FRESH HERBS (TRY THYME OR OREGANO) MAY BE SUBSTITUTED. SERVES 4.

> ¾ cup kosher salt *or* 6 tablespoons table
>   salt, plus more to taste
> ¾ cup sugar
> 1 chicken (3 to 3½ pounds), rinsed, patted
>   dry, and cut into 8 pieces (see "Cutting
>   Up a Whole Chicken," page 10)
> 2 tablespoons minced fresh tarragon
>   leaves
> 1 medium garlic clove, minced
> Pepper
> 1 teaspoon vegetable oil
> 2 tablespoons Dijon mustard
> 2 tablespoons butter, softened
> ¼ cup plain bread crumbs

1. If brining the chicken pieces: In a gallon-size sealable plastic bag, dissolve the ¾ cup salt and sugar in 1 quart of water. Add the chicken, pressing out as much air as possible; seal and refrigerate until fully seasoned, about 1½ hours.

2. Rinse the chicken pieces well and pat dry. Mix the tarragon, garlic, and salt and pepper to taste (use salt sparingly if chicken was brined) in a small bowl. Rub this paste under the skin of each chicken piece.

3. Arrange the chicken pieces on a broiler pan, skin side up, so that the wings and legs are around the perimeter of the pan and the thicker breasts and thighs are in the center. Brush the chicken with oil and lightly season with salt and pepper (be generous with salt if you have not brined the chicken). Adjust the oven rack so that the chicken will be no closer than 8 inches from the heating element and preheat the broiler. Mix the mustard, butter, and bread crumbs in a small bowl with a fork until the mixture resembles coarse meal; set aside.

4. Broil the chicken until the skin is a rich brown color, about 12 minutes. Turn the chicken over; continue to broil until the juices run clear. The wings and legs should be done in about 7 minutes; remove them to a plate, cover with foil, and continue to broil the thighs and breasts for an additional 3 to 5 minutes.

5. When the remaining pieces are cooked, remove the broiler pan from the oven, turn the thighs and breasts skin side up, return the wings and legs to the pan skin side up. Wearing an oven mitt, carefully lift up the top of the broiler pan and brush each piece of chicken with a little of the pan drippings. Sprinkle the chicken with the bread crumb mixture. Return it to the oven; broil until the topping turns golden brown, about 3 minutes. Serve.

◆

Spicy Broiled Chicken with Toasted Peanut Crust

FINELY CHOPPED PEANUTS MIXED WITH SCALLIONS AND A LITTLE SOY SAUCE GIVE THIS CHICKEN A SAVORY ASIAN CRUNCH. INCREASE OR DECREASE THE AMOUNT OF HOT RED PEPPER FLAKES ACCORDING TO TASTE. SERVES 4.

¾ cup kosher salt *or* 6 tablespoons table
    salt, plus more to taste
¾ cup sugar
1 chicken (3 to 3½ pounds), rinsed,
    patted dry, and cut into 8 pieces
    (see "Cutting Up a Whole Chicken,"
    page 10)
2 tablespoons minced fresh cilantro leaves
2 medium garlic cloves, minced
1 tablespoon finely chopped fresh
    gingerroot
½ teaspoon hot red pepper flakes
Pepper
1 teaspoon vegetable oil
¼ cup finely chopped unsalted peanuts
2 scallions, white and light green parts,
    finely chopped
2 teaspoons soy sauce

1. If brining the chicken pieces: In a gallon-size sealable plastic bag, dissolve the ¾ cup salt and sugar in 1 quart of water. Add the chicken, pressing out as much air as possible; seal and refrigerate until fully seasoned, about 1½ hours.

2. Rinse the chicken pieces well and pat dry. Mix the cilantro, garlic, ginger, red pepper flakes, and salt and pepper to taste (use salt sparingly if chicken was brined) in a small bowl. Rub this paste under the skin of each chicken piece.

3. Arrange the chicken pieces on a broiler pan, skin side up, so that the wings and legs are around the perimeter of the pan and the thicker breasts and thighs are in the center. Brush the chicken with oil and lightly season with salt and pepper (be generous with salt if you have not brined the chicken). Adjust the oven rack so that the chicken will be no closer than 8 inches from the heating element and preheat the broiler. Combine the peanuts, scallions, and soy sauce in a small bowl; set aside.

4. Broil the chicken until the skin is a rich brown color, about 12 minutes. Turn the chicken over; continue to broil until the juices run clear. The wings and legs should be done in about 7 minutes; remove them to a plate, cover with foil, and continue to broil the thighs and breasts for an additional 3 to 5 minutes.

5. When the remaining pieces are cooked, remove the broiler pan from the oven, turn the thighs and breasts skin side up, return the wings and legs to the pan skin side up. Wearing an oven mitt, carefully lift up the top of the broiler pan and brush each piece of chicken with a little of the pan drippings. Sprinkle the chicken with the peanut mixture. Return the chicken to the oven; broil until the topping turns golden brown, about 3 minutes. Serve.

CHAPTER 15

BUTTERFLIED
CHICKEN

/I\

REMOVING THE BACKBONE FROM A WHOLE CHICKEN

SO THAT IT CAN BE OPENED UP AND FLATTENED—A

PROCESS KNOWN AS BUTTERFLYING—MAY SEEM LIKE

AN UNNECESSARY AND TIME-CONSUMING PROCESS.

BUT WE HAVE FOUND THAT THIS RELATIVELY QUICK

AND SIMPLE PROCEDURE—BECAUSE IT LEAVES THE

BIRD WITH A MORE EVEN THICKNESS—PROVIDES MANY

BENEFITS. ◆ A FLATTENED 3-POUND CHICKEN COOKS

in half an hour or less, versus the hour or more for a traditionally roasted bird. In addition, since the breast isn't sticking out exposed to the heat while the legs are tucked under away from it, all the parts of a flattened bird get done at the same time. Finally, unlike a whole roasted chicken, the butterfly cut is a breeze to separate into sections when carving. One cut down the breast with the kitchen shears, a quick snip of the skin holding the legs, and the job is done (see figures 1–2, page 210).

Won over by the virtues of this technique, we set out to test various methods by which butterflied chicken can be cooked. Our aims were to work out the kinks in each method and determine if there were some general rules that applied to all of them.

The first question to ask is, where should the chicken be split? Most recipes called for the bird to be split down the back, but a few said to split the breast. Was it necessary to cut slits on either side of the breast for each leg? And did we really need to pound the chicken after we butterflied it, or was it enough to just flatten it with our hands? Was it possible to season the chicken with herbs and garlic without these burning when cooked at high heat?

We also wanted to consider weighting the chicken, a step advocated in many recipes. We wondered if pressing the bird down with a weight would provide enough benefits to justify the extra work when sautéing or grilling butterflied chicken. And if weighting was better, what was the simplest way to do it? Most recipes recommended bricks or a large can. Was there a better solution than scrounging the basement for dirty bricks or searching the cabinets for 10 pounds of cans?

We began our research with the butterflying technique itself. To find out if the chicken should be split at the breast or the back, we prepared one each way for roasting. From the start, the breast-split chicken looked unnatural. The back, now the center of the bird, was flanked by two towering chicken breasts. During cooking, the bird bowed and the breasts overshadowed the back, which caused the juices to puddle in the middle and prevented the chicken from browning evenly. The bird split down the back was much more attractive; it stayed flat during cooking and browned evenly.

We also discovered that tucking the chicken legs under was worth the effort, if only for visual appeal. This was particularly true for the roasted and broiled chicken, where holding the legs in place with weights was not possible. Chickens cooked with untucked legs tended to bow and warp. In any case, tucking under the chicken legs makes the presentation nicer. Even the weighted birds looked more attractive with tucked legs, and tucking the legs into the breast takes just seconds.

We thought pounding the chicken might decrease cooking time, but it made no noticeable difference. However, it was easier to weight a chicken that had been pounded to a uniform thickness. We also liked the look of the really flattened chicken. We used a mallet with a flat side for this purpose, but whatever tool you use, make sure it is has a smooth face. A rough-textured mallet will tear the chicken and give it a pockmarked appearance.

Seasoning the outside of the chicken with herbs or garlic, regardless of the cooking method, proved to be pointless. Because each technique required high heat, the herbs charred and the garlic burned. But butterflied chickens are especially easy to season under the skin. Since the backs had been removed, access to the legs and thighs was easy. In fact, stuffing the seasoning under the skin worked beautifully for all the cooking techniques. We included salt and pepper in the seasoning mixture, and also started by adding a bit of oil or butter, but soon realized that this wasn't necessary. The garlic gave the seasoning mixture the pasty quality necessary for easy spreading. And once the cooking process began, there was enough fat from the skin and juice from the meat to moisten and transport the flavorings.

With our general work done, we turned our attention to the specifics of each cooking method.

Roasting is the simplest of the cooking methods. Once the chicken is butchered (and seasonings rubbed under the skin, if you like), it goes in the oven, and you can forget about it until it's done.

Many of the recipes for grilling, broiling, and sautéing butterflied chicken were a bit more complicated, calling for turning the chicken several times. If possible, we wanted to turn the bird just once (especially the weighted birds).

Sautéing chicken with only one turn in a skillet was a bit tricky. Our first attempts produced skin that was too dark and meat that was too pink near the bone. Two things overcame these problems: first, not heating the skillet too high before putting in the chicken (it has, after all, thirty minutes to brown); and second, reducing the heat from medium-high to a strong medium, which allowed the chicken to cook through before it became too brown.

We also decided to explore the effect of weighting the birds during cooking, so we cooked two chickens —one weighted, the other simply covered. The weighted chicken browned more evenly and got done a few minutes faster than the unweighted bird. But we hated using cans and bricks as weights. For sautéing, we found that we could just as easily use a pot of water to flatten the cooking chickens. We dug out a soup kettle with a diameter slightly smaller than the sauté pan, covered its bottom with foil to protect it from spattering fat, and filled it with 5 quarts of water (about 10 pounds). Not only was the soup kettle easier to find than bricks or cans, but it was simple to use. When it came time to turn the chicken, we just lifted the pot by its handles, flipped the bird, and returned the pot to its spot.

Finding a weight for grilling offered other problems. Any pot would have to fit under the grill cover, and it was destined to be damaged by smoke. We had

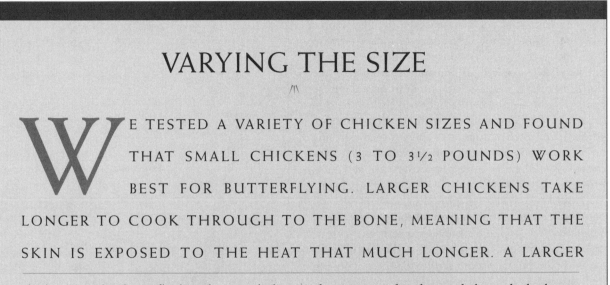

VARYING THE SIZE

E TESTED A VARIETY OF CHICKEN SIZES AND FOUND THAT SMALL CHICKENS (3 TO 3½ POUNDS) WORK BEST FOR BUTTERFLYING. LARGER CHICKENS TAKE LONGER TO COOK THROUGH TO THE BONE, MEANING THAT THE SKIN IS EXPOSED TO THE HEAT THAT MUCH LONGER. A LARGER

chicken can be butterflied and roasted, but sautéing, grilling, and broiling all present problems because the skin can char while the meat is still bloody.

While larger chickens are best cooked by other methods, Cornish game hens are excellent candidates for butterflying, especially when there are only two people for dinner. The cooked hen can be cut along the breast into two pieces, each sufficient as a main course serving, especially if side dishes are plentiful.

Use a 1½-pound Cornish game hen in any of the recipes in this chapter, halving the herb paste and adjusting the cooking times as follows:

◆ **Broil** for 12 minutes with the skin side up, followed by 10 minutes with the skin side down.

◆ **Grill** for 12 minutes with the skin side down, followed by 10 minutes with the skin side up.

◆ **Sauté** for 12 minutes with the skin side down, followed by 12 minutes with the skin side up.

◆ **Roast** with the skin side up for 20 to 25 minutes; for good browning, finish by broiling for 5 minutes.

to resort to using a beat-up jelly-roll pan and two bricks. Since the chicken was to cook over direct heat, we thought grease fires might be a problem, but we cooked a half dozen chickens this way without a single flare-up. We suspect the combination of the grill cover and the jelly-roll pan prevented oxygen from feeding the fire. As with the sautéing, we found that one turn was enough—twelve minutes breast side up, and about fifteen minutes breast side down produced a stunning chicken.

Broiling, our last method, took some fine-tuning. Our first attempts consistently set off smoke alarms. After experimenting, we found that the key to good chicken broiling is oven rack position. The chicken must be far enough from the heating element to cook through without burning, which means the top of the chicken must be about 8 inches from the heat source (so the oven rack should be about 12 inches away to take into account the height of the broiler pan and chicken itself). As with grilling and sautéing, only one turn is necessary. But a bread crumb or grated cheese coating to broiled butterflied chicken makes the skin especially delicious and is worth an extra turn. So, when the chicken is done, it is again turned skin side up. The crumbs or other coating are sprinkled over the skin, and the chicken broiled just until the crumbs brown.

The following recipes provide examples of each cooking technique, but they're just to get you started. Virtually any grilled, broiled, roasted, or sautéed chicken recipe (excluding boneless, skinless chicken breast) can be tailored to one of these cooking methods.

WEIGHTING A BUTTERFLIED CHICKEN

1. To weight a butterflied chicken while it grills, find an old jelly-roll pan or cookie sheet and set it on top of the chicken. Put 2 bricks on the pan.

2. To weight a butterflied chicken while it sautés, cover the bottom of a soup kettle with foil and fill it with 5 quarts of water; set the kettle on top of the chicken.

Grilled Butterflied Chicken

SERVES 4

W E TESTED THIS recipe several times with a 3-pound chicken. Although grilling conditions vary, each time we cooked the chicken, it was done in less than 30 minutes—12 minutes on the skin side and 12 to 15 minutes on the other side. For chickens that weigh closer to 3½ pounds, plan on the full 15 minutes once the chicken has been turned. Avoid checking the chicken except when turning, or the coals will cool, increasing the grilling time. Besides, cooking a chicken this way is like grilling a steak—one turn should do it.

1 teaspoon minced lemon zest
1 teaspoon minced fresh rosemary leaves
1 large garlic clove, minced
½ teaspoon salt
¼ teaspoon pepper

1 chicken (3 to 3½ pounds), butterflied
(see figures 1–5, page 208)
3 tablespoons fresh lemon juice
3 tablespoons olive oil

1. Mix the lemon zest, rosemary, garlic, salt, and pepper in a small bowl. Rub the garlic paste under the skin of the chicken. Place the chicken in a gallon-size sealable plastic bag with the lemon juice and olive oil. Seal and refrigerate, turning occasionally, from 2 to 24 hours; return to room temperature before cooking.

2. If using a charcoal grill, prepare the fire (see figure 1–4, page 156), spreading the hot coals evenly across the bottom of the grill. Set the grill rack in place. Cover and let the grill rack heat about 5 minutes. Test the heat level by holding your hand 5 inches above the rack. For a medium fire, you should be able to hold it there for about 3 seconds. If using a gas grill, light the grill and set on high; let it heat for 10 minutes and then turn the heat down to medium.

3. Place the chicken, skin side down, on the grill rack. Set a jelly-roll or other flat pan on top of chicken; put 2 bricks in the jelly-roll pan (see figure 1, opposite). Cover and grill until the chicken skin is deep brown and shows grill marks, about 12 minutes. Turn the chicken with tongs. Replace the jelly-roll pan, bricks, and grill lid, and continue cooking until the chicken juices run clear, about 15 more minutes.

4. Remove the chicken from grill; cover with foil and let rest 10 to 15 minutes. Carve following figures 1 and 2 on page 210, and serve.

BUTTERFLYING A CHICKEN

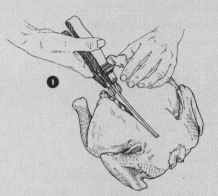

1. Position the chicken breast side down, with the tail of the chicken facing you; use poultry shears to cut along one side of the backbone down its entire length.

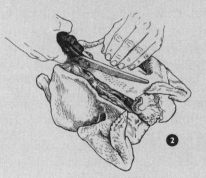

2. Place the poultry shears on the other side of the backbone and slice along the other side. Discard the bone.

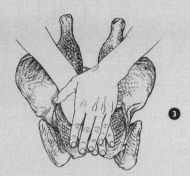

3. Turn the chicken breast side up; open the chicken out on the work surface. Use the palms of your hands to flatten it.

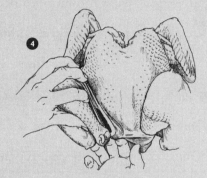

4. Make ½-inch slits on either side of each breast about 1 inch from the tip; tuck the legs into these openings.

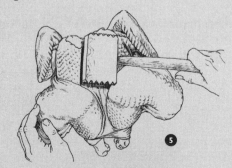

5. Use the smooth face of a mallet to pound the chicken to approximately even thickness.

Grilled Butterflied Chicken with Ginger and Orange

CHINESE SESAME CREPES (PAGE 409) WOULD MAKE A NICE ACCOMPANIMENT TO THIS ASIAN-FLAVORED DISH. SERVES 4.

1 teaspoon minced orange zest
1 tablespoon peeled and minced fresh gingerroot
1 large garlic clove, minced
½ teaspoon salt
¼ teaspoon pepper
1 chicken (3 to 3½ pounds), butterflied (see figures 1–5, opposite)
1 tablespoon soy sauce
3 tablespoons fresh orange juice
3 tablespoons olive oil

1. Mix the orange zest, ginger, garlic, salt, and pepper in a small bowl. Rub the paste under the skin of the chicken. Place the chicken in a gallon-size sealable plastic bag with the soy sauce, orange juice, and olive oil. Seal and refrigerate, turning occasionally, from 2 to 24 hours; return to room temperature before cooking.

2. If using a charcoal grill, prepare the fire (see figures 1–4, page 156), spreading the hot coals evenly across the bottom of the grill. Set the grill rack in place. Cover and let the grill rack heat about 5 minutes. Test the heat level by holding your hand 5 inches above the rack. For a medium fire, you should be able to hold it there for about 3 seconds. If using a gas grill, light the grill and set on high; let it heat for 10 minutes and then turn the heat down to medium.

3. Place the chicken, skin side down, on the grill rack. Set a jelly-roll or other flat pan on top of chicken; put 2 bricks in the jelly-roll pan. Cover and grill until the chicken skin is deep brown and shows grill marks, about 12 minutes. Turn the chicken with tongs. Replace the jelly-roll pan, bricks, and grill lid, and continue cooking until the chicken juices run clear, about 15 more minutes.

4. Remove the chicken from grill; cover with foil and let rest 10 to 15 minutes. Carve and serve.

Grilled Butterflied Chicken with Curry and Mint

YOGURT, RATHER THAN CITRUS JUICE, IS THE ACIDIC COMPONENT OF THE MARINADE HERE. IT GIVES THE CHICKEN A MILD, TANGY FLAVOR AND COOKS UP INTO A GOLDEN CRUST. SERVES 4.

1 teaspoon curry powder
1 tablespoon chopped fresh mint leaves
1 large garlic clove, minced
½ teaspoon salt
¼ teaspoon pepper
¼ cup plain yogurt
3 tablespoons olive oil
1 chicken (3 to 3½ pounds), butterflied (see figures 1–5, opposite)

1. Mix the curry powder, mint, garlic, salt, and pepper in a small bowl. Rub the paste under the skin of the chicken. Whisk together the yogurt and olive oil in a small bowl. Place the chicken in a gallon-size sealable plastic bag with the yogurt and oil. Seal and refrigerate, turning occasionally, from 2 to 24 hours; return to room temperature before cooking.

2. If using a charcoal grill, prepare the fire (see figures 1–4, page 156), spreading the hot coals evenly across the bottom of the grill. Set the grill rack in place. Cover and let the grill rack heat about 5 minutes. Test the heat level by holding your hand 5 inches above the rack. For a medium fire, you should be able to hold it there for about 3 seconds. If using a gas grill, light the grill and set on high; let it heat for 10 minutes and then turn the heat down to medium.

3. Place the chicken, skin side down, on the grill rack. Set a jelly-roll or other flat pan on top of chicken; put 2 bricks in the jelly-roll pan. Cover and grill until the chicken skin is deep brown and shows grill marks, about 12 minutes. Turn the chicken with tongs. Replace the jelly-roll pan, bricks, and grill lid, and continue cooking until the chicken juices run clear, about 15 more minutes.

4. Remove the chicken from grill; cover with foil and let rest 10 to 15 minutes. Carve and serve.

CARVING A BUTTERFLIED CHICKEN

1. To carve the butterflied chicken, place chicken skin side down and use kitchen shears to cut through the breastbone. (Since the breastbone is broken and the meat is flattened during pounding, this should be easy.)

2. Once the breast has been split, only the skin holds the portions together. Separate each leg and thigh from each breast and wing.

Grilled Butterflied Chicken with Southwestern Flavors

SERVE THIS CHICKEN WITH FLOUR OR CORN TORTILLAS TOASTED ON THE GRILL AFTER THE CHICKEN COMES OFF. SERVES 4.

> 1 teaspoon chili powder
> 1 teaspoon ground cumin
> 1 tablespoon chopped fresh cilantro leaves
> ½ teaspoon salt
> ¼ teaspoon pepper
> 1 chicken (3 to 3½ pounds), butterflied (see figures 1–5, page 208)
> 3 tablespoons fresh lime juice
> 3 tablespoons olive oil

1. Mix the chili powder, cumin, cilantro, salt, and pepper in a small bowl. Rub the paste under the skin of the chicken. Place the chicken in a gallon-size sealable plastic bag with the lime juice and oil. Seal and refrigerate, turning occasionally, from 2 to 24 hours; return to room temperature before cooking.

2. If using a charcoal grill, prepare the fire (see figures 1–4, page 156), spreading the hot coals evenly across the bottom of the grill. Set the grill rack in place. Cover and let the grill rack heat about 5 minutes. Test the heat level by holding your hand 5 inches above the rack. For a medium fire, you should be able to hold it there for about 3 seconds. If using a gas grill, light the grill and set on high; let it heat for 10 minutes and then turn the heat down to medium.

3. Place the chicken, skin side down, on the grill rack. Set a jelly-roll or other flat pan on top of chicken; put 2 bricks in the jelly-roll pan. Cover and grill until the chicken skin is deep brown and shows grill marks, about 12 minutes. Turn the chicken with tongs. Replace the jelly-roll pan, bricks, and grill lid, and continue cooking until the chicken juices run clear, about 15 more minutes.

4. Remove the chicken from grill; cover with foil and let rest 10 to 15 minutes. Carve and serve.

Broiled Butterflied Chicken

SERVES 4

A PARMESAN AND BREAD CRUMB mixture gives this chicken a quick, crunchy crust. Keep a close eye on the chicken while browning the cheese mixture—it's a matter of seconds between a golden crust and a blackened one.

  1 teaspoon minced lemon zest
  1 large garlic clove, minced
  Salt
  ¼ teaspoon hot red pepper flakes
  1 chicken (3 to 3½ pounds), butterflied
    (see figures 1–5, page 208)
  1 teaspoon vegetable oil
  Pepper
  2 tablespoons grated Parmesan cheese
  1 tablespoon plain bread crumbs

1. Mix the lemon zest, garlic, ½ teaspoon salt, and red pepper flakes in a small bowl. Rub this paste under the skin of the chicken. Transfer the chicken to a broiler pan, skin side up; brush with oil and lightly season with salt and pepper to taste; let stand while the broiler heats. Mix the cheese and bread crumbs; set aside.

2. Adjust the oven rack so that the chicken will be no closer than 8 inches from the heating element and preheat the broiler. Broil the chicken until the skin is a rich brown, about 12 minutes. Turn the chicken over; continue to broil until the juices run clear, about 15 minutes longer. Remove from the oven and turn chicken skin side up. Wearing an oven mitt, carefully lift up the top of the broiler pan and brush chicken with pan drippings. Sprinkle the chicken with the cheese mixture. Return to the oven; broil until the topping turns golden brown, about 3 minutes longer.

3. Remove the chicken from the oven, cover with foil, and let rest 10 to 15 minutes. Carve and serve.

◆

Broiled Butterflied Chicken with Feta and Oregano

FRESH OREGANO, LEMON, AND FETA CHEESE GIVE THIS CHICKEN A GREEK FLAVOR. SERVE WITH COMPLEMENTARY VEGETABLES LIKE EGGPLANT OR ZUCCHINI DRESSED WITH LEMON JUICE AND OLIVE OIL. SERVES 4.

  1 teaspoon minced lemon zest
  1 tablespoon chopped fresh oregano leaves
  1 large garlic clove, minced
  Salt
  1 chicken (3 to 3½ pounds), butterflied
    (see figures 1–5, page 208)
  1 teaspoon vegetable oil
  Pepper
  2 tablespoons finely crumbled feta cheese
  1 tablespoon plain bread crumbs

1. Mix the lemon zest, oregano, garlic, and ½ teaspoon salt in a small bowl. Rub this paste under the skin of the chicken. Transfer the chicken to a broiler pan, skin side up; brush with oil and lightly season with salt and pepper to taste; let stand while the broiler heats. Mix the cheese and bread crumbs; set aside.

2. Adjust the oven rack so that the chicken will be no closer than 8 inches from the heating element and preheat the broiler. Broil the chicken until the skin is a rich brown, about 12 minutes. Turn the chicken over; continue to broil until the juices run clear, about 15 minutes longer. Remove from the oven and turn

(continued on next page)

chicken skin side up. Wearing an oven mitt, carefully lift up the top of the broiler pan and brush chicken with pan drippings. Sprinkle the chicken with the cheese mixture. Return to the oven; broil until the topping turns golden brown, about 3 minutes longer.

3. Remove the chicken from the oven, cover with foil, and let rest 10 to 15 minutes. Carve and serve.

◆

Broiled Butterflied Chicken with Spicy Bread Crumbs

PAPRIKA AND CHILI POWDER ENLIVEN THE BREAD CRUMB TOPPING FOR THIS CHICKEN. SERVE WITH FRESH CORN AND A SALAD OF ROMAINE LETTUCE WITH A CREAMY AVOCADO DRESSING. **SERVES 4.**

1 teaspoon minced lime zest
1 large garlic clove, minced
Salt
1 chicken (3 to 3½ pounds), butterflied
    (see figures 1–5, page 208)
1 teaspoon vegetable oil
Pepper
¼ teaspoon paprika
¼ teaspoon chili powder
1 tablespoon plain bread crumbs

1. Mix the lime zest, garlic, and ½ teaspoon salt in a small bowl. Rub this paste under the skin of the chicken. Transfer the chicken to a broiler pan, skin side up; brush with oil and lightly season with salt and pepper to taste; let stand while the broiler heats. Mix the paprika, chili powder, and bread crumbs; set aside.

2. Adjust the oven rack so that the chicken will be no closer than 8 inches from the heating element and preheat the broiler. Broil the chicken until the skin is a rich brown, about 12 minutes. Turn the chicken over; continue to broil until the juices run clear, about 15 minutes longer. Remove from the oven and turn chicken skin side up. Wearing an oven mitt, carefully lift up the top of the broiler pan and brush chicken with pan drippings. Sprinkle the chicken with the bread crumb mixture. Return to the oven; broil until the topping turns golden brown, about 3 minutes longer.

3. Remove the chicken from the oven, cover with foil, and let rest 10 to 15 minutes. Carve and serve.

◆

Broiled Butterflied Chicken with Aromatic Bread Crumbs

A BASMATI RICE PILAF (SEE PAGE 132) WOULD GO VERY NICELY WITH THIS DISH. **SERVES 4.**

1 tablespoon chopped fresh cilantro leaves
1 large garlic clove, minced
Salt
1 chicken (3 to 3½ pounds), butterflied
    (see figures 1–5, page 208)
1 teaspoon vegetable oil
Pepper
¼ teaspoon ground cumin
¼ teaspoon ground cinnamon
Pinch ground cloves
1 tablespoon bread crumbs

1. Mix the cilantro, garlic, and ½ teaspoon salt in a small bowl. Rub this paste under the skin of the chicken. Transfer the chicken to a broiler pan, skin side up; brush with oil and lightly season with salt and pepper to taste; let stand while the broiler heats. Mix the cumin, cinnamon, ¼ teaspoon pepper, the cloves, and bread crumbs; set aside.

2. Adjust the oven rack so that the chicken will be no closer than 8 inches from the heating element and preheat the broiler. Broil the chicken until the skin is a rich brown, about 12 minutes. Turn the chicken over; continue to broil until the juices run clear, about 15 minutes longer. Remove from the oven and turn chicken skin side up. Wearing an oven mitt, carefully lift up the top of the broiler pan and brush chicken with pan drippings. Sprinkle the chicken with the bread crumb mixture. Return to the oven; broil until the topping turns golden brown, about 3 minutes longer.

3. Remove the chicken from the oven, cover with foil, and let rest 10 to 15 minutes. Carve and serve.

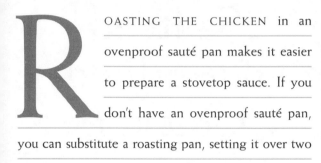

Roasted Butterflied Chicken

SERVES 4

ROASTING THE CHICKEN in an ovenproof sauté pan makes it easier to prepare a stovetop sauce. If you don't have an ovenproof sauté pan, you can substitute a roasting pan, setting it over two burners to make the sauce.

2 teaspoons minced fresh tarragon leaves
1 medium garlic clove, minced
Salt and pepper
1 chicken (3 to 3½ pounds), butterflied
    (see figures 1–5, page 208)
1 teaspoon vegetable oil
1 cup chicken stock or low-sodium
    canned broth
1 tablespoon Dijon mustard
1 tablespoon softened butter

1. Mix the tarragon, garlic, ½ teaspoon salt, and ¼ teaspoon pepper in a small bowl. Rub this paste under the skin of the chicken. Transfer the chicken to a large ovenproof sauté pan, skin side up; rub with oil and lightly season with salt and pepper to taste. Let stand at room temperature while you heat the oven to 500 degrees.

2. Roast the chicken until the skin is nicely browned and the juices run clear, about 30 minutes. Transfer to a plate, cover with foil, and let rest while making the sauce.

3. Spoon off all the fat from the sauté pan. Place the pan on a burner set at medium-high; add the stock and simmer until reduced by half, scraping up the drippings that have stuck to bottom, 3 to 4 minutes. Remove the pan from the heat. Whisk in the mustard, swirl in the butter with a wooden spoon, and season with salt and pepper to taste. Carve the chicken and serve with pan sauce.

◆

Roasted Butterflied Chicken with Mushrooms and Marsala

BROWNED MUSHROOMS IN A RICH MARSALA WINE SAUCE MAKE A NATURAL ACCOMPANIMENT TO ROASTED CHICKEN. SERVE WITH MASHED POTATOES. **SERVES 4.**

1 tablespoon minced fresh parsley leaves
1 medium garlic clove, minced
Salt and pepper
1 chicken (3 to 3½ pounds), butterflied
    (see figures 1–5, page 208)
1 teaspoon vegetable oil
1 shallot, minced
10 ounces white button mushrooms,
    trimmed and thinly sliced
¾ cup marsala
1 tablespoon softened butter

1. Mix the parsley, garlic, ½ teaspoon salt, and ¼ teaspoon pepper in a small bowl. Rub this paste under the skin of the chicken. Transfer the chicken to a large ovenproof sauté pan, skin side up; rub with oil and lightly season with salt and pepper to taste. Let stand at room temperature while you heat the oven to 500 degrees.

2. Roast the chicken until the skin is nicely browned and the juices run clear, about 30 minutes. Transfer to a plate, cover with foil, and let rest while making the sauce.

(continued on next page)

3. Spoon off all the fat from the sauté pan. Place the pan on a burner set at medium-high; add the shallot and sauté until softened, 2 to 3 minutes. Add the mushrooms and sauté until they release their juices, about 3 minutes. Add the marsala and simmer until reduced by half, scraping up the drippings that have stuck to bottom, 3 to 4 minutes. Remove from the heat, swirl in the butter with a wooden spoon, and season with salt and pepper to taste. Carve the chicken and serve with pan sauce.

◆

Roasted Butterflied Chicken with Sherry Vinegar and Peppers

SAUTEED SWEET PEPPERS CONTRAST NICELY WITH A TART VINEGAR SAUCE HERE. A SAFFRON RICE PILAF OR RISOTTO WOULD PAIR WELL WITH THIS DISH. **SERVES 4**.

> 2 teaspoons minced fresh thyme leaves
> 1 medium garlic clove, minced
> Salt and pepper
> 1 chicken (3 to 3½ pounds), butterflied
>   (see figures 1–5, page 208)
> 1 teaspoon vegetable oil
> 1 medium shallot, finely chopped
> 2 red bell peppers, cored, seeded, and
>   sliced thin
> ¼ cup chicken stock or low-sodium
>   canned broth
> 2 tablespoons sherry vinegar
> 1 tablespoon softened butter

1. Mix the thyme, garlic, ½ teaspoon salt, and ¼ teaspoon pepper in a small bowl. Rub this paste under the skin of the chicken. Transfer the chicken to a large ovenproof sauté pan, skin side up; rub with oil and lightly season with salt and pepper to taste. Let stand at room temperature while you heat the oven to 500 degrees.

2. Roast the chicken until the skin is nicely browned and the juices run clear, about 30 minutes. Transfer to a plate, cover with foil, and let rest while making the sauce.

3. Spoon off all the fat from the sauté pan. Place the pan on a burner set at medium-high; add the shallot and sauté until softened, 2 to 3 minutes. Add the peppers and cook until they release their juices and become soft, 7 to 10 minutes. Add the stock and vinegar and simmer until reduced by half, scraping up the drippings that have stuck to bottom, 3 to 4 minutes. Remove from the heat, swirl in the butter with a wooden spoon, and season with salt and pepper to taste. Carve the chicken and serve with pan sauce.

MASTER RECIPE

Sautéed Butterflied Chicken

SERVES 4

WILD MUSHROOMS AND fresh sage give this pan sauce a woodsy flavor. White button mushrooms may be substituted if wild ones are unavailable.

> 4 teaspoons minced fresh sage leaves
> 1 medium garlic clove, minced
> Salt and pepper
> 1 chicken (3 to 3½ pounds), butterflied
>   (see figures 1–5, page 208)
> 1 tablespoon vegetable oil
> 2 medium shallots, minced

5 ounces assorted wild mushrooms,
   trimmed and sliced (about 2 cups)
2 tablespoons dry vermouth
½ cup chicken stock
1 tablespoon butter

1. Mix 2 teaspoons sage, the garlic, ½ teaspoon salt, and ¼ teaspoon pepper in small bowl. Rub this paste under the skin of the chicken. Lightly season the chicken with salt and pepper to taste. Let stand at room temperature about 15 minutes to allow flavors to meld.

2. Heat the oil in an 11- or 12-inch sauté pan set over medium-high heat. Cover the bottom of a soup kettle that has a diameter slightly smaller than the sauté pan with foil and fill with 5 quarts of water. Lay the chicken, skin side down, in the sauté pan. Set the kettle on top to hold flat (see figure 2, page 206); cook over a strong medium heat until the skin is nicely browned, about 12 minutes. Remove the soup kettle; turn the chicken skin side up. Replace the kettle and continue cooking until the juices run clear, about 18 minutes. Transfer the chicken to a plate; cover with foil while making the sauce.

3. Remove all but 1 tablespoon fat from the pan; return the pan to the burner and increase the heat to medium-high. Add the shallots; sauté until softened, about 2 minutes. Add the mushrooms; sauté until their juices release and the mushrooms soften, about 2 minutes. Add the vermouth; cook until the liquid has almost evaporated, about 1 minute. Add the chicken stock; simmer until thickened, about 2 minutes. Stir in the remaining sage. Remove from the heat and swirl in the butter with a wooden spoon. Carve the chicken and serve with the pan sauce.

Sautéed Butterflied Chicken with Lemon-Basil Pan Sauce

SERVE THIS VARIATION WITH ORZO, COUSCOUS, OR RICE ON THE SIDE. SERVES 4.

2 medium garlic cloves, minced
3 tablespoons minced basil leaves
Salt and pepper
1 chicken (3 to 3½ pounds), butterflied
   (see figures 1–5, page 208)
1 tablespoon vegetable oil
2 medium shallots, minced
2 tablespoons fresh lemon juice
½ cup chicken stock or low-sodium
   canned broth
1 tablespoon butter

1. Mix the garlic, 1 tablespoon basil, ½ teaspoon salt, and ¼ teaspoon pepper in a small bowl. Rub this paste under the skin of the chicken. Lightly season the chicken with salt and pepper to taste. Let stand at room temperature about 15 minutes to allow flavors to meld.

2. Heat the oil in an 11- or 12-inch sauté pan set over medium-high heat. Cover the bottom of a soup kettle that has a diameter slightly smaller than the sauté pan with foil and fill with 5 quarts of water. Lay the chicken, skin side down, in the sauté pan. Set the kettle on top to hold flat; cook over a strong medium heat until the skin is nicely browned, about 12 minutes. Remove the soup kettle; turn the chicken skin side up. Replace the kettle and continue cooking until the juices run clear, about 18 minutes. Transfer the chicken to a plate; cover with foil while making the sauce.

3. Remove all but 1 tablespoon fat from the pan; return the pan to the burner and increase the heat to medium-high. Add the shallots; sauté until softened, about 2 minutes. Add the lemon juice and chicken stock; simmer until thickened, about 2 minutes. Remove from the heat, stir in the remaining 2 tablespoons basil, and swirl in the butter. Carve the chicken and serve with the pan sauce.

Sautéed Butterflied Chicken with Tomato, Olive, and Caper Pan Sauce

SERVE THIS CHICKEN WITH CRUSTY BREAD FOR MOP-PING UP THE MEDITERRANEAN-INSPIRED PAN SAUCE. SERVES 4.

2 tablespoons chopped fresh parsley
   leaves
1 medium garlic clove, minced
Salt and pepper
1 chicken (about 3 to 3½ pounds),
   butterflied (see figures 1–5, page 208)
1 tablespoon vegetable oil
1 cup canned crushed tomatoes
12 black olives, pitted and coarsely
   chopped
1 tablespoon capers
¼ cup dry white wine

1. Mix 1 tablespoon parsley, the garlic, ½ teaspoon salt, and ¼ teaspoon pepper in a small bowl. Rub this paste under the skin of the chicken. Lightly season the chicken with salt and pepper to taste. Let stand at room temperature about 15 minutes to allow flavors to meld.

2. Heat the oil in an 11- or 12-inch sauté pan set over medium-high heat. Cover the bottom of a soup kettle that has a diameter slightly smaller than the sauté pan with foil and fill with 5 quarts of water. Lay the chicken, skin side down, in the sauté pan. Set the kettle on top to hold flat; cook over a strong medium heat until the skin is nicely browned, about 12 minutes. Remove the soup kettle; turn the chicken skin side up. Replace the kettle and continue cooking until the juices run clear, about 18 minutes. Transfer the chicken to a plate; cover with foil while making the sauce.

3. Remove all but 1 tablespoon fat from the pan; return the pan to the burner and increase the heat to medium-high. Add the tomatoes, olives, capers, and wine; simmer until thickened, about 5 minutes. Stir in the remaining tablespoon of parsley. Carve the chicken and serve with the pan sauce.

Sautéed Butterflied Chicken with Green Peppercorn and Mustard Pan Sauce

IF USING CANNED PEPPERCORNS, BE SURE TO RINSE THEM WELL TO REMOVE EXCESS SALT FROM THE BRIN-ING MIXTURE. SERVES 4.

2 tablespoons chopped fresh parsley leaves
1 medium garlic clove, minced
Salt and pepper
1 chicken (3 to 3½ pounds), butterflied
   (see figures 1–5, page 208)
1 tablespoon vegetable oil
½ cup dry white wine
¼ cup heavy cream
1 tablespoon Dijon mustard
1 tablespoon green peppercorns, crushed
   with the back of a chef's knife

1. Mix 1 tablespoon parsley, the garlic, ½ teaspoon salt, and ¼ teaspoon pepper in a small bowl. Rub this paste under the skin of the chicken. Lightly season the chicken with salt and pepper to taste. Let stand at room temperature about 15 minutes to allow flavors to meld.

2. Heat the oil in an 11- or 12-inch sauté pan set over medium-high heat. Cover the bottom of a soup kettle that has a diameter slightly smaller than the sauté pan with foil and fill with 5 quarts of water. Lay the chicken, skin side down, in the sauté pan. Set the kettle on top to hold flat; cook over a strong medium heat until the skin is nicely browned, about 12 minutes. Remove the soup kettle; turn the chicken skin side up. Replace the kettle and continue cooking until the juices run clear, about 18 minutes. Transfer the chicken to a plate; cover with foil while making the sauce.

3. Remove all but 1 tablespoon fat from the pan; return the pan to the burner and increase the heat to medium-high. Add the wine and cream. Whisk in the mustard; simmer until thickened, about 3 minutes. Stir in the peppercorns and the remaining tablespoon of parsley. Carve the chicken and serve with the pan sauce.

CHAPTER 16

CHICKEN

WINGS

/|\

CHICKEN WINGS—ONCE CONSIDERED FIT ONLY

FOR THE STOCKPOT—HAVE BECOME RESPECTABLE

IN RECENT YEARS. THEIR WIDE AVAILABILITY AT FAST-

FOOD RESTAURANTS HAS CERTAINLY INCREASED THEIR

APPEAL, AS HAS THE PROLIFERATION OF ASIAN REST-

AURANTS, WHERE WINGS ARE OFTEN STUFFED AND

SERVED AS ELEGANT APPETIZERS OR USED IN SIMPLE

PREPARING WINGS FOR GRILLING OR ROASTING

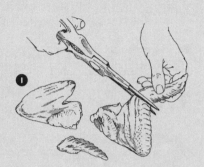

1. With poultry shears or a chef's knife, sever the wing tip. Discard the tips or use them to make stock.

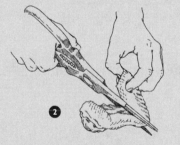

2. We find it easier to cook and eat chicken wings if they have been cut into separate parts—the meaty "drumstick" and the longer double-boned section. Cut through the joint of the remaining wing with poultry shears or a chef's knife to produce these 2 parts.

wing tips before cooking. After one test with the wing tips on, it was clear why. Because it is so fatty and thin, the wing tip will char long before the rest of the wing is done. Our next question was whether to separate the remaining wing into two pieces—the meaty drumsticklike portion that is attached to the bird and the double-boned section between the drumstick and tip. We cooked wings both ways and found that the skin browned better (especially near the joint) and the meat cooked more evenly (and quickly) if the wing was separated at the joint into two pieces before cooking. Separating the wing also made it easier to eat since there was no tricky joint to nibble around.

With the preparation issues settled, we focused on cooking methods. The possible choices include grilling, broiling, roasting, deep-frying, and stir-frying. Deep-frying and stir-frying (see "Stir-Frying Chicken Wings," page 227) are specialty methods, which we would deal with later, but we do not consider them to be appropriate as an all-purpose method for cooking chicken wings. We attempted several times to broil chicken wings, each time moving them farther and farther from the heating element. However, owing to their high fat content, we set off smoke alarms each time and eventually gave up on broiling.

Roasting was much easier to perfect. The only issues here were temperature and turning. Like broiling, roasting can lead to excessive smoking. However, we found that as long as the oven temperature is kept at 375 degrees, the wings will brown nicely and the kitchen air will stay fresh. We attempted to cook the wings at 400 degrees and at 425 degrees, but the thick smoke is not worth the minimal time savings.

We found that cooking the wings right in the pan was problematic since the wings were sitting in their own fat and the skin remained flabby. To make sure that the skin crisps nicely, elevate the wings on a rack. As for turning, we had the best results when starting the wings skin side down and then turning them halfway through the cooking and brushing the wings with a basting sauce at the same time.

While we like roasted chicken wings, we do find them a tad greasy. Wings have a lot of fat and there is only so much that can be rendered in the oven without terrible smoking. We had high hopes when we switched our focus to grilling and our first test

stir-fries. Our goals for this chapter were to develop an all-purpose cooking method for wings and to figure out how to re-create (and simplify if possible) the best Asian dishes we sampled when eating out.

Our first question when cooking wings was preparation. Many restaurants remove the skinny, meatless outside did not disappoint. As with many foods, grilled wings develop a rich, dark skin over hot coals. In addition, the intense grill heat does a better job of rendering fat than the oven. One danger on the grill is that the skin will burn. For this reason, we found it best to use a medium fire and to turn the wings often, at least four or five times as they cook, to make sure that they don't spend too much time over any particular hot spot on the grill.

In terms of adding flavor, we tried marinating and basting, and found that marinating offered no advantages and, of course, took extra time. We had excellent results when we simply mixed the sauce ingredients, added the wings to the bowl with the sauce, then grilled or roasted, basting either constantly if grilling or after twenty minutes if roasting.

Wings seem like an indulgence, better suited to small portions, so we like them best as an appetizer for six or more people; however, they can be served as a main course for four. Serve the wings hot, or let them cool slightly and eat them when just warm.

With our all-purpose method for preparing chicken wings done, we turned to specialty recipes like deep-fried buffalo wings. As with any deep-frying, it is imperative to get the oil hot (we found 360 degrees to be the best temperature) and then cook in small batches so that the temperature does not drop too much.

For Asian-style deep-fried stuffed wings, it is necessary to remove the drumstick and then bone the middle section of the wing. In this case, the wing tips are kept attached, since they provide a natural handle for eating stuffed wings. Once the wing is boned, it can be stuffed with any finely chopped, fairly moist stuffing. We prefer a stuffing made with ground chicken (its mild flavor works well with the wings), although ground veal, beef, and pork can also be used. A little cornstarch added to the filling helps to bind it together. Chilling the filling in the refrigerator also ensures that it will be quite firm and hold up in the fryer. Stuffed deep-fried wings should be served with a dipping sauce.

Given the richness of deep-fried wings, we feel that they are best served as an hors d'oeuvre. Boning and stuffing wings is also fairly time-consuming—you would not want to prepare 6 pounds of wings this way. However, as an occasional treat for a small crowd, the effort is surely justified.

Charcoal-Grilled Chicken Wings

SERVES 4 TO 6

WE LIKE TO TURN THE wings several times during cooking to ensure even browning and prevent the skin from burning. Cook the wings over a medium fire (you should be able to hold your hand 5 inches from the grill for 3 to 4 seconds) so that they'll cook through without burning.

2 tablespoons extra-virgin olive oil
2 tablespoons fresh lemon juice
Salt and pepper
18 chicken wings (about 3 pounds), wing tips removed and remaining wing separated into 2 parts at the joint (see figures 1 and 2, opposite)
1 tablespoon minced fresh herb leaves (parsley, basil, oregano, mint, or cilantro)

(continued on next page)

1. Light 5 quarts of charcoal (1 chimney starter heaped full) and allow to burn until the flames have died down and all the charcoal is covered with a layer of fine gray ash. Return the grill rack to position; cover the grill and let the rack heat for 5 minutes.

2. Combine 1 tablespoon of the oil, the lemon juice, and salt and pepper to taste in a large bowl. Add the chicken wings and toss to coat. Combine the remaining tablespoon oil and the herbs in a small bowl and set it aside.

3. Grill the wings over medium heat, uncovered, extinguishing any flames with a squirt bottle. Turn them every 3 or 4 minutes, brushing with the oil and herb mixture, until the chicken is dark and fully cooked, 15 to 20 minutes. Transfer to a platter and serve immediately, or cool slightly and serve warm.

MASTER RECIPE

Gas-Grilled Chicken Wings

SERVES 4 TO 6

E'VE FOUND that medium-high heat is the best setting for gas-grilled wings, although temperatures may vary from grill to grill. Cook the wings uncovered. Such small pieces might burn with the lid down.

2 tablespoons extra-virgin olive oil
2 tablespoons fresh lemon juice
Salt and pepper
18 chicken wings (about 3 pounds), wing tips removed and remaining wing separated into 2 parts at the joint (see figures 1 and 2, page 218)
1 tablespoon minced fresh herb leaves (parsley, basil, oregano, mint, or cilantro)

1. Light the gas grill, set at high heat, and cover. Heat for 10 to 15 minutes.

2. Combine 1 tablespoon of the oil, the lemon juice, and salt and pepper to taste in a large bowl. Add the chicken wings and toss to coat. Combine the remaining tablespoon oil and the herbs in a small bowl and set aside.

3. Grill the chicken wings, uncovered, over medium-high heat, extinguishing any flames with a squirt bottle. Turn them every 3 or 4 minutes, brushing with the oil and herb mixture, until the chicken is dark and fully cooked, 15 to 20 minutes. Transfer to a platter and serve immediately, or cool slightly and serve warm.

Roasted Chicken Wings

SERVES 4 TO 6

PLACE THE WINGS on a rack so that fat can drip down, and line the roasting pan beneath with foil for easy cleanup. Herbs and additional olive oil are brushed on midway through the 40-minute cooking time so that the herbs will flavor the chicken without burning.

2 tablespoons extra-virgin olive oil
2 tablespoons fresh lemon juice
Salt and pepper
18 chicken wings (about 3 pounds), wing
   tips removed and remaining wing
   separated into 2 parts at the joint (see
   figures 1 and 2, page 218)
1 tablespoon minced fresh herb leaves
   (parsley, basil, oregano, mint, or cilantro)

1. Preheat the oven to 375 degrees. Line a 9-by-13-inch roasting pan with aluminum foil and place a roasting rack inside the pan.

2. Combine 1 tablespoon oil, the lemon juice, and salt and pepper to taste in a large bowl. Add the chicken wings and toss to coat. Combine the remaining tablespoon oil and the herbs in a small bowl and set aside.

3. Place the chicken wings, skin side down, on the rack. Bake for 20 minutes, turn, and brush with the oil and herb mixture. Continue to bake until well browned, another 20 to 25 minutes. Transfer to a platter and serve immediately, or cool slightly and serve warm.

◆

Hoisin Chicken Wings

HOISIN SAUCE GIVES THESE WINGS A GLOSSY FINISH. SERVE THEM WITH DRINKS, OR WITH SEVERAL OTHER DISHES AS PART OF A FAMILY-STYLE ASIAN MEAL. **SERVES 4 TO 6.**

½ cup hoisin sauce
3 tablespoons soy sauce
3 tablespoons rice wine
2 tablespoons sugar
4 garlic cloves, minced
18 chicken wings (about 3 pounds), wing
   tips removed and remaining wing
   separated into 2 parts at the joint (see
   figures 1 and 2, page 218)

1. Light a charcoal or gas fire or preheat the oven according to the instructions in one of the Master Recipes, pages 219–21.

2. Combine the hoisin sauce, soy sauce, rice wine, sugar, and garlic in a large bowl. Reserve ¼ cup of the mixture for basting the chicken wings as they cook. Add the chicken wings to the remaining sauce and toss to coat.

3. Grill or roast according to the relevant Master Recipe, brushing the chicken wings after every turn with the reserved sauce, until the chicken is dark and fully cooked. Transfer to a platter and serve immediately, or cool slightly and serve warm.

Garlic and Spice Chicken Wings

CINNAMON GIVES THESE GARLICKY WINGS A MIDDLE EASTERN FLAVOR. SERVE THEM AS PART OF A MEDITERRANEAN OR MIDDLE EASTERN MEAL, MAYBE WITH SOME GRILLED EGGPLANT AND COUSCOUS ON THE SIDE. IF YOU DON'T OWN A GARLIC PRESS, MINCE THE GARLIC FINE, SPRINKLE IT WITH A LITTLE SALT, AND THEN USE THE SIDE OF A CHEF'S KNIFE TO WORK IT INTO A SMOOTH PUREE (SEE FIGURES 1 AND 2, PAGE 129). SERVES 4 TO 6.

   10 garlic cloves, peeled and pureed
   ¼ cup extra-virgin olive oil
   ¼ cup fresh lemon juice
   ½ teaspoon ground cinnamon
   ¼ teaspoon cayenne pepper
   ½ teaspoon ground allspice
   Salt and pepper
   18 chicken wings (about 3 pounds), wing tips removed and remaining wing separated into 2 parts at the joint (see figures 1 and 2, page 218)

1. Light a charcoal or gas fire or preheat the oven according to the instructions in one of the Master Recipes, pages 219–21.

2. Combine the garlic, oil, lemon juice, cinnamon, cayenne, allspice, and salt and pepper to taste in a large bowl. Reserve 2 tablespoons of the mixture for basting the chicken wings as they cook. Add the chicken wings to the remaining sauce and toss to coat.

3. Grill or roast according to the relevant Master Recipe, brushing the chicken wings after every turn with the reserved sauce, until the chicken is dark and fully cooked. Transfer to a platter and serve immediately, or cool slightly and serve warm.

Honey-Mustard Chicken Wings

HONEY AND MUSTARD GIVE THESE WINGS EXCELLENT COLOR AND FLAVOR. MOLASSES OR MAPLE SYRUP CAN BE SUBSTITUTED FOR THE HONEY IF YOU LIKE A MORE ASSERTIVE SWEETENER. SERVES 4 TO 6.

   ¾ cup honey
   ¼ cup soy sauce
   2 tablespoons Dijon mustard
   2 tablespoons vegetable oil
   4 garlic cloves, minced
   18 chicken wings (about 3 pounds), wing tips removed and remaining wing separated into 2 parts at the joint (see figures 1 and 2, page 218)

1. Light a charcoal or gas fire or preheat the oven according to the instructions in one of the Master Recipes, pages 219–21.

2. Combine the honey, soy sauce, mustard, oil, and garlic in a large bowl. Reserve ¼ cup of the mixture for basting the chicken wings as they cook. Add the chicken wings to the remaining sauce and toss to coat.

3. Grill or roast according to the relevant Master Recipe, brushing the chicken wings after every turn with the reserved sauce, until the chicken is dark and fully cooked. Transfer to a platter and serve immediately, or cool slightly and serve warm.

◆

Sweet and Sour Chicken Wings

BROWN SUGAR MAKES FOR A WELL-CARAMELIZED CRUST ON THESE WINGS. JUST MAKE SURE TO HAVE YOUR SQUIRT BOTTLE OF WATER READY IN CASE OF FLARE-UPS IF YOU ARE GRILLING, SINCE SUGARED WINGS TEND TO BURN QUICKLY IF NOT CAREFULLY WATCHED. SERVES 4 TO 6.

   ½ cup ketchup
   ½ cup packed brown sugar
   ¼ cup rice vinegar
   3 tablespoons soy sauce
   2 tablespoons Asian sesame oil

4 garlic cloves, minced

18 chicken wings (about 3 pounds), wing tips removed and remaining wing separated into 2 parts at the joint (see figures 1 and 2, page 218)

1. Light a charcoal or gas fire or preheat the oven according to the instructions in one of the Master Recipes, pages 219–21.

2. Combine the ketchup, brown sugar, vinegar, soy sauce, sesame oil, and garlic in a large bowl. Reserve ¼ cup of the mixture for basting the chicken wings as they cook. Add the chicken wings to the remaining sauce and toss to coat.

3. Grill or roast according to the relevant Master Recipe, brushing the chicken wings after every turn with the reserved sauce, until the chicken is dark and fully cooked. Transfer to a platter and serve immediately, or cool slightly and serve warm.

◆

Hot Wings

MANY PEOPLE LIKE THEIR WINGS SPICY. THE PRODI-GIOUS AMOUNT OF HOT SAUCE COATING THESE WINGS PROMISES TO SATISFY HEAT ADDICTS. IF YOU LIKE YOUR WINGS HOT BUT NOT BLAZING, DON'T BASTE THEM WITH THE ADDITIONAL SAUCE AS THEY COOK. SERVE WITH BLUE CHEESE DRESSING (PAGE 224) IF YOU WANT BUFFALO WINGS FLAVOR BUT DON'T WANT TO DEEP-FRY. SERVES 4 TO 6.

¾ cup Tabasco or other hot sauce

¼ cup fresh lime juice

¼ cup soy sauce

2 tablespoons olive oil

Salt and pepper

18 chicken wings (about 3 pounds), wing tips removed and remaining wing separated into 2 parts at the joint (see figures 1 and 2, page 218)

1. Light a charcoal or gas fire or preheat the oven according to the instructions in one of the Master Recipes, pages 219–21.

2. Combine the Tabasco, lime juice, soy sauce, oil, and salt and pepper to taste in a large bowl. Reserve ¼ cup of the mixture for basting the chicken wings as they cook. Add the chicken wings to the remaining sauce and toss to coat.

3. Grill or roast according to the relevant Master Recipe, brushing the chicken wings after every turn with the reserved sauce, until the chicken is dark and fully cooked. Transfer to a platter and serve immediately or cool slightly and serve warm.

◆

Buffalo Chicken Wings

THE IDEA OF DEEP-FRIED CHICKEN WINGS TOSSED WITH HOT SAUCE AND MARGARINE, AND SERVED WITH CARROTS, CELERY, AND A BLUE CHEESE DIPPING SAUCE ON THE SIDE, ORIGINATED IN UPSTATE NEW YORK, BUT THIS HAS BECOME STANDARD BAR FOOD ALL OVER THE COUNTRY. TOSS OUR VERSION WITH THE HOT SAUCE JUST BEFORE SERVING SO THAT THE WINGS RETAIN THEIR FRIED CRUNCH. SERVES 6 TO 8 AS AN APPETIZER.

1 to 2 quarts vegetable oil, for frying

18 chicken wings (about 3 pounds), wing tips removed and remaining wing separated into 2 parts at the joint (see figures 1 and 2, page 218)

Salt and pepper

2 tablespoons Tabasco or other hot sauce, or to taste

Carrot and celery sticks

Blue Cheese Dressing (recipe follows)

1. Heat several inches of oil to 360 degrees in an electric fryer or large, deep kettle. Sprinkle the chicken wings with salt and pepper. Fry the chicken in batches until golden, 10 to 12 minutes. Keep the chicken warm in a 200-degree oven until serving.

2. Place the warm, cooked wings in a large bowl and toss with the Tabasco sauce. Transfer to a platter and serve with the carrots, celery, and Blue Cheese Dressing on the side.

Blue Cheese Dressing

WE USE SEMISOFT BLUE CHEESE LIKE SAGA BLUE FOR AN EXTRA-CREAMY DRESSING, BUT ROQUEFORT OR ANOTHER SHARP BLUE CHEESE MAY BE SUBSTITUTED FOR A DRESSING WITH MORE BITE. MAKES ABOUT 1 1/2 CUPS.

1 1/2 cups sour cream
1 cup crumbled Saga Blue or other
    semisoft blue cheese, rind trimmed
1 small garlic clove, coarsely chopped
Salt and pepper

Combine the sour cream, cheese, and garlic in the work bowl of a food processor. Process until smooth. Scrape into a small bowl and season with salt and pepper to taste. Cover and refrigerate until ready to use, up to several days.

◆

Boned and Stuffed Thai-Style Chicken Wings

BONING THE "MIDDLE" SECTION OF A CHICKEN WING TAKES A LITTLE PRACTICE, BUT IT IS WELL WORTH THE EFFORT IF YOU WANT AN ELEGANT HORS D'OEUVRE. THE TRICK IS TO SEPARATE THE MEAT AND SKIN FROM THE BONE WITHOUT TEARING THE SKIN, SO THAT YOU HAVE AN INTACT POCKET TO HOLD THE STUFFING. HERE WE COMBINE GROUND CHICKEN AND MUSHROOMS. A FIERY CHILE DIPPING SAUCE COMPLEMENTS THE MILD FILLING. LOOK FOR FISH SAUCE IN SUPERMARKETS WITH AN ASIAN FOOD SECTION OR IN GOURMET STORES. SERVES 6 AS AN APPETIZER.

1 pound ground chicken
1/4 pound mushrooms, stems trimmed, minced
2 scallions, white and light green parts, minced
1 garlic clove, minced
1 1/2-inch piece fresh gingerroot, peeled
    and finely chopped
1 tablespoon Thai fish sauce
1/2 teaspoon vegetable oil, plus 1 to
    2 quarts for deep-frying
2 teaspoons cornstarch
12 chicken wings (about 2 pounds)

1. Combine the ground chicken, mushrooms, scallions, garlic, ginger, fish sauce, 1/2 teaspoon vegetable oil, and cornstarch in a medium bowl. Refrigerate the stuffing until firm, at least 30 minutes.

2. Cut each wing with a sharp knife or poultry shears at the joint that separates the drumstick from the double-boned section (see figure 1, opposite). Set aside the drumstick portion and reserve for another use.

3. To bone the double-boned portion of each wing, loosen the meat around the exposed joint with a sharp knife (see figure 2, opposite). Hold the wing in one hand and with the other hand push the skin and meat down the bone until it touches the small wing tip (see figure 3, opposite). If necessary, with a sharp knife loosen the tough ligaments connecting the meat to the bone. Sever the double bone with a sharp knife or poultry shears. You should have a pocket of skin and meat attached to a wing tip (see figure 4, opposite).

4. Heat several inches of oil to 360 degrees in an electric fryer or large, deep kettle. Insert about 1 tablespoon of the stuffing into each pocket, packing it in firmly with your fingers (see figure 5, opposite). The wings should be very full and the stuffing visible. Fry the chicken in batches until golden, 10 to 12 minutes. Keep the chicken warm in a 200-degree oven until serving. Serve with Chile Dipping Sauce.

◆

Chile Dipping Sauce

IF FRESH CHILES ARE UNAVAILABLE, SUBSTITUTE 1/4 TO 1/2 TEASPOON CRUSHED RED PEPPER FLAKES. MAKES ABOUT 3/4 CUP.

1 jalapeño or small hot red chile,
    stemmed, seeded, and finely chopped
1/4 cup fish sauce
1/4 cup fresh lime juice
1/4 cup sugar
1 small carrot, finely shredded
1 garlic clove, minced

Combine all the ingredients in a small bowl. Stir to dissolve the sugar. Refrigerate until ready to use.

BONING AND STUFFING CHICKEN WINGS

1. Cut each wing with a sharp knife or poultry shears at the joint that separates the drumstick from the double-boned section and wing tip. Reserve the drumsticks for another use.

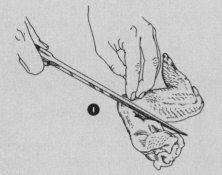

2. To bone the double-boned portion of each wing, loosen the meat around the exposed joint with the tip of a sharp knife.

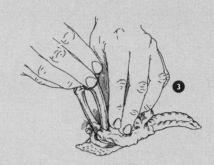

3. Hold the wing in one hand and, with the other hand, push the skin and meat down the bone until it touches the wing tip. Use the tip of a knife to cut away connective tissue attached to the bone.

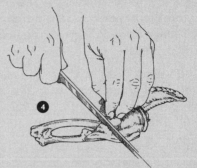

4. Sever the double bone with a sharp knife or poultry shears. You should have a pocket of skin and meat attached to a wing tip.

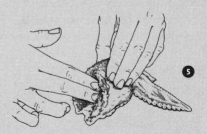

5. Firmly pack the stuffing into the pocket with your fingers. The stuffing should be visible at the top of the pocket.

Boned and Stuffed Southwestern Chicken Wings

THIS GROUND CHICKEN FILLING IS FLAVORED WITH CUMIN, GARLIC, AND CILANTRO. SERVE WITH CLASSIC RED SALSA (PAGE 148). **SERVES 6 AS AN APPETIZER.**

> 1 pound ground chicken
> 2 shallots, minced
> 3 garlic cloves, minced
> 2 teaspoons ground cumin
> ¼ cup minced fresh cilantro leaves
> 2 teaspoons cornstarch
> Salt and pepper
> 12 chicken wings (about 2 pounds)
> 1 to 2 quarts vegetable oil, for deep-frying

1. Combine the ground chicken, shallots, garlic, cumin, cilantro, cornstarch, and salt and pepper to taste in a medium bowl. Refrigerate the stuffing until firm, at least 30 minutes.

2. Cut each wing with a sharp knife or poultry shears at the joint that separates the "drumstick" from the double-boned section (see figure 1, page 225). Set aside the drumstick portion and reserve for another use.

3. To bone the double-boned portion of each wing, loosen the meat around the exposed joint with a sharp knife (see figure 2, page 225). Hold the wing in one hand and with the other hand push the skin and meat down the bone until it touches the small wing tip (see figure 3, page 225). If necessary, with a sharp knife loosen the tough ligaments connecting the meat to the bone. Sever the double bone with a sharp knife or poultry shears. You should have a pocket of skin and meat attached to a wing tip; see figure 4, page 225.

4. Heat several inches of oil to 360 degrees in an electric fryer or large, deep kettle. Insert about 1 tablespoon of the stuffing into each pocket, packing it in firmly with your fingers. The wings should be very full and the stuffing visible. Fry the chicken in batches until golden, 10 to 12 minutes. Keep the chicken warm in a 200-degree oven until serving.

Stir-Fried Chicken Wings

SERVES 4

THE KEY TO THIS RECIPE is to cook the wings through and then drain off excess fat before adding the vegetables. For more information on stir-frying, see chapter 7.

> 1½ pounds chicken wings, wing tips removed and remaining wing separated into 2 parts at the joint (see figures 1 and 2, page 218)
> 1 tablespoon soy sauce
> 1 tablespoon dry sherry
> 2 to 3 tablespoons peanut or vegetable oil
> 1½ pounds prepared vegetables, cut into small pieces and divided into several batches based on cooking times (see "Pointers for Success" on pages 88–89)
> 2 tablespoons minced scallions, white parts only
> 1 tablespoon minced garlic
> 1 tablespoon minced fresh gingerroot
> 1 recipe from Ten Sauces for Stir-Fry (pages 92–94)

1. Toss the chicken wings with the soy sauce and sherry in a medium bowl; set aside for 15 minutes, tossing once or twice.

STIR-FRYING
CHICKEN WINGS

/I\

CHICKEN WINGS CAN BE SUBSTITUTED FOR BONELESS CHICKEN CHUNKS IN ANY OF THE STIR-FRY RECIPES IN CHAPTER 7 (SEE PAGES 84–100). REPLACE THE ¾ POUND OF BONELESS CHICKEN WITH 1½ POUNDS OF WINGS TO MAKE FOUR MAIN-COURSE SERVINGS. THE WINGS TAKE LONGER TO COOK

(about 10 minutes) than boneless chicken, and much more fat is rendered in the process. Excess fat should be poured off before the vegetables and aromatics are cooked so that the finished dish won't be greasy. (Stir-fried chicken wings also make a good appetizer for six to eight people.)

2. Heat a 12- or 14-inch skillet over high heat for 3 to 4 minutes. The pan should be so hot you can hold an outstretched hand 1 inch over the pan for only 3 seconds. Add 1 tablespoon oil and swirl it so the oil evenly coats the bottom of the pan. Heat the oil until it just starts to shimmer and smoke. Check the heat with your hand as before.

3. Drain the chicken and add it to the pan. Stir-fry until well browned and cooked through, 10 to 12 minutes. Use a slotted spoon to transfer the cooked wings to a bowl. Cover and keep warm. Pour off excess fat from the pan.

4. Let the pan come back up to temperature, 1 to 2 minutes. When it is hot, drizzle in 2 teaspoons oil. When the oil just starts to smoke, add the first batch of long-cooking vegetables. Stir-fry until the vegetables are just tender-crisp, 1 to 2 minutes. Leaving the first batch in the pan, repeat with the remaining vegetables,

adding 1 teaspoon oil for each batch and cooking each set until crisp-tender, or wilted for leafy greens.

5. Clear the center of the pan and add the scallions, garlic, and ginger. Drizzle with ½ teaspoon oil. Mash into the pan with the back of a spatula. Cook until fragrant but not colored, about 10 seconds. Remove the pan from heat and stir the scallions, garlic, and ginger into the vegetables for 20 seconds.

6. Return the pan to the heat and add the cooked chicken wings. Stir in the sauce and stir-fry until the ingredients are well coated with sauce and sizzling hot, about 1 minute. Serve immediately with rice.

GROUND CHICKEN

/l\

THE GROWING POPULARITY OF POULTRY, AND CHICK-

EN IN PARTICULAR, HAS LED TO THE CREATION OF

NEW PRODUCTS THAT DID NOT EXIST ALL THAT

LONG AGO. GROUND CHICKEN IS ONE OF THESE. IN

PAST DECADES, ANY BUTCHER COULD HAVE GROUND

BONELESS CHICKEN—BUT NO ONE DID. IN AN ERA

WHEN FAT WAS NOT AN ISSUE, GROUND BEEF WAS KING.

Of course, all that has changed in recent times. With less than half the fat of lean beef, ground chicken is an excellent alternative for people who want to eat less fat but still enjoy spaghetti and meatballs, burritos, and meat loaf.

A couple of notes about buying ground chicken. Fat content can vary from brand to brand depending on the ratio of light to dark meat and how much skin is added. Good ground chicken needs some fat. (All white-meat chicken without any skin cooks up very dry and tasteless.) We tested several brands of ground chicken sold in our local supermarket against a combination of white and dark meat that our butcher ground for us. Frankly, we could not tell much difference among the samples, especially since most recipes call for adding spices and other flavorings to the ground chicken. Therefore, we developed all of the recipes in this chapter with Perdue ground chicken, which is the leading brand in most parts of the country. According to the package label, Perdue ground chicken contains 12 grams of fat per 4 ounces. If you prefer to control the fat content in ground chicken, ask your butcher to grind it to your specifications.

A few general notes about working with supermarket ground chicken. First, given the low fat content, you do not want to overcook it. Of course, it must lose all hint of pinkness and turn opaque throughout, but this will take just a few minutes over high heat, no more. Second, ground chicken is softer than ground beef and will not hold its shape as well. When making meatballs, for instance, firm them up in the refrigerator for an hour or so before trying to cook them.

While supermarket ground chicken is our choice for the vast majority of recipes in this chapter, there are a few cases where we prefer to grind our own chicken. For instance, French dumplings called quenelles should be made with all white meat for the most delicate texture. We recommend buying boneless, skinless breasts and grinding them in a food processor. Since the texture of the dumplings should be smooth, there is little danger of overprocessing them.

We also like to grind our own chicken for sausage. In this case, we recommend using thighs because of their higher fat content. (Sausage made with white meat is unpalatably dry.) We bone the thighs and then grind the meat and skin separately. Unlike for que-

nelles, chicken sausage requires ground meat with texture. Sausage made with coarse ground meat not only has a better mouth-feel but also larger pieces do a better job of holding on to moisture, a key factor in making good poultry sausages. Careful pulsing in the food processor will yield ⅜-inch pieces; the skin should be ground finer, to about ⅛ inch. We find that freezing the meat and skin for fifteen minutes makes it less likely to turn into a puree when processed.

If you like, use ground turkey in any of the recipes that follow, except the quenelles and sausages. Ground turkey is generally leaner than ground chicken and can cook up a bit dry. It does have a slightly firmer texture, which is one reason it is so popular when making burgers. For burgers and other recipes developed specifically for ground turkey, see chapter 29.

◆

Fusilli with Chicken Bolognese Sauce

THIS IS A LIGHTENED, STREAMLINED VERSION OF A FAVORITE MEAT SAUCE FOR PASTA. WE CHOSE FUSILLI, LITTLE CORKSCREW SHAPES, BECAUSE THEY CATCH THE BITS OF GROUND CHICKEN AND MUSHROOM, BUT OTHER SHAPES WITH PLACES TO CATCH THE SAUCE—TRY ORECCHIETTE OR RIGATONI—WORK EQUALLY WELL. SERVES 4 TO 6.

> 1 tablespoon olive oil
> 1 pound ground chicken
> ½ pound white button mushrooms, stems trimmed, sliced thin
> Salt and pepper
> 2 garlic cloves, minced
> 1 tablespoon chopped fresh oregano leaves or ½ teaspoon dried oregano
> 1 28-ounce can crushed tomatoes
> 1 pound fusilli or other dried pasta
> Grated Parmesan cheese, for the table

1. Heat the oil over medium-high heat in a large skillet and add the chicken. Cook, stirring frequently to break up the meat, until it loses its pink color, 3 to 4 minutes. Add the mushrooms and salt and pepper to taste and cook for 3 minutes. Add the garlic and oregano, and cook, stirring frequently, until the mushrooms release their juices, about 2 minutes. Add the tomatoes and simmer, stirring occasionally, until the sauce thickens, about 15 minutes longer. Taste for salt and pepper.

2. While the sauce is cooking, bring 4 quarts of water to a boil in a large pot or soup kettle. Add salt to taste and the fusilli and cook until al dente. Drain the pasta, toss it with the sauce, and serve with grated cheese passed at the table.

◆

Lasagne Cacciatore

CHUNKS OF CHICKEN MAKE SMOOTH LAYERING DIFFICULT, SO WE PREFER GROUND CHICKEN TO LARGER CHUNKS IN OUR LASAGNA. GROUND CHICKEN IS GENERALLY LOWER IN FAT THAN GROUND BEEF; TO FURTHER LIGHTEN THIS DISH, USE PART-SKIM MOZZARELLA CHEESE. THIS RECIPE CALLS FOR CONVENTIONAL DRIED LASAGNA NOODLES, NOT NO-BOIL NOODLES. SERVES 6 TO 8.

4 tablespoons olive oil
1 pound ground chicken
Salt and pepper
2 medium onions, halved and sliced thin
4 garlic cloves, minced
10 ounces white button mushrooms,
  stems trimmed, sliced thin
1 large red bell pepper, cored, seeded,
  and cut into ½-inch dice
1 28-ounce can crushed tomatoes
¼ cup finely chopped fresh parsley leaves
18 dried lasagna noodles (about 1 pound)
1 pound mozzarella cheese, shredded

1. Heat 2 tablespoons olive oil in a large saucepan over medium heat. Add the chicken, sprinkle generously with salt and pepper to taste, and cook, stirring frequently to break up the meat, until it is cooked through, 3 to 4 minutes. Remove the chicken from the pan and set aside.

2. Add the remaining 2 tablespoons olive oil to the pan along with the onions. Cook until the onions soften and begin to brown, about 10 minutes. Stir in the garlic and mushrooms and cook for 5 more minutes. Add the bell pepper and sauté for 2 minutes. Stir in the tomatoes, parsley, 1 teaspoon salt, and ½ teaspoon pepper. Add the chicken and simmer over low heat for 10 minutes. Taste for salt and pepper.

3. Meanwhile, preheat the oven to 400 degrees and bring 5 quarts of water to a boil in a large kettle or stockpot. Add salt to taste and the noodles and cook until almost al dente. Drain the noodles in a colander and then plunge them into a large bowl of ice water to stop the cooking. Drain the noodles on clean, dry cloth towels.

4. Grease a 13-by-9-inch lasagne pan. Smear several tablespoons of tomato sauce (without large chunks of chicken or vegetables) across the bottom. Line the bottom with a layer of pasta, making sure the noodles touch but do not overlap. Spread 1 cup of sauce over the pasta and sprinkle with ⅙ of mozzarella. Repeat the layering of pasta, sauce, and cheese 4 more times. For the sixth layer, sprinkle the remaining cheese over the noodles.

5. Bake the lasagne until the cheese turns golden brown in spots and the sauce is bubbling, about 25 minutes. Remove the pan from the oven, let the lasagne settle for 5 minutes, cut into squares, and serve immediately.

Spaghetti and Chicken Meatballs

BREAD SOAKED IN BUTTERMILK GIVES THESE MEATBALLS A TANGY FLAVOR AND PREVENTS THEM FROM DRYING OUT DURING COOKING. MEATBALLS MADE FROM CHICKEN ARE SOFTER THAN ONES MADE FROM BEEF OR PORK, SO THEY SHOULD BE REFRIGERATED FOR AN HOUR BEFORE FRYING TO PREVENT STICKING AND FALLING APART. BUILDING THE TOMATO SAUCE IN THE SAME PAN USED TO FRY THE MEATBALLS ADDS FLAVOR AND DEPTH. SIMPLY DRAIN OFF THE COOKING FAT, LEAVING BEHIND ANY BROWN BITS, THEN ADD FRESH OIL AND START THE SAUCE. SERVES 4 TO 6.

> 2 slices white sandwich bread, crusts removed, torn into small pieces
> 1/2 cup buttermilk *or* 6 tablespoons plain yogurt thinned with 2 tablespoons milk
> 1 pound ground chicken
> 1/4 cup grated Parmesan cheese, plus extra for the table
> 2 tablespoons finely minced fresh parsley leaves
> 1 large egg yolk
> 2 garlic cloves, minced
> Salt and pepper
> About 1 1/4 cups vegetable oil, for pan-frying
> 2 tablespoons extra-virgin olive oil
> 1 28-ounce can crushed tomatoes
> 1 tablespoon finely chopped fresh basil leaves
> 1 pound spaghetti

1. Combine the bread and buttermilk in a small bowl, mashing occasionally with a fork, until the buttermilk is absorbed and the mixture becomes a smooth paste, about 10 minutes (see figure 1, opposite).

2. Place the ground chicken, cheese, parsley, egg yolk, half of the garlic, and salt and pepper to taste in a medium bowl. Add the bread mixture and combine with a fork and then your hands until evenly mixed (see figure 2, opposite). Shape 3 tablespoons of the mixture into 1 1/2-inch round meatballs (you should get about 14 meatballs). Place meatballs on platter, cover with plastic wrap, and refrigerate until firm, about 1 hour.

3. Bring 4 quarts of water to a boil in a large kettle or soup pot.

4. Meanwhile, pour the vegetable oil into a 10- or 11-inch sauté pan to a depth of 1/4 inch. Turn the heat to medium-high. After several minutes, test the oil with the edge of a meatball. When the oil sizzles, add the meatballs in a single layer. Fry, turning several times, until nicely browned on all sides, about 10 minutes (see figure 3, opposite). Transfer the browned meatballs to a plate lined with paper towels.

5. Discard the oil in the pan but leave behind any browned bits. Add the olive oil along with the remaining garlic and sauté, scraping up any browned bits, just until the garlic is golden, about 30 seconds. Add the tomatoes, bring to a boil, and simmer gently until the sauce thickens, about 10 minutes. Stir in the basil and salt and pepper to taste. Add the meatballs and simmer, turning them occasionally, until heated through, about 5 minutes. Keep warm over low heat.

6. When the meatballs are returned to the sauce, add salt to taste and pasta to the boiling water. Cook until al dente, drain, and return to the pot. Ladle several large spoonfuls of tomato sauce (without meatballs) over the spaghetti and toss until the noodles are well coated. Divide the pasta among individual bowls and top each with a little more tomato sauce and several meatballs. Serve immediately, with grated cheese passed separately.

PREPARING MEATBALLS

1. Mash the bread cubes and buttermilk together with a fork. Let stand, mashing occasionally, until a smooth paste forms, about 10 minutes.

2. Once all the ingredients for the meatballs are in the bowl, mix with a fork to roughly combine. At this point, use your hands to make sure that the flavorings are evenly distributed throughout the mixture.

3. Meatballs must be browned well on all sides. This may involve standing meatballs on their sides near the end of the cooking process. If necessary, use tongs to lean them up against each other to get the final sides browned.

Chicken Picadillo

THIS CUBAN DISH IS TRADITIONALLY MADE WITH GROUND BEEF, BUT ADAPTS WELL TO GROUND CHICKEN. SERVE CHICKEN PICADILLO OVER FLUFFY WHITE RICE WITH BLACK BEANS ON THE SIDE. IT MAY ALSO BE USED AS A FILLING FOR EMPANADAS. **SERVES 6 TO 8.**

- ¼ cup olive oil
- 1 green bell pepper, cored, seeded, and cut into ¼-inch dice
- 1 medium onion, cut into ¼-inch dice
- 3 garlic cloves, minced
- 1 teaspoon ground cumin
- ½ teaspoon cayenne pepper
- 2 pounds ground chicken
- 1 28-ounce can whole tomatoes, drained, seeded, and coarsely chopped (see figure on page 107)
- ½ cup dry white wine
- ¼ cup raisins
- 2 tablespoons drained capers
- Salt and pepper

1. Heat the oil in a large skillet over medium-high heat. Add the bell pepper, onion, and garlic and sauté until softened, 3 to 4 minutes. Add the cumin, cayenne, and chicken; stir frequently, breaking up the meat into small chunks, until it is cooked through, 4 to 5 minutes.

2. Add the tomatoes, wine, raisins, capers, and salt and pepper to taste; bring to a simmer and cook until most of the liquid has evaporated, 8 to 10 minutes. Adjust the seasonings and serve.

Spicy Szechwan Chicken

A LIBERAL SPRINKLING OF GROUND SZECHWAN PEPPER-CORNS GIVES THIS GROUND CHICKEN STIR-FRY ITS DISTINCTIVE, AROMATIC FLAVOR. SPICY ASIAN CHILI OIL ADDS HEAT. LOOK FOR BOTH OF THESE ITEMS IN THE ASIAN SECTION OF YOUR SUPERMARKET OR AT ASIAN FOOD STORES. SERVE OVER STEAMED WHITE RICE OR FRESH (OR FROZEN) ASIAN EGG NOODLES. **SERVES 4.**

- 1 pound ground chicken
- ¼ cup soy sauce
- 2 tablespoons peanut oil
- 4 garlic cloves, minced
- 2 tablespoons finely chopped fresh gingerroot
- 8 scallions, white and light green parts, finely chopped
- 2 tablespoons smooth peanut butter
- 2 tablespoons chili oil
- 1 cup chicken stock or low-sodium canned chicken broth
- 1 tablespoon ground Szechwan peppercorns

1. Combine the chicken and soy sauce in a medium bowl and mix well.

2. Heat 1 tablespoon of peanut oil over medium-high heat in a large skillet and add the chicken. Cook, stirring frequently to break up the meat, until it loses its pink color, 3 to 4 minutes. Remove the chicken to a bowl with a slotted spoon.

3. Heat the remaining tablespoon of peanut oil in the pan. Add the garlic, ginger, and scallions and stir-fry for 30 seconds. Add the peanut butter, chili oil, and chicken stock, stirring well to dissolve the peanut butter. Simmer for 3 minutes and then return the chicken to the pan. Sprinkle the Szechwan peppercorns over the chicken, stir well, cook until heated through, another minute. Serve immediately with steamed white rice or noodles.

Spicy Thai Basil Chicken

SUPERMARKET-GROUND CHICKEN WORKS WELL IN THIS VERY QUICK THAI DISH. VERY SPICY, TINY THAI HOT PEPPERS ARE BEST HERE, BUT ANY FRESH HOT PEPPER WILL DO. SWEET THAI BASIL HAS A VERY DISTINCTIVE, AROMATIC FLAVOR (CILANTRO IS A BETTER SUBSTITUTE THAN REGULAR ITALIAN BASIL). SERVE WITH PLENTY OF STEAMED WHITE RICE TO OFFSET THE HEAT OF THE PEPPERS. A MILD VEGETABLE SIDE DISH, SUCH AS GRILLED OR BROILED SLICES OF EGGPLANT, IS ALSO A GOOD IDEA. **SERVES 4.**

¼ cup peanut oil
3 garlic cloves, minced
4 to 6 fresh hot peppers, stemmed,
   seeded, and finely chopped
1 pound ground chicken
1 tablespoon Thai fish sauce
1 teaspoon sugar
1 tablespoon soy sauce
2 tablespoons water
½ red bell pepper, cored, seeded, and cut
   into ¼-inch dice
¼ cup finely chopped fresh Thai basil or
   cilantro leaves

1. Heat a 12- or 14-inch skillet over high heat for 3 to 4 minutes. The pan should be so hot you can hold an outstretched hand 1 inch over the pan for only 3 seconds. Add the oil and swirl so that it evenly coats the bottom of the pan. Heat the oil until it just starts to shimmer and smoke.

2. Add the garlic and hot peppers and stir-fry for 30 seconds. Add the chicken and stir-fry until it is in small chunks and cooked through, about 2 minutes. Add the fish sauce, sugar, soy sauce, and water and stir-fry for another 30 seconds. Add the bell pepper and basil and stir-fry until the peppers begin to soften, about 2 minutes. Serve immediately.

Quick Ground Chicken Curry

HERE, STIR-FRIED GROUND CHICKEN IS SUBSTITUTED FOR CHICKEN THIGHS AND THE ACID USUALLY PROVIDED BY TOMATOES OR YOGURT IS SUPPLIED BY A SPRINKLE OF LIME JUICE AT THE END. THE DISH TAKES LESS THAN 15 MINUTES, START TO FINISH. SERVE WITH BASMATI RICE, PILAF STYLE (PAGE 132) OR STEAMED WHITE RICE. **SERVES 4.**

¼ cup flavorless (vegetable or canola) oil
1 medium onion, halved and sliced thin
4 large garlic cloves, pureed (see figures 1
   and 2, page 129)
1 ½ inch-piece fresh gingerroot, peeled
   and pureed (see page 129)
1 pound ground chicken
2 teaspoons ground cumin
2 teaspoons ground coriander
1 teaspoon ground turmeric
1 jalapeño chile, stemmed and minced
½ teaspoon salt, plus more to taste
¼ cup chopped fresh cilantro leaves
3 tablespoons fresh lime juice

1. Heat the oil in a large skillet, preferably nonstick, over medium-high heat until hot, but not smoking. Add the onion to the skillet; sauté until softened, 3 to 4 minutes.

2. Stir in the garlic, ginger, chicken, ground spices, jalapeño, and ½ teaspoon of salt. Cook, stirring almost constantly to break up the meat, until the chicken is cooked through, 3 to 4 minutes. Stir in the cilantro and the lime juice. Serve immediately.

Steamed Curried Chicken Dumplings

THESE PYRAMID-SHAPED DUMPLINGS CAN BE STEAMED OR PAN-FRIED TO MAKE POTSTICKERS. STEAMED DUMPLINGS WILL BE MOIST BUT RESILIENT WITH CHEWY SKINS. PAN-FRIED DUMPLINGS COMBINE CRISPY AND CHEWY TEXTURES WITH THE FLAVOR ASSOCIATED WITH BROWNING. WITH EITHER METHOD, SERVE THE DUMPLINGS AS SOON AFTER COOKING AS POSSIBLE, WITH SOY-GINGER DIPPING SAUCE. WONTON WRAPPERS ARE SOLD IN THE REFRIGERATED CASES OF MOST SUPERMARKETS. IF RED CURRY PASTE IS UNAVAILABLE FROM YOUR LOCAL GOURMET STORE OR ASIAN MARKET, INCREASE THE CURRY POWDER TO 1½ TEASPOONS AND ADD A PINCH OF CAYENNE PEPPER. MAKES 32 DUMPLINGS.

1 tablespoon vegetable oil
1 small onion, finely chopped
½ small celery stalk, minced
1 small garlic clove, minced
2 medium carrots, shredded (about 1 cup)
½ teaspoon Thai red curry paste
3 tablespoons unsweetened coconut milk
6 ounces ground chicken
2 teaspoons Thai fish sauce
½ teaspoon curry powder
2 tablespoons shredded fresh basil leaves
32 square wonton wrappers

FOR PAN-FRYING
½ cup chicken stock or low-sodium
   canned chicken broth or water
2 tablespoons vegetable oil

Soy-Ginger Dipping Sauce (recipe
   follows)

1. Heat the oil in a large skillet. Add the onion, celery, garlic, and carrots and sauté over medium heat until the vegetables soften, about 2 minutes longer. Add the curry paste and coconut milk; cook over medium-high heat, stirring to incorporate the curry paste, until most of the coconut milk has been absorbed. Transfer the vegetable mixture to a bowl; cool to room temperature.

2. Mix in the ground chicken, fish sauce, curry powder, and basil. Refrigerate to firm up texture, at least 30 minutes or up to 1 day.

3. Place 2 level teaspoons of the filling in the center of a wonton wrapper (see figure 1, opposite). Moisten the edges lightly with water. Bring up 2 opposite corners of the wrapper and join them over the filling (see figure 2, opposite). Bring up the 2 other corners and pinch all 4 together in a point to make a pyramid-shaped parcel. Pinch the seams firmly together to seal (see figure 3, opposite).

4. *If steaming*, grease a collapsible steamer basket (cooking spray works best). Fill a large soup kettle with enough water to come to the bottom of the basket. Bring to a simmer over medium-low heat. Arrange the dumplings ½ inch apart in the basket and lower the basket into the kettle. Increase the heat to high; cover and steam until the dumplings are cooked through, about 5 minutes.

If pan-frying, bring the chicken stock to a simmer in a small saucepan. Meanwhile, heat 2 tablespoons vegetable oil in a very large skillet over medium heat. When the oil is hot and hazy, add the dumplings, flat sides down, to the pan. Fry until the bottoms are browned, about 2 minutes. Add the simmering broth to the skillet, pouring around the dumplings. Cover and cook until the liquid is absorbed, 3 minutes longer. Uncover and let the dumplings fry until the bottoms are crisp again, about 1 minute.

5. Serve immediately with Soy-Ginger Dipping Sauce.

Soy-Ginger Dipping Sauce

DUMPLINGS, WITH THEIR RATHER BLAND DOUGH WRAP-
PERS, BENEFIT FROM A TANGY DIPPING SAUCE LIKE THIS
ONE. MAKES 1 CUP.

1/4 cup soy sauce
1/4 cup rice vinegar
2 1/2 teaspoons sugar
1/2 medium scallion, finely chopped
2 teaspoons finely shredded fresh
    gingerroot
1/2 teaspoon Asian sesame oil
1/2 teaspoon chili oil

Bring the soy sauce, vinegar, sugar, and 1/4 cup water to boil over medium heat, stirring briefly, until sugar dissolves. Pour into a bowl; stir in the scallion, ginger, and sesame and chili oils. The sauce can be covered and refrigerated overnight.

STEP-BY-STEP

FORMING DUMPLINGS

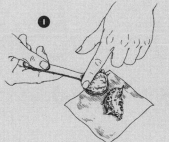

1. Place 2 level teaspoons of the filling in the center of a wonton wrapper.

2. Moisten the edges of the wrapper lightly with water. Bring up the 2 opposite corners of the wrapper and join them over the filling.

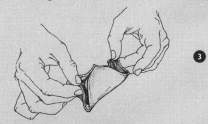

3. Bring up the 2 other corners and pinch all 4 together in a point to make a pyramid-shaped parcel. Pinch the seams firmly together to seal.

Ground Chicken Burritos

SUPERMARKET GROUND CHICKEN, WELL SEASONED
AND QUICKLY SAUTEED, MAKES A GREAT BURRITO
FILLING. THESE BURRITOS ARE MUCH LIGHTER AND
FRESHER TASTING THAN TYPICAL RESTAURANT FARE;
INSTEAD OF HIGH-FAT REFRIED BEANS, WE SIMPLY
REHEAT PLAIN BLACK BEANS IN A SKILLET AND MASH
THEM WITH A LITTLE OLIVE OIL. THE OPTIONAL PICK-
LED JALAPEÑOS ADD A VINEGARY BLAST OF MILD HEAT.
LOOK FOR THEM IN A SUPERMARKET NEAR OTHER
MEXICAN FOODS. SERVES 4.

    3 tablespoons olive oil
    2 15-ounce cans black beans, drained and
        rinsed
    Salt and pepper
    ¾ pound ground chicken
    1 garlic clove, minced
    1 teaspoon ground cumin
    ½ teaspoon chili powder
    ¼ teaspoon cayenne pepper
    ¼ cup chopped fresh cilantro leaves
    4 large flour tortillas
    4 large romaine lettuce leaves, cut
        crosswise into ¼-inch strips
    1 avocado, peeled and cut into ¼-inch
        dice
    2 medium tomatoes, cored, seeded, and
        cut into ¼-inch dice
    2 tablespoons fresh lime juice
    ½ cup sour cream (optional)
    4 pickled jalapeño chiles, coarsely
        chopped (optional)

1. Heat 2 tablespoons of oil and the black beans in a
medium skillet set over medium heat, lightly mashing
them with a fork. Season with salt and pepper to taste.
Cover and keep warm.

2. Heat the remaining tablespoon of oil over high
heat in a medium skillet. Add the chicken, garlic,
cumin, chili powder, and cayenne and stir-fry until the
chicken is cooked through and in small chunks, about
2 minutes. Stir in the cilantro, scrape the cooked
chicken into a bowl, season with salt and pepper to
taste, and cover with aluminum foil to keep warm.

FOLDING UP A BURRITO

1. Spoon filling in 4-inch-wide column down the
center of each tortilla. Fold the bottom quarter,
then the left side, of each tortilla up over the filling.

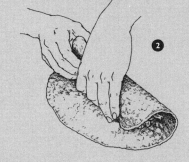

2. Starting at the left side, roll the tortilla into a
fairly tight cylinder.

3. Lay the tortillas on a work surface. Spoon a 4-inch-
wide column of warmed beans onto each tortilla. Top
with the chicken, lettuce, avocado, and tomatoes.
Sprinkle each burrito with the lime juice and season
with salt and pepper to taste.

4. Fold the bottom quarter of each tortilla up over the
filling, and then roll from the side into a cylinder (see
above) and place the burritos on individual serving
plates. Serve with a dollop of sour cream topped with
some jalapeños on each plate.

Indian Chicken Patties in Pita Pockets

BROILING THESE HIGHLY SPICED PATTIES GIVES THEM A NICE CRUST WITHOUT ADDING FAT. SPOON SOME CUCUMBER RAITA OR PLAIN YOGURT INTO THE PITA POCKETS ALONG WITH CHICKEN PATTIES. IF YOU LIKE, ADD SOME SHREDDED LETTUCE AND DICED TOMATOES AS WELL. SERVES 4.

- 1 1-inch piece fresh gingerroot, peeled and coarsely chopped
- 2 garlic cloves, peeled and coarsely chopped
- 2 jalapeño chiles, stemmed, seeded, and coarsely chopped
- ¼ cup tightly packed fresh mint leaves
- 1 small onion, peeled and quartered
- 2 teaspoons ground cumin
- 1 teaspoon salt
- 1 pound ground chicken
- 4 large pita pockets
- Cucumber Raita (page 133) or plain yogurt

1. Combine the ginger, garlic, jalapeños, mint, onion, cumin, and salt in the work bowl of a food processor. Process until everything is finely chopped, scraping down the sides of the bowl once or twice as necessary. Add the chicken and pulse once or twice to mix, being careful not to overprocess.

2. Preheat the broiler and adjust the oven rack so that the patties will be about 4 inches from the heating element. Form the chicken into 8 patties each, about 3 inches in diameter. Transfer the patties to a broiler pan and broil, turning once, until they are browned on both sides and cooked all the way through, 6 to 8 minutes.

3. Place 2 patties inside each pita pocket and spoon some cucumber raita or plain yogurt on top of the patties. Serve immediately.

Chicken and Apple Meat Loaf with Mushroom Gravy

GROUND CHICKEN CAN MAKE A GREAT LIGHTER MEAT LOAF, AS LONG AS A MOISTENING INGREDIENT (WE FOUND THAT CHOPPED APPLES WORK ESPECIALLY WELL) IS ADDED TO THE MIX. WE SUGGEST EITHER SHAPING THE MEAT MIXTURE INTO A FREE-FORM LOAF (IF YOU LIKE A LOT OF CRISPY CRUST) OR BAKING IT IN A PERFORATED MEAT LOAF PAN TO PREVENT IT FROM STEWING IN ITS OWN JUICES. SERVE WITH QUICK MUSHROOM GRAVY (RECIPE FOLLOWS) AND PERFECT MASHED POTATOES (PAGE 147). SERVES 6 TO 8.

- 2 teaspoons vegetable oil
- 1 medium onion, chopped
- 2 garlic cloves, minced
- 2 large eggs
- 1 teaspoon dried thyme
- 1 teaspoon salt
- ½ teaspoon pepper
- 2 teaspoons Dijon mustard
- 2 teaspoons Worcestershire sauce
- ½ cup whole milk or plain yogurt
- 1 tart apple, such as Granny Smith, peeled and grated
- 2 pounds ground chicken
- 1⅓ cups fresh bread crumbs
- ¼ cup finely chopped fresh parsley leaves

1. Heat the oven to 350 degrees. Heat the oil in a medium skillet. Add the onion and garlic; sauté until softened, about 5 minutes. Set aside to cool.

2. Mix the eggs with the thyme, salt, pepper, mustard, Worcestershire sauce, milk, and apple. Combine the egg mixture with the meat in a large bowl, along with the bread crumbs, parsley, and cooked onion and garlic. Mix with a fork until evenly blended and meat mixture does not stick to the bowl. (If the mixture sticks, add additional milk or yogurt, a couple tablespoons at a time, until the mix no longer sticks.)

(continued on next page)

3. Turn the meat mixture onto a foil-lined (for easy cleanup) shallow baking pan (see figure 1). With wet hands, pat the mixture into approximately a 9-by-5-inch loaf shape. Or, turn the meat mixture into a special meat loaf pan with a perforated bottom and drip pan (see figures 2 and 3). Bake the loaf until it registers 160 degrees on an instant-read thermometer, about 1 hour 15 minutes. Cool at least 20 minutes. Slice the meat loaf and serve with Quick Mushroom Gravy.

◆

Quick Mushroom Gravy

THIS FLAVORFUL GRAVY, RELATIVELY LOW IN FAT, MAKES A GOOD QUICK ACCOMPANIMENT TO EITHER THE CHICKEN AND APPLE MEAT LOAF OR THE CHICKEN CROQUETTES (OPPOSITE PAGE). TRY SUBSTITUTING SHIITAKE OR CREMINI MUSHROOMS FOR A MORE REFINED FLAVOR. MAKES ABOUT 2 CUPS.

> 2 tablespoons butter
> 1 medium onion, finely chopped
> ½ pound white button mushrooms, stems trimmed, sliced thin
> ¼ teaspoon dried thyme
> 1 ½ tablespoons cornstarch
> 1 cup chicken stock or low-sodium canned chicken broth
> ½ cup white wine
> Salt and pepper

1. Heat the butter in a medium saucepan. Add the onion and cook until softened, 3 to 4 minutes. Add the mushrooms and thyme and cook until they release their juices, 5 to 7 minutes.

2. In a small bowl, dissolve the cornstarch in 3 tablespoons of stock. Add the remaining stock and wine to the pan and bring to a boil; simmer for 2 or 3 minutes. Add the cornstarch mixture and cook, stirring, until the gravy thickens, about 1 minute. Season with salt and pepper to taste. Serve immediately or keep warm over low heat.

SHAPING MEAT LOAF

☙

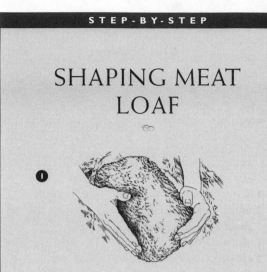

1. With wet hands, pat mixture into approximately a 9-by-5-inch loaf shape on a foil-lined shallow baking dish.

2. A special meat loaf pan is actually 2 pans that fit together. The first pan, which holds the meat loaf, has a perforated bottom, which allows fat to flow into the drip pan below. When baked in this kind of pan, meat loaf is crustless and soft.

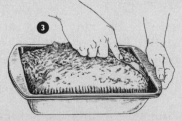

3. If using a perforated loaf pan, before baking the meat loaf use a fork to pull the mixture away from the pan sides to allow fat to drip down into the bottom pan.

Chicken Croquettes

THESE CROQUETTES ARE AN ALTERNATIVE TO CHICKEN MEAT LOAF, MADE A LITTLE MORE DELICATE BECAUSE OF THE EGG WHITES FOLDED INTO THE MIXTURE. THEY MAY ALSO BE SERVED WITH QUICK MUSHROOM GRAVY (OPPOSITE PAGE). SERVES 6 TO 8.

 3 slices white sandwich bread, crusts
 removed, torn into small pieces
 ¼ cup heavy cream
 1¾ pounds ground chicken
 2 eggs, separated, plus 1 whole egg for
 dipping
 1 shallot, finely chopped
 2 tablespoons chopped fresh tarragon
 leaves
 Salt and pepper
 1 cup plain bread crumbs
 4 tablespoons butter
 4 tablespoons vegetable oil
 1 lemon, cut into wedges (optional)

1. Combine the bread and cream in a small bowl and set aside for several minutes.

2. Combine the bread mixture, chicken, egg yolks, shallot, tarragon, and salt and pepper to taste in the work bowl of a food processor. Pulse 3 or 4 times to blend, but do not overblend to the point of pureeing it. Transfer to a large bowl.

3. Beat the egg whites until they hold stiff peaks. Fold them into the meat mixture. Cover and refrigerate until firm enough to form into patties, 2 to 3 hours.

4. Place the remaining egg in a shallow bowl or pie plate and lightly beat it. Place the bread crumbs in another shallow bowl or pie plate; season with salt and pepper if desired. With wet hands, shape the meat mixture into 12 oval croquettes. One at a time, dip the croquettes into the beaten egg, and then coat with the bread crumbs.

5. Preheat oven to 200 degrees. Heat 2 tablespoons of oil and 2 tablespoons of butter in a large skillet over medium-high heat. Fry half of the croquettes, turning once, until brown and crisp, about 15 minutes. Remove them from the pan with a slotted spoon and drain on paper towels. Transfer them to a baking sheet and keep warm in the oven. Add the remaining butter and oil to the pan, heat, and fry the remaining croquettes. Serve immediately with lemon wedges, if desired.

◆

Chicken Quenelles in Chicken and Escarole Broth

QUENELLES ARE LIGHT BUT RICH DUMPLINGS OFTEN MADE FROM GROUND VEAL, FISH, OR CHICKEN. FOR THE MOST DELICATE AND SMOOTHEST CHICKEN DUMPLINGS, WE GRIND OUR OWN BONELESS, SKINLESS BREASTS IN THE FOOD PROCESSOR, ALONG WITH CREAM, EGG, AND SEASONINGS. THE MIXTURE IS REFRIGERATED UNTIL FIRM AND THEN DROPPED BY SPOONFULS INTO SIMMERING STOCK. THE RICHNESS OF THE QUENELLES IS OFFSET BY THE ESCAROLE, WHICH IS SIMMERED IN THE SAME BROTH USED TO COOK THE DUMPLINGS. SERVES 6 TO 8.

 ½ pound boneless, skinless
 chicken breasts
 1 egg
 1 cup heavy cream
 ½ teaspoon salt
 Pinch pepper
 Pinch ground nutmeg
 2 quarts Long-Cooked Traditional
 Chicken Stock (page 285)
 1 small head escarole, core and tough
 outer leaves discarded; inner leaves
 separated

1. Combine the chicken, egg, cream, salt, pepper, and nutmeg in the work bowl of a food processor. Process until finely ground, about 30 seconds. Scrape the mixture into a bowl, cover with plastic wrap, and refrigerate until firm, 2 to 3 hours.

(continued on next page)

2. Bring the stock to a boil in a large kettle or stock-pot and lower the heat so the stock remains at a gentle simmer. Drop heaping tablespoonfuls of the dumpling mixture into the simmering stock (see figure below). Cook the dumplings, turning them gently with a spoon for about 5 minutes; continue until completely opaque, 8 to 10 minutes. Remove the dumplings with a slotted spoon and set aside on a plate.

3. Add the escarole to the simmering stock and cook until the leaves are tender, about 10 minutes. Taste the stock for salt and pepper and return the quenelles to the stock to reheat. Ladle the broth, quenelles, and escarole into soup bowls. Serve immediately.

STEP-BY-STEP

MAKING QUENELLES

To form quenelles, scoop a heaping tablespoonful of the mixture onto a wet spoon. Moisten your finger and use it to roll the mixture into the gently simmering stock.

Chicken Sausage with Apples and Sage

WE LIKE TO MAKE A LARGE BATCH OF SAUSAGE AND THEN DIVIDE IT INTO SMALL PACKAGES THAT CAN BE FROZEN. THIS SAUSAGE IS A GOOD FLAVORING FOR BEAN OR RICE DISHES OR AS PART OF A STUFFING. YOU CAN ALSO SHAPE THIS BREAKFAST SAUSAGE INTO THIN 2-INCH PATTIES AND COOK THEM IN AN UNGREASED NONSTICK SKILLET OVER MEDIUM HEAT UNTIL NICELY BROWNED ON BOTH SIDES, ABOUT 10 MINUTES. EACH 1/2-POUND PACKAGE WILL MAKE FOUR PATTIES. WHETHER USING THE SAUSAGE IN BULK OR TO MAKE PATTIES, IT'S A GOOD IDEA TO FRY A LITTLE OF IT RIGHT AWAY, SO YOU CAN ADJUST SEASONINGS BEFORE FREEZING IT. MAKES 7 SMALL PACKAGES, EACH ABOUT 1/2 POUND.

> 1 cup apple cider
> 4 1/2 pounds chicken thighs with bones and skin
> 3 ounces dried apples, finely chopped
> 2 teaspoons pepper
> 2 teaspoons dried sage
> 1 teaspoon salt
> 1/4 teaspoon ground ginger
> 1/8 teaspoon ground cinnamon
> 1/8 teaspoon ground nutmeg

1. Boil down the cider in a nonreactive saucepan almost to a syrup, 2 to 3 tablespoons. Let cool and set aside.

2. Bone and grind the chicken, grinding the skin separately (see figures 1–6, opposite page).

3. Combine the cider, chicken, skin, and remaining ingredients in a large bowl. Blend thoroughly but gently with your hands. (Don't overmix, or the fat will melt.) Shape several tablespoons of the mixture into a small patty. Fry the patty in an ungreased nonstick skillet set over medium heat until cooked through. Taste and adjust the seasonings in the remaining sausage as needed.

4. Divide the sausage into 1/2-pound portions, wrap tightly in plastic or aluminum foil, and refrigerate for 2 days or freeze for several months.

PREPARING SAUSAGE

1. Remove the skin from the chicken thighs and set it aside. Cut along the bone with a sharp paring knife to expose it.

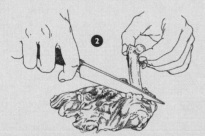

2. After loosening the meat from one end, lift the bone up so that it is perpendicular to the thigh and continue to cut the meat away from the bone. The boned meat should weigh about 3½ pounds.

3. Use a chef's knife to dice the meat into 1-inch pieces.

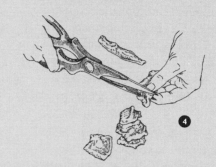

4. Snip the skin into 1-inch pieces. Freeze the skin and meat for 15 minutes to firm it up.

5. Process the meat in 1-pound batches into ⅜-inch pieces. Do not overprocess the meat into a slurry.

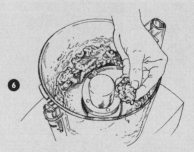

6. Process the skin into ⅛-inch pieces. (The fat should be fairly smooth.) Pick through and discard any large pieces.

Mediterranean Chicken Sausage

THIS AROMATIC SAUSAGE IS NOT OVERLY SPICY BUT HAS PLENTY OF FLAVOR. IT IS PARTICULARLY GOOD WITH LENTILS, GREENS, SEAFOOD SOUPS, OR PASTA DISHES. IF YOU WANT TO USE THIS SAUSAGE TO MAKE BREAKFAST PATTIES, FOLLOW THE SHAPING AND COOKING INSTRUCTIONS ON PAGE 242. MAKES 7 SMALL PACKAGES, EACH ABOUT ½ POUND.

2 tablespoons olive oil
2 medium onions, sliced
4½ pounds chicken thighs with bones and skin
1 tablespoon tomato paste
4 large garlic cloves, minced
2 tablespoons paprika
2 teaspoons fennel seeds, coarsely ground
2 teaspoons ground cumin
2 teaspoons ground coriander
2 teaspoons pepper
1 teaspoon salt
1 teaspoon ground turmeric
1 teaspoon sugar
½ teaspoon ground allspice
½ teaspoon cayenne pepper
2 teaspoons minced lemon zest
1 tablespoon fresh lemon juice
¼ cup minced fresh parsley leaves
2 tablespoons minced fresh mint leaves *or* 2 teaspoons dried mint

1. Heat the oil in a medium skillet over medium heat. Add the onions; sauté until soft but not colored, about 7 minutes. Transfer to food processor fitted with the steel blade; pulse until the onions are ground coarse. Set aside.

2. Bone and grind the chicken, grinding the skin separately (see figures 1–6, page 243).

3. Combine the onions, chicken, skin, and remaining ingredients in a large bowl. Blend thoroughly but gently with your hands. (Don't overmix, or the fat will melt.) Shape several tablespoons of the mixture into a small patty. Fry the patty in an ungreased nonstick skillet set over medium heat until cooked through. Taste and adjust the seasonings in the remaining sausage as needed.

4. Divide the sausage into ½-pound portions, wrap tightly in plastic or aluminum foil, and refrigerate for 2 days or freeze for several months.

CHAPTER 18

CHICKEN AND
DUMPLINGS

/I\

DESPITE AMERICA'S ONGOING LOVE AFFAIR WITH

COMFORT FOOD, CHICKEN AND DUMPLINGS HASN'T

MADE A COMEBACK LIKE ITS BAKED COUSIN, CHICKEN

POT PIE. AFTER MAKING SEVERAL DOZEN BATCHES OF

DUMPLINGS, WE KNOW WHY. AS TRICKY AS PIE PASTRY

AND BISCUITS ARE FOR POT PIE, DUMPLINGS ARE FAR

MORE TEMPERAMENTAL. DRY OVEN HEAT AND RICH

SAUCE CAMOUFLAGE MINOR BISCUIT AND PASTRY

flaws in pot pie. In contrast, moist steam heat tends to make dumplings gummy or leaden.

We wanted to develop a dumpling that was light yet substantial, tender yet durable. But which style of dumpling to explore? In the South, dumplings are either rolled thin and cut into noodlelike strips or rolled thick and stamped out like biscuits. In other parts of the country, especially the Midwest and East, dumplings are shaped by hand into round, puffy balls. Could these three styles come from the same dough, or would we need to develop separate doughs to accommodate each style?

Most flour-based dumplings are made of flour, salt, and one or more of the following ingredients: butter, eggs, milk, and baking powder. Depending on the ingredient list, dumplings are usually mixed in one of three ways.

The most common mixing method is a biscuit or pastry style in which cold butter is cut into the dry ingredients, then cold milk and/or eggs are stirred in until just mixed. Other dumplings are made by simply mixing wet into dry ingredients. Also, many of the eggier dumplings are made *pâte à choux* style, adding flour to hot water and butter, then whisking in eggs, one at a time.

We made batch after batch of dumplings in some combination of the above ingredients and following one of the three mixing methods. (We even made a yeast-based dumpling that, when cooked, tasted like soggy bread!) After our first day of testing, we hadn't made a single dumpling that we really liked. In short, we found dumplings made with eggs tended to be tough and chewy, while dumplings made without eggs tended to be fragile, often disintegrating into the cooking liquid. Dumplings made without enough liquid tended to be leaden while those made with too much liquid were particularly prone to disintegrate.

We finally made progress when we tried cutting butter into flour, baking powder, and salt. Instead of the usual cold liquid into the dry ingredients, we added hot liquid to the flour-butter mixture. Dumplings made according to this method were light and fluffy, yet they held up beautifully during cooking. These were the firm yet tender dumplings we were looking for. There turns out to be a scientific reason behind our finding. Hot liquids, unlike cold ones,

expand and set the starch in the flour, keeping it from absorbing too much of the cooking liquid.

Because we were adding hot milk, we questioned why it was necessary to cut in the cold butter. Why couldn't we simply heat the milk and butter together and dump it into the dry ingredients? A side-by-side tasting of dumplings made from the two different mixing techniques made us realize that cutting the butter into the flour was indeed an unnecessary step. The simpler route of adding the hot milk and melted butter to the dry ingredients actually yielded more substantial, better-textured dumplings.

Now that we had the technique down, it was time to test the formula. Would a dumpling made with cake flour be more tender than one made with all-purpose? Was butter the best fat, or would dumplings made with shortening or chicken fat taste better? Which liquid offered the best flavor and texture: milk, buttermilk, chicken stock, or water?

We thought that cake flour dumplings would be even lighter textured than those made with all-purpose. In fact, just the opposite was true. They were tight, spongy little dumplings with a metallic, acidic aftertaste. The process by which cake flour is chlorinated leaves it acidic and so sets eggs faster in baking, resulting in a smoother, finer-textured cake. The acidic flavor is masked in a batter rich with butter, sugar, and eggs, but it really comes through in a simple dumpling dough.

Although we were pretty sure the dumplings made with vegetable shortening wouldn't taste as good as those made with butter, we had high hopes for the ones made with chicken fat. After a side-by-side test of dumplings made with butter, shortening, and chicken fat, we selected those made with butter. The shortening dumplings tasted flat, like cooked flour and chicken stock, while the ones made with chicken fat tasted like flour and strongly flavored chicken stock. Butter gave the dumplings that extra flavor dimension and richness they needed.

Liquids were simple. Dumplings made with chicken stock, much like those made with chicken fat, tasted too similar to the broth. Those made with water were pretty dull. Whole milk dumplings were tender with a pleasant biscuity flavor and are our first choice.

Having decided on dumplings made with all-purpose flour, butter, milk, baking powder, and salt, we tested the formula by shaping them into balls, cutting them into biscuit shapes, and rolling them thin and cutting them into strips. Regardless of shape, we got the same consistent results: tender yet sturdy dumplings. The only difference among the three shapes is cooking time.

After refining the dumpling, we turned our energies to updating the chicken part of the dish. Our first few attempts were disastrous. To make the dish clean and sleek, we left the chicken pieces on the bone, cut the vegetables into long, thin strips and thickened the broth ever so slightly. As we ate the finished product, we realized that we needed a knife (to cut the chicken off the bone), a fork (to eat the vegetables, dumplings, and meat), and a spoon (for the broth). Although we wanted the dish to look beautiful, it had to be eater-friendly. In order for the dish to work, the chicken had to come off the bone, the vegetables needed to be cut a little smaller, and the broth required reducing and thickening. As the dish evolved, we worked toward making it not only a one-dish but also a one-utensil meal.

Chicken and dumplings and chicken pot pie share common ingredients and similar techniques, but each dish has a unique feel. Chicken pot pie is more casserole-like, while chicken and dumplings is more like a stew. So even though we thought boneless, skinless chicken breasts were a wonderful timesaving substitute for a whole chicken in chicken pot pie, the breasts didn't seem quite right for this dish. We preferred large, uneven chunks of light and dark meat, which meant we needed to start with a whole chicken. However, we did develop a variation using boneless, skinless breasts; it takes much less time but loses some of the flavor and character of the Master Recipe.

Because we wanted this dish to serve six to eight, and because we preferred bigger chunks of meat, we chose the larger oven roasters over the small fryer hens. We also preferred oven roasters over the stewing hens called for in many recipes. Although we loved the flavor of the hen's broth, it had to simmer for two hours before becoming tender. And once tender, the meat was dry.

We found that our quick stock-making method (see chapter 21) was perfectly suited to this dish since this method yields rich, flavorful chicken broth and perfectly poached chicken parts. We remove and cut the back, the wings, and the giblets (excluding liver) of an oven roaster into 2-inch pieces. The remaining parts —legs, thighs, and breasts—are set aside for poaching. We sauté the bony chicken pieces with onion until they loose their raw color. The heat is turned down, the pot is covered, and the pieces cook until all their liquid is released, in just twenty minutes.

Once the chicken pieces have "sweated," the meaty chicken parts and water are added. This step allows the cook to finish the stock and poach the chicken at the same time, the rich poaching liquid infusing the chicken while the bony chicken parts further enrich the broth. In twenty minutes, the parts are perfectly cooked and the stock is incredibly potent. Once this step is complete, the dish can be made in less than a half-hour.

Our updated chicken and dumplings needed vegetables, but where and how to cook them? In an attempt to streamline the process, we tried cooking the vegetables along with the poaching chicken parts. After fishing out hot, slightly overcooked vegetables from among the chicken parts and pieces, we decided this little shortcut wasn't worth it. So we simply washed the pot, returned it to the stove, and steamed the vegetables for ten minutes while removing the meat from the bone, straining the stock, and making the dumpling dough. Because the vegetables would cook again for a short time in the sauce, we wanted them slightly undercooked at this point. Steaming them separately gave us more control.

With our meat poached and off the bone, our stock degreased and strained, and our vegetables steamed to perfection, we were ready to complete the dish, like someone ready to stir-fry. We chose thickening at the beginning of this final phase, rather than at the end. (Once the chicken, vegetables, and dumplings are added to the pot, it's hard to stir in and evenly distribute any thickener.)

To a roux of flour and chicken fat (once again, using every bit of the chicken to make the dish), we added our homemade stock and stirred until thickened. Although we needed 6 cups of stock to poach the chicken parts, we found this quantity of liquid made the dish much too saucy, more like chicken and

FIVE DUMPLINGS, THREE SHAPES

/|\

THE SIMPLE MASTER RECIPE FOR DUMPLINGS IS NOTHING MORE THAN FLOUR, BAKING POWDER, AND SALT MIXED WITH MELTED BUTTER AND HOT MILK. THE DOUGH IS MIXED WITH A FORK OR KNEADED BRIEFLY BY HAND JUST UNTIL IT COMES TOGETHER. THE DOUGH MAY BE FORMED INTO THREE

shapes (see illustrations). Note that cooking times for the thin strip dumplings will be less than for larger balls or biscuit rounds. The dumplings should be made while the chicken is cooling and the vegetables are steaming.

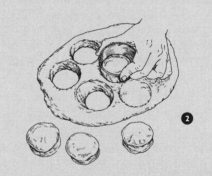

2. For biscuitlike dumplings, roll the dough to a thickness of ½ inch. Use a 2-inch biscuit cutter or a round drinking glass top to cut out dough rounds.

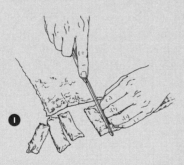

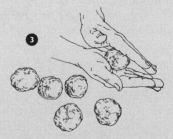

1. For flat noodlelike dumplings, roll the dough to a thickness of ⅛ inch. Cut the dough into strips that measure about 2 inches long and ½ inch across.

3. For round, puffy dumplings, divide the dough into 18 pieces. Roll each piece into a 1½-inch round ball.

Baking Powder Dumplings

MAKES ENOUGH DUMPLINGS
FOR 6 TO 8 SERVINGS

THIS BASIC RECIPE may be flavored with herbs, cornmeal, or even raisins.

> 2 cups all-purpose flour
> 1 tablespoon baking powder
> ¾ teaspoon salt
> 3 tablespoons unsalted butter
> 1 cup milk

1. Mix the flour, baking powder, and salt in a medium bowl. Heat the butter and milk to a simmer and add to the dry ingredients.

2. Mix with a fork until the mixture just comes together. Following the instructions with the illustrations on the opposite page, form the dough into the desired shape. Set aside and cook according to recipe instructions.

Herb Dumplings

Make Baking Powder Dumplings, mixing ¼ cup minced fresh parsley, chives, tarragon, or scallion greens with the dry ingredients.

◆

Dill Dumplings

Make Baking Powder Dumplings, mixing ¼ cup minced fresh dill with the dry ingredients.

◆

Cornmeal Dumplings

Make Baking Powder Dumplings, replacing ½ cup flour with ½ cup yellow cornmeal.

◆

Raisin Dumplings

Make Baking Powder Dumplings, mixing ¼ cup coarsely chopped raisins with the dry ingredients.

dumpling soup. Pulling off and reserving 2 cups of stock solved the problem.

To the thickened liquid, we added our shaped dough for steaming. But when it came time to add the meat and vegetables to the pot, we found it difficult to stir them in among all those fragile little dumplings. With the major meat and vegetable additions, the dish cooled down dramatically and required additional cooking. So we switched the order, adding chicken and vegetables to the thickened sauce, then steaming the dumplings. Not only did the dumplings remain undisturbed but also the chicken and vegetables had an opportunity to mingle with one another and the sauce.

A few peas and a little parsley made the dish beautiful, and a little dry sherry or vermouth, as we found with chicken pot pie, heightened the flavor. A touch of cream enriches and beautifies, but the dish is equally good without it.

The final dish looks good, tastes great, and is simple to make. Best of all, it can be eaten with just a fork.

Chicken and Dumplings

SERVES 6 TO 8

A TOUCH OF HEAVY CREAM gives the dish a more refined look and rich flavor, but you may want to omit it. For best results, prepare and shape the dumplings while the vegetables steam in step 2. We like boiling onions—small yellow or white onions about 2 inches in diameter—in this recipe.

You may substitute a dozen pearl onions in their place. Use the same Dutch oven to make the stock, steam the vegetables, and assemble the final dish.

1 large roasting chicken (6 to 7 pounds), rinsed, patted dry, and cut into 8 pieces (see "Cutting Up a Whole Chicken," page 10); wings, neck, and back hacked into 2-inch pieces (see figures 1–3, pages 278–279)
1 large onion, cut into large chunks (not necessary to peel)
2 bay leaves
Salt
3 celery stalks, trimmed and cut into 1-by-½-inch pieces
4 carrots, peeled and cut into 1-by-½-inch pieces
6 boiling onions, peeled and halved
4 tablespoons butter or chicken fat skimmed from strained stock
6 tablespoons all-purpose flour
1 teaspoon dried thyme
2 tablespoons dry sherry or vermouth
¼ cup heavy cream (optional)
1 recipe Baking Powder Dumplings (page 249), shaped
¾ cup frozen peas, thawed
¼ cup minced fresh parsley leaves
Pepper

1. Heat a 5- or 6-quart Dutch oven over medium-high heat. Add the hacked-up chicken pieces (wings, neck, and back) and the onion chunks; sauté until the onion softens and the chicken loses its raw color, about 5 minutes. Reduce the heat to low, cover, and continue to cook until the chicken pieces give up most of their liquid, about 20 minutes. Increase the heat to medium-high, add 6 cups of hot water, the chicken legs, thighs, and breasts, bay leaves, and ¾ teaspoon salt, then bring to a low boil. Reduce the heat; continue to simmer, partially covered, until the broth is flavorful and the chicken parts are just cooked through, about 20 minutes longer. Remove the chicken parts and set aside. When cool enough to handle, remove the meat from bones in 2- to 3-inch chunks. Strain the broth, discarding the hacked chicken pieces. Skim and reserve the fat from the broth and set aside 4 cups of broth, reserving extra for another use. Wipe the Dutch oven clean with a paper towel.

2. Meanwhile, bring ½ inch of water to a simmer in the cleaned Dutch oven fitted with a steamer basket. Add the celery, carrots, and boiling onions; cover and steam until just tender, about 10 minutes. Remove and set aside. Wipe the Dutch oven dry.

3. Heat the butter in the empty Dutch oven over medium-high heat. Whisk in the flour and thyme; cook, whisking constantly, until the flour turns golden, 1 to 2 minutes. Continuing to whisk constantly, gradually add the sherry or vermouth, then the reserved 4 cups of chicken stock; simmer until the gravy thickens slightly, 2 to 3 minutes. Stir in the optional cream, the chicken, and the steamed vegetables; return to a simmer.

4. Lay the formed dumplings on the surface of the chicken mixture; cover and simmer until the dumplings are cooked through, about 10 minutes for strip dumplings and 15 minutes for balls and biscuit rounds. Gently stir in the peas and parsley. Adjust the seasonings, including generous amounts of salt and pepper. Ladle portions of meat, sauce, vegetables, and dumplings into soup plates and serve immediately.

Chicken and Herb Dumplings with Spring Vegetables

ASPARAGUS AND LEEKS ARE ADDED TO THE STEW FOR A SPRINGTIME VARIATION. THE LEEKS ARE STEAMED ALONG WITH THE CARROTS, BUT THE ASPARAGUS ARE ADDED RAW RIGHT BEFORE THE DUMPLINGS ARE STEAMED TO PREVENT THEIR OVERCOOKING. ANY COMBINATION OF PARSLEY, CHIVES, AND TARRAGON IN THE DUMPLINGS WILL GIVE THEM A GARDEN-FRESH FLAVOR AND AROMA. SERVES 6 TO 8.

1 large roasting chicken (6 to 7 pounds), rinsed, patted dry, and cut into 8 pieces (see "Cutting Up a Whole Chicken," page 10); wings, neck, and back hacked into 2-inch pieces (see figures 1–3, pages 278–279)

1 large onion, cut into large chunks (not necessary to peel)

2 bay leaves

Salt

3 celery stalks, trimmed and cut into 1-by-½-inch pieces

4 carrots, peeled and cut into 1-by-½-inch pieces

3 large leeks, white and light green parts, trimmed and cut into 1-inch lengths

4 tablespoons butter or chicken fat skimmed from strained stock

6 tablespoons all-purpose flour

1 teaspoon dried thyme

2 tablespoons dry sherry or vermouth

¼ cup heavy cream (optional)

24 asparagus stalks, trimmed and cut into 2-inch lengths

1 recipe Herb Dumplings (page 249), shaped

¾ cup frozen peas, thawed

¼ cup minced fresh parsley leaves

Pepper

1. Heat a 5- or 6-quart Dutch oven over medium-high heat. Add the hacked-up chicken pieces (wings,

(continued on next page)

neck, and back) and the onion chunks; sauté until the onion softens and the chicken loses its raw color, about 5 minutes. Reduce the heat to low, cover, and continue to cook until the chicken pieces give up most of their liquid, about 20 minutes. Increase the heat to medium-high, add 6 cups of hot water, the chicken legs, thighs, and breasts, bay leaves, and ¾ teaspoon salt, then bring to a low boil. Reduce the heat; continue to simmer, partially covered, until the broth is flavorful and the chicken parts are just cooked through, about 20 minutes longer. Remove the chicken parts and set aside. When cool enough to handle, remove the meat from bones in 2- to 3-inch chunks. Strain the broth, discarding the hacked chicken pieces. Skim and reserve the fat from the broth and set aside 4 cups of broth, reserving extra for another use. Wipe the Dutch oven clean with a paper towel.

2. Meanwhile, bring ½ inch of water to a simmer in the cleaned Dutch oven fitted with a steamer basket. Add the celery, carrots, and leeks; cover and steam until just tender, about 10 minutes. Remove and set aside. Wipe the Dutch oven dry.

3. Heat the butter in the empty Dutch oven over medium-high heat. Whisk in the flour and thyme; cook, whisking constantly, until the flour turns golden, 1 to 2 minutes. Continuing to whisk constantly, gradually add the sherry, then the reserved 4 cups of chicken stock; simmer until the gravy thickens slightly, 2 to 3 minutes. Stir in the optional cream, the chicken, the steamed vegetables, and the raw asparagus; return to a simmer.

4. Lay the formed dumplings on the surface of the chicken mixture; cover and simmer until the dumplings are cooked through, about 10 minutes for strip dumplings and 15 minutes for balls and biscuit rounds. Gently stir in the peas and parsley. Adjust the seasonings, including generous amounts of salt and pepper. Ladle portions of meat, sauce, vegetables, and dumplings into soup plates and serve immediately.

Chicken and Dill Dumplings with Kohlrabi

KOHLRABI IS A LESS COMMON RELATIVE OF BROCCOLI, CAULIFLOWER, AND CABBAGE. LOOK FOR SMALL, YOUNG KOHLRABI WITH SMOOTH BULBS AND GREEN, UNBLEMISHED LEAVES. CRUNCHY PALE GREEN KOHLRABI SLICES MAKE THIS VARIATION ON CHICKEN AND DUMPLINGS PARTICULARLY FRESH-TASTING. BABY CARROTS, A SPRINKLING OF PARSLEY, AND DILL DUMPLINGS CONTRIBUTE TO THE CLEAN, BRIGHT LOOK AND FLAVOR OF THIS DISH. SERVES 6 TO 8.

1 large roasting chicken (6 to 7 pounds), rinsed, patted dry, and cut into 8 pieces (see "Cutting Up a Whole Chicken," page 10); wings, neck, and back hacked into 2-inch pieces (see figures 1–3, pages 278–279)
1 large onion, cut into large chunks (not necessary to peel)
2 bay leaves
Salt
3 young kohlrabi (about 1½ pounds), peeled, quartered, and cut into ½-inch-thick slices (see figures 1 through 3, page 253)
¾ pound baby carrots, trimmed, *or* 4 carrots, peeled and cut into 1-by-½-inch pieces
4 tablespoons butter or chicken fat skimmed from strained stock
6 tablespoons all-purpose flour
1 teaspoon dried thyme
2 tablespoons dry sherry or vermouth
¼ cup heavy cream (optional)
1 recipe Dill Dumplings (page 249), shaped
¼ cup minced fresh parsley leaves
Pepper

1. Heat a 5- or 6-quart Dutch oven over medium-high heat. Add the hacked-up chicken pieces (wings, neck, and back) and the onion chunks; sauté until the onion softens and the chicken loses its raw color, about 5 minutes. Reduce the heat to low, cover, and continue to cook until the chicken pieces give up most of their liquid, about 20 minutes. Increase the heat to medium-high, add 6 cups of hot water, the chicken legs, thighs, and breasts, bay leaves, and ¾ teaspoon salt, then bring to a low boil. Reduce the heat; continue to simmer, partially covered, until the broth is flavorful and the chicken parts are just cooked through, about 20 minutes longer. Remove the chicken parts and set aside. When cool enough to handle, remove the meat from bones in 2- to 3-inch chunks. Strain the broth, discarding the hacked chicken pieces. Skim and reserve the fat from the broth and set aside 4 cups of broth, reserving extra for another use. Wipe the Dutch oven clean with a paper towel.

2. Meanwhile, bring ½ inch of water to a simmer in the cleaned Dutch oven fitted with a steamer basket. Add the kohlrabi and carrots; cover and steam until just tender, about 10 minutes. Remove and set aside. Wipe the Dutch oven dry.

3. Heat the butter in the empty Dutch oven over medium-high heat. Whisk in the flour and thyme; cook, whisking constantly, until the flour turns golden, 1 to 2 minutes. Continuing to whisk constantly, gradually add the sherry, then the reserved 4 cups of chicken stock; simmer until the gravy thickens slightly, 2 to 3 minutes. Stir in the optional cream, the chicken, and the steamed vegetables; return to a simmer.

4. Lay the formed dumplings on the surface of the chicken mixture; cover and simmer until the dumplings are cooked through, about 10 minutes for strip dumplings and 15 minutes for balls and biscuit rounds. Gently stir in the parsley. Adjust the seasonings, including generous amounts of salt and pepper. Ladle portions of meat, sauce, vegetables, and dumplings into soup plates and serve immediately.

PREPARING KOHLRABI

1. Trim the leafy greens and stems from each kohlrabi knob. Slice the ends off of each knob.

2. Peel away the tough skin and the fibrous layer just underneath the skin with a vegetable peeler.

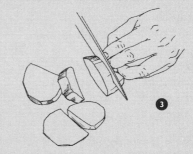

3. Quarter each knob and cut each quarter into ½-inch-thick slices.

Chicken and Cornmeal Dumplings with Sweet Potatoes and Bacon

SWEET POTATOES STAND IN FOR THE CARROTS AND CORNMEAL IS ADDED TO THE DUMPLING RECIPE FOR A SOUTHERN-STYLE DISH. TWO SLICES OF BACON COOK ALONG WITH THE CHICKEN TO GIVE THE BROTH A SALTY, SMOKY FLAVOR. SERVES 6 TO 8.

1 large roasting chicken (6 to 7 pounds), rinsed, patted dry, and cut into 8 pieces (see "Cutting Up a Whole Chicken," page 10); wings, neck, and back hacked into 2-inch pieces (see figures 1–3, pages 278–279)

2 slices bacon

1 large onion, cut into large chunks (not necessary to peel)

2 bay leaves

Salt

3 celery stalks, trimmed and cut into 1-by-½-inch pieces

2 medium sweet potatoes (about 1½ pounds), peeled and cut into ½-inch cubes

4 tablespoons butter or chicken fat skimmed from strained stock

6 tablespoons all-purpose flour

1 teaspoon dried thyme leaves

2 tablespoons dry sherry or vermouth

¼ cup heavy cream (optional)

1 recipe Cornmeal Dumplings (page 249), shaped

¾ cup frozen peas, thawed

¼ cup minced fresh parsley leaves

Pepper

1. Heat a 5- or 6-quart Dutch oven over medium-high heat. Add the hacked-up chicken pieces (wings, neck, and back), bacon, and onion chunks; sauté until the onion softens and the chicken loses its raw color, about 5 minutes. Reduce the heat to low, cover, and continue to cook until the chicken pieces give up most of their liquid, about 20 minutes. Increase the heat to medium-high, add 6 cups of hot water, the chicken legs, thighs, and breasts, bay leaves, and ¾ teaspoon salt, then bring to a low boil. Reduce the heat; continue to simmer, partially covered, until the broth is flavorful and the chicken parts are just cooked through, about 20 minutes longer. Remove the chicken parts and set aside. When cool enough to handle, remove the meat from bones in 2- to 3-inch chunks. Strain the broth, discarding the hacked chicken pieces and the bacon. Skim and reserve the fat from the broth and set aside 4 cups of broth, reserving extra for another use. Wipe the Dutch oven clean with a paper towel.

2. Meanwhile, bring ½ inch of water to a simmer in the cleaned Dutch oven fitted with a steamer basket. Add the celery and sweet potatoes; cover and steam until just tender, about 10 minutes. Remove and set aside. Wipe the Dutch oven dry.

3. Heat the butter in the empty Dutch oven over medium-high heat. Whisk in the flour and thyme; cook, whisking constantly, until the flour turns golden, 1 to 2 minutes. Continuing to whisk constantly, gradually add the sherry, then the reserved 4 cups of chicken stock; simmer until the gravy thickens slightly, 2 to 3 minutes. Stir in the optional cream, the chicken, and the steamed vegetables; return to a simmer.

4. Lay the formed dumplings on the surface of the chicken mixture; cover and simmer until the dumplings are cooked through, about 10 minutes for strip dumplings and 15 minutes for balls and biscuit rounds. Gently stir in the peas and parsley. Adjust the seasonings, including generous amounts of salt and pepper. Ladle portions of meat, sauce, vegetables, and dumplings into soup plates and serve immediately.

Chicken and Raisin Dumplings

RAISINS MAKE THE DUMPLINGS A BIT SWEET; CURRY POWDER ADDS SOME GENTLE HEAT AND SPICE TO THE SAUCE. FOR A MORE EXOTIC FLAVOR, REPLACE THE PARSLEY WITH AN EQUAL AMOUNT OF MINCED CILANTRO. SERVES 6 TO 8.

- 1 large roasting chicken (6 to 7 pounds), rinsed, patted dry, and cut into 8 pieces (see "Cutting Up a Whole Chicken," page 10); wings, neck, and back hacked into 2-inch pieces (see figures 1–3, pages 278–279)
- 1 large onion, cut into large chunks (not necessary to peel)
- 2 bay leaves
- Salt
- 3 celery stalks, trimmed and cut into 1-by-1/2-inch pieces
- 1 pound red potatoes, peeled and cut into 1/2-inch chunks
- 3/4 pound baby carrots, trimmed, *or* 4 carrots, peeled and cut into 1-by-1/2-inch pieces
- 4 tablespoons butter or chicken fat skimmed from strained stock
- 6 tablespoons all-purpose flour
- 2 teaspoons curry powder
- 2 tablespoons dry sherry or vermouth
- 1/4 cup heavy cream (optional)
- 1 recipe Raisin Dumplings (page 249), shaped
- 1/4 cup minced fresh parsley leaves
- Pepper

1. Heat a 5- or 6-quart Dutch oven over medium-high heat. Add the hacked-up chicken pieces (wings, neck, and back) and the onion chunks; sauté until the onion softens and the chicken loses its raw color, about 5 minutes. Reduce the heat to low, cover, and continue to cook until the chicken pieces give up most of their liquid, about 20 minutes. Increase the heat to medium-high, add 6 cups of hot water, the chicken legs, thighs, and breasts, bay leaves, and 3/4 teaspoon salt, then bring to a low boil. Reduce the heat; continue to simmer, partially covered, until the broth is flavorful and the chicken parts are just cooked through, about 20 minutes longer. Remove the chicken parts and set aside. When cool enough to handle, remove the meat from bones in 2- to 3-inch chunks. Strain the broth, discarding the hacked chicken pieces. Skim and reserve the fat from the broth and set aside 4 cups of broth, reserving extra for another use. Wipe the Dutch oven clean with a paper towel.

2. Meanwhile, bring 1/2 inch of water to a simmer in the cleaned Dutch oven fitted with a steamer basket. Add the celery, potatoes, and carrots; cover and steam until just tender, about 10 minutes. Remove and set aside. Wipe the Dutch oven dry.

3. Heat the butter in the empty Dutch oven over medium-high heat. Whisk in the flour; cook, whisking constantly, until the flour turns golden, 1 to 2 minutes. Whisk in the curry powder. Continuing to whisk constantly, gradually add the sherry, then the reserved 4 cups of chicken stock; simmer until the gravy thickens slightly, 2 to 3 minutes. Stir in the optional cream and the chicken and the steamed vegetables; return to a simmer.

4. Lay the formed dumplings on the surface of the chicken mixture; cover and simmer until the dumplings are cooked through, about 10 minutes for strip dumplings and 15 minutes for balls and biscuit rounds. Gently stir in the parsley. Adjust the seasonings, including generous amounts of salt and pepper. Ladle portions of meat, sauce, vegetables, and dumplings into soup plates and serve immediately.

Quick Chicken and Dumplings

SERVES 6 TO 8

I F BUTCHERING AND COOKING a whole chicken are too time-consuming, or if you prefer an all-white-meat chicken and dumplings, try this variation. Boneless, skinless breasts don't produce as rich a stock as a whole roaster, but the time saved—almost an hour of preparation and cooking—may be worth it. This streamlined method may be used in any of the variations in this chapter. As with the other Master Recipe, prepare and shape the dumplings while the vegetables steam.

2 whole boneless, skinless chicken breasts, split and trimmed of excess fat

4 cups chicken stock or 2 15-ounce cans low-sodium chicken broth with water added to equal 4 cups

3 celery stalks, trimmed and cut into 1-by-½-inch pieces

4 carrots, peeled and cut into 1-by-½-inch pieces

6 boiling onions, peeled and halved

4 tablespoons butter

6 tablespoons all-purpose flour

1 teaspoon dried thyme

2 tablespoons dry sherry or vermouth

¼ cup heavy cream (optional)

1 recipe Baking Powder Dumplings (page 249), shaped

¾ cup frozen peas, thawed

¼ cup minced fresh parsley leaves

Salt and pepper

1. Put the chicken and stock in a 5- or 6-quart Dutch oven over medium-high heat. Cover, bring to a simmer; simmer until chicken is just done, 8 to 10 minutes. Transfer the meat to a large bowl, reserving 4 cups of stock in a measuring cup. When cool enough to handle, tear the meat into 2- to 3-inch chunks. Wipe the Dutch oven clean with a paper towel.

2. Meanwhile, bring ½ inch of water to a simmer in the cleaned Dutch oven fitted with a steamer basket. Add the celery, carrots, and boiling onions; cover and steam until just tender, about 10 minutes. Remove and set aside. Wipe the Dutch oven dry.

3. Heat the butter in the empty Dutch oven over medium-high heat. Whisk in the flour and thyme; cook, whisking constantly, until the flour turns golden, 1 to 2 minutes. Continuing to whisk constantly, gradually add the sherry, then the reserved 4 cups of chicken stock; simmer until the gravy thickens slightly, 2 to 3 minutes. Stir in the optional cream, the chicken, and the steamed vegetables; return to a simmer.

4. Lay the formed dumplings on the surface of the chicken mixture; cover and simmer until the dumplings are cooked through, about 10 minutes for strip dumplings and 15 minutes for balls and biscuit rounds. Gently stir in the peas and parsley. Adjust the seasonings, including generous amounts of salt and pepper. Ladle portions of meat, sauce, vegetables, and dumplings into soup plates and serve immediately.

CHICKEN POT PIE

/|\

MOST EVERYONE LOVES A GOOD CHICKEN POT PIE.

UNFORTUNATELY, MOST POT PIES ARE TIRED AND

STODGY; EVEN WHEN MADE WITH FRESH INGREDIENTS,

THEY TASTE LIKE LEFTOVERS. IN DEVELOPING OUR POT

PIE RECIPE, WE WANTED TO AVOID TWO COMMON

PROBLEMS. THE FIRST IS OVERCOOKED VEGETABLES. A

FILLING CHOCK-FULL OF BRIGHT, FRESH VEGETABLES

GOING INTO THE OVEN LOOKS COMPLETELY DIFFERENT

after forty minutes of high-heat baking under a blanket of dough. Carrots become mushy and pumpkin colored, while peas and fresh herbs fade from fresh spring to drab green. The second problem is overly juicy fillings. Before baking, the filling may appear thick and creamy. After baking, however, pies look like chicken soup en croute. We wanted moist and saucy pie, but we also wanted it thick enough to eat with a fork.

Like a lot of satisfying dishes, traditional pot pie takes time. Before the pie even makes it to the oven, the cook must poach a chicken; take the meat off the bone and cut it up; strain the broth; prepare and blanch vegetables; make a sauce; and mix and roll out biscuit or pie dough. Our goal was to simplify the process (pot pie, after all, is supper food) without sacrificing quality.

We began our tests by focusing on the chicken. In addition to making pies with roast chicken and poached chicken parts, we steamed and roasted whole chickens, and braised chicken parts. Steaming the chicken was time-consuming, requiring about one hour, and the steaming liquid wasn't a strong enough broth for the pot pie sauce. Roast chicken also required an hour in the oven, and by the time we took off the skin and mixed the meat in with the sauce and vegetables, the roasted flavor was lost. We had similar results with braised chicken: it lost its delicious flavor once the browned skin was removed, and the sauce made from the braising liquid tasted too pronounced, distracting us from the meat, vegetables, and crust.

Next we tried poaching, the most traditional cooking method. Of the two poaching liquids we tried, we preferred the chicken poached in white wine and broth to the one poached in broth alone. The wine infused the meat and made for a richer, more full-flavored sauce. To our disappointment, however, the acidity of the wine-broth sauce caused the green peas and fresh herbs to lose their bright green color in the oven. Vegetables baked in the broth-only sauce kept their bright color, though the bland sauce needed perking up—a problem we'd have to deal with later. Now we were ready to test this method against quicker-cooking boneless, skinless chicken breasts.

Because boneless, skinless breasts cook so quickly, sautéing was another possible cooking method. Before comparing poached parts to breasts, we tried cooking the breasts three different ways. We cut raw breast meat into bite-size pieces and sautéed them; we sautéed whole breasts, shredding the breast meat once cool enough to handle; and we poached whole breasts in canned broth, also shredding the meat.

Once again, poaching was our favorite method. The resulting tender, irregularly shaped chicken pieces mixed well with the vegetables and, much like textured pasta, caused the sauce to cling. The sautéed chicken pieces, however, floated independently in the sauce, their surfaces too smooth to attract sauce. We had hoped to like the sautéed whole breasts. Unfortunately, sautéing caused the outer layer of the meat to turn crusty, a texture we did not like in the pie.

Our only concern with the poached boneless, skinless breasts was the quality of the broth. Though both the parts and the breasts were poached in canned broth, we thought the long-simmered poaching liquid of the parts would be significantly better. But in our comparison of the pies, we found no difference in quality, and we were able to shave a half hour off the cooking time (ten minutes to cook the breasts compared with forty minutes to cook the parts). For those who like either dark or a mix of dark and white meat in the pie, boneless, skinless chicken thighs can be used as well.

With the chicken element decided, we made pies with raw vegetables, sautéed vegetables, and parboiled vegetables. The vegetables sautéed before baking held their color and flavor best, the parboiled ones less so. The raw vegetables were not fully cooked at the end of baking time and gave off too much liquid, watering down the flavor and thickness of the sauce.

Of course, the other means of keeping the vegetables fresh is not overcooking them in the oven. To keep the pie from becoming overly rich and complicated, we had ruled out a double crust. The vegetables became another reason for keeping the pie single-crusted. To get a bottom crust fully cooked, the pie would have to cook for at least forty-five minutes, at which point the peas and carrots would be lifeless.

Our final task was to develop a sauce that was flavorful, creamy, and of the proper consistency. Chicken pot pie sauce is traditionally based on a roux (a mixture of butter and flour sautéed together briefly), thinned with chicken broth and often enriched with cream.

Because of the dish's inherent richness, we wanted to see how little cream we could get away with using. We

ASSEMBLING A POT PIE

1. If using pie dough, lay the rectangle of dough for the large pie or the dough rounds for the individual pies over the pot pie filling, trimming the dough to within ¾ inch of the pan lip.

2. For a double-crust effect, simply tuck the overhanging dough down into the pan side. This tucked crust will become soft in the oven, like the bottom crust on a pie.

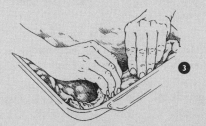

3. For a more finished look, tuck the overhanging dough back under itself so the folded edge is flush with the lip of the pan.

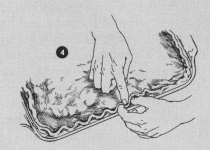

4. Holding the dough with thumb and index finger of one hand, push the dough with the index finger of the other hand to form a pleated edge. Repeat all around the edge to flute the dough.

5. Cut at least four 1-inch vent holes in a large pot pie or one 1-inch vent hole in each individual pie.

6. If using biscuits to top a pot pie, simply arrange the dough rounds over the warm filling before baking.

tried three different pot pie fillings—with ¼ cup of cream, ¼ cup of half-and-half, and 1½ cups of milk, respectively. Going into the oven, all the fillings seemed to have the right consistency and creaminess; when they came out, however, it was a different story. Vegetable and meat juices diluted the consistency and creaminess of the cream and half-and-half sauces. To achieve a creamy-looking sauce, we would have needed to increase the cream dramatically. Fortunately, we didn't have to try it, because we actually liked the milk-enriched sauce. The larger quantity of milk kept the sauce creamy in both color and flavor. To keep the sauce from becoming too liquid, we simply added more flour. A sauce that looks a little thick before baking will become the perfect consistency after taking on the chicken and vegetable juices that release during baking.

We had worked out the right consistency, but because we had been forced to abandon the wine for the vegetables' sake, the sauce tasted a little bland. Lemon juice had the same dulling effect on the color of the vegetables as the wine. Sherry turned out to be the secret. Because sherry is more intensely flavored and less acidic than wine, we were able to use less and still get the flavor boost we wanted without affecting the color of the vegetables.

Chicken Pot Pie

SERVES 6 TO 8

YOU CAN MAKE the filling ahead of time, but remember to heat it on top of the stove before topping it. As for the topping, it can be made up to 2 hours in advance and refrigerated on a floured baking sheet. The pot pie can be baked in one large pan (a standard 13-by-9-inch pan is ideal, but feel free to use any baking dish with a similar surface area) or six individual ceramic baking dishes.

1½ pounds boneless, skinless chicken breasts and/or thighs
2 cups chicken stock *or* 1 can (15 ounces) low-sodium broth with water added to equal 2 cups
1½ tablespoons vegetable oil
1 medium-large onion, finely chopped
3 medium carrots, peeled and cut crosswise ¼ inch thick
2 small celery stalks, cut crosswise ¼ inch thick
Salt and pepper
4 tablespoons unsalted butter
½ cup all-purpose flour
1½ cups milk
½ teaspoon dried thyme

STEP-BY-STEP

SHREDDING CHICKEN BY HAND

While the vegetables are sautéing, shred the meat by hand into bite-size pieces. Do not use a knife. Irregular surfaces caused by hand-shredding help the sauce to coat and cling to the chicken.

3 tablespoons dry sherry
¾ cup frozen green peas, thawed
3 tablespoons minced fresh parsley leaves
1 recipe Rich, Flaky Pie Dough or Fluffy
   Buttermilk Biscuits (pages 266–267)

1. Adjust the oven rack to low-center position; heat the oven to 400 degrees. Put the chicken and stock in a small Dutch oven or soup kettle over medium heat. Cover, bring to a simmer; simmer until the chicken is just done, 8 to 10 minutes. Transfer the meat to a large bowl, reserving the broth in a measuring cup for easy pouring later.

2. Increase the heat to medium-high; heat the oil in the now-empty pot. Add the onion, carrots, and celery; sauté until just tender, about 5 minutes. Season to taste with salt and pepper. While the vegetables are sautéing, shred the meat into bite-size pieces (see figure opposite). Transfer the cooked vegetables to the bowl with the chicken.

3. Heat the butter over medium heat in the again-empty pot. When the foaming subsides, add the flour; cook about 1 minute, stirring. Whisk in the chicken broth, the milk, any accumulated chicken juices, and the thyme. Bring to a simmer, then continue to simmer until the sauce fully thickens, about 1 minute. Season to taste with salt and pepper; stir in the sherry.

4. Pour the sauce over the chicken mixture; stir to combine. Stir in the peas and parsley. Adjust the seasonings. (The filling can be covered and refrigerated overnight; reheat before topping with the pie dough or biscuits.) Pour the mixture into a 13-by-9-inch pan or six 12-ounce ovenproof dishes. Top with the pie dough (see figures 1–5, page 259) or biscuits (see figure 6, page 259); bake until the topping is golden brown and the filling is bubbly, 30 minutes for a large pie and 20 to 25 minutes for individual pies. Serve hot.

Chicken and Corn Pot Pie
with Cornmeal Biscuit Topping

IN THIS VARIATION ON THE BASIC POT PIE, CORN KERNELS REPLACE PEAS AND A CORNMEAL CRUST REPLACES THE PLAIN BISCUIT FOR A TRADITIONAL SOUTHERN FLAVOR. SERVES 6 TO 8.

1 ½ pounds boneless, skinless chicken
   breasts and/or thighs
2 cups chicken stock *or* 1 can (15 ounces)
   low-sodium broth with water added to
   equal 2 cups
¼ pound bacon, cut crosswise into
   ½-inch-wide strips
6 whole scallions, finely chopped
3 medium carrots, peeled and cut crosswise ¼ inch thick
2 small celery stalks, cut crosswise ¼ inch thick
Salt and pepper
4 tablespoons unsalted butter
½ cup flour
1 ½ cups milk
½ teaspoon dried thyme
3 tablespoons dry sherry
2 cups fresh whole corn kernels, *or*
   1 10-ounce package frozen whole corn
   kernels, thawed
3 tablespoons minced fresh parsley leaves
1 recipe Cornmeal Biscuits (page 267)

1. Adjust the oven rack to low-center position; heat the oven to 400 degrees. Put the chicken and stock in a small Dutch oven or soup kettle over medium heat. Cover, bring to a simmer; simmer until the chicken is just done, 8 to 10 minutes. Transfer the meat to a large bowl, reserving the broth in a measuring cup for easy pouring later.

2. Increase the heat to medium and cook the bacon in the now-empty pot, stirring frequently, until the fat is rendered and bacon is crisp, about 10 minutes. Remove the bacon from the pan with a slotted spoon and drain on paper towels. Discard all but 2 tablespoons of the rendered fat.

(continued on next page)

3. Increase the heat to medium-high; heat the bacon fat in the again-empty pot. Add the scallions, carrots, and celery; sauté until just tender, about 5 minutes. Season to taste with salt and pepper. While the vegetables are sautéing, shred the meat into bite-size pieces. Add the cooked and drained bacon to the bowl with the chicken. Transfer the cooked vegetables to the bowl.

4. Heat the butter over medium heat in the again-empty pot. When the foaming subsides, add the flour; cook about 1 minute, stirring. Whisk in the chicken broth, the milk, any accumulated chicken juices, and the thyme. Bring to a simmer, then continue to simmer until the sauce fully thickens, about 1 minute. Season to taste with salt and pepper; stir in the sherry.

5. Pour the sauce over the chicken mixture; stir to combine. Stir in the corn and parsley. Adjust the seasonings. (The filling can be covered and refrigerated overnight; reheat before topping with the biscuits.) Pour the mixture into a 13-by-9-inch pan or six 12-ounce ovenproof dishes. Top with the biscuits; bake until the biscuits are golden brown and the filling is bubbly, 30 minutes for a large pie and 20 to 25 minutes for individual pies. Serve hot.

◆

Spring Vegetable and Chicken Pot Pie with Herb Biscuit Topping

MAKE THIS VARIATION WHEN SPRING VEGETABLES BEGIN TO ARRIVE AT THE MARKET. BECAUSE THE ASPARAGUS ARE NOT BLANCHED BUT SAUTEED, THE STALKS SHOULD BE AS SLENDER AND FRESH AS POSSIBLE. SERVES 6 TO 8.

1 ½ pounds boneless, skinless chicken
    breasts and/or thighs
2 cups chicken stock *or* 1 can (15 ounces)
    low-sodium broth with water added to
    equal 2 cups
1 ½ tablespoons vegetable oil
6 whole scallions, finely chopped
3 medium carrots, peeled and cut cross-
    wise ¼ inch thick

18 slender asparagus stalks, tough ends
    trimmed, halved lengthwise, and cut
    into 1-inch pieces (see figures 1 and 2,
    opposite)
Salt and pepper
4 tablespoons unsalted butter
½ cup flour
1 ½ cups milk
½ teaspoon dried thyme
3 tablespoons dry sherry
1 cup frozen peas, thawed
3 tablespoons minced fresh parsley leaves
1 recipe Herb Biscuits (page 267)

1. Adjust the oven rack to low-center position; heat the oven to 400 degrees. Put the chicken and stock in a small Dutch oven or soup kettle over medium heat. Cover, bring to a simmer; simmer until the chicken is just done, 8 to 10 minutes. Transfer the meat to a large bowl, reserving the broth in a measuring cup for easy pouring later.

2. Increase the heat to medium-high; heat the oil in the now-empty pot. Add the scallions and carrots; sauté for 2 or 3 minutes. Add the asparagus and cook for another 3 or 4 minutes, until the vegetables begin to soften. Season to taste with salt and pepper. While the vegetables are sautéing, shred the meat into bite-size pieces. Transfer the cooked vegetables to the bowl with the chicken.

3. Heat the butter over medium heat in the again-empty pot. When the foaming subsides, add the flour; cook about 1 minute, stirring. Whisk in the chicken broth, the milk, any accumulated chicken juices, and the thyme. Bring to a simmer, then continue to simmer until the sauce fully thickens, about 1 minute. Season to taste, and stir in the sherry.

4. Pour the sauce over the chicken mixture; stir to combine. Stir in the peas and parsley. Adjust the seasonings. (The filling can be covered and refrigerated overnight; reheat before topping with the biscuits.) Pour the mixture into a 13-by-9-inch pan or six 12-ounce ovenproof dishes. Top with the biscuits; bake until the biscuits are golden brown and the filling is bubbly, 30 minutes for a large pie and 20 to 25 minutes for individual pies. Serve hot.

TRIMMING AND SLICING ASPARAGUS

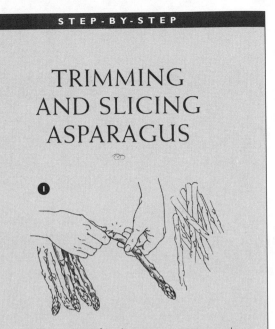

❶

1. The tough part of each asparagus spear can be easily removed by this method: Hold the asparagus about halfway down the stalk. With the other hand, hold the cut end between the thumb and index finger about an inch or so up the stalk. Bend the stalk until it snaps.

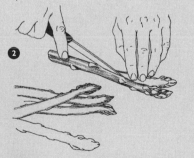

❷

2. Once the tough ends have been trimmed, slice each asparagus spear lengthwise. The halved asparagus spears are then cut into 1-inch-long pieces.

Spinach, Tomato, and Chicken Pot Pie with Parmesan Biscuit Topping

A PARMESAN BISCUIT TOPPING COMPLEMENTS THE ITALIAN FLAVORS OF SPINACH AND TOMATO. THE TOMATOES MUST BE SEEDED AND THE COOKED SPINACH WELL DRAINED SO THAT THE FINISHED PIE IS NOT WATERY. SERVES 6 TO 8.

> 1 1/2 pounds boneless, skinless chicken breasts and/or thighs
> 2 cups chicken stock *or* 1 can (15 ounces) low-sodium broth with water added to equal 2 cups
> 1 1/2 tablespoons vegetable oil
> 1 medium-large onion, finely chopped
> 3 medium carrots, peeled and cut crosswise 1/4 inch thick
> 2 small celery stalks, cut crosswise 1/4 inch thick
> 3 plum tomatoes, cored, seeded, and chopped
> Salt and pepper
> 1 pound spinach, stemmed and washed
> 4 tablespoons unsalted butter
> 1/2 cup flour
> 1 1/2 cups milk
> 1/2 teaspoon dried oregano
> 3 tablespoons dry sherry
> 3 tablespoons minced fresh basil leaves
> 1 recipe Parmesan Biscuits (page 267)

1. Adjust the oven rack to low-center position; heat the oven to 400 degrees. Put the chicken and stock in a small Dutch oven or soup kettle over medium heat. Cover, bring to a simmer; simmer until the chicken is just done, 8 to 10 minutes. Transfer the meat to a large bowl, reserving the broth in a measuring cup for easy pouring later.

2. Increase the heat to medium-high; heat the oil in the now-empty pot. Add the onion, carrots, celery, and tomatoes; sauté until just tender, about 5 min-

(continued on next page)

utes. Season to taste with salt and pepper. While the vegetables are sautéing, shred the meat into bite-size pieces. Transfer the cooked vegetables to the bowl with the chicken.

3. Add the spinach to the again-empty pot and cook until completely limp, 2 to 3 minutes. Transfer the cooked spinach to a bowl and cool slightly. Place the cooked spinach between layers of paper towel and squeeze to remove excess water (see figure). Coarsely chop the drained spinach and add it to the bowl with the chicken and vegetables.

4. Heat the butter over medium heat in the again-empty pan. When the foaming subsides, add the flour; cook about 1 minute, stirring. Whisk in the chicken broth, the milk, any accumulated chicken juices, and the oregano. Bring to a simmer, then continue to simmer until the sauce fully thickens, about 1 minute. Season to taste with salt and pepper; stir in the sherry.

5. Pour the sauce over the chicken mixture; stir to combine. Stir in the basil. Adjust the seasonings. (The filling can be covered and refrigerated overnight; reheat before topping with the biscuits.) Pour the mixture into a 13-by-9-inch pan or six 12-ounce ovenproof dishes. Top with the biscuits; bake until the biscuits are golden brown and the filling is bubbly, 30 minutes for a large pie and 20 to 25 minutes for individual pies. Serve hot.

REMOVING EXCESS LIQUID FROM COOKED SPINACH

It's imperative that the cooked spinach be drained of excess moisture that could otherwise make the pot pie sauce watery. Let the cooked spinach cool slightly and then place it between 2 layers of paper towels. Squeeze down on the top layer of paper towels to expel moisture from the spinach. Once the spinach is dry, it can be coarsely chopped and added to the bowl with the other cooked vegetables.

Wild Mushroom and Chicken Pot Pie

DRIED PORCINI MUSHROOMS, IMPORTED FROM ITALY AND AVAILABLE IN MOST SUPERMARKETS AND GOURMET STORES, ARE ADDED TO WHITE MUSHROOMS TO GIVE THIS POT PIE A MORE INTENSE FLAVOR. THE SOAKING LIQUID USED TO REHYDRATE THE MUSHROOMS REPLACES SOME OF THE CHICKEN STOCK USED TO POACH THE CHICKEN AND THEN TO ENRICH THE SAUCE. SERVES 6 TO 8.

- 1 ounce dried porcini mushrooms
- 1½ pounds boneless, skinless chicken breasts and/or thighs
- 1 cup chicken stock or low-sodium canned broth
- 1½ tablespoons vegetable oil
- 1 medium onion, finely chopped
- 3 medium carrots, peeled and cut cross-wise ¼ inch thick
- 2 small celery stalks, cut crosswise ¼ inch thick
- 12 ounces white button mushrooms, stems trimmed, sliced thin
- Salt and pepper
- 4 tablespoons unsalted butter
- ½ cup flour
- 1½ cups milk
- ½ teaspoon dried thyme
- 3 tablespoons dry sherry
- ¾ cup frozen peas, thawed
- 3 tablespoons minced fresh parsley leaves
- 1 recipe Rich, Flaky Pie Dough (page 266) or Fluffy Buttermilk Biscuits (page 267)

1. Place the porcini in a small bowl and cover with 2 cups warm tap water. Let stand 20 minutes to allow the mushrooms to rehydrate. Lift the mushrooms from the liquid with a slotted spoon and pat dry on paper towels. Chop coarsely. Strain the liquid through a sieve lined with a paper towel and reserve 1 cup.

2. Adjust the oven rack to low-center position; heat the oven to 400 degrees. Put the chicken, stock, and mushroom liquid in a small Dutch oven or soup kettle over medium heat. Cover, bring to a simmer; simmer until the chicken is just done, 8 to 10 minutes. Transfer the meat to a large bowl, reserving the poaching liquid in a measuring cup for easy pouring later.

3. Increase the heat to medium-high; heat the oil in the now-empty pot. Add the onion, carrots, celery, and both kinds of mushrooms; sauté until just tender, about 5 minutes. Season to taste with salt and pepper. While the vegetables are sautéing, shred the meat into bite-size pieces. Transfer the cooked vegetables to the bowl with the chicken.

4. Heat the butter over medium heat in the again-empty pot. When the foaming subsides, add the flour; cook about 1 minute, stirring. Whisk in the poaching broth, the milk, any accumulated chicken juices, and the thyme. Bring to a simmer, then continue to simmer until the sauce fully thickens, about 1 minute. Season to taste with salt and pepper; stir in the sherry.

5. Pour the sauce over the chicken mixture; stir to combine. Stir in the peas and parsley. Adjust the seasonings. (The filling can be covered and refrigerated overnight; reheat before topping with the pie dough or biscuits.) Pour the mixture into a 13-by-9-inch pan or six 12-ounce ovenproof dishes. Top with the pie dough or biscuits; bake until the topping is golden brown and the filling is bubbly, 30 minutes for a large pie and 20 to 25 minutes for individual pies. Serve hot.

TOPPINGS FOR POT PIES

∧

THERE ARE TWO BASIC CHOICES FOR TOPPING A POT PIE:

FLAKY PIE PASTRY OR TENDER BISCUITS. (BISCUITS ARE EAS-

IER TO MAKE, BUT GOOD PIE PASTRY IS WORTH THE EFFORT,

ESPECIALLY IF YOU ARE TRYING TO MAKE THE DISH MORE ELEGANT

FOR COMPANY.) WE FIND THAT A COMBINATION OF BUTTER AND

shortening delivers the best texture and flavor for pie pastry. Use a food processor to cut the fat into the flour. Once the mixture resembles coarse cornmeal, turn it into a bowl and add just enough ice water to bring the dough together. When making fluffy buttermilk biscuits, we again use the food processor to cut the butter into the dry ingredients. We then scrape this mixture into a bowl and stir in the buttermilk. Do not overwork the biscuits. Unlike pie pastry, biscuits take to a number of different flavorings. Three of our favorite variations follow.

◆

Rich, Flaky Pie Dough

IF YOU LIKE A BOTTOM CRUST IN YOUR POT PIE, YOU CAN DUPLICATE THAT SOFT CRUST TEXTURE BY TUCK-ING ANY OVERHANGING DOUGH DOWN INTO THE PAN SIDE RATHER THAN FLUTING IT. ENOUGH TO COVER ONE 13-BY-9-INCH (OR THE EQUIVALENT) PAN OR SIX 12-OUNCE OVENPROOF BAKING DISHES.

1½ cups all-purpose flour
½ teaspoon salt
8 tablespoons (½ cup) unsalted chilled
   butter, cut into ¼-inch pieces

4 tablespoons chilled all-vegetable
   shortening
3 to 4 tablespoons ice-cold water

1. Mix the flour and salt in the work bowl of a food processor fitted with the steel blade. Scatter the butter pieces over the flour mixture, tossing to coat the butter with a little of the flour. Cut the butter into the flour with five 1-second pulses. Add the shortening; continue pulsing until the flour is pale yellow and resembles coarse corn-meal, keeping some butter bits the size of small peas, about four more 1-second pulses. Turn the mixture into a medium bowl.

2. Sprinkle 3 tablespoons of ice-cold water over the mixture. Using a rubber spatula, fold the water into the flour mixture. Then press down on the dough mixture with the broad side of the spatula until the dough sticks together, adding up to 1 tablespoon more cold water if the dough will not come together. Shape the dough into a ball, then flatten into a 4-inch disk. Wrap the dough in plastic and refrigerate for 30 minutes while preparing the pie filling.

3. On a floured surface, roll the dough into a 15-by-11-inch rectangle, about ⅛ inch thick. If making individual pies, roll the dough ⅛ inch thick and cut 6 dough rounds about 1 inch larger than the pan circumference. Lay the dough over the warm pot pie filling, trimming the dough to ½ inch of pan lip. Tuck the overhanging dough back under itself so the folded edge is flush with the lip of the pan. Flute the edges all around. Or don't trim the dough and simply tuck the overhanging dough down into the pan side. Cut at least four 1-inch vent holes in a large pot pie or one 1-inch vent hole in the smaller pies. Proceed with the pot pie recipe.

◆

Fluffy Buttermilk Biscuits

IF YOU LIKE, SUBSTITUTE AN 8-OUNCE CONTAINER OF LOW-FAT OR WHOLE-MILK PLAIN YOGURT FOR THE BUTTERMILK. IF THE DOUGH DOES NOT QUITE COME TOGETHER, ADD 1 OR 2 TABLE-SPOONS REGULAR MILK. ENOUGH TO COVER ONE 13-BY-9-INCH (OR THE EQUIVALENT) PAN OR SIX 12-OUNCE OVENPROOF BAKING DISHES.

- 1 cup all-purpose flour
- 1 cup cake flour (not self-rising)
- 2 teaspoons baking powder
- ¼ teaspoon baking soda
- 1 teaspoon sugar
- ½ teaspoon salt
- 8 tablespoons (½ cup) chilled unsalted butter, quartered lengthwise and cut crosswise into ¼-inch pieces
- ¾ cup cold buttermilk, plus 1 to 2 tablespoons extra, if needed

1. Pulse the flours, baking powder, baking soda, sugar, and salt in the work bowl of a food processor fitted with the steel blade. Add the butter pieces; pulse until the mixture resembles coarse cornmeal with a few slightly larger butter lumps.

2. Transfer the mixture to a medium bowl; add ¾ cup buttermilk; stir with a fork until the dough gathers into moist clumps. Add the remaining 1 or 2 tablespoons buttermilk if the dough is too dry. Transfer the dough to a floured work surface and form into a rough ball, then roll the dough ½ inch thick. Using a 2 ½- or 3-inch pastry cutter, stamp out 8 rounds of dough. If making individual pies, cut the dough slightly smaller than the circumference of each dish. (Dough rounds can be refrigerated on a lightly floured baking sheet covered with plastic wrap up to 2 hours.)

3. Arrange the dough rounds over the warm filling and proceed with the pot pie recipe.

◆

Parmesan Biscuits

Make Fluffy Buttermilk Biscuits, decreasing the butter to 5 tablespoons. After the fat has been processed into the flour and transferred to a medium bowl, add 1½ cups grated Parmesan cheese (4 ounces); toss lightly, then stir in the liquid.

◆

Herb Biscuits

Make Fluffy Buttermilk Biscuits, adding 3 tablespoons minced parsley or 2 tablespoons minced fresh parsley leaves and 1 tablespoon minced fresh tarragon or dill leaves after the fat has been processed into the flour.

◆

Cornmeal Biscuits

Make Fluffy Buttermilk Biscuits, replacing the cake flour with 1 cup yellow cornmeal.

Chicken Pot Pie with Rosemary and Potatoes

THE POTATOES ARE BOILED FIRST AND THEN CUT INTO SMALL PIECES IN THIS STICK-TO-YOUR-RIBS RECIPE FLAVORED WITH ROSEMARY AND GARLIC. SERVES 6 TO 8.

¾ pound small red potatoes
1½ pounds boneless, skinless chicken breasts and/or thighs
2 cups chicken stock *or* 1 can (15 ounces) low-sodium broth with water added to equal 2 cups
1½ tablespoons vegetable oil
2 medium garlic cloves, minced
1 medium-large onion, finely chopped
3 medium carrots, peeled and cut crosswise ¼ inch thick
2 small celery stalks, cut crosswise ¼ inch thick
Salt and pepper
4 tablespoons unsalted butter
½ cup flour
1½ cups milk
1 tablespoon finely chopped fresh rosemary leaves
3 tablespoons dry sherry
¾ cup frozen peas, thawed
3 tablespoons minced fresh parsley leaves
1 recipe Rich, Flaky Pie Dough (page 266) or Fluffy Buttermilk Biscuits (page 267)

1. Bring several quarts of water to a boil in a medium saucepan. Add the potatoes and simmer until the potatoes are tender, about 20 minutes. Drain the potatoes, cool slightly, and cut them into ½-inch cubes.

2. Adjust the oven rack to low-center position; heat the oven to 400 degrees. Put the chicken and stock in a small Dutch oven or soup kettle over medium heat. Cover, bring to a simmer; simmer until the chicken is just done, 8 to 10 minutes. Transfer the meat to a large bowl, reserving the broth in a measuring cup for easy pouring later.

3. Increase the heat to medium-high; heat the oil in the now-empty pot. Add the garlic, onion, carrots, and celery; sauté until just tender, about 5 minutes. Season to taste with salt and pepper. While the vegetables are sautéing, shred the meat into bite-size pieces. Transfer the cooked vegetables to the bowl with the chicken.

4. Heat the butter over medium heat in the again-empty pot. When the foaming subsides, add the flour; cook about 1 minute, stirring. Whisk in the chicken broth, the milk, any accumulated chicken juices, and the rosemary. Bring to a simmer, then continue to simmer until the sauce fully thickens, about 1 minute. Season to taste with salt and pepper; stir in the sherry.

5. Pour the sauce over the chicken mixture; stir to combine. Stir in the potatoes, peas, and parsley. Adjust the seasonings. (The filling can be covered and refrigerated overnight; reheat before topping with the pie dough or biscuits.) Pour the mixture into a 13-by-9-inch pan or six 12-ounce ovenproof dishes. Top with the pie dough or biscuits; bake until the topping is golden brown and the filling is bubbly, 30 minutes for a large pie and 20 to 25 minutes for individual pies. Serve hot.

CHICKEN AND RICE

PERHAPS CLOSEST TO JAMBALAYA OR PAELLA,

"CHICKEN AND RICE" IS NOTHING MORE THAN

CHICKEN PIECES SAUTEED UNTIL WELL BROWNED

AND THEN COOKED ON TOP OF THE STOVE IN

CASSEROLE FASHION WITH SAUTEED ONIONS AND

GARLIC, A LIQUID (STOCK, WATER, OR WINE), AND

RICE. THE APPEAL IS OBVIOUS: IT'S A ONE-DISH

SUPPER, IT'S EASY, AND IT'S EMINENTLY VARIABLE.

Yet, after having made a dozen attempts at perfecting this recipe, we found two major problems. The white meat tends to dry out before the dark meat is cooked and the rice is often heavy and greasy. Besides solving these problems, we also wanted to devise a Master Recipe that lends itself to variations, perhaps a blend of Indian spices or a version with Latin overtones.

First, we tackled the problem of overcooked breast meat. The solution was rather simple: By adding the breast meat to the dish ten minutes after the thighs and legs (the pieces are browned together but the dark meat goes back into the pot with the rice and liquid earlier), both cooked perfectly. Of course, one could make this dish with just dark or light meat but, like most cooks, we are most likely to have a whole chicken on hand rather than just thighs or breasts. Buying a whole chicken also allows you to buy a higher-quality bird, since precut parts usually come from mass-market poultry operations. In addition, most family members have distinct and different taste preferences encompassing both kinds of meat.

The texture of the rice, however, was a more vexing issue. Our first thought was to reduce the amount of olive oil—from 2 tablespoons to 1—used to sauté the chicken and onion. This simply was not enough fat to get the job done and the resulting rice was only fractionally less greasy. We thought that perhaps the chicken skin was the culprit. But after making this dish with skinless chicken pieces, we were surprised to find that the rice was still heavy and the chicken, as we suspected, was tough and chewy. The skin is effective at maintaining succulent meat especially during heavy sautéing.

We then thought that reducing the amount of liquid in the recipe would produce less sodden rice. We were using 1½ cups of long-grain white rice to 1½ cups of chicken stock plus 2 cups of water. By reducing the stock to a mere ½ cup, we had better results. The rice was indeed lighter, but the top layer of rice was undercooked and dried out. This was solved by stirring the dish once when adding the breast meat so that the rice on top was stirred into the bottom, producing more even cooking.

We then made four different batches using four different liquids: chicken stock (heavy, greasy rice), water (bland, flat tasting), a combination of wine and water (the acidity of the wine cuts through the fat, producing clean, clear flavors), and a combination of water, chopped canned tomatoes, and tomato liquid (the acid in the tomatoes punches up and enriches flavor). We then used a combination of white wine, water, chopped tomatoes, and tomato liquid with excellent results. For the freshest flavor, use only chopped or diced tomatoes *not* packed in a puree or sauce. Tomatoes packed in juice will result in a cleaner, brighter flavor.

Finally, we tested different varieties of rice to see which held up best to this sort of cooking. A basic long-grain white rice was fine, with good flavor and decent texture; a medium-grain rice was creamy with a risotto-like texture and excellent flavor (some testers found this version too heavy, but others on the tasting panel forgave the dense texture for the improved flavor); basmati rice was nutty, with separate, light grains (by far the lightest version, but basmati seemed somewhat out of place in such a pedestrian dish); and converted rice, which was absolutely tasteless although virtually indestructible. So basic long-grain white rice is a fine all-purpose solution, although both medium-grain and basmati rices can also be used with different but good results.

Chicken and Rice

SERVES 4

THIS IS THE BASIC CHICKEN and rice dish. Although we rarely suggest stirring rice during cooking, it is necessary here to ensure that the top layer of rice does not undercook and dry out. If you prefer, you can make this dish with packaged breast meat parts or boneless chicken thighs, using a total of eight pieces. Be sure to use canned tomatoes that are packed in their own juices rather than in a puree or sauce.

1 chicken (3 to 3 1/2 pounds), rinsed, patted dry, and cut into 8 pieces (see "Cutting Up a Whole Chicken," page 10)
Salt and pepper
2 tablespoons olive oil
1 medium onion, chopped
3 garlic cloves, minced
1 1/2 cups long-grain or medium-grain white rice or basmati rice
1 cup chopped canned tomatoes, plus 1/2 cup packing liquid
1/2 cup white wine
1/4 cup chopped fresh parsley leaves

1. Season the chicken liberally with salt and pepper. Heat the oil in a heavy Dutch oven over medium-high heat. When the oil is hot, add the chicken parts, skin side down, and brown, turning several times, until very dark, about 12 minutes. Remove the chicken to a bowl and pour off all but 2 tablespoons of the fat from the pot.

2. Lower the heat to medium. Add the onion and cook, stirring frequently, until softened, 3 to 4 minutes. Add the garlic and continue to cook for 1 minute. Stir in the rice and cook, stirring, for an additional minute. Add the tomatoes and their liquid, the wine, and 2 cups water. Scrape the bottom of the pot with a wooden spoon to loosen any browned bits.

3. Add back the chicken thighs and legs (the breasts will be added later), and bring to a boil. Cover the pot and simmer gently for 15 minutes. Add the chicken breasts, stir ingredients gently so that the rice is thoroughly mixed, cover, and continue to cook for 10 to 15 minutes, or until rice is done. Stir in the parsley and serve immediately.

Chicken and Rice with Indian Spices

THIS VARIATION HAS SEVERAL OF THE SPICES TRADI-
TIONALLY USED IN INDIAN COOKING INCLUDING CIN-
NAMON, TURMERIC, CUMIN, AND CORIANDER. IT IS
PARTICULARLY GOOD WHEN MADE WITH BASMATI RICE.
SERVES 4.

  1 chicken (3 to 3½ pounds), rinsed, patted
    dry, and cut into 8 pieces (see "Cutting
    Up a Whole Chicken," page 10)
  Salt and pepper
  2 tablespoons olive oil
  1 3-inch piece cinnamon stick
  1 medium onion, chopped
  2 green bell peppers, cored, seeded, and
    cut into ½-inch dice
  3 garlic cloves, minced
  1 teaspoon ground turmeric
  1 teaspoon ground coriander
  1 teaspoon ground cumin
  1½ cups long-grain white rice or basmati rice
  1 cup chopped canned tomatoes, plus
    ½ cup packing liquid
  ½ cup white wine
  ¼ cup chopped fresh parsley leaves

1. Season the chicken liberally with salt and pepper.
Heat the oil in a heavy Dutch oven over medium-
high heat. When the oil is hot, add the chicken
parts, skin side down, and brown, turning several
times, until very dark, about 12 minutes. Remove the
chicken to a bowl and pour off all but 2 tablespoons
of the fat from the pot.

2. Lower the heat to medium. Add the cinnamon
stick and stir with a wooden spoon until it unfurls,
about 10 seconds. Add the onion and bell peppers and
cook, stirring frequently, until softened, 5 to 6 minutes. Add the garlic and ground spices and cook for 1
minute. Stir in the rice and cook, stirring, for an additional minute. Add the tomatoes and their liquid, the
wine, and 2 cups water. Scrape the bottom of the pot
with a wooden spoon to loosen any browned bits.

3. Add back the chicken thighs and legs (the breasts
will be added later), and bring to a boil. Cover the pot
and simmer gently for 15 minutes. Add the chicken
breasts, stir ingredients gently so that the rice is thoroughly mixed, cover, and continue to cook for 10 to
15 minutes, or until rice is done. Discard the cinnamon stick, stir in the parsley, and serve immediately.

◆

Chicken and Rice with Saffron, Peas, and Paprika

THE SAFFRON GIVES THE RICE AN EARTHY FLAVOR AND
BRILLIANT YELLOW COLOR IN THIS SPANISH-STYLE
CASSEROLE. YOU MAY USE FRESH PEAS IN THIS RECIPE,
BUT THEY MUST BE BLANCHED BEFORE BEING ADDED TO
THE POT. FROZEN PEAS WILL DELIVER GOOD RESULTS
AND CAN BE USED WITHOUT PRECOOKING OR THAW-
ING. SERVES 4.

  1 chicken (3 to 3½ pounds), rinsed,
    patted dry, and cut into 8 pieces (see
    "Cutting Up a Whole Chicken," page
    10)
  Salt and pepper
  2 tablespoons olive oil
  1 medium onion, chopped
  2 green bell peppers, cored, seeded, and
    cut into ½-inch dice
  3 garlic cloves, minced
  4 teaspoons paprika
  ¼ teaspoon saffron threads
  1½ cups long-grain or medium-grain
    white rice
  1 cup chopped canned tomatoes, plus
    ½ cup packing liquid
  ½ cup white wine
  1 cup frozen peas
  ¼ cup minced fresh parsley leaves

1. Season the chicken liberally with salt and pepper. Heat the oil in a heavy Dutch oven over medium-high heat. When the oil is hot, add the chicken parts, skin side down, and brown, turning several times, until very dark, about 12 minutes. Remove the chicken to a bowl and pour off all but 2 tablespoons of the fat from the pot.

2. Lower the heat to medium. Add the onion and bell peppers and cook, stirring frequently, until softened, 5 to 6 minutes. Add the garlic, paprika, and saffron and continue to cook for 1 minute. Stir in the rice and cook, stirring, for an additional minute. Add the tomatoes and their liquid, the wine, and 2 cups water. Scrape the bottom of the pot with a wooden spoon to loosen any browned bits.

3. Add back the chicken thighs and legs (the breasts will be added later), and bring to a boil. Cover the pot and simmer gently for 15 minutes. Add the chicken breasts, stir ingredients gently so that the rice is thoroughly mixed, cover, and continue to cook for 10 to 15 minutes, or until rice is done. Stir in the peas and parsley and set aside, covered, for 5 minutes. Serve immediately.

◆

Chicken and Rice with Jalapeño, Cilantro, and Lime Juice

FOR MORE FLAVOR, TOAST 2 TEASPOONS OF CUMIN SEEDS IN A NONSTICK SKILLET SET OVER MEDIUM HEAT FOR 3 TO 4 MINUTES AND THEN PROCESS IN AN ELECTRIC SPICE GRINDER. SERVES 4.

> 1 chicken (3 to 3½ pounds), rinsed, patted dry, and cut into 8 pieces (see "Cutting Up a Whole Chicken," page 10)
> Salt and pepper
> 2 tablespoons olive oil
> 1 medium onion, chopped
> 2 jalapeño chiles, stemmed, seeded, and minced
> 3 garlic cloves, minced
> 2 teaspoons ground cumin

2 teaspoons ground coriander
1 teaspoon chili powder
1½ cups long-grain white rice or basmati rice
1 cup chopped canned tomatoes, plus ½ cup packing liquid
½ cup white wine
¼ cup chopped fresh cilantro leaves
3 tablespoons fresh lime juice

1. Season the chicken liberally with salt and pepper. Heat the oil in a heavy Dutch oven over medium-high heat. When the oil is hot, add the chicken parts, skin side down, and brown, turning several times, until very dark, about 12 minutes. Remove the chicken to a bowl and pour off all but 2 tablespoons of the fat from the pot.

2. Lower the heat to medium. Add the onion and jalapeños and cook, stirring frequently, until softened, 3 to 4 minutes. Add the garlic and ground spices and continue to cook for 1 minute. Stir in the rice and cook, stirring, for an additional minute. Add the tomatoes and their liquid, the wine, and 2 cups water. Scrape the bottom of the pot with a wooden spoon to loosen any browned bits.

3. Add back the chicken thighs and legs (the breasts will be added later), and bring to a boil. Cover the pot and simmer gently for 15 minutes. Add the chicken breasts, stir ingredients gently so that the rice is thoroughly mixed, cover, and continue to cook for 10 to 15 minutes, or until rice is done. Stir in the cilantro and lime juice and set aside, covered, for 5 minutes. Serve immediately.

Chicken and Rice with Anchovies, Olives, and Lemon

KALAMATA OR OTHER BRINE-PACKED BLACK OLIVES WILL WORK BEST IN THIS RECIPE. THE ITALIAN FLAVORS IN THIS DISH CALL OUT FOR A SIMPLE LEAFY GREEN SALAD TO ROUND OUT THE MEAL. **SERVES 4.**

> 1 chicken (3 to 3½ pounds), rinsed, patted dry, and cut into 8 pieces (see "Cutting Up a Whole Chicken," page 10)
> Salt and pepper
> 2 tablespoons olive oil
> 1 medium onion, chopped
> 5 anchovy fillets, chopped
> 3 garlic cloves, minced
> 1½ cups long-grain or medium-grain white rice
> 1 cup chopped canned tomatoes, plus ½ cup packing liquid
> ½ cup white wine
> 1 teaspoon grated lemon zest
> 1 tablespoon fresh lemon juice
> ½ cup black olives, pitted and chopped
> ¼ cup chopped fresh parsley leaves

1. Season the chicken liberally with salt and pepper. Heat the oil in a heavy Dutch oven over medium-high heat. When the oil is hot, add the chicken parts, skin side down, and brown, turning several times, until very dark, about 12 minutes. Remove the chicken to a bowl and pour off all but 2 tablespoons of the fat from the pot.

2. Lower the heat to medium. Add the onion and anchovies and cook, stirring frequently, until softened, 3 to 4 minutes. Add the garlic and continue to cook for 1 minute. Stir in the rice and cook, stirring, for an additional minute. Add the tomatoes and their liquid, the wine, and 2 cups water. Scrape the bottom of the pot with a wooden spoon to loosen any browned bits.

3. Add back the chicken thighs and legs (the breasts will be added later), and bring to a boil. Cover the pot and simmer gently for 15 minutes. Add the chicken breasts, stir ingredients gently so that the rice is thoroughly mixed, cover, and continue to cook for 10 to 15 minutes, or until rice is done. Stir in the lemon zest and juice, olives, and parsley and set aside, covered, for 5 minutes. Serve immediately.

◆

Chicken and Rice with Curry

THIS CURRIED CASSEROLE CONTAINS TWO JALAPEÑOS AND IS FAIRLY SPICY. YOU CAN ADJUST THE HEAT LEVEL AS DESIRED. THIS DISH IS PARTICULARLY GOOD WHEN MADE WITH BASMATI RICE. **SERVES 4.**

> 1 chicken (3 to 3½ pounds), rinsed, patted dry, and cut into 8 pieces (see "Cutting Up a Whole Chicken," page 10)
> Salt and pepper
> 2 tablespoons olive oil
> 1 medium onion, chopped
> 2 jalapeño chiles, stemmed, seeded, and minced
> 3 garlic cloves, minced
> 1 tablespoon curry powder
> 1½ cups long-grain white rice or basmati rice
> 1 cup chopped canned tomatoes, plus ½ cup packing liquid
> ½ cup white wine
> ¼ cup chopped fresh cilantro leaves

1. Season the chicken liberally with salt and pepper. Heat the oil in a heavy Dutch oven over medium-high heat. When the oil is hot, add the chicken parts, skin side down, and brown, turning several times, until very dark, about 12 minutes. Remove the chicken to a bowl and pour off all but 2 tablespoons of the fat from the pot.

2. Lower the heat to medium. Add the onion and jalapeños and cook, stirring frequently, until softened, 3 to 4 minutes. Add the garlic and curry powder and continue to cook for 1 minute. Stir in the rice and cook, stirring, for an additional minute. Add the tomatoes and their liquid, the wine, and 2 cups water. Scrape the bottom of the pot with a wooden spoon to loosen any browned bits.

3. Add back the chicken thighs and legs (the breasts will be added later), and bring to a boil. Cover the pot and simmer gently for 15 minutes. Add the chicken breasts, stir ingredients gently so that the rice is thoroughly mixed, cover, and continue to cook for 10 to 15 minutes, or until rice is done. Stir in the cilantro and serve immediately.

◆

Chicken and Rice with Ginger, Soy Sauce, and Scallions

THE ASIAN FLAVORINGS IN THIS DISH ARE AN EXCELLENT MATCH WITH BOTH THE CHICKEN AND THE RICE. SERVE WITH STEAMED BROCCOLI OR SNOW PEAS. **SERVES 4.**

> 1 chicken (3 to 3 1/2 pounds), rinsed, patted
>   dry, and cut into 8 pieces (see "Cutting
>   Up a Whole Chicken," page 10)
> Salt and pepper
> 2 tablespoons olive oil
> 1 medium onion, chopped
> 3 garlic cloves, minced
> 1 tablespoon minced fresh gingerroot
> 1 1/2 cups long-grain or medium-grain
>   white rice or basmati rice
> 1 cup chopped canned tomatoes, plus
>   1/2 cup packing liquid
> 1/2 cup white wine
> 2 tablespoons soy sauce
> 1/4 cup chopped scallions

1. Season the chicken liberally with salt and pepper. Heat the oil in a heavy Dutch oven over medium-high heat. When the oil is hot, add the chicken parts, skin side down, and brown, turning several times, until very dark, about 12 minutes. Remove the chicken to a bowl and pour off all but 2 tablespoons of the fat from the pot.

2. Lower the heat to medium. Add the onion and cook, stirring frequently, until softened, 3 to 4 minutes. Add the garlic and ginger and continue to cook for 1 minute. Stir in the rice and cook, stirring, for an additional minute. Add the tomatoes and their liquid, the wine, and 2 cups water. Scrape the bottom of the pot with a wooden spoon to loosen any browned bits.

3. Add back the chicken thighs and legs (the breasts will be added later), and bring to a boil. Cover the pot and simmer gently for 15 minutes. Add the chicken breasts, stir ingredients gently so that the rice is thoroughly mixed, cover, and continue to cook for 10 to 15 minutes, or until rice is done. Stir in the soy sauce and scallions and set aside, covered, for 5 minutes. Serve immediately.

CHAPTER 21

CHICKEN STOCK

/|\

CHICKEN STOCK OR BROTH (ALTHOUGH THE WORDS

ARE USED INTERCHANGEABLY, TECHNICALLY STOCK IS

MADE WITH MEATY BONES AND BROTH IS MADE WITH

A WHOLE CHICKEN OR PARTS) IS THE BASIS FOR MANY

RECIPES IN THE BOOK—EVERYTHING FROM CHICKEN

NOODLE SOUP TO CHICKEN POT PIE. AS THE FRENCH

MASTER CHEF ESCOFFIER PROCLAIMED, "STOCK IS

EVERYTHING . . . WITHOUT IT NOTHING CAN BE DONE."

HACKING UP A CHICKEN FOR STOCK

/٨\

WHEN MAKING OUR MASTER RECIPE OR THE VARIATION WITH BREAST MEAT, YOU WILL NEED TO CUT THE CHICKEN INTO SMALL PIECES SO THAT THEY WILL RELEASE THEIR FLAVOR AS QUICKLY AS POSSIBLE. (SINCE THE CHICKEN SIMMERS FOR SUCH A LONG TIME IN THE TRADITIONAL STOCK

recipes, there is no need to cut up the parts.) We prefer to use a meat cleaver to hack the chicken into 2-inch pieces.

If using a whole chicken, start by removing the whole legs and wings from the body; set them aside. Separate the back from the breast, then split the breast and set the halves aside. Hack the back crosswise into three or four pieces, then halve each of these pieces. Cut the wing at each joint to yield three pieces. Leave the wing tip whole, then halve each of the remaining joints. Because of the larger bones, the legs and thighs are most difficult to cut. Start by splitting the leg and thigh at the joint, then hack each to yield three to four pieces. If using just backs, wing tips, or whole legs, follow the directions outlined above for that part.

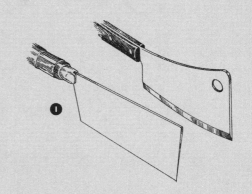

1. Chinese cleavers can be used to hack up poultry parts. The cleaver on the left is designed for chopping vegetables. It gently tapers to a slender cutting edge while the meat cleaver on the right is more like a wedge, tapering within the last 2 centimeters. The hole at the top corner of the meat cleaver is for hanging the cleaver on a hook.

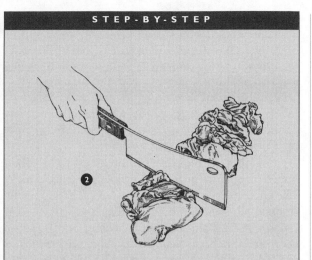

2. To hack through bone, place your hand near the far end of the meat cleaver's handle, curling your fingers securely around like a fist. Handle the meat cleaver the way you would a hammer, with the motion in the arm rather than the wrist, and the weight of the blade's front tip leading the force of the chop.

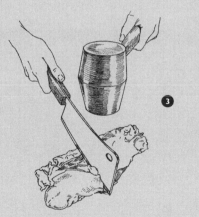

3. If you cannot chop the bone in one strike, place the cleaver in the groove of the first chop, then strike the blade's blunt edge with a heavy mallet or hammer wrapped in a kitchen towel.

Preparing your own stock is one of the best culinary investments you can make. Of course, most Americans buy canned broths, but these thin, insipid liquids cannot compete with the genuine article. (For information on getting the most from canned broth, see "The Canned Broth Dilemma," page 284.) Homemade stock has a richness, body, and flavor that canned versions never will have.

When developing stock recipes, we had two goals. We wanted to extract as much pure chicken flavor as possible from the meat and/or bones. We also wanted to keep the technique as simple and quick as possible.

The most common technique for making stock is to place all the ingredients (chicken, vegetables, aromatics, and water) into a pot, simmer, strain, and defat. We tested a tremendous number of ingredients—everything from thyme and parsley to carrots and parsnips—and found that we preferred stock with fewer ingredients. Onions, salt, and bay leaves complement the flavor of the chicken; everything else is a distraction. The exceptions are garlic and ginger, which we like to use in place of the onion and bay leaves when making stock for an Asian soup.

We tried a cut-up chicken as well as the more traditional necks and backs with the simmering method. The necks and backs are bony and yield a richer, more full-bodied stock. If your supermarket does not stock necks and bones, whole legs work just as well.

Some other tips emerged during our testing. For example, skim any impurities that rise to the surface as the water comes to a simmer. We found that removing the foam gave our stock a cleaner, clearer chicken flavor.

Don't let the stock boil too vigorously. Boiling breaks the fat into tiny droplets that a gravy skimmer will not be able to trap. The result is greasy stock. Allowing the fat to congeal while the stock chills in the refrigerator will fix this problem, but we often want to use stock right away. Keep the stock at a gentle simmer to avoid this whole issue.

Lastly, let the stock simmer as long as possible—up to five hours. We tried simmering stocks from one to six hours. When we tasted the various stocks, it was clear that more time yields a better stock. In fact, our favorite stock simmered for five hours. (After that we could not taste any improvement; evidently the bones were spent, having given up all their flavor to the stock.) The Long-Cooked Traditional Chicken Stock has a rich, intense chicken flavor—just what you want when making a simple chicken soup with a few dumplings or matzoh balls.

On other occasions, the Short-Cooked Traditional Chicken Stock, which simmers for two and one-half hours, is fine. Although the chicken flavor is not quite as intense, it is still good. We tried to cut back on the simmering time, but we were disappointed with the results.

Our testing had produced some good recipes so far, and we had reached some interesting conclusions about traditional stock making, but we wondered if we could find a quicker route to good stock. While throwing everything into the pot and letting it simmer for hours is easy (the hands-on work is no more than ten minutes), you do need to be around the house. Of course, there are times when you need stock in a hurry or don't want to hang around the house for five hours. We were willing to try almost anything.

We tried blanching a whole chicken under the theory that blanching keeps the chicken from releasing foam during cooking. The blanched chicken was then partially covered with water and placed in a heatproof bowl over a pan of simmering water. Cooked this way, the chicken never simmered, and the resulting broth was remarkably clear, refined, and full-flavored. The only problem was that it took four hours for the broth to take on sufficient flavor. We also noted that our 4-pound chicken was good for nothing but the compost heap after being cooked so long.

A number of recipes promote roasting chicken bones or parts and then using them to make stock. The theory, at least, is that roasted parts will flavor stock in minutes, not hours. We gave it a try several times, roasting chicken backs, necks, and bones—with and without vegetables. We preferred the roasted-parts stock with vegetables. The resulting stock was dark in color and had a nice caramelized onion flavor, but it still wasn't the full-flavored stock we were looking for. While the roasted notes were quite strong, the actual chicken flavor was too tame.

At last, we tried sautéing a chicken, hacked into small pieces, with an onion until the chicken lost its raw color. The pot was then covered and the chicken

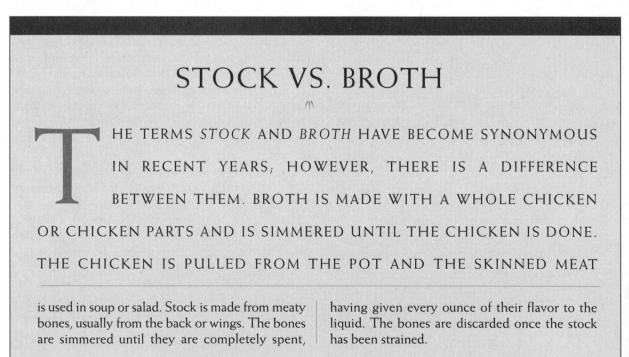

STOCK VS. BROTH

THE TERMS *STOCK* AND *BROTH* HAVE BECOME SYNONYMOUS IN RECENT YEARS; HOWEVER, THERE IS A DIFFERENCE BETWEEN THEM. BROTH IS MADE WITH A WHOLE CHICKEN OR CHICKEN PARTS AND IS SIMMERED UNTIL THE CHICKEN IS DONE. THE CHICKEN IS PULLED FROM THE POT AND THE SKINNED MEAT

is used in soup or salad. Stock is made from meaty bones, usually from the back or wings. The bones are simmered until they are completely spent, having given every ounce of their flavor to the liquid. The bones are discarded once the stock has been strained.

and onion cooked over low heat until they released their rich, flavorful juices, which took about twenty minutes. Only at that point was the water added, and the broth was simmered for just twenty minutes longer.

We knew we were onto something as we smelled the chicken and onions sautéing, and the finished broth confirmed what our noses had detected. The broth tasted pleasantly sautéed, not boiled. We had some refining to do, though. For once, we had made too strong a broth.

We substituted chicken backs and wing tips for the whole chicken and used more water. The broth was less intense, but just the right strength to make a base for some of the best chicken soup we've ever tasted. We made the stock twice more—once without the onion and once with onion, celery, and carrot. The onion added a flavor dimension we liked; the extra vegetables neither added to nor detracted from the final soup, so we left them out.

After much trial and error, we had a Master Recipe that delivered liquid gold in just forty minutes. While this recipe requires more hands-on work (hacking up parts, browning an onion, then chicken parts), it is ready in a fraction of the time required to make stock by traditional methods.

So how do you come up with the useless chicken parts for stock? The Buffalo chicken wing fad has made wings more expensive than legs and thighs. For those who can buy chicken backs, this is clearly an inexpensive way to make stock for soup. Our local grocery store usually sells them for almost nothing, but in many locations they may be difficult to get.

Luckily, we found that relatively inexpensive whole legs make incredibly full-flavored broths for soup. In a side-by-side comparison of a stock made from backs and broth made from whole legs, we found the whole leg broth was actually more full-flavored than the all-bone stock. For the less frugal, broth made from legs and thighs is, in fact, superior; just don't try to salvage the meat. After five minutes of sautéing, twenty minutes of sweating, and another twenty minutes of simmering, the meat is void of flavor.

If you are making a soup that needs some chicken meat, use a whole chicken as directed in Chicken Broth with Sautéed Breast Meat. The breast is removed in two pieces, sautéed briefly, and then added with the water to finish cooking. The rest of the bird —the legs, back, wings, and giblets—are sweated with the onions and discarded when the stock is done. However, the breast meat is perfectly cooked, ready to be skinned and shredded when cool. We particularly liked the tidiness of this method: one chicken yields one pot of soup. One note about this method. We found it necessary to cut the chicken into pieces small enough to release their flavorful juices in a short period of time (see "Hacking Up a Chicken for Stock," pages 278–279).

Stock freezes beautifully and you should always have some on hand. Try freezing stock in small airtight containers; we find portions of 1 cup or so allow us the most flexibility in the kitchen. If freezer space is at a premium, try reducing the defatted stock. (The fat can be discarded or refrigerated in an airtight container for several days and used in place of butter or oil in any poultry recipe.) Simply place the stock in a saucepan and simmer until it is reduced by half or more. The concentrated stock can be frozen in ice cube trays and then transferred to a sealable plastic bag. When you need stock, add the cube to some hot water.

When making stock, we generally keep the salt to a minimum. It's always possible to add more salt when it's time to use the stock. Use an especially light hand with the salt if you plan on reducing the stock significantly. Driving off water in the stock will intensify the saltiness as well as the chicken flavor.

SKIMMING AND DEFATTING STOCK

⌒

1. Chicken stock should be defatted before being used. The easiest way to do this is to refrigerate the stock until the fat rises to the surface and congeals. Use a spoon to scrape the fat off the surface of the stock.

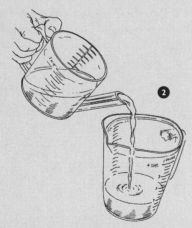

2. If you don't have time to refrigerate the stock and allow the fat to congeal, use a gravy skimmer. Pour the stock into the gravy skimmer. Pour the stock out the spout attached to the bottom of the skimmer. The fat will stay floating on top.

Chicken Stock

MAKES ABOUT 2 QUARTS

C HICKEN PIECES ARE sautéed and then sweated before being cooked in water for a rich but very quick stock. This is our favorite all-purpose stock. It also takes less than an hour to prepare.

1 tablespoon vegetable oil
1 medium onion, cut into medium dice
4 pounds chicken backs and wing tips or whole legs, cut into 2-inch pieces (see figures 1–3, pages 278–279)
2 quarts boiling water
2 teaspoons salt
2 bay leaves

1. Heat the oil in a large stockpot or soup kettle. Add the onion; sauté until colored and softened slightly, 2 to 3 minutes. Transfer the onion to a large bowl.

2. Add half of the chicken pieces to the pot; sauté until no longer pink, 4 to 5 minutes. Transfer the cooked chicken to the bowl with the onion. Sauté the remaining chicken pieces. Return the onion and chicken pieces to the pot. Reduce the heat to low, cover, and cook until the chicken releases its juices, about 20 minutes.

3. Increase the heat to high; add the boiling water, salt, and bay leaves. Return to a simmer, then cover and barely simmer until the broth is rich and flavorful, about 20 minutes.

4. Strain the broth; discard the solids. Skim the fat (see left). (The broth can be covered and refrigerated up to 2 days or frozen for several months.)

Chicken Broth with Sautéed Breast Meat

CHOOSE THIS BROTH WHEN YOU WANT TO HAVE SOME BREAST MEAT TO ADD TO SOUP. **MAKES ABOUT 2 QUARTS.**

1 tablespoon vegetable oil
1 whole chicken (about 3½ pounds),
    breast removed, split, and reserved;
    remaining chicken cut into 2-inch pieces
    (see figures 1–3, pages 278–279)
1 medium onion, cut into medium dice
2 quarts boiling water
2 teaspoons salt
2 bay leaves

1. Heat the oil in a large stockpot or soup kettle. When the oil shimmers and starts to smoke, add the chicken breast halves; sauté until brown on both sides, about 5 minutes. Remove the chicken breast pieces and set aside. Add the onion to the pot; sauté until colored and softened slightly, 2 to 3 minutes. Transfer the onion to a large bowl.

2. Add half of the chicken pieces to the pot; sauté until no longer pink, 4 to 5 minutes. Transfer the cooked chicken to the bowl with the onion. Sauté the remaining chicken pieces. Return the onion and chicken pieces (excluding the breasts) to the pot. Reduce the heat to low, cover, and cook until the chicken releases its juices, about 20 minutes.

3. Increase the heat to high; add the boiling water, the chicken breasts, salt, and bay leaves. Return to a simmer, then cover and barely simmer until the chicken breasts are cooked through and the broth is rich and flavorful, about 20 minutes.

4. Remove the chicken breasts from pot; when cool enough to handle, remove the skin from the breasts, then remove the meat from the bones and shred into bite-size pieces; discard the skin and bone. Strain the broth into a separate container; discard the solids. Skim the fat (see figures 1 and 2, opposite) and reserve for later use, if desired. (The shredded chicken and broth can be covered and refrigerated separately up to 2 days.)

DEFATTING CANNED BROTH

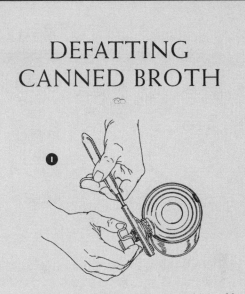

1. Most canned chicken stock contains a blob of fat that should be removed. While you can try to skim the fat off with a small spoon, the spoon can sometimes break the fat into smaller pieces. We find the following method is foolproof: Using a manual can opener, punch a small hole in the top of the can without turning. Rotate the can 180 degrees and make a second opening about ½ to 1 inch long.

2. Pour the stock through the larger opening. The liquid will pass through, but the more viscous fat will remain trapped in the can.

THE CANNED
BROTH DILEMMA

/I\

CANNED BROTH IS A SHORT-CUT WE WANT TO LIKE—IF ONLY IT TASTED BETTER. IN A BLIND TASTING OF A DOZEN CANNED BROTHS, WE FOUND LITTLE TO CHEER ABOUT. ALTHOUGH THE LOW-SODIUM PRODUCTS WERE GENERALLY PRE-FERRED, NO ONE WAS EXCITED ABOUT ANYTHING HE OR SHE TESTED.

Brands with MSG were singled out as having an odd chemical flavor. If you are going to use canned broth, try simmering it with some vegetables. If you have stray chicken parts around, such as clipped wing tips or a single back, add it as well.

◆

Improved Canned Chicken Broth

THIS BROTH CAN BE USED WITHOUT HESITATION IN MANY DISHES CALLING FOR CHICKEN STOCK—EVERYTHING FROM A STIR-FRY SAUCE TO RISOTTO OR CHICKEN POT PIE. IT'S ALSO FINE IN A CHICKEN SOUP WITH PLENTY OF OTHER FLAVORFUL INGRE-DIENTS. THE SHORTCOMINGS OF CANNED BROTH ARE QUITE NOTICEABLE IN A SOUP WHERE THE BROTH TAKES CENTER STAGE. WE DO NOT RECOM-MEND CANNED BROTHS, EVEN WHEN DOCTORED UP, IN WONTON SOUP, FOR INSTANCE. **MAKES ABOUT 3 CUPS.**

2 15-ounce cans low-sodium chicken
  broth, defatted (see figures 1 and 2,
  page 283)
1 carrot, peeled and sliced thin
1 medium onion, cut into medium dice
1 celery stalk, cut into chunks
Several sprigs fresh parsley

1. Place all the ingredients in a medium sauce-pan. Bring to a simmer. Simmer gently for 15 minutes.

2. Strain the broth; discard the solids. Use the stock as soon as possible; the improvement offered by the vegetables is temporary.

Short-Cooked Traditional Chicken Stock

THIS IS A SIMPLE, STANDARD CHICKEN STOCK. IT TAKES 2½ HOURS (MUCH LONGER THAN OUR MASTER RECIPE), BUT REQUIRES NO WORK OTHER THAN THROWING THE INGREDIENTS IN A POT. IF YOU WOULD RATHER NOT STAND OVER THE STOVE AND BROWN PARTS, THIS METHOD IS IDEAL. THE STOCK TASTES MORE LIKE BOILED CHICKEN THAN THE MASTER RECIPE, WHICH HAS A SLIGHTLY SAUTEED CHICKEN FLAVOR. **MAKES ABOUT 2 QUARTS.**

> 4 pounds chicken backs and wing tips or
> whole legs
> 1 medium onion, cut into medium dice
> 3 quarts water
> 2 teaspoons salt
> 2 bay leaves

1. Place all the ingredients in a large stockpot or soup kettle. Bring to a simmer, using a mesh skimmer to remove any foam that rises to surface. Simmer gently for 2½ hours.

2. Strain the broth; discard the solids. Skim the fat (see figures 1 and 2, page 282) and reserve for later use, if desired. (The broth can be covered and refrigerated up to 2 days or frozen for several months.)

Long-Cooked Traditional Chicken Stock

LONG-COOKED STOCK IS SIMPLE, BUT REQUIRES 5 HOURS OF COOKING TIME. THIS METHOD PRODUCES THE MOST FLAVORFUL STOCK OF ALL—EVEN MORE THAN THE MASTER RECIPE. IT REQUIRES A LARGE INVESTMENT OF TIME, BUT NOT EFFORT. SOUPS THAT RELY PRIMARILY ON STOCK FOR FLAVOR—MATZOH BALL OR WONTON, FOR EXAMPLE—BENEFIT FROM THE USE OF LONG-COOKED STOCK. THE SUBTLETIES IN THIS STOCK WILL BE LOST IN SOUPS WITH A LOT OF INGREDIENTS OR IN OTHER DISHES REQUIRING STOCK, SO USE THE MASTER RECIPE OR SHORT-COOKED STOCK INSTEAD. **MAKES ABOUT 2 QUARTS.**

> 4 pounds chicken backs and wing tips or
> whole legs
> 3½ quarts water
> 1 medium onion, cut into medium dice
> 2 teaspoons salt
> 2 bay leaves

1. Place the chicken and water in a large stockpot or soup kettle. Bring to a simmer, using a mesh skimmer to remove any foam that rises to surface. Simmer gently for 3 hours.

2. Add the onion, salt, and bay leaves and simmer for another 2 hours.

3. Strain the broth; discard the solids. Skim the fat (see figures 1 and 2, page 282) and reserve for later use, if desired. (The broth can be covered and refrigerated up to 2 days or frozen for several months.)

◆

Asian Stock

USE THIS STOCK FOR ANY ASIAN SOUP OR OTHER DISH WITH ASIAN FLAVORS. THE GINGER AND GARLIC FLAVORS ARE NOTICEABLE BUT NOT OVERPOWERING. **MAKES ABOUT 2 QUARTS.**

Follow any stock recipe, replacing the onion and bay leaves with a thinly sliced ½-inch chunk of unpeeled fresh gingerroot and 3 peeled and crushed garlic cloves.

CHICKEN

SOUP

/Λ\

WE'VE ALWAYS MADE GOOD VEGETABLE SOUP—UNFOR-

TUNATELY, IT WAS OFTEN THE PRODUCT OF A FAILED

CHICKEN SOUP. WE WOULD START OFF BY ADDING A

STANDARD HOMEMADE CHICKEN BROTH TO SAUTEED

CELERY, CARROTS, AND ONIONS. TO THE SIMMERING

BROTH AND VEGETABLES WE WOULD ADD SOME DICED

CHICKEN AND RICE OR NOODLES. THE RESULTING

"chicken soup" was so weak and characterless that we invariably added a can of tomatoes, a few potatoes, a turnip or two, and a package of green peas or mixed vegetables. It took all that to make the soup finally taste satisfying. Thus, chicken soup became vegetable soup.

Clearly, good chicken soup starts with robust stock that tastes like chicken. After much trial and error we developed several techniques for making stocks for soup. These broths are so rich and flavorful, you may long to be sick. The secret to intense chicken stock is the extra-long simmering of traditional recipes (with ingredients thrown into the pot and cooked over low heat) or a shortcut method that calls for browning an onion and hacked-up chicken parts to release their flavor and then adds water and cooks for twenty minutes. (For more information on making stock, see chapter 21.)

If the soup will not contain any chicken meat, the Master Recipe for stock or either of the traditional simmered stocks is fine. The first part of this chapter gives plenty of examples of these lighter soups, such as egg drop, matzoh ball, or wonton. These are first-course or luncheon soups.

The second part of this chapter focuses on soups with chicken meat in them. For these soups, our Chicken Broth with Sautéed Breast Meat is the only choice. The addition of the chicken meat, as well an array of vegetables, pasta, and/or rice, makes these soups much sturdier, suitable for a winter meal with a leafy salad and good bread.

Most of these soups should be served as soon as they are ready. Soups with eggs, pasta, or rice certainly cannot hold. Soups with just chicken and vegetables can be refrigerated for a day or two and then reheated, but we find that flavors are freshest when the soup is just made. We do suggest that you make the stock at least a day in advance. That way the stock can chill in the refrigerator and the fat can be easily removed.

Soup is open to tremendous variation and improvisation. While the recipes that follow are adaptable, we have carefully timed the addition of vegetables, noodles, grains, and other ingredients to make sure that each item is perfectly cooked, but not over-cooked. You may make adjustments if you keep in mind general cooking times for additional ingredients or substitutions.

◆

Straciatella

STRACIATELLA IS A SORT OF FRITTATA SOUP—A SIMPLE CHICKEN BROTH WITH BITS OF PARMESAN AND EGG FLOATING IN IT. FRESH BASIL IS DELICIOUS HERE, BUT PARSLEY MAY BE SUBSTITUTED. SERVES 6 TO 8.

 1 recipe (about 2 quarts) any traditional
     chicken stock (pages 282 and 285)
 4 eggs
 ¼ cup freshly grated Parmesan cheese
 ¼ cup finely chopped fresh basil leaves
 Pinch freshly grated nutmeg
 Salt and pepper

1. Bring the stock to a simmer in a large saucepan over medium-high heat. Whisk together the eggs, cheese, basil, and nutmeg in a medium bowl.

2. Swirl the pan so that the broth is moving in a circle. Pour the egg mixture into the broth in a slow, steady stream so that ribbons of coagulated egg form (see figure opposite). Let the eggs stand in the broth without mixing until they are set, less than 1 minute. Once they have set, break them up with a fork. Season with salt and pepper and serve immediately.

MAKING EGG DROP SOUP

Whisk the broth so that it is moving in a circle. Pour the eggs into the broth in a slow, steady stream so that ribbons of coagulated egg form.

Egg Drop Soup

THIS SIMPLE SOUP, A STANDARD IN CHINESE RESTAURANTS, IS EASILY MADE AT HOME. WITH HOMEMADE STOCK AND NO MSG, IT IS ALSO FAR SUPERIOR TO MOST TAKEOUT VARIETIES. SERVES 6 TO 8.

1 recipe (about 2 quarts) Asian Stock
   (page 285)
1 tablespoon soy sauce
Salt
2 tablespoons cornstarch
4 whole scallions, chopped fine
2 tablespoons finely chopped fresh
   cilantro leaves
4 eggs, beaten

1. Bring the stock to a simmer in a large saucepan set over medium-high heat. Add the soy sauce and salt to taste.

2. Combine the cornstarch and 2 tablespoons water in a small bowl and stir until smooth. Whisk the cornstarch mixture into the broth until it thickens slightly, about 1 minute. Stir in the scallions and cilantro.

3. Swirl the pan so that the broth is moving in a circle. Pour the eggs into the broth in a slow, steady stream so that ribbons of coagulated egg form (see figure, left). Let the eggs stand in the broth without mixing until they are set, less than 1 minute. Once they have set, break them up with a fork. Serve immediately.

Avgolemono

AVGOLEMONO IS A CLASSIC GREEK CHICKEN SOUP THICKENED WITH EGGS AND RICE AND FLAVORED WITH LEMON AND PARSLEY. WE LIKE CREAMY ARBORIO RICE HERE, BUT LONG-GRAIN WHITE RICE MAY ALSO BE USED. SERVES 6 TO 8.

1 recipe (about 2 quarts) any traditional
   chicken stock (pages 282 and 285)
1 cup arborio or long-grain white rice
4 eggs
1 cup fresh lemon juice
1/3 cup chopped fresh parsley leaves
Salt and pepper

1. Bring the stock to a simmer in a large saucepan set over medium-high heat. Add the rice and return to a simmer; lower the heat and cook, partially covered, until the rice is tender, about 20 minutes.

2. Whisk together the eggs, lemon juice, and parsley. Whisk the egg mixture into the kettle and continue whisking to break up clumps of rice and incorporate the eggs. Heat the soup through, but do not allow it to come to a boil. Season with salt and pepper to taste and serve immediately.

SHAPING WONTONS

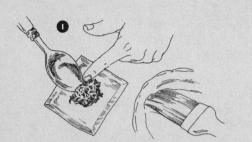

1. Position a wonton skin with one corner facing you and one pointing away from you. Brush the skin with beaten egg and place 1 teaspoon of filling in the center.

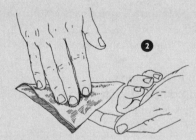

2. Fold the wonton in half, away from you, making a triangle. Press the edges firmly to seal.

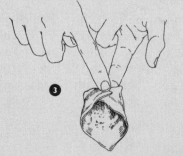

3. Brush the 2 corners nearest to you with egg, fold them in, and press them together to seal.

Chicken Broth with Pork Wontons

COMPARED TO TAKEOUT VERSIONS, HOMEMADE WON-TONS ARE A REVELATION—AND SURPRISINGLY SIMPLE TO MAKE. PORK IS THE TRADITIONAL FILLING, BUT BONELESS, SKINLESS CHICKEN THIGHS MAY BE SUBSTI-TUTED. THE FOLLOWING RECIPE MAKES 50 WONTONS. USE THEM ALL, OR PLACE THE EXTRAS ON A TRAY, WRAP IN PLASTIC, AND FREEZE THEM FOR LATER USE. WON-TON SKINS ARE AVAILABLE IN MANY SUPERMARKETS AND ASIAN GROCERIES. THE WONTONS ARE COOKED SEPARATELY IN BOILING WATER AND THEN ADDED TO THE BROTH. TRY TO TIME IT SO THAT THE BROTH IS ALREADY SIMMERING WHEN YOU COOK THE WONTONS. SERVES 6 TO 8.

> 10 ounces spinach, stemmed and washed
> 2 small boneless loin pork chops (about ¾ pound), trimmed of fat and cut into ½-inch chunks
> 1 teaspoon coarsely chopped fresh gingerroot
> 1 garlic clove, coarsely chopped
> 1 tablespoon soy sauce
> ½ teaspoon Asian sesame oil
> Salt and pepper
> 50 wonton skins
> 1 egg, beaten
> 1 recipe (about 2 quarts) Asian Stock (page 285)
> 6 scallions, finely chopped
> 6 large spinach leaves, stemmed and shredded

1. Bring 2 quarts of water to boil in a large soup kettle. Add the 10 ounces of spinach and cook for 1 minute. Drain the spinach and cool slightly. Squeeze the excess water from the cooked spinach (see figure on page 264) and coarsely chop.

2. Combine the spinach, pork, ginger, garlic, soy sauce, sesame oil, 1 teaspoon salt, and ½ teaspoon pepper in the work bowl of a food processor. Process until smooth and well combined. Scrape the filling into a medium bowl and adjust seasonings.

3. Place a wonton skin on a flat work surface. Brush with beaten egg and place a teaspoon of filling in the center of the skin (see figure 1, opposite). Fold the wonton in half, away from you, making a triangle (see figure 2, opposite). Press the edges firmly to seal. Brush the 2 corners nearest to you with egg, fold them in, and press them together to seal (see figure 3, opposite). Place the wontons on a large baking sheet and let them dry uncovered for 20 minutes.

4. Bring 4 quarts of water to a boil in a large pot. Salt the water and add the wontons. Cook 3 to 4 minutes, until the wontons are tender. Lift the wontons from the water with a slotted spoon and set them aside in a large bowl.

5. In the meantime, bring the stock to a simmer in a large soup kettle. Add the scallions and spinach leaves and cook 3 to 4 minutes, or until the spinach is wilted. Add the cooked wontons and simmer another 2 minutes, until they are heated through. Season with salt and pepper and serve immediately.

◆

Chicken Soup with Matzoh Balls

THIS SOUP IS BEST MADE WITH LONG-COOKED STOCK SINCE IT DEPENDS ON A STRONG, HEARTY CHICKEN FLAVOR. MATZOH BALLS MADE WITH CHICKEN FAT WILL BE MORE FLAVORFUL THAN THOSE MADE WITH VEGETABLE OIL. CARROTS AND DILL ADD COLOR TO THE FINISHED DISH. **SERVES 6 TO 8.**

4 eggs, beaten
½ cup water
¼ cup chicken fat or vegetable oil
1 cup matzoh meal
Salt and pepper
1 recipe (about 2 quarts) Long-Cooked
   Traditional Chicken Stock (page 285)
4 medium carrots, peeled, trimmed, halved
   lengthwise, and cut into 2-inch lengths
2 tablespoons finely chopped fresh dill
   (optional)

1. Combine the eggs, water, and chicken fat in a medium bowl. Stir in the matzoh meal. Season with salt and pepper to taste. Refrigerate the mixture for at least 1 hour or up to 4 hours.

2. Bring 4 quarts of water to a simmer in a wide pot. With moistened hands, form the matzoh mixture into balls the size of large walnuts. Drop the balls into the gently simmering water and cook, covered, for 15 minutes, turning them once so they cook evenly.

3. While the matzoh balls are cooking, bring the stock to a simmer in a large saucepan. Add the carrots and cook until tender, about 10 minutes. Add the cooked matzoh balls, stir in the dill if desired, and serve immediately.

◆

Passatelli

PASSATELLI IS THE ITALIAN VERSION OF MATZOH BALL SOUP, WITH DUMPLINGS MADE OF CHEESE AND BREAD CRUMBS. TRADITIONALLY, THE CHEESE AND DUMPLING MIXTURE IS PUSHED THROUGH A POTATO RICER TO MAKE PASTALIKE THREADS, BUT WE LIKE TO SHAPE THE MIXTURE INTO SMALL DUMPLINGS BECAUSE THERE IS LESS DANGER THAT THE DUMPLINGS WILL DISINTEGRATE IN THE SIMMERING SOUP. HOMEMADE BREAD CRUMBS ARE ESSENTIAL HERE AS IS THE BEST CHEESE, PREFERABLY PARMIGIANO-REGGIANO. FOR THE BREAD CRUMBS, GRIND 2 SLICES OF WHITE BREAD IN THE FOOD PROCESSOR AND THEN DRY OUT THE CRUMBS FOR 5 MINUTES IN A 300-DEGREE OVEN. **SERVES 6 TO 8.**

½ cup homemade bread crumbs
2 eggs
1 cup freshly grated Parmesan cheese,
   plus more for garnish
Pinch freshly grated nutmeg
Salt and pepper
1 recipe (about 2 quarts) any traditional
   chicken stock (pages 282 and 285)
2 tablespoons chopped fresh parsley leaves (optional)

(continued on next page)

1. Combine the bread crumbs, eggs, cheese, nutmeg, and salt and pepper to taste in a medium bowl. Refrigerate for 15 minutes to firm up.

2. Bring the stock to a simmer over medium heat.

3. With moistened hands, roll teaspoonfuls of the dumpling mixture into grape-size balls. Drop the dumplings into the gently simmering broth and cook until they float to the surface, 3 to 4 minutes. Stir in the parsley and serve with extra cheese.

◆

Chicken Noodle Soup with Chicken Livers and Peas

BITS OF CHICKEN LIVER RATHER THAN COOKED CHICKEN FLOAT IN CHICKEN BROTH. THIS ITALIAN SOUP IS SEASONED WITH GRATED PARMESAN CHEESE AND BRIGHTENED BY THE ADDITION OF FRESH OR FROZEN PEAS. WE CALL FOR EGG PASTINA FOR EXTRA RICHNESS, BUT ANY TINY PASTA SHAPE—STARS, ORZO, EVEN ALPHABETS—MAY BE SUBSTITUTED. SERVES 6 TO 8.

1 tablespoon butter
½ pound chicken livers
Salt and pepper
1 recipe (about 2 quarts) any chicken
    stock (pages 282 and 285)
½ cup egg pastina
½ cup frozen peas, thawed
¾ cup freshly grated Parmesan cheese

1. Melt the butter in a small skillet set over medium heat. Add the chicken livers and cook until firm and cooked through, 7 to 8 minutes. Transfer to a cutting board and cool slightly. Coarsely chop the livers, place them in a small bowl, and season with salt and pepper to taste.

2. Bring the stock to a simmer in a large soup kettle. Add the pastina and cook until tender, about 5 minutes. Stir in the livers, peas, and Parmesan and heat through for a minute or two. Season with salt and pepper and serve.

Hearty Chicken Noodle Soup

THIS IS A BASIC CHICKEN NOODLE SOUP RECIPE. FEEL FREE TO VARY OR ADD VEGETABLES AND EXPERIMENT WITH NOODLE SHAPES. SERVES 6 TO 8.

3 tablespoons vegetable oil or reserved
    chicken fat
1 medium onion, cut into medium dice
1 large carrot, peeled and sliced ¼ inch
    thick
1 celery stalk, sliced ¼ inch thick
½ teaspoon dried thyme
1 recipe (about 2 quarts) Chicken Broth
    with Sautéed Breast Meat (page 283),
    broth and meat separated
2 cups (3 ounces) hearty, wide egg
    noodles
¼ cup minced fresh parsley leaves
Salt and pepper

1. Heat the oil in a large soup kettle set over medium-high heat. Add the onion, carrot, and celery; sauté until softened, about 5 minutes. Add the thyme and broth; simmer until the vegetables are tender and flavors meld, 10 to 15 minutes.

2. Add the chicken meat and noodles and cook until just tender, about 10 minutes. Stir in the parsley and taste for salt and pepper. Serve immediately.

Chicken Soup with Leeks, Wild Rice, and Mushrooms

WILD RICE AND WILD MUSHROOMS LEND A WOODSY FLAVOR TO THIS LUXURIOUS TAKE ON BASIC CHICKEN NOODLE SOUP. WILD RICE TAKES MUCH LONGER TO COOK THAN REGULAR RICE OR PASTA, SO IT IS COOKED BEFORE BEING ADDED TO THE SOUP. SERVES 6 TO 8.

- 1 recipe (about 2 quarts) Chicken Broth with Sautéed Breast Meat (page 283), broth and meat separated
- 1/2 ounce dried wild mushrooms, such as porcini or shiitakes
- 1/2 cup wild rice
- 3 tablespoons vegetable oil or reserved chicken fat
- 1 medium leek, rinsed thoroughly, quartered lengthwise, then sliced thin crosswise (see page 105)
- 1 large carrot, peeled and sliced 1/4 inch thick
- 1/3 pound sliced fresh button or wild mushrooms
- 1/2 teaspoon dried thyme
- 1/4 cup minced fresh parsley leaves
- Salt and pepper

1. Heat 1 cup of chicken broth in a small saucepan. Stir in the dried mushrooms. Let sit 30 minutes, until the mushrooms are soft and rehydrated.

2. While the mushrooms are softening, combine the wild rice and 1 cup water in a small saucepan set over medium-high heat. Bring to a boil, cover, turn the heat to low, and cook until tender, 40 to 45 minutes.

3. Heat the oil in a large soup kettle set over medium-high heat. Add the leek and carrot; sauté until softened, about 5 minutes. Add the fresh mushrooms and continue to sauté until the mushrooms are softened, about 5 minutes.

4. Drain and chop the dried wild mushrooms; reserve the soaking broth. Pour the soaking broth through a strainer lined with a paper towel or coffee filter to remove any grit. Add this liquid, the dried mushrooms, the thyme, and remaining broth, to the kettle; simmer until the vegetables are tender and flavors meld, 10 to 15 minutes.

5. Add the chicken meat and wild rice and cook for 5 minutes. Stir in the parsley and taste for salt and pepper. Serve immediately.

◆

Italian Chicken Soup with Shells, Tomatoes, and Zucchini

ZUCCHINI, TOMATOES, AND PASTA SHELLS INSTEAD OF EGG NOODLES GIVE CHICKEN NOODLE SOUP AN ITALIAN FLAVOR. PASS GRATED PARMESAN CHEESE AT THE TABLE, IF DESIRED. SERVES 6 TO 8.

- 3 tablespoons vegetable oil or reserved chicken fat
- 1 medium onion, cut into medium dice
- 1 large carrot, peeled and sliced 1/4 inch thick
- 1 celery stalk, sliced 1/4 inch thick
- 1 medium zucchini, cut into medium dice
- 1/2 teaspoon dried thyme
- 1 recipe (about 2 quarts) Chicken Broth with Sautéed Breast Meat (page 283), broth and meat separated
- 1/2 cup chopped fresh or canned tomatoes
- 1 cup small shells or macaroni
- 1/4 cup minced fresh basil leaves
- Salt and pepper

1. Heat the oil in a large soup kettle set over medium-high heat. Add the onion, carrot, celery, and zucchini; sauté until softened, about 7 minutes. Add the thyme, broth, and tomatoes; simmer until the vegetables are tender and flavors meld, 10 to 15 minutes.

2. Add the chicken meat and shells and cook until just tender, about 10 minutes. Stir in the basil and taste for salt and pepper. Serve immediately.

Chicken Soup with Orzo and Spring Vegetables

HERE IS A SPRINGTIME VARIATION ON BASIC CHICKEN NOODLE SOUP. ORZO IS A RICE-SHAPED PASTA THAT IS PERFECT FOR SOUPS SINCE IT FITS EASILY ON A SPOON. SERVES 6 TO 8.

3 tablespoons vegetable oil or reserved chicken fat

1 medium leek, rinsed thoroughly, quartered lengthwise, then sliced thin crosswise (see figures 1 and 2, page 105)

1 large carrot, peeled and sliced 1/4 inch thick

1 celery stalk, sliced 1/4 inch thick

1/2 teaspoon dried thyme

1 recipe (about 2 quarts) Chicken Broth with Sautéed Breast Meat (page 283), broth and meat separated

1/2 cup orzo

1/4 pound trimmed asparagus, cut into 1-inch lengths (see figures 1 and 2, page 263)

1/4 cup fresh or frozen peas

2 tablespoons minced fresh tarragon leaves

Salt and pepper

1. Heat the oil in a large soup kettle set over medium-high heat. Add the leek, carrot, and celery; sauté until softened, about 5 minutes. Add the thyme and broth; simmer until the vegetables are tender and flavors meld, 10 to 15 minutes.

2. Add the chicken meat, orzo, asparagus, and peas and cook until just tender, about 8 minutes. Stir in the tarragon and taste for salt and pepper. Serve immediately.

Chicken Soup with Basil-Garlic Mayonnaise Toasts

AÏOLI, A FRENCH GARLIC MAYONNAISE, IS OFTEN USED TO FLAVOR SOUPS. THIS VERSION HAS SOME BASIL FOR COLOR AND FRESH FLAVOR. SPOON A LITTLE INTO EACH BOWL AND USE THE REST TO SPREAD ON ADDITIONAL BREAD. CAUTION: THIS RECIPE CONTAINS RAW EGG. (SEE PAGE 305.) SERVES 6 TO 8.

BASIL-GARLIC MAYONNAISE

3 garlic cloves, peeled

1/4 cup tightly packed fresh basil leaves

1 egg

2 tablespoons fresh lemon juice

1 cup extra-virgin olive oil

1/2 teaspoon salt, or to taste

3 tablespoons olive oil

1 small fennel bulb, stems, fronds, and base trimmed; bulb cored and cut into medium dice (see page 97)

1 medium onion, cut into medium dice

1 large carrot, peeled and sliced 1/4 inch thick

1 recipe (about 2 quarts) Chicken Broth with Sautéed Breast Meat (page 283), broth and meat separated

1 cup cooked or canned cannellini beans, drained

Salt and pepper

12 to 16 pieces lightly toasted French or Italian bread

1. For the mayonnaise, place the garlic and basil in the work bowl of a food processor. Process until coarsely chopped, scraping down the sides of the bowl several times as necessary. Add the egg and the lemon juice to the work bowl and pulse 2 or 3 times to break up. With the machine running, pour the extra-virgin olive oil through the feed tube in a thin stream. Process the mayonnaise about 1 minute, until it becomes thick and emulsified. Scrape the mayonnaise into a small bowl and stir in the salt. Refrigerate in an airtight container until ready to use.

2. Heat the olive oil in a large soup kettle set over medium-high heat. Add the fennel, onion, and carrot; sauté until softened, about 5 minutes. Add the broth; simmer until the vegetables are tender and flavors meld, 10 to 15 minutes. Add the chicken meat and beans and simmer until heated through, 3 or 4 minutes. Taste for salt and pepper.

3. Place 2 slices of toasted bread at the bottom of each soup bowl. Ladle some soup over the bread, top with a dollop of mayonnaise, and serve immediately with extra toasted bread and mayonnaise.

◆

Thai Chicken Soup with Cellophane Noodles

CELLOPHANE NOODLES, THAI FISH SAUCE, AND PICK-LED GINGER—AVAILABLE AT MANY SUPERMARKETS AND ASIAN GROCERIES—TURN CHICKEN BROTH INTO A QUICK, EXOTIC NOODLE SOUP. SERVES 6 TO 8.

- 1 recipe (about 2 quarts) Asian Stock (page 285) made according to directions for Chicken Broth with Sautéed Breast Meat (page 283), broth and meat separated
- ¼ pound dried cellophane noodles
- 2 ounces pickled ginger, sliced into ¼-inch slivers
- 2 tablespoons Thai fish sauce
- 3 whole scallions, finely chopped
- ¼ cup chopped fresh cilantro leaves
- Salt

1. Bring the stock to a boil in a large soup kettle set over medium-high heat. Add the noodles and cook until tender, 2 to 3 minutes. Remove the noodles from the pot with a slotted spoon and transfer them directly to the 6 or 8 soup bowls.

2. Add the chicken, pickled ginger, fish sauce, scallions, and cilantro to the soup kettle. Simmer until the flavors meld, about 2 minutes. Season with salt to taste. Ladle the soup over the noodles and serve immediately.

Chicken Velouté

THIS IS A CLASSIC FRENCH CREAM OF CHICKEN SOUP FLAVORED WITH SHERRY. IT CAN BE MADE WITH MILK, HALF-AND-HALF, OR HEAVY CREAM, DEPENDING ON THE DESIRED RICHNESS. SERVES 6 TO 8.

- 6 tablespoons unsalted butter
- 3 medium shallots, finely chopped
- 6 tablespoons all-purpose flour
- 1 teaspoon dried thyme
- 1 cup dry sherry
- 1 recipe (about 2 quarts) Chicken Broth with Sautéed Breast Meat (page 283), broth and meat separated
- 2 cups milk, half-and-half, or heavy cream
- Salt and pepper
- 2 tablespoons finely chopped fresh chives, for garnish

1. Melt the butter in a large soup kettle set over medium heat. Add the shallots and cook until soft, about 5 minutes. Do not brown. Stir in the flour and cook, stirring, until the floury smell has dissipated, 2 or 3 minutes.

2. Whisk in the thyme, sherry, and broth and continue to whisk for a minute to break up any lumps. Bring the soup to a simmer and cook for 15 minutes, skimming any foam that comes to the surface.

3. Add the milk and the chicken pieces and simmer for 1 minute. Season with salt and pepper, garnish with chives, and serve immediately.

Chicken Gumbo with Andouille Sausage and Okra

GUMBO IS TRADITIONALLY THICKENED WITH FILE—POWDERED SASSAFRAS LEAVES—BUT IT CAN ALSO BE THICKENED WITH A ROUX. WE CHOOSE THE ROUX BECAUSE FILE POWDER CAN BE DIFFICULT TO FIND OUTSIDE OF LOUISIANA. IF YOU CAN'T FIND ANDOUILLE SAUSAGE, SUBSTITUTE KIELBASA OR ANOTHER SMOKED SAUSAGE. SERVES 6 TO 8.

- ¾ pound andouille sausage, sliced into ¼-inch-thick rounds
- 1 medium onion, coarsely chopped
- 1 celery stalk, coarsely chopped
- 1 green bell pepper, stemmed, seeded, and cut into ¼-inch dice
- 4 scallions, white and light green parts, finely chopped
- 2 garlic cloves, finely chopped
- 4 tablespoons all-purpose flour
- 1 teaspoon Tabasco sauce
- 1 large ripe tomato, cored and chopped, *or* 1 cup chopped canned tomatoes
- 1 recipe (about 2 quarts) Chicken Broth with Sautéed Breast Meat (page 283), broth and meat separated
- 1 cup okra, trimmed and sliced into ¼-inch disks
- ½ cup long-grain white rice
- Salt and pepper

1. Set a large soup kettle over medium-high heat. Add the sausage and cook until brown, 7 to 8 minutes. Remove the sausage with a slotted spoon and drain on paper towels. Drain all but 2 tablespoons of the fat from the pot and add the onion, celery, bell pepper, scallions, and garlic. Cook until soft, about 5 minutes.

2. Stir in the flour and cook, stirring constantly, until the flour turns golden, 3 to 4 minutes. Add the Tabasco and tomato and bring to a simmer. Add the broth and okra and return to a simmer. Add the chicken, sausage, and rice and cook, partially covered, until the rice is tender, about 20 minutes. Taste for salt and pepper and serve.

Hearty Chicken Soup with Tomato, Jalapeño, and Avocado

A WHOLE HEAD OF GARLIC INFUSES THIS SOUP WITH A GENTLE GARLIC FLAVOR. THE CHILES, AVOCADO, AND LIME ARE CHARACTERISTIC OF MEXICAN HOME COOKING. SERVE THIS SOUP WITH WARM FLOUR TORTILLAS, OR FLOAT PIECES OF FRIED CORN TORTILLAS IN EACH BOWL. SERVES 6 TO 8.

- 1 recipe (about 2 quarts) Chicken Broth with Sautéed Breast Meat (page 283), broth and meat separated
- 1 garlic head, unpeeled, sliced in half crosswise
- 2 jalapeño chiles, stemmed, seeded, and cut into thin strips
- 1 medium onion, cut into ¼-inch dice
- Salt
- 2 medium ripe tomatoes (about ¾ pound), cored, seeded, and cut into ¼-inch dice
- ¼ cup chopped fresh cilantro leaves
- 2 small ripe avocados, peeled, pitted, and cut into ¼-inch dice
- 1 lime, cut into 6 to 8 wedges

1. Heat the broth and garlic in a large soup kettle set over medium-high heat. Bring to a simmer; lower the heat and cook, partially covered, for 20 minutes. Strain the stock and discard the garlic.

2. Return the stock to the pot. Add the jalapeños, onion, and salt to taste and bring to a simmer; cook for about 7 minutes. Add the tomatoes, cilantro, and chicken and simmer another 3 minutes. Ladle the soup into bowls and garnish with the avocado. Serve the lime wedges on the side.

Mulligatawny

MULLIGATAWNY IS A TRADITIONAL ANGLO-INDIAN SOUP, SPICED WITH CURRY. FINELY GRATED UNSWEET-ENED COCONUT (LOOK FOR THIS INGREDIENT AT NAT-URAL FOODS STORES AND INDIAN MARKETS) GIVES THE SOUP BODY AND CONTRASTS WELL WITH THE HOT CURRY. GARNISH BOWLS OF THIS SOUP WITH DOLLOPS OF YOGURT, OR SERVE CUCUMBER RAITA (PAGE 133) ON THE SIDE. SERVES 6 TO 8.

3 tablespoons vegetable oil
1 medium onion, cut into medium dice
1 large carrot, peeled and sliced ¼ inch thick
1 celery stalk, sliced ¼ inch thick
½ cup dried unsweetened grated coconut
4 tablespoons all-purpose flour
1½ tablespoons curry powder
1 teaspoon ground cumin
1 recipe (about 2 quarts) Chicken Broth with Sautéed Breast Meat (page 283), broth and meat separated
¾ cup chopped fresh cilantro leaves
Salt and pepper
1 cup low-fat yogurt (optional)

1. Heat the oil in a large soup kettle set over medium-high heat. Add the onion, carrot, and celery; sauté until softened, about 5 minutes. Add the coconut and cook another 2 minutes. Add the flour, curry powder, and cumin, and cook, stirring constantly, another 2 minutes. Add the broth and bring to a simmer; cook, partially covered, for 20 minutes.

2. Carefully pour half the hot soup into a blender. Place a towel over the blender lid and hold it in place while pureeing the soup. Return the pureed soup to the pot. Add the chicken, cilantro, and salt and pepper to taste. Cook until heated through, 2 to 3 minutes. Adjust the seasonings. Serve immediately, with dollops of yogurt, if desired.

Sweet and Sour Chicken and Shallot Soup

LEMON JUICE, SUGAR, AND FISH SAUCE MAKE THIS SOUP SWEET, SALTY, AND SOUR. SWEET THAI BASIL, AVAILABLE IN MANY ASIAN GROCERIES, IS AUTHENTIC, BUT IF IT IS UNAVAILABLE, REGULAR BASIL OR EVEN MINT MAY BE SUBSTITUTED. SERVES 6 TO 8.

1 tablespoon vegetable oil
8 medium shallots, peeled and sliced thin
½ teaspoon hot red pepper flakes, or to taste
1 recipe (about 2 quarts) Asian Stock (page 285) made according to directions for Chicken Broth with Sautéed Breast Meat (page 283), broth and meat separated
3 tablespoons Thai fish sauce
2 tablespoons fresh lemon juice
2 teaspoons sugar
¼ cup chopped fresh sweet Thai basil leaves
Salt

1. Heat the oil in a large soup kettle set over medium-high heat. Add the shallots and red pepper flakes; sauté until softened, about 5 minutes.

2. Add the stock and bring to a simmer. Stir in the chicken, fish sauce, lemon juice, sugar, and basil. Cook just until flavors meld, about 3 minutes. Season with salt to taste and serve immediately.

Mexican Chicken Soup with Chicken Meatballs

INSTEAD OF CHICKEN PIECES, THIS SOUP FEATURES GARLICKY, CILANTRO-SPIKED MEATBALLS. IF GROUND CHICKEN IS UNAVAILABLE, GROUND TURKEY MAY BE SUBSTITUTED. YOU NEED TO ADD SOME OIL TO THE MEATBALLS TO KEEP THEM MOIST. MOST OF THE REMAINING OIL IN THIS RECIPE IS USED TO FRY THE MEATBALLS AND IS DISCARDED ONCE THE MEATBALLS ARE COOKED. SERVES 6 TO 8.

10 tablespoons vegetable oil
8 garlic cloves, peeled
1 cup tightly packed cilantro leaves
Salt and pepper
1 pound ground chicken or turkey
1 egg, beaten
¾ cup bread crumbs
1 recipe (about 2 quarts) any chicken stock (pages 282 and 285)
2 jalapeño chiles, stemmed, seeded, and sliced thin
2 medium tomatoes (about ¾ pound), cored, seeded, and cut into ¼-inch dice
2 tablespoons fresh lime juice

1. Combine 4 tablespoons vegetable oil, the garlic, cilantro, ½ teaspoon salt, and pepper to taste in the work bowl of a food processor. Process until smooth, scraping down the sides of the bowl as necessary.

2. Combine the ground chicken, egg, bread crumbs, and cilantro mixture in a large bowl and mix until just combined. Roll the chicken mixture into balls the size of walnuts and refrigerate for at least 30 minutes or up to 2 hours.

3. Bring the stock to a simmer in a large soup kettle. Add the jalapeños and tomatoes and cook for 5 minutes.

4. Heat the remaining 6 tablespoons of oil in a wide skillet set over medium-high heat until hot but not smoking. Cook the meatballs in batches, shaking the pan occasionally and turning them once or twice until they are brown on all sides and are cooked through, 7 to 10 minutes. Drain the meatballs on a plate lined with paper towels.

5. Add the meatballs to the simmering soup and cook for 5 minutes. Stir in the lime juice and serve immediately.

CHICKEN
SALAD

/|\

CHICKEN SALAD IS NOT A COMPLEX OR COMPLICATED

RECIPE: TENDER BREAST MEAT IS PULLED APART BY

HAND (NOT CUBED WITH A KNIFE), AND BOUND

LOOSELY WITH A DRESSING, USUALLY MAYONNAISE. IN

THE CLASSIC RECIPE, THERE'S A LITTLE CELERY FOR

TEXTURE, SOME PARSLEY AND SCALLIONS FOR FLAVOR,

AND A SQUEEZE OF LEMON JUICE FOR FRESHNESS. WE

OFTEN MAKE THIS SALAD FROM LEFTOVER ROAST OR

poached chicken, and put it together by taste and sight.

But what if you don't have any leftover chicken in the refrigerator? How should the chicken be cooked for use specifically in a salad? We identified several possibilities before going into the kitchen. Poaching is the method usually cited in cookbooks. Steaming, roasting, and baking in foil are other less common choices. In addition to these methods, research uncovered yet another technique, a sort of cousin to poaching: the chicken breasts are dropped into simmering aromatic water, the pot is covered and removed from the heat, and the chicken sits in the liquid for two hours as it cools from a near boil to almost room temperature.

Because we prefer an all white-meat chicken salad, we ran our tests with whole chicken breasts. We decided to start with bone-in, skin-on breasts, but we were also ready to try boneless, skinless chicken breasts if poaching proved the favored method.

Our tests results were consistent and conclusive. Wet-cooked chicken breasts—those steamed, poached, simmered, or roasted in foil—all had a bland, unmistakably boiled flavor that the tasters didn't like. Allowing the chicken breast to cook in the gradually cooling liquid yielded juicy, tender meat, but with that now-familiar moist-cooked chicken flavor. We repeated this technique, substituting a flavorful chicken broth for the aromatic water; the resulting meat was more flavorful, but clearly wet-cooked. Not surprisingly, chicken cooked in the microwave also had that watery taste.

Salads made with oven-roasted chicken breasts were our hands-down favorite. Even after the skin and bones were removed, the meat tasted roasted and the resulting chicken salad was superb. Try one of the following recipes, or if you have your own favorite salad recipe, roast rather than poach the chicken and experience the difference firsthand. Dry heat is clearly the answer.

Simple Roasted Chicken Breasts

MAKES ENOUGH FOR 1 RECIPE CHICKEN SALAD

LINING A JELLY-ROLL PAN or other baking pan with foil makes cleanup a breeze. We find that whole breasts cook up slightly juicier than split breasts, but the latter may be used in this recipe, reducing the baking time by 5 or 10 minutes.

2 large, whole bone-in, skin-on chicken
  breasts (at least 1½ pounds each)
1 tablespoon vegetable oil
Salt

Adjust the oven rack to the middle position and heat the oven to 400 degrees. Set the chicken breasts on a small, foil-lined baking pan. Brush with the oil and sprinkle generously with salt. Roast until a meat thermometer inserted into the thickest part of breast registers 160 degrees, 35 to 40 minutes. Cool the chicken to room temperature, remove the skin, and continue with one of the chicken salad recipes that follow. (The chicken breasts can be wrapped in plastic and refrigerated for 2 days.)

REMOVING MEAT FROM A ROASTED BREAST

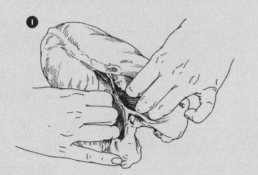

1. Once the roasted chicken breasts have cooled to room temperature, remove the skin and pull each side of the breast away from the bone in a single piece.

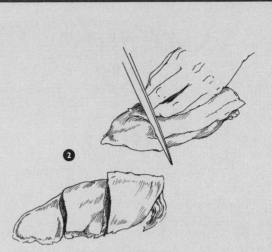

2. Cut each breast half into thirds with a chef's knife.

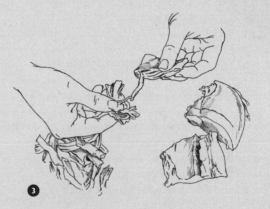

3. Shred the meat by hand into small pieces to guarantee a rough surface to which the dressing may adhere. Do not chop the chicken with a knife; the cut surfaces will be too smooth.

Creamy Chicken Salad

SERVES 6

THIS IS THE CLASSIC all-American recipe, with mayonnaise, celery, and scallions. In addition to the parsley leaves, you can flavor the salad with 2 tablespoons of minced fresh tarragon or basil leaves. See figures 1 through 3 (page 301) for information on removing the meat from the roasted chicken breasts. Two whole bone-in breasts will yield about 5 cups of shredded meat.

 1 recipe Simple Roasted Chicken Breasts
   (page 300), skinned and boned, meat
   shredded into bite-size pieces
 2 medium celery stalks, cut into small dice
 2 whole scallions, minced
 ¾ to 1 cup mayonnaise
 1 ½ to 2 tablespoons fresh lemon juice
 2 tablespoons minced fresh parsley leaves
   Salt and pepper

Mix all the salad ingredients in a large bowl, including salt and pepper to taste. Serve. (The chicken salad can be covered and refrigerated overnight.)

Chicken Salad with Hoisin Dressing

TRY SERVING THIS ASIAN-STYLE SALAD ON A BED OF YOUNG SPINACH LEAVES, SLICED CUCUMBER, AND RADISHES OR ROLL IT UP IN A FLOUR TORTILLA WITH SHREDDED ICEBERG LETTUCE OR WATERCRESS. SERVES 6.

 ⅓ cup rice wine vinegar
 1 ½ tablespoons soy sauce
 3 tablespoons hoisin sauce
 1 tablespoon minced fresh gingerroot
 1 tablespoon Asian sesame oil
 3 tablespoons vegetable oil
 1 recipe Simple Roasted Chicken Breasts
   (page 300), skinned and boned, meat
   shredded into bite-size pieces
 2 medium celery stalks, cut into small dice
 2 whole scallions, minced
 2 tablespoons minced fresh cilantro or
   parsley leaves

1. Whisk the vinegar, soy sauce, hoisin sauce, and ginger together in a small bowl; whisk in both oils and set the dressing aside.

2. Mix the remaining salad ingredients in a large bowl. Add the dressing; toss to coat. Serve. (The chicken salad can be covered and refrigerated overnight.)

◆

Waldorf Chicken Salad

THIS AMERICAN CLASSIC FEATURES CRISP APPLES AND TOASTED WALNUTS IN A MAYONNAISE-BASED CHICKEN SALAD. SERVE OVER SALAD GREENS—ICEBERG IF YOU WANT TO BE FAITHFUL TO THE ORIGINAL, OR, BETTER STILL, TENDER DARK GREENS LIKE BABY SPINACH OR ARUGULA. SERVES 6.

 6 tablespoons chopped walnuts
 1 recipe Simple Roasted Chicken Breasts
   (page 300), skinned and boned, meat
   shredded into bite-size pieces

1 large, firm apple such as Granny Smith,
   cored and cut into medium dice
2 medium celery stalks, cut into small dice
2 whole scallions, minced
¾ to 1 cup mayonnaise
1½ to 2 tablespoons fresh lemon juice
2 tablespoons minced fresh parsley leaves
Salt and pepper

1. Place the walnuts in a small skillet over medium heat. Toast, shaking the pan occasionally, until fragrant, about 5 minutes.

2. Mix all the salad ingredients in a large bowl, including salt and pepper to taste. Serve. (The chicken salad can be covered and refrigerated overnight.)

◆

Chicken Salad with Chipotle Vinaigrette

CHIPOTLE CHILES IN ADOBO ARE SMOKY, WITH MILD TO MEDIUM HEAT. THEY ARE AVAILABLE IN LATIN GROCERIES AND MANY SUPERMARKETS. YELLOW CHERRY TOMATOES ADD NICE COLOR AND ACIDITY TO THE SALAD, BUT IF THEY ARE UNAVAILABLE, RED ARE FINE. SERVES 6.

¼ cup olive oil
¼ cup fresh lime juice
2 chipotle chiles in adobo
Salt and pepper
1 recipe Simple Roasted Chicken Breasts
   (page 300), skinned and boned, meat
   shredded into bite-size pieces
2 small avocados, peeled, seeded, and cut
   into ¼-inch dice
12 yellow or red cherry tomatoes, halved
2 tablespoons finely chopped red onion
2 tablespoons minced fresh cilantro leaves

1. Combine the oil, lime juice, and chiles in the work bowl of a food processor or blender; process until blended. Scrape the dressing into a small bowl and season with salt and pepper to taste.

2. Combine the remaining ingredients in a large bowl. Pour the dressing over the salad and toss to combine. Serve. (The chicken salad can be covered and refrigerated overnight.)

◆

Chicken Salad with Moroccan Spices

CUMIN, PAPRIKA, CAYENNE, AND SMALL BLACK MOROCCAN OLIVES GIVE THIS SALAD ITS NORTH AFRICAN FLAVOR. IF YOU CAN'T FIND MOROCCAN OLIVES, ANY OTHER SMALL BLACK VARIETY, SUCH AS NIÇOISE, WILL DO. SERVES 6.

1 teaspoon ground cumin
1 teaspoon sweet paprika
½ teaspoon cayenne pepper
2 garlic cloves, finely chopped
¼ cup olive oil
¼ cup fresh lemon juice
¼ cup chopped fresh cilantro leaves
Salt and pepper
1 recipe Simple Roasted Chicken Breasts
   (page 300), skinned and boned, meat
   shredded into bite-size pieces
1 red bell pepper, stemmed, seeded, and
   cut into ¼-inch dice
2 whole scallions, minced
20 Moroccan, Niçoise, or other small
   black olives, pitted and coarsely
   chopped

1. Whisk the cumin, paprika, cayenne, garlic, olive oil, lemon juice, cilantro, and salt and pepper to taste together in a small bowl; set the dressing aside.

2. Mix the remaining salad ingredients in a large bowl. Add the dressing; toss to coat. Serve. (The chicken salad can be covered and refrigerated overnight.)

MAKING YOUR OWN MAYONNAISE

/\

MAYONNAISE IS A THICK, CREAMY EMULSION OF EGG YOLK AND OIL WITH A LITTLE ACID AND SOME SEASONINGS. AN EMULSION IS A MIXTURE OF TWO THINGS THAT DON'T ORDINARILY MIX, SUCH AS OIL AND WATER, OR OIL AND VINEGAR. THE ONLY WAY TO MIX THEM IS TO STIR OR WHISK SO

strenuously that the two ingredients break down into tiny droplets. Many of these droplets will continue to find each other and recoalesce into pure fluid. (This is what happens when the emulsion breaks.) Eventually one of the fluids will break entirely into droplets so tiny that they remain separated by the opposite fluid.

The liquid in droplet form is called the *dispersed phase* because the droplets are dispersed throughout the emulsion. The liquid that surrounds the droplets is the *continuous phase.* Because the continuous phase forms the surface of the emulsion, that's what the mouth and tongue feel and taste first.

The science of mayonnaise is fairly complex and unusual. In this case, whisking transforms three thin liquids—vegetable oil, lemon juice, and egg yolk—into a thick, creamy sauce. In this sauce, the egg yolk and lemon juice are the continuous phase (that's why something that is 95 percent oil doesn't taste greasy) and the oil is the dispersed phase that must be broken into tiny droplets.

Mayonnaise works because an egg yolk is such

a good emulsifier and stabilizer. But sometimes mayonnaise can "break," as the ingredients revert back to their original liquid form. To keep mayonnaise from breaking, it is first necessary to whisk the egg yolk and lemon juice thoroughly (the egg yolk itself contains liquid and fat materials that must be emulsified). It is equally important to add the oil *slowly* to the egg yolk. Remember, 2 tablespoons of yolk and lemon juice are being "stretched" around ¾ cup of oil.

In terms of oil, we like the flavor of corn oil in our basic mayonnaise. It produces a dressing that is rich and eggy with good body. Canola oil makes a slightly lighter, more lemony mayo. We find that extra-virgin olive oil can be harsh and bitter, especially if used alone in mayonnaise. Pure olive oil produces a mellower mayonnaise but is more costly than corn or canola oil and does not deliver better results.

Homemade mayo makes an especially delicious chicken salad, but many cooks prefer the convenience and safety of commercial brands made without raw eggs. In our tasting of major brands, Hellmann's (sold under the Best Foods label in the

West) came out on top. Among light or reduced-calorie brands, Hellmann's again beat out Kraft, which is its main competition in the marketplace.

◆

Classic Mayonnaise

EACH TIME YOU ADD OIL, MAKE SURE TO WHISK UNTIL IT IS THOROUGHLY INCORPORATED. MAYONNAISE SHOULD HAVE A SMOOTH, UNIFORM CONSISTENCY. IF IT APPEARS GRAINY OR BEADED AFTER THE LAST ADDITION OF OIL, CONTINUE TO WHISK AND IT SHOULD EMULSIFY. TO KEEP THE BOWL STABLE WHILE WHISKING, TRY SETTING IT ON A WET DISHCLOTH. MAKES ABOUT 1 CUP.

> 1 large egg yolk
> 1 1/2 teaspoons salt
> 1/4 teaspoon Dijon mustard
> 1 1/2 teaspoons fresh lemon juice
> 1 teaspoon white wine vinegar
> 3/4 cup corn oil

1. Whisk the egg yolk vigorously in a medium bowl for 15 seconds. Add all the remaining ingredients except for the oil and whisk until the yolk thickens and color brightens, about 30 seconds.

2. Add 1/4 cup oil in a slow, steady stream, continuing to whisk vigorously until the oil is incorporated completely and the mixture thickens, about 1 minute. Add another 1/4 cup oil in the same manner, whisking until it is incorporated completely, about another 30 seconds. Add last 1/4 cup oil all at once and whisk until it is incorporated completely, about 30 seconds more. Use immediately or refrigerate in an airtight container for several days.

Food Processor Mayonnaise

A YOLK-ONLY MAYONNAISE WILL BECOME TOO THICK IN A FOOD PROCESSOR. SINCE YOU ARE USING THE WHOLE EGG, THE OTHER INGREDIENTS MUST BE DOUBLED. MAKES ABOUT 1 1/2 CUPS.

> 1 large egg
> 1 tablespoon salt
> 1/2 teaspoon Dijon mustard
> 1 tablespoon fresh lemon juice
> 2 teaspoons white wine vinegar
> 1 1/2 cups corn oil

Place all of the ingredients except for the oil in the work bowl of a food processor fitted with the metal blade and pulse 3 or 4 times to combine. With the machine running, add the oil in a thin, steady stream through the open feed tube until it is incorporated completely. Use immediately or refrigerate in an airtight container for several days.

CAUTION: These recipes contain raw egg. Because of the threat of salmonella, food safety experts advise against serving raw eggs to the very young, the elderly, and those whose immune systems are compromised. The rest of us eat them at our own risk.

Jicama and Chicken Salad with Ginger Vinaigrette

JICAMA IS A STARCHY, SLIGHTLY SWEET ROOT VEG-
ETABLE THAT LOOKS A LITTLE LIKE A TURNIP AND
TASTES A LITTLE BIT LIKE A WATER CHESTNUT. PEELED,
CHOPPED (¼-INCH PIECES ARE THE RIGHT SIZE FOR
THIS SALAD), AND UNCOOKED, IT GIVES THIS SALAD
DRESSED WITH A GINGER VINAIGRETTE SOME CRUNCH.
SERVES 6.

> ¼ cup/olive oil
> 1 tablespoon Dijon mustard
> Grated zest of 1 lemon
> 2 tablespoons fresh lemon juice
> 1 tablespoon finely chopped fresh
>   gingerroot
> ¼ cup finely chopped fresh cilantro leaves
> Salt and pepper
> 1 recipe Simple Roasted Chicken Breasts
>   (page 300), skinned and boned, meat
>   shredded into bite-size pieces
> 2 cups peeled, diced jicama (see figures
>   1–4, page 168)
> 3 whole scallions, sliced into thin rounds

1. Whisk the oil, mustard, lemon zest and juice, ginger, cilantro, and salt and pepper to taste together in a
small bowl; set the dressing aside.

2. Mix the remaining salad ingredients in a large
bowl. Add the dressing; toss to coat. Serve. (The
chicken salad can be covered and refrigerated
overnight.)

Curried Chicken Salad with Raisins and Honey

THIS SWEET AND SPICY CHICKEN SALAD IS EXCELLENT
OVER SALAD GREENS OR SPOONED INTO A CRUSTY
ROLL. SERVES 6.

> 1 recipe Simple Roasted Chicken Breasts
>   (page 300), skinned and boned, meat
>   shredded into bite-size pieces
> 2 medium celery stalks, cut into small dice
> 2 whole scallions, minced
> 2 tablespoons minced fresh cilantro or
>   parsley leaves
> ¾ to 1 cup mayonnaise
> 1½ to 2 tablespoons fresh lemon juice
> 6 tablespoons golden raisins
> 2 teaspoons curry powder
> 1 tablespoon honey
> Salt and pepper

Mix all the salad ingredients in a large bowl, including
salt and pepper to taste. Serve. (The chicken salad can
be covered and refrigerated overnight.)

◆

Vietnamese Chicken Salad

FISH SAUCE, AVAILABLE IN ASIAN GROCERIES AND MANY
SUPERMARKETS, GIVES THIS SALAD ITS DISTINCTIVE
FLAVOR. NAPA CABBAGE MAY SUBSTITUTE FOR THE BOK
CHOY HERE. TRY THIS SALAD OVER RICE NOODLES,
ALSO AVAILABLE AT ASIAN GROCERIES. SERVES 6.

> ¼ cup vegetable oil
> 2 tablespoons fresh lime juice
> 1 tablespoon Vietnamese or Thai fish
>   sauce
> 1 teaspoon sugar
> 2 garlic cloves, finely chopped
> 1 small fresh hot red pepper or jalapeño
>   chile, seeded and minced (optional)

1 recipe Simple Roasted Chicken Breasts
(page 300), skinned and boned, meat
shredded into bite-size pieces
½ head bok choy, cored, outer leaves
trimmed, and leaves cut crosswise into
thin strips
1 carrot, peeled and shredded
2 whole scallions, minced
2 tablespoons minced fresh mint leaves
2 tablespoons chopped unsalted peanuts

1. Whisk the oil, lime juice, fish sauce, sugar, garlic, and hot pepper together in a small bowl; set the dressing aside.

2. Mix the chicken, bok choy, carrot, scallions, and mint in a large bowl. Add the dressing; toss to coat. Garnish with peanuts. Serve. (The chicken salad can be covered and refrigerated for several hours.)

◆

Chicken and Mango Salad with Curry-Lime Dressing

WHITE MEAT CHICKEN, NEUTRAL IN FLAVOR, IS OFTEN THE PERFECT FOIL FOR HIGHLY FLAVORED AND SPICED SALAD INGREDIENTS. HERE CHICKEN SERVES AS A BACK-DROP FOR A SURPRISING BUT DELICIOUS COMBINATION OF SWEET MANGOES, PEPPERY ARUGULA, AND CURRY POWDER. SERVES 6.

2 teaspoons curry powder
¼ cup olive oil
2 tablespoons fresh lime juice
¼ teaspoon hot red pepper flakes,
or to taste
Salt and pepper
1 recipe Simple Roasted Chicken Breasts
(page 300), skinned and boned, meat
shredded into bite-size pieces
1 bunch arugula, stemmed and washed
2 ripe mangoes, peeled, pitted, and cut
into ½-inch dice (see figures 1–4,
page 121)

1. Whisk the curry powder, oil, lime juice, red pepper flakes, and salt and pepper to taste together in a small bowl; set the dressing aside.

2. Mix the remaining ingredients in a large bowl. Add the dressing; toss to coat. Serve. (The chicken salad can be covered and refrigerated overnight.)

◆

Chicken Salad with Yogurt-Dill Dressing

YOGURT, CUCUMBER, AND DILL ARE CLASSIC FLAVOR-INGS FOR MILD, CREAMY CHICKEN SALAD. MIX WELL BEFORE SERVING, AS THE YOGURT AND CUCUMBER MIGHT RELEASE SOME WATER IF ALLOWED TO STAND FOR ANY LENGTH OF TIME. SERVES 6.

1 recipe Simple Roasted Chicken Breasts
(page 300), skinned and boned, meat
shredded into bite-size pieces
1 cucumber, peeled, seeded, and cut into
¼-inch dice
1 cup plain low-fat yogurt
1 tablespoon fresh lemon juice
2 tablespoons minced fresh dill
Salt and pepper

Mix all the salad ingredients in a large bowl, including salt and pepper to taste. Serve. (The chicken salad can be covered and refrigerated overnight.)

Chicken and Orange Salad

SHERRY VINEGAR HAS AN OAKY, SLIGHTLY SWEET FLA-
VOR. RED WINE VINEGAR MAY BE SUBSTITUTED FOR A
MORE ACIDIC DRESSING. SERVES 6.

> ¼ cup olive oil
> 2 tablespoons sherry vinegar
> 1 recipe Simple Roasted Chicken Breasts
>   (page 300), skinned and boned, meat
>   shredded into bite-size pieces
> 2 navel oranges, peeled, separated into
>   sections, and cut into ½-inch dice
> 2 tablespoons finely chopped red onion
> ¼ cup chopped fresh parsley leaves
> Salt and pepper

1. Whisk the oil and vinegar together in a small bowl.

2. Mix all the salad ingredients and dressing in a large bowl, including salt and pepper to taste. Serve. (The chicken salad can be covered and refrigerated overnight.)

◆

Chicken and Escarole Salad

TO MAKE YOUR OWN FAT-FREE CROUTONS, CUT DAY-
OLD COUNTRY WHITE BREAD INTO ½-INCH CUBES,
PLACE THEM ON A BAKING SHEET, AND BAKE IN A 350-
DEGREE OVEN UNTIL GOLDEN AND CRISP, ABOUT 10
MINUTES. IF YOU PREFER, USE THE GARLIC CROUTONS
FROM THE CHICKEN CAESAR SALAD RECIPE (OPPOSITE
PAGE) OR STORE-BOUGHT CROUTONS. SERVES 6.

> ¼ cup olive oil
> 2 tablespoons red wine vinegar
> 1 garlic clove, chopped fine
> 1 recipe Simple Roasted Chicken Breasts
>   (page 300), skinned and boned, meat
>   shredded into bite-size pieces
> 1 medium head escarole, cored, tough
>   outer leaves removed, and torn into
>   bite-size pieces
> 1 cup croutons
> Salt and pepper

1. Whisk the oil, vinegar, and garlic together in a small bowl.

2. Mix all the salad ingredients and dressing in a large bowl, including salt and pepper to taste. Serve immediately.

◆

Chicken Salad with Bacon and Potatoes

IF YOU COOK THE CHICKEN AHEAD OF TIME, LET IT
COME TO ROOM TEMPERATURE BEFORE MAKING THE
SALAD SO THAT THE WARM DRESSING WON'T BECOME
CHILLED WHEN POURED FROM THE SKILLET. SERVES 6.

> 12 small red potatoes (about ¾ pound)
> 4 slices bacon
> 1 recipe Simple Roasted Chicken Breasts
>   (page 300), skinned and boned, meat
>   shredded into bite-size pieces
> 1 bunch arugula, trimmed and washed
> 2 whole scallions, minced
> 3 tablespoons olive oil
> 2 tablespoons balsamic vinegar
> Salt and pepper

1. Bring 2 quarts of water to a boil in a medium saucepan. Cook the potatoes until they are tender but not falling apart, about 15 minutes. Drain, cool, and quarter them. Set the potatoes aside.

2. Cook the bacon in a small skillet over medium-high heat until crisp, 6 to 8 minutes. Lift the bacon from the pan, drain on paper towels, crumble, and set aside. Leave 2 tablespoons of bacon drippings in the pan; discard the rest. Set the pan aside.

3. Combine the potatoes, bacon, chicken, arugula, and scallions in a large bowl. Add the oil and vinegar to the pan with the bacon drippings and set over medium-high heat until boiling, about 1 minute. Pour over the salad ingredients, season with salt and pepper to taste, and serve immediately.

Chicken Caesar Salad

CODDLING (COOKING THE EGG IN THE SHELL FOR
ABOUT A MINUTE) SETS SOME OF THE PROTEINS AND
HELPS THE EGG TO CREATE A THICK, SMOOTH DRESS-
ING. CODDLING, HOWEVER, DOES NOT HEAT THE EGG
SUFFICIENTLY TO KILL ANY BACTERIA THAT MAY BE
PRESENT. (SEE CAUTION, PAGE 305.) SERVES 6.

GARLIC CROUTONS

2 large garlic cloves, pureed through a
  press or by hand (see figures 1 and 2,
  page 129)
¼ teaspoon salt
3 tablespoons extra-virgin olive oil
2 cups ½-inch white bread cubes (from a
  baguette or country loaf)

CAESAR DRESSING

3 tablespoons fresh lemon juice
1 teaspoon Worcestershire sauce
¼ teaspoon salt
8 grindings fresh black pepper
1 small garlic clove, pureed through a
  press or by hand (see figures 1 and 2,
  page 129)
4 anchovy fillets, minced fine
1 large egg
⅓ cup extra-virgin olive oil

2 medium heads romaine lettuce or 2
  large romaine hearts
⅓ cup freshly grated Parmesan cheese
1 recipe Simple Roasted Chicken Breasts
  (page 300), skinned and boned, meat
  shredded

1. For the croutons, preheat the oven to 350 degrees. Combine the garlic, salt, and oil in a small bowl; set aside for 20 minutes. Spread the bread cubes out over a small baking sheet. Pour the oil through a fine-mesh strainer and drizzle it directly onto the bread. Toss to coat the bread evenly with oil. Bake until golden, about 12 minutes. Cool on a baking sheet to room temperature. Store the croutons in an airtight container for up to 1 day.

2. For the dressing, whisk the lemon juice, Worcestershire, salt, pepper, garlic, and anchovies together in a medium bowl. Bring several cups of water to a boil in a small saucepan. Carefully place the egg in the boiling water and cook for 45 seconds. Remove the egg with a slotted spoon and cool very briefly. Crack the egg into the bowl with the other ingredients and whisk until smooth. Add the oil in a slow, steady stream, whisking constantly until smooth. Adjust the seasonings. The dressing may be refrigerated in an airtight container for 1 day; shake before using.

3. Discard any bruised outer leaves from the romaine heads, if using. Tear the large crisp inner leaves crosswise into 4 pieces; tear the smaller leaves into 3 pieces. Wash the lettuce in a bowl of cold water until free of grit. Spin dry. There should be about 10 cups. (The lettuce may be refrigerated in sealable plastic bag for up to 4 hours.)

4. When ready to serve, place the lettuce in a large bowl. Drizzle with half of the dressing and toss to lightly coat the leaves. Sprinkle with the cheese, drizzle with the remaining dressing, and add the chicken. Toss until the leaves are well coated with dressing and cheese. Add the croutons, toss several times, and divide the salad among individual plates. Serve immediately.

ROASTED CORNISH GAME HENS

/|\

EVEN THOUGH CORNISH HENS ARE RELATIVELY CHEAP

(TWO FOR $5 IN MOST SUPERMARKETS) AND COOK

QUICKLY ENOUGH FOR A WEEKNIGHT SUPPER (LESS

THAN THIRTY MINUTES UNSTUFFED), MOST PEOPLE

THINK OF THEM AS "COMPANY FOOD." AND FOR GOOD

REASON. THEY STUFF BEAUTIFULLY AND MAKE AN

impressive presentation when served one to a guest.

However, cooking Cornish hens to perfection is not easy. If roasted breast side up, the breast will surely overcook before the legs and thighs are done. Getting the birds to brown properly with such a short stay in the oven is difficult, especially if you have crowded six birds into one large pan. And a 500-degree oven is not the answer to any of these problems. Six little birds dripping fat onto an overheated roasting pan will set off smoke alarms all over the neighborhood.

Stuffing also presents some challenges. Because the cavity is the last spot to heat up, getting the stuffing to reach a safe internal temperature of 160 degrees means overcooking the meat in many cases.

One final problem: After roasting a few batches, we thought the flavor of these birds was unremarkable. Most Cornish hens are mass produced (companies that specialize in free-range or boutique chickens have not entered this market) and are lacking in flavor. Our mission then was clear: to stuff and roast six grocery-store quality Cornish hens in a way that they looked good (the skin had to brown) and tasted great (we

would have to up the flavor in the meat), without overcooking them or smoking up the kitchen.

You may as well steam Cornish hens as roast six of them in a high-sided roasting pan. The pan sides shield the birds from oven heat, and their snug fit in the pan further prevents browning. So our first move was to get the birds up out of the pan and onto a wire rack set over the pan. We also switched to a large roasting pan that measured 19 by 13 inches. Our second step was to space the birds as far apart as possible on the rack to ensure even cooking and good browning.

From our initial tests, we determined that rotating the birds was crucial for moist, juicy breast meat. Because Cornish hens are in the oven for such a short time, we opted for just one turn, as opposed to the two turns we favor when roasting a regular chicken. We found that one turn, from breast side down to breast side up, kept the breast meat from becoming dry or coarse-textured and was not too much of a hassle.

After roasting Cornish hens at temperatures ranging from 350 to 500 degrees, as well as roasting high and finishing low and roasting low and finishing high, we

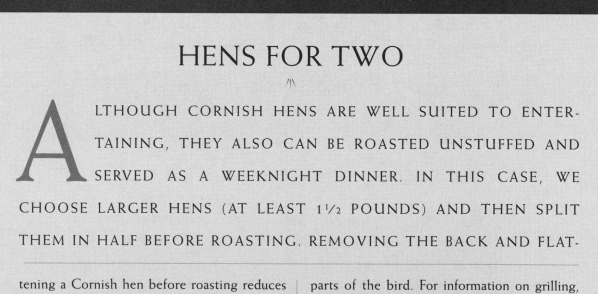

HENS FOR TWO

/|\

ALTHOUGH CORNISH HENS ARE WELL SUITED TO ENTER-
TAINING, THEY ALSO CAN BE ROASTED UNSTUFFED AND
SERVED AS A WEEKNIGHT DINNER. IN THIS CASE, WE
CHOOSE LARGER HENS (AT LEAST 1 1/2 POUNDS) AND THEN SPLIT
THEM IN HALF BEFORE ROASTING. REMOVING THE BACK AND FLAT-

tening a Cornish hen before roasting reduces the cooking time to just twenty-five minutes and promotes even cooking among the various parts of the bird. For information on grilling, broiling, and sautéing butterflied Cornish hens, see page 205.

found that all oven temperatures have their problems. We finally settled on 400 degrees, cranking up the oven to 450 degrees during the last few minutes. This roasting temperature was high enough to encourage browning while low enough to prevent excessive smoking. Adding water to the roasting pan once the chicken fat starts to render and the juices flow guarantees a smokeless kitchen. Another perk: the pan is automatically deglazed in the oven. Once the birds are roasted, you can pour the pan juices into a saucepan without having to deglaze the roasting pan over two burners.

Even at these relatively high temperatures, the skin was not quite as brown as we might have liked. Forty-five minutes, no matter what the oven temperature, is not enough time to get a dark mahogany skin on any bird. We decided to see if we could improve the appearance of the skin with a glaze of some sort. We tested balsamic vinegar, soy sauce, and jam thinned with a little soy sauce. All three glazes worked beautifully. The balsamic glaze was our favorite, giving the hens a pleasing spotty brown, barbecued look.

With the cooking and skin issues resolved, we turned our attention to boosting the flavor in the bland meat. Two hours in a saltwater bath transformed mediocre-tasting birds into something special. Much like koshering, brining draws out the blood, giving the birds a clean, fresh flavor. The salt flavor permeates the birds, making each bite, rather than just the skin, taste seasoned.

Our final challenge was to roast the birds, stuffed, without overcooking. Starting the hens breast side down was a help, since it slowed down the cooking in the heat-sensitive breast meat. Heating the stuffing in a microwave before spooning it into each hen also helped. By the time the stuffing reached 160 degrees (a temperature sufficient to kill any salmonella), the breast was 172 degrees and the thigh 176 degrees. As we expected, the thigh was nice and juicy at this temperature. Surprisingly, the breast meat—which we usually think is ideally cooked to 165 to 170 degrees—was still nice and juicy at this higher temperature and not at all dry, like birds that had been filled with room temperature stuffing.

Although we were aware that trussing would slow down the roasting of the hens' legs and thighs, we

COMPARING CHICKEN, CORNISH HENS, AND POUSSIN

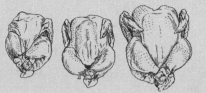

A standard broiler/fryer chicken (right) weighs between 3½ and 4 pounds and will feed 4 people. A standard supermarket Cornish hen (middle) weighs at least 1½ pounds, maybe 2 pounds, enough to feed 2 people. A poussin (left) weighs about 1 pound, ideal for a single serving.

knew we had to do something. With their more fragile, loose frame, Cornish hens are unsightly with their dangling legs. Stuffing the birds further increases the need to close the cavity. We discovered that simply tying the legs together improved the look of our hens and secured the stuffing without impeding roasting.

One final note about buying Cornish hens. It is becoming increasingly difficult to find small Cornish hens. Not long ago, these dwarfed birds hovered around a pound, but for economic reasons, producers started growing them bigger. Now the consumer is lucky to find them under 1½ pounds.

Larger hens can serve two (each bird will yield at least 12 ounces of meat and skin), but small hens (under 1½ pounds) are best for individual presentation.

You may want to look for poussin at your local butcher shop. These baby chickens usually weigh just 1 pound—the perfect size for an individual portion. Poussin are generally more flavorful than mass-produced Cornish hens. You can skip the brining step; just make sure to season them well before stuffing.

Roasted Stuffed Cornish Hens

SERVES 6

B RINING THE BIRDS breast side down ensures that the meatiest portions are fully submerged. Pouring a little water into the roasting pan at the 25-minute mark, once the birds have been turned, both prevents them from smoking during cooking and makes instant *jus*, eliminating the need to deglaze the pan over two burners. To enrich the flavor of the *jus* to use as a sauce, pour it into a small saucepan, spoon off the fat that collects on the surface, and simmer it with a little vermouth or white wine.

- 2 cups kosher *or* 1 cup table salt
- 6 Cornish hens (each less than 1½ pounds if possible), trimmed of extra fat, giblets removed and reserved for another use or for stuffing, rinsed well
- 1 recipe stuffing (see pages 316–320), heated until very hot in a microwave
- 6 tablespoons balsamic vinegar
- 3 tablespoons olive oil
- ¼ cup dry vermouth or white wine

1. Dissolve the salt in 5 quarts of cold water in a small, clean bucket or large bowl. Add the hens breast side down; refrigerate 2 to 3 hours. Remove, rinse thoroughly, pat dry, and prick skin all over the breast and legs with the point of a paring knife (see figure 1, opposite).

2. Adjust the oven rack to the middle position and heat the oven to 400 degrees. Spoon ½ cup of hot stuffing into the cavity of each hen (see figure 2, opposite); tie its legs together with a 10-inch piece of kitchen twine (see figure 3, opposite). Leaving as much space as possible between each bird, arrange them breast side down and wings facing out on a large (at least 19 by 13 inches) wire rack set over an equally large roasting or jelly-roll pan. Whisk the vinegar and oil in a small bowl; set aside.

3. Roast until the backs are golden brown, about 25 minutes. Remove the pan from the oven, brush the bird backs with the vinegar and oil glaze (reblending before each bird), turn the hens breast side up and the wings facing out, and brush the breast and leg areas with additional glaze. Return the pan to the oven, add 1 cup of water, and roast until a meat thermometer inserted into the stuffed cavity registers about 150 degrees, 15 to 20 minutes longer. Remove the pan from the oven again, brush the birds with the reblended glaze, return the pan to the oven, add ½ cup water to the pan, and increase the oven temperature to 450 degrees. Roast until the birds are spotty brown and the stuffed cavity registers 160 degrees, 5 to 10 minutes longer, depending on the bird size. Remove the birds from the oven, brush with the remaining glaze, and let rest for 10 minutes.

4. Meanwhile, pour the hen *jus* from the roasting pan into a small saucepan, spoon off excess fat, add the vermouth, and simmer over medium-high heat until the flavors blend, 2 to 3 minutes. Drizzle about ¼ cup of the sauce over each hen and serve, passing the remaining sauce separately.

PREPARING STUFFED CORNISH HENS

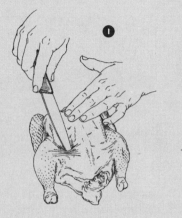

1. To prevent the skin from "ballooning" when juices build up, carefully prick the skin (but not the meat) on the breast and legs with the tip of a knife before roasting.

2. Spoon about ½ cup of hot stuffing into the cavity of each hen.

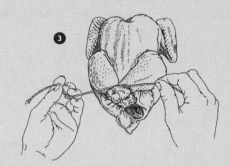

3. Tie the legs of the hen together with a 10-inch piece of kitchen twine.

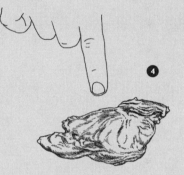

4. Hen livers can be a delicious addition to stuffings. Look for them in the plastic pouches packed into the cavity of most Cornish hens. The liver is dark, smooth, and about the size of a half-dollar.

NINE GREAT STUFFINGS
FOR CORNISH HENS

/I\

WHILE ANY STUFFING, INCLUDING THOSE FOR TURKEY (SEE PAGES 334–341), CAN BE USED TO FILL THE CAVITY OF A CORNISH HEN, THE FOLLOWING RECIPES MATCH BEAUTIFULLY THE DELICATE FLAVOR OF A HEN. A THANKSGIVING TURKEY MIGHT CALL FOR A TRADITIONAL BREAD STUFFING,

but hens can be filled with a variety of grains, including rice, couscous, quinoa, and barley.

Any of these stuffings may be prepared a day in advance, placed in a microwave-safe bowl, wrapped tightly with plastic, and refrigerated. Microwave the stuffing until it is quite hot just before stuffing it into the hens.

◆

Wild Rice Stuffing
with Carrots, Mushrooms,
and Thyme

THE WILD RICE BLEND (A MIXTURE OF REGULAR LONG-GRAIN AND WILD RICE) IN THIS STUFFING HOLDS TOGETHER WHEN PRESSED WITH A FORK. LOOK FOR WILD RICE BLENDS IN THE SUPERMARKET. YOU CAN USE ALL WILD RICE, BUT THE COOKED GRAINS WILL REMAIN SEPARATE. MAKES ABOUT 3 CUPS, ENOUGH TO STUFF 6 CORNISH HENS.

1 ounce dried porcini mushrooms, rehydrated in 1 cup hot tap water for 20 minutes
1¼ cups chicken stock or low-sodium chicken broth, or more if necessary
1 cup wild rice blend
2 tablespoons butter
1 small onion, minced
1 small carrot, minced
½ small celery stalk, minced
4 ounces fresh shiitake mushrooms, stemmed and sliced thin
2 teaspoons minced fresh thyme leaves
2 tablespoons minced fresh parsley leaves
Salt and pepper

1. Lift the rehydrated porcini from the liquid, squeeze dry, and chop coarse. Set aside. Strain the rehydrating liquid into a large measuring cup through a sieve lined with a paper towel or coffee filter. Add enough chicken stock to the mushroom liquid to equal 2 cups. Bring the liquid to a boil in a medium saucepan, add the rice blend, and return to a boil. Reduce the heat to low, cover, and simmer until the rice is fully cooked, 40 to 45 minutes. Turn the rice into a medium microwave-safe bowl; fluff with a fork.

2. Meanwhile, heat the butter in a medium skillet over medium heat. Add the onion, carrot, and celery; sauté until slightly softened, 3 to 4 minutes. Add the shiitake mushrooms; sauté until tender and liquid evaporates, about 5 minutes. Add the porcini mushrooms and the thyme; cook, stirring until well coated and blended with the other ingredients, 1 to 2 minutes longer. Add this mixture to the rice; toss to combine. Add the parsley and season with salt and pepper to taste.

◆

Wild Rice Stuffing with Cranberries and Toasted Pecans

RAISINS, CURRANTS, OR EVEN DRIED BLUEBERRIES MAY BE SUBSTITUTED FOR THE CRANBERRIES HERE. MAKES ABOUT 3 CUPS, ENOUGH TO STUFF 6 CORNISH HENS.

> 2 cups chicken stock or low-sodium canned chicken broth
> 1 cup wild rice blend
> 2 tablespoons butter
> 1 small onion, minced
> ½ small celery stalk, minced
> ¼ cup toasted pecans, coarsely chopped
> ¼ cup dried cranberries
> 2 tablespoons minced fresh parsley leaves
> 2 teaspoons minced fresh thyme leaves
> Salt and pepper

1. Bring the chicken stock to a boil in a medium saucepan. Add the rice blend; return to a boil. Reduce the heat to low, cover, and simmer until the rice is fully cooked, 40 to 45 minutes. Turn the rice into a medium microwave-safe bowl; fluff with a fork.

2. Meanwhile, heat the butter in a medium skillet over medium heat. Add the onion and celery; sauté until softened, 3 to 4 minutes. Add this mixture, as well as the pecans, cranberries, parsley, and thyme, to the rice; toss to coat. Season with salt and pepper to taste.

◆

Mashed Potato Stuffing

MASHED POTATOES ARE MOISTENED AND ENRICHED BY THE JUICES OF THE HENS WHEN THEY ARE USED AS STUFFING INSTEAD OF AS A SIDE DISH. SCALLIONS GIVE THE POTATOES AN ESPECIALLY APPEALING FLAVOR. MAKES ABOUT 3 CUPS, ENOUGH TO STUFF 6 CORNISH HENS.

> 4 large russet or Yukon Gold potatoes (about 2 pounds), peeled and cut in half
> 2 tablespoons butter
> 1 tablespoon heavy cream
> 8 scallions, white and light green parts, finely chopped
> Salt and pepper

1. Place the potatoes in a medium saucepan, cover with cold water, and bring to a boil. Cook the potatoes until soft and falling apart, about 30 minutes.

2. Drain and mash the potatoes with a potato masher in a microwave-safe bowl until fairly smooth. Stir in the butter, cream, scallions, and salt and pepper to taste.

Couscous Stuffing with Currants, Apricots, and Pistachios

TOASTED SLIVERED ALMONDS CAN BE SUBSTITUTED FOR THE PISTACHIOS. MAKES ABOUT 3 CUPS, ENOUGH TO STUFF 6 CORNISH HENS.

2 tablespoons butter
1 small onion, minced
2 medium garlic cloves, minced
¼ teaspoon ground cinnamon
⅛ teaspoon ground ginger
⅛ teaspoon ground turmeric
1 cup couscous
1⅓ cups chicken stock or low-sodium canned chicken broth
¼ cup dried apricots (8 to 9 whole), finely chopped
3 tablespoons currants
¼ cup shelled, toasted pistachio nuts, chopped
2 tablespoons minced fresh parsley leaves
1 teaspoon fresh lemon juice
Salt and pepper

1. Heat the butter over medium heat in a medium saucepan. Add the onion, garlic, cinnamon, ginger, and turmeric; sauté until the onion softens, 3 to 4 minutes. Add the couscous; stir until well coated, 1 to 2 minutes.

2. Add the chicken stock, bring to a simmer, remove from heat, cover, and let stand until the couscous has fully rehydrated, about 5 minutes. Fluff the couscous with a fork; stir in the dried fruit, nuts, parsley, and lemon juice. Season with salt and pepper to taste. Transfer the mixture to a microwave-safe bowl.

Brown Rice Stuffing with Dried Cherries

NUTTY, CHEWY BROWN RICE MAKES A HEARTY BUT NOT HEAVY STUFFING FOR CORNISH HENS. DRIED CHERRIES AND CINNAMON CONTRIBUTE TO THE EARTHY FLAVOR OF THE STUFFING. IF YOU LIKE, USE ONE 15-OUNCE CAN OF BROTH AND DILUTE IT WITH WATER TO EQUAL 2½ CUPS. MAKES ABOUT 3 CUPS, ENOUGH TO STUFF 6 CORNISH HENS.

2½ cups chicken stock or low-sodium canned chicken broth
1 cup brown rice
2 tablespoons butter
2 shallots, finely chopped
1 garlic clove, minced
½ cup dried cherries
¼ cup toasted walnuts, coarsely chopped
2 tablespoons minced fresh parsley leaves
¼ teaspoon ground cinnamon
Salt and pepper

1. Bring the chicken stock to a boil in a medium saucepan. Add the rice; return to a boil. Reduce the heat to low, cover, and simmer until the rice is fully cooked, 40 to 45 minutes. Turn the rice into a medium microwave-safe bowl; fluff with a fork.

2. Meanwhile, heat the butter in a medium skillet over medium heat. Add the shallots and garlic; sauté until softened, 3 to 4 minutes. Add this mixture, as well as the cherries, walnuts, parsley, cinnamon, and salt and pepper to taste, to the rice; toss to mix.

Bread Stuffing with Prunes, Port, and Ham

WHITE BREAD BINDS TOGETHER THIS SWEET-AND-SAVORY COMBINATION OF PRUNES AND HAM. IF NOT ALREADY STALE, TOAST THE BREAD CUBES IN A 350-DEGREE OVEN FOR 5 TO 7 MINUTES TO DRY THEM OUT. MAKES ABOUT 3 CUPS, ENOUGH TO STUFF 6 CORNISH HENS.

- 1/2 cup pitted prunes, chopped
- 1/4 cup port
- 2 ounces Virginia or other baked ham, finely chopped
- 1/4 cup toasted almonds, coarsely chopped
- 2 tablespoons butter
- 1 small onion, finely chopped
- 1 small celery stalk, finely chopped
- 2 tablespoons minced fresh parsley leaves
- 10 chopped fresh sage leaves
- 3 cups stale white bread cut into 1/2-inch cubes, crusts on
- 2 tablespoons chicken stock or water
- Salt and pepper

1. Combine the prunes and port in a small saucepan. Bring to a simmer and cook until the prunes are soft and have absorbed most of the liquid, about 15 minutes. Combine the prunes, ham, and almonds in a microwave-safe bowl; set aside.

2. Heat the butter in a medium skillet over medium heat. Add the onion and celery; sauté until softened, 3 to 4 minutes. Add this mixture, as well as the parsley, sage, bread, stock, and salt and pepper to taste, to the prune mixture; toss to mix.

Quinoa Stuffing with Lemon and Rosemary

QUINOA, AN ANCIENT SOUTH AMERICAN GRAIN NOW WIDELY AVAILABLE IN SUPERMARKETS AND NATURAL FOODS STORES, GROWS WITH A BITTER PROTECTIVE COATING CALLED SAPONIN THAT IS MOSTLY REMOVED DURING PROCESSING. HOWEVER, IT'S STILL A GOOD IDEA TO RINSE QUINOA WELL BEFORE COOKING. RICH IN IRON AND PROTEIN, THIS GRAIN HAS A LIGHT, CRUNCHY TEXTURE AND NUTTY FLAVOR, MAKING IT PERFECT FOR STUFFING SMALL HENS. MAKES ABOUT 3 CUPS, ENOUGH TO STUFF 6 CORNISH HENS.

- 1 1/2 cups quinoa
- 3 cups chicken stock or low-salt canned chicken broth
- 2 tablespoons butter
- 1 small onion, finely chopped
- 1 garlic clove, finely chopped
- 4 sun-dried tomatoes packed in oil, drained, patted dry, and coarsely chopped
- 1 teaspoon grated lemon zest
- 1 teaspoon chopped fresh rosemary leaves
- Salt and pepper

1. Rinse the quinoa in a strainer. Combine the quinoa and the stock in a saucepan and bring to a boil. Reduce the heat to low and simmer until all the liquid is absorbed, 10 to 15 minutes. Spoon the quinoa into a microwave-safe bowl.

2. Meanwhile melt the butter in a small skillet over medium heat. Add the onion and garlic; sauté until softened, 3 to 4 minutes. Add this mixture, along with the sun-dried tomatoes, zest, rosemary, and salt and pepper to taste, to quinoa; toss to mix.

Orzo Stuffing with Red Pepper, Liver, and Fresh Herbs

THE LIVER (SEE FIGURE 4, PAGE 315) IS USUALLY PACKED WITH THE NECK AND REST OF THE GIBLETS IN A SMALL PLASTIC BAG THAT IS STUFFED INTO THE BODY CAVITY OF MOST BRANDS OF CORNISH HEN. MAKES ABOUT 3 CUPS, ENOUGH TO STUFF 6 CORNISH HENS.

> 1 cup orzo
> 2 tablespoons butter
> 6 Cornish hen livers
> ¼ small red bell pepper, cored, seeded, and diced fine (about ¼ cup)
> 3 medium scallions, white and light green parts, sliced thin
> 2 tablespoons minced fresh parsley leaves
> 2 tablespoons minced fresh basil leaves
> 1 teaspoon fresh lemon juice
> Salt and pepper

1. Bring 2 quarts of water to a boil in a large saucepan. Add the orzo; boil over medium-high heat until al dente, 9 to 11 minutes. Drain, then cool under cold running water. Turn into a medium microwave-safe bowl; set aside.

2. Meanwhile, heat 1 tablespoon butter in a medium skillet over medium heat. Add the livers; sauté until just cooked, about 5 minutes. Remove the livers from the pan; cut into small dice when cool enough to handle; add to the orzo.

3. Heat the remaining 1 tablespoon butter in the now empty skillet. Add the bell pepper; sauté until almost softened, about 2 minutes.

Add the scallions; continue to sauté until the vegetables soften, 2 to 3 minutes longer. Add this mixture, as well as the parsley, basil, and lemon juice, to the orzo; toss to coat. Season with salt and pepper to taste.

◆

Barley with Basil Pesto

BARLEY SUBSTITUTES FOR PASTA HERE AS A MEDIUM FOR PESTO. COOKED ORZO TOSSED WITH PESTO MIGHT ALSO BE USED AS A STUFFING. MAKES ABOUT 3 CUPS, ENOUGH TO STUFF 6 CORNISH HENS.

> 1 cup pearl barley
> 2¾ cups chicken stock or low-salt canned chicken broth
> 3 tablespoons Classic Basil Pesto (page 196)
> Salt and pepper

1. Combine the barley and stock in a medium saucepan and bring to a boil. Reduce heat, cover, and simmer until all the liquid is absorbed, about 30 minutes.

2. Transfer the barley to a microwave-safe bowl. Toss with the pesto and salt and pepper to taste; set aside.

Simple Roasted Butterflied Cornish Hens

SERVES 4

THERE'S PROBABLY no time to brine hens during the week (although you certainly can), so lift the skin and season the meat directly with salt, pepper, and herbs. See the figures that follow for instructions on butterflying Cornish hens.

2 Cornish hens (1 ½ to 2 pounds each)
Salt and pepper
Minced fresh or dried herbs, such as
    thyme, basil, or tarragon, for sprinkling
2 teaspoons butter, softened

1. Adjust the oven rack to the lower-middle position and heat the oven to 400 degrees. Remove the backbone from each hen with a pair of kitchen shears (see figure 1, page 322) and flatten the bird, breast side facing up, with the palm of your hand (see figure 2, page 322). Loosen the skin around legs/thighs and on either side of the breastbone to expose the meat. Generously season the meat with salt, pepper, and the herb of choice (see figure 3, page 322); return the skin to its original position. Pierce the skin in 4 or 5 places to prevent bubbling. Rub the skin side of each hen with the softened butter. Place the hens on a large (at least 19 by 13 inches) wire rack set over an equally large roasting or jelly-roll pan.

2. Roast the hens 20 to 25 minutes, until golden brown and juices run clear. Turn the oven setting from bake to broil; broil until nicely browned, about 5 minutes. Remove from the pan and split each hen down the breastbone with a chef's knife or kitchen shears. Serve.

BUTTERFLYING CORNISH HENS

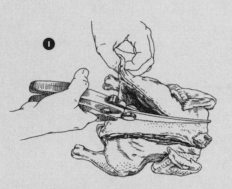

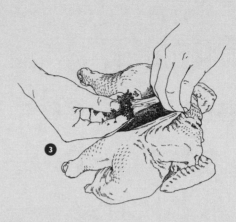

3. Loosen the skin around legs/thighs and on either side of the breastbone to expose the meat. Generously season the meat under the skin with salt, pepper, and herb of choice; return the skin to its original position.

1. Before roasting large, unstuffed Cornish hens, butterfly them—split each hen by cutting on either side of the backbone and removing it.

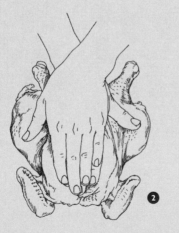

2. Flatten the bird, breast side facing up, with the palms of your hands.

ROASTED TURKEY

/I\

ALTHOUGH TURKEY HAS BECOME COMMONPLACE IN

SUPERMARKETS, MOST COOKS ROAST WHOLE BIRDS

ONLY AT HOLIDAY TIME. WE ALL KNOW WHY THIS IS,

TOO: THE BIRD MAY LOOK LOVELY ON THE PLATTER,

BUT MORE OFTEN THAN NOT IT'S TERRIBLY BLAND

AND VERY DRY, SALVAGED ONLY BY GOOD GRAVY AND

WONDERFUL SIDE DISHES. ◆ IS IT POSSIBLE TO ROAST

a turkey perfectly? Usually juicy breast meat comes with a price—shocking pink legs and thighs. You have some leeway with the dark meat, which is almost impossible to dry out during normal roasting times. The trick is that the breast, which is exposed to direct heat and finishes cooking at a lower temperature, becomes parched while the legs and thighs take their time creeping to doneness. Nearly every roasting method in existence tries to compensate for this; few succeed.

There are literally hundreds of different methods of roasting turkey; we tested a dozen or so fairly different ones, from traditional to idiosyncratic. Our goals were to end up with an attractive bird, to determine the ideal internal temperature, and to find a method that would finish both legs and breasts simultaneously.

There were other issues as well. We like stuffing, but wondered whether, by necessitating longer cooking times, it leads to drier meat. Is basting a pointless ritual or is it time well spent? Is stuffing the cavity with herbs and vegetables a waste of good thyme, not to mention celery, carrots, and onions? Perhaps roasting these same vegetables alongside the turkey makes for more flavorful pan juices and therefore better gravy? These were our original questions for research. Once we started roasting, we realized there were others we hadn't yet known to ask.

We are fans of brining chicken before cooking (see "The Science of Brining," page 7) and hoped that a saltwater bath would improve turkey as well. When we first removed the brined turkey from the refrigerator, we found a beautiful, milky-white bird. When roasted, the texture of the breast was different from that of the other birds we had cooked; the meat was firm and juicy at the same time. And the turkey tasted seasoned all the way through; with other birds, the seasoning stayed at the skin level.

We experimented with the brining time, and found that twelve hours in the refrigerator produces pleasantly seasoned turkeys and not overly salty pan juices. Brining was our first real breakthrough; we now believe it to be essential in achieving perfect taste and texture.

Our first roasting experiments used the method most frequently promoted by the National Turkey Federation, the United States Department of Agricul-

ture, and legions of cookbook authors and recipe writers. This, of course, features a moderate (325-degree) oven, a breast-up bird, and an open pan. We tried this method twice, basting one turkey and leaving the other alone. The basted turkey acquired a beautifully tanned skin, while the unbasted bird remained quite pale. Both were cooked to 170 degrees in the leg/thigh. Despite the fact that this was 10 degrees lower than recommended by the USDA and most producers, the breasts still registered a throat-catchingly dry 180 degrees.

We quickly determined that almost all turkeys roasted in the traditional breast-up manner produced breast meat that was consistently 10 degrees ahead of the leg/thigh meat (tenting the breast with heavy-duty foil was the exception; read on). Because white meat is ideal at 160 degrees, and dark thigh meat just loses its last shades of pink at about 170 degrees, you might conclude, as we did, that roasting turkeys with their breasts up is a losing proposition.

Still, we pressed on, next trying a two-hour turkey—essentially braising the bird at 425 degrees in airtight heavy-duty foil for the first hour, then removing the foil and roasting at a slightly lower temperature for the second. Like all of the other breast-up methods, this produced white meat that was 10 degrees hotter than dark meat, but at least this turkey seemed a bit juicier than those cooked with purely dry heat. However, the turkey's spotty brown skin, which looked sticky, thin, and translucent, was a definite drawback. And because the pan juices sweated along with the bird for the first hour of cooking, the liquid added to the pan finished thin and brothy—great for turkey soup, but not intense enough to make a good pan gravy. A related technique—turkey roasted in a chemical-free brown bag atop carrots, celery, and onions—received a high score for its beautiful brown skin. Its taste and texture, however, were only average; the bird was typically dry and bland.

One recipe instructed us to make a paste of flour and butter, then rub it onto the turkey skin before roasting. The ensuing crust would theoretically seal in the juices and roast the turkey to perfection. The results were disappointing; the turkey's skin was swelled and soggy and the breast meat was dry and chalky, leaving only a flavorless pasty feeling in the mouth.

A number of recipes call for placing butter-soaked cheesecloth over the breast for most of the roasting time, augmented by occasional basting. The cheesecloth is removed during the last minutes of cooking to allow the skin to brown. This technique produces magazine-cover turkey, but does nothing to lower the temperature of the breast meat or to improve the flavor. It joined most of the others in the reject pile.

Injecting butter into the turkey was another logical-sounding attempt to keep it juicy and make it flavorful. But while the skin ballooned during roasting, it deflated once out of the oven, and much of the injected butter wound up in the bird's cavity; the rest of it formed pockets at injection sites rather than infusing the whole bird as we had hoped. Even though the meat surrounding the pockets was nicely seasoned, the overall results were inconsistent, and the technique felt contrived.

We also discovered that stuffing a bird makes overcooked meat more likely. Because it slows interior cooking (our tests showed a nearly 30-degree difference in internal temperature after an hour in the oven), stuffing means longer oven times, which can translate to bone-dry surface meat. We eventually developed a method for roasting a stuffed turkey (see "When Stuffing Is a Must," page 338), but if the turkey is your priority we recommend cooking the dressing separately.

ARE POP-UP TIMERS RELIABLE?

MORE THAN A DECADE AGO, SOME POULTRY SUPPLIERS BEGAN INSERTING AUTOMATIC POP-UP TIMERS IN THEIR BIRDS. THE TECHNOLOGY BEHIND THIS DEVICE IS QUITE SIMPLE. A COMPOUND WITH A KNOWN MELTING TEMPERATURE IS LIQUEFIED IN THE BOTTOM OF THE TIMER DEVICE. A SPRING

is compressed into the molten material as it cools and hardens. The timer is then inserted in the thickest part of the breast. When the material at the bottom of the timer melts again during cooking, the spring is freed, it expands, and the plastic stem rises.

While frequent basting can sometimes clog the spring mechanism or cause it to pop up too quickly (the very hot liquid may melt the base material too early), there is a more basic problem with pop-up timers. Volk Enterprises in California, the only American producer of the devices, calibrates theirs to "pop" at 178 degrees, a temperature chosen to guarantee that the legs will be well done—but that also ensures that the breast meat will be way overcooked. (The company's timers for turkey breasts sold separately are calibrated at 163 degrees, a temperature that is much more friendly to delicate white meat.) Our advice: ignore the timer that comes with your holiday turkey and rely on your own thermometer.

INTERNAL TEMPERATURE— HOW MUCH IS ENOUGH?

/I\

INDUSTRY STANDARDS DEVELOPED BY THE UNITED STATES DEPARTMENT OF AGRICULTURE AND THE NATIONAL TURKEY FEDERATION CALL FOR WHOLE BIRDS TO BE COOKED TO AN INTERNAL THIGH TEMPERATURE OF 180 TO 185 DEGREES. THE BREAST TEMPERATURE, ACCORDING TO THESE STANDARDS, SHOULD BE 170 DEGREES.

Our kitchen tests showed, however, that breast temperature rarely drops below that of the thigh, no matter how you cook the bird. And no meat is at its best at a temperature of 180 or 185 degrees.

While the USDA might have us believe that the only safe turkey is a dry turkey, this just isn't true. The two main bacterial problems in turkey are salmonella and campylobacter. According to USDA standards, salmonella in meat is killed at 160 degrees. Turkey is no different. So why the higher safety standard of 180 degrees?

Part of the problem is that stuffing must reach an internal temperature of 165 degrees to be considered safe. (Carbohydrates such as bread provide a better medium for bacterial growth than do proteins such as meat; hence, the extra safety margin of 5 degrees). Since the temperature of the stuffing often lags behind the bird, the USDA recommends waiting until thigh meat reaches 180 degrees.

Since we recommend roasting a turkey *without* bread-based stuffing, a finished temperature of 160 to 165 degrees is more than adequate to kill possible pathogens, even according to USDA standards. A number of food scientists all confirmed the safety of this recommendation. Killing salmonella depends on a complex relation between temperature and time. To rid foods of bacteria, the industry uses two common methods, "fast" and "slow." In the slow method, food is held at 143 degrees for thirty minutes, eliminating the salmonella. Salmonella will also be killed when the food maintains a temperature of 160 degrees for fifteen seconds; this is the fast method.

Because home conditions are imprecise, experts don't recommend the slow method. But as long as meat temperature is properly measured in the deepest part of the thigh and away from the bone, a reading of 160 degrees will certainly last for 15 seconds and indicate that any possible salmonella bacteria have been killed. And campylobacter, the other important bacterial contaminant, is even more sensitive to heat than salmonella.

The final word on poultry safety is this: as long as your thermometer reaches 160 degrees, all unstuffed meat (including turkey) should be bacteria free. Since home thermometers may vary by a couple of degrees, you may want to wait until the thermometer registers 165 degrees, just to be safe (we found that dark meat also tastes better at this temperature). A temperature of 165 degrees (in the thigh and the stuffing) also guarantees that stuffed turkeys are safe. Bacteria in meat cooked to 180 or 185 degrees is long gone—but so, too, moistness and flavor.

Of all the breast-up methods, tenting the bird's breast and upper legs with foil—as suggested by numerous authors—worked the best. The foil deflects some of the oven's heat, reducing the ultimate temperature differential between white and dark meat from 10 to 6 degrees. The bird is roasted at a consistent 325-degree temperature, and during the last forty-five minutes of roasting the foil is removed, allowing enough time for lovely browning. If you're partial to open-pan roasting and don't care to follow the technique we developed, try the foil shield; it certainly ran a close second.

Many people resort to butchery in an attempt to compensate for the fact that white meat roasts more quickly than dark. A friend roasts his turkey whole, removes the breast, and returns the legs to the oven while he carves white meat at the table. Guests enjoy white meat the first time around and dark meat for seconds. This is fine for those who like both parts of the bird, but an informal poll revealed that dark-meat-only lovers do not take to this method.

Then there were the really unusual methods, such as Julia Child's clever technique of roasting breast and legs/thighs separately. You might think dismantling a turkey is difficult, but cutting out the backbone and separating the whole legs from the breast takes less than ten minutes. We liked how quickly the turkey parts roasted: the legs cooked more quickly than the breast, and were done in forty-five minutes, and the breast followed with a temperature of 160 to 165 about ten minutes later. In an attempt to make the bird appear whole, we secured the legs to the breast with skewers, put it on a serving platter, and garnished it with garlands of herbs. Although not quite what we wanted, this method does have two advantages: it is quick, and you can easily roast each portion perfectly.

A related but somewhat less drastic technique is to remove the backbone of the bird before cooking, on the theory that the portions of meat nearest the cavity take the longest to cook. Although this technique reduced the temperature variation between breast and leg and produced juicy meat, the bird looked fat, stubby, and unnatural at the table. After dissecting a number of birds in various ways, we decided that,

TAKING THE TEMPERATURE OF A TURKEY

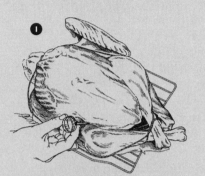

1. Be sure that you measure the temperature of the thickest part of the thigh.

2. This cutaway shows the actual point to which the tip of the thermometer should penetrate.

although these techniques are perfectly acceptable at other times during the year, the holiday turkey should be spared the knife until it reaches the table.

Our most successful attempt at achieving equal temperatures in leg and breast came when we followed James Beard's technique of turning the turkey as it roasts. In this method, the bird begins breast side down on a V-rack, then spends equal time on each of its sides before being turned breast side up. The V-rack is important not just to hold the turkey in place but also to elevate the turkey, affording some protection from the heat of the roasting pan. This combination of rack and technique produced a turkey with a breast temperature as low as, and sometimes lower than, that of the legs.

Because we were using smaller turkeys than Beard had used—12 pounds rather than 18 pounds—we had to fine-tune his method. Large turkeys spend enough time in the oven to brown at 350 degrees; ours were cooking in as little as 1½ hours, yielding quite pale skin. Clearly, we needed higher heat.

Reviewing our notes, we noticed that the basted birds were usually the evenly browned, beautiful ones. So we turned up the heat to 400 degrees, basted faithfully, and got what we wanted. In an effort to streamline, we tried to skip the leg-up turns, roasting only breast side down, then breast side up. But these two extra turns were necessary for the turkey to brown all over. Brining, turning, and basting are work, yes, but the combination produces the best turkey we've ever had.

During our first few tests, we discovered that filling the cavity with aromatic herbs and vegetables made for a subtle but perceptible difference in flavor. This was especially noticeable in the inner meat of the leg and thigh; turkeys with hollow cavities, by contrast, tasted bland.

Roasted alongside the turkey, the same combination of carrot, celery, onion, and thyme also did wonders for the pan juices. But these vegetables dry up fairly quickly, burning rather than caramelizing over the two-hour-plus roasting period. We added just enough stock to keep the vegetables moist until the turkey juices started to flow.

Best Roasted Turkey with Giblet Pan Gravy

SERVES 10 TO 12

I F YOU PREFER, you can double the amount of salt in the brine and cut brining time to just 4 hours. This hurry-up brine works with large turkeys as well. A V-rack (see "Buying a Roasting Rack," pages 32–33) keeps the turkey elevated off the hot roasting pan and is essential.

Turkey
2 cups kosher salt *or* 1 cup table salt
1 turkey (12 to 14 pounds), rinsed thoroughly, giblets, neck, and tail piece removed and reserved
3 medium onions, coarsely chopped
1 ½ medium carrots, peeled and coarsely chopped
1 ½ celery stalks, coarsely chopped
6 fresh thyme sprigs
3 tablespoons unsalted butter, melted
Oil for rack

Giblet Pan Gravy
1 tablespoon vegetable oil
Reserved turkey giblets, neck, and tail piece

1 medium onion, including skin, chopped
1 ½ quarts turkey or chicken stock *or* 1 quart low-sodium canned chicken broth plus 2 cups water
2 fresh thyme sprigs
8 fresh parsley stems
3 tablespoons unsalted butter
¼ cup all-purpose flour
1 cup dry white wine
Salt and pepper

1. If brining the turkey: Dissolve the salt in 2 gallons of cold water in a large stockpot or clean bucket. Add the turkey and refrigerate or set in a very cool (40 degrees or less) spot for 12 hours.

2. To start the gravy: Heat the oil in a soup kettle over medium heat; add the giblets, neck, and tail, then sauté until golden and fragrant, about 5 minutes. Add the onion; continue to sauté until softened, 3 to 4 minutes longer. Reduce the heat to low; cover and cook until the turkey and onion release their juices, about 20 minutes. Add the stock, thyme, and parsley; bring to boil, then adjust the heat to low. Simmer, skimming any scum that may rise to the surface, until the broth is rich and flavorful, about 30 minutes longer. Strain the broth (you should have about 5 cups) and reserve neck, heart, and gizzard. When cool enough to handle, shred the neck meat, remove the gristle from the gizzard, then dice the reserved heart and gizzard. Refrigerate the giblets and broth separately in covered containers until ready to use.

3. To roast the turkey: Adjust the oven rack to the lowest position and heat the oven to 400 degrees. Remove the turkey from the salt water and rinse inside and out under cool running water for several minutes, until all traces of salt are gone. Pat dry inside and out with paper towels. Toss one-third of the onions, carrots, celery, and thyme with 1 tablespoon of melted butter and place this mixture in the body cavity. Bring the turkey legs together and perform a simple truss (see page 330).

4. Scatter the remaining vegetables and thyme over a shallow roasting pan. Pour 1 cup water over vegetables. Set an oiled V-rack adjusted to the widest setting in the pan. Brush the entire breast side of the turkey with half
(continued on next page)

SIMPLE TRUSSING FOR AN UNSTUFFED TURKEY

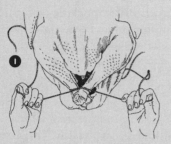

1. Using the center of a 5-foot length of cooking twine, tie the legs together at the ankles.

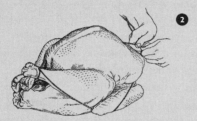

2. Run the twine around the thighs and under the wings on both sides of the bird, pulling tightly.

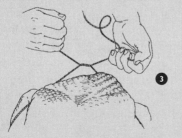

3. Keeping the twine pulled snug, tie a firm knot around the excess flesh at the neck of the bird. Snip off excess twine.

of the remaining butter, then place the turkey, breast side down, on the V-rack. Brush the entire back side of the turkey with the remaining butter.

5. Roast for 45 minutes. Remove the pan from the oven (close the oven door); baste. With a wad of paper towels or a turkey lifter (see figure, page 334) in each hand, turn the turkey, leg/thigh side up. If the liquid in the pan has totally evaporated, add an additional ½ cup water. Return the turkey to the oven and roast 15 minutes. Remove the turkey from the oven again, baste, and again use the paper toweling or a turkey fork to turn the other leg/thigh side up; roast for another 15 minutes. Remove the turkey from the oven for the final time, baste, and turn it breast side up; roast until the breast registers 160 to 165 and the thigh registers 170 to 175 degrees on an instant-read thermometer, 30 to 45 minutes (see page 328). Transfer the turkey to a platter and let rest 20 to 30 minutes. Reserve the pan with the juices and vegetables.

6. To thicken the gravy: While the turkey is roasting, return the reserved giblet broth to a simmer. Heat the butter in a large heavy-bottomed saucepan over medium-low heat. Vigorously whisk in the flour (the roux will froth and then thin out again). Cook slowly, stirring constantly, until nutty brown and fragrant, 10 to 15 minutes. Vigorously whisk all but 1 cup of the hot broth into roux. Bring to a boil, then reduce to a simmer for about 30 minutes, until the gravy is lightly thickened and very flavorful.

7. To finish the gravy: Spoon out and discard as much fat as possible from the roasting pan, leaving the caramelized herbs and vegetables. Place the roasting pan over 2 burners at medium-high heat (if the drippings are not a dark brown, cook, stirring constantly, until they caramelize). Return the gravy to a simmer. Add the wine to the roasting pan of caramelized vegetables, scraping up any browned bits with wooden spoon and boiling until reduced by half, about 5 minutes. Add the remaining 1 cup broth, stir, then strain the pan juices into the gravy, pressing as much juice as possible out of the vegetables. Stir the giblets into the gravy; return to a boil. Adjust the seasonings Add salt and pepper to taste if necessary.

8. Carve the turkey (see page 15); serve with gravy.

Large Roasted Turkey with Giblet Pan Gravy

SMALLER TURKEYS COOK FASTER AND ARE GENERALLY MORE TENDER, BUT SOMETIMES YOU NEED A BIGGER BIRD FOR A LARGE HOLIDAY CROWD. BY TINKERING WITH OUR ORIGINAL RECIPE, WE FOUND IT WASN'T NECESSARY TO ROAST THE BIRD ON EACH SIDE. LOWERING THE OVEN TEMPERATURE HELPS PRODUCE A BEAUTIFUL LARGE TURKEY, WITHOUT SACRIFICING JUICINESS AND FLAVOR. SERVES 18 TO 20.

For an 18- to 20-pound turkey (we don't recommend larger birds; it's too hard to cook them evenly), follow the Master Recipe, roasting the turkey breast down in a 250-degree oven for 3 hours, basting every hour. Then turn breast side up and roast another hour, basting once or twice. Increase the temperature to 400 degrees and roast until done, about 1 hour longer.

◆

Stuffed Roast Turkey with Giblet Pan Gravy

COOKING A TURKEY WITHOUT STUFFING IS EASY (THE MEAT COOKS MORE EVENLY), BUT MANY PEOPLE SIMPLY CAN'T IMAGINE ROAST TURKEY WITHOUT THE STUFFING. AFTER MUCH TRIAL AND ERROR, WE PERFECTED THE FOLLOWING METHOD. YOUR BEST BET IS TO START WORKING ON THIS THE NIGHT BEFORE THE BIG MEAL, COMPLETING STEPS 1–2. THE BREAD FOR THE STUFFING, HOWEVER, CAN BE DRIED SEVERAL DAYS IN ADVANCE. ALL THAT WILL BE LEFT FOR THE BIG DAY ARE STEPS 3–10: STUFFING AND ROASTING THE BIRD AND ENRICHING THE GRAVY BASE WITH THE ROASTING PAN DRIPPINGS. A 12- TO 15-POUND TURKEY WILL ACCOMMODATE APPROXIMATELY HALF OF THE STUFFING. BAKE THE REMAINDER IN A CASSEROLE AS THE BIRD RESTS BEFORE CARVING. SERVES 10 TO 12.

TURKEY

- 2 cups kosher *or* 1 cup table salt
- 1 turkey (12 to 15 pounds), rinsed thoroughly, giblets, neck, and tail piece removed and reserved
- 2 medium onions, coarsely chopped
- 1 medium carrot, peeled and coarsely chopped
- 1 celery stalk, coarsely chopped
- 4 fresh thyme sprigs
- Oil for rack
- 2 tablespoons unsalted butter, melted

GIBLET PAN GRAVY

- 1 tablespoon vegetable oil
- Reserved turkey giblets, neck, and tail piece
- 1 medium onion, including skin, chopped
- 1½ quarts turkey or chicken stock *or* 1 quart low-sodium canned chicken broth plus 2 cups water
- 2 fresh thyme sprigs
- 8 fresh parsley stems
- 3 tablespoons unsalted butter
- ¼ cup all-purpose flour
- 1 cup dry white wine
- Salt and pepper

STUFFING

- 1 recipe (12 cups) prepared stuffing (pages 334–341)
- 1 tablespoon butter, plus extra to grease casserole dish and foil
- ¼ cup turkey or chicken stock or low-sodium canned chicken broth

1. If brining the turkey: Dissolve the salt in 2 gallons of cold water in a large stockpot or clean bucket. Add the turkey and refrigerate or set in a very cool (40 degrees or less) spot for 12 hours.

2. To start the gravy: Heat the oil in a soup kettle over medium heat; add the giblets, neck, and tail, then sauté until golden and fragrant, about 5 minutes. Add the onion; continue to sauté until softened, 3 to 4 minutes longer. Reduce the heat to low; cover and cook until the turkey and onion release their juices, about 20 minutes. Add the stock, thyme, and parsley; bring to boil, then adjust the heat to low. Simmer, skimming any scum that may rise to the surface, until the broth is rich and flavorful, about 30 minutes longer. Strain the broth (you should have about 5 cups) and reserve

(continued on next page)

neck, heart, and gizzard. When cool enough to handle, shred the neck meat, remove the gristle from the gizzard, then dice the reserved heart and gizzard. Refrigerate the giblets and broth separately in covered containers until ready to use.

3. To stuff and roast the turkey: Adjust the oven rack to the lowest position and heat the oven to 400 degrees. Remove the turkey from the salt water and rinse inside and out under cool water for several minutes until all traces of salt are gone. Pat dry inside and out with paper towels; set aside. Scatter the onions, carrot, celery, and thyme over a shallow roasting pan. Pour 1 cup of water over the vegetables. Set an oiled V-rack adjusted to the widest setting in the pan.

4. Place 6 cups of the stuffing in a buttered medium casserole, dot the surface with 1 tablespoon butter, cover with buttered foil, and refrigerate while the turkey roasts. Microwave the remaining stuffing on full power, stirring 2 or 3 times, until very hot (120 to 130 degrees), 6 to 8 minutes (if you can handle the stuffing your with hands, it is not hot enough). Spoon 4 to 5 cups of the stuffing into the turkey cavity until very loosely packed. Secure the skin flap over the cavity opening with turkey lacers or skewers (see figures 1–5, opposite). Tuck the wings behind the back, brush entire breast side with half the melted butter, then place the turkey breast side down on the V-rack. Fill the neck cavity with the remaining heated stuffing and secure the skin flap (figure 6, opposite). Brush the back with the remaining butter.

5. Roast 1 hour, then reduce the temperature to 250 degrees and roast 2 hours longer, adding additional water if the pan becomes dry. Remove the pan from the oven (close the oven door) and with a wad of paper towels or a turkey lifter (see figure, page 334) in each hand, turn breast side up and baste. Increase the oven temperature to 400 degrees; continue roasting until the breast registers 160 to 165 degrees, the thigh registers 170 to 175 degrees, and the stuffing registers 165 degrees on an instant-read thermometer, 1 to 1½ hours longer (see figures 1 and 2, page 328). Transfer the turkey from the roasting pan to a platter and let rest 20 to 30 minutes. Reserve the pan with the juices and vegetables. Leave the oven on.

6. To thicken the gravy: While the turkey is roasting, return the reserved giblet broth to a simmer. Heat the butter in a large, heavy-bottomed saucepan over medium-low heat. Vigorously whisk in the flour (the roux will froth and then thin out again). Cook slowly, stirring constantly, until nutty brown and fragrant, 10 to 15 minutes. Vigorously whisk all but 1 cup of the hot broth into roux. Bring to a boil, then reduce to a simmer for about 30 minutes, until the gravy is lightly thickened and very flavorful.

7. For the remaining stuffing: When the turkey comes out of the oven, add the ¼ cup stock to the dish of reserved stuffing, replace the foil, and bake at 400 degrees until a knife inserted into the stuffing comes out hot, about 20 minutes. Remove the foil; continue to bake until the stuffing forms a golden brown crust, about 15 minutes longer.

8. To finish the gravy: Spoon out and discard as much fat as possible from the roasting pan, leaving the caramelized herbs and vegetables. Place the roasting pan over 2 burners at medium-high heat (if the drippings are not a dark brown, cook, stirring constantly, until they caramelize). Return the gravy to a simmer. Add the wine to the roasting pan of caramelized vegetables, scraping up any browned bits with wooden spoon and boiling until reduced by half, about 5 minutes. Add the remaining 1 cup broth, stir, then strain the pan juices into the gravy, pressing as much juice as possible out of the vegetables. Stir the giblets into the gravy; return to a boil. Add salt and pepper to taste if necessary.

9. Carve the turkey (see page 15); serve with stuffing and gravy.

STUFFING AND TRUSSING A TURKEY

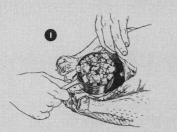

1. Placing the preheated stuffing in the cavity of the bird. Since it's hot, a measuring cup or spoon is needed to handle the stuffing.

2. Alternatively, a canvas stuffing bag (sold in the equipment aisle at many supermarkets) makes the job a lot easier. Fill the bag with the stuffing and then slide the bag into the cavity of the turkey.

3. To keep the stuffing in the cavity, use metal skewers (or cut bamboo skewers) and thread them through the skin on either side of the cavity.

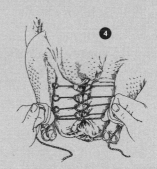

4. Use a 2-foot piece of kitchen twine to close up the cavity, as if you were lacing up boots. Center the twine on the top skewer and then simply cross the twine as you wrap each end of the string around and under the skewers.

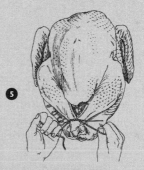

5. Loosely tie the legs together with another short piece of kitchen twine.

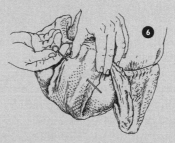

6. Flip bird over onto its breast. Stuff the neck cavity loosely with approximately 1 cup of stuffing. Pull skin flap over and use a skewer to pin flap to turkey.

TURNING A ROASTING TURKEY

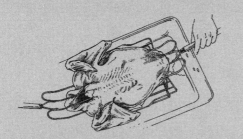

Use wads of paper towels or roast turkey lifters to turn the bird as it roasts. Built like small pitchforks, turkey lifters cost about $4 and are one gadget worth buying.

Fig and Chestnut Stuffing

THIS STUFFING IS QUITE RICH WITH DRIED FRUIT AND CHESTNUTS, WHICH GIVE IT A MEATY CONSISTENCY. MAKES ABOUT 12 CUPS.

- 3 tablespoons unsalted butter
- 4 medium onions, coarsely chopped
- 4 celery stalks, coarsely chopped
- ½ cup port
- 6 ounces dried figs (about 15), chopped
- 2 tablespoons minced fresh thyme leaves
- 2 tablespoons minced fresh sage leaves
- 1¼ pounds French, country, or Pepperidge Farm White bread, cut into ½-inch cubes and dried (about 12 cups)
- 1¾ cups turkey or chicken stock or low-sodium canned chicken broth
- 2 eggs, beaten
- 2 16-ounce cans chestnuts, drained and coarsely chopped
- ½ cup chopped fresh parsley leaves
- Salt and pepper

Heat the butter in a large skillet over medium-high heat. Add the onions and celery; sauté until softened, 7 to 8 minutes. Add the port, figs, thyme, and sage; boil until the port is almost evaporated, 1 to 2 minutes. Mix with all the remaining ingredients, including salt and pepper to taste, in a large, microwave-safe bowl.

◆

Cranberry-Pecan Stuffing

CRANBERRIES AND PECANS ARE AN ALL-AMERICAN COMBINATION, BUT ANY OTHER NUTS MAY BE SUBSTITUTED HERE; TRY CHOPPED WALNUTS OR SLIVERED ALMONDS. YOU CAN CHOP CRANBERRIES WITH A KNIFE BUT IT'S EASIER TO PULSE THEM SEVERAL TIMES IN THE WORK BOWL OF A FOOD PROCESSOR. MAKES ABOUT 12 CUPS.

- 3 tablespoons unsalted butter
- 4 medium onions, coarsely chopped
- 4 celery stalks, coarsely chopped
- 2 garlic cloves, minced
- ½ cup brandy
- 6 ounces fresh or frozen cranberries (about 2 cups), coarsely chopped
- 2 tablespoons minced fresh thyme leaves
- 2 tablespoons minced fresh sage leaves
- 1¼ pounds French, country, or Pepperidge Farm White bread, cut into ½-inch cubes and dried (about 12 cups)
- 1¾ cups turkey or chicken stock or low-sodium canned chicken broth
- 2 eggs, beaten
- 1½ cups toasted pecans, coarsely chopped
- ½ cup chopped fresh parsley leaves
- Salt and pepper

Heat the butter in a large skillet over medium-high heat. Add the onions and celery; sauté until softened, 7 to 8 minutes. Add the garlic and sauté another minute. Add the brandy, cranberries, thyme, and sage; boil until the brandy is almost evaporated, 1 to 2 minutes. Mix with all the remaining ingredients, including salt and pepper to taste, in a large, microwave-safe bowl.

Oyster Stuffing

IF YOU ARE HAVING YOUR FISHMONGER SHUCK THE OYSTERS FOR YOU, MAKE SURE THAT HE PACKS THEM IN AMPLE OYSTER LIQUOR FOR USE IN THE RECIPE. BOTTLED CLAM JUICE CAN BE USED IN A PINCH. CORNBREAD CAN BE SUBSTITUTED FOR THE WHITE BREAD HERE, IF YOU LIKE. MAKES ABOUT 12 CUPS.

3 tablespoons unsalted butter
4 medium onions, coarsely chopped
4 celery stalks, coarsely chopped
1/2 cup dry sherry
2 tablespoons minced fresh thyme leaves
2 tablespoons minced fresh sage leaves
1 1/4 pounds French, country, or Pepperidge Farm White bread, cut into 1/2-inch cubes and dried (about 12 cups)
3 dozen oysters, shucked
1/2 cup oyster liquor
1 1/4 cups turkey or chicken stock or low-sodium canned chicken broth
2 eggs, beaten
1/2 cup chopped fresh parsley leaves
Salt and pepper

Heat the butter in a large skillet over medium-high heat. Add the onions and celery; sauté until softened, 7 to 8 minutes. Add the sherry, thyme, and sage; boil until the sherry is almost evaporated, 1 to 2 minutes. Mix with all the remaining ingredients, including salt and pepper to taste, in a large, microwave-safe bowl.

DRYING BREAD FOR STUFFING

ANY GOOD-QUALITY WHITE BREAD MAY BE USED TO MAKE STUFFING. WE FOUND THAT FRENCH BREAD WORKS WELL, AS DOES A ROUND COUNTRY BREAD. FIRM, SLICED WHITE BREAD MAY ALSO BE USED. THE BREAD ABSORBS THE MOST LIQUID AND FLAVOR IF DRIED FIRST. TRIM the bread or not, as you prefer, before cutting it into 1/2-inch cubes. Spread the cubes in a single layer over several baking sheets and dry at room temperature for 2 to 3 days, or in a 225-degree oven for 25 to 40 minutes to prepare for use.

Bacon and Apple Stuffing

THE CLASSIC FLAVORS OF BACON AND APPLE STUFFING COMPLEMENT A TRADITIONAL THANKSGIVING MEAL OF TURKEY, CRANBERRY SAUCE, AND PUMPKIN PIE. **MAKES ABOUT 12 CUPS.**

- ½ pound sliced bacon, cut into ½-inch pieces
- 4 medium onions, coarsely chopped
- 4 celery stalks, coarsely chopped
- 6 medium-firm, tart apples, such as Granny Smith, peeled, cored, and diced
- ½ cup white wine
- 2 tablespoons minced fresh thyme leaves
- 2 tablespoons minced fresh sage leaves
- 1¼ pounds French, country, or Pepperidge Farm White bread, cut into ½-inch cubes and dried (about 12 cups)
- 1¾ cups turkey or chicken stock or low-sodium canned chicken broth
- 2 eggs, beaten
- ½ cup chopped fresh parsley leaves
- Salt and pepper

Fry the bacon in a large skillet over medium-high heat until crisp and brown, about 5 minutes. Transfer the bacon with a slotted spoon to a paper towel–lined plate; pour off all but 3 tablespoons fat from the pan. Add the onions, celery, and apples; sauté until softened, about 15 minutes. Add the wine, thyme, and sage; boil until the wine is almost evaporated, 1 to 2 minutes. Mix with all the remaining ingredients, including the reserved bacon and salt and pepper to taste, in a large, microwave-safe bowl.

Cornbread Stuffing with Sausage

CORNBREAD, SAUSAGE, AND A LITTLE BIT OF BOURBON GIVE THIS STUFFING A COUNTRY FLAVOR. ONE CUP OF CHOPPED DRIED FRUIT (PRUNES, APRICOTS, RAISINS) MAY BE ADDED TO THE MIX IF YOU DESIRE A LITTLE SWEETNESS. **MAKES ABOUT 12 CUPS.**

- 1 tablespoon olive oil
- 1 pound sweet sausage, casings removed and crumbled
- 1 to 2 tablespoons butter (if necessary)
- 4 medium onions, coarsely chopped
- 4 celery stalks, coarsely chopped
- ½ cup bourbon
- 2 tablespoons minced fresh thyme leaves
- 2 tablespoons minced fresh sage leaves
- 12 cups dried, crumbled cornbread (see page 339)
- 1¾ cups turkey or chicken stock or low-sodium canned chicken broth
- 2 eggs, beaten
- 1 cup pecans, coarsely chopped
- ½ cup chopped fresh parsley leaves
- 2 teaspoons salt (assuming a brined bird)
- Pepper

Heat the oil in a 10-inch skillet and fry the sausage over medium-high heat until the meat loses its raw color, 5 to 7 minutes; remove with a slotted spoon to a small bowl. If necessary, add enough butter to the rendered sausage fat to equal 3 tablespoons. Add the onions and celery; sauté until softened, 7 to 8 minutes. Add the bourbon, thyme, and sage; boil until the bourbon is almost evaporated, 1 to 2 minutes. Mix with all the remaining ingredients, including the sausage and salt and pepper to taste, in a large, microwave-safe bowl.

Cornbread and Chorizo Stuffing

CHORIZO IS A SPICY SPANISH-STYLE SAUSAGE. IF UNAVAILABLE, ANOTHER SPICY SMOKED SAUSAGE SUCH AS ANDOUILLE CAN BE SUBSTITUTED. KIELBASA CAN BE USED AS WELL. MAKES ABOUT 12 CUPS.

- 1 tablespoon olive oil
- 1 pound chorizo or other spicy smoked sausage, cut into 1/2-inch dice
- 1 to 2 tablespoons butter (if necessary)
- 4 medium onions, coarsely chopped
- 4 celery stalks, coarsely chopped
- 2 garlic cloves, finely chopped
- 1 red bell pepper, cored, seeded, and cut into 1/2-inch dice
- 1/2 cup tequila
- 2 tablespoons minced fresh thyme leaves
- 12 cups dried, crumbled cornbread (see page 339)
- 1 3/4 cups turkey or chicken stock or low-sodium canned chicken broth
- 2 eggs, beaten
- 2 cups fresh or frozen corn kernels
- 6 scallions, white and light green parts, finely chopped
- Salt and pepper

Heat the olive oil in a 10-inch skillet. Fry the chorizo over medium-high heat until browned, 5 to 7 minutes; remove with a slotted spoon to a small bowl. If necessary, add enough butter to the rendered sausage fat to equal 3 tablespoons. Add the onions and celery; sauté until slightly softened, 4 to 5 minutes. Add the garlic and bell pepper and sauté until softened, about 5 minutes. Add the tequila and thyme; boil until the tequila is almost evaporated, 1 to 2 minutes. Mix with all the remaining ingredients, including the sausage and salt and pepper to taste, in a large, microwave-safe bowl.

Cornbread-Pear Stuffing

APPLES MAY BE SUBSTITUTED FOR PEARS. MAKES ABOUT 12 CUPS.

- 1/2 pound sliced bacon, cut into 1/2-inch pieces
- 2 medium onions, coarsely chopped
- 2 small celery stalks, coarsely chopped
- 3 medium-large ripe but firm pears, peeled, cored, and cut into 1/2-inch chunks (about 3 cups)
- 3 tablespoons minced fresh thyme leaves
- 2 tablespoons minced fresh sage leaves
- 2/3 pound French, country, or Pepperidge Farm White bread, cut into 1/2-inch cubes and dried (about 6 cups)
- 6 cups dried, crumbled cornbread (see page 339)
- 1 3/4 cups turkey or chicken stock or low-sodium canned chicken broth
- 1 cup pecans, toasted and coarsely chopped
- 2 large eggs, lightly beaten
- 1/4 cup minced fresh parsley leaves
- Salt and pepper

Fry the bacon in a large skillet over medium-high heat until crisp and brown, about 5 minutes. Transfer the bacon with a slotted spoon to a paper towel–lined plate; pour off all but 3 tablespoons fat from pan. Add the onions and celery; sauté until softened, about 5 minutes. Add the pears, thyme, and sage; sauté until the pears begin to soften, 5 to 7 minutes longer. Mix with all the remaining ingredients, including the bacon and salt and pepper to taste, in a large, microwave-safe bowl.

WHEN STUFFING
IS A MUST

/|\

FOR SOME COOKS, THE STUFFING IS THE BEST PART OF THE
HOLIDAY MEAL AND FOR BEST FLAVOR THEY WANT TO COOK
AT LEAST SOME OF THE STUFFING IN THE BIRD. THIS CAUSES
ALL KINDS OF COOKING PROBLEMS SINCE THE STUFFING CAN BE
SLOW TO HEAT UP. THE STUFFING ENTHUSIASTS IN OUR TEST

kitchen developed a method that gets the stuffing hot enough to kill any bacteria without causing the delicate breast meat to dry out (see the recipe on page 331).

Getting the perfect recipe took a lot of work. At the outset, we limited our turkey to a maximum of 15 pounds because it is just too difficult to safely stuff and roast larger birds and have the meat remain moist and flavorful. From initial tests with both fast and slow cooking methods, we saw that the stuffing generally lagged at least 10 degrees behind the breast and leg. Since the stuffing must reach a temperature of 165 degrees according to USDA standards, our breast meat was at a bone-dry 175 degrees in these early experiments.

Clearly, we were going to have to heat the stuffing before putting it into the turkey. When we heated stuffing to 120 degrees in a microwave

and then roasted the bird at a constant 325 degrees, we cut forty-five minutes off the roasting time, as compared to using cold stuffing. The breast was still overcooked, but this method was promising.

We pursued the pre-warming technique in further tests and found that the stuffing hits its lowest temperature in the birds usually at the one-hour mark, dropping approximately 20 degrees. By heating the stuffing to 120 or even 130 degrees in the microwave, we were able to get the stuffing out of the so-called danger zone of 40 to 140 degrees in which bacteria grow most quickly in about two and one-half hours, a time that experts say is safe.

With the stuffing issue resolved, we now focused on the roasting technique to ensure juicy breast meat when the bird is stuffed. It had become clear to us that high heat and even constant moderate heat wreak havoc on the turkey, resulting in parched breast meat. The low and slow method was, well, too low and slow, and not a safe method for a stuffed turkey. A combination of low heat with high or moderate heat seemed like it would be the answer.

We also determined that, regardless of temperature, roasting the bird breast down for only one hour was not sufficient. The breast needed to be shielded for most of the cooking time. We also abandoned roasting leg side up because the turns were too awkward with a stuffed bird.

We roasted two stuffed turkeys, both started breast down. One cooked at a low 250 degrees for three hours, was rotated breast up, cooked for an additional fifteen minutes, and the temperature was then increased to 400 degrees. The breast was overcooked as the thigh creeped to the proper temperature. The other turkey we roasted at 400 degrees for one hour, reduced the temperature to 250 degrees, flipped the breast up after a total of three hours, and then turned the heat back to 400 degrees until done. The bird finished as close to perfection as possible: 163 degrees in the breast, 180 in the thigh, and 165 degrees in the stuffing. Clearly, the thigh meat benefited from the initial blast of heat. The spotty browning of the skin was a disappointment, but a few minor adjustments to the time spent breast up fixed this problem. Finally, a perfectly roasted stuffed turkey.

Cornbread

THIS CORNBREAD IS MOIST AND LIGHT, WITH THE RICH TASTE OF CORN. USE STONE-GROUND OR WATER-GROUND CORNMEAL FOR THE BEST TASTE AND TEXTURE. THIS RECIPE WILL MAKE MORE THAN YOU NEED FOR THE STUFFINGS IN THIS CHAPTER. RESERVE THE EXTRA (WITHOUT DRYING) FOR SNACKING. MAKES 2 9-INCH SQUARES.

> 2 cups yellow or white cornmeal
> 2 cups all-purpose flour
> 4 teaspoons baking powder
> 1 teaspoon baking soda
> 3 tablespoons sugar
> 1 teaspoon salt
> 4 large eggs
> 1 ⅓ cups buttermilk
> 1 ⅓ cups milk
> 4 tablespoons unsalted butter, melted,
> plus extra for greasing pan

1. Adjust the oven rack to the center position and heat to 425 degrees. Grease two 9-by-9-by-2-inch metal pans.

2. Stir the cornmeal, flour, baking powder, baking soda, sugar, and salt together in a large bowl. Push the dry ingredients up the side of the bowl to make a well.

3. Crack the eggs into the well and stir them lightly with a wooden spoon. Add the buttermilk and milk to the eggs. Stir the wet and dry ingredients quickly until almost combined. Add the melted butter; stir until the ingredients are just combined.

4. Divide the batter between the greased pans. Bake until the top is golden brown and lightly cracked and the edges have pulled away from the sides of the pans, about 25 minutes.

5. Transfer the pans to a wire rack to cool slightly, 5 to 10 minutes. Cut the cornbread into squares and remove from pans. Each pan will yield about 8 cups of crumbled cornbread when dried. Reserve extra squares for another use. For use in stuffing, spread the squares in a single layer on a baking sheet and dry in a 225-degree oven for 25 to 40 minutes; cool and coarsely crumble.

Herb and Mushroom Stuffing

MUSHROOMS AND HEAVY CREAM GIVE THIS STUFFING A PARTICULARLY RICH, MOIST TEXTURE. IF YOU LIKE, USE WHOLE WHEAT BREAD IN PLACE OF WHITE BREAD. MAKES ABOUT 12 CUPS.

- 3 tablespoons butter
- 4 medium celery stalks, coarsely chopped
- 3 medium onions, coarsely chopped
- 10 ounces fresh button or wild mushrooms, sliced thin
- 2 teaspoons dried sage
- 2 teaspoons dried thyme
- 1 teaspoon dried rosemary
- 1 teaspoon dried marjoram
- ¼ cup sweet sherry
- 1¼ pounds French, country, or Pepperidge Farm White bread, cut into ½-inch cubes and dried (about 12 cups)
- 1 cup chicken or turkey stock or low-sodium canned broth
- ½ cup heavy cream
- 2 large eggs, lightly beaten
- ½ cup minced fresh parsley leaves
- Salt and pepper

Heat the butter in a large skillet over medium-high heat. Add the celery and onions; sauté until softened, about 5 minutes. Add the mushrooms; sauté until lightly golden and liquid evaporates, about 7 minutes. Add the sage, thyme, rosemary, and marjoram; sauté to blend flavors, 2 to 3 minutes. Add the sherry; cook until reduced by half. Mix with all the remaining ingredients, including salt and pepper to taste, in a large, microwave-safe bowl.

Rich Meat and Potato Stuffing

SAUSAGE AND GROUND BEEF ARE COMBINED WITH BUTTERY MASHED POTATOES IN THIS HOLIDAY INDULGENCE. BECAUSE IT DOES NOT CONTAIN EGGS, THIS STUFFING CAN BE MADE ONE DAY AHEAD AND REFRIGERATED. MAKES ABOUT 12 CUPS.

- 1 tablespoon olive oil
- 1 pound sweet sausage, casings removed and crumbled
- 2 pounds lean ground beef
- 2 teaspoons ground coriander
- 1 teaspoon dried thyme
- 1 teaspoon pepper
- ¼ teaspoon cayenne
- 3 pounds baking or russet potatoes, peeled and quartered
- 4 tablespoons unsalted butter
- ½ cup finely chopped fresh parsley leaves
- Salt

1. Heat the oil in a 10-inch skillet. Fry the sausage over medium-high heat until it loses its raw color, 5 to 7 minutes; remove with a slotted spoon to a large, microwave-safe bowl. Drain all but 1 tablespoon of fat from the skillet and add the beef, coriander, thyme, pepper, and cayenne; sauté until meat loses its raw color, breaking up the pieces with a wooden spoon, about 5 minutes. Remove with a slotted spoon and add to the sausage.

2. Meanwhile, put the potatoes in a large saucepan and add cold water to cover. Bring to a boil and continue to cook over medium heat until the potatoes are tender when pierced with a knife, about 20 minutes. Drain and mash the potatoes and butter with a potato masher. Add the potatoes and the parsley to the meat and mix well; season with salt to taste.

Italian Rice and Sausage Stuffing

THIS STUFFING USES ITALIAN INGREDIENTS AND FLA-VORS. BECAUSE THE BASE IS STARCHY ARBORIO RICE, THIS STUFFING HAS A CREAMY CONSISTENCY, AKIN TO RISOTTO. MAKES ABOUT 12 CUPS.

3½ cups turkey or chicken stock or low-sodium canned broth
2½ cups water
3 tablespoons butter
3 cups arborio rice
1 tablespoon olive oil
1 pound sweet Italian sausage, casings removed and crumbled
2 medium onions, finely chopped
2 eggs, lightly beaten
1 cup raisins
½ cup pine nuts, toasted
½ cup finely chopped fresh parsley leaves
½ cup grated Parmesan cheese
Salt and pepper

1. Combine the stock, water, and butter in a large saucepan and bring to a boil. Stir in the rice and turn the heat to low. Cook, covered, until all the liquid has been absorbed, 15 to 20 minutes. Remove the pan from the heat and stir with a fork to separate the rice grains.

2. Heat the oil in a 10-inch skillet. Fry the sausage over medium-high heat until the meat loses its raw color, 5 to 7 minutes; remove with a slotted spoon to a large microwave-safe bowl. Drain all but 2 table-spoons of fat from the pan and sauté the onions until softened, 7 to 8 minutes.

3. Add the onions, rice, and all the remaining ingredients, including salt and pepper to taste, to the sausage and mix well.

Cranberry Sauce

THIS SIMPLE SAUCE MARRIES WELL WITH A VARIETY OF STUFFING FLAVORS. IF YOU LIKE, YOU CAN ADD ½ CUP EACH OF CHOPPED NUTS AND CELERY ALONG WITH THE ORANGE ZEST. MAKES 5 CUPS.

2 cups sugar
1½ pounds (about 8 cups) fresh or frozen cranberries
2 tablespoons grated orange zest

Combine 3 cups water and the sugar in a medium saucepan and bring to a boil. Boil the syrup for 5 minutes and then add the cranberries. Turn the heat to medium-low and simmer, skimming off any foam, until the cranberries are translucent, about 5 minutes. Remove from heat, stir in the orange zest, and refrigerate until firm and well chilled, at least 5 hours or overnight.

GRILL-ROASTED WHOLE TURKEY

/|\

GRILL-ROASTING A WHOLE TURKEY—COOKING IT IN A

COVERED GRILL OVER INDIRECT HEAT AT A TEMPERA-

TURE BETWEEN 350 AND 400 DEGREES—IS AN IMPRES-

SIVE FEAT. WHILE THIN CUTS OF MEAT ARE GRILLED

DIRECTLY OVER HOT COALS, LARGE ROASTS—SUCH AS

A WHOLE TURKEY—WILL BURN BEFORE THEY COOK

through if exposed to such heat high. However, by building the fire on just one side of the grill and then cooking the turkey indirectly on the cooler side, the meat roasts to perfection.

As with a grill-roasted chicken (see chapter 12), grill-roasted turkey develops a beautifully bronzed and very crisp skin, something that can be hard to achieve in the oven. Because the turkey cooks in just two hours on the grill, the meat stays moist and juicy. The issues for grill-roasting a chicken and turkey are pretty much the same, but the size of the turkey presents some added challenges.

First, we found it imperative to choose a small turkey (12 to 14 pounds gross weight, 11 to 13 pounds once the giblets have been removed and the turkey drained). Mammoth 18-pound birds won't fit in most grills and are difficult to cook through without burning the skin.

Second, we found it helpful to elevate the bird a bit off the grill rack by placing it in a V-rack, just as if it were in the oven (see "Buying a Roasting Rack," pages 32–33). The slight elevation of the V-rack keeps the skin from sticking to the rack or burning and promotes even circulation of heat within the grill. We also position a drip pan underneath the grill rack to collect fat and prevent flare-ups. We recommend using a disposable aluminum pan. You can make your own drip pan by turning up the sides on a large piece of heavy-duty foil. However, don't use regular foil; it's too flimsy to withstand the heat of the grill.

Even with a small turkey, a charcoal fire will die out before the meat is cooked through. For this reason, we found it necessary to build a large fire (with 5 pounds of charcoal) and then add more hot coals halfway through the cooking time. Of course, using a gas grill guarantees a constant source of heat and eliminates this issue.

As we did with grill-roasted chicken, we prefer to flavor the turkey with wood chips added twice during the roasting process—at the start and again when adding more charcoal. Given the larger size of the bird, it's no surprise that we found we needed to use twice as much chips (6 cups in total) when grill-roasting a turkey.

We conducted several tests to see if turning and basting were necessary. We found that starting the turkey breast side down and then turning it after one hour kept the breast juicy and was worth the effort. We tested two more turns—putting the turkey on either side—but too much heat was lost from the grill and we had to add even more charcoal. Even more important, the turkey did not taste any juicier for the extra effort.

As for basting, we found that basting with butter before grilling can speed the browning of the skin too much and spice rubs tend to burn if added at the start. We also wanted to conserve heat in the grill. Since the grill must be opened in order to turn the bird, we used that opportunity to baste with butter or brush on a spice paste and had excellent results.

Like an oven-roasted turkey, a grill-roasted one benefits mightily from brining (for more information, see chapter 25). If you decide to omit this step, season the turkey well with salt before putting it on the grill and add salt to any spice rub you are using to baste the bird.

Grill-Roasted Turkey

SERVES 10 TO 12

A S WITH OVEN-ROASTING, we find brining before grill-roasting improves the flavor and texture of the turkey. In addition, some wood chips thrown onto the coals give the bird a strong but not overpowering smoky flavor. Grill-roasted turkey is a great choice for summer entertaining. The usual summer poultry accompaniments—salsa, potato salad, corn on the cob—can replace Thanksgiving standbys like cranberry sauce, stuffing, and squash.

2 cups kosher salt *or* 1 cup table salt
1 turkey (12 to 14 pounds), rinsed thoroughly, giblets and tail removed
1 medium onion, coarsely chopped
1 small carrot, coarsely chopped
1 celery stalk, coarsely chopped
3 fresh thyme sprigs
3 tablespoons unsalted butter, melted
6 cups hickory or other wood chips, soaked in cold water to cover for 30 minutes and drained

1. If brining the turkey: Dissolve the salt in 2 gallons of cold water in a large stockpot or clean bucket. Add the turkey and refrigerate or set in a very cool (40 degrees or less) spot for 12 hours.

2. When the turkey is almost finished brining, set up a gas or charcoal grill for indirect cooking (see figures on pages 346–347 and 350). Remove the turkey from the salt water and rinse inside and out under cool running water for several minutes until all traces of salt are gone.

3. Toss the onion, carrot, celery, and thyme with 1 tablespoon butter and place the mixture in the cavity of the turkey.

4. Add half the chips to the fire. Grill-roast the turkey breast side down in a V-rack for 1 hour. Add the additional coals, if using, and the second batch of chips; baste the turkey with the remaining butter, turn breast side up, and continue to grill-roast until an instant-read thermometer inserted into the thigh registers between 165 and 170 degrees, 1 to 1¼ hours longer, depending on the grill temperature. Remove the turkey from the grill, let rest for 20 to 30 minutes, carve (see page 15), and serve.

SETTING UP A GAS GRILL FOR INDIRECT COOKING OF A WHOLE TURKEY

/!\

MAKE SURE YOUR GRILL LID IS TALL ENOUGH TO ACCOMMODATE BOTH YOUR TURKEY AND A V-RACK. ALSO, MAKE SURE YOUR GRILL HAS 2 BURNERS, EACH CONTROLLED BY A SEPARATE TEMPERATURE DIAL. ONCE THE GRILL IS PREHEATED, YOU WILL HAVE TO TURN THE HEAT OFF ON ONE SIDE OF THE GRILL.

Start by soaking 6 cups of wood chips for 30 minutes. Next, put a disposable aluminum pan or piece of heavy-duty aluminum foil, with sides turned up to form a shallow lip, under the grill rack, on the side that will eventually be turned off to act as drip pan. Turn both burners to high and heat the grill to about 400 degrees; this will take about 15 minutes. Turn off the heat on the side with the drip pan. Use tongs to lift up the rack and toss a large handful of soaked and drained chips on the side opposite the drip pan. Place a V-rack positioned on the widest setting on the grill rack over the drip pan. Place the turkey breast side down in the V-rack. Grill-roast the turkey, covered, for 1 hour.

Remove the turkey from the grill and place it in a large roasting pan or on a large carving board. Use tongs to lift up the grill rack and toss the remaining soaked chips over the hot lava rocks on the side opposite the drip pan. Baste the back side of the turkey with melted butter or the selected spice rub, then with a wad of paper toweling in each hand, turn the turkey breast side up and baste. Return the turkey breast side up to the V-rack; quickly replace the lid and continue grill-roasting until the turkey is done, 1 to 1¼ hours longer.

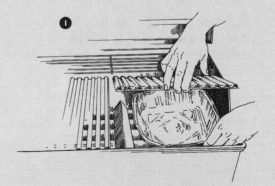

1. Put a disposable aluminum pan or piece of heavy-duty foil with sides turned up under the grill rack to act as drip pan on the side that will eventually be turned off.

Apple-Smoked Turkey

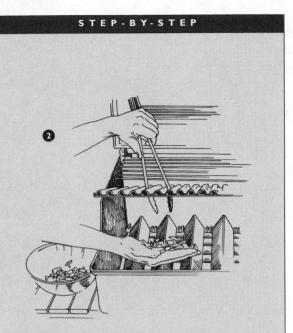

ONIONS AND APPLES PLACED INSIDE THE TURKEY COM-
PLEMENT THE SMOKY FLAVOR FROM THE CHIPS. USE
FRUITWOOD CHIPS, ESPECIALLY APPLE WOOD, OR HICK-
ORY. A SIMPLE RUB OF CUMIN AND GARLIC GIVES THE
SKIN GREAT COLOR AND FLAVOR. **SERVES 10 TO 12.**

2 cups kosher salt *or* 1 cup table salt
1 turkey (12 to 14 pounds), rinsed
    thoroughly, giblets and tail removed
1 medium onion, coarsely chopped
2 Granny Smiths or other tart apples,
    cored and cut into ¼-inch dice
3 fresh thyme sprigs
3 tablespoons olive oil
4 garlic cloves, minced
3 tablespoons ground cumin
6 cups apple or other wood chips, soaked
    in cold water to cover for 30 minutes
    and drained

2. Turn both burners to high and heat the grill to
about 400 degrees; this will take about 15 minutes.
Turn off the heat on the side with the drip pan. Use
tongs to lift up the rack and toss a large handful of
soaked chips on the flames on the side opposite the
drip pan.

1. If brining the turkey: Dissolve the salt in 2 gallons
of cold water in a large stockpot or clean bucket. Add
the turkey and refrigerate or set in a very cool (40
degrees or less) spot for 12 hours.

2. When the turkey is almost finished brining, set up
a charcoal or gas grill for indirect cooking. Remove
the turkey from the salt water and rinse inside and out
under cool running water for several minutes until all
traces of salt are gone.

3. Toss the onion, apples, and thyme with 1 tablespoon oil and place this mixture in the cavity of the
turkey. Combine the remaining 2 tablespoons oil, the
garlic, and cumin in a small bowl; set aside for basting.

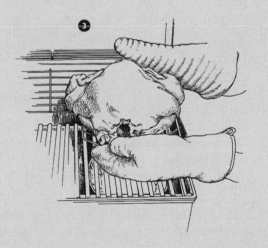

3. Place the turkey breast side down in a V-rack. Set
the turkey and the V-rack on the grill over the drip
pan.

4. Add half the chips to the fire. Grill-roast the
turkey breast side down in a V-rack for 1 hour. Add
the additional coals, if using, and the second batch of
chips; baste the turkey, turn breast side up, and continue to grill-roast until an instant-read thermometer
inserted into the thigh registers between 165 and
170 degrees, 1 to 1¼ hours longer, depending on the
grill temperature. Remove the turkey from the grill,
let rest for 20 to 30 minutes, carve (see page 15), and
serve.

SETTING UP A CHARCOAL GRILL FOR INDIRECT COOKING OF A WHOLE TURKEY

/|\

MAKE SURE YOUR GRILL LID IS TALL ENOUGH TO ACCOMMODATE BOTH YOUR TURKEY AND A V-RACK. SINCE YOU WILL ADD CHARCOAL DURING THE GRILL-ROASTING PROCESS, YOU WILL NEED A CHIMNEY STARTER. A TOTAL OF 6½ POUNDS OF CHARCOAL IS REQUIRED TO KEEP

the fire going long enough to cook the turkey through.

Start the fire with 5 pounds of charcoal. Fill the chimney to the brim with charcoal (you should be able to get about 4 pounds of charcoal into the starter) and place the remaining 1 pound or so of charcoal in 2 piles on opposite sides of the grill, leaving enough room in the middle for the drip pan, which is added later. Light the charcoal in the starter. When the coals at the top of the

Mesquite and Chili Grill-Roasted Turkey

MESQUITE CHIPS ARE MILDER THAN HICKORY CHIPS AND GIVE GRILLED FOOD A PLEASANT, WOODSY FLAVOR. SERVE THIS TURKEY WITH CRANBERRY–RED PEPPER RELISH (PAGE 353). SERVES 10 TO 12.

- 2 cups kosher salt *or* 1 cup table salt
- 1 turkey (12 to 14 pounds), rinsed thoroughly, giblets and tail removed
- 1 lime
- 1 medium onion, coarsely chopped
- 3 fresh cilantro sprigs
- 3 tablespoons olive oil
- 2 tablespoons chili powder
- 2 tablespoon sweet paprika
- 6 cups mesquite wood chips, soaked in cold water to cover for 30 minutes and drained

1. If brining the turkey: Dissolve the salt in 2 gallons of cold water in a large stockpot or clean bucket. Add the turkey and refrigerate or set in a very cool (40 degrees or less) spot for 12 hours.

chimney starter are covered with a thin layer of white ash, divide the hot coals between the 2 piles of unheated charcoal and wait several minutes for all the coals to become red-hot. While the charcoal is heating up, soak 6 cups of wood chips for 30 minutes.

Use long-handled tongs to place a disposable aluminum roasting pan or piece of heavy-duty aluminum foil, with sides turned up to form a shallow lip, in the center of the grill to act as a drip pan. Put the grill rack in place. You may also want to place an oven or grill thermometer on the grill rack (over the drip pan, not on the coals) to keep track of the temperature. Put on the grill lid, open the bottom and lid vents halfway, and heat the grill to about 400 degrees. This should take about 5 minutes.

Remove the grill lid. Use tongs to lift the rack halfway off the grill and toss a handful of soaked chips onto each pile of coals. Put the grill rack back in position. Place a V-rack positioned on the widest setting on the grill rack over the drip pan. Place the turkey breast side down in the V-rack. Grill-roast the turkey, covered, for about 1 hour.

About 40 minutes into roasting, light an additional 1½ pounds of charcoal in a chimney starter. When the charcoal is hot (the turkey will have been grill-roasting for about 1 hour), remove the turkey from the grill and place it in a large roasting pan or on a large carving board. Working as quickly as possible, remove the V-rack and grill rack, stir up the coals, and add half the new hot coals to each pile along with the remaining chips; replace the grill rack, V-rack, and lid. Baste the back side of the turkey with melted butter or the selected spice rub, then with a wad of paper toweling in each hand, turn the turkey breast side up and baste. Return the turkey to the V-rack breast side up; quickly replace the lid and continue grill-roasting until the turkey is done, about 1 to 1¼ hours longer.

2. When the turkey is almost finished brining, set up a charcoal or gas grill for indirect cooking. Remove the turkey from the salt water and rinse inside and out under cool running water for several minutes until all traces of salt are gone.

3. Halve and juice the lime. Place the lime halves in the cavity of the turkey. Toss the onion and cilantro with 1 tablespoon oil and place this mixture in the cavity with the lime. Combine the remaining 2 tablespoons oil, the chili powder, paprika, and lime juice in a small bowl; set aside for basting.

4. Add half the chips to the fire. Grill-roast the turkey breast side down in a V-rack for 1 hour. Add the additional coals, if using, and the second batch of chips; baste the turkey, turn breast side up, and continue to grill-roast until an instant-read thermometer inserted into the thigh registers between 165 and 170 degrees, 1 to 1¼ hours longer, depending on the grill temperature. Remove the turkey from the grill, let rest for 20 to 30 minutes, carve (see page 15), and serve.

SETTING UP A COVERED KETTLE GRILL FOR INDIRECT COOKING OF A WHOLE TURKEY

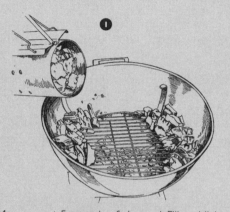

1. Measure out 5 pounds of charcoal. Fill and light the chimney starter. Place remaining charcoal in 2 piles on either side of the grill, leaving room in the middle for the drip pan. When the coals in chimney are covered with a thin layer of white ash, divide them between the 2 piles of unheated charcoal and wait several minutes for all the coals to become red-hot.

2. Use long-handled tongs to place a disposable aluminum pan or piece of heavy-duty foil with sides turned up in the center of the grill to act as drip pan.

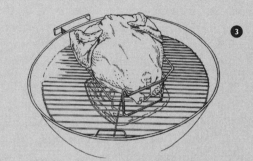

3. Place a V-rack on the grill rack over the drip pan. Place the turkey breast side down in the V-rack.

4. Partway through grill-roasting, add more charcoal and turn the turkey. With a wad of paper towels in each hand, turn turkey breast side up.

Grill-Roasted Turkey with Indian Spice Rub

MIXING PRE-GROUND SPICES IS THE QUICKEST WAY TO FLAVOR THE OUTSIDE OF A TURKEY. THE SPICES BELOW CAN BE VARIED ACCORDING TO TASTE AND WHAT YOU HAVE ON HAND IN YOUR PANTRY. FOR MAXIMUM FLAVOR AND FRESHNESS, TRY TOASTING AND GRINDING WHOLE SPICES. SERVE THIS TURKEY WITH CURRIED APPLE-CRANBERRY CHUTNEY (PAGE 353). SERVES 10 TO 12.

> 2 cups kosher salt *or* 1 cup table salt
> 1 turkey (12 to 14 pounds), rinsed thoroughly, giblets and tail removed
> 1 medium onion, coarsely chopped
> 1 medium carrot, coarsely chopped
> 1 celery stalk, coarsely chopped
> 3 fresh thyme sprigs
> 3 tablespoons olive oil
> 2 tablespoons curry powder
> 2 tablespoons chili powder
> 1 tablespoon ground allspice
> 1 teaspoon ground cinnamon
> 6 cups hickory or other wood chips, soaked in cold water to cover for 30 minutes and drained

1. If brining the turkey: Dissolve the salt in 2 gallons of cold water in a large stockpot or clean bucket. Add the turkey and refrigerate or set in a very cool (40 degrees or less) spot for 12 hours.

2. When the turkey is almost finished brining, set up a charcoal or gas grill for indirect cooking. Remove the turkey from the salt water and rinse inside and out under cool running water for several minutes until all traces of salt are gone.

3. Toss the onion, carrot, celery, and thyme with 1 tablespoon oil and place this mixture in the cavity of the turkey. Combine the remaining 2 tablespoons oil, the curry powder, chili powder, allspice, and cinnamon in a small bowl; set aside for basting.

4. Add half the chips to the fire. Grill-roast the turkey breast side down in a V-rack for 1 hour. Add the additional coals, if using, and the second batch of chips; baste the turkey, turn breast side up, and continue to grill-roast until an instant-read thermometer inserted into the thigh registers between 165 and 170 degrees, 1 to 1¼ hours longer, depending on the grill temperature. Remove the turkey from the grill, let rest for 20 to 30 minutes, carve (see page 15), and serve.

◆

Charcoal Grill-Roasted Turkey with Pan Gravy

IF YOU WANT TO GRILL A TURKEY FOR THANKSGIVING AND WANT SOME GRAVY FOR THE TABLE, THEN CHOOSE THIS RECIPE. SINCE THE TURKEY IS COOKED IN A V-RACK PLACED DIRECTLY IN A ROASTING PAN ON TOP OF THE GRILL RACK, THERE IS NO NEED FOR A DRIP PAN UNDER THE GRILL RACK. GRILLING WILL DAMAGE GOOD PANS, SO CHOOSE A BEAT-UP ROASTING PAN OR A HEAVY-DUTY DISPOSABLE PAN FOR THIS RECIPE. THIS RECIPE CAN BE MADE ONLY OVER A CHARCOAL FIRE. THE PAN WITH THE VEGETABLES AND PAN DRIPPINGS DEFLECTS TOO MUCH HEAT IN A GAS GRILL AND PREVENTS THE TURKEY FROM COOKING PROPERLY. SERVES 10 TO 12.

> 2 cups kosher salt *or* 1 cup table salt
> 1 turkey (12 to 14 pounds), rinsed thoroughly, giblets and tail removed
> 3 medium onions, coarsely chopped
> 1½ medium carrots, coarsely chopped
> 1½ celery stalks, coarsely chopped
> 6 fresh thyme sprigs
> 1 bay leaf
> 3 tablespoons unsalted butter, melted
> 3 tablespoons cornstarch

1. If brining the turkey: Dissolve the salt in 2 gallons of cold water in a large stockpot or clean bucket. Add the turkey and refrigerate or set in a very cool (40 degrees or less) spot for 12 hours.

2. Meanwhile, put the giblets, neck, and tail piece (reserve the liver), as well as one-third of the onions, carrots, celery, and thyme sprigs, and the bay leaf in a

(continued on next page)

large saucepan. Add 6 cups of water and bring to a boil, skimming the foam from the surface as necessary. Simmer, uncovered, for 1 hour; add the liver and simmer another 5 minutes. Strain the broth (you should have about 4½ cups; if not, add water); set the neck, tail, and giblets aside. Cool the broth to room temperature and refrigerate until ready to use. Remove the meat from the neck and tail. Remove the gristle from the gizzard and cut the giblets into a medium dice. Refrigerate the meat and giblets in a covered container until ready to use.

3. When the turkey is almost finished brining, set up a charcoal grill for indirect cooking but without the drip pan below the grill rack. Remove the turkey from the salt water and rinse inside and out under cool running water for several minutes until all traces of salt are gone.

4. Toss another one-third of the onions, carrots, celery, and thyme with 1 tablespoon butter and place this mixture in the cavity of the turkey. Scatter the remaining vegetables and thyme over a 15 by 10-inch (disposable, if you like) roasting pan; pour 1 cup of the reserved broth over the vegetables. Cover the pan with an 18-by-12-inch piece of heavy-duty foil, crimping the edges to secure the foil to the pan. Cut out a rectangular piece from the center of the foil just large enough to allow the V-rack, adjusted to its widest setting, to rest in the bottom of the pan. Position the turkey, breast side down, in the V-rack. The foil and the turkey itself should be covering the pan juices to prevent them from evaporating.

5. Add half the chips to the fire. Grill-roast the turkey for 1 hour. Add the additional coals and the second batch of chips; baste the turkey with the remaining 2 tablespoons butter, turn breast side up, and check the pan drippings; add an additional ½ cup broth if the vegetables are dry and starting to burn. Continue to grill-roast until an instant-read thermometer inserted into the thigh registers between 165 and 170 degrees, 1 to 1¼ hours longer, depending on the grill temperature. Remove the turkey from the grill and let rest for 20 to 30 minutes.

6. Meanwhile, strain the pan drippings into a large saucepan (discard the solids) and skim the fat. Bring the roasting pan to the stove and place it over 2 burners set to medium heat. Add 3 cups of the reserved broth to the roasting pan and, using a wooden spoon, stir to loosen any brown bits. When the pan juices start to simmer, strain them into the saucepan with the pan drippings. Mix the cornstarch with ½ cup water and gradually stir into the saucepan. Add the reserved neck and tail meat and giblets and bring to a boil. Simmer until the sauce thickens slightly. Carve the turkey (see page 15) and serve with the gravy.

SPICY CRANBERRY RELISHES

⁄\\

TRADITIONAL CRANBERRY SAUCE DOES NOT REALLY WORK ALL THAT WELL WITH A SPICE-RUBBED GRILL-ROASTED TURKEY AND SUMMER FOODS. HOWEVER, TART CRANBERRIES CAN BE USED TO MAKE SPICY RELISHES MORE AT HOME WITH SUMMER FOODS, INCLUDING GRILLED TURKEY. FRESH CRANBERRIES are not available in the summer, but frozen cranberries can be used successfully in either recipe.

◆

Cranberry–Red Pepper Relish

FOR A SPICIER RELISH, INCREASE THE HOT RED PEPPER FLAKES. MAKES ABOUT 5 CUPS.

- 4 red bell peppers, cored, seeded, and cut into small dice
- 4 cups cranberries, picked through and coarsely chopped
- 2 medium onions, finely chopped
- 1 cup apple cider vinegar
- 1 ½ cups sugar
- 2 jalapeño chiles, stemmed, seeded, and minced
- ½ teaspoon salt
- ½ teaspoon hot red pepper flakes

Mix all the ingredients in a medium saucepan. Bring to a boil, then simmer, stirring occasionally, until the mixture thickens to a jamlike consistency, about 30 minutes. Cool to room temperature. (The relish can refrigerated in an airtight container for 2 weeks.)

Curried Apple-Cranberry Chutney

THE CURRY POWDER IN THIS CHUTNEY IS ADDED FOR COMPLEXITY, NOT HEAT. MAKES ABOUT 5 CUPS.

- 4 large Golden Delicious apples (about 2 pounds), peeled, quartered, cored, and cut into medium dice (about 5 cups)
- 3 cups cranberries, picked through and coarsely chopped
- 1 ½ cups firmly packed light brown sugar
- 8 ounces golden raisins
- 1 medium onion, minced
- 2 tablespoons minced crystallized ginger
- 2 tablespoons yellow mustard seeds
- 4 medium garlic cloves, minced
- 2 teaspoons grated lemon zest
- 2 teaspoons curry powder
- ½ teaspoon salt
- ¼ teaspoon cayenne pepper

Mix all the ingredients in a medium saucepan. Bring to a boil; cover and simmer, stirring occasionally, until the apples are tender and most of the liquid is absorbed, about 30 minutes. Cool to room temperature. (The chutney can be refrigerated in an airtight container for 2 weeks.)

ROASTED TURKEY BREAST

THE GROWING POPULARITY OF TURKEY HAS TRANS-

LATED INTO SEVERAL NEW PRODUCTS IN THE SUPER-

MARKET. WHOLE BONE-IN TURKEY BREASTS, PERFECT

FOR A FAMILY MEAL OR SMALL CELEBRATION, ARE NOW

FOUND EITHER FRESH OR FROZEN IN ALMOST EVERY

MARKET. OUR GOAL FOR THIS CUT IS THE SAME AS FOR

a whole roast turkey—crisp skin and juicy meat.

Since there is so little literature about these relatively new cuts, we started our testing with few guidelines. At the outset, we roasted one fresh and one frozen breast at 325 degrees on a wire rack set in a roasting pan to an internal temperature of 170 degrees. Neither breast was seasoned beforehand or basted while roasting.

Both cooked breasts had a flat, dusty flavor with anemic, rubbery skin. The frozen breast was also stringy, tough, dry, and chewy. The fresh breast was moister and more tender. Clearly, the fresh breasts are better options and we set about to fix the flavor issues.

We like to brine a whole turkey (see page 324) and found that this technique worked equally well with a bone-in breast. We tested salt-only and salt-sugar brines. We liked the effects of the sugar (it adds sweetness, as might be expected, and helps balance the saltiness). After much trial and error we came up with a formula that works well for a bone-in breast weighing between 6 and 8 pounds: 1½ cups *each* kosher salt and sugar dissolved in 6 quarts of cool water.

For cooks in a rush, we found it was possible to brine in a double-strength solution for two hours. The five-hour brine offers a slightly gentler flavor, but in each case the turkey is delicately seasoned, with room for further seasonings at the table if you like.

With the flavor of the meat vastly improved, we focused on roasting techniques. Our first area of concern was the final internal temperature. Most sources say to roast a whole turkey to 170 or even 180 degrees. This temperature may be necessary for legs and thighs, but tender white meat dries out at these temperatures. Brining had significantly improved both the flavor and juiciness, but the meat was still a tad dry when cooked to 170 degrees.

We roasted three more breasts in a 325-degree oven, testing internal temperatures of 165 degrees, 160 degrees, and 155 degrees. Initially, we thought the breast roasted to 155 degrees was the best sample. However, as we cut down to the bone we noticed some pink, mushy meat that clearly had been undercooked. The breasts cooked to 160 and 165 degrees did not have this problem and still were plenty juicy. A temperature of 160 degrees or higher also ensures that any possible bacteria have been killed.

With the final internal temperature issue settled, we confronted the issue of crisp skin. At a constant 325 degrees, the skin remained rubbery and pale. Slow roasting was delivering perfectly cooked meat, but clearly some sort of compromise was needed.

The best method turned out to be roasting at 450 degrees for thirty minutes, then reducing the temperature to 325 degrees for the remaining roasting time, thirty to forty-five minutes more. Higher initial temperatures caused the skin to burn; lower initial temperatures did not get the skin brown enough. By blasting the turkey at high heat for only thirty minutes, we also protected the meat from becoming dry.

We did notice one slight problem. The skin was not browning as evenly as the skin on a whole turkey that spends several hours in the oven. We brushed some melted butter on the turkey breast before it went into the oven and then basted every fifteen minutes throughout the roasting period. The skin was golden but limp. We tried again, brushing the skin with butter just once—before it went into the oven. The skin was evenly golden and slightly crisp. It was at this point that we made an important observation.

The crispest part of the skin was where the skin touched no meat; a small section that stretches across the two halves of the breast, where the extra flap of skin from the neck rests. We wondered: if all the skin were released from the meat, might it become even crisper, as it had with roast chicken?

Most turkey breasts come with an excessive flap of neck skin that dangles uselessly and remains rubbery and inedible. We removed all but one inch of it and realized that it would be perfectly suited for elevating the skin while larding the meat. After carefully lifting up the skin all over the surface of the breast without breaking the thin membrane attached to the meat, we divided the fatty neck skin into two pieces and tucked each under the released skin on either side of the breastbone point, the narrowest and most exposed part of the breast. We spread the seasoned butter under the rest of the released skin and then brushed the exterior with a little melted butter.

A little more than an hour later, we had a perfectly roasted bone-in turkey breast. The meat trickled juice when sliced, while the texture was firm but still tender and moist. The flavor was rich, while the skin was crisp and deeply bronzed.

SHOPPING FOR A TURKEY BREAST

/𝖨\

WHEN BUYING A TURKEY BREAST, THERE ARE TWO OPTIONS IN MANY SUPERMARKETS. EACH OPTION CONTAINS A SLIGHTLY DIFFERENT CUT. ◆ REGULAR, OR "TRUE CUT," IS THE MOST READILY AVAILABLE STYLE OF TURKEY BREAST, EITHER FRESH OR FROZEN. IT IS A WHOLE TURKEY BREAST,

bone in, with skin and usually with ribs, a portion of wing meat, and a portion of back and neck skin. The best ones are USDA Grade A and are minimally processed. Try to avoid those that have been injected with a saline solution, often called "self-basters," as the solution masks the natural flavor of the turkey. (If these are the only turkeys available, omit the brining step since these birds are already quite salty.)

Also best avoided are those sold with a pop-up timer; it won't pop up until the turkey is overcooked, but it does break the skin and allow juices to escape. If you have no choice, leave the timer in place until the turkey breast is fully roasted—according to internal temperature, *not* the timer—and pull it out just before carving.

Removing the timer earlier will accelerate the loss of juices.

Although a "true cut" breast is excellent carved at the table, it lacks the wings, neck, and giblets that are essential for making a good gravy (although these parts can always be bought separately). This style, therefore, is best when gravy is not desired.

A bit harder to locate, hotel, or "country-style," turkey breasts usually are sold only fresh. They often cost a little more, but come with wings, neck, and giblets. It may be a way for the store to make a little more profit on parts they would normally sell for less, but this style presents well at the table, especially with a giblet gravy or pan sauce on the side.

PREPARING A WHOLE TURKEY BREAST FOR ROASTING

4. Being careful not to tear the delicate membrane around the perimeter of the breast, release the skin on either side of the breastbone to form 2 pockets.

1. Use a boning knife to cut out the remaining portion of the neck and reserve it for another use.

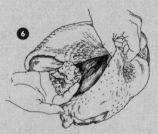

5. Insert a piece of reserved skin flap under the released skin on either side of the breastbone point, pushing it as far into the breast as possible.

2. To facilitate carving, scrape the meat away from the wishbone with a boning knife to expose it. Pull the wishbone out with your hands.

6. Rub seasoned butter under the released skin; brush the breast skin with melted butter.

3. Cut off the extra flap of skin at the neck end, leaving a 1-inch overhang. Cut the flap in half and set it aside.

7. Place the prepared turkey, skin side up, on a lightly oiled adjustable V-rack set in a roasting pan. Position the breast so that the narrow pointed end sits lower in the rack than the larger neck end.

Roasted Turkey Breast

SERVES 6 TO 8

1 1/2 cups kosher salt *or* 3/4 cup table salt
1 1/2 cups sugar
1 6- to 8-pound fresh, whole, bone-in, skin-on turkey breast, rinsed and prepared according to figures 1 and 2, opposite
4 tablespoons unsalted butter, 3 tablespoons softened, 1 tablespoon melted
1/4 teaspoon pepper

I
F PRESSED FOR TIME, use twice as much salt and sugar in the brine and cut the soaking time to just 2 hours. If you are unable to purchase a turkey breast without a pop-up timer, leave it in place and ignore it. If removed, the timer will leave a gaping hole for juices to escape during roasting. If you want to make traditional gravy to accompany a roasted turkey breast, buy a hotel or country-style breast that comes with wings, neck, and giblets, or buy these parts separately. Make sure to scatter some chopped onion, carrot, and celery, as well as some whole garlic cloves and thyme branches, in the pan under the turkey. (Follow instructions for making gravy in the roasted turkey recipe on page 329.) Some liquid is required in the pan to keep the drippings from burning. If you plan on making gravy, use white wine or chicken stock. Otherwise, water is fine.

1. If brining the turkey: Mix the salt and sugar in 1 1/2 gallons of cool water in a large, clean stockpot until completely dissolved. Set the turkey breast in the brine, making sure it is submerged. Cover and refrigerate for 5 hours.

2. Twenty minutes before roasting, adjust the oven rack to the middle position and heat the oven to 450 degrees. Mix the softened butter with the pepper in a small bowl. Set aside.

3. Remove the turkey breast from the brine, rinse inside and out under cool running water, and pat dry. Following figures 3 through 7, opposite, prepare the breast for roasting—larding with the neck skin, rubbing the seasoned butter under the breast skin, and brushing the skin with the melted butter.

4. Place the turkey breast in the oven, wide neck end toward the oven rear. Pour 1/2 cup water (or white wine or stock if you are making gravy) over the pan bottom to prevent the drippings from burning. Roast 15 minutes, then rotate the roasting pan. Roast until the skin turns golden, 15 minutes longer. Reduce the oven temperature to 325 degrees; continue to roast the breast, rotating the pan once, about halfway through cooking, until the internal temperature in the deepest part of the breast registers 160 to 165 degrees (depending on preference), 30 to 45 minutes longer.

5. Remove the turkey breast from the oven. Let stand 20 minutes. Carve and serve.

BONELESS TURKEY BREAST

⁄Ι\

AN EVEN NEWER CUT NOW SOLD FRESH AND FROZEN IN MANY SUPERMARKETS IS A BONELESS, SKINLESS TURKEY BREAST. MOST BRANDS CONTAIN TWO PIECES PER PACKAGE, EACH THE BREAST FROM ONE SIDE OF THE BIRD IN A SINGLE SLAB. WE FIND THAT THIS CUT CAN BE BUTTERFLIED, STUFFED, ROLLED, AND

tied. It's an excellent alternative to pork or veal.

A couple of caveats about buying this cut. Many supermarkets carry only frozen boneless breasts that have been injected with saline solution. These are not our first choices since they taste more like salt than turkey. Second, it's hard to tell how these breasts have been butchered. Some are fully intact, but other packages we opened had one good breast and another that was in tatters.

Our advice is to buy this cut fresh (it's easier to see the quality of the butchering and the pieces are less likely to have been injected) or take a fresh regular bone-in breast over to the butcher counter and ask them to bone it for you. You can also bone a whole breast yourself.

You may cook both pieces from a single turkey at once—each mini-roast will feed three or four—or use one for a smaller meal and freeze the other.

Lemon-Thyme Roasted Turkey Breast with Quick Pan Gravy

IT IS EASY ENOUGH TO MAKE A PAN REDUCTION GRAVY TO ACCOMPANY A ROASTED TURKEY BREAST AND THERE'S NO NEED TO MAKE TURKEY STOCK. THIS RECIPE IS IDEAL WHEN SHORT ON TIME OR IF THE TURKEY BREAST YOU BOUGHT DID NOT COME WITH GIBLETS. IN THIS RECIPE, WE FLAVOR THE TURKEY WITH GARLIC AND HERBS. THE PAN JUICES FORM THE BASE FOR THE GRAVY AND SOME LEMON JUICE ADDS SOME NEEDED ACIDITY. OTHER HERBS AND FLAVORINGS MAY BE SUBSTITUTED—ORANGE JUICE AND OREGANO OR LEMON WITH EITHER TARRAGON OR ROSEMARY, FOR EXAMPLE. **SERVES 6 TO 8.**

1 ½ cups kosher salt *or* ¾ cup table salt
1 ½ cups sugar
1 6- to 8-pound fresh, whole, bone-in, skin-on turkey breast, rinsed and prepared according to figures 1 and 2 on page 358
4 tablespoons unsalted butter, 3 tablespoons softened, 1 tablespoon melted
¼ teaspoon pepper
2 garlic cloves, minced
1 ½ tablespoons minced fresh thyme leaves *or* 2 teaspoons dried thyme
2 cups chicken stock or low-sodium canned broth
1 tablespoon fresh lemon juice
1 ½ tablespoons cornstarch

1. If brining the turkey: Mix the salt and sugar in 1½ gallons of cool water in a large, clean stockpot until completely dissolved. Set the turkey breast in brine, making sure it is submerged. Cover and refrigerate for 5 hours.

2. Twenty minutes before roasting, adjust the oven rack to the middle position and heat the oven to 450 degrees. Mix the softened butter with the pepper, garlic, and thyme in a small bowl. Set aside.

3. Remove the turkey breast from the brine, rinse inside and out under cool running water, and pat dry. Following figures 3 through 7 on page 358, prepare the breast for roasting—larding with the neck skin, rubbing the garlic and herb butter under the breast skin, and brushing the skin with the melted butter.

4. Place the turkey breast in the oven, wide neck end toward the oven rear. Pour ½ cup stock over the pan bottom to prevent the drippings from burning. Roast 15 minutes, then rotate the roasting pan. Roast until the skin turns golden, 15 minutes longer. Reduce the oven temperature to 325 degrees; continue to roast the breast, rotating the pan once, about halfway through cooking, until the internal temperature in the deepest part of the breast registers 160 to 165 degrees (depending on preference), 30 to 45 minutes longer.

5. Remove the turkey breast from the oven and transfer to a cutting board. Let stand 20 minutes.

6. Meanwhile, combine the lemon juice and cornstarch in a small bowl and stir well to dissolve any lumps. Place the roasting pan on a burner over medium-high heat. Add the remaining 1½ cups chicken stock and bring to a simmer, scraping the bottom of the pan with a wooden spoon to remove any browned bits. Bring to a boil and add the lemon juice and cornstarch mixture; boil, stirring frequently, until the gravy thickens, about 1 minute. Taste for salt and pepper. Carve the turkey breast and serve with the gravy on the side.

BONING A WHOLE TURKEY BREAST

1. Place a boning knife on one side of the breastbone at the tail end, opposite the wishbone. Cut down along the breastbone, pulling the meat off the bone as you cut further down, until the wishbone is reached.

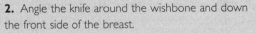

2. Angle the knife around the wishbone and down the front side of the breast.

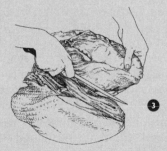

3. Slice any remaining tendons at the bottom of the breast that are keeping the meat attached to the carcass. Remove the breast in a single piece. Repeat the process on the other side of the breastbone to remove the other piece of breast meat.

Chili-Rubbed Roasted Turkey Breast with Eggplant and Tomato Relish

A SIMPLE SPICE RUB COLORS AND FLAVORS THE SKIN OF THIS ROASTED BREAST. THE RELISH, SERVED WARM OR AT ROOM TEMPERATURE, IS A COMBINATION CONDIMENT AND SIDE DISH TO THE TURKEY. SERVES 6 TO 8.

- 1½ cups kosher salt *or* table salt
- 1½ cups sugar
- 1 6- to 8-pound fresh, whole, bone-in, skin-on turkey breast, rinsed and prepared according to figures 1 and 2 on page 358
- 4 tablespoons unsalted butter, 3 tablespoons softened, 1 tablespoon melted
- ¼ teaspoon pepper
- 2 teaspoons ground cumin
- 1 teaspoon chili powder

1. If brining the turkey: Mix the salt and sugar in 1½ gallons of cool water in a large, clean stockpot until completely dissolved. Set the turkey breast in brine, making sure it is submerged. Cover and refrigerate for 5 hours.

2. Twenty minutes before roasting, adjust the oven rack to the middle position and heat the oven to 450 degrees. Mix the softened butter with the pepper in a small bowl. Set aside.

3. Remove the turkey breast from the brine, rinse inside and out under cool running water, and pat dry. Following illustrations 3 through 7 on page 358, prepare the breast for roasting: larding with the neck skin, rubbing the seasoned butter under the breast skin, and brushing the skin with the melted butter. Sprinkle the turkey with the cumin and chili powder.

4. Place the turkey breast in the oven, wide neck end toward the oven rear. Pour ½ cup water over the pan bottom to prevent the drippings from burning. Roast 15 minutes, then rotate roasting pan. Roast until the skin turns golden, 15 minutes longer. Reduce the oven temperature to 325 degrees; continue to roast the breast, rotating the pan once, about halfway through cooking, until the internal temperature in the deepest part of the breast registers 160 to 165 degrees (depending on preference), 30 to 45 minutes longer.

5. Remove the turkey breast from the oven. Let stand 20 minutes. Carve and serve with the relish on the side.

◆

Eggplant and Tomato Relish

YOU CAN TOSS DICED EGGPLANT WITH ¼ CUP OF SALT IN A LARGE BOWL. TRANSFER TO A COLANDER AND LET STAND 1 HOUR. LIGHTLY PRESS THE EGGPLANT WITH PAPER TOWELS TO REMOVE EXCESS LIQUID. RINSE WELL AND PAT DRY. MAKES ABOUT 6 CUPS.

- 6 tablespoons extra-virgin olive oil
- 2 medium eggplants (about 2½ pounds), peeled and cut into ½-inch dice
- 1 medium onion, finely chopped
- 1 tablespoon minced fresh gingerroot
- 4 garlic cloves, minced
- 1 jalapeño or other fresh hot chile, seeded and finely chopped
- ½ cup raisins
- 1 cup red wine vinegar
- ¼ cup packed brown sugar
- 6 medium tomatoes (about 2 pounds), cored, seeded, and cut into ¼-inch dice
- ¼ cup minced fresh cilantro leaves
- Salt and pepper

1. Heat ¼ cup of oil over medium-high heat in a large skillet. Add the eggplant and cook, stirring occasionally, until golden and soft, 6 to 8 minutes. Transfer the cooked eggplant to a bowl and set aside.

2. Heat 2 tablespoons of oil over medium-high heat and add the onion; sauté until soft and golden, about 5 minutes. Reduce heat to medium and add the ginger, garlic, and jalapeño; sauté another minute.

3. Add the eggplant, the raisins, vinegar, brown sugar, and tomatoes to the pan. Bring to a simmer and cook, stirring frequently, until eggplant and tomatoes soften, about 5 minutes. Stir in the cilantro and adjust the seasonings. Serve hot or at room temperature.

Roasted Butterflied Boneless Turkey Breast

SERVES 6 TO 8

2 tablespoons olive oil
1 pound fresh spinach leaves, washed and stemmed
1 small onion, minced
2 garlic cloves, minced
¼ cup toasted pine nuts, coarsely chopped
½ cup grated Parmesan cheese
Salt and pepper
1 boneless, skinless turkey breast, split (about 3 pounds total)
1 tablespoon melted butter

FOR TRADITIONAL roasted turkey flavor, we recommend cooking the breast on the bone. However, many companies sell boneless turkey breast that can be stuffed. Lay this flat piece of meat out on a work surface, cover with cooked greens, as in this recipe, or other stuffing, roll up in a cylinder, and tie with string to secure. Boneless breasts are split before they're packaged, so the following recipes make two small stuffed roasts each. You will need between ½ cup and 1 cup of stuffing—the amount varies depending on the richness of the stuffing—for each roast. You can halve this recipe, using only one side of the breast if you like. See page 361 if you want to bone a whole turkey breast yourself.

1. Adjust the oven rack to the middle position and heat the oven to 325 degrees. Heat 1 tablespoon of oil over medium-high heat in a large saucepan. Add the spinach and cook, stirring frequently, until it is very limp, 6 to 8 minutes. Remove the spinach from the pot and place it in a colander. Cool slightly and press down on the cooked spinach with paper towels to remove the excess water. Coarsely chop the spinach and place it in a medium bowl.

2. Heat the remaining tablespoon oil over medium-high heat in a small skillet; sauté the onion and garlic until softened, 2 to 3 minutes. Add them to the bowl along with the pine nuts and cheese and mix well. Stir in salt and pepper to taste.

3. Butterfly the turkey breast halves, following the figures on page 365. Cover the surface of each half with the spinach mixture. Roll the turkey breast halves, jelly-roll style, and tie in 3 or 4 places with kitchen twine (see figures, page 365). Brush the rolled turkey breast halves with the melted butter and sprinkle with salt and pepper to taste.

4. Place the turkey breast halves on a rack in a roasting pan. Roast until the internal temperature in the deepest part of the rolls registers 160 to 165 degrees, about 1½ hours.

5. Remove the turkey breast halves from the oven. Let stand 10 minutes. Slice crosswise into ½-inch-thick pieces (see figure, page 365) and serve.

Roasted Butterflied Boneless Turkey Breast with Pancetta and Rosemary

THIS ROLLED BREAST BORROWS ITS FLAVORS FROM A CLASSIC ITALIAN RECIPE FOR PORK ROAST, BUT WITH MUCH LESS FAT. SAUTEED LEAFY GREENS AND ROASTED POTATOES WOULD COMPLEMENT THE DISH NICELY. SERVES 6 TO 8.

> 1 boneless, skinless turkey breast, split (about 3 pounds)
> ¼ pound thinly sliced pancetta
> 2 garlic cloves, minced
> 1 teaspoon chopped fresh rosemary leaves or ¼ teaspoon dried
> 1 tablespoon melted butter
> Salt and pepper

1. Adjust the oven rack to the middle position and heat the oven to 325 degrees.

2. Butterfly the turkey breast halves, following the figures, opposite. Cover the surface of each half with the sliced pancetta. Sprinkle with the garlic and rosemary. Roll the turkey breast halves, jelly-roll style, and tie in 3 or 4 places with kitchen twine (see figures, opposite). Brush the rolled turkey breast halves with the melted butter and sprinkle with salt and pepper to taste.

3. Place the turkey breast halves on a rack in a roasting pan. Roast until the internal temperature in the deepest part of the rolls registers 160 to 165 degrees, about 1½ hours.

4. Remove the turkey breast halves from the oven. Let stand 10 minutes. Slice crosswise into ½-inch-thick pieces (see figure, opposite) and serve.

Roasted Butterflied Boneless Turkey Breast with Chiles and Raisins

A RICH PASTE MADE OF RAISINS AND ANCHO CHILES FLAVORS THIS BONELESS BREAST. EITHER CORNBREAD (SEE PAGE 339) OR SOFT POLENTA WOULD MAKE A GOOD ACCOMPANIMENT. SERVES 6 TO 8.

> 1 cup raisins
> 2 dried ancho chiles
> 4 garlic cloves, coarsely chopped
> ¼ cup chopped fresh parsley leaves
> Salt and pepper
> 1 boneless, skinless turkey breast, split (about 3 pounds)
> 1 tablespoon melted butter

1. Place the raisins and chiles in a heatproof bowl and cover with boiling water. Let soak until plumped and softened, 20 to 30 minutes. Remove the raisins and chiles from the water. Stem, seed, and coarsely chop the chiles. Combine the raisins, chiles, garlic, parsley, and salt and pepper to taste in the work bowl of a food processor. Process until a smooth paste forms. Set aside.

2. Adjust the oven rack to the middle position and heat the oven to 325 degrees.

3. Butterfly the turkey breast halves, following figures, opposite. Cover the surface of each half with the raisin-chile mixture. Roll the turkey breast halves, jelly-roll style, and tie in 3 or 4 places with kitchen twine (see figures, opposite). Brush the rolled turkey breast halves with the melted butter and sprinkle with salt and pepper to taste.

4. Place the turkey breast halves on a rack in a roasting pan. Roast until the internal temperature in the deepest part of the rolls registers 160 to 165 degrees, about 1½ hours.

5. Remove the turkey breast halves from the oven. Let stand 10 minutes. Slice crosswise into ½-inch-thick pieces (see figure, opposite) and serve.

BUTTERFLYING A BONELESS TURKEY BREAST

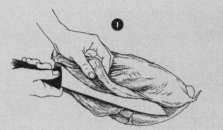

1. A packaged boneless turkey breast is actually just half of the entire breast. The meat is at least 1½ inches thick, except for a thinner portion attached to one side. Where the thick and thin portions meet, make a horizontal cut into the larger side of the breast, slicing through to within ½ inch of the other side.

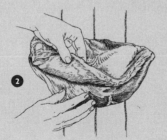

2. Position 3 strands of kitchen twine underneath the meat. Lift the top piece of meat and fold it back as if opening a book to make a large, flat piece of meat. Lay the stuffing on top of the meat, leaving a ½-inch space around the edges.

TYING AND CARVING A BUTTER-FLIED BONELESS TURKEY BREAST

1. Roll the turkey breast jelly-roll style, making sure to keep the filling from falling out the sides of the turkey breast.

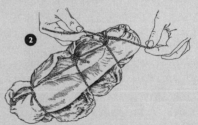

2. Secure the turkey breast in 3 places around the circumference and once around the length of the roll with kitchen twine.

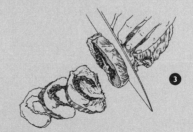

3. Slice each turkey breast piece crosswise into ½-inch-thick rounds. Each slice should contain some filling in the center, with meat wrapped around it. Make sure to remove any strings that may be attached to the slices.

Deep-Fried Boneless Turkey Breast

OVER THE LAST FEW YEARS WE'VE BEEN INTRIGUED BY A NUMBER OF RECIPES FOR DEEP-FRIED TURKEY, BUT THE 60-GALLON DRUM, BUCKETS OF OIL, AND LARGE OUTDOOR FIRE REQUIRED TO DEEP-FRY A WHOLE TURKEY HAVE SCARED US AWAY. WE DECIDED TO SEE WHAT A BONED, SPLIT TURKEY BREAST WOULD TASTE LIKE DEEP-FRIED, HOWEVER, AND WERE PLEASED WITH THE RESULTS. THE MEAT DEVELOPS A CRUNCHY CRUST AND THE INSIDE REMAINS INCREDIBLY JUICY. ONLY 1 GALLON OF OIL, A PERFECTLY SAFE AMOUNT FOR INDOOR COOKING, IS REQUIRED TO COMPLETELY SURROUND THIS 3-POUND CUT. WE TESTED VARIOUS OILS, INCLUDING PEANUT, SAFFLOWER, AND VEGETABLE OIL, AND COULD NOT TELL MUCH DIFFERENCE IN FLAVOR. SINCE VEGETABLE OIL IS THE CHEAPEST, WE RECOMMEND THAT YOU USE IT HERE. TO ENSURE GOOD RESULTS, USE A DEEP-FAT THERMOMETER TO CHECK THE TEMPERATURE OF THE OIL. DEEP-FRIED TURKEY BREAST IS EXCELLENT ON SANDWICHES (TRY MAKING A CLUB SANDWICH WITH IT—THE TURKEY HAS SO MUCH FLAVOR YOU CAN EVEN DO WITHOUT THE BACON) AND IN SALADS (REPLACE THE CHICKEN WITH DEEP-FRIED TURKEY IN THE RECIPE FOR CHICKEN CAESAR SALAD, PAGE 309) OR TRY USING DEEP-FRIED TURKEY IN A CHEF'S OR COBB SALAD. **SERVES 6 TO 8.**

1 gallon vegetable oil, for frying
1 boneless, skinless turkey breast, split
   (about 3 pounds)
Salt and ground black pepper

1. Heat the oil to 350 degrees in a large, deep pot, at least 8 quarts.

2. Butterfly the turkey breast halves, following the figures on page 365. Sprinkle with salt and pepper. Roll the turkey breast halves, jelly-roll style, and tie in 3 or 4 places with kitchen twine (see page 365).

3. With long tongs, carefully lower one breast half into the oil. Fry the breast half until it is cooked through and golden (an instant-read thermometer carefully inserted into the thickest part of the breast should read 160 to 165 degrees), 15 to 20 minutes. Carefully remove the turkey from the oil, transfer to a plate lined with paper towels, and cover with aluminum foil. Repeat with the second breast half.

4. Let both pieces rest uncovered for 10 minutes. Remove kitchen twine and slice crosswise into thin rounds for sandwiches or carve into strips for salad.

SAUTEED TURKEY CUTLETS

ONE OF THE MOST POPULAR "NEW" TURKEY CUTS TO

EMERGE IN RECENT YEARS IS THE CUTLET. THINLY

SLICED PIECES OF BREAST MEAT, USUALLY FOUR TO A

PACKAGE, HAVE BECOME A POPULAR ITEM IN MOST

SUPERMARKETS. ONE LOOK AT THE NUTRITIONAL

LABEL TELLS THE STORY. EACH 4-OUNCE CUTLET HAS

just 130 calories and less than 1 gram of fat, as compared to nearly 200 calories and 4 grams of fat in a chicken cutlet that is the same size. Both are low in calories and fat, but the turkey numbers are about as low as any meat or seafood gets.

Ultra-lean turkey cutlets can pose some challenges in the kitchen. The biggest threat is overcooking. Misjudge the timing by a minute or two and this delicate meat can resemble shoe leather. But there are some factors that make turkey cutlets remarkably easy to prepare. Unlike chicken breasts, turkey cutlets are an even thickness, usually about ¼ inch. There are no tendons or floppy tenderloins to contend with (turkey cutlets are breast slices, not the entire breast half as with chicken cutlets) and no chance that part of the cutlet will overcook while part remains bloody. Also, because the cutlets are so thin, they are a lot less messy to prepare. The fat does not have time to smoke and splatter as it can when sautéing chicken cutlets.

In many regards, turkey cutlets look and cook more like veal scaloppine than any chicken part. In fact, they can be used in recipes where you might use veal scaloppine. If you are avoiding veal because of ethical reasons or price (turkey cutlets cost half as much as veal), this trendy poultry item is an excellent alternative. The flavor is a bit milder and never has the milky sweetness found in really good veal, but since supermarket veal is rather disappointing and bland, turkey cutlets more than hold their own in terms of flavor, texture, and ease of preparation.

We had several questions at the outset of our testing. We wanted to devise a foolproof method for cooking turkey cutlets that would keep them as tender and moist as possible. We wondered if turkey cutlets could be cooked in such a way as to promote the development of a crust, one of our favorite things about sautéed chicken cutlets. Could we get these thin cutlets to brown before they overcooked? Would flour help? What about the choice of fat and cooking temperature?

We started by testing the role of flour. We sautéed two batches of cutlets—one seasoned with just salt and pepper, the other seasoned and then lightly coated on both sides with flour. Although the internal texture of both batches was similar, the exterior was quite different. The floured cutlets developed a light brown crust in places, making a nice contrast to the tender, white interior meat. The unfloured cutlets were less flavorful (browning adds flavor) and we missed the pleasing crunch added by a nicely browned exterior.

We then examined fat. As with chicken cutlets (see chapter 5), we found that a mixture of butter and oil is the best medium for cooking turkey cutlets. The butter promotes browning and adds flavor, while the oil helps keep the fat from burning in the pan. Since turkey cutlets are so mild tasting, we like to use olive oil along with the butter, but other cooking oils will certainly work as well. In these early tests, we also noticed it was imperative to pat dry the cutlets before flouring them. We usually rinse poultry to remove any stickiness, but if the cutlets are not blotted dry with paper towels, the flour won't cling properly and the cutlets won't brown.

We found that medium-high heat produced the best crust without burning the fat. The timing proved remarkably simple—two minutes on the first side and another minute or two on the second. Don't try to brown both sides or you run the risking of overcooking. Once the meat feels firm and the second side has lost it raw pink color, take the turkey out of the pan. Serve the cutlets, browned side up. Also, use tongs to turn the meat and remove it from the pan. Pricking the meat with a fork can cause precious juices to escape.

Although most poultry companies put four 4-ounce cutlets in a package and claim that this amount serves four, we think this is a bit skimpy. Six cutlets is a more realistic amount for four people. (Serve each person a whole cutlet and cut the remaining two cutlets in half after cooking to yield four more smaller pieces.) In any case, you will have to cook these large, flat cutlets in batches to prevent overcrowding in the pan. Keep the first batch warm on a plate in a low oven while cooking the second batch. Given the short cooking time, the cutlets won't dry out during their brief stay in the oven.

Once the second batch is out of the pan, it's time to make a sauce. Turkey cutlets are not nearly as juicy as thicker chicken cutlets, so a pan sauce is imperative. Also, given the less meaty nature of this cut, the sauce will take extra prominence, giving the dish most of its flavor. If you are interested in keeping the fat in check, thicken the sauce with chopped tomatoes as directed in several of the recipes that follow. Otherwise, butter swirled into the pan just before serving does an excellent job of enriching the texture and flavor of a quick pan sauce.

The following recipes illustrate just some of the possible pan sauces. For other ideas, see chapter 5 and adapt any of the sauces for sautéed chicken cutlets.

Sautéed Turkey Cutlets

SERVES 4

Because they are so thin, turkey cutlets cook quickly—3 to 4 minutes total. The technique is more like that for veal scaloppine than for chicken cutlets. Keep a close eye on them, since these thin and delicate pieces of meat will dry out quickly if overcooked.

Salt and pepper
6 turkey cutlets (about 1 1/2 pounds),
    rinsed and thoroughly dried
1/4 cup all-purpose flour
1 1/2 tablespoons unsalted butter, softened
1 1/2 tablespoons olive oil

1. Preheat the oven to the lowest possible temperature. Place a plate in the oven for keeping the cooked cutlets warm while you make the sauce.

2. Sprinkle 1 teaspoon salt and 1/4 to 1/2 teaspoon pepper on both sides of the cutlets. Measure the flour onto a plate or pie tin. Working with 1 cutlet at a time, press both sides into the flour. Shake gently to remove excess flour.

3. Heat half the butter and oil in a heavy-bottomed skillet measuring at least 9 inches across the bottom. Swirl the skillet over high heat until the butter has melted. Continue to heat until the butter stops foaming and has just begun to color. Lay half the cutlets in the skillet.

4. Maintain medium-high heat, so the fat sizzles but does not smoke, and sauté the cutlets until browned on one side, about 2 minutes. Turn the cutlets with tongs; cook on the other side until the meat feels firm when pressed, 1 to 2 minutes. Transfer the cutlets to the plate in the oven; repeat the process with the remaining butter, oil, and cutlets. Keep warm in the oven until ready to serve.

◆

Sautéed Turkey Cutlets with Lemon Sauce

LEMON JUICE, WHITE WINE, GARLIC, AND THYME MAKE THE SIMPLEST, AND SOMETIMES THE MOST SATISFYING, SEASONING FOR POULTRY, INCLUDING TURKEY CUTLETS. THE BUTTER SWIRLED INTO THE FINISHED SAUCE GIVES IT A RICH FLAVOR AND TEXTURE. IF YOU ARE CHOOSING TURKEY CUTLETS FOR HEALTH REASONS, YOU CAN USE LESS BUTTER—THE SAUCE WILL BE THINNER BUT STILL TASTY. SERVES 4.

Salt and pepper
6 turkey cutlets (about 1 1/2 pounds),
    rinsed and thoroughly dried
1/4 cup all-purpose flour
4 1/2 tablespoons unsalted butter, softened
1 1/2 tablespoons olive oil
2 medium garlic cloves, minced
1 cup dry white wine
3 tablespoons fresh lemon juice
1 tablespoon fresh thyme leaves

(continued on next page)

1. Preheat the oven to the lowest possible temperature. Place a plate in the oven for keeping the cooked cutlets warm while you make the sauce.

2. Sprinkle 1 teaspoon salt and ¼ to ½ teaspoon pepper on both sides of the cutlets. Measure the flour onto a plate or pie tin. Working with 1 cutlet at a time, press both sides into the flour. Shake gently to remove excess flour.

3. Heat ¾ tablespoon butter and ¾ tablespoon oil in a heavy-bottomed skillet measuring at least 9 inches across the bottom. Swirl the skillet over high heat until the butter has melted. Continue to heat until the butter stops foaming and has just begun to color. Lay half the cutlets in the skillet.

4. Maintain medium-high heat, so the fat sizzles but does not smoke, and sauté the cutlets until browned on one side, about 2 minutes. Turn the cutlets with tongs; cook on the other side until the meat feels firm when pressed, 1 to 2 minutes. Transfer the cutlets to the plate in the oven; repeat the process with another ¾ tablespoon butter and the remaining ¾ tablespoon oil and cutlets. Keep warm until ready to serve.

5. Without discarding the fat, set the skillet over medium heat. Add the garlic; sauté until softened, about 1 minute. Increase the heat to high, add the wine and lemon juice, and scrape the skillet bottom with a wooden spatula or spoon to loosen any browned bits. Boil until the liquid reduces to about ⅓ cup, about 3 minutes. Add any accumulated turkey juices from the plate with the cutlets; reduce the sauce again to ⅓ cup. Add the thyme and season with salt and pepper to taste. Off the heat, swirl in the remaining 3 tablespoons butter until it melts and thickens the sauce. Spoon the sauce over the cutlets; serve immediately.

Sautéed Turkey Cutlets with Chorizo and Peppers

CHORIZO, A SPANISH-STYLE SMOKED SAUSAGE, GIVES THIS DISH A BASQUE FLAVOR. SERVE WITH YELLOW RICE UNDERNEATH OR ON THE SIDE TO SOAK UP THE TOMATO JUICES. OTHER FRESH HERBS, ESPECIALLY PARSLEY, WOULD BE APPROPRIATE IN THIS DISH. **SERVES 4**.

> Salt and pepper
> 6 turkey cutlets (about 1½ pounds), rinsed and thoroughly dried
> ¼ cup all-purpose flour
> 1½ tablespoons unsalted butter, softened
> 1½ tablespoons olive oil
> 1 small onion, finely chopped
> 2 medium garlic cloves, minced
> 1 green bell pepper, cored, seeded, and cut into ¼-inch dice
> 2 ounces chorizo sausage, cut into ¼-inch dice
> ½ cup dry sherry
> ½ cup chicken stock or low-sodium canned chicken broth
> 1 medium-large ripe tomato (about ½ pound), cored, seeded, and chopped
> 2 teaspoons fresh thyme leaves

1. Preheat the oven to the lowest possible temperature. Place a plate in the oven for keeping the cooked cutlets warm while you make the sauce.

2. Sprinkle 1 teaspoon salt and ¼ to ½ teaspoon pepper on both sides of the cutlets. Measure the flour onto a plate or pie tin. Working with 1 cutlet at a time, press both sides into the flour. Shake gently to remove excess flour.

3. Heat ¾ tablespoon butter and ¾ tablespoon oil in a heavy-bottomed skillet measuring at least 9 inches across the bottom. Swirl the skillet over high heat until the butter has melted. Continue to heat until the butter stops foaming and has just begun to color. Lay half the cutlets in the skillet.

4. Maintain medium-high heat, so the fat sizzles but does not smoke, and sauté the cutlets until browned on one side, about 2 minutes. Turn the cutlets with tongs; cook on the other side until the meat feels firm when pressed, 1 to 2 minutes. Transfer the cutlets to the plate in the oven; repeat the process with the remaining butter, oil, and cutlets. Keep warm until ready to serve.

5. Without discarding the fat, set the skillet over medium heat. Add the onion; sauté until softened, 3 to 4 minutes. Add the garlic and sauté another minute. Add the pepper and sauté until it begins to soften, about 4 minutes. Add the chorizo and cook until it starts to brown, about 2 minutes. Increase the heat to high, add the sherry, stock, and tomato, and scrape the skillet bottom with a wooden spatula or spoon to loosen any browned bits. Boil until the sauce is chunky and thickened, about 3 minutes. Add any accumulated turkey juices from the plate with the cutlets; reduce the sauce again. Add the thyme and season with salt and pepper to taste. Spoon the sauce over the cutlets; serve immediately.

◆

Sautéed Turkey Cutlets with Cranberries and Chives

CRANBERRIES ARE A NATURAL MATCH WITH TURKEY AND THIS DISH, WHICH USES DRIED CRANBERRIES, LETS YOU ENJOY THIS HOLIDAY COMBINATION WITH A MERE 20 MINUTES' WORK. SERVES 4.

    ½ cup dried cranberries
    Salt and pepper
    6 turkey cutlets (about 1½ pounds),
        rinsed and thoroughly dried
    ¼ cup all-purpose flour
    4½ tablespoons unsalted butter, softened
    1½ tablespoons olive oil
    2 shallots, minced
    2 medium garlic cloves, minced
    1 cup chicken stock or low-sodium
        canned chicken broth
    ¼ cup snipped fresh chives

1. Place the cranberries in a heatproof bowl and cover with boiling water. Soak until plump and softened, about 20 minutes. Drain, reserving the cranberries.

2. Meanwhile, preheat the oven to the lowest possible temperature. Place a plate in the oven for keeping the cooked cutlets warm while you make the sauce.

3. Sprinkle 1 teaspoon salt and ¼ to ½ teaspoon pepper on both sides of the cutlets. Measure the flour onto a plate or pie tin. Working with 1 cutlet at a time, press both sides into the flour. Shake gently to remove excess flour.

4. Heat ¾ tablespoon butter and ¾ tablespoon oil in a heavy-bottomed skillet measuring at least 9 inches across the bottom. Swirl the skillet over high heat until the butter has melted. Continue to heat until the butter stops foaming and has just begun to color. Lay half the cutlets in the skillet.

5. Maintain medium-high heat, so the fat sizzles but does not smoke, and sauté the cutlets until browned on one side, about 2 minutes. Turn the cutlets with tongs; cook on the other side until the meat feels firm when pressed, 1 to 2 minutes. Transfer the cutlets to the plate in the oven; repeat the process with another ¾ tablespoon butter and the remaining ¾ tablespoon oil and cutlets. Keep warm until ready to serve.

6. Without discarding the fat, set the skillet over medium heat. Add the shallots; sauté until softened, 3 to 4 minutes. Add the garlic; sauté another minute to soften. Increase the heat to high, add the stock and drained cranberries, and scrape the skillet bottom with a wooden spatula or spoon to loosen any browned bits. Boil until the sauce becomes thick and chunky, about 3 minutes. Add any accumulated turkey juices from the plate with the cutlets; reduce the sauce again. Add the chives and season with salt and pepper to taste. Off the heat, swirl in the remaining 3 tablespoons butter until it melts and thickens the sauce. Spoon the sauce over the cutlets; serve immediately.

Sautéed Turkey Cutlets with Asparagus and Cherry Tomatoes

THIN ASPARAGUS SPEARS AND CHERRY TOMATOES MAKE A COLORFUL AND FRESH-TASTING ACCOMPANIMENT TO SAUTEED CUTLETS. THE ASPARAGUS SPEARS ARE CUT INTO SMALL PIECES THAT WILL COOK THROUGH WHILE THE SAUCE REDUCES. IF ONLY THICKER ASPARAGUS ARE AVAILABLE, SLICE THE TRIMMED SPEARS IN HALF LENGTHWISE BEFORE CUTTING INTO SMALL LENGTHS. IF YOU PREFER A LESS BUTTERY TOMATO-BASED SAUCE, SUBSTITUTE 1 MEDIUM-LARGE TOMATO, SEEDED AND CHOPPED, FOR THE CHERRY TOMATOES AND OMIT THE FINAL 3 TABLESPOONS OF BUTTER SWIRLED IN AT THE END. SERVES 4.

Salt and pepper
6 turkey cutlets (about 1 1/2 pounds),
    rinsed and thoroughly dried
1/4 cup all-purpose flour
4 1/2 tablespoons unsalted butter, softened
1 1/2 tablespoons olive oil
2 medium garlic cloves, minced
1/2 cup chicken stock or low-sodium
    canned chicken broth
1/2 cup white wine
12 thin asparagus spears, tough ends
    snapped off and cut into 1-inch lengths
    (see figures 1 and 2, page 263)
12 cherry tomatoes, halved
1 tablespoon chopped fresh tarragon or
    basil leaves

1. Preheat the oven to the lowest possible temperature. Place a plate in the oven for keeping the cooked cutlets warm while you make the sauce.

2. Sprinkle 1 teaspoon salt and 1/4 to 1/2 teaspoon pepper on both sides of the cutlets. Measure the flour onto a plate or pie tin. Working with 1 cutlet at a time, press both sides into the flour. Shake gently to remove excess flour.

3. Heat 3/4 tablespoon butter and 3/4 tablespoon oil in a heavy-bottomed skillet measuring at least 9 inches across the bottom. Swirl the skillet over high heat until the butter has melted. Continue to heat until the butter stops foaming and has just begun to color. Lay half the cutlets in the skillet.

4. Maintain medium-high heat, so the fat sizzles but does not smoke, and sauté the cutlets until browned on one side, about 2 minutes. Turn the cutlets with tongs; cook on the other side until the meat feels firm when pressed, 1 to 2 minutes. Transfer the cutlets to the plate in the oven; repeat the process with another 3/4 tablespoon butter and the remaining 3/4 tablespoon oil and cutlets. Keep warm until ready to serve.

5. Without discarding the fat, set the skillet over medium heat. Add the garlic; sauté until softened, about 1 minute. Increase the heat to high, add the stock, wine, asparagus, and tomatoes and scrape the skillet bottom with a wooden spatula or spoon to loosen any browned bits. Boil until the sauce becomes thick and chunky, about 3 minutes. Add any accumulated turkey juices from the plate with the cutlets; reduce the sauce again. Add the tarragon and season with salt and pepper to taste. Off the heat, swirl in the remaining 3 tablespoons butter until it melts and thickens the sauce. Spoon the sauce over the cutlets; serve immediately.

◆

Sautéed Turkey Cutlets with Leeks and Mushrooms

PLAIN BUTTON MUSHROOMS ARE FINE IN THIS RECIPE, BUT WOODSY CREMINI WILL MAKE THE SAUCE MORE FLAVORFUL IF YOU CAN FIND THEM. THE CHOPPED BLACK OLIVES ADDED AT THE END OF THE COOKING TIME GIVE THE FINISHED DISH A PLEASING PUNGENCY. SERVES 4.

Salt and pepper
6 turkey cutlets (about 1 1/2 pounds),
    rinsed and thoroughly dried
1/4 cup all-purpose flour
4 1/2 tablespoons unsalted butter, softened
1 1/2 tablespoons olive oil
3 leeks, white and light green parts,
    washed, patted dry, and thinly sliced
    (see page 105)
6 ounces mushrooms, stem ends trimmed,
    sliced thin

1 cup dry white wine
1 tablespoon fresh lemon juice
8 Kalamata or other large brine-packed black olives, pitted and coarsely chopped
1 tablespoon minced fresh parsley leaves

1. Preheat the oven to the lowest possible temperature. Place a plate in the oven for keeping the cooked cutlets warm while you make the sauce.

2. Sprinkle 1 teaspoon salt and ¼ to ½ teaspoon pepper on both sides of the cutlets. Measure the flour onto a plate or pie tin. Working with 1 cutlet at a time, press both sides into the flour. Shake gently to remove excess flour.

3. Heat ¾ tablespoon butter and ¾ tablespoon oil in a heavy-bottomed skillet measuring at least 9 inches across the bottom. Swirl the skillet over high heat until the butter has melted. Continue to heat until the butter stops foaming and has just begun to color. Lay half the cutlets in the skillet.

4. Maintain medium-high heat, so the fat sizzles but does not smoke, and sauté the cutlets until browned on one side, about 2 minutes. Turn the cutlets with tongs; cook on the other side until the meat feels firm when pressed, 1 to 2 minutes. Transfer the cutlets to the plate in the oven; repeat the process with another ¾ tablespoon butter and the remaining ¾ tablespoon oil and cutlets. Keep warm until ready to serve.

5. Without discarding the fat, set the skillet over medium heat. Add the leeks; sauté until softened, about 5 minutes. Add the mushrooms and sauté until they release their juices and begin to brown, about 5 minutes. Increase the heat to high, add the wine and lemon juice, and scrape the skillet bottom with a wooden spatula or spoon to loosen any browned bits. Boil until the sauce becomes thick and chunky, about 3 minutes. Add any accumulated turkey juices from the plate with the cutlets; reduce the sauce again. Add the olives and parsley and season with salt and pepper to taste. Off the heat, swirl in the remaining 3 tablespoons butter until it melts and thickens the sauce. Spoon the sauce over the cutlets; serve immediately.

Sautéed Turkey Cutlets with Quick Pan Salsa

MILD-FLAVORED TURKEY CUTLETS COMBINE WELL WITH HIGHLY SEASONED SAUCES. HERE WE MAKE A SIMPLE TOMATO SALSA FLAVORED WITH CHILI POWDER AND PICKLED JALAPEÑOS. FRESH CHILES AND OTHER GROUND SPICES, INCLUDING CUMIN, GINGER, OR PAPRIKA, CAN BE USED IN A SIMILAR FASHION. SERVES 4.

Salt and pepper
6 turkey cutlets (about 1½ pounds), rinsed and thoroughly dried
¼ cup all-purpose flour
1½ tablespoons unsalted butter, softened
1½ tablespoons olive oil
1 small red onion, finely chopped
½ cup chicken stock or low-sodium canned chicken broth
2 medium-large tomatoes (about 1 pound), cored, seeded, and chopped
2 tablespoons red wine vinegar
1 teaspoon chili powder
1 or 2 pickled jalapeño chiles, finely chopped
2 tablespoons chopped fresh cilantro leaves

1. Preheat the oven to the lowest possible temperature. Place a plate in the oven for keeping the cooked cutlets warm while you make the sauce.

2. Sprinkle 1 teaspoon salt and ¼ to ½ teaspoon pepper on both sides of the cutlets. Measure the flour onto a plate or pie tin. Working with 1 cutlet at a time, press both sides into the flour. Shake gently to remove excess flour.

3. Heat ¾ tablespoon butter and ¾ tablespoon oil in a heavy-bottomed skillet measuring at least 9 inches across the bottom. Swirl the skillet over high heat until the butter has melted. Continue to heat until the butter stops foaming and has just begun to color. Lay half the cutlets in the skillet.

4. Maintain medium-high heat, so the fat sizzles but does not smoke, and sauté the cutlets until browned on one side, about 2 minutes. Turn the cutlets with

(continued on next page)

tongs; cook on the other side until the meat feels firm when pressed, 1 to 2 minutes. Transfer the cutlets to the plate in the oven; repeat the process with the remaining butter, oil, and cutlets. Keep warm until ready to serve.

5. Without discarding the fat, set the skillet over medium heat. Add the onion; sauté until it just begins to soften, 1 to 2 minutes. Increase the heat to high; add the stock, tomatoes, vinegar, chili powder, and jalapeño, and scrape the skillet bottom with a wooden spatula or spoon to loosen any browned bits. Boil until the sauce is chunky and thickened, about 3 minutes. Add any accumulated turkey juices from the plate with the cutlets; reduce the sauce again. Add the cilantro and season with salt and pepper to taste. Spoon the sauce over the cutlets; serve immediately.

◆

Sautéed Turkey Cutlets with Celery and Orange

THE CELERY SHOULD BE COOKED UNTIL YIELDING BUT NOT MUSHY. LEMON ZEST AND 2 TABLESPOONS OF LEMON JUICE MAY BE SUBSTITUTED FOR THE ORANGE ZEST AND JUICE; INCREASE THE CHICKEN STOCK TO 1 CUP. SERVES 4.

Salt and pepper
6 turkey cutlets (about 1 1/2 pounds), rinsed and thoroughly dried
1/4 cup all-purpose flour
4 1/2 tablespoons unsalted butter, softened
1 1/2 tablespoons olive oil
1 onion, finely chopped
6 celery stalks, trimmed and sliced thin
1/2 cup chicken stock or low-sodium canned chicken broth
1 tablespoon grated orange zest
1/2 cup fresh orange juice
1 tablespoon minced fresh parsley or thyme leaves

1. Preheat the oven to the lowest possible temperature. Place a plate in the oven for keeping the cooked cutlets warm while you make the sauce.

2. Sprinkle 1 teaspoon salt and 1/4 to 1/2 teaspoon pepper on both sides of the cutlets. Measure the flour onto a plate or pie tin. Working with 1 cutlet at a time, press both sides into the flour. Shake gently to remove excess flour.

3. Heat 3/4 tablespoon butter and 3/4 tablespoon oil in a heavy-bottomed skillet measuring at least 9 inches across the bottom. Swirl the skillet over high heat until the butter has melted. Continue to heat until the butter stops foaming and has just begun to color. Lay half the cutlets in the skillet.

4. Maintain medium-high heat, so the fat sizzles but does not smoke, and sauté the cutlets until browned on one side, about 2 minutes. Turn the cutlets with tongs; cook on the other side until the meat feels firm when pressed, 1 to 2 minutes. Transfer the cutlets to the plate in the oven; repeat the process with another 3/4 tablespoon butter and the remaining oil and cutlets. Keep warm until ready to serve.

5. Without discarding the fat, set the skillet over medium heat. Add the onion and celery; sauté until softened, about 6 minutes. Increase the heat to high, add the stock and the orange zest and juice, and scrape the skillet bottom with a wooden spatula or spoon to loosen any browned bits. Boil until the sauce becomes thick and chunky, about 3 minutes. Add any accumulated turkey juices from the plate with the cutlets; reduce the sauce again. Add the parsley and season with salt and pepper to taste. Off the heat, swirl in the remaining 3 tablespoons butter until it melts and thickens the sauce. Spoon the sauce over the cutlets; serve immediately.

◆

Sautéed Turkey Cutlets with Artichokes

BOTTLED MARINATED ARTICHOKE HEARTS MAKE THIS ONE OF THE QUICKEST RECIPES IN THIS CHAPTER. SIMPLY RINSE, PAT DRY, AND SLICE THEM FOR A SIMPLE BUT SATISFYING VEGETABLE SAUCE FOR TURKEY CUTLETS. SERVES 4.

Salt and pepper
6 turkey cutlets (about 1 ½ pounds),
   rinsed and thoroughly dried
¼ cup all-purpose flour
4 ½ tablespoons unsalted butter, softened
1 ½ tablespoons olive oil
1 garlic clove, minced
1 cup chicken stock or low-sodium
   canned chicken broth
2 tablespoons fresh lemon juice
1 6-ounce jar marinated artichoke hearts,
   drained, rinsed, and cut lengthwise into
   ¼-inch-thick slices
1 tablespoon minced fresh parsley leaves

1. Preheat the oven to the lowest possible temperature. Place a plate in the oven for keeping the cooked cutlets warm while you make the sauce.

2. Sprinkle 1 teaspoon salt and ¼ to ½ teaspoon pepper on both sides of the cutlets. Measure the flour onto a plate or pie tin. Working with 1 cutlet at a time, press both sides into the flour. Shake gently to remove excess flour.

3. Heat ¾ tablespoon butter and ¾ tablespoon oil in a heavy-bottomed skillet measuring at least 9 inches across the bottom. Swirl the skillet over high heat until the butter has melted. Continue to heat until the butter stops foaming and has just begun to color. Lay half the cutlets in the skillet.

4. Maintain medium-high heat, so the fat sizzles but does not smoke, and sauté the cutlets until browned on one side, about 2 minutes. Turn the cutlets with tongs; cook on the other side until the meat feels firm when pressed, 1 to 2 minutes. Transfer the cutlets to the plate in the oven; repeat the process with another ¾ tablespoon butter and the remaining ¾ tablespoon oil and cutlets. Keep warm until ready to serve.

5. Without discarding the fat, set the skillet over medium heat. Add the garlic; sauté until softened, about 1 minute. Increase the heat to high, add the stock and lemon juice, and scrape the skillet bottom with a wooden spatula or spoon to loosen the browned bits. Boil until the sauce thickens, about 3 minutes. Add any accumulated turkey juices from the

plate with the cutlets; reduce the sauce again. Add the artichokes and season with salt and pepper to taste; cook another minute to heat the artichokes. Stir in the parsley. Off the heat, swirl in the remaining 3 tablespoons butter until it melts and thickens the sauce. Spoon the sauce over the cutlets; serve immediately.

◆

Sautéed Turkey Cutlets with Caper-Anchovy Sauce

A SAUCE OF HAM, CAPERS, AND ANCHOVIES MAKES FOR A RICH AND WELL-SEASONED TURKEY CUTLET DISH. YOU PROBABLY WON'T NEED TO ADD ANY SALT AT THE END, SINCE THESE INGREDIENTS ALREADY CONTAIN PLENTIFUL AMOUNTS. SERVES 4.

Salt and pepper
6 turkey cutlets (about 1 ½ pounds),
   rinsed and thoroughly dried
¼ cup all-purpose flour
1 ½ tablespoons unsalted butter,
   softened
1 ½ tablespoons olive oil
2 ounces thinly sliced ham, cut into
   ¼-inch dice
4 flat anchovy fillets, minced
1 ½ tablespoons capers, rinsed, dried, and
   coarsely chopped
½ cup brandy
¼ cup heavy cream

1. Preheat the oven to the lowest possible temperature. Place a plate in the oven for keeping the cooked cutlets warm while you make the sauce.

2. Sprinkle 1 teaspoon salt and ¼ to ½ teaspoon pepper on both sides of the cutlets. Measure the flour onto a plate or pie tin. Working with 1 cutlet at a time, press both sides into the flour. Shake gently to remove excess flour.

3. Heat ¾ tablespoon butter and ¾ tablespoon oil in a heavy-bottomed skillet measuring at least 9 inches across the bottom. Swirl the skillet over high heat

(continued on next page)

until the butter has melted. Continue to heat until the butter stops foaming and has just begun to color. Lay half the cutlets in the skillet.

4. Maintain medium-high heat, so the fat sizzles but does not smoke, and sauté the cutlets until browned on one side, about 2 minutes. Turn the cutlets with tongs; cook on the other side until the meat feels firm when pressed, 1 to 2 minutes. Transfer the cutlets to the plate in the oven; repeat the process with another ¾ tablespoon butter and the remaining ¾ tablespoon oil and cutlets. Keep warm until ready to serve.

5. Without discarding the fat, set the skillet over medium heat. Add the ham, anchovies, and capers and cook until heated through, about 1 minute. Increase the heat to high, add the brandy, and bring to a boil, scraping the skillet bottom with a wooden spatula or spoon to loosen any browned bits. Add the cream and boil until the liquid reduces to about ⅓ cup, about 3 minutes. Add any accumulated turkey juices from the plate with the cutlets; reduce the sauce again to ⅓ cup. Spoon the sauce over the cutlets; serve immediately.

Turkey "Saltimbocca"

WE'VE ADAPTED A CLASSIC ITALIAN RECIPE FOR VEAL CUTLETS WRAPPED IN PROSCIUTTO. A QUICK TOMATO PAN SAUCE ADDS SOME MOISTURE TO THE FLAVORFUL COMBINATION. WARN DINERS ABOUT THE TOOTHPICKS USED TO SECURE THE HAM TO THE TURKEY, OR REMOVE THEM YOURSELF JUST BEFORE SAUCING THE CUTLETS. SERVES 4.

Salt and pepper
6 turkey cutlets (about 1½ pounds), rinsed and thoroughly dried
¼ cup all-purpose flour
12 fresh sage leaves, minced
6 thin slices prosciutto
1½ tablespoons unsalted butter, softened
1½ tablespoons olive oil
1 shallot, minced
2 medium garlic cloves, minced
½ cup dry white wine
1 medium-large ripe tomato (about ½ pound), cored, seeded, and chopped
2 tablespoons chopped fresh parsley leaves

1. Preheat the oven to the lowest possible temperature. Place a plate in the oven for keeping the cooked cutlets warm while you make the sauce.

2. Sprinkle 1 teaspoon salt and ¼ to ½ teaspoon pepper on both sides of the cutlets. Measure the flour onto a plate or pie tin and stir in the sage. Working with 1 cutlet at a time, press both sides into the flour. Shake gently to remove excess flour.

3. Wrap a piece of prosciutto around the center of each cutlet. Secure the prosciutto by threading a toothpick through both the cutlet and the prosciutto.

4. Heat ¾ tablespoon butter and ¾ tablespoon oil in a heavy-bottomed skillet measuring at least 9 inches across the bottom. Swirl the skillet over high heat until the butter has melted. Continue to heat until the butter stops foaming and has just begun to color. Lay half the cutlets in the skillet.

5. Maintain medium-high heat, so the fat sizzles but does not smoke, and sauté the cutlets until browned on one side, about 2 minutes. Turn the cutlets with tongs; cook on the other side until the meat feels firm when pressed, 1 to 2 minutes. Transfer the cutlets to the plate in the oven; repeat the process with the remaining butter, oil, and cutlets. Keep warm until ready to serve.

6. Without discarding the fat, set the skillet over medium heat. Add the shallot; sauté until softened, 3 to 4 minutes. Add the garlic; sauté another minute. Increase the heat to high, add the wine and tomato, and scrape the skillet bottom with a wooden spatula or spoon to loosen any browned bits. Boil until the sauce becomes thick and chunky, about 3 minutes. Add any accumulated turkey juices from the plate with the cutlets; reduce the sauce again. Add the parsley and season with salt and pepper to taste. Spoon the sauce over the cutlets; serve immediately.

CHAPTER 29

GROUND TURKEY

/|\

LIKE GROUND CHICKEN, GROUND TURKEY IS ANOTHER

RELATIVELY NEW PRODUCT IN SUPERMARKETS. WHILE

GROUND CHICKEN IS VERY SOFT AND HAS A HARD

TIME HOLDING ITS SHAPE, GROUND TURKEY IS FIRMER

AND DRIER, MAKING IT WELL SUITED TO BURGERS AND

CHILI, WHERE WE LIKE LARGE CHUNKS OF MEAT.

GROUND TURKEY WILL NEVER TASTE JUST LIKE BEEF,

but when seasoned and cooked properly it can make good burgers and chili, especially for those people concerned about their fat intake.

We ran some initial tests and found out pretty quickly that a lean, fully cooked pan-fried turkey burger, seasoned simply with salt and pepper, was a weak stand-in for an all-beef burger. Simply put, it was dry, tasteless, and colorless. Clearly, we were going to have to alter the formula we use with ground beef to get a turkey burger with beef burger qualities—dark and crusty on the outside, full-flavored and juicy with every bite. The lower fat content of ground turkey along with the fact that turkey burgers must be cooked through (no rare meat here) were going to be a challenge.

We figured that finding the right kind of ground turkey would be crucial. According the National Turkey Federation, there are three options: white meat (consisting of 1 to 2 percent fat), dark meat (15 percent fat, or more), and a blend of the two (ranging from 7 to 15 percent fat). The latter is the most common choice in markets.

At the grocery store, we found multiple variations on the white meat/dark meat theme. Did we want our turkey frozen and packed in a tubelike canister? Or did we want it refrigerated on a Styrofoam tray like hamburger? Would pre-formed patties—refrigerated or frozen—offer quality as well as convenience? Or, would we get better results buying individual turkey parts and grinding them ourselves in the food processor? To find out for sure, we bought them all, and fired up a skillet.

The higher-fat (15 percent) ground turkey—available both frozen in a tube or fresh on a Styrofoam tray—cooked up relatively flavorful and reasonably juicy, with a decent burgerlike crust. Frankly, these burgers didn't need much help. On the other hand, we didn't see much point in eating them, either. Given that a great beef burger contains only 20 percent fat, a mere 5 percent fat savings didn't seem worth it for the real thing. Our challenges lay ahead.

At the other extreme was ground turkey breast. This ultra-lean meat was a long shot, but we had to try it. After all, somebody was selling this grind, and somebody was buying it. As we were mixing and forming these patties, we knew we had about as much chance

of making these look, taste, and feel like real burgers as we did making vanilla wafers taste like chocolate chip cookies. They needed binder to keep them from falling apart. They needed extra fat to keep them from parching and extra fat in the pan to keep them from sticking. And they needed flavor to save them from blandness. A fool's task we didn't want to take on.

With 7 percent fat, lean ground turkey was the most popular style at all the grocery stores we checked. Burgers made from this mix were dry, rubbery-textured, and mild-flavored. With a little help, however, these leaner patties were meaty enough to have real burger potential.

We tested pre-formed lean patties—refrigerated and frozen—and found them mediocre. To varying degrees, the frozen ones all had a week-old roast turkey taste to them. A few bites from one of the refrigerated varieties turned up significant turkey debris—ground up gristle, tendon, and bonelike chips.

For all the obvious reasons, we swore that even if we liked it, we weren't going to make grind-your-own turkey a part of the Master Recipe. We suspected the temptation might be great, given how much we liked grind-your-own-chuck-beef burgers. Sure enough, the food processor-ground burgers made from a boned and skinned turkey thigh were far superior to any commercially ground turkey. Since they were made from all thigh meat rather than a mix of light and dark, they were especially meaty-flavored. And since they were pulsed in a food processor rather than pushed through a grinder, they actually had a beeflike chew.

At first we ground the turkey skin with the meat, but it ground up inconsistently, and we ended up picking a lot of it out anyway. We left it out of the next batch and found the skinless ground thigh meat equally flavorful and clearly lower in fat. As a matter of fact, our butcher declared our home-ground skinless turkey under 90 percent lean when tested in his Univex Fat Analyzer, a device used in supermarkets to gauge fat content in ground meat. As with beef, we found that turkey grinds best when it is cut into small chunks, partially frozen, and pulsed in small batches.

If you are willing to take the time, food processor–ground turkey thighs cook up into low-fat turkey burgers with great flavor and texture. (See the recipe on page 381.) For those with little time or energy for this process, we decided to see what we could do to improve the flavor and texture of the lean commercially ground turkey. We wanted a Master Recipe that could be prepared without the food processor.

To improve texture and juiciness, we started with the obvious milk-soaked soft bread crumbs. For comparison we also made burgers with buttermilk- and yogurt-soaked bread. With these additions, all three burgers felt more like meat loaf than burger. The dairy and bread diluted the already weak meaty flavor of the turkey. In addition, the bread and milk lightened the meat's color, while the sugar in both these ingredients caused the burgers to easily burn. Developing a good thick crust on these burgers was impossible.

We tried other fillers to improve texture, including cornmeal mush, mashed pinto beans, and minced tempeh, all of which tasted too distinct. Heat-and-serve mashed potatoes from the grocery store refrigerator case didn't mix well with the meat, resulting in a fall-apart textured burger with noticeable potato pockets.

With turkey sausage slightly higher in fat and flavor, a small amount mixed in with the ground turkey moderately improved our burger, but buying a whole package of turkey sausage for such a small improvement was like buying a half pint of cream for just 1 tablespoon.

Among all the lackluster candidates, two successful fillers emerged. Dried mushrooms—rehydrated and minced—added a moist, chewy texture that the burgers desperately needed. Additionally, they offered an earthy, meaty flavor without tasting too distinct. Minced sautéed fresh mushrooms improved texture as well, but for us, their milder flavor made them less attractive than the dried ones. Moist and thick ricotta cheese, our other winner, helped keep the burgers moist as they cooked. Since ricotta cheese can be used right from the container, we decided to use it as the binder in our Master Recipe and offer the mushrooms in a variation.

For turkey burger flavorings, we wanted only those that enhanced the burger's taste without drawing attention to themselves. After trying over twenty-five different flavorings (fermented black beans, drained salsa, sun-dried tomatoes, smoked mozzarella and cheddar, olive paste, canned black olives, prepared caponata, tomato paste, teriyaki marinade, A-1 steak sauce, ketchup, Worcestershire sauce, Dijon mustard, anchovy paste, Parmesan cheese, annatto, teriyaki, miso, soy sauce, paprika, fresh thyme, fresh rosemary, sautéed onions, and garlic), only four fit our criteria. Many of the listed flavorings were wonderful but too distinct.

Miso, a fermented soybean paste often used as a soup base, offered a subtle savoriness to the turkey that we liked. Worcestershire and Dijon mustard, more common pantry items, flavored the burger almost equally well. While fresh rosemary was a little too distinct an herb, fresh thyme flavored the burgers nicely.

Since turkey burgers must be well done, cooking them all the way through can be a bit tricky—too high and they burn before they've cooked through; too low and they look pale and steamed. Although we tried several cooking methods—broiling, roasting, pan-frying—nothing compared in quality and ease to our stove-top method. Browning the burgers in a heavy-bottomed skillet over medium heat, then finishing them partially covered over low heat gave us a rich-crusted burger that was cooked all the way through.

Of course these burgers grill well, too. Just build a two-tier fire—one medium-hot, the other low. Cook the burgers over the hotter fire until browned on both sides, then move them to the low fire and cook, covered with a disposable pan, until cooked through. (See a discussion of this technique on page 155.) Our generous cooking times should ensure a fully cooked burger. As an extra precaution, however, you may want to test them for doneness by sticking an instant-read thermometer through the side of one of the burgers into its center. The burger is done at 160 degrees.

Making great turkey chili turns out to be a much simpler proposition than burgers. When we used ground turkey in a favorite beef chili recipe, the results were excellent. Because the ground turkey is cooked in so much liquid, there is little danger of it drying out. Therefore, you can use lean ground turkey, even all white-meat ground turkey with just 2 percent fat.

A couple of notes about our chili recipe. We find that toasting and grinding your own chiles is worth the minimal effort. The powders sold in bottles just don't have the same depth of flavor and richness. We recommend using 2 tablespoons of chili powder per pound of ground meat, although this amount can be altered if you like chili that is especially mild or hot. Sautéing the chili powder helps bring out its warm, earthy flavor, although we add a little water to the spices first to make sure that they don't scorch or burn. We also like to use a combination of dried and fresh chiles for flavor and bite. Jalapeños should be added along with the garlic.

Our chili recipe has one other unusual feature—a thickener. We prefer the sauce to be smooth and silky, not watery, and therefore tested an array of thickeners that could be added at the end of the cooking time. Cornstarch or masa harina (a flour ground from lime-treated hulled corn) were our favorites.

Pan-Seared Turkey Burgers

SERVES 4

RICOTTA CHEESE IS THE secret to keeping burgers made with pre-ground turkey moist. Our basic recipe is seasoned with Worcestershire and mustard. The variations with miso and mushrooms require a trip to the natural foods store or some extra prep time, but are delicious.

½ cup ricotta cheese
2 teaspoons Worcestershire sauce
2 teaspoons Dijon mustard
½ teaspoon salt
½ teaspoon pepper
1 teaspoon minced fresh thyme leaves (optional)
1¼ pounds 93% lean ground turkey
1 tablespoon vegetable or canola oil

1. Mix the ricotta, Worcestershire sauce, mustard, salt, pepper, and thyme in a medium bowl. Add the ground turkey; lightly mix to combine. Divide the meat into 4 portions. Working one at a time, lightly toss each portion of meat from hand to hand to form a ball. With fingertips, lightly flatten each ball into a 1-inch-thick patty.

2. Heat a large, heavy-bottomed skillet (cast-iron works well) over medium heat until well heated, 4 to 5 minutes. Add the oil, then the burgers. Cook over medium heat until the bottom side of each burger has developed a medium brown crust, 3 to 4 minutes. Turn the burgers over; continue to cook until the other side of each burger starts to brown, 3 to 4 minutes longer. Reduce the heat to low and partially cover with a lid so that steam can escape. Continue to cook, turning once more to ensure even browning, until a meat thermometer inserted from the side into burger center registers 160 degrees, 8 to 10 minutes longer. Remove the burgers from the pan and serve immediately.

◆

Grilled Turkey Burgers

THE CRUST ON GRILLED BURGERS IS ESPECIALLY THICK AND BROWN. YOU MAY ALSO GRILL ANY OF THE VARIATIONS THAT FOLLOW. SERVES 4.

Follow the Master Recipe through step 1. Prepare a 2-level grill fire (see figures 1–4, page 156). Cook the burgers over the hotter part of the fire, turning once, until well browned on both sides, 8 to 10 minutes total. Slide the burgers to the cooler part of the grill, cover them with a disposable aluminum roasting pan, and continue grilling until cooked through, another 5 to 7 minutes.

Turkey Burgers
with Dried Mushrooms

RECONSTITUTED DRIED MUSHROOMS GIVE TURKEY BURGERS A PARTICULARLY MEATY FLAVOR. WE LIKE DRIED PORCINI OR SHIITAKE MUSHROOMS IN THIS RECIPE. SERVES 4.

Follow the Master Recipe, replacing the Worcestershire sauce and mustard with 1 ounce dried mushrooms that have been rehydrated in 1 cup hot water for 15 minutes, squeezed dry, and minced fine. You may also add 1 teaspoon miso, thinned with 1 teaspoon mushroom liquid for extra flavor.

◆

Turkey Burgers
with Miso

MISO IS A FERMENTED SOYBEAN PASTE WITH A PUNGENT, EARTHY FLAVOR. IT IS USED TO MAKE SOUP IN JAPAN AND IS SOLD IN ORIENTAL AND NATURAL FOODS STORES. IT COMES IN SEVERAL COLORS, ANY OF WHICH CAN BE USED IN THIS RECIPE. SERVES 4.

Follow the Master Recipe, replacing the Worcestershire sauce and mustard with 2 teaspoons miso thinned with 2 teaspoons water.

◆

Ultimate Turkey Burger

GRINDING YOUR OWN TURKEY WILL TAKE SOME TIME, BUT THE REWARD IS A RICH, BEEFY TEXTURE. IF DESIRED, FLAVOR WITH MUSHROOMS AND/OR MISO AS IN VARIATION ABOVE. SERVES 4.

- 1 turkey thigh (about 2 pounds) skinned, boned, and cut into 1-inch chunks (about 1½ pounds)
- 2 teaspoons Worcestershire sauce
- 2 teaspoons Dijon mustard
- ½ teaspoon salt
- ½ teaspoon pepper
- 1 teaspoon minced fresh thyme leaves (optional)
- 1 tablespoon vegetable or canola oil

1. Place the turkey chunks on a platter in the freezer, tossing them occasionally, until semifrozen, about 30 minutes.

2. Working in 3 batches, place the semifrozen turkey cubes in the work bowl of a food processor fitted with the steel blade; process until it resembles ground burger meat, 12 to 14 one-second pulses.

3. Transfer the ground meat to a medium bowl; season with Worcestershire sauce, mustard, salt, pepper, and thyme. Divide the meat into 4 portions. Working one at a time, lightly toss each portion of meat from hand to hand to form a ball. With fingertips, lightly flatten each ball into a 1-inch-thick patty.

4. Heat a large, heavy-bottomed skillet (cast-iron works well) over medium heat until well heated, 4 to 5 minutes. Add the oil, then the burgers. Cook over medium heat until the bottom side of each burger has developed a dark brown crust, about 5 minutes. Turn the burgers over; continue to cook until the burgers start to brown, 4 to 5 minutes longer. Reduce the heat to low and partially cover with a lid so that steam can escape. Continue to cook, turning the burgers once more to ensure even browning, until a meat thermometer inserted from the side into the burger center registers 160 degrees, 5 to 6 minutes longer. Remove the burgers from the pan and serve immediately.

Turkey Chili

SERVES 6

WITH A MINI-CHOPPER or coffee grinder dedicated for spices, it takes a maximum of 10 minutes to toast and grind your own chili powder. Likewise, for the best flavor, toast cumin seeds in a dry skillet over medium heat until fragrant, about 4 minutes, before grinding them. When buying dried chiles, go for specimens that are moist and pliant, like dried fruit. Although the chili tastes great fresh from the pot, the flavor will develop and mellow with time, so consider refrigerating it for a night and reheating to serve. Serve it with sides of warm pinto or kidney beans, cornbread or chips, corn tortillas or tamales, rice, biscuits, or just plain crackers. Or, add four 15-ounce cans of rinsed and drained beans (black, red, or white, according to taste and what you have on hand) to the cooked chili. Possible garnishes include minced white onion, diced avocado, shredded cheddar or jack cheese, sour cream, or chopped fresh cilantro leaves.

3 medium ancho chiles (about ½ ounce)
  or 3 tablespoons ancho chili powder
3 medium New Mexico chiles (about ¾ ounce)
  or 3 tablespoons New Mexico chili powder
2 tablespoons ground cumin
2 teaspoons dried oregano, preferably
  Mexican
¼ cup vegetable oil
3 pounds ground turkey
Salt
1 medium onion, minced
5 medium garlic cloves, minced
4 or 5 small jalapeño chiles, stemmed,
  seeded, and minced
1 cup canned crushed tomatoes
2 tablespoons fresh lime juice
3 tablespoons cornstarch dissolved in 3
  tablespoons water or 5 tablespoons
  masa harina dissolved in ⅔ cup water
Pepper
Cayenne, hot pepper sauce, or pequin
  chiles (optional)

1. If starting with whole chiles, adjust the oven rack to the center position and heat the oven to 350 degrees. Rinse and dry the chiles and bake until puffed, fragrant, and toasted, about 6 minutes. When cool enough to handle, remove the stems and seeds, rip into coin-size pieces, and process in the work bowl of a mini-chopper/grinder or spice-dedicated coffee grinder until pulverized and powdery, 30 to 45 seconds. Whether grinding chiles into powder or starting with pre-ground, measure the chili powder, cumin, and oregano into a small bowl and mix in ½ cup water to form a thick paste; set aside.

2. Heat 2 tablespoons oil in a large, heavy soup kettle or Dutch oven over medium-high heat; add the turkey and 2 teaspoons salt to the pot and cook, stirring frequently, until the meat loses its raw color, 10 to 12 minutes. Spoon the turkey and cooking juices into a large bowl and set aside. Adjust heat to medium and add the remaining 2 tablespoons oil and the onion; cook, stirring frequently, until the onion becomes soft and translucent, 5 to 6 minutes. Add the garlic and jalapeños; cook 1 minute longer. Add the reserved chile spice paste; sauté until fragrant, 2 to 3 minutes.

Add the meat with accumulated juices, 7 cups water, the tomatoes, and lime juice; cover the pot and bring to a simmer. Adjust the heat to the lowest possible setting, remove the cover from the pot, and simmer slowly for about 2 hours.

3. To thicken the juices to gravy consistency, gradually stir in one-third of the cornstarch paste into the chili; simmer until thickened, 5 to 10 minutes. Continue adding the paste in increments and simmering until the desired consistency is achieved. Adjust seasoning with salt and pepper, as well as a pinch of cayenne, a dash of hot pepper sauce, or crumbled chile pequins to add heat, if desired.

◆

Smoky Chipotle Chili

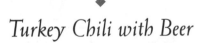

CHIPOTLE CHILES, AVAILABLE IN LATIN GROCERIES AND MANY SUPERMARKETS, GIVE THIS VARIATION A SMOKY, RATHER THAN HOT, FLAVOR. **SERVES 6.**

Follow the Master Recipe, substituting 5 minced canned chipotle peppers in adobo sauce for the jalapeños.

◆

Turkey Chili with Beer

PURISTS PREFER CHILI COOKED WITH WATER BECAUSE THEY BELIEVE THAT THE FLAVORS OF THE CHILES ARE CLEARER. BUT BEER ADDS A CERTAIN DIMENSION TO THE DISH. ANY BEER WILL DO, BUT DARKER BREWS MAKE ESPECIALLY POTENT CHILI. **SERVES 6.**

Follow the Master Recipe, substituting five 12-ounce bottles of beer for the water.

◆

Turkey Chili with Cornmeal Dumplings

CORNMEAL DUMPLINGS STEAMED DIRECTLY ON TOP OF A COMPLETED POT OF CHILI ARE A NICE CHANGE FROM CORNBREAD OR RICE. THE DUMPLINGS CAN BE FORMED SEVERAL HOURS IN ADVANCE AND REFRIGERATED ON A BAKING SHEET BEFORE STEAMING. **SERVES 6.**

1 recipe for turkey chili (opposite page)
1 ½ cups all-purpose flour
½ cup yellow cornmeal
1 tablespoon baking powder
¾ teaspoon salt
3 tablespoons unsalted butter
1 cup milk

1. While the chili is simmering, mix the flour, cornmeal, baking powder, and salt in a medium bowl. Bring the butter and milk to a simmer and add to the dry ingredients. Mix with a fork or knead by hand 2 to 3 times until the mixture just comes together. Following figures 1 through 3 on page 248, form the dough into the desired shape. Refrigerate formed dumplings until ready to use.

2. When the chili is done, reduce the heat to a bare simmer. Lay the dumplings on the surface of the chili; cover and simmer until the dumplings are cooked through, about 10 minutes for strip dumplings and 15 minutes for balls and biscuit rounds. Ladle portions of chili and dumplings into soup plates and serve immediately.

◆

Cincinnati-Style Turkey Chili

CINCINNATI-STYLE CHILI IS SWEETER THAN TEXAS-STYLE, WITH MORE TOMATOES AND THE ADDED FLAVORS OF ALLSPICE, CINNAMON, CORIANDER, AND CARDAMOM. IF YOU WANT TO SERVE IT AS THEY DO IN CINCINNATI, LADLE IT OVER BOWLS OF SPAGHETTI OR EGG NOODLES. **SERVES 6.**

Follow the Master Recipe, adding ½ teaspoon ground allspice, ½ teaspoon ground cinnamon, ½ teaspoon ground coriander, and ½ teaspoon ground cardamom to the spice paste. Omit the jalapeños. Reduce the water to 6 cups, increase the tomatoes to 2 cups, and replace the lime juice with ½ cup red wine vinegar.

CHAPTER 30

LEFTOVER TURKEY

AND CHICKEN

/|\

LEFTOVERS CAN BE RECYCLED IN SANDWICHES,

SOUPS, SALADS, STIR-FRIES, OR EVEN ENCHILADAS.

(FOR MORE INFORMATION ON CHICKEN SALADS, SEE

CHAPTER 23.) THERE ARE A FEW THINGS TO REMEMBER

WHEN USING LEFTOVER TURKEY OR OTHER POULTRY.

IF POSSIBLE, STORE IN WHOLE PIECES OR LARGE

chunks. If chopped or shredded, the meat will dry out quickly so wait to cut the turkey or chicken until it is needed. While it is a good idea to keep the skin on pieces in the refrigerator (it helps seal in moisture), you should discard the skin before chopping or shredding the meat. If stored in an airtight container, leftover turkey or chicken should stay fresh for two or three days.

◆

Turkey Club Sandwich

THE CLASSIC SANDWICH IS MADE WITH LETTUCE, TOMATO, TURKEY, AND BACON LAYERED IN BETWEEN SLICES OF TOASTED BREAD THAT HAVE BEEN SPREAD WITH MAYONNAISE. WE LIKE TO ADD A LITTLE HEAT TO THE MAYO, BUT THE TABASCO CAN BE OMITTED. THIN SLICES OF AVOCADO CAN BE LAYERED IN WITH THE OTHER INGREDIENTS TO MAKE A "CALIFORNIA" CLUB. SERVES 4.

    1/2 cup mayonnaise
    1/2 teaspoon Tabasco or other hot sauce
    12 slices good-quality white bread,
       toasted
    8 small lettuce leaves
    2 cups thinly sliced leftover turkey breast
    12 slices crisp-cooked bacon
    1 medium tomato, cored and sliced thin

1. Combine the mayonnaise and Tabasco in a small bowl. Spread a thin layer of the dressing on one side of each piece of toast.

2. Place 4 slices of toast, dressing side up, on a work surface. Top each of the toast slices with a lettuce leaf, some turkey, 1 1/2 slices of bacon, and a slice of tomato. Top each sandwich with another slice of toast, dressing side up. Divide the remaining lettuce, turkey, bacon, and tomato among the sandwiches, and top with the remaining toast, dressing side down.

3. Slice each sandwich diagonally into quarters and secure each quarter with a toothpick.

Turkey, Avocado, and Cheddar Melt

A PICKLED JALAPEÑO STIRRED INTO THE DRESSING GIVES THIS SANDWICH SOME HEAT. ONE TABLESPOON OF PICKLE RELISH MAY BE SUBSTITUTED FOR A MILDER TASTE. SERVE 2 OPEN-FACED SANDWICHES PER PERSON. SERVES 2.

    1/4 cup mayonnaise
    2 tablespoons ketchup
    1 pickled jalapeño chile, finely chopped
    2 cups sliced leftover turkey
    4 slices good-quality white bread, lightly
       toasted
    1/2 ripe avocado, peeled, halved, and
       sliced thin
    4 ounces cheddar cheese, cut into 4 slices

1. Preheat the broiler. Combine the mayonnaise, ketchup, and jalapeño in a small bowl.

2. Place some turkey on top of each piece of toast. Spread the dressing on top of the turkey. Place the avocado slices on top of the dressed turkey. Place a slice of cheese on top of each sandwich.

3. Place the sandwiches on a broiler pan and broil 3 inches from the heat until the cheese has melted, 1 to 2 minutes. Serve immediately.

◆

Turkey Tetrazzini

TETRAZZINI IS GREAT WITH LEFTOVER CHICKEN, AS WELL. USING A SHALLOW BAKING DISH, NO COVER, AND A VERY HOT OVEN BENEFITS BOTH TEXTURE AND FLAVOR. DON'T BE STINGY WITH THE SALT AND PEPPER. THIS DISH NEEDS AGGRESSIVE SEASONING. SERVES 8.

    TOPPING
    1/2 cup fresh bread crumbs
    Pinch salt
    1 1/2 tablespoons unsalted butter, melted
    1/4 cup grated Parmesan cheese

FILLING
Salt
¾ pound spaghetti or other long-strand pasta
6 tablespoons butter, plus extra for
    greasing baking dish
10 ounces white button mushrooms,
    wiped clean, stems trimmed, sliced thin
2 medium onions, minced
Pepper
¼ cup all-purpose flour
2 cups chicken stock or canned low-
    sodium chicken broth
3 tablespoons dry sherry
½ cup grated Parmesan cheese
¼ teaspoon grated nutmeg
2 teaspoons fresh lemon juice
2 teaspoons minced fresh thyme leaves
4 cups leftover turkey or chicken, cut into
    ¼-inch dice
2 cups frozen peas

1. For the topping: Set the oven rack to the middle position and heat the oven to 350 degrees. Mix the bread crumbs, salt, and butter in a small baking dish; bake until golden brown and crisp, 15 to 20 minutes. Cool to room temperature, transfer to a bowl, and mix with ¼ cup grated Parmesan.

2. For the filling: Increase the oven temperature to 450 degrees. Butter a shallow casserole or baking dish. Bring a large quantity of water to a boil in large stockpot. Salt the water, snap the spaghetti in half, and cook until al dente. Reserve ¼ cup of the cooking water, drain the spaghetti, and return to the pot with the reserved liquid.

3. Meanwhile, heat 2 tablespoons butter in a large skillet over medium heat until the foaming subsides; add the mushrooms and onions and sauté, stirring frequently, until the onions soften and the mushroom liquid evaporates, 7 to 10 minutes. Season to taste with salt and pepper; transfer to a medium bowl and set aside.

4. Melt the remaining 4 tablespoons butter in the now cleaned skillet over medium heat. When the foam subsides, whisk in the flour and cook, whisking constantly, until the flour turns golden, 1 to 2 minutes.

Whisking constantly, gradually add the chicken stock. Adjust the heat to medium-high and simmer until the mixture thickens, 3 to 4 minutes. Off the heat, whisk in the sherry, Parmesan, nutmeg, ½ teaspoon salt, lemon juice, and thyme. Add sauce, mushroom mixture, turkey, and peas to the spaghetti and mix well, adjusting seasonings to taste.

5. Turn the mixture into the buttered baking dish, sprinkle evenly with the reserved bread crumbs, and bake until the bread crumbs brown and the mixture is bubbly, about 8 minutes. Serve immediately.

◆

Chicken and Bulgur Salad with Olives, Raisins, and Pine Nuts

BULGUR REQUIRES NO COOKING, JUST REHYDRATING IN WATER, MAKING THIS AN ESPECIALLY EASY WAY TO USE LEFTOVERS. SERVES 4.

1 cup fine bulgur
2 tablespoons fresh lemon juice
2 tablespoons extra-virgin olive oil
2 cups chopped leftover chicken
⅓ cup green olives, pitted and coarsely
    chopped
¼ cup pine nuts
¼ cup raisins
2 tablespoons chopped fresh parsley
    leaves
Salt

1. Combine the bulgur, 1 cup water, the lemon juice, and oil in a medium bowl. Let sit until the liquid is absorbed, about 30 minutes. Fluff the mixture with a fork.

2. Stir in the chicken, olives, pine nuts, raisins, parsley, and salt to taste. The salad, covered in plastic, may be refrigerated for several hours before serving. Let the salad come to room temperature before serving.

Penne with Chicken, Asparagus, and Lemon

OTHER VEGETABLES, SUCH AS BLANCHED BROCCOLI OR GREEN BEANS, MAY BE SUBSTITUTED FOR THE ASPARAGUS HERE. SERVES 4 TO 6.

    12 asparagus spears, trimmed and cut into
        1-inch lengths
    1 pound penne
    6 tablespoons extra-virgin olive oil
    4 medium garlic cloves, finely chopped
    1 teaspoon grated lemon zest
    1 teaspoon salt
    1½ cups shredded leftover chicken

1. Bring a large pot of salted water to a boil for cooking the pasta. Bring a small pot of salted water to a boil and blanch the asparagus until tender, 2 to 3 minutes. Drain and set the asparagus aside.

2. Add the pasta to the boiling water. While the pasta is cooking, heat the olive oil in a large skillet over medium heat. Add the garlic and sauté until golden, about 2 minutes. Add the lemon zest and salt and cook for another minute. Stir in the asparagus and chicken and heat through, another minute.

3. Reserve ½ cup of the cooking liquid and drain the pasta when al dente. Toss the pasta and sauce until well coated. If the pasta seems dry, add the cooking liquid 1 tablespoon at a time until the desired consistency is achieved. Serve immediately.

◆

Fusilli with Chicken and Pesto

USE THE PESTO RECIPE ON PAGE 196, OR YOUR OWN FAVORITE RECIPE, IN THIS SIMPLE DISH OF PASTA AND LEFTOVER CHICKEN. SERVES 4 TO 6.

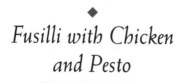

    1 pound fusilli
    2 cups shredded leftover chicken
    ¾ cup pesto

1. Bring a large pot of salted water to a boil and cook the fusilli until al dente. Reserve ½ cup of the cooking liquid and drain the pasta.

2. In a large bowl, toss the pasta and chicken with the pesto until well coated. If the pasta seems dry, add the cooking liquid 1 tablespoon at a time until the desired consistency is achieved. Serve immediately.

◆

Chicken and Goat Cheese Quesadillas

LEFTOVER CHICKEN MAKES A GREAT QUESADILLA FILLING. INGREDIENTS MAY BE VARIED ACCORDING TO TASTE AND WHAT YOU HAVE ON HAND. TRY SUBSTITUTING CHEDDAR AND HALF A CHOPPED CHIPOTLE CHILE IN ADOBO SAUCE FOR THE GOAT CHEESE AND SUN-DRIED TOMATOES. SERVES 2.

    6 sun-dried tomatoes packed in oil,
        drained and coarsely chopped
    1 garlic clove, minced
    2 tablespoons minced fresh parsley leaves
    2 ounces crumbled goat cheese
    Salt and pepper
    4 8-inch flour tortillas
    1 cup shredded leftover chicken

1. Combine the tomatoes, garlic, parsley, and goat cheese in a medium bowl. Season with salt and pepper to taste.

2. Spread the goat cheese mixture on top of 2 of the tortillas. Scatter the chicken over the cheese and then press it lightly into the cheese mixture. Top with the remaining 2 tortillas.

3. Heat an 8-inch skillet over medium-high heat. Cook the quesadillas one at a time until the cheese is melted and the tortillas are toasted, 2 to 3 minutes per side. Serve immediately.

Turkey Enchiladas with Chili Sauce

THE RECIPE CALLS FOR A LOT OF CHILI POWDER, BUT THIS AMOUNT GIVES THE SAUCE A RICH, WARM FLAVOR THAT IS SPICY BUT NOT OVERWHELMING. SERVES 4 TO 6.

- 12 6-inch corn tortillas
- 1/2 cup chili powder
- 3 tablespoons olive oil
- 2 garlic cloves, minced
- 3 cups chicken stock or low-sodium canned broth
- Salt and pepper
- 1 medium onion, sliced thin
- 2 cups shredded leftover turkey
- 1/4 cup minced fresh cilantro leaves
- 1 1/2 cups shredded Monterey jack or cheddar cheese

1. Preheat the oven to 350 degrees. Divide the tortillas into 2 stacks and wrap each in aluminum foil. Bake until heated through, 10 minutes. Remove from the oven and set aside.

2. In a small bowl, combine the chili powder and 1/4 cup water. Heat 1 tablespoon oil in a large saucepan. Sauté the garlic over medium heat until golden, about 2 minutes. Add the chili paste and cook, stirring constantly, for 1 minute. Whisk in the chicken stock, bring to a simmer, and cook until thickened, 8 to 10 minutes. Season with salt and pepper to taste.

3. Heat the remaining 2 tablespoons oil in another large skillet. Sauté the onion over medium heat until softened, 5 to 7 minutes. Stir in the turkey, cilantro, and salt and pepper to taste.

4. Grease a 9-by-13-inch baking dish. Place 2 tablespoons of the turkey mixture in each tortilla, roll up, and place each tortilla seam side down in the dish. Pour the chili sauce over the rolled tortillas. Sprinkle the cheese over the top. Bake until the enchiladas are heated through and the cheese is melted and bubbling, 20 to 25 minutes. Serve immediately.

Turkey Soup with Cheese Tortellini and Swiss Chard

WHEN ALL THE TURKEY MEAT IS GONE, YOU'VE STILL GOT ONE MORE MEAL LEFT IN THE TURKEY—SOUP MADE FROM THE CARCASS. HERE, WE ADD TORTELLINI AND SWISS CHARD TO THE BROTH; OTHER PASTAS (OR OTHER COOKED GRAINS) AND GREENS MAY BE SUBSTITUTED. USE A CLEAVER TO CHOP THE CLEANED CARCASS INTO SEVERAL PIECES THAT WILL FIT INTO A STOCKPOT. SERVES 6 TO 8.

- 1 carcass from 12-pound turkey, chopped into 4 or 5 pieces
- 1 carrot, coarsely chopped
- 1 celery stalk, coarsely chopped
- 1 medium onion, coarsely chopped
- 1 bay leaf
- 1/2 teaspoon dried thyme
- 1 teaspoon fennel seeds
- 1/2 pound fresh cheese tortellini
- Salt and pepper
- 4 cups coarsely chopped Swiss chard (leaves only)

1. Combine 4 quarts water, the turkey carcass, carrot, celery, onion, bay leaf, thyme, and fennel seeds in a large stockpot and bring to a boil. Lower the heat and simmer for 1 1/2 hours. Lift out the turkey carcass pieces and reserve. Strain the liquid through a sieve into another large pot, pressing on the solids to extract as much flavor as possible. Remove any meat from the carcass and chop fine; add the meat to the broth.

2. Bring the soup to a boil, add the tortellini, then salt and pepper to taste, and cook until the tortellini are tender, 5 to 7 minutes. Add the Swiss chard and cook until wilted, another 1 to 2 minutes. Serve immediately.

Turkey and Black Bean Soup

CHOPPED LEFTOVER TURKEY TURNS BLACK BEAN SOUP INTO A HEARTY MAIN COURSE. IF DESIRED, GARNISH WITH SOUR CREAM AND MORE MINCED CILANTRO LEAVES OR SLICED SCALLIONS. **SERVES 8 TO 10.**

- 1 pound dried black beans, rinsed and picked over
- 3 tablespoons olive oil
- 1 medium onion, minced
- 4 garlic cloves, minced
- ¼ teaspoon Tabasco or other hot sauce, or to taste
- 2 teaspoons ground cumin
- 1 teaspoon ground coriander
- 10 cups chicken stock *or* 5 cups low-sodium canned broth mixed with 5 cups water
- ¼ cup sherry vinegar
- Salt and pepper
- 3 cups chopped leftover turkey
- ¼ cup minced fresh cilantro leaves

1. Place the beans in a large bowl, add enough water to cover by 2 inches, soak overnight, and drain. Or, place the beans and water to cover in a large pot, bring to a boil, simmer for 1 minute, remove from heat, cover, let stand 1 hour, and drain.

2. Heat the oil in a large soup kettle. Add the onion and sauté over medium heat until softened, 5 to 7 minutes. Add the garlic, Tabasco, cumin, and coriander and cook for another minute. Add the stock and beans to the pot, bring to a boil, and simmer until the beans are softened, about 1½ hours.

3. Ladle 4 cups of the soup into a blender or food processor and puree until smooth. Return to the pot along with the vinegar and salt and pepper to taste. Stir in the turkey and cilantro and heat through, 4 to 5 minutes.

Turkey Hash with Spicy Tomato Sauce

SERVE AS IS OR TOP EACH PORTION OF TURKEY HASH WITH A POACHED EGG. MAKE SURE TO CUT THE POTA-TOES AS DIRECTED. LARGER PIECES WILL NOT COOK THROUGH. **SERVES 4.**

- 3 tablespoons extra-virgin olive oil
- 1 garlic clove, minced
- 1 jalapeño chile, seeded and minced
- 1 cup canned crushed tomatoes
- 2 tablespoons minced fresh parsley leaves
- Salt and pepper
- 2 medium russet or Yukon Gold potatoes, peeled and cut into ¼-inch dice
- 1 small onion, finely chopped
- ½ green bell pepper, cored, seeded, and cut into ¼-inch dice
- 1½ cups chopped leftover turkey
- 3 slices bacon, cooked crisp and crumbled

1. Heat 1 tablespoon oil in a medium skillet. Add the garlic and sauté over medium heat until golden, 2 to 3 minutes. Add the jalapeño and cook another minute. Add the tomatoes, bring to a simmer, and cook until thickened, 7 to 10 minutes. Stir in the parsley, season with salt and pepper to taste, and set aside.

2. Heat the remaining 2 tablespoons oil in a large skillet. Add the potatoes and sauté over medium-high heat, stirring frequently, until they begin to soften, about 10 minutes. Add the onion and bell pepper and continue to cook until the potatoes are browned and fully cooked, another 10 minutes. Stir in the turkey and bacon and heat through, another 2 minutes. Serve with the warm tomato sauce on the side.

Leftover Turkey Croquettes

THESE PATTIES GO WELL WITH REHEATED LEFTOVER GRAVY AND/OR CRANBERRY SAUCE. USE THE FOOD PROCESSOR TO MIX THE INGREDIENTS FOR THE CROQUETTES BUT DO NOT PUREE. THESE CROQUETTES SHOULD CONTAIN TINY CHUNKS OF TURKEY MEAT. SERVES 4.

3 slices good-quality white bread, crusts removed
¼ cup milk
2 cups coarsely chopped leftover turkey
1 small onion, coarsely chopped
2 eggs
1 tablespoon fresh parsley leaves
Salt and pepper
2 cups bread crumbs
¼ teaspoon cayenne pepper
4 tablespoons unsalted butter

1. Tear the bread into small pieces, place it in a small bowl, and pour in the milk. Let stand 10 minutes until the milk is absorbed.

2. Combine the bread, turkey, onion, eggs, parsley, and salt and pepper to taste in the work bowl of a food processor. Pulse several times until the mixture is well blended. Do not overprocess or puree.

3. Shape the turkey mixture into 8 round patties. Combine the bread crumbs, cayenne, and salt to taste in a pie plate or shallow bowl and coat the patties with the bread crumb mixture. Refrigerate until firm, about 1 hour.

4. Heat the butter in a large skillet. Cook the patties over medium heat until browned on both sides, about 5 minutes per side. Serve immediately.

Cobb Salad

WE LIKE TO ASSEMBLE COBB SALAD IN INDIVIDUAL SALAD BOWLS. THERE'S NO MESSY TOSSING THAT MIGHT BREAK APART DELICATE INGREDIENTS LIKE HARD-COOKED EGGS. SIMPLY DRIZZLE THE DRESSING OVER EACH PORTION AND SERVE. TO PREPARE THE EGGS, PLACE THEM AND COLD WATER TO COVER IN A MEDIUM SAUCEPAN, TURN THE HEAT TO MEDIUM, BRING TO A BOIL, AND SIMMER FOR 10 MINUTES. DRAIN AND PLACE THE EGGS IN A BOWL OF COLD WATER UNTIL COOL ENOUGH TO PEEL. SERVES 4.

1 large head romaine or iceberg lettuce, tough outer leaves discarded, washed, dried, and torn into bite-size pieces (9 cups total)
2 avocados, peeled, pitted, and cut into ¼-inch dice
4 small ripe tomatoes, cored and cut into 8 wedges each
2 cups chopped leftover turkey
4 hard-cooked eggs, peeled and cut into 8 wedges each
½ pound crisp-cooked bacon, crumbled
½ pound blue cheese, crumbled
1½ tablespoons red wine vinegar
¼ teaspoon salt
⅛ teaspoon pepper
6 tablespoons extra-virgin olive oil

1. Divide the lettuce among 4 oversized individual salad bowls. Layer the avocadoes, tomatoes, turkey, eggs, bacon, and blue cheese into the bowls.

2. Whisk together the vinegar, salt, and pepper in a small bowl. Slowly whisk in the oil until the dressing is smooth and emulsified. Drizzle some dressing over each portion and serve immediately.

Turkey Fried Rice

THIS QUICK STIR-FRY GIVES LEFTOVER TURKEY A NEW FLAVOR. OTHER VEGETABLES—INCLUDING SLICED MUSH-ROOMS, CHOPPED ONION, FROZEN PEAS, AND COOKED BROCCOLI—CAN BE USED ALONG WITH OR INSTEAD OF THE BELL PEPPER. SERVES 4.

- 4 tablespoons peanut oil
- 2 eggs, lightly beaten
- 1 red bell pepper, cored, seeded, and cut into ¼-inch dice
- 2 medium garlic cloves, minced
- 1 tablespoon chopped fresh gingerroot
- 6 scallions, white and light green parts, sliced thin
- 4 cups cooked white rice
- 2 tablespoons soy sauce
- 2 teaspoons Asian sesame oil
- 2 cups chopped leftover turkey

1. Heat 1 tablespoon of the peanut oil in a large skillet or wok over medium-high heat. Add the eggs and cook until the bottom is solidified and beginning to brown. Use a spatula to slice the partially cooked egg into thin strips and cook, stirring frequently, until cooked all the way through. Transfer the egg pieces to a bowl.

2. Heat another tablespoon of peanut oil in the same skillet over medium-high heat and add the bell pepper. Stir-fry until partially tender, about 2 minutes. Transfer the pepper to the bowl with the eggs.

3. Heat the remaining 2 tablespoons of peanut oil in the same skillet over medium-high heat. Add the garlic, ginger, and scallions and stir-fry until fragrant, about 30 seconds. Add the rice, soy sauce, and sesame oil and stir-fry until bits of the rice begin to crisp, 2 to 3 minutes.

4. Return the egg and bell pepper to the skillet along with the turkey. Stir-fry until heated through, 1 to 2 minutes. Serve immediately.

CHAPTER 31

ROASTED
DUCK

/Ι\

ALTHOUGH A DUCK MAY RESEMBLE A CHICKEN OR

TURKEY (THERE IS A BREAST, TWO LEGS AND TWO

WINGS), THE COOKING CHALLENGES ARE QUITE DIF-

FERENT. IN LEAN BIRDS, THE TRICK IS TO KEEP THE

DELICATE WHITE MEAT FROM DRYING OUT WHILE

GETTING THE THICKER LEGS AND THIGHS COOKED

THROUGH TO THE BONE. THE SKIN MUST ALSO BE

crisped, but this is simply a function of finding the right oven temperature to promote even browning.

A duck does not have any white meat. The breast is dark (although the legs are even darker and gamier) and there is a thick layer of fat between the skin and meat that keeps everything fairly moist. There is little danger of overcooking the breast. The challenge in roasting a duck is getting rid of this fat layer so that the skin can crisp up and the meat is not too fatty. If the fat remains, the skin will be thick and soft (not thin and crisp as desired) and the meat will be greasy.

There are two styles of duck roasting, each with countless variations. In general, European cooks use various roasting regimens—changing the temperature, turning the bird in the oven, and sometimes pricking the skin—to rid the duck of excess fat. In contrast, Chinese recipes often call for a two-step cooking method that starts with boiling or steaming to melt the fat and then finishes with roasting to crisp up and brown the bird.

We started our testing with simple Western roasting methods. Many sources recommend starting the duck in a hot oven to render the fat as quickly as possible. We had our doubts but proceeded to roast a duck at 425 degrees. As we suspected, our kitchen filled with smoke fairly quickly. For the next test, we lowered the oven temperature to 375 degrees, but the smoking persisted.

At this point, we decided to try slow-roasting. The theory here is that over several hours the duck fat will slowly render. A final application of high heat can be used if needed to brown the skin. At 275 degrees, things progressed quite slowly and after three hours and a quick high-temperature browning, the meat was still greasy. The lower temperature was not rendering the fat as well as the higher temperatures we had been using in our initial tests.

Clearly, some sort of compromise was needed. We next tried roasting the duck at 350 degrees. While there had been some smoking of pan drippings at 375 degrees, there was none at 350 degrees. After nearly two hours, the bird was giving off very little fat so we raised the temperature to 500 degrees to crisp up the somewhat splotchy skin. Fifteen minutes later, we had a pretty good duck.

We had discovered a couple of refinements along the way. First, pricking the skin with the tip of a paring knife, being careful just to pierce the fat layer and not the flesh, helps the fat to escape from the bird. Second, it is imperative to spoon or pour off some of the fat while the duck roasts. After 1¼ hours, we found it necessary to drain the roasting pan. At this time, vegetables could be added to the pan and roasted for another 40 minutes at the low temperature and then the final 15 minutes at 500 degrees. Third, using a rack kept the duck up away from the fat in the pan and helped get the skin on the thighs and legs nicely browned. Finally, we tried various turning regimens, but found that they were unnecessary (there's no danger of the breast meat drying out) and could hinder the browning and crisping of the all-important breast skin.

At this point in our testing, we liked our results (and have included it as an option in the recipes that follow), but we wondered if the two-step cooking methods advocated by so many Asian chefs and cookbooks would be better suited to a fatty duck. When we talked with California chef Bruce Cost, he was a passionate advocate for steaming then roasting the duck. With his help, we developed a regimen for coating the duck with seasoned salt, curing it for four hours to dry out the skin, followed by steaming to render the fat and cook the meat, and a final quick roasting (no more than forty minutes) to brown the skin.

Although this Chinese method takes all day (the work is actually more convenient if broken up over two days), we felt the effort was justified by the results. The skin was crackling crisp without a trace of fat. Our roasted duck was good, but our steamed-then-roasted duck was great. Not only is the skin crisper, but also the meat is moister and juicier, no doubt because of the steaming and the shorter roasting period.

After much experimentation, we came up with the following recipe for steaming-then-roasting a duck. We start by rubbing the duck with a mixture of toasted spices and salt. The duck is then set on a rack over a deep roasting pan (air must be able to circulate underneath the duck) and cured for four hours. During this time, the seasonings penetrate into the duck and the skin dries out. While we found that this step is not absolutely necessary, we recommend curing the duck unless pressed for time.

The next step is steaming. A 16-inch wok or large Dutch oven fitted with a rack are the best options. The duck is placed on the rack above boiling water. After about one hour, the skin becomes taut as the fat underneath melts into the simmering water below. When the skin begins to pull away from the joints on the wings, the meat is fully cooked and well seasoned. At this point, the bird is cooled to room temperature. (It can be wrapped in plastic and refrigerated overnight.) When ready to serve, the duck is brushed with soy sauce or balsamic vinegar (depending on whether Asian or European seasonings have been used) and then roasted in a 400-degree oven until crisp, no more than forty minutes.

Asian-style duck is highly seasoned owing to the spice rub. The duck is flavorful enough to serve as is or a sauce can be added if desired. Vegetable side dishes and/or Chinese pancakes are the natural accompaniments.

While we think this two-step cooking method produces the best duck we have ever tasted, there are some tradeoffs here. A steamed duck gives off almost no fat when roasted and the roasting time is really too short to cook any vegetables in the pan. The process also takes all day.

Our traditional roasted duck recipe takes just two hours start to finish and therefore we have included it as well. Adding vegetables or fruits to the pan is easy and delicious. Potatoes, shallots, pears, turnips, and more can cook in the duck fat and help turn a roast duck into a complete dinner. Also, a roasted duck works well with a variety of sauces. In fact, we think a sauce is required since the bird is not seasoned with anything more than salt and pepper.

We find that pan sauces are often greasy, which is no surprise given the fatty nature of a duck. Although we have included a recipe for the classic duck à l'orange, which minimizes this problem, in general we avoid using the pan drippings and rely on a reduction sauce made from a basic duck stock. The duck stock, which gets its flavor from the neck and giblets, can be made while the bird roasts and then flavored in the last minutes of cooking with apple cider, port, orange juice, or blueberries.

With either Master Recipe, there are two carving possibilities. A traditional Western carving follows the method for a chicken and removes the parts of the bird intact. Chinese cooks usually take the meat off the legs and thighs and cut the breast into small pieces for a boneless presentation. (See page 17 for more details.)

Despite the fact that duck starts out weighing a pound more than an average chicken, the yield is actually less. The bones are heavier and much of the initial weight is fat that will be rendered during cooking. With abundant side dishes, a duck will serve four. If side dishes are skimpy or diners are particularly hungry, a duck will yield only three servings.

PREPARING TWICE-COOKED DUCK

I. Rub half of the seasoned salt mixture over the skin and inside the cavity of the duck.

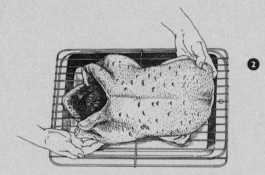

2. Set a flat rack on top of a deep roasting pan. Place the duck on top, making sure that air can circulate underneath. Set aside in a cool, airy place for 4 hours to dry out the skin and allow the seasonings to penetrate.

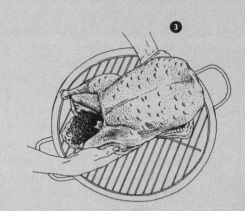

3. Set a flat rack in a 16-inch wok or wide, deep pot. Fill the bottom with water and bring it to a boil. Place the duck breast side up on the rack, making sure the duck rests 1 inch above the water.

4. After the duck has steamed for 50 to 60 minutes, the skin will become taut. Look at the drumsticks to see if the duck has steamed long enough. The skin should have started to pull away from joints, and the meat will be exposed.

Twice-Cooked Duck

SERVES 3 TO 4

STEAMING THEN ROASTING a duck produces the moistest bird with the least amount of fat. In general, we prefer to cure the duck with a seasoned salt before steaming (see following recipes). However, if pressed for time, you may simply salt the duck and then steam it right away. You will want to serve this duck with a sauce as it is a bit bland.

> 1 duck (about 4½ pounds), thawed, rinsed, and patted dry (giblets reserved for another use)
> Salt
> 1 tablespoon dark soy sauce or balsamic vinegar

1. Rub the outside and inside cavity of the duck generously with salt (see figure 1, opposite).

2. Bring several inches of water to a boil in a 16-inch wok or wide, deep pot fitted with a rack 1 inch above water level. Place the duck, breast side up, on the rack (figure 3, opposite). Cover the pot and steam over high heat, adding more boiling water if necessary, until the skin becomes taut and starts to pull away from the joints on the drumsticks, 50 to 60 minutes (figure 4, opposite).

3. Cool to room temperature and brush the skin with soy sauce. (The duck can be wrapped in plastic and refrigerated up to 1 day. Bring to room temperature before roasting.)

4. Heat the oven to 400 degrees. Place the duck on a rack inside a roasting pan. Roast until the skin is crisp and quite brown, 35 to 40 minutes. Remove from the oven, tent with foil, and let rest for 10 to 20 minutes. Carve (see page 17) and serve.

◆

Twice-Cooked Duck with Asian Flavorings

CALIFORNIA CHEF BRUCE COST FIRST SHOWED US THIS TRADITIONAL CHINESE METHOD FOR COOKING A DUCK. IN ADDITION TO STEAMING AND ROASTING, THE DUCK IS RUBBED WITH A SEASONED SALT AND AIR-DRIED TO HELP CRISP UP THE SKIN. ALTHOUGH THIS METHOD INVOLVES SEVERAL STEPS THAT REQUIRE SOME MINIMAL ATTENTION FROM MORNING THROUGH TO DINNERTIME, THE RESULTS ARE SUPERIOR. THE SKIN IS ESPECIALLY CRISP AND THE MEAT IS TENDER AND PER-FECTLY COOKED. THOSE WHO DO NOT HAVE KOSHER SALT CAN SUBSTITUTE 1 TABLESPOON OF REGULAR TABLE SALT. IF YOU WANT TO USE THESE FLAVORS BUT DON'T HAVE THE TIME TO CURE THE DUCK, RUB THE SEASONED SALT OVER THE BIRD AND THEN STEAM IMME-DIATELY AS IN THE MASTER RECIPE. SERVES 3 TO 4.

> 4 whole star anise
> 2 teaspoons Szechwan peppercorns
> 1 small cinnamon stick
> 2 tablespoons kosher salt
> 1 duck (about 4½ pounds), thawed, rinsed, and patted dry (giblets reserved for another use)
> 4 thick slices unpeeled fresh gingerroot
> 1 cup fresh cilantro leaves
> 1 tablespoon dark soy sauce

(continued on next page)

1. Toast the star anise, peppercorns, and cinnamon stick in a dry skillet until they start to smoke. Grind in a spice mill and combine with salt. Rub half the mixture over the outside and inside cavity of the duck (see figure 1, page 396). Set aside the remaining mixture.

2. Place the ginger slices and cilantro in the duck cavity. Set the duck on a rack above a roasting pan and leave uncovered in a cool, airy place for 4 hours (figure 2, page 396).

3. Bring several inches of water to a boil in a 16-inch wok or wide, deep pot fitted with a rack 1 inch above water level. Place the duck, breast side up, on the rack (figure 3, page 396). Cover the pot and steam over high heat, adding more boiling water if necessary, until the skin becomes taut and starts to pull away from the joints on the wings, 50 to 60 minutes (figure 4, page 396).

4. Cool to room temperature and brush the skin with soy sauce. (The duck can be wrapped in plastic and refrigerated up to 1 day. Bring to room temperature before roasting.)

5. Heat the oven to 400 degrees. Place the duck on a rack inside a roasting pan. Roast until the skin is crisp and quite brown, 35 to 40 minutes. Remove from the oven, tent with foil, and let rest for 10 to 20 minutes. Carve (see page 17) and serve, using the reserved portion of the spice mixture as a condiment at the table for duck.

◆

Twice-Cooked Duck with Rosemary and Sage

TWICE-COOKED DUCK CAN BE SEASONED WITH A VARIETY OF MIXTURES. HERE, WE REPLACE THE ASIAN SPICES WITH AN HERBED SALT. OTHER HERBS MAY BE SUBSTITUTED, ACCORDING TO TASTE. EITHER APPLE CIDER SAUCE (PAGE 400) OR PORT SAUCE (PAGE 401) WOULD ENHANCE THE FLAVORS OF THE DUCK. SERVES 3 TO 4.

Follow Twice-Cooked Duck with Asian Flavorings (page 397), replacing the spice mixture with 2 tablespoons each of minced fresh rosemary leaves and sage leaves mixed with 2 tablespoons kosher salt and 2 teaspoons pepper. Rub half the mixture over the outside and inside cavity of the duck; reserve the other half for use at the table. Dry, steam, and roast according to the recipe, placing fresh rosemary sprigs in the cavity instead of ginger and cilantro, and brushing with balsamic vinegar instead of soy sauce.

◆

Twice-Cooked Duck with Lemon and Thyme

BLUEBERRY SAUCE WORKS WELL WITH THIS LEMONY DUCK. SERVES 3 TO 4.

Follow Twice-Cooked Duck with Asian Flavorings (page 397), replacing the spice mixture with 2 tablespoons each of minced fresh thyme leaves and minced lemon zest mixed with 2 tablespoons kosher salt and 2 teaspoons pepper. Rub half the mixture over the outside and inside cavity of the duck; reserve the other half for use at the table. Dry, steam, and roast according to the recipe, placing fresh thyme sprigs in the cavity instead of ginger and cilantro, and brushing with balsamic vinegar instead of soy sauce.

◆

Twice-Cooked Duck with Three-Seed Salt

THIS VARIATION PRODUCES A DUCK WITH HIGHLY SPICED SKIN AND AROMATIC MEAT. SERVE WITH A BASMATI RICE, PILAF STYLE (PAGE 132) AND ORANGE SAUCE (PAGE 401). SERVES 3 TO 4.

Follow Twice-Cooked Duck with Asian Flavorings (page 397), replacing the spice mixture with the following: Toast 1 tablespoon *each* of cumin, coriander, and fennel seeds in a dry skillet until they start to smoke; grind toasted seeds and combine with 2 tablespoons kosher salt. Rub half the mixture over the outside and inside cavity of the duck; reserve the other half for use at the table. Dry, steam, and roast according to the recipe, placing ginger and cilantro leaves in the cavity and brushing with soy sauce.

Simple Roasted Duck with Potatoes and Turnips

SERVES 3 TO 4

WHEN WE HAVE THE time, we prefer the twice-cooked duck for its moist-ness and extra-crisp skin. However, there are times when we want to prepare a duck and get it in and out of the oven in under 2 hours. The following Western-style recipe allows us to do this. ◆ Unlike twice-cooked duck, a roasted duck releases abundant amounts of fat that must be drained from the roasting pan periodically. Not all of the fat goes to waste, however. Potatoes and turnips added to the pan during the last hour of cooking benefit from being cooked in the drip-pings and produce a hearty side dish for the duck. Any of the sauces would work here.

1 duck (about 4½ pounds), thawed,
    rinsed, and patted dry (giblets reserved)
Salt and pepper
1 pound small red potatoes, cut in half
1 pound small turnips, peeled and cut in half

1. Preheat the oven to 350 degrees. Prick the skin of the duck with the point of a sharp paring knife, being careful to pierce just the fat layer and not the flesh (see figure). Season the cavity and rub the skin generously with salt and pepper. Place the duck breast side up in a large rack placed inside a roasting pan. Roast for 1 hour and 15 minutes.

2. Remove the pan from the oven and drain off the fat. Scatter the potatoes and turnips around the edges of the pan, sprinkle with salt and pepper, and return the pan to the oven. Roast for 20 minutes, turn the vegetables to coat with any newly rendered fat, and roast another 20 minutes.

3. Raise the oven temperature to 500 degrees. Roast until the skin is crisp and quite brown, about 15 min-utes longer. Remove from the oven; lift the potatoes and turnips from the pan with a slotted spoon, place them in a serving bowl, and cover with foil. Tent the duck with foil and let rest for 10 to 20 minutes. Carve (see page 17) and serve with vegetables.

PREPARING SIMPLE ROASTED DUCK

Prick the skin of the duck with the point of a sharp paring knife, being careful to pierce just the fat layer and not the flesh.

FOUR SAUCES
FOR DUCK

/|\

PAN DRIPPINGS FROM A ROASTED DUCK ARE VERY GREASY

AND WE DON'T LIKE TO USE THEM WHEN MAKING SAUCES.

A DUCK STOCK REDUCTION GIVES THE FOLLOWING FOUR

SAUCES A STRONG DUCK FLAVOR WITHOUT ADDING ANY FAT. IT IS

OUR PREFERRED METHOD FOR SAUCING A ROASTED DUCK.

Duck Stock Reduction

USE THIS QUICK STOCK, MADE FROM THE NECK
AND GIBLETS OF THE DUCK YOU WILL BE ROAST-
ING, TO MAKE ANY OF THE SAUCES BELOW, OR ONE
OF YOUR OWN DEVISING. **MAKES ABOUT** ½ **CUP.**

> **Neck and giblets from 1 duck**
> ½ **teaspoon salt**
> **8 black peppercorns**

Combine all the ingredients in a medium
saucepan; cover with water and bring to a boil.
Turn the heat down and cook at a bare simmer 1
hour. Strain into a small saucepan and reduce over
medium heat until ½ cup remains, 10 to 15 minutes. Proceed with one of the following sauces.

Apple Cider Sauce

THE TART-SWEET FLAVOR OF REDUCED APPLE CIDER
COMPLEMENTS THE SLIGHTLY GAMY FLAVOR OF
ROASTED DUCK VERY WELL. **MAKES ABOUT** ½ **CUP.**

> **2 cups apple cider**
> ½ **cup Duck Stock Reduction**
> **Salt and pepper**

1. Bring 1½ cups apple cider to boil in a small
saucepan. Reduce over high heat until ¼ cup
remains, 10 to 15 minutes. Set aside.

2. Bring the stock and the remaining ½ cup
cider to a boil in another small saucepan. Reduce
over medium-high heat until ½ cup remains,
about 10 minutes.

3. Stir in the reduced cider and cook until
syrupy, 3 to 4 minutes. Remove from heat and
season with salt and pepper to taste. Set aside and
reheat when ready to serve with the roasted duck.

Port Sauce

A GOOD QUALITY TAWNY PORT WORKS WELL HERE.
MAKES ABOUT ½ CUP.

> **2 cups port**
> **½ cup Duck Stock Reduction**
> **Salt and pepper**

1. Bring 1½ cups port to a boil in a small saucepan. Reduce over high heat until ¼ cup remains, 10 to 15 minutes. Set aside.

2. Bring the stock and the remaining ½ cup port to a boil in another small saucepan. Reduce over medium-high heat until ½ cup remains, about 10 minutes.

3. Stir in the reduced port and cook until syrupy, 3 to 4 minutes. Remove from heat and season with salt and pepper to taste. Set aside and reheat when ready to serve with the roasted duck.

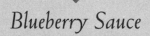

Blueberry Sauce

DEPENDING ON THE SWEETNESS OF THE BERRIES, DECREASE OR INCREASE THE AMOUNT OF SUGAR TO TASTE. RASPBERRIES OR BLACKBERRIES MAY BE SUBSTITUTED. MAKES ABOUT ⅔ CUP.

> **1 cup blueberries**
> **2 tablespoons sugar**
> **½ cup Duck Stock Reduction**
> **Salt and pepper**

1. Combine the blueberries, ½ cup water, and the sugar in a small saucepan. Bring to a boil over medium-high heat until the mixture is thick and syrupy, about 15 minutes. Push the berry mixture through a fine strainer.

2. Combine the stock and the berry mixture in a clean saucepan and bring to a boil. Reduce over medium-high heat until ⅔ cup remains, about 10 minutes. Remove from heat and season with salt and pepper to taste. Set aside and reheat when ready to serve with the roasted duck.

Orange Sauce

IF YOU LIKE THE FLAVOR OF DUCK À L'ORANGE BUT WOULD RATHER NOT USE THE PAN DRIPPINGS TO MAKE A SAUCE, TRY THIS RECIPE, WHICH STARTS WITH REDUCED DUCK STOCK AND ADDS ORANGE JUICE, SUGAR, AND A LITTLE LIME JUICE TO CUT THE SWEETNESS. MAKES ABOUT ½ CUP.

> **1¾ cups fresh orange juice**
> **¼ cup fresh lime juice**
> **2 tablespoons sugar**
> **½ cup Duck Stock Reduction**
> **Salt and pepper**

1. Combine the juices and sugar. Bring 1½ cups of the juice and the sugar to a boil in a small saucepan. Reduce over high heat until ¼ cup remains, 10 to 15 minutes. Set aside.

2. Bring the stock and the remaining ½ cup juice to a boil in another small saucepan. Reduce over medium-high heat until ½ cup remains, about 10 minutes.

3. Stir in the reduced juice and cook until syrupy, 3 to 4 minutes. Remove from heat and season with salt and pepper to taste. Set aside and reheat when ready to serve with the roasted duck.

Roasted Duck with Pears and Carmelized Shallots

PEARS AND SHALLOTS CARAMELIZE WITH A LITTLE SUGAR AS THEY ROAST IN THE BOTTOM OF THE PAN. NO SAUCE IS NECESSARY SINCE THE FRUIT PROVIDES A JAMLIKE ACCOMPANIMENT. **SERVES 3 TO 4.**

    1 duck (about 4½ pounds), thawed,
       rinsed, and patted dry (giblets reserved
       for another use)
    Salt and pepper
    4 pears, peeled, halved, cored, and cut
       into ¼-inch-thick slices
    10 shallots, peeled and sliced thin
    2 tablespoons brown sugar

1. Preheat the oven to 350 degrees. Prick the skin of the duck with the point of a sharp paring knife, being careful to pierce just the fat layer and not the flesh. Season the cavity and rub the skin generously with salt and pepper. Place the duck breast side up on a large roasting rack placed inside a roasting pan. Roast for 1 hour and 15 minutes. Remove the pan from the oven and drain off the fat. Return to the oven and roast 20 minutes longer.

2. Remove the pan from the oven and drain off the fat. Scatter the pears and shallots around the edges of the pan and return the pan to the oven. Roast for 20 minutes, sprinkle the pears and shallots with the brown sugar, turn the pears and shallots to coat with any newly rendered fat, and roast another 20 minutes.

3. Raise the oven temperature to 500 degrees. Roast until the skin is crisp and quite brown, about 15 minutes longer. Remove from the oven; lift the pears and shallots from the pan with a slotted spoon, place them in a serving bowl, and cover with foil. Tent the duck with foil and let rest for 10 to 20 minutes. Carve (see page 17) and serve with the pears and shallots.

Roasted Duck with Tomatoes, Olives, and Artichokes

TOMATOES ARE ROASTED ON THE BOTTOM OF THE PAN ALONG WITH ARTICHOKE HEARTS AND OLIVES FOR A RICH VEGETABLE SIDE DISH. NO SAUCE IS NECESSARY, SINCE THE TOMATOES MOISTEN THE COOKED DUCK. **SERVES 3 TO 4.**

    1 duck (about 4½ pounds), thawed,
       rinsed, and patted dry (giblets reserved
       for another use)
    Salt and pepper
    1 6-ounce jar artichoke hearts, rinsed and
       drained
    ½ cup plump black olives such as
       Kalamatas, pitted and coarsely chopped
    8 small plum tomatoes, halved

1. Preheat the oven to 350 degrees. Prick the skin of the duck with the point of a sharp paring knife, being careful to pierce just the fat layer and not the flesh. Season the cavity and rub the skin generously with salt and pepper. Place the duck breast side up on a large roasting rack placed inside a roasting pan. Roast for 1 hour and 15 minutes. Remove the pan from the oven and drain off the fat. Return to the oven and roast 25 minutes longer.

2. Combine the artichokes, olives, and tomatoes in a medium bowl and toss with a little salt and pepper (you may want to go lightly on the salt since the artichokes and olives are already quite salty). Remove the pan from the oven and drain off the fat again. Add the artichokes, olives, and tomatoes to the pan and roast 15 minutes longer. Turn the vegetables to coat with any newly rendered fat.

3. Raise the oven temperature to 500 degrees. Roast until the skin is crisp and quite brown, about 15 minutes longer. Remove from the oven; lift the vegetables from the pan with a slotted spoon, place them in a serving bowl, and cover with foil. Tent the duck with foil and let rest for 10 to 20 minutes. Carve (see page 17) and serve with vegetables.

Roasted Duck à l'Orange

ROASTED DUCK WITH ORANGE SAUCE IS A CLASSIC.
TRADITIONAL ORANGE SAUCES CAN BE CLOYINGLY
SWEET AND GREASY; WE ADD LEMON JUICE AND WHITE
VINEGAR TO CUT THE SWEETNESS. THIS SAUCE IS
ENRICHED WITH THE BROWNED BITS FROM THE BOT-
TOM OF THE ROASTING PAN FOR FLAVOR. HOWEVER,
THE DRIPPINGS ARE QUITE GREASY AND SHOULD BE
REMOVED BEFORE THE PAN IS DEGLAZED WITH SOME OF
THE SAUCE. SERVES 3 TO 4.

> 1 duck (about 4½ pounds), thawed,
>   rinsed, and patted dry (giblets reserved
>   for another use)
> Salt and pepper
> 2 oranges
> 2 lemons
> ½ cup Grand Marnier or other orange-
>   flavored liqueur
> 1 tablespoon cornstarch
> ¼ cup sugar
> ⅓ cup white wine vinegar
> 2 cups chicken stock or low-sodium
>   canned broth

1. Preheat the oven to 350 degrees. Prick the skin of
the duck with the point of a sharp paring knife, being
careful to pierce just the fat layer and not the flesh.
Season the cavity and rub the skin generously with
salt and pepper. Place the duck breast side up on a
large roasting rack placed inside a roasting pan. Roast
for 1 hour and 15 minutes. Remove the pan from the
oven and drain off the fat. Add ½ cup water to the
pan and roast another 40 minutes.

2. Raise the oven temperature to 500 degrees. Roast
until the skin is crisp and quite brown, about 15 minutes longer.

3. While the duck is roasting, prepare the sauce:
Remove the zest from 1 orange and 1 lemon with a
grater. Set aside. Juice all the oranges and lemons and
set the juice aside. In a small bowl, combine the Grand
Marnier and cornstarch, stirring to dissolve any lumps,
and set aside.

4. Place the sugar and ¼ cup water in a medium
saucepan over high heat. Cook until the sugar dissolves and the mixture comes to a boil. Add the juices,
vinegar, and stock and bring to a boil; turn the heat to
medium and reduce to 2 cups, 15 to 20 minutes. Stir
in the grated zests.

5. When the duck is done, remove it from the oven.
Tent the duck with foil and let rest for 10 to 20 minutes. Drain the fat from the roasting pan. Place the
pan on a burner over high heat, add ½ cup of the
sauce, and scrape the brown bits from the bottom of
the pan with a wooden spoon. Pour the liquid back
into the saucepan, bring to a boil, and stir in the cornstarch mixture. Simmer 2 to 3 minutes until the sauce
thickens. Carve the duck (see page 17) and serve with
the orange sauce.

PEKING DUCK

/ʌ\

THERE IS ALWAYS A REASON WHY A DISH REMAINS POP-

ULAR FOR CENTURIES. IN THE CASE OF PEKING DUCK,

WHICH DATES BACK AT LEAST FOUR HUNDRED YEARS,

IT IS THE ALLURING COMBINATION OF CRACKLING

PIECES OF CRISP SKIN AND JUICY (BUT NOT FATTY)

SLICES OF MEAT. MOST AMERICANS KNOW THIS DISH

AS A CHINESE RESTAURANT CLASSIC. HOWEVER, WITH

a few simple modifications, an excellent Peking duck can be prepared at home with minimal fuss.

California chef David SooHoo worked with our test kitchen to help develop this method. It calls for equipment rarely seen in the kitchen—an electric fan and a metal hanger from the dry cleaners—but we found that these modern tools cut drying time from three days to several hours. Best of all, this streamlined preparation (which takes less than thirty minutes of hands-on time) guarantees that the duck will have crisp, dark skin and moist, flavorful meat.

In addition to the drying process, there are two steps that will be unfamiliar to most American cooks. The first is part of the traditional recipe and involves pumping air into the bird to separate the skin from the meat. The idea is to lift the skin from the meat so it will crisp when cooked, not to make a balloon. Use a basketball pump or even a straw for the task and do not worry if the air escapes once it has done the job.

The second unfamiliar step is a quick dip in simmering water and vinegar. Ladling hot liquid over the duck's skin opens the pores—look for goose bumps as you do this—and allows some of the fat to escape. With less fat, the skin will crisp up better.

When the bird is done, carve separate slices of skin and meat and serve them with Chinese pancakes and hoisin sauce.

Peking Duck

SERVES 4

TRADITIONAL RECIPES CALL for a duck with both the head and feet still attached. Our version is for a supermarket duck, without the head and feet. To make 2 ducks, double the amount of marinade, cilantro, and scallions but keep the ingredients for the wok bath the same.

GARLIC-GINGER MARINADE

4 garlic cloves, peeled
2 1/2-inch slices fresh gingerroot, peeled
1 tablespoon salt
2 tablespoons sugar
1/2 teaspoon five-spice powder *or* 1 whole
  star anise
2 tablespoons rice wine or white wine

PEKING DUCK

1 4- to 5-pound duck
1 small bunch cilantro, leaves and stems
  (about 1 cup)
2 whole scallions, roots trimmed
1/2 cup distilled white vinegar
1/2 cup cornstarch
1 tablespoon Kitchen Bouquet
1/2 cup sugar or honey

1. Puree the marinade ingredients in a blender or food processor until smooth.

2. Pull out the fat that lines the sides of the duck's back cavity and discard. Pour the marinade into the open cavity and stuff the bird with cilantro and scallions.

3. Bring the excess skin around the neck up over the open cavity. Thread skewers through the skin to seal the cavity. Tie kitchen twine around the skewers to pinch the skin tightly shut (see figure 1, page 408). Repeat the process at the tail end to seal that cavity as well.

4. Insert the needle of a basketball pump (or a thin straw) between the 2 flaps of skin and into the back cavity. Pump several times to lift the skin from the meat (figure 2, page 408). Do not overinflate. As long as skin has visibly detached from meat, you have completed this step; it does not matter if the air slowly escapes from the duck.

5. Fold up both ends of a metal hanger from the dry cleaners. Slide ends of hanger under the wings of the bird (figure 3, page 408). Secure the hanger by tying a 3-foot piece of wet string through the ends of the hanger and around the bird (figure 4, page 408).

6. Bring 1 gallon of water and ½ cup vinegar to a boil in a large wok or stockpot. Use the hanger to hold the duck above the wok and ladle the hot liquid over the surface of the duck until goose bumps are visible on the skin, 1 to 2 minutes (figure 5, page 408). Do not let the duck rest for long periods in the water or it will begin to cook. Set the duck aside and discard all but 2 quarts of liquid from the wok. Dissolve the cornstarch in 1 cup cold water and whisk the mixture into the liquid in the wok. Whisk in the Kitchen Bouquet and sugar and stir until the mixture is smooth and the sugar dissolves. Use the hanger to hold the duck above the wok and ladle the hot paste over skin. Make sure that all parts of the duck are coated with the thick brown liquid.

7. Hang the duck away from the sunlight in a cool, dry place (either over a work sink or a covering of newspaper.) Place an electric fan set to high about 1 foot from the duck. Blow-dry, turning the duck once, until the skin between the leg and belly is translucent, 4 to 8 hours depending on the heat and humidity. (The duck can be dried overnight and then refrigerated during the day until cooking time.)

8. Preheat the oven to 350 degrees. Untie the string that secures the hanger, discard the string and hanger. Wrap the legs and wings with aluminum foil to prevent them from burning. Place the duck on a rack set in a roasting pan.

9. Roast the duck for 1 hour. Remove the foil and continue cooking until the meat juices from leg run clear and the temperature registers 180 degrees on an instant-read thermometer, 15 to 30 minutes more depending on the size of the duck.

10. Remove and discard all strings and skewers. Detach the legs and wings (see page 17) and carve the skin and then meat from both. Slice the skin and then the meat from the body and place all carvings on a large platter.

PREPARING A DUCK FOR AIR-DRYING

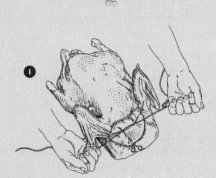

1. Bring the excess skin around the neck up over the open cavity. Thread skewers through the skin to seal the cavity. Tie kitchen twine around the skewers to pinch the skin tightly shut. Repeat the process at the tail end to seal that cavity as well.

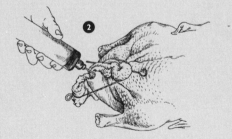

2. Insert the needle of a basketball pump or a thin straw into the sealed tail cavity by sliding it between the flaps of skin. Pump several times to lift the skin from the meat.

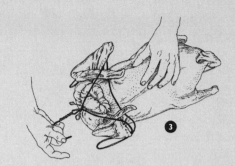

3. Fold both ends of a metal clothes hanger up and slide them under the wings of the bird.

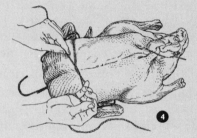

4. To secure the hanger, tie a 3-foot piece of wet string through the ends of the hanger and around the bird.

5. Hold the duck above the wok bath by the hanger and ladle hot liquid over the surface of the duck until goose bumps are visible on the skin.

Chinese Sesame Crepes

TRADITIONALLY, THIS CHINESE PANCAKE IS QUITE STURDY (IT WAS OFTEN CARRIED INTO THE FIELD BY FARMERS FOR MIDDAY MEALS) AND THUS VERY CHEWY. WE PREFER A MORE DELICATE CREPE THAT IS NOT NEARLY AS DOUGHY OR TOUGH. WE SPIKE A EUROPEAN-TYPE BATTER WITH SESAME OIL AND SESAME SEEDS TO GIVE THE PANCAKES THEIR ASIAN CHARACTER. MAKES ABOUT 18.

   1¼ cups all-purpose flour
   ¼ teaspoon salt
   2 eggs
   1¼ cups milk
   2 tablespoons Asian sesame oil
   2 tablespoons sesame seeds
   Vegetable oil, for coating the pan

1. Whisk together the flour, salt, eggs, milk, sesame oil, and sesame seeds in a medium bowl.

2. Set a 6- to 8-inch nonstick skillet over medium-high heat; brush the pan with vegetable oil. Pour 2 to 3 tablespoons of batter into the center of the pan; swirl until the bottom is coated. Cook until the crepe edges start to brown, about 1 minute. Turn and brown the other side, about 30 seconds longer. Remove the crepe from the pan and set aside. Repeat, oiling the pan as necessary, until all the batter is used, stacking the finished crepes on top of one another. Wrap crepes in a kitchen towel to keep warm.

Hoisin Sauce

BOTTLED HOISIN SAUCE CAN BE HARSH AND FLOURY. WE COOK AWAY THE OFF FLAVORS BY BOILING THE BOTTLED SAUCE WITH A LITTLE GARLIC, RICE WINE, AND CHICKEN STOCK. THE RESULT IS A PURER TASTING SAUCE TO ACCOMPANY A HOMEMADE PEKING DUCK. MAKES ABOUT 1¼ CUPS.

   1 tablespoon peanut oil
   2 garlic cloves, finely chopped
   1 8-ounce jar hoisin sauce (about ¾ cup)
   2 tablespoons Asian sesame oil
   ¼ cup rice wine
   1 tablespoon balsamic vinegar
   ¼ cup chicken stock or low-sodium
      canned chicken broth

1. Heat the peanut oil over medium in a small saucepan. Add the garlic and cook until golden, about 2 minutes.

2. Increase the heat to high and add the hoisin sauce and sesame oil. Bring to a boil and cook, stirring constantly, for 3 minutes. Add the rice wine and vinegar and cook, stirring constantly, for another 3 minutes.

3. Reduce the heat to low and add the stock. Cook at a barest simmer, stirring occasionally, until thick, 12 to 15 minutes. Hoisin sauce can be refrigerated in an airtight container for several weeks.

DUCK

BREASTS

/I\

THE DEMAND FOR DUCK BREASTS HAS BEEN FUELED BY

THEIR POPULARITY WITH CHEFS. IN RESPONSE TO

RESTAURANT PATRONS WHO WANTED TO RE-CREATE

CHEF DISHES AT HOME, BONELESS DUCK BREASTS

HAVE BECOME A STANDARD ITEM IN MANY SUPERMAR-

KETS AND MOST BUTCHER SHOPS. UNFORTUNATELY,

CHEF RECIPES RARELY WORK FOR HOME COOKS

(professional cooking equipment for meat, such as a salamander or indoor grill, is completely different from the home options) and there are few duck breast recipes in cookbooks. With little good information to begin with, we wanted to figure out which cooking methods make the most sense for the home cook.

Depending on the variety of duck, an entire breast can weigh anywhere from 12 to 20 ounces. The most commonly available size is 12 ounces, which splits neatly into two breast halves, each weighing about 6 ounces—an ideal serving for one person.

Duck breast meat is firm and flavorful and tastes best when cooked to a medium-rare stage, 140 degrees measured on an instant-read thermometer. Although health experts recommend cooking all poultry, including duck, to at least 160 degrees, we find that duck breast cooked to this stage is akin to eating a well-done steak. If you are concerned about eating medium-rare duck breast, roast a whole duck, which is cooked to an internal temperature well above 160 in order to render the fat.

Speaking of fat, the skin on a duck breast adds flavor and a pleasantly crisp texture when prepared correctly. However, when we prepared many recipes in the past, the skin has been flabby or chewy and there has been way too much of it. We knew the skin was going to be a central theme in our testing.

We decided to focus on the three cooking methods that held the most promise—grilling, sautéing, and braising. (We eliminated broiling because the skin was prone to spontaneous combustion.) For each cooking method we wanted to develop a foolproof technique, while figuring out how to deal with the skin.

First, we simply seasoned a duck breast with a little salt and pepper and grilled it. As might be expected, the flare-ups soon were out of control. We tried to rescue the meat, but by the time we contained the inferno the duck breasts were charred. This failure clearly illustrated the need to remove some of the fat.

When we removed the excess fat (bits hanging off the meat itself), the results were better. The skin that remained became fairly crisp and there were no flare-ups. Several sources suggest scoring the skin with a sharp knife to help render more fat. When we scored the skin, we found that it cooked up crisper and with very little chewiness. Several of our testers still thought the skin was overpowering the meat. It was delicious,

but the meat seemed like an afterthought. When we removed all but a 2-inch-wide strip of skin from the center of the duck breast, everyone reacted positively. The balance between skin and meat was just right.

With the skin issue settled, we next focused on the heat level. We wondered if duck breast would respond best to high heat, or if indirect or medium heat might render more fat and cook the breast more evenly. Indirect heat did not work because the skin did not crisp up. The same thing happened over a medium-low fire. Clearly, we needed a fairly hot (but not scorching) fire to cook the breast quickly before it had time to dry out. A hot fire would also make the skin crisp.

We stumbled upon one last trick. We let one batch go skin side down too long. Thinking that we had ruined them, we turned them back over and finished cooking for a few minutes. To our surprise, the meat was perfectly cooked and the skin even crisper than before. Upon reflection, it makes sense to cook duck breast longer on the skin side. The extra cooking time renders more fat and the meat is protected from the heat and thus has less chance of drying.

A final set of tests revolved around flavoring duck breast before grilling. We tried several marinades but were unimpressed. Unlike chicken, duck has so much intrinsic flavor that it does not need a boost. Salt and pepper is adequate, although a spice rub is certainly appropriate as well.

With our grilling technique perfected, we moved on to sautéing. We figured the issues would be pretty much the same. We still wanted to render most of the fat from the skin, but were unwilling to strip the skin totally away from the meat.

Our first few tests revealed an initial problem. A duck breast is thinner around the edges and thicker down the middle. While the difference is not so great as to cause cooking problems in the meat (it's fine if the center is a bit undercooked, that's really the definition of medium-rare anyway), the skin was another matter. The skin over the thick middle of each breast was crisp and delicious but the skin around the edges was not. While we had removed excess skin so as not to overpower the meat when grilling, we had no choice but to remove all but a thin strip of the skin when sautéing, since only the center portion was in direct contact with the pan and becoming crisp and brown.

PREPARING A DUCK BREAST FOR GRILLING AND SAUTEING

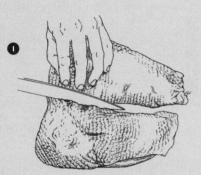

I. To prepare a whole boneless duck breast for grilling or sautéing, first separate the breast into halves.

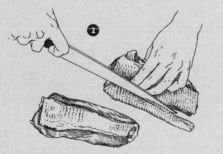

2. With a sharp chef's knife, trim any overhanging skin and fat from around each half. Slide fingers under the remaining skin along the length of the breast half to release it from the meat. Turn the breast half on its side and slice off some of the fat so that only a strip of skin 1½ to 2 inches remains in the center of each breast half.

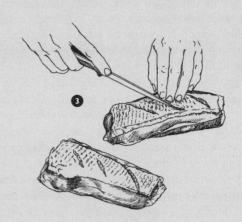

3. Use a paring knife to score the skin on each breast half diagonally 3 or 4 times to allow the fat to melt during cooking.

CARVING A DUCK BREAST

Use a sharp carving knife to slice cooked breast halves on the diagonal into ½-inch-thick pieces. Fan slices out over a serving plate.

As with grilling, we found that scoring the remaining skin helped to render more fat. One main problem remained—the fat in the pan. When grilling, rendered fat drips down onto the coals. However, on top of the stove, the cooking process was quickly becoming pan-frying, not sautéing. We found it necessary to drain the fat from the pan halfway through the cooking time and again just before making a sauce.

Braising had shown some initial promise. We tried a couple of recipes with the skin on, but were disgusted by the results. The braising liquid, which we wanted to use as a sauce over starches like mashed potatoes or rice, was greasy, and the skin on the breasts was rubbery. For our next tests, we removed the skin. The result was much improved. The meat cooks up firm and moist, almost like a prime rib. If you miss the crisp skin, make cracklings (see page 421).

We found that an initial searing of the skinless duck breasts was necessary for flavor when braising. After the meat is browned, we take it out of the pan and start assembling the braising liquid, which will eventually become a sauce. Shallots, garlic, onions, and the like can be sautéed in a little fat, as if making a regular pan sauce. However, once the liquid—wine, juice, and/or stock—is added and comes to a boil, we return the meat to the pan and let it finish cooking as the sauce reduces. We found there was no need to cover the pan as the meat simmered in the sauce. In fact, covering the pan lengthened the time needed to reduce the sauce and is not recommended.

When the meat is cooked through, simply transfer it to a plate and reduce the sauce to the desired consistency. We prefer to keep the sauce for braised duck breasts fairly thin so it can be used to moisten mashed potatoes, couscous, rice, or noodles.

A few final thoughts. It's best to let cooked duck breast rest several minutes (either under foil if grilling, or on a plate in the oven if making a pan sauce for sautéed or braised duck recipes) before carving. Like beef, the meat holds on to its juices better if allowed to rest. As for carving, we like to cut the breast on the diagonal into ½-inch-thick slices and then fan the slices out over a plate. Of course, you can serve the duck breast halves whole (like a chicken cutlet) and let diners cut their own meat, but the sliced presentation is attractive and works especially well with sauces.

MASTER RECIPE

Grilled Duck Breasts

SERVES 4

TRIMMED AND SCORED duck breasts may be rubbed with a mixture of spices (see the variations that follow) or simply sprinkled with salt and pepper before being placed on the grill.

2 whole boneless duck breasts, about
12 ounces each, split, trimmed of
excess skin and fat, and scored 3 or 4
times diagonally (see figures 1–3, page
413)
Salt and pepper

1. Prepare a charcoal fire (see figures 1–4, page 156) or preheat a gas grill. Sprinkle the duck breasts with salt and pepper to taste. Place the duck breasts skin side down on the grill. Grill the duck breasts over a medium-hot fire (you should be able to keep your hand 5 inches above the fire for 3 to 4 seconds) for 8 minutes. Turn the duck breasts and cook another 3 to 4 minutes, until medium-rare (an instant-read thermometer inserted into the thickest part of the breast will read 140 degrees). Remove the breasts from the grill, tent with foil, and let rest for 5 minutes.

2. Slice the breasts diagonally into ½-inch-thick pieces (see page 413) and fan a sliced breast half on each dinner plate.

Grilled Duck Breasts with Apple-Onion Chutney

MAKE THIS DISH IN THE FALL, DURING THE APPLE HAR-VEST, WHEN IT'S STILL WARM ENOUGH TO GRILL. PEARS MAY SUBSTITUTE FOR APPLES HERE. **SERVES 4.**

2 tablespoons extra-virgin olive oil
1 medium onion, finely chopped
3 tart apples, peeled, cored, and cut into
   ½-inch dice
¼ cup raisins
¼ cider vinegar
¼ cup packed brown sugar
Pinch ground allspice
Pinch ground cloves
Salt and pepper
2 whole boneless duck breasts, about 12
   ounces each, split, trimmed of excess
   skin and fat, and scored 3 or 4 times
   diagonally (see figures 1–3, page 413)

1. Prepare a charcoal fire (see figures 1–4, page 156) or preheat a gas grill.

2. Heat the oil in a large skillet. Add the onion and sauté until softened, 5 to 7 minutes. Add the apples and sauté, stirring frequently, until they begin to brown, about 5 minutes.

3. Add the raisins, vinegar, brown sugar, allspice, cloves, and salt and pepper to taste. Bring to a simmer, turn the heat to low, and cook another 10 minutes. Cover to keep warm.

4. Sprinkle the duck breasts with salt and pepper to taste. Place the duck breasts skin side down on the grill. Grill the duck breasts over a medium-hot fire (you should be able to keep your hand 5 inches above the fire for 3 to 4 seconds) for 8 minutes. Turn the duck breasts and cook another 3 to 4 minutes, until medium-rare (an instant-read thermometer inserted into the thickest part of the breast will read 140 degrees). Remove the breasts from the grill, tent with foil, and let rest for 5 minutes.

5. Slice the breasts diagonally into ½-inch-thick pieces (see page 413) and fan a sliced breast half on each dinner plate. Serve with the warm chutney.

◆

Spice-Rubbed Grilled Duck Breasts

WE'VE ADAPTED OUR SIMPLE SPICE RUB FOR CHICKEN PARTS HERE, ADDING A LITTLE SALT SINCE WE'RE NOT BRINING DUCK. ANY OTHER FAVORITE SPICE RUB MAY BE SUBSTITUTED; SEE PAGES 194–195 FOR IDEAS. **SERVES 4.**

1 teaspoon ground cumin
1 teaspoon curry powder
1 teaspoon chili powder
½ teaspoon ground allspice
½ teaspoon pepper
¼ teaspoon ground cinnamon
½ teaspoon salt
2 whole boneless duck breasts, about 12
   ounces each, split, trimmed of excess
   skin and fat, and scored 3 or 4 times
   diagonally (see figures 1–3, page 413)

1. Prepare a charcoal fire (see figures 1–4, page 156) or preheat a gas grill. Combine the cumin, curry powder, chili powder, allspice, pepper, cinnamon, and salt in a small bowl. Rub the duck breasts with the spice mixture. Place the duck breasts skin side down on the grill. Grill the duck breasts over a medium-hot fire (you should be able to keep your hand 5 inches above the fire for 3 to 4 seconds) for 8 minutes. Turn the duck breasts and cook another 3 to 4 minutes, until medium-rare (an instant-read thermometer inserted into the thickest part of the breast will read 140 degrees). Remove the breasts from the grill, tent with foil, and let rest for 5 minutes.

2. Slice the breasts diagonally into ½-inch-thick pieces (see page 413) and fan a sliced breast half on each dinner plate.

Grilled Duck Breasts with White Bean Puree

SIMPLY GRILLED DUCK BREAST MARRIES WELL WITH THIS SLIGHTLY PIQUANT WHITE BEAN PUREE. DEPENDING ON THE TEXTURE OF YOUR BEANS, YOU MIGHT WANT TO THIN THEM WITH WATER. THE BEANS MAY BE PREPARED SEVERAL HOURS IN ADVANCE AND REHEATED IN THE MICROWAVE. SERVES 4.

- ¼ cup extra-virgin olive oil
- 2 garlic cloves, minced
- 2 fresh rosemary sprigs
- 3 cups cooked *or* 2 15-ounce cans white beans, drained and rinsed
- 1 tablespoon red wine vinegar
- 1 tablespoon finely chopped fresh parsley leaves
- Salt and pepper
- 2 whole boneless duck breasts, about 12 ounces each, split, trimmed of excess skin and fat, and scored 3 or 4 times diagonally (see figures 1–3, page 413)

1. Prepare a charcoal fire (see figures 1–4, page 156) or preheat a gas grill.

2. Heat 2 tablespoons of oil in a large skillet over medium-high heat. Add the garlic and rosemary and sauté just until the garlic begins to color, 2 to 3 minutes. Add the beans and cook until heated through, 5 to 7 minutes. Remove the rosemary sprigs and discard. Scrape the beans into a blender or the work bowl of a food processor. Add the remaining 2 tablespoons of oil and the vinegar and puree. If the puree is very thick, thin it by adding up to ¼ cup water, a tablespoon at a time, through the feed tube as the food processor is running. Return the beans to the pan, stir in the parsley, and season with salt and pepper to taste. Cover to keep warm.

3. Sprinkle the duck breasts with salt and pepper to taste. Place the duck breasts skin side down on the grill. Grill the duck breasts over a medium-hot fire (you should be able to keep your hand 5 inches above the fire for 3 to 4 seconds) for 8 minutes. Turn the

duck breasts and cook another 3 to 4 minutes, until medium-rare (an instant-read thermometer inserted into the thickest part of the breast will read 140 degrees). Remove the breasts from the grill, tent with foil, and let rest for 5 minutes.

4. Place a portion of the bean puree on each of 4 dinner plates. Slice the breasts diagonally into ½-inch-thick pieces (see page 413) and fan a sliced breast half on top of each portion of puree. Serve immediately.

MASTER RECIPE

Sautéed Duck Breasts

SERVES 4

IN THIS MASTER RECIPE, we make a quick pan sauce with wine or vermouth and crushed green peppercorns. Other liquids and flavorings may be substituted according to taste. See the variations that follow or adapt any of the pan sauces for sautéed chicken cutlets (see chapter 5).

- 2 whole boneless duck breasts, about 12 ounces each, split, trimmed of excess skin and fat, and scored 3 or 4 times diagonally (see figures 1–3, page 413)
- Salt and pepper
- 2 tablespoons butter
- 1 medium shallot, finely chopped
- 1 cup dry white wine or vermouth
- 1 tablespoon green peppercorns, rinsed, drained, and crushed

1. Preheat the oven to the lowest possible temperature. Place a plate in the oven for keeping the cooked breasts warm while you make a sauce.

2. Sprinkle the breasts with salt and pepper to taste. Heat 1 tablespoon butter in a heavy-bottomed skillet measuring at least 9 inches across the bottom. Swirl the skillet over high heat until the butter has melted. Continue to heat until the butter stops foaming and has just begun to color. Lay the duck breasts in the skillet, skin side down.

3. Maintain medium-high heat, so the fat sizzles but does not smoke, and sauté the breasts until the skin is crisp and well browned, 8 to 10 minutes. If the skin starts to brown too quickly, turn the heat down to medium. Quickly drain all but 1 tablespoon of the fat from the pan. Turn the breasts with tongs; cook on other side until the meat is medium-rare, 4 to 5 minutes. Transfer the breasts to the plate in the oven; keep warm until ready to serve.

4. Discard all but 1 tablespoon of the fat remaining in the pan, being careful to leave the browned bits behind. Add the shallot and sauté until softened, 2 to 3 minutes. Increase the heat to high, add the wine, and scrape the skillet bottom with a wooden spatula or spoon to loosen any browned bits. Boil until the liquid reduces to about ⅓ cup, about 3 minutes. Add any accumulated juices from the plate with the duck breasts; reduce the sauce again to ⅓ cup. Add the peppercorns and season with salt and pepper to taste. Off the heat, swirl in the remaining tablespoon butter until it melts and thickens the sauce. Remove the breasts from the oven, slice (see page 413), and spoon the sauce over them; serve immediately.

Sautéed Duck Breasts with Asian Flavors

FIVE-SPICE POWDER GIVES THIS SAUTE A SLIGHTLY EXOTIC FLAVOR. SERVE WITH RICE AND STEAMED VEGETABLES. SERVES 4.

> 2 whole boneless duck breasts, about 12 ounces each, split, trimmed of excess skin and fat, and scored 3 or 4 times diagonally (see figures 1–3, page 413)
> 2 teaspoons five-spice powder
> Salt and pepper
> 2 tablespoons butter
> 1 garlic clove, minced
> 1 1-inch-piece fresh gingerroot, minced
> 3 scallions, white and light green parts, finely chopped
> 1 cup rice wine
> 2 teaspoons soy sauce

1. Preheat the oven to the lowest possible temperature. Place a plate in the oven for keeping the cooked breasts warm while you make a sauce.

2. Sprinkle the breasts with five-spice powder and salt and pepper to taste. Heat 1 tablespoon butter in a heavy-bottomed skillet measuring at least 9 inches across the bottom. Swirl the skillet over high heat until the butter has melted. Continue to heat until the butter stops foaming and has just begun to color. Lay the duck breasts in the skillet, skin side down.

3. Maintain medium-high heat, so the fat sizzles but does not smoke, and sauté the breasts until the skin is crisp and well browned, 8 to 10 minutes. If the skin starts to brown too quickly, turn the heat down to medium. Quickly drain all but 1 tablespoon of the fat from the pan. Turn the breasts with tongs; cook on other side until meat is medium-rare, 4 to 5 minutes. Transfer the breasts to the plate in the oven; keep warm until ready to serve.

4. Discard all but 1 tablespoon of the fat remaining in the pan, being careful to leave the browned bits behind. Add the garlic, ginger, and scallions and sauté

(continued on next page)

until fragrant, about 1 minute. Increase the heat to high, add the rice wine and soy sauce, and scrape the skillet bottom with a wooden spatula or spoon to loosen any browned bits. Boil until the liquid reduces to about ⅓ cup, about 3 minutes. Add any accumulated juices from the plate with the duck breasts; reduce the sauce again to ⅓ cup. Season with salt and pepper to taste. Off the heat, swirl in the remaining tablespoon butter until it melts and thickens the sauce. Remove the breasts from the oven, slice (see page 413), and spoon the sauce over them; serve immediately.

◆

Sautéed Duck Breasts with Rum and Dried Cherry Sauce

WE LIKE THE SWEETNESS OF RUM WITH THE SLIGHTLY TART CHERRIES. DRIED CRANBERRIES OR EVEN DRIED BLUEBERRIES MIGHT BE SUBSTITUTED HERE; ADJUST THE QUANTITY OF SUGAR TO TASTE. SERVES 4.

> ½ cup dried cherries
> 2 whole boneless duck breasts, about 12 ounces each, split, trimmed of excess skin and fat, and scored 3 or 4 times diagonally (see figures 1–3, page 413)
> Salt and pepper
> 1 tablespoon butter
> 1 medium shallot, minced
> 1 teaspoon sugar
> ½ cup dark rum
> ½ cup chicken stock or low-sodium canned broth
> ¼ cup heavy cream

1. Place the cherries in a small heatproof bowl and cover with boiling water. Let stand until softened, about 15 minutes; drain and set aside.

2. Preheat the oven to the lowest possible temperature. Place a plate in the oven for keeping the cooked breasts warm while you make a sauce.

3. Sprinkle the breasts with salt and pepper to taste. Heat the butter in a heavy-bottomed skillet measuring at least 9 inches across the bottom. Swirl the skillet over high heat until the butter has melted. Continue

to heat until the butter stops foaming and has just begun to color. Lay the duck breasts in the skillet, skin side down.

4. Maintain medium-high heat, so the fat sizzles but does not smoke, and sauté the breasts until the skin is crisp and well browned, 8 to 10 minutes. If the skin starts to brown too quickly, turn the heat down to medium. Quickly drain all but 1 tablespoon of the fat from the pan. Turn the breasts with tongs; cook on other side until meat is medium-rare, 4 to 5 minutes. Transfer the breasts to the plate in the oven; keep warm until ready to serve.

5. Discard all but 1 tablespoon of the fat remaining in the pan, being careful to leave the browned bits behind. Add the shallot, cherries, and the sugar, and sauté until the shallot is softened, 2 to 3 minutes. Increase the heat to high, add the rum and stock, and scrape the skillet bottom with a wooden spatula or spoon to loosen any browned bits. Add the cream and boil until the liquid reduces to about ⅓ cup, about 3 minutes. Add any accumulated juices from the plate with the duck breasts; reduce the sauce again to ⅓ cup. Remove the breasts from the oven, slice (see page 413), and spoon the sauce over them; serve immediately.

◆

Sautéed Duck Breasts with Wild Mushrooms

GAMY DUCK AND WOODSY MUSHROOMS COMBINE WELL IN THIS SIMPLE PAN SAUCE. FEEL FREE TO MIX VARIETIES OF MUSHROOMS ACCORDING TO TASTE AND AVAILABILITY. SERVES 4.

> 2 whole boneless duck breasts, about 12 ounces each, split, trimmed of excess skin and fat, and scored 3 or 4 times diagonally (see figures 1–3, page 413)
> Salt and pepper
> 2 tablespoons butter
> 2 garlic cloves, minced
> 1 medium shallot, finely chopped

10 ounces fresh wild mushrooms such as
    shiitake, chanterelle, or morel, wiped
    clean and sliced thin
½ cup white wine
½ cup chicken stock or low-sodium
    canned broth
1 tablespoon minced fresh parsley leaves

1. Preheat the oven to the lowest possible temperature. Place a plate in the oven for keeping the cooked
breasts warm while you make a sauce.

2. Sprinkle the breasts with salt and pepper to taste.
Heat 1 tablespoon butter in a heavy-bottomed skillet
measuring at least 9 inches across the bottom. Swirl
the skillet over high heat until the butter has melted.
Continue to heat until the butter stops foaming and
has just begun to color. Lay the duck breasts in the
skillet, skin side down.

3. Maintain medium-high heat, so the fat sizzles but
does not smoke, and sauté the breasts until the skin is
crisp and well browned, 8 to 10 minutes. If the skin
starts to brown too quickly, turn the heat down to
medium. Quickly drain all but 1 tablespoon of the fat
from the pan. Turn the breasts with tongs; cook on
other side until meat is medium-rare, 4 to 5 minutes.
Transfer the breasts to the plate in the oven; keep
warm until ready to serve.

4. Discard all but 1 tablespoon of the fat remaining
in the pan, being careful to leave the browned bits
behind. Add the garlic and shallot and sauté until
softened, 2 to 3 minutes. Add the mushrooms and
sauté, stirring frequently, until they begin to give up
their juices, 3 to 4 minutes. Increase the heat to high,
add the wine and stock, and scrape the skillet bottom
with a wooden spatula or spoon to loosen any
browned bits. Boil until the liquid reduces to about ⅓
cup, about 3 minutes. Add any accumulated juices
from the plate with duck breasts; reduce the sauce
again to ⅓ cup. Add the parsley and season with salt
and pepper to taste. Off the heat, swirl in the remaining tablespoon butter until it melts and thickens the
sauce. Remove the breasts from the oven, slice (see
page 413), and spoon the sauce over them; serve
immediately.

Braised Duck Breasts

SERVES 4

THE LIQUID USED TO BRAISE the
duck breasts becomes an abundant
sauce, wonderful poured over both
the meat and an accompaniment like
rice, couscous, or mashed potatoes. Use duck cracklings as a garnish, if desired.

2 whole boneless duck breasts, about
    12 ounces each, split and skin removed
    (see figure, page 420)
Salt and pepper
2 tablespoons butter
1 cup red wine
2 cups chicken stock or low-sodium
    canned broth

1. Preheat the oven to the lowest possible temperature. Place a plate in the oven for keeping the cooked
breasts warm while you finish the sauce.

2. Sprinkle the breasts with salt and pepper to taste.
Heat 1 tablespoon of butter in a large sauté pan over
high heat. When the butter stops foaming, add the
duck breasts and brown quickly, about 1 minute on
each side. Remove the breasts and set aside.

3. Increase the heat to high, add the wine, and scrape
the skillet bottom with a wooden spatula or spoon to
loosen any browned bits. Add the stock and bring to a

(continued on next page)

boil. Lower the heat and add the duck breasts; cook, uncovered, at a simmer for 5 minutes, turn, and cook another 5 to 6 minutes. Transfer the breasts to the plate in the oven.

4. Bring the cooking liquid to a boil and reduce to 1 cup. Off the heat, swirl in the remaining tablespoon of butter until it melts and thickens the sauce. Season with salt and pepper to taste. Remove the breasts from the oven, slice (see page 413), and spoon the liquid over them; serve immediately.

◆

Braised Duck Breasts with Olive Sauce

WE LIKE THE LOOK AND FLAVOR OF GREEN OLIVES WITH RED WINE, BUT BLACK OLIVES LIKE KALAMATA MAY BE SUBSTITUTED TO MAKE AN ATTRACTIVE DARK PURPLE SAUCE. **SERVES 4.**

> 2 whole boneless duck breasts, about 12 ounces each, split and skin removed (see figure)
> Salt and pepper
> 2 tablespoons butter
> 1 garlic clove, minced
> ½ cup green olives, pitted and coarsely chopped
> 1 cup red wine
> 2 cups chicken stock or low-sodium canned broth
> 1 tablespoon minced fresh parsley leaves

1. Preheat the oven to the lowest possible temperature. Place a plate in the oven for keeping the cooked breasts warm while you finish the sauce.

2. Sprinkle the breasts with salt and pepper. Heat 1 tablespoon of butter in a large sauté pan over high heat. When the butter stops foaming, add the duck breasts and brown quickly, about 1 minute on each side. Remove the breasts and set aside.

3. Turn the heat down to medium. Add the garlic and olives to the pan and sauté, stirring frequently, until the garlic just begins to color. Turn the heat back to high. Add the wine, and scrape the skillet bottom with a wooden spatula or spoon to loosen any browned bits. Add the stock and bring to a boil. Lower the heat and add the duck breasts; cook, uncovered, at a simmer for 5 minutes, turn, and cook another 5 to 6 minutes. Transfer the breasts to the plate in the oven.

4. Bring the cooking liquid to a boil and reduce to 1 cup. Stir in the parsley. Off the heat, swirl in the remaining tablespoon of butter until it melts and thickens the sauce. Season with salt and pepper to taste. Remove the breasts from the oven, slice (see page 413), and spoon the liquid over them; serve immediately.

STEP-BY-STEP

PREPARING A DUCK BREAST FOR BRAISING

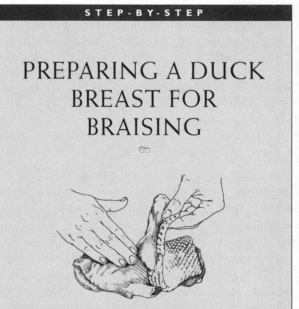

To braise duck breast, all the skin must be removed. Start by splitting the duck breast, as in figure 1 on page 413. Then, carefully remove the skin and fat by separating the membrane from the meat with your fingers. Discard the skin and fat or use to make cracklings.

Braised Duck Breasts with Prunes and Orange

THE PRUNES AND ORANGE JUICE GIVE THE BRAISING LIQUID A RICH, SYRUPY CONSISTENCY. SERVE OVER BUTTERED NOODLES. SERVES 4.

2 whole boneless duck breasts, about 12 ounces each, split and skin removed (see figure, opposite)
Salt and pepper
2 tablespoons butter
1 shallot, minced
1 garlic clove, minced
12 prunes, pitted and coarsely chopped
½ cup brandy
½ cup fresh orange juice
2 cups chicken stock or low-sodium canned broth
1 teaspoon minced fresh thyme leaves

1. Preheat the oven to the lowest possible temperature. Place a plate in the oven for keeping the cooked breasts warm while you finish the sauce.

2. Sprinkle the breasts with salt and pepper to taste. Heat 1 tablespoon of butter in a large sauté pan over high heat. When the butter stops foaming, add the duck breasts and brown quickly, about 1 minute on each side. Remove the breasts and set aside.

3. Turn the heat down to medium. Add the shallot and garlic to the pan and sauté, stirring frequently, until the garlic just begins to color. Turn the heat back to high. Add the prunes and brandy, and scrape the skillet bottom with a wooden spatula or spoon to loosen any browned bits. Add the juice and stock and bring to a boil. Lower the heat and add the duck breasts; cook, uncovered, at a simmer for 5 minutes, turn, and cook another 5 to 6 minutes. Transfer the breasts to the plate in the oven.

4. Bring the cooking liquid to a boil and reduce to 1 cup. Stir in the thyme. Off the heat, swirl in the remaining tablespoon of butter until it melts and thickens the sauce. Season with salt and pepper to taste. Remove the breasts from the oven, slice (see page 413), and spoon the liquid over them; serve immediately.

◆

Duck Cracklings

DUCK CRACKLINGS (SMALL PIECES OF CRISPED SKIN) MAKE A NICE GARNISH ON A PLATE OF BRAISED DUCK AND MASHED POTATOES MOISTENED BY THE BRAISING LIQUID. DUCK CRACKLINGS MAY BE MADE SEVERAL HOURS AHEAD OF TIME AND CRISPED IN A 350-DEGREE OVEN FOR 5 MINUTES BEFORE SERVING. IN OUR TESTING, WE FOUND THAT BAKING THE CRACKLINGS IN THE OVEN WAS MORE RELIABLE THAN SAUTEING IN THE SKILLET, WHERE BURNING WAS A CONSTANT THREAT. SERVES 4.

Skin and fat removed from 2 whole boneless duck breasts
Salt and pepper

Preheat the oven to 350 degrees. Slice the skin and fat lengthwise into ¼-inch-thick strips. Place in a shallow baking dish and bake, stirring 2 or 3 times, until the cracklings are crisp and golden, 25 to 30 minutes. Drain the cracklings on paper towels and sprinkle with salt and pepper to taste.

ROASTED
GOOSE

/|\

THOSE WHO HAVE NEVER COOKED A GOOSE ARE IN

FOR A TREAT. THE MEAT IS SURPRISINGLY FIRM,

ALMOST CHEWY TO THE BITE, YET IT IS ALSO MOIST

AND NOT AT ALL TOUGH OR STRINGY. BOTH THE

BREAST AND LEGS ARE DARK, IN THE MANNER OF

DUCK, BUT UNLIKE DUCK, GOOSE HAS NO GAMY OR

TALLOWY UNDERTONES. ACTUALLY, THE FIRST IMPRES-

SION OF MANY PEOPLE IS THAT GOOSE TASTES A LOT

like roast beef, and perhaps it is this rich, beefy quality that makes the bird so satisfying and festive.

Goose, however, does have a problem. Although the meat itself is not fatty, a very thick layer of fat lies just below the skin. As a consequence, the skin, which looks so tempting, often turns out to be too soft and greasy to eat. To make a good roast goose, it is imperative to rid the bird of this fat.

Most cookbooks and chefs suggest periodic basting with chicken stock or wine to dissolve the fat and promote a handsome brown color. But this method does not work. A considerable amount of subcutaneous fat always remains, and worse, the basting seriously softens the skin. We tried a variation on this technique. During the last hour of roasting, we turned the oven heat up to 450 degrees and stopped basting. We were hoping to get crispy skin, but what we actually got was a smoky kitchen. And to no purpose—the skin was still chewy and fatty.

Among all the goose-cooking methods we had read about, we were most intrigued by the steam-roasting and closed-cover techniques recommended by various authorities. Since the best way to render fat is to simmer it in water, steaming sounded like a promising procedure.

So we set a goose on a rack over an inch of water and steamed it on top of the stove in a covered roaster for about an hour. Then we poured the water out of the pan and put the goose into a 325-degree oven, covered. After one hour we checked on the goose, and seeing that the skin was very flabby and not in the least bit brown, we removed the cover of the pan and turned the heat up to 350 degrees. Alas, an hour later the skin was still soft and only a little browner. Even though the goose tested done at this point, we let it stay in the oven for another thirty minutes, but the skin did not improve.

Despite its shortcomings, this method melted out a good deal of the subcutaneous fat, so we decided to modify it and try again. This time we poured only a few cups of water into the pan, and we put the goose directly into the oven rather than starting it on top of the stove. Our plan was to roast the goose covered for about one and one half hours, and then uncover the pan, raise the oven heat, and roast for about one and one half hours longer. During the first phase, we reasoned, the goose would steam and the fat would melt; and during the second phase the dry heat of the oven would evaporate the juices in the pan and crisp the skin. Or so we hoped.

What actually happened was that we got a goose much like the first, with unsatisfactorily soft, pale skin. And in tasting the goose, we realized that there was yet another problem: steaming had perhaps made the meat a tad juicier, but it had also made the texture a little rubbery and imparted a boiled, stewish flavor. The goose no longer tasted the way we thought goose should. So we abandoned steaming.

Since liquid basting and steaming had both proved unsuccessful, we thought it was time to try a simple dry roast. Some of the geese that we had bought came with instructions to roast at 500 degrees for thirty minutes and then to turn the oven down to 300 degrees and roast several hours longer. The directions said to cover the pan during the second phase of roasting, but having had poor results with covered cooking, we decided to ignore that recommendation and roast uncovered throughout. We stuffed the goose, dried and pricked the skin, and popped it into the scorching oven. As we should have guessed, within fifteen minutes the goose had begun to drip, and the kitchen had filled with smoke. We quickly turned the oven thermostat down and let the bird roast until it tested done, about three hours. Then we increased the oven temperature to 400 degrees, transferred the goose to a large jelly-roll pan, and returned it to the oven for about fifteen minutes to brown and crisp the skin. The results surprised us. This method, the simplest of all, yielded a beautifully brown, crisp-skinned bird, with moist meat and surprisingly little unmelted fat.

Dry, open roasting looked like the way to proceed, but we wondered if the technique could be further improved. We thought about adapting a classic technique often used with duck. The duck is immersed in boiling water for one minute and then allowed to dry, uncovered, in the refrigerator for twenty-four hours. The boiling and drying were supposed to tighten the skin, so that during roasting, the fat would be squeezed out. We tried the method with duck and found it highly effective, so we were emboldened to roast a goose using the same procedure. We loved the results. The skin was papery-crisp and defatted to the point where it could be eaten with pleasure—and without guilt.

As it happened, we wanted to do a bit more work on the stuffing, and we also needed to refine our recommendations with respect to timing and doneness. So we had to roast another goose. We boiled the bird and put it in the refrigerator, planning to roast it the next day, but something came up that prevented us from cooking it until the day after. The delay proved to be a lucky happenstance. Dried for a full two days, the goose was even crisper and less greasy than the one dried for twenty-four hours. It was perfect.

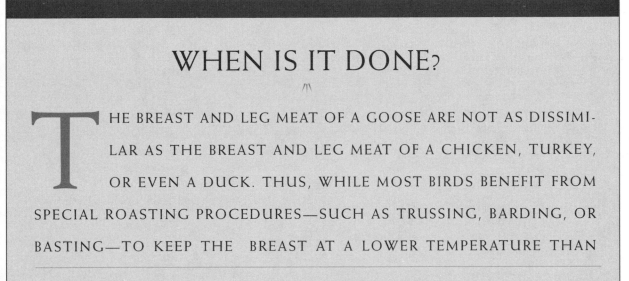

WHEN IS IT DONE?

THE BREAST AND LEG MEAT OF A GOOSE ARE NOT AS DISSIMILAR AS THE BREAST AND LEG MEAT OF A CHICKEN, TURKEY, OR EVEN A DUCK. THUS, WHILE MOST BIRDS BENEFIT FROM SPECIAL ROASTING PROCEDURES—SUCH AS TRUSSING, BARDING, OR BASTING—TO KEEP THE BREAST AT A LOWER TEMPERATURE THAN

the legs and to prevent it from drying out, a goose can simply be put in the oven and left alone except for turning it over at the halfway mark to ensure even cooking.

Unlike these other birds, the doneness of goose cannot be judged solely by the internal temperature of the meat. The length of the cooking time is also an important factor. Goose generally reaches an internal temperature of 170 degrees in the thigh cavity (the usual indicator of well done) after less than two hours of roasting. Yet the meat turns out to be tough, especially around the thighs, if the bird is removed from the oven at this point. At least forty-five minutes of additional roasting are required. The most reliable indicator of doneness, is the feel of the drumsticks. When the skin has puffed and the meat

inside feels soft and almost shredded when pressed—like well-done stew meat—the rest of the bird should be just right.

Another good way to test for doneness is to make a small slit in the skin at the base of the thigh, where it joins the body. If the juices are pinkish rather than clear, the bird needs more cooking. If, on the other hand, there are no juices, the goose has been cooked enough and may even be verging on overdone. Don't panic though. One of the nicest things about goose is that it is tolerant of a little overcooking and does not readily dry out and turn stringy. This is because the particular proteins in goose tend to turn soft and gelatinous during cooking, so goose remains moist and tender even when thoroughly cooked.

PREPARING AND STUFFING A GOOSE

1. Use tweezers or small pliers to remove any remaining quills from the goose skin.

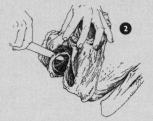

2. Pull back the skin at the neck end and locate the wishbone. Scrape along the outside of the wishbone with a paring knife until the bone is exposed; then cut the bone free of the flesh.

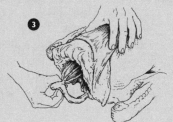

3. Pull down on the wishbone, freeing it from the carcass; add the bone to the stockpot.

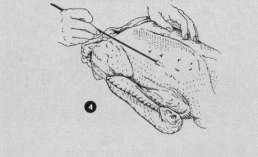

4. With a trussing needle or thin skewer, prick the goose skin all over, especially around the breast and thighs, holding the needle nearly parallel to the bird to avoid pricking the meat. Pricking the skin helps render the fat during cooking.

5. Using rubber gloves to protect your hands from possible splashes of boiling water, lower the goose, neck end down, into the water, submerging as much of the goose as possible until "goose bumps" appear, about 1 minute. Repeat this process, submerging the goose tail end down.

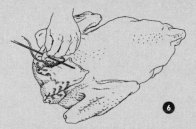

6. Pack a small handful of stuffing into the neck cavity; sew the opening shut with a trussing needle and heavy white twine.

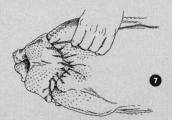

7. Pack the remaining stuffing in the body cavity, pressing it in firmly with your hands or a large spoon; sew the body vent shut.

Roasted Goose

SERVES 8 TO 10

WE USED BOTH FRESH and frozen geese in testing and found no difference in the final result. This is fortunate, as most geese come to the market frozen, even at holiday time. To thaw, simply leave the goose in the refrigerator for 24 hours or more. Turning the goose in the boiling water may not be necessary if you have a stockpot large enough for the goose to be fully submerged. To make sure there is plenty of meat to go around, make up the plates in the kitchen rather than passing platters at the table. Mound a big spoonful of stuffing on the plate and bank three to four slices of meat against it. Moisten both stuffing and meat with gravy, and lay a strip or two of skin over the top.

1 roasting goose (10 to 12 pounds gross weight), neck, giblets, wing tips, and excess fat removed, rinsed, patted dry, and reserved; wishbone removed and skin pricked all over (see figures 1–4, opposite)
1 recipe Prune and Apple Stuffing (page 428) or Pork and Chestnut Stuffing (page 429), warmed
Salt and pepper
1 recipe Red Wine Giblet Gravy or Plum and Port Gravy (page 430)

1. Fill a large stockpot two-thirds of the way with water and bring to a rolling boil. Following figure 5 (opposite), submerge the goose in boiling water for about 2 minutes total. Drain the goose and dry thoroughly, inside and out, with paper towels. Set the goose, breast side up, on a rack in a roasting pan and refrigerate, uncovered, for 24 to 48 hours.

2. Adjust the oven rack to the low-center position and heat oven to 325 degrees. Following figures 6 and 7 (opposite), stuff and truss goose. Season the goose skin liberally with salt and pepper.

3. Place the goose, breast down, on a heavy-duty wire rack set over a deep roasting pan; roast for 1½ hours. Remove the goose from the oven and bail out most of the fat from the roasting pan, being careful not to disturb the browned bits at the bottom. Turn the goose breast up, and return to the oven to roast until the flesh of the drumsticks feels soft and broken up (like well-done stew meat) and the skin has puffed up around the breast bone and tops of thighs, from 1¼ to 1½ hours longer. Increase the oven temperature to 400 degrees; transfer the goose, still on its rack, to a large jelly-roll pan. Return to the oven to further brown and fully crisp the skin, about 15 minutes longer. Let stand, uncovered, about ½ hour before carving.

4. Remove the trussing, and spoon the stuffing into a serving bowl. Carve the goose following the instructions on page 18. Serve the stuffing and carved goose immediately; pass the gravy separately.

Brown Goose Stock

THE GOOSE STOCK CAN BE COOLED TO ROOM TEMPER-
ATURE AND REFRIGERATED IN AN AIRTIGHT CONTAINER
FOR UP TO 3 DAYS. MAKES ABOUT 1 1/2 CUPS.

- 3 tablespoons goose fat, patted dry and
  chopped
- Goose neck and wing tips, cut into 1-inch
  pieces; heart and gizzard left whole, all
  parts patted dry
- 1 medium onion, peeled and chopped
- 1 medium carrot, peeled and chopped
- 1 medium celery stalk, chopped
- 2 teaspoons sugar
- 2 cups full-bodied red wine
- 1/2 cup chicken stock or low-salt canned
  chicken broth
- 6 large fresh parsley stems
- 1 large bay leaf
- 1 teaspoon black peppercorns
- 1/2 teaspoon dried thyme

1. Heat the fat over medium heat in a large saucepan until it melts, leaving small browned bits. Increase the heat to medium-high; heat the fat until it just begins to smoke. Add the goose pieces and giblets to the fat; sauté, stirring frequently, until the meat turns a deep mahogany color, about 10 minutes.

2. Add the onion, carrot, and celery; sauté, stirring frequently, until the vegetables brown around the edges, about 10 minutes longer. Stir in the sugar; continue to cook, stirring continuously, until the sugar caramelizes and begins to smoke. Pour in the wine, scraping the pan bottom with a wooden spoon to dissolve any browned bits.

3. Add the chicken stock, parsley, bay leaf, peppercorns, and thyme. Bring to a simmer, then adjust the heat so that the liquid barely bubbles. Simmer, partially covered, until the stock is dark and rich, about 2 hours, adding a little water if the solids become exposed.

Prune and Apple Stuffing

THIS STUFFING CAN BE COVERED AND REFRIGERATED A
DAY AHEAD. MAKES ABOUT 8 CUPS.

- 6 ounces (about 1 cup) pitted prunes, cut
  into 1/2-inch pieces
- 1/3 cup sweet sherry (cream or amontillado)
- 8 ounces homemade-style white bread,
  cut into 1/2-inch cubes (about 4 cups
  lightly packed)
- 1/3 cup reserved goose fat, patted dry and
  chopped
- 3 medium onions, finely chopped (about
  3 cups)
- 3 medium celery stalks, finely chopped
  (about 1 1/2 cups)
- 3 medium-large Granny Smith apples, peeled
  and cut into 1/2-inch chunks (about 3 cups)
- 6 ounces Black Forest ham, minced (about
  1 cup)
- 2 tablespoons minced fresh sage or
  1 1/2 teaspoons rubbed dried sage
- Salt and pepper
- 1/4 teaspoon ground cloves
- 1/4 teaspoon grated nutmeg or ground mace

1. Soak the prunes in the sherry in a small bowl for at least 2 hours, preferably overnight.

2. Heat the oven to 400 degrees. Spread the bread cubes over a large baking sheet; bake, stirring occasionally, until the cubes are lightly toasted but still soft inside, about 10 minutes.

3. Heat the fat in a 12-inch skillet over medium heat until it melts, leaving small browned bits. Leaving 2 tablespoons fat in the skillet, remove and set aside the remaining fat. Increase the heat to medium-high. Add the onions and celery; sauté until the vegetables soften, 5 to 7 minutes. Scrape the vegetables into a large mixing bowl.

4. Return the skillet to the burner; heat 2 tablespoons of the reserved fat. Add the apples; sauté until golden and soft but not mushy, 5 to 7 minutes. Add the apples to the onions and celery. Stir in the ham, sage, 1 tea-

THE SHAPE OF THE GOOSE

/\

THOUGH DRESSED GEESE CAN WEIGH AS MUCH AS 14 POUNDS, WEIGHTS OVER 12 POUNDS ARE RARE IN AMERICAN MARKETS. IN ANY CASE, IT HAS BEEN OUR EXPERIENCE THAT HEAVIER GEESE GAIN MUCH MORE IN FAT AND BONE THAN THEY DO IN MEAT. FURTHERMORE, THE BREAST MEAT OF LARGE GEESE

tends to be coarse and not very appealing.

Geese vary considerably in shape, some being long and slim, with thighs that protrude above the breast bone, and others being wide and squat, with thighs tucked along the body. We expected the long ones to have less breast meat, but this proved not to be the case. Nor did shape seem to appreciably affect cooking times. According to the man at our market, there is no rhyme or reason to the differences in shape. Geese simply vary.

spoon each salt and pepper or to taste, the cloves, nutmeg, the prunes, unabsorbed sherry, and bread cubes. Turn the mixture into a 13-by-9-inch or comparably sized microwave-safe pan and heat in a 325-degree oven or microwave until stuffing is warmed through before packing it into the goose.

◆

Pork and Chestnut Stuffing

GRINDING YOUR OWN PORK MAKES FOR A LESS FATTY STUFFING—WHICH IS ESPECIALLY IMPORTANT BECAUSE THE GOOSE WILL SATURATE THE STUFFING WITH ITS OWN FAT. THIS STUFFING CAN BE MADE A DAY IN ADVANCE AND REHEATED BEFORE PACKING IT INTO THE GOOSE. MAKES ABOUT 8 CUPS.

1½ pounds boneless pork chops, trimmed
    and cut into ½-inch chunks
2 tablespoons olive oil
1 fresh rosemary sprig
2 medium onions, finely chopped
2 garlic cloves, finely chopped
1 cup dry white wine
¾ pound breakfast sausage links
2 16-ounce cans chestnuts, drained and
    coarsely chopped
¼ cup finely chopped fresh parsley leaves
Salt and pepper

1. Place half the pork cubes in the work bowl of a food processor and process until coarsely chopped. Scrape into a bowl and repeat with the remaining pork.

2. Heat the olive oil and rosemary in a large skillet over medium-high heat. Add the chopped pork and cook, stirring to break up the big chunks, until the meat loses its raw color, 7 to 10 minutes. Stir in the onions and garlic and cook until the onions begin to soften, about 10 minutes. Add the wine and cook, stirring occasionally, until the liquid is evaporated, another 10 minutes.

(continued on next page)

3. Meanwhile, heat a skillet over medium-high and cook the sausage links until browned on all sides, about 15 minutes. Drain on paper towels, cool, and cut into ½-inch-thick rounds.

4. Combine the cooked pork, sausages, chestnuts, and parsley in a large bowl. Season with salt and pepper to taste. Turn the mixture into a 13-by-9-inch or comparably sized microwave-safe pan and heat in a 325-degree oven or microwave until stuffing is warmed through before packing it into the goose.

◆

Red Wine Giblet Gravy

THIS SIMPLE GRAVY STARTS WITH THE GOOSE STOCK AND THEN USES SHERRY TO DEGLAZE THE ROASTING PAN WITH THE BROWNED BITS FROM THE GOOSE. THIS GRAVY WORKS BEST WITH THE SWEET PRUNE AND APPLE STUFFING (PAGE 428). **MAKES ABOUT 2 CUPS.**

> 1 recipe Brown Goose Stock (page 428)
> ½ cup sweet sherry (cream or amontillado)
> ½ cup chicken stock or low-salt canned
>   broth, if needed
> 2½ tablespoons melted goose fat from
>   the roasting pan
> 2½ tablespoons all-purpose flour
> 1 goose liver, cut into small dice
> Salt and pepper

1. Bring the reserved goose stock to a simmer. Spoon most of the fat out of the roasting pan, leaving behind all the brown roasting particles. Set the pan over 2 burners on low heat. Add the sherry; scrape with a wooden spoon until all of the brown glaze in the pan is dissolved. Pour the mixture into the goose stock and simmer to blend flavors, about 5 minutes.

2. Strain the mixture into a 4-cup glass measure, pressing down on the solids with the back of a spoon; let the liquid stand until the fat rises to the top. Skim the fat, and if necessary add enough chicken stock to make up to 2 cups. Rinse out the goose stockpot and return the strained stock to it. Take the gizzard and heart from the strainer, cut into tiny dice, and add to the goose stock. Return the stock to a boil.

3. Heat the goose fat and flour over medium-low heat in a heavy-bottomed medium saucepan, stirring constantly with a wooden spoon until the roux just begins to color, about 5 minutes; remove from heat. Beating constantly with a whisk, pour the boiling stock, all at once, into the brown roux. Return the saucepan to low heat; simmer 3 minutes. Add the liver; simmer 1 minute longer. Taste, and adjust seasoning, adding salt and lots of fresh black pepper.

◆

Plum and Port Gravy

THIS GRAVY'S SWEETNESS COMPLEMENTS THE GAMY FLAVOR OF GOOSE AND IS A GOOD MATCH FOR SAVORY PORK AND CHESTNUT STUFFING (PAGE 429). HERE, PORT IS USED TO DEGLAZE THE ROASTING PAN AND PLUM PRESERVES ARE ADDED TO THE GRAVY FOR BODY, COLOR, AND SWEETNESS. **MAKES ABOUT 1 ½ CUPS.**

> 1 recipe Brown Goose Stock (page 428)
> ½ cup port
> ½ cup chicken stock or low-salt canned
>   broth, if needed
> ½ cup plum preserves
> Salt and pepper
> 2 tablespoons butter

1. Bring the reserved goose stock to a simmer. Spoon most of the fat out of the roasting pan, leaving behind all the brown roasting particles. Set the pan over 2 burners on low heat. Add the port; scrape with a wooden spoon until all of the brown glaze in the pan is dissolved. Pour the mixture into the goose stock; simmer to blend flavors, about 5 minutes.

2. Strain the mixture into a 4-cup glass measure, pressing down on the solids with the back of a spoon; let the liquid stand until the fat rises to the top. Skim the fat, and if necessary add enough chicken stock to make up to 2 cups. Rinse out the goose stockpot and return the strained stock to it. Add the preserves. Return the stock to a boil; lower the heat to medium and reduce to 1½ cups, about 15 minutes.

3. Taste and adjust seasoning. Remove from heat and swirl in butter.

QUAIL

/I\

THESE TINY BIRDS HAVE A RICH FLAVOR THAT IS MEATY

BUT NOT GAMY. THE MEAT ON THE BREAST AS WELL AS

THE LEGS IS UNIFORMLY THE COLOR OF DARK-MEAT

CHICKEN WHEN COOKED. ALTHOUGH BOBWHITE

QUAIL ARE NATIVE TO THIS COUNTRY (THAT'S WHAT

HUNTERS SHOOT), MOST COMMERCIAL OPERATIONS

RAISE AN ASIAN VARIETY CALLED CORTURNIX. THEY

RANGE IN SIZE FROM 4 TO 6 OUNCES EACH, DEPEND-

ING ON THE FARM AND AGE AT SLAUGHTER. WE PREFER

larger quail, at least 5 ounces, since they are less bony and easier to eat. Like most game birds, quail are expensive, usually $3 or $4 per bird, with two birds needed for each serving.

Once you get the quail home, you may need to remove the feet and pluck out a few remaining feathers. A thorough rinsing and drying with paper towels is also required. In our testing, we found that quail take well to high-heat cooking methods. Whether grilling, roasting, sautéing, or braising, you want to cook them fairly quickly to crisp the skin and protect the delicate meat from becoming dry. Because they are so small, quail do not take well to slow cooking. By the time the skin has browned, the meat has lost too much moisture.

We tried boning the quail and found that they are too small for this less-than-delicate operation. Besides, quail taste better when cooked on the bone. Eating quail can be a bit messy, making this activity better suited to the home than in a restaurant, where struggling with tiny bones might seem like a chore.

When grilling or sautéing, we found it best to split the birds along the backbone so that the bird can lie flat on the grill in the pan. When braising or roasting the birds, we like to tie the legs together with kitchen twine to keep them from splaying to the sides. Tying the legs against the breast also helps shield it from overcooking.

All four cooking methods deliver excellent, if somewhat different, results. Braising ensures juicy birds along with enough sauce for accompanying starch. Although an initial browning develops flavor, the skin is not very crisp, especially compared to other cooking methods. Roasting at a high temperature produces a browned skin (at lower temperatures the meat cooks through before the skin becomes crisp) and does not require much attention during cooking. Grilling and sautéing result in the crispest skin and shortest cooking times.

With all four cooking methods, we find that cooking the meat until slightly pink is best. The meat is juicier and more flavorful than when the meat is cooked through like chicken or turkey. Although it is hard to measure the temperature in the tiny thighs or breasts on these birds, we found that an internal temperature of 140 to 145 degrees was ideal. Of course, if

you prefer, you may cook quail until all signs of pinkness are gone. Add a few extra minutes to the cooking times in the recipes that follow in order to boost the internal temperature to 160 or 165 degrees. In any case, never cook quail as thoroughly as chicken or turkey. A temperature of 180 degrees will produce an expensive culinary disaster.

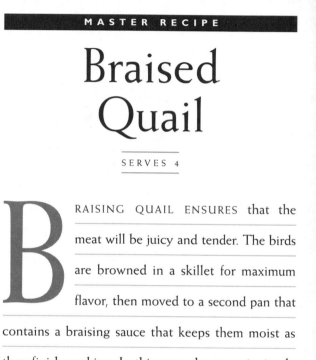

MASTER RECIPE

Braised Quail

SERVES 4

BRAISING QUAIL ENSURES that the meat will be juicy and tender. The birds are browned in a skillet for maximum flavor, then moved to a second pan that contains a braising sauce that keeps them moist as they finish cooking. In this case, the sauce is simply white wine and chicken stock.

>   3 tablespoons olive oil
>   4 tablespoons butter
>   1 medium onion, minced
>   1 cup dry white wine
>   1 cup chicken stock or low-sodium
>   canned broth
>   8 whole quail (about 5 ounces each),
>   rinsed and patted dry
>   Salt and pepper
>   2 tablespoons minced fresh parsley leaves

1. Heat 1 tablespoon oil and 1 tablespoon butter in a large skillet. Add the onion and cook until softened, about 5 minutes. Add the wine and stock; bring to a boil and reduce until slightly thickened, 5 to 7 minutes. Cover the pan to keep the sauce warm.

2. Tie the legs of each quail together with kitchen twine (see figure). Sprinkle each quail liberally with salt and pepper. Heat the remaining 2 tablespoons oil and 2 tablespoons butter in another large skillet. Cook the quail in batches over high heat until browned on all sides, about 6 minutes total. Transfer the browned quail to the pan with the sauce; bring to a simmer, cover, and cook the quail until the juices run clear when the thighs are pierced with a fork, about 7 minutes.

3. Remove the pan from the heat. Transfer the cooked quail to a platter and cover with foil to keep warm. Swirl in the remaining tablespoon of butter and the parsley. Season with salt and pepper to taste.

4. Remove and discard the string from each quail. Place 2 quail on each of 4 dinner plates, spoon some sauce over the quail, and serve immediately.

STEP-BY-STEP

PREPARING QUAIL FOR BRAISING AND ROASTING

Pull the legs back over the breast and use a 10-inch length of kitchen twine to tie the legs together on each quail. This helps keep the quail from losing its shape as it cooks and also helps protect the delicate breast meat.

Braised Quail with Figs

THE SAUCE IN THIS RECIPE CONSISTS OF FIGS AND GAR-LIC ALONG WITH WHITE WINE, CHICKEN STOCK, AND SHERRY VINEGAR. TO SOFTEN DRIED FIGS, PLACE THEM IN A HEATPROOF BOWL, COVER WITH BOILING WATER, AND LET STAND FOR 15 MINUTES. DRAIN AND PAT THE FIGS DRY WITH PAPER TOWELS, CUT OFF THE TOUGH STEMS, AND THEN CUT THEM IN HALF FROM TOP TO BOTTOM. WE LIKE THIS SWEET AND SAVORY DISH OVER BUTTERED COUSCOUS. SERVES 4.

> 3 tablespoons olive oil
> 4 tablespoons butter
> 16 dried figs, rehydrated, stemmed, and halved (see above)
> 2 medium garlic cloves, minced
> 1 cup dry white wine
> 1 cup chicken stock or low-sodium canned broth
> ¼ cup sherry vinegar
> 2 tablespoons sugar
> 8 whole quail (about 5 ounces each), rinsed and patted dry
> Salt and pepper
> 2 tablespoons minced fresh parsley leaves

1. Heat 1 tablespoon oil and 1 tablespoon butter in a large skillet. Add the figs and cook over medium heat until lightly browned, 1 minute. Add the garlic and cook until softened, about 2 minutes. Add the wine, stock, vinegar, and sugar; bring to a boil and reduce until slightly thickened, 5 to 7 minutes. Cover the pan to keep the sauce warm.

2. Tie the legs of each quail together with kitchen twine. Sprinkle each quail liberally with salt and pepper. Heat the remaining 2 tablespoons oil and 2 tablespoons butter in another large skillet. Cook the quail in batches over high heat until browned on all sides, about 6 minutes total. Transfer the browned quail to the pan with the sauce; bring to a simmer, cover, and cook the quail until the juices run clear when the thighs are pierced with a fork, about 7 minutes.

(continued on next page)

3. Remove the pan from the heat. Transfer the cooked quail to a platter and cover with foil to keep warm. Swirl in the remaining tablespoon of butter and the parsley. Season with salt and pepper to taste.

4. Remove and discard the string from each quail. Place 2 quail on each of 4 dinner plates, spoon some sauce over the quail, and serve immediately.

◆

Braised Quail with Mushroom Sauce

A HEARTY TOMATO AND MUSHROOM SAUCE PROVIDES AN EXCELLENT FOIL TO THE DELICATE QUAIL MEAT. IF YOU LIKE, USE CREMINI MUSHROOMS, ALTHOUGH REGULAR BUTTON MUSHROOMS WILL BE FINE AS WELL. SERVE THE QUAIL AND SAUCE OVER STEAMED RICE OR BUTTERED NOODLES. **SERVES 4.**

3 tablespoons olive oil
5 tablespoons butter
4 ounces mushrooms, stem ends trimmed and coarsely chopped (about 2 cups)
1 shallot, finely chopped
6 small plum tomatoes (about 1 pound), peeled, seeded, and coarsely chopped
1 cup dry white wine
1 cup chicken stock or low-sodium canned broth
8 whole quail (about 5 ounces each), rinsed and patted dry
Salt and pepper
2 tablespoons minced fresh tarragon leaves

1. Heat 2 tablespoons oil and 2 tablespoons butter in a large skillet. Add the mushrooms and cook over medium-high heat until lightly browned, 3 to 4 minutes. Add the shallot and cook until softened, 2 to 3 minutes. Add the tomatoes and simmer until they release their juices, about 5 minutes. Add the wine and stock; bring to a boil and reduce until slightly thickened, 5 to 7 minutes. Turn off the heat and cover the pan to keep the sauce warm.

2. Tie the legs of each quail together with kitchen twine. Sprinkle each quail liberally with salt and pepper. Heat the remaining 2 tablespoons oil and 2 tablespoons butter in another large skillet. Cook the quail in batches over high heat until browned on all sides, about 6 minutes total. Transfer the browned quail to the pan with the sauce; bring to a simmer, cover, and cook the quail until the juices run clear when the thighs are pierced with a fork, about 7 minutes.

3. Remove the pan from the heat. Transfer the cooked quail to a platter and cover with foil to keep warm. Swirl in the remaining tablespoon of butter and the tarragon. Season with salt and pepper to taste.

4. Remove and discard the string from each quail. Place 2 quail on each of four dinner plates, spoon some sauce over the quail, and serve immediately.

Roasted Quail

SERVES 4

IN ORDER TO KEEP the quail moist but give them a well-browned skin, the oven temperature is turned up to 500 degrees during the last 10 minutes of roasting. Serve with a pilaf of brown and wild rice.

2 tablespoons butter
1 teaspoon chopped fresh thyme leaves
8 whole quail (about 5 ounces each), rinsed and patted dry
Salt and pepper
½ cup white wine

1. Place a shallow roasting pan in the oven and preheat to 425 degrees. Melt the butter and combine with the thyme. Sprinkle each quail liberally with salt and pepper. Brush with melted butter inside and out. Tie the legs of each bird together with kitchen twine (see figure on page 433).

2. Remove the hot roasting pan and add the quail, breast side down. Roast 15 minutes, turn the quail breast side up, and baste with the pan juices. Turn the oven up to 500 degrees. Roast until the juices run clear when the thighs are pierced with a fork, 8 to 10 minutes more.

3. Transfer the cooked quail to a platter. Cover with foil to keep warm. Add the wine to the roasting pan. Bring the liquid to a boil on the stovetop, scraping the pan bottom with a wooden spatula or spoon to loosen any browned bits. Boil until the sauce thickens, about 3 minutes. Season with salt and pepper to taste. Place 2 quail on each of 4 dinner plates. Spoon some sauce over the quail and serve immediately.

◆

Roasted Quail with Shiitakes and Port Sauce

THE QUAIL ARE BRUSHED WITH A PORT REDUCTION BEFORE GOING INTO THE OVEN, FOR COLOR AND FLAVOR. THE QUAIL ARE ROASTED WITH MUSHROOMS, WHICH BECOME A VEGETABLE ACCOMPANIMENT TO THE BIRDS. SERVE WITH A PILAF OF BROWN AND WILD RICE. SERVES 4.

    1 cup port
    6 fresh thyme sprigs
    3 tablespoons butter
    8 ounces shiitake mushrooms, stems
        discarded and caps sliced thin
    1 teaspoon chopped fresh thyme leaves
    Salt and pepper
    8 whole quail (about 5 ounces each),
        rinsed and patted dry

1. Place a shallow roasting pan in the oven and preheat to 425 degrees. Meanwhile, bring the port and thyme sprigs to a boil in a small saucepan and reduce to ½ cup. Remove the pan from the heat and stir in 2 tablespoons butter. Strain the mixture into a small bowl and discard the thyme sprigs.

2. Melt the remaining tablespoon butter and toss with the mushrooms, chopped thyme, and salt and pepper to taste. Sprinkle each quail liberally with salt and pepper. Brush with half the port sauce inside and out; reserve the remainder. Tie the legs of each bird together with kitchen twine.

3. Remove the hot roasting pan from the oven and scatter the mushroom mixture across the bottom of the pan. Place the quail on top of the mushrooms, breast side down. Roast 15 minutes, turn the quail breast side up, and baste with the pan juices. Turn the oven up to 500 degrees. Roast until the juices run clear when the thighs are pierced with a fork, 8 to 10 minutes more.

4. Transfer the cooked quail to a platter. Cover with foil to keep warm. Add the remaining port glaze to the roasting pan. Bring the liquid to a boil on the stovetop, scraping the pan bottom with a wooden spatula or spoon to loosen the mushrooms and browned bits. Boil until the sauce thickens, about 3 minutes. Season with salt and pepper to taste. Place 2 quail on each of 4 dinner plates. Spoon some mushroom and port sauce over the quail and serve immediately.

Roasted Quail with Spinach and Pine Nut Stuffing

USE FROZEN SPINACH HERE TO SAVE WORK. TOAST THE PINE NUTS ON A BAKING SHEET IN A 375-DEGREE OVEN UNTIL GOLDEN, ABOUT 5 MINUTES. TO PREVENT SMOKING DURING THE FINAL HIGH HEAT COOKING, COOK THE STUFFED QUAIL ON A RACK AND ADD WATER TO THE BOTTOM OF THE ROASTING PAN. SERVES 4.

½ cup balsamic vinegar
2 tablespoons butter
½ cup raisins
2 tablespoons olive oil
2 shallots, minced
1 10-ounce package frozen chopped spinach, thawed and squeezed to remove excess water (see figure on page 264)
½ cup pine nuts, toasted
Salt and pepper
8 whole quail (about 5 ounces each), rinsed and patted dry

1. Preheat the oven to 425 degrees. Bring the vinegar to a boil in a small saucepan and reduce to ¼ cup. Remove from heat and stir in the butter. Set aside.

2. Combine the raisins and ¼ cup water in a small saucepan and bring to a boil. Cover, remove from heat, and let steep for 10 minutes to plump the raisins. Drain and set aside.

3. Heat the olive oil in a medium skillet. Add the shallots and cook over medium heat until softened, 2 to 3 minutes. Add the spinach, pine nuts, and raisins. Season with salt and pepper to taste. Cool the stuffing to room temperature.

4. Place a shallow roasting pan in the hot oven for 10 minutes. Sprinkle each quail liberally with salt and pepper. Brush with the vinegar glaze. Fill each cavity with 2 tablespoons of the spinach mixture. Tie the legs of each bird together with kitchen twine.

5. Remove the hot roasting pan from the oven. Place the quail, breast side down, on a rack in the pan. Roast 15 minutes, turn the quail breast side up, and baste with the pan juices. Add ½ cup water to the bottom of the roasting pan to prevent smoking. Turn the oven up to 500 degrees. Roast until the juices run clear when the thighs are pierced with a fork, 8 to 10 minutes more. Serve immediately.

MASTER RECIPE

Grilled Quail

SERVES 4

THE TINY WING TIPS of quail tend to burn on the grill, so it's best to clip them off before cooking. It is important to oil the grill rack before placing the birds on the grill; use a pair of tongs to rub a wad of paper towels that have been dipped in oil over the hot grate. Cook the quail over a medium-hot fire, taking care to douse any flames with a squirt bottle and/or move the quail to a cooler part of the grill if flare-ups occur.

8 whole quail (about 5 ounces each), rinsed and patted dry; wing tips removed, butterflied (see figures 1–3, page 438)
2 tablespoons extra-virgin olive oil
Salt and pepper

1. Prepare the fire for grilling (see figures 1–4, page 156). Oil the grill rack (see page 438). Brush the quail with oil and sprinkle with salt and pepper to taste.

2. Place the quail on the grill skin side down. Cook over a medium-hot fire until well browned, 5 to 7 minutes. Turn and cook the quail until the juices run clear when the thighs are pierced with a fork, about 5 minutes. Serve immediately.

◆

Grilled Quail
with Molasses Glaze

MOLASSES GIVES THESE GRILLED QUAIL A GREAT FLA-VOR AND SHEEN. WATCH THE BIRDS CAREFULLY TO MAKE SURE THE SUGARY MARINADE DOESN'T BURN. SERVE THESE BIRDS WITH POTATO SALAD OR PERHAPS SWEET POTATO FRIES. SERVES 4.

    ¼ cup vegetable oil
    Grated zest of 1 orange
    ¾ cup fresh orange juice
    ¼ cup molasses
    2 teaspoons juniper berries, crushed with
        the back of a chef's knife
    1 teaspoon hot red pepper flakes
    3 medium garlic cloves, finely chopped
    1½ teaspoons salt
    8 whole quail (about 5 ounces each),
        rinsed and patted dry; wing tips
        removed, butterflied (see figures 1–3,
        page 438)

1. Combine the oil, zest and juice, molasses, juniper berries, red pepper flakes, garlic, and salt in a medium bowl. Divide the quail between 2 large sealable plastic bags and pour half the marinade into each bag. Refrigerate for 3 hours, turning once or twice.

2. Prepare the fire for grilling (see figures 1–4, page 156). Oil the grill rack. Remove the quail from the marinade and place them on the grill skin side down. Cook over medium-hot fire until well browned, 5 to 7 minutes. Turn and cook the quail until the juices run clear when the thighs are pierced with a fork, about 5 minutes.

Grilled Quail
with Asian Flavors

BECAUSE THEY ARE SO SMALL, QUAIL CAN BENEFIT FROM SOAKING IN A POTENT MARINADE. HERE, A COMBINATION OF ASIAN SESAME OIL, LIME JUICE AND ZEST, HONEY, GAR-LIC, GINGER, AND FISH SAUCE IS USED. THE LEFTOVER MARINADE CAN BE BOILED FOR A FEW MINUTES UNTIL SLIGHTLY THICKENED, AND THEN USED AS A SAUCE FOR ACCOMPANYING RICE OR ASIAN NOODLES. SERVES 4.

    2 tablespoons Asian sesame oil
    2 tablespoons peanut oil
    Grated zest of 2 limes
    ½ cup fresh lime juice
    ½ cup honey
    ½ cup Thai fish sauce
    2 medium garlic cloves, minced
    1 1-inch piece fresh gingerroot, peeled
        and minced
    8 whole quail (about 5 ounces each),
        rinsed and patted dry; wing tips
        removed, butterflied (see figures 1–3,
        page 438)

1. Combine the oils, lime zest and juice, honey, fish sauce, garlic, and ginger in a medium bowl. Divide the quail between 2 large sealable plastic bags and pour half the marinade into each bag. Refrigerate for 3 hours, turning once or twice.

2. Prepare the fire for grilling (see figures 1–4, page 156). Oil the grill rack. Remove the quail from the marinade and place them on the grill skin side down. Cook over a medium-hot fire until well browned, 5 to 7 minutes. Turn and cook the quail until the juices run clear when the thighs are pierced with a fork, about 5 minutes. Serve immediately.

PREPARING QUAIL FOR GRILLING AND SAUTEING

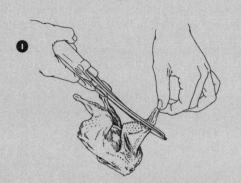

1. The tiny wing tips will singe on the grill or in a hot skillet. Use poultry scissors or a chef's knife to remove the tip from each wing.

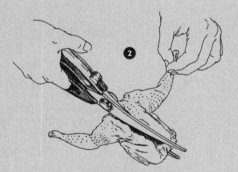

2. Butterflied quail will cook more evenly when grilled or sautéed. To butterfly quail, insert a poultry or kitchen shears inside the cavity and cut along one side of the backbone. The backbone is so small, there is no need to cut along the other side of the bone to remove it, as is necessary for a chicken.

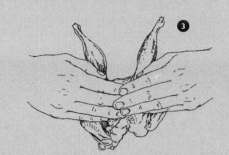

3. Turn the butterflied bird skin side up and flatten it by pressing down with your hands.

KEEPING QUAIL FROM STICKING TO THE GRILL

Quail skin is thin and delicate, and you don't want it to stick. Just before placing the quail on the grill, dip a large wad of paper towels into vegetable oil, grab it with tongs, and wipe the hot grill thoroughly to lubricate it.

Sautéed Quail

SERVES 4

WE BUTTERFLY quail before sautéing for even cooking. By the time the quail has browned on both sides, the meat should be perfectly done. Use a 12-inch skillet to cook all eight quail at one time.

8 whole quail (about 5 ounces each), rinsed and patted dry; wing tips removed, butterflied (see figures 1–3, opposite)
Salt and pepper
2 tablespoons olive oil
2 tablespoons butter
1 medium onion, minced
1 cup white wine

1. Sprinkle each quail liberally with salt and pepper to taste. Heat the oil and butter in a large skillet over medium-high heat. When the foaming subsides, add the quail to the pan and sauté skin side down until golden brown, about 5 minutes. Turn and sauté until tender and still juicy, another 3 or 4 minutes. Remove the birds to a platter and cover with foil.

2. Drain all but 1 tablespoon of the fat from the skillet. Add the onion and sauté over medium-high heat until golden, about 3 minutes. Turn the heat to high and add the wine. Scrape the brown bits from the bottom of the pan. Reduce the sauce to ½ cup, about 3 minutes. Season with salt and pepper to taste. Place 2 quail on each plate and serve immediately with sauce.

Sautéed Quail on Warm Lentils

A TART BALSAMIC VINEGAR SAUCE IS A QUICK WAY TO ENLIVEN BOTH THE FLAVORFUL SAUTEED QUAIL AND THE EARTHY LENTILS. AND ANY PAN SAUCE FROM CHAPTER 5 CAN BE ADAPTED FOR QUAIL. SERVES 4.

1 cup lentils
1 tablespoon chopped fresh sage leaves
3 tablespoons olive oil
Salt and pepper
16 whole fresh sage leaves
8 whole quail (about 5 ounces each), rinsed and patted dry; wing tips removed, butterflied (see figures 1–3, opposite)
4 tablespoons unsalted butter
2 medium garlic cloves, minced
½ cup chicken stock or low-sodium canned broth
½ cup balsamic vinegar

1. Bring 6 cups of water to a boil in a medium saucepan. Add the lentils and cook until tender, about 20 minutes. Drain, transfer to a bowl, and toss with the chopped sage, 1 tablespoon oil, and salt and pepper to taste. Cover with foil to keep warm.

2. While the lentils are cooking, prepare the quail: Place 1 sage leaf under the skin of each quail breast half. Sprinkle each quail liberally with salt and pepper. Heat remaining 2 tablespoons oil and 2 tablespoons butter in a large skillet over medium-high heat. When the foaming subsides, add the quail to the pan and sauté skin side down until golden brown, about 5 minutes. Turn and sauté until tender and still juicy, another 3 or 4 minutes. Remove the birds to a platter and cover with foil.

3. Drain all but 1 tablespoon of the fat. Add the garlic and sauté over medium-high heat until golden, about 1 minute. Turn the heat to high, and add stock and vinegar. Scrape the brown bits from the bottom of the pan. Reduce the sauce to ¾ cup, 2 to 3 minutes. Swirl in 2 tablespoons butter and season with salt and pepper to taste. Spoon some lentils onto 4 dinner plates. Place 2 quail on top of the lentils, and pour the sauce over the quail. Serve immediately.

CHAPTER 36

SQUAB

/I\

MEATY SQUAB—A YOUNG PIGEON THAT CANNOT FLY

BECAUSE ITS FEATHERS HAVE NOT DEVELOPED FULLY—

BEARS LITTLE RESEMBLANCE TO OTHER FEATHERED

BIRDS. THE FLESH IS RICH AND GAMY, MORE LIKE VENI-

SON OR BEEF THAN CHICKEN. ABOUT THE SAME SIZE

AS A SMALL CORNISH GAME HEN (ROUGHLY 1 POUND),

IT IS IDEAL FOR ENTERTAINING SINCE ONE BIRD SERVES

ONE PERSON. ◆ GIVEN THE STRONG FLAVOR OF THE

MEAT, WE FIND THAT STRONG SEASONINGS—SUCH AS

chiles, garlic, ham, and sage—work best with squab. As with quail, we prefer to cook squab to a medium-rare stage. The meat will still be pink and an instant-read thermometer stuck into the thigh or breast will read 140 to 145 degrees. As with quail, if you prefer not to see red when eating poultry, cook the birds a few minutes longer to an internal temperature of 160 degrees. Above that temperature, the meat will dry out considerably and lose its juiciness. The flavor will also become somewhat livery, like overcooked beef.

Whole squab are usually roasted or braised. When roasting, it is easy to overcook the birds, especially if you wait for the skin to brown. We experimented with various roasting temperatures and found that a fairly hot oven (set at 425 degrees) was necessary to get the skin golden brown during the short time it takes to cook through such a small bird. We found that browning was promoted by several turns. We start the birds on one wing, turned them to the other wing, and then finished roasting the birds breast side up. This turning regimen ensures that all parts of the skin are nicely browned by the time the squab is done, after no more than 30 minutes in the oven.

When braising, we found that browning the birds helped developed flavor. Wine, either white or red, makes an excellent braising liquid since it helps moderate the richness of the meat and can be reduced to a sauce for the cooked birds.

In addition to roasting and braising, squab takes well to high-heat cooking methods like grilling and sautéing. In this case, you want to purchase boneless squab. The wings and legs will still be on the bone, but the rest of the bird will be freed from the back, breast, and thigh bones. We find that the wings prevent the boned birds from lying flat on the grill or in a pan, so we clip them off before cooking. The tiny leg bones remain but do not pose such a problem.

Since sautéing more than two or three birds at a time is difficult (you need a *very* large skillet), we generally prefer to grill squab. However, when conditions do not permit cooking outside, sautéing is a decent alternative (brown the squab in batches), especially for cooks who like crisp skin and fairly rare meat. With either grilling or sautéing, don't expect to cook the meat until all traces of pink are gone. By the time that happens, the skin will be charred.

PREPARING SQUAB FOR GRILLING OR SAUTEING

The wings are not terribly meaty on a squab and can prevent the breast from cooking properly when grilling or sautéing. We prefer to use a chef's knife or poultry scissors to remove them before cooking.

BONING SQUAB

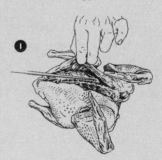

1. We recommend that you buy boneless squab (the wing and drumstick bones will remain) if you can. If not, use a sharp boning knife to do the job yourself. Start by inserting the tip of a boning knife at the top of the back and cut down the middle of the back. Scrape the meat away from the backbone, along the rib bones, being careful not to tear the skin.

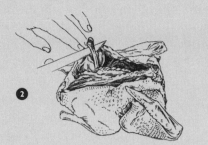

2. Scrape the meat away from the thigh bones, slicing away the meat and skin under the bone to free it.

3. Cut through the joint that connects the thigh and leg bone. Remove the thigh bone, but leave the leg bones in place since it's very difficult to remove them without tearing up the meat.

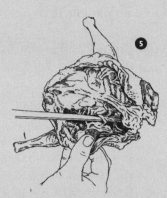

5. Use the boning knife to cut around the rib cage and scrape the meat away from the bones. Turn the squab over and lift the meat off the breastbone. Discard the bone structure.

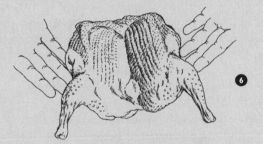

6. The boneless squab (with the 2 drumstick bones still in the bird) has 2 meaty lobes of breast meat plus boneless thigh meat attached to the legs.

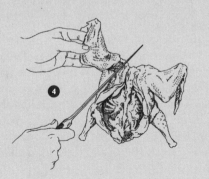

4. Slice off the wings and discard them.

Grilled Squab

SERVES 4 AS A MAIN COURSE,
8 AS AN APPETIZER

BONELESS SQUAB ARE necessary when grilling. Squab may be purchased boneless or see figures 1 through 6 (pages 442–443) for instructions on boning squab at home. For eight appetizer portions, use kitchen shears to split the squab after grilling. Serve with a salsa or other sauce to perk up the flavor.

> 4 boneless squab (about 10 ounces each),
>   rinsed and patted dry; wings removed
>   (see page 442)
> 1 tablespoon extra-virgin olive oil
> Salt and pepper

1. Prepare the fire for grilling (see figures 1–4, page 156). Brush the squab with oil and sprinkle liberally with salt and pepper.

2. Place the squab on the grill breast side down and cook over a medium-hot fire until well browned, 5 to 7 minutes. Turn and cook until the juices run clear when the thigh is pierced with a fork, 4 to 5 minutes. Remove the squab from the grill and serve immediately.

Grilled Squab with Mesclun and Curry Vinaigrette

FOR EIGHT APPETIZER PORTIONS, USE KITCHEN SHEARS TO SPLIT THE SQUAB AFTER GRILLING AND SERVE WITH A HALF PORTION OF GREENS. MESCLUN, A SALAD MIX OF BABY GREENS, IS AVAILABLE AT MOST SUPERMARKETS AND PRODUCE STORES. AN ASSORTMENT OF OTHER LEAFY GREENS MAY BE SUBSTITUTED, IF DESIRED. SERVES 4 AS A MAIN COURSE, 8 AS AN APPETIZER.

> 4 boneless squab (about 10 ounces each),
>   rinsed and patted dry; wings removed
>   (see page 442)
> 1/2 cup plus 1 tablespoon extra-virgin
>   olive oil
> Salt and pepper
> 2 tablespoons fresh lime juice
> 1/2 teaspoon curry powder
> 1 tablespoon chopped fresh cilantro
>   leaves
> 10 cups mesclun or other salad greens

1. Prepare the fire for grilling (see figures 1–4, page 156). Brush the squab with 1 tablespoon olive oil and sprinkle liberally with salt and pepper. Place on the grill breast side down and cook over a medium-hot fire until well browned, 5 to 7 minutes. Turn and cook until the juices run clear when the thigh is pierced with a fork, 4 to 5 minutes. Remove the squab from the grill and cover with foil to keep warm.

2. While the squab are on the grill, whisk the lime juice, 1/2 teaspoon salt, the curry powder, and cilantro together in a small bowl. Whisk in the remaining 1/2 cup oil until the dressing is emulsified. Place the greens in a large bowl and toss with half the dressing. Divide the dressed greens among 4 plates and top each plate with 1 grilled squab. Drizzle remaining dressing over the birds and serve immediately.

Grilled Squab with Red Chile–Pumpkin Seed Sauce

THE STRONG, ALMOST BEEFY FLAVOR OF SQUAB IS A GOOD MATCH FOR POTENT MARINADES. IN THIS RECIPE, THE MEXICAN-STYLE MARINADE CONTAINS PUMPKIN SEEDS, ANCHO CHILES, AND SPICES. THE MARINADE MAY BE MADE IN ADVANCE AND REFRIGERATED FOR SEVERAL DAYS. SERVES 4.

½ cup hulled pumpkin seeds
4 dried ancho chiles
¼ cup olive oil
1 small onion, finely chopped
2 medium garlic cloves, finely chopped
1 cup canned crushed tomatoes
2 tablespoons maple syrup
1 tablespoon white wine vinegar
½ teaspoon ground cumin
¼ teaspoon ground cinnamon
¼ teaspoon ground coriander
Salt and pepper
4 boneless squab (about 10 ounces each),
    rinsed and patted dry; wings removed
    (see page 442)

1. Preheat the oven to 350 degrees. Place the pumpkin seeds on a baking sheet and toast in the oven until golden, 7 to 10 minutes. Set the toasted seeds aside in a small bowl. Rinse and dry the chiles. Place them on the empty baking sheet and roast in the oven until puffed, fragrant, and toasted, about 6 minutes. Remove the chiles from the oven and cool. When the chiles are cool enough to handle, remove the stems and seeds, rip into coin-size pieces, and process in a spice grinder until pulverized and powdery, 30 to 45 seconds.

2. Heat the olive oil in a large skillet. Add the onion and cook over medium heat until softened, 4 to 5 minutes. Add the garlic and cook another minute. Add the ground chiles, the tomatoes, 1 cup water, the maple syrup, vinegar, cumin, cinnamon, coriander, and salt and pepper to taste and cook until thickened, 5 to 7 minutes.

3. Transfer the tomato sauce to a blender, along with the pumpkin seeds, and puree until smooth. Transfer to a bowl and cool completely.

4. Place the squab in a large sealable plastic bag and pour half the sauce in the bag. Refrigerate for 3 hours, turning occasionally.

5. Prepare the fire for grilling (see figures 1–4, page 156). Brush the excess sauce off of the birds and discard. Place the squab on the grill skin side down and cook over a medium-hot fire until well browned, 5 to 7 minutes. Turn and cook until the juices run clear when the thigh is pierced with a fork, 4 to 5 minutes. Remove the squab from the grill and cover with foil to keep warm.

6. While the squab is on the grill, bring the remaining sauce to a boil in a small saucepan, lower the heat, and simmer for 3 to 4 minutes. Serve the squab with the warm sauce.

Sautéed Squab

SERVES 4

Boneless squab can be sautéed just like chicken cutlets, although they should be cooked only to medium rare. As with grilled squab, we clip the wings off to promote even cooking.

Salt and pepper
4 boneless squab (about 10 ounces each),
   rinsed and patted dry; wings removed
   (see page 442)
¼ cup all-purpose flour
4½ tablespoons unsalted butter, softened
1½ tablespoons olive oil
2 medium garlic cloves, minced
1 cup white wine
2 tablespoons minced fresh parsley leaves

1. Preheat the oven to the lowest possible temperature. Place a plate in the oven for keeping the cooked squab warm while you make the sauce.

2. Sprinkle 1 teaspoon salt and ¼ to ½ teaspoon pepper on both sides of the squab. Measure the flour onto a plate or pie tin. Working with 1 squab at a time, press both sides into the flour. Shake gently to remove excess flour.

3. Heat ¾ tablespoon butter and ¾ tablespoon oil in a heavy-bottomed skillet measuring at least 9 inches across the bottom. Swirl the skillet over high heat until the butter has melted. Continue to heat until the butter stops foaming and has just begun to color. Lay 2 squab skin side down in the skillet.

4. Maintain medium-high heat, so the fat sizzles but does not smoke, and sauté the squab until browned on one side, 5 to 7 minutes. Turn the squab with tongs; cook on other side until meat feels firm when pressed, 3 to 5 minutes. Transfer the squab to the plate in the oven; repeat with another ¾ tablespoon butter and the remaining ¾ tablespoon oil and the remaining 2 squab. Keep the squab warm until ready to serve.

5. Without discarding the fat, set the skillet over medium heat. Add the garlic; sauté until golden, about 1 minute. Increase the heat to high, add the wine, and scrape the skillet bottom with a wooden spatula or spoon to loosen any browned bits. Boil until the liquid reduces to about ⅓ cup, about 3 minutes. Add any accumulated juices from the plate with the squab; reduce the sauce again to ⅓ cup. Add the parsley and season to taste with salt and pepper. Off the heat, swirl in the remaining 3 tablespoons butter until it melts and thickens the sauce. Spoon the sauce over the squab and serve immediately.

◆

Sautéed Squab with Orange-Cumin Sauce

A QUICK PAN SAUCE MADE FROM THE COOKING JUICES COMPLETES THIS DISH. ANY RECIPE FOR SAUTEED CHICKEN CUTLETS (SEE CHAPTER 5) CAN BE ADAPTED FOR USE WITH BONELESS SQUAB. **SERVES 4.**

Salt and pepper
4 boneless squab (about 10 ounces each),
   rinsed and patted dry; wings removed
   (see page 442)
¼ cup all-purpose flour
4½ tablespoons unsalted butter, softened
1½ tablespoons olive oil
2 shallots, minced
2 medium garlic cloves, minced
1 cup fresh orange juice
1 teaspoon ground cumin
1 tablespoon fresh thyme leaves

1. Preheat the oven to the lowest possible temperature. Place a plate in the oven for keeping the cooked squab warm while you make the sauce.

2. Sprinkle 1 teaspoon salt and ¼ to ½ teaspoon pepper on both sides of the squab. Measure the flour onto a plate or pie tin. Working with 1 squab at a time, press both sides into the flour. Shake gently to remove excess flour.

3. Heat ¾ tablespoon butter and ¾ tablespoon oil in a heavy-bottomed skillet measuring at least 9 inches across the bottom. Swirl the skillet over high heat until the butter has melted. Continue to heat until the butter stops foaming and has just begun to color. Lay 2 squab skin side down in the skillet.

4. Maintain medium-high heat, so the fat sizzles but does not smoke, and sauté the squab until browned on one side, 5 to 7 minutes. Turn the squab with tongs; cook on other side until meat feels firm when pressed, 3 to 5 minutes. Transfer the squab to the plate in the oven; repeat with another ¾ tablespoon butter and the remaining ¾ tablespoon oil and the remaining 2 squab. Keep the squab warm until ready to serve.

5. Without discarding the fat, set the skillet over medium heat. Add the shallots; sauté until softened, about 1 minute. Add the garlic; sauté another minute. Increase the heat to high, add the juice and cumin, and scrape the skillet bottom with a wooden spatula or spoon to loosen any browned bits. Boil until the liquid reduces to about ⅓ cup, about 3 minutes. Add any accumulated juices from the plate with the squab; reduce the sauce again to ⅓ cup. Add the thyme and season to taste with salt and pepper. Off the heat, swirl in the remaining 3 tablespoons butter until it melts and thickens the sauce. Spoon the sauce over the squab and serve immediately.

Roasted Squab

SERVES 4

I N ORDER TO PROMOTE good browning, roast the squab on each side for 5 minutes, then turn breast side up and roast until the juices run clear, another 15 to 20 minutes. Deglaze with white wine to make a quick pan sauce.

> 4 whole squab (about 1 pound each), rinsed and patted dry
> 2 tablespoons olive oil
> Salt and pepper
> 1 cup dry white wine
> 2 tablespoons butter

1. Preheat the oven to 425 degrees.

2. Tie the legs of the squab together loosely with kitchen twine (see figure, page 449). Brush the squab with oil, and sprinkle with salt and pepper to taste. Place squab wing side down in a large roasting pan and roast for 5 minutes; turn to the other side and roast another 5 minutes. Turn the squab breast side up and roast until the juices run clear when the thigh is pierced with a fork, 15 to 20 minutes. Transfer the squab to a platter and cover with foil.

3. Drain the excess fat from the roasting pan. Place the pan on the stovetop over high heat, add the wine, bring to a boil, and scrape any browned bits from the bottom of the pan. Simmer until the sauce reduces to about ½ cup, about 3 minutes. Remove the pan from the heat and swirl in the butter.

4. Place each squab on a dinner plate and serve immediately with the pan sauce.

Roasted Squab with Green Grapes

THE RICH, MEATY FLAVOR OF SQUAB MARRIES WELL WITH THIS SWEET SAUCE OF WHITE GRAPE JUICE AND GRAPES. PEELED GRAPES MAKE FOR AN ESPECIALLY SMOOTH FINISHED DISH, BUT UNPEELED ONES ARE FINE ALSO. SERVE WITH BUTTERED ORZO. SERVES 4.

4 whole squab (about 1 pound each), rinsed and patted dry
2 tablespoons olive oil
Salt and pepper
1 cup dry white wine
1 cup white grape juice
2 cups seedless green grapes (peeled if desired), quartered
2 tablespoons unsalted butter

1. Preheat the oven to 425 degrees. Tie the legs of the squab together loosely with kitchen twine. Brush the squab with oil, and sprinkle with salt and pepper to taste. Place the squab wing side down in a large roasting pan and roast for 5 minutes; turn to the other side and roast another 5 minutes. Turn the squab breast side up and roast until the juices run clear when the thigh is pierced with a fork, 15 to 20 minutes. Transfer the squab to a platter and cover with foil.

2. Drain the excess fat from the roasting pan. Place the pan on the stovetop over high heat, add the wine, bring to a boil, and scrape any browned bits from the bottom of the pan. Add the grape juice and reduce to ¾ cup, 5 to 7 minutes. Add the grapes and cook until heated through, about 1 minute. Remove the pan from the heat and swirl in the butter.

3. Place each squab on a dinner plate. Drizzle sauce over each portion and serve immediately.

Roast Squab with Cornbread Dressing

CORNBREAD DRESSING IS PREPARED SEPARATELY AND SERVED ALONGSIDE THE BIRDS, MOISTENED WITH A GRAVY MADE FROM THE PAN JUICES. USE DAY-OLD HOMEMADE (SEE PAGE 339) OR STORE-BOUGHT CORN-BREAD THAT WON'T FALL APART WHEN SAUTEED. THE DRESSING CAN BE MADE A DAY IN ADVANCE, REFRIGER-ATED, AND REHEATED IN THE MICROWAVE. TOAST THE PINE NUTS IN A DRY SKILLET SET OVER MEDIUM HEAT UNTIL GOLDEN, ABOUT 5 MINUTES. SERVES 4.

6 tablespoons unsalted butter
1 shallot, finely chopped
3 ounces prosciutto, cut into 1 thick slice and diced
2 scallions, white and light green parts, finely chopped
3 cups cornbread, cut into ½-inch cubes
2 tablespoons chopped fresh parsley leaves
½ cup pine nuts, toasted
Salt and pepper
8 medium garlic cloves, crushed
4 whole squab (about 1 pound each), rinsed and patted dry
2 tablespoons olive oil
1 cup dry white wine
1 cup chicken stock or low-sodium canned broth

1. Preheat the oven to 425 degrees. Heat 4 table-spoons butter in a medium skillet. Add the shallot and prosciutto and sauté over medium heat until the shal-lot softens, 2 to 3 minutes. Add the scallions, corn-bread, parsley, and pine nuts; sauté until the cornbread is lightly browned, about 1 minute. Season with salt and pepper to taste. Cover to keep warm. (Dressing can be refrigerated overnight. Reheat in microwave before serving.)

2. Place 2 garlic cloves inside the cavity of each squab. Tie the legs of the squab together loosely with kitchen twine. Brush the squab with oil, and sprinkle with salt and pepper to taste. Place squab wing side down in a large roasting pan and roast for 5 minutes; turn to the other side and roast another 5 minutes. Turn the squab breast side up and roast until the juices run clear when the thigh is pierced with a fork, 15 to 20 minutes. Transfer the squab to a platter and cover with foil.

3. Drain the excess fat from the roasting pan. Place the pan on the stovetop over high heat, add the wine, bring to a boil, and scrape the browned bits from the bottom of the pan. Add the stock and reduce to ¾ cup, 5 to 7 minutes. Remove the pan from the heat and swirl in the remaining 2 tablespoons butter.

4. Place each squab on a dinner plate alongside a portion of stuffing. Drizzle the sauce over each portion and serve immediately.

Braised Squab

SERVES 4

B RAISING TAKES MORE time than grilling or sautéing, and results in a more well-done but tender and juicy bird. Here, pancetta and sage perfume the meat. Bacon or prosciutto and other herbs may be substituted according to taste.

> 4 squab (about 1 pound each), rinsed and patted dry
> Salt and pepper
> 8 fresh sage leaves
> 4 ¼-inch-thick pancetta slices, about 6 ounces total
> 2 tablespoons unsalted butter
> 2 tablespoons olive oil
> 1 cup dry white wine

1. Sprinkle the cavity of each squab with salt and pepper to taste. Place 2 sage leaves and 1 piece of pancetta in the cavity of each squab. Sprinkle the birds with salt and pepper to taste.

2. Heat the butter and oil in a large sauté pan over medium-high heat. When the foaming subsides, add the squab to the pan and sauté, turning several times, until browned on all sides, 10 to 12 minutes.

(continued on next page)

PREPARING SQUAB FOR ROASTING

Use a 10-inch length of kitchen twine to tie the legs of the squab together.

3. Turn the heat to high, add ¾ cup wine to the pan, and bring to a boil. Reduce the heat to low, cover the pan, and simmer, turning the birds several times, until tender and done, about 45 minutes. Remove the birds to a platter and cover with foil.

4. Spoon off as much fat from the skillet as you can, turn the heat to high, and add the remaining ¼ cup wine. Scrape any brown bits from the bottom of the pan and simmer for 1 minute. Pour the juices over the squab and serve immediately.

◆

Braised Squab with Red Wine Sauce

RED WINE AT THE BOTTOM OF THE PAN GIVES THESE SQUAB AN EXCEPTIONALLY ATTRACTIVE DARK COLOR. PRUNES, CURRANTS, OR EVEN DRIED CHERRIES MIGHT BE SUBSTITUTED FOR THE RAISINS. **SERVES 4.**

> 4 squab (about 1 pound each), rinsed and
>   patted dry
> Salt and pepper
> 4 fresh thyme sprigs
> 4 large garlic cloves, crushed
> 2 tablespoons unsalted butter
> 2 tablespoons olive oil
> 1 cup dry red wine
> ⅓ cup raisins

1. Sprinkle the cavity of each squab with salt and pepper to taste. Place 1 thyme sprig and 1 garlic clove in the cavity of each squab. Sprinkle the birds with salt and pepper to taste.

2. Heat the butter and oil in a large sauté pan over medium-high heat. When the foaming subsides, add the squab to the pan and sauté, turning several times, until browned on all sides, 10 to 12 minutes.

3. Turn the heat to high, add ¾ cup wine and the raisins to the pan, and bring to a boil. Reduce the heat to low, cover the pan, and simmer, turning the birds several times, until tender and done, about 45 minutes. Remove the birds to a platter and cover with foil.

4. Spoon off as much fat from the skillet as you can, turn the heat to high, and add the remaining ¼ cup wine. Scrape any brown bits from the bottom of the pan and simmer for 1 minute. Pour over the squab and serve immediately.

CHAPTER 37

PHEASANT

/I\

DOMESTICATED PHEASANT IS AKIN TO CHICKEN, OR

AT LEAST CHICKEN THE WAY IT USED TO BE. NOWA-

DAYS SO MUCH COMMERCIAL CHICKEN IS BLAND

THAT FARM-RAISED PHEASANT TASTES MORE LIKE A

GOOD FREE-RANGE OR ORGANIC CHICKEN. FARM-

RAISED PHEASANT IS NOT BLAND, BUT IT IS NOT GAMY,

EITHER. WHILE WILD PHEASANT CAN BE DARK AND

OVERPOWERING, DOMESTICATED PHEASANT SOLD BY

BUTCHERS IS LIGHT COLORED AND MILD. A WHOLE

PHEASANT—AVAILABLE FRESH FROM MANY BUTCHERS

but almost always frozen—weighs about 2½ pounds and can be cooked much like a chicken. A pheasant is ideal for two people.

Unlike wild pheasant, domesticated pheasant can be cooked whole. (The sinewy legs and thighs on wild pheasant require much longer cooking.) Also, wild pheasant is usually barded because it is so lean. Farm-raised birds are only slightly leaner than chickens and this extra step is not required.

Since the birds weigh just 2½ pounds, we find it necessary to use a moderately hot oven (set at 400 degrees) to get the skin brown during the short roasting time. Lower oven temperatures resulted in skin that was too pale. In our tests, we found that turning the birds so that they spend time on either side as well as breast side up facilitated even cooking and browning. If roasted breast side up for the entire cooking time, the sides were too pale. By putting the wings and side of the breast in direct contact with the hot pan they browned better.

Since pheasant is a bit leaner than chicken, it can dry out when roasted. For this reason, we suggest removing it from the oven when an instant-read thermometer stuck into the thigh or breast registers 155 degrees. (The internal temperature will rise to 160 degrees while the bird rests before carving.) At this stage, the meat has a slight pink tinge and is still juicy. Pheasant can be cooked to 160 or 165 degrees if you are worried about the dangers of undercooking, but there is some sacrifice in texture.

In addition to roasting, pheasant can be butterflied and grilled like any small chicken. When grilling, we particularly like to coat the skin with a spice rub or let the bird marinate in a flavorful liquid. We also found that pheasant takes well to braising. We cut the bird into six pieces (the leg/thigh is best cooked together since it is so small). In our testing, we found it useful to leave the leg/thigh pieces in the pan longer. This way the tender breast meat is protected and the dark meat has time to cook through and soften.

Simple Roasted Pheasant

SERVES 4

ILD PHEASANT SHOULD be cut into pieces before cooking so that the tough legs and thighs can be cooked longer than the breast and wings. However, farm-raised birds are tender enough to simply roast whole. Here, smaller pheasant (about 2½ pounds each) are stuffed with aromatic vegetables, simply trussed, and roasted in a hot oven. The pan juices become a savory sauce for the cooked birds.

1 small onion, sliced thin
1 small carrot, sliced thin
1 small celery stalk, sliced thin
2 garlic cloves, peeled
2 fresh thyme sprigs
2 tablespoons unsalted butter
2 pheasant (about 2½ pounds each), rinsed and patted dry
2 tablespoons vegetable oil
Salt and pepper
1½ cups chicken stock or low-sodium canned broth

1. Preheat the oven to 400 degrees. Place half the onion, carrot, celery, garlic, thyme, and butter into the cavity of each pheasant. Tie together the legs of each pheasant with kitchen twine (see figure). Rub each bird with 1 tablespoon oil, ½ teaspoon salt, and ¼ teaspoon pepper.

2. Place the birds on their sides in a large roasting pan; roast 15 minutes, turn each bird onto the other side, and roast another 15 minutes. Turn the birds breast side up, baste with the pan juices, and roast until a meat thermometer inserted into the thickest part of the thigh registers 155 degrees, 15 to 20 minutes.

3. Remove the pheasant from the oven and transfer to a carving board. Transfer the vegetables from both cavities to a medium saucepan. Cover the pheasant with foil to keep warm.

4. Skim the fat from the pan juices. Place the roasting pan on top of the stove, turn the heat to high, and add the stock, scraping the bottom of the pan with a wooden spoon to loosen any brown bits. Pour the stock and pan juices into the saucepan with the vegetable mixture. Bring to a boil and simmer until reduced to ¾ cup, about 10 minutes. Strain the sauce through a fine sieve and discard the solids. Season with salt and pepper to taste.

5. Carve the pheasant as you would a chicken (see page 13). Serve with the sauce on the side.

◆

Roasted Pheasant with Wild Rice and Pecans

ONIONS AND GARLIC ROASTED INSIDE THE BIRDS ADD FLA-VOR TO A SIDE DISH OF WILD RICE WITH PECANS. **SERVES 4.**

> 1 cup wild rice
> Salt and pepper
> 1 small onion, finely chopped
> 4 fresh rosemary sprigs
> 2 garlic cloves, finely chopped
> 4 tablespoons unsalted butter
> 2 pheasant (about 2½ pounds each), rinsed and patted dry
> 2 tablespoons vegetable oil
> 1 cup pecans, coarsely chopped
> 1 cup chicken stock or low-sodium canned broth
> ¼ cup chopped fresh parsley leaves

1. Rinse the rice and combine with 4 cups water in a medium saucepan. Bring to a boil, reduce to a simmer, and cook partially covered until the water is absorbed and the rice is tender, 45 minutes to 1 hour. Remove from heat, stir in ½ teaspoon salt, and set aside.

2. Meanwhile, preheat the oven to 400 degrees. Divide the onion, rosemary, garlic, and 2 tablespoons butter and place into the cavity of each pheasant. Tie together the legs of each pheasant with kitchen twine. Rub each bird with 1 tablespoon vegetable oil, ½ teaspoon salt, and ¼ teaspoon pepper.

3. Place the birds on their sides in a large roasting pan; roast 15 minutes, turn each bird onto the other side, and roast another 15 minutes. Turn the birds breast side up, baste with the pan juices, and roast until a meat thermometer inserted into the thickest part of the thigh registers 155 degrees, 15 to 20 minutes.

(continued on next page)

TYING THE LEGS FOR ROASTING

Use a 10-inch length of kitchen twine to tie the legs on the pheasant together before roasting.

4. Remove the pheasant from the oven and transfer to a carving board. Transfer the onion mixture from both cavities to a small bowl and set aside. Cover the pheasant with foil to keep warm.

5. Melt the remaining 2 tablespoons butter in a large skillet. Add the pecans and sauté over medium heat until they begin to brown, about 2 minutes. Add the stock and bring to a boil; simmer until reduced to a thick syrup, about 10 minutes. Add the rice, onion mixture, the parsley, and ½ cup water and cook, stirring several times, until heated through, about 5 minutes. Season with salt and pepper to taste.

6. Carve the pheasant as you would a chicken (see page 13). Serve with the wild rice on the side.

MASTER RECIPE

Grilled Spice-Rubbed Pheasant

SERVES 4

PHEASANT CAN BE butterflied and grilled in the same manner as a whole chicken. Here, we use a simple spice rub of curry powder, cumin, and cinnamon; any of the preparations for Grilled Butterflied Chicken (see pages 207–210) may be adapted for pheasant.

2 tablespoons curry powder
1 teaspoon ground cumin
½ teaspoon ground cinnamon
1 teaspoon salt
½ teaspoon pepper
2 pheasant (about 2½ pounds each), rinsed, patted dry, and butterflied (see figures 1 and 2, opposite)
3 tablespoons olive oil

1. Combine the curry powder, cumin, cinnamon, salt, and pepper in a small bowl. Rub each pheasant all over with the mixture and refrigerate for 1 hour.

2. Prepare the fire for grilling (see figures 1–4, page 156). Brush the spice-rubbed birds with the olive oil and place breast side down on the grill. Cook over a medium-hot fire until well browned, 7 to 10 minutes; turn and continue to cook until a meat thermometer inserted into the thickest part of the thigh registers 155 degrees, another 7 to 10 minutes. Remove from the grill, let rest 10 minutes, halve each bird by cutting along one side of the breastbone, and serve.

◆

Grilled Pheasant with Pear and Currant Chutney

APPLES AND RAISINS MAY BE SUBSTITUTED HERE. THE CHUTNEY CAN BE MADE AHEAD, REFRIGERATED, AND BROUGHT TO ROOM TEMPERATURE OR WARMED BEFORE BEING SERVED. **SERVES 4.**

1½ cups pear brandy or regular brandy
10 juniper berries, crushed
1 tablespoon chopped fresh tarragon leaves
½ teaspoon grated lemon zest
1 teaspoon fresh lemon juice
¼ cup olive oil
Salt and pepper

2 pheasant (about 2½ pounds each),
   rinsed, patted dry, and butterflied (see
   figures 1 and 2)
1 small red onion, finely chopped
2 pears, peeled, cored, and cut into
   ¼-inch dice
½ cup currants
1 tablespoon honey
1 tablespoon cider vinegar

1. Combine 1 cup brandy, the juniper berries, tarragon, lemon zest and juice, 2 tablespoons oil, 1 teaspoon salt, and 1 teaspoon pepper in a small bowl. Place each pheasant in a large sealable plastic bag and pour half the marinade into each bag. Refrigerate for 3 hours.

2. Heat the remaining 2 tablespoons oil in a large skillet. Cook the onion over medium heat until it begins to soften, 3 to 4 minutes. Add the pears and cook until they begin to soften and brown, 10 to 12 minutes. Add the remaining ½ cup brandy, the currants, honey, and vinegar, bring to a simmer, and cook, stirring constantly, until the pears are very soft, 12 to 15 minutes. Set aside.

3. Prepare the fire for grilling (see figures 1–4, page 156). Remove the pheasant from the refrigerator and let stand at room temperature for 15 minutes. Place the pheasant breast side down on the grill. Cook over a medium-hot fire until well browned, 7 to 10 minutes; turn and continue to cook until a meat thermometer inserted into the thickest part of the thigh registers 155 degrees, another 7 to 10 minutes. Remove from the grill, let rest 10 minutes, halve each bird by cutting down along one side of the breastbone, and serve with the pear chutney.

BUTTERFLYING A PHEASANT FOR GRILLING

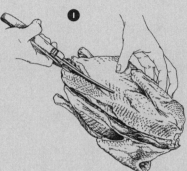

1. To butterfly a pheasant, use poultry scissors to cut along one side of the backbone from the tail to the neck. Cut along the other side of the backbone, separating it entirely from the bird. Reserve the backbone for use in stock, or discard.

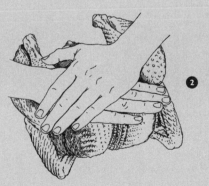

2. Place the bird on a work surface, skin side up. With the palms of your hands, push down on the breast to break the breastbone and allow the pheasant to lie flat.

CUTTING UP A PHEASANT FOR BRAISING

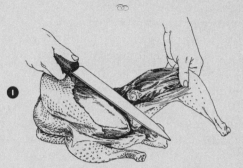

1. Using a sharp chef's knife cut through the skin around the leg where it attaches to the body. Pop the leg/thigh out of its socket and then use your chef's knife, to cut through the flesh and skin to detach the leg/thigh from the body. Repeat on the other side of the bird. Because the pieces are so small, keep the legs attached to the thighs.

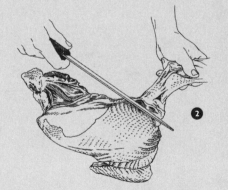

2. Turn the pheasant on its side and pull the wing away from the body. Cut around and through the joint that attaches the wing to the breast. Repeat with the second wing.

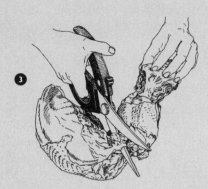

3. Using poultry shears, cut down the ribs between the back and the breast, first on one side of the bird and then on the other. The back and breast should be neatly separated. Reserve the back for stock, or discard.

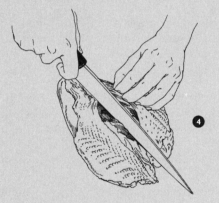

4. Place the breast piece skin side up on a cutting board. Press down on the breast with both hands to crack the breastbone. Split the breast down the breastbone, cutting right through the bone with a chef's knife. Because the pheasant is smaller than a chicken, it's possible to cut right through the bone, rather than alongside it.

Braised Pheasant

SERVES 2

IT IS POSSIBLE TO BRAISE only one cut-up pheasant at a time in a large skillet on top of the stove, so use this recipe when cooking for two. (If you are willing to cook in two pans at one time, you can double the recipe.) The braising liquid—a combination of white wine and chicken stock—is reduced once the pheasant pieces are cooked and then enriched with a little butter.

> 1 pheasant (about 2 1/2 pounds), rinsed, patted dry, and cut into 6 pieces (see figures 1–4, opposite)
> Salt and pepper
> 2 tablespoons olive oil
> 1 medium onion, minced
> 1 cup white wine
> 1/2 cup chicken stock or low-sodium canned broth
> 2 tablespoons butter
> 1 tablespoon minced fresh parsley leaves

1. Preheat the oven to the lowest possible temperature. Place a plate in the oven for keeping the cooked pheasant warm. Sprinkle the pheasant pieces with salt and pepper to taste.

2. Heat the oil in a large skillet over medium heat. Add the pheasant and cook until browned on one side, about 5 minutes. Turn and cook until browned on the other side, another 5 minutes. Remove the browned pheasant pieces and set aside.

3. Add the onion to the pan and cook over medium heat, stirring occasionally, until golden, about 5 minutes. Add the wine and stock and bring the liquid to a boil. Reduce the heat to a simmer, add the pheasant, and cook, partially covered, until the breast meat is cooked, 12 to 15 minutes. Remove the breasts to the plate in the oven and cover with foil. Continue to cook the remaining parts until done, another 20 to 25 minutes. Remove the remaining pheasant pieces to the plate in the oven and again cover with foil.

4. Bring the liquid in the pan to a boil, reduce the heat to medium, and cook until thickened, 7 to 10 minutes. Remove the pan from the heat and stir in the butter and parsley until the sauce is smooth and thick. Arrange the pheasant pieces on plates and spoon the sauce over the pheasant. Serve immediately.

◆

Pheasant Braised in Tomato Sauce

SERVE THIS JUICY BRAISE OVER RICE, BUTTERED NOODLES, OR SOFT POLENTA. SERVES 2.

> 1 pheasant (about 2 1/2 pounds), rinsed, patted dry, and cut into 6 pieces (see figures 1–4, opposite)
> Salt and pepper
> 2 tablespoons olive oil
> 1 medium onion, finely chopped
> 2 ounces prosciutto, cut into one 1/4-inch-thick slice and then cut into 1/4-inch dice
> 1 fresh rosemary sprig
> 6 whole cloves
> 1 bay leaf
> 1 cup canned crushed tomatoes
> 1 cup dry white wine
> 1 cup chicken stock or low-sodium canned broth

(continued on next page)

1. Preheat the oven to the lowest possible temperature. Place a plate in the oven for keeping the cooked pheasant warm. Sprinkle the pheasant pieces with salt and pepper to taste.

2. Heat the oil in a large skillet over medium heat. Add the pheasant and cook until browned on one side, about 5 minutes. Turn and cook until browned on the other side, another 5 minutes. Remove the browned pheasant pieces and set aside. Drain off all but 1 tablespoon of the fat at the bottom of the pan.

3. Add the onion, prosciutto, rosemary, cloves, and bay leaf to the pan and cook, stirring frequently, over medium heat until the onion softens, about 5 minutes. Add the tomatoes, wine, and stock and bring to a boil. Reduce the heat to a simmer, add the pheasant, and cook, partially covered, until the breast meat is cooked, 12 to 15 minutes. Remove the breasts to the plate in the oven and cover with foil. Continue to cook the remaining parts until done, another 20 to 25 minutes. Remove the remaining pheasant pieces to the plate in the oven and again cover with foil.

4. Bring the liquid in the pan to a boil, reduce the heat to medium, and cook until thickened, 7 to 10 minutes. Remove the bay leaf, arrange the pheasant pieces on plates, and spoon the sauce over the pheasant. Serve immediately.

◆

Pheasant Braised with Red Wine and Red Cabbage

RED CABBAGE PROTECTS THE PHEASANT PIECES FROM DIRECT HEAT AND MAKES A HEARTY ACCOMPANIMENT IN THIS SIMPLE BRAISE. BECAUSE OF THE VEGETABLES, THIS DISH CAN BE STRETCHED TO SERVE THREE PEOPLE. SERVES 2 TO 3.

> 1 pheasant (about 2½ pounds), rinsed, patted dry, and cut into 6 pieces (see figures 1–4, page 456)
> Salt and pepper
> 2 tablespoons olive oil

> 1 small red cabbage (about 2½ pounds), cored and shredded
> 4 garlic cloves, finely chopped
> 1 cup dry red wine
> ½ cup chicken stock or low-sodium canned broth
> ¼ cup soy sauce
> 2 tablespoons balsamic vinegar

1. Preheat the oven to the lowest possible temperature. Place a plate in the oven for keeping the cooked pheasant warm. Sprinkle the pheasant pieces with salt and pepper to taste.

2. Heat the oil in a large skillet over medium heat. Add the pheasant and cook until browned on one side, about 5 minutes. Turn and cook until browned on the other side, another 5 minutes. Remove the browned pheasant pieces and set aside.

3. Add the cabbage and garlic to the pan and cook, stirring occasionally, over medium heat until the cabbage is wilted, 7 to 10 minutes. Add the wine, stock, soy sauce, and vinegar and bring to a boil. Reduce the heat to a simmer, add the pheasant, and cook, partially covered, until the breast meat is cooked, 12 to 15 minutes. Remove the breasts to the plate in the oven and cover with foil. Continue to cook the remaining parts until done, another 20 to 25 minutes. Remove the remaining pheasant pieces to the plate in the oven and again cover with foil.

4. Cook the cabbage, uncovered, until it is very soft and most of the liquid has evaporated, about 5 minutes. Season with salt and pepper to taste. Mound portions of cabbage on each individual plate and arrange the pheasant pieces on top of the cabbage.

CHAPTER 38

SMOKED POULTRY

/|\

SMOKING IS NOT AN EXACT SCIENCE. EXTREMELY LOW

COOKING TEMPERATURES (OFTEN JUST ABOVE 200

DEGREES) AND LONG COOKING TIMES (UP TO TEN

HOURS) TRANSLATE INTO UNPREDICTABILITY. THE

COOKING TIME FOR THE SAME RECIPE MADE ON THE

SAME SMOKER ON TWO SEPARATE OCCASIONS CAN

VARY BY AN HOUR OR TWO. THAT'S BECAUSE SMOKERS

are greatly affected by ambient conditions (wind and temperature) and minor changes in procedure, such as how often and how long the smoker is opened to check on the food or add wood.

While it is possible to smoke in a kettle-style grill (see pages 462–463 for more information), a specially designed water smoker is much easier to use. Water smokers are shaped like a torpedo (or a giant coffee can) and are made of thin metal. An electric coil (or area for charcoal) rests on the bottom of the smoker. Some models come with a side door for adding wood chunks, which should be placed around the coil. A metal water pan rests several inches above the coil. Most smokers come with two cooking racks. One rests on or just above the water pan, the other is close to the top of the body. A domed lid fits on top of the body of the smoker and may contain vents for releasing heat.

During the course of our testing recipes for this chapter, we developed the following list of tips to ensure good results when smoking. See the sidebar on pages 468–469 for information on setting up and using a water smoker.

◆ Line the water pan with heavy-duty aluminum foil. It will make cleanup much easier.

◆ Fill the lined water pan with hot tap water. Cold water will increase the cooking time significantly. If the cooking time is more than three or four hours, be prepared to add more hot water to keep the pan from running dry.

◆ Don't bother with flavorings in the water pan. We tried using beer instead of water, or adding herbs and spices to the water and couldn't taste the difference. Season birds in advance with spice rubs or pastes. Although two hours is usually enough time for the flavors to penetrate into the meat, birds can be rubbed and then refrigerated overnight before smoking.

◆ For a medium smoke flavor, add three tennis ball–size wood chunks every three hours. To slow down the rate at which they burn, soak all chunks in cold water for at least thirty minutes, and preferably longer. For a smokier flavor or for foods that will smoke three hours or less, add four or five chunks every two hours.

◆ Place an oven thermometer on the cooking rack so that you can see what the temperature is inside the smoker when checking on the bird. We found that a temperature of 200 to 250 degrees worked best. On electric smokers, the vents can be used to lower the temperature if it gets too hot. On charcoal smokers, opening the vents boosts the temperature at first because the fire is fed by more air, but then causes the temperature to drop as the fire burns out faster.

◆ On windy or cool days, plan on longer cooking times. The metal on most smokers is fairly thin and radiates heat. If the temperature is cool or there is a lot of wind to carry that heat away, expect the smoker to have trouble maintaining a particular heat level. Compensate by raising the temperature—set the dial as high as it will go or add more charcoal.

◆ When smoking, it is necessary to cook all foods by internal temperature, not time. When you think something is done, insert an instant-read thermometer in the thickest part of the meat, away from the bone. Insert the thermometer on an angle into boneless breasts or into the thigh on whole birds.

◆ Since smoking is accomplished at such low temperatures and in a moist environment, there is little danger of the breast meat drying out before the thigh is cooked through in whole chickens or turkeys. With the exception of duck breasts and quail (which we like medium-rare), other birds should be cooked until well done—180 degrees for whole chicken and turkey and 165 degrees for chicken and turkey breasts.

In addition to the birds and parts covered in this chapter, we tested several other kinds of poultry in the smoker and did not like the results. Goose, duck, and squab are quite fatty and must be cooked at temperatures much higher than 200 or 250 degrees in order to make them palatable. (Skinned duck breasts, however, are delicious when smoked.) We couldn't tell much difference between a smoked pheasant and a smoked chicken. The smoke flavor obliterated the subtle gaminess that makes pheasant such a treat. Given the difficulty of obtaining pheasant (not to mention the cost), we don't recommend smoking them. Among game birds, we think only quail and Cornish hens are worth smoking.

EQUIPMENT
FOR SMOKING

/l\

THEORETICALLY, A KETTLE GRILL CAN BE USED TO SMOKE ANY-
THING. HOWEVER, SINCE THE FIRE WILL LAST ONLY AN HOUR
OR SO, WE RECOMMEND THAT YOU STICK WITH BONELESS
CHICKEN BREASTS, DUCK BREASTS, QUAIL, OR OTHER QUICK-
COOKING ITEMS. YOU CAN LIGHT MORE CHARCOAL IN A CHIMNEY

and keep the fire going, but the process is messy (ashes may fly up onto the food) and doesn't make all that much sense for a turkey that will take eight or more hours to cook.

For items that require a longer smoking time, such as a turkey breast or a whole turkey or chicken, a water smoker is essential. It also works well with shorter-cooking items like chicken or duck breasts. We prefer electric water smokers since they require far less tending than charcoal models (you must add more charcoal every hour and risk having the fire die out if you're not attentive), and they work faster and deliver more consistent results.

When shopping for an electric water smoker, look for a model with vents on the lid to regulate the heat, a side door for adding wood chunks, a heat regulator dial on the plug to adjust the temperature inside the smoker, and an external thermometer that lets you know the smoker is at the proper temperature without having to remove the lid. Even if your smoker comes with an external thermometer, it still makes sense to use a thermometer on the cooking rack, at least until you have worked with the smoker for some time and can judge the reliability of the external gauge. Several companies manufacture inexpensive electric water smokers. We have had good results with smokers made by Meco and they generally cost less than $100.

In addition to a water smoker or kettle grill, you will need wood chunks. Chips are fine when grilling and you want a quick burst of smoke. However, smoking a whole turkey can take ten hours and slow-burning wood chunks will deliver the best results. To slow down the rate at which the chunks burn, soak them in cold water for at least thirty minutes (and preferably longer) before placing them in the smoker. We had good results with hickory and mesquite chunks, both of which are available at hardware stores and other shops that sell grilling equipment.

HOW TO SMOKE-COOK WITH A KETTLE-STYLE GRILL

⋏

AT LEAST AN HOUR BEFORE YOU PLAN TO START COOKING, PLACE WOOD CHUNKS, EACH THE SIZE OF A TENNIS BALL, IN A BOWL OF COLD WATER. FOR A MILD SMOKY FLAVOR, USE 3 CHUNKS. FOR A STRONGER FLAVOR, USE 4 OR 5. ◆ THIRTY MINUTES BEFORE YOU PLAN TO COOK, LIGHT A CHIMNEY FULL OF CHAR-

coal. Remove the top grate from the kettle grill. Line a standard-size loaf pan with heavy-duty aluminum foil, fill it two-thirds with hot tap water, and place it on one side of the bottom grate of the grill. When the charcoal is covered with white ash, place the charcoal along the opposite side of the bottom grate. Use long-handled tongs to position the charcoal as needed (see figure 1). Close all vents underneath the grill except the one directly under the charcoal. Place the soaked wood chunks on top of the charcoal (see figure 2, opposite).

Replace the top grate and set the food on the rack, directly over the pan with the water (see figure 3, opposite). Cover the grill with the lid, making sure the top vent is open and positioned directly above the food. Insert the probe end of a grill thermometer into the vent (see figure 4, opposite). Use the thermometer to make sure that the temperature registers between 200 and 250 degrees. To lower the temperature, partially close the vent beneath the charcoal. Do not open the grill more than is necessary or you will

slow down the cooking process. Use an instant-read thermometer to judge when food is done.

1. Place the charcoal in a single layer along one side of the bottom grate, opposite the water pan. Use long-handled tongs to position the charcoal as needed.

2. Place the soaked wood chunks on top of the charcoal.

3. Replace the top grate and set the food on the grate, directly over the water pan.

4. If you own a grill thermometer (sold at most hardware stores), insert the probe end of a grill thermometer into one of the vents on the grill lid. Check frequently and adjust the vents to maintain a temperature of 200 to 250 degrees. You can also place an oven thermometer directly on the rack (it's more accurate than a grill thermometer stuck in the lid), but you should only check this gauge when opening the grill for another reason (to baste birds, for instance). There is precious little heat inside a kettle grill when smoking and you don't want the fire to die out before the bird is done.

Whole Smoked Turkey

SERVES 10 TO 12

SMOKING A WHOLE TURKEY may take half a day, but is actually very simple. To prevent drying out, the bird is wrapped in damp cheesecloth for the first several hours of cooking. This recipe is very plain—the turkey is just seasoned with salt and pepper. It's fine when served with a relish or salsa. The more highly seasoned variations can stand on their own.

> 1 10- to 12-pound turkey, rinsed and patted dry
> 1 tablespoon salt
> 1 tablespoon pepper

1. Set up the smoker and soak the wood chunks (see "How to Smoke-Cook with a Water Smoker," pages 468–469). Rub the turkey inside and out with salt and pepper.

2. Dampen a 7-foot length of cheesecloth and wrap it around the bird, tying the ends together (see figure). Transfer the turkey to the smoker, breast side down. Spray the cheesecloth with more water at 1½-hour intervals to keep it damp. After 5 hours, remove the cheesecloth with a scissors, turn the turkey breast side up, and continue smoking until the internal temperature in the thigh reaches 180 degrees, 3 to 6 hours longer, depending on the size of the bird and the temperature of your smoker.

3. When the turkey is cooked, remove and let stand for 15 minutes. (The turkey can be cooled to room temperature, wrapped in foil, and refrigerated up to 3 days.) Carve (see page 15) and serve.

STEP-BY-STEP

PREPARING A WHOLE TURKEY FOR SMOKING

To prevent a whole turkey from drying out during the long smoking process, it is necessary to wrap it in cheesecloth for part of the cooking time. Dampen a 7-foot length of cheesecloth and wrap it around the bird, tying the ends together.

Cranberry-Glazed Whole Smoked Turkey

THIS CRANBERRY PASTE GIVES THE TURKEY A FRUITY-SMOKY FLAVOR. FOR MAXIMUM IMPACT, ALLOW THE GLAZED TURKEY TO MARINATE IN THE REFRIGERATOR OVERNIGHT BEFORE SMOKING. THIS FESTIVE SMOKED TURKEY MAKES A DELICIOUS CENTERPIECE FOR A HOLIDAY MEAL. SERVES 10 TO 12.

1 8-ounce can jellied cranberry sauce
1 small onion, coarsely chopped
4 garlic cloves, coarsely chopped
4 tablespoons butter, softened
1 tablespoon ground cumin
1 tablespoon salt
1 tablespoon pepper
1 10- to 12-pound turkey, rinsed and patted dry

1. Combine the cranberry sauce, onion, garlic, butter, cumin, salt, and pepper in the work bowl of a food processor. Process until smooth. Rub the paste liberally underneath the skin of the turkey and inside the cavity. Place the turkey in a large plastic bag and refrigerate overnight.

2. Remove the turkey from the refrigerator and let sit at room temperature for 45 minutes. Set up the smoker and soak the wood chunks (see "How to Smoke-Cook with a Water Smoker," pages 468–469).

3. Dampen a 7-foot length of cheesecloth and wrap it around the bird, tying the ends together. Transfer the turkey to the smoker, breast side down. Spray the cheesecloth with more water at 1½-hour intervals to keep it damp. After 5 hours, remove the cheesecloth with a scissors, turn the turkey breast side up, and continue smoking until the internal temperature in the thigh reaches 180 degrees, 3 to 6 hours longer, depending on the size of the bird and the temperature of your smoker.

4. When the turkey is cooked, remove and let stand for 15 minutes. (The turkey can be cooled to room temperature, wrapped in foil, and refrigerated up to 3 days.) Carve (see page 15) and serve.

Whole Smoked Turkey with Chile-Cumin Rub

A WHOLE TURKEY MAY BE RUBBED WITH ANY NUMBER OF SPICE PASTES AND THEN SMOKED. WE LIKE THE EARTHY, SPICY COMBINATION OF CHILI POWDER AND CUMIN, BUT ANY OF THE SPICE RUBS IN THIS CHAPTER ARE APPROPRIATE. THIS SPICY, SMOKY TURKEY IS PERFECT FOR A SUMMER PARTY. SERVES 10 TO 12.

1 10- to 12-pound turkey, rinsed and patted dry
½ cup Chile-Cumin Rub (page 467)
1 tablespoon salt

1. Rub the turkey all over with the spice rub, then sprinkle with salt. Place the turkey in a large plastic bag and refrigerate for at least 2 hours. (The turkey can be refrigerated overnight for stronger flavor.)

2. Remove the turkey from the refrigerator and let sit at room temperature for 45 minutes. Set up the smoker and soak the wood chunks (see "How to Smoke-Cook with a Water Smoker," pages 468–469).

3. Dampen a 7-foot length of cheesecloth and wrap it around the bird, tying the ends together. Transfer the turkey to the smoker, breast side down. Spray the cheesecloth with more water at 1½-hour intervals to keep it damp. After 5 hours, remove the cheesecloth with a scissors, turn the turkey breast side up, and continue smoking until the internal temperature in the thigh reaches 180 degrees, 3 to 6 hours longer, depending on the size of the bird and the temperature of your smoker.

4. When the turkey is cooked, remove and let stand for 15 minutes. (The turkey can be cooled to room temperature, wrapped in foil, and refrigerated up to 3 days.) Carve (see page 15) and serve.

Smoked Turkey Breast with Ginger-Cardamom Rub

SERVES 10 TO 12

HERE, WE PAIR A MEATY turkey breast with a strongly flavored mixture dominated by ginger and cardamom. Depending on your taste and what else you plan to serve with your smoke-cooked poultry, you may substitute any of the rubs in this chapter or any for grilled chicken parts in chapter 11.

1 6- to 8-pound fresh, whole, bone-in, skin-on turkey breast, rinsed and prepared according to figures 1 and 2 on page 358
¼ cup Ginger-Cardamom Rub (page 467)
1 teaspoon salt

1. Rub the turkey breast all over with the spice rub, then sprinkle with salt. Cover and refrigerate the rubbed turkey breast for at least 2 hours. (The turkey breast can be refrigerated overnight for stronger flavor.)

2. Set up the smoker and soak the wood chunks (see "How to Smoke-Cook with a Water Smoker," pages 468–469).

3. Smoke the turkey breast until a meat thermometer registers 165 degrees, 6 to 7 hours. Remove from the grill or smoker and let it rest at least 15 minutes. (The turkey can be cooled to room temperature, wrapped in foil, and refrigerated up to 3 days.) Carve and serve.

◆

Chipotle-Garlic Smoked Turkey Breast

A WET MIXTURE OF CHIPOTLE CHILES AND GARLIC IS RUBBED UNDER THE SKIN OF THE TURKEY, SO THAT THE MEAT IS INFUSED WITH A SMOKY, SPICY FLAVOR, AS WELL AS THE FLAVOR OF SMOKE. SERVES 8 TO 10.

4 canned chipotle chiles in adobo, chopped fine
4 garlic cloves, finely chopped
2 tablespoons minced fresh cilantro leaves
1 teaspoon ground cumin
1 teaspoon salt
1 6- to 8-pound fresh, whole, bone-in, skin-on turkey breast, rinsed and prepared according to figures 1 and 2 on page 358

1. Combine the chiles, garlic, cilantro, cumin, and salt in a small bowl. Rub the mixture underneath the skin of the turkey breast. Cover and refrigerate the rubbed turkey breast for at least 2 hours. (The turkey breast can be refrigerated overnight for stronger flavor.)

2. Set up the smoker and soak the wood chunks (see "How to Smoke-Cook with a Water Smoker," pages 468–469).

3. Smoke the turkey breast until a meat thermometer registers 165 degrees, 6 to 7 hours. Remove from the grill or smoker and let it rest at least 15 minutes. (The turkey can be cooled to room temperature, wrapped in foil, and refrigerated up to 3 days.) Carve and serve.

THREE RUBS FOR
SMOKED POULTRY

Ginger-Cardamom Rub

EACH OF THE SPICES IN THIS RUB ADDS A LAYER OF
FLAVOR, BUT IF YOU'VE RUN OUT OF ONE OR TWO,
YOU CAN COMPENSATE BY INCREASING THE
AMOUNTS OF THE ONES YOU DO HAVE, ACCORD-
ING TO TASTE. MAKES ABOUT 1¼ CUPS.

> 3 tablespoons ground cardamom
> 3 tablespoons ground ginger
> 3 tablespoons pepper
> 3 tablespoons ground fenugreek
>   (optional)
> 2 tablespoons ground turmeric
> 2 tablespoons ground cumin
> 2 tablespoons ground coriander
> 2 tablespoons cayenne pepper
> 1 tablespoon ground allspice
> 1 teaspoon ground cloves

Mix all the ingredients in a small bowl. Place the
spice rub in an airtight container and store in the
pantry for up to 6 weeks.

◆

Chile-Cumin Rub

THIS RUB IS A LITTLE SWEET AND A LITTLE HOT,
WITH JUST A HINT OF CLOVES. MAKES ABOUT 1 CUP.

> ½ cup sweet paprika
> 2 tablespoons ground cumin
> 2 tablespoons mild chili powder
> 2 tablespoons pepper

1 teaspoon cayenne pepper
½ teaspoon ground cloves

Mix all ingredients in a small bowl. Place the
spice rub in an airtight container and store in the
pantry for up to 6 weeks.

◆

Mustard Rub

IF YOU PREFER A HOTTER RUB, INCREASE THE MUS-
TARD TO 3 TABLESPOONS. MAKES ABOUT 1 CUP.

> ¼ cup fennel seeds
> ¼ cup cumin seeds
> ¼ cup coriander seeds
> 1 tablespoon ground cinnamon
> 2 tablespoons dry mustard
> 2 tablespoons brown sugar

1. Toast the fennel, cumin, and coriander over
medium heat in a small skillet, shaking the pan
occasionally to prevent burning, until the first
wisps of smoke appear, 3 to 5 minutes. Remove
from heat, cool to room temperature, then mix
with the remaining ingredients.

2. Grind the mixture to a powder in a spice
grinder or with a mortar and pestle. Place the
spice rub in an airtight container and store in the
pantry for up to 6 weeks.

HOW TO SMOKE-COOK
WITH A WATER SMOKER

T LEAST AN HOUR BEFORE YOU PLAN TO START COOKING, PLACE WOOD CHUNKS, EACH THE SIZE OF A TENNIS BALL, IN A BOWL OF COLD WATER. FOR FOODS THAT WILL SMOKE LESS THAN 3 HOURS, USE 3 CHUNKS. FOR FOODS THAT REQUIRE LONGER SMOKING TIMES, USE 3 CHUNKS FOR EVERY 3 HOURS OF

estimated cooking time. If you want foods to have a smokier flavor, soak extra wood chunks as desired.

Thirty minutes before you plan to cook, plug in the smoker. Line the water pan with heavy-duty aluminum foil. When the smoker is hot, place the soaked wood chunks in the smoker, avoiding the electric coil (see figure 1). Position the water pan in the smoker and fill it with hot tap water (see figure 2, opposite). Set the top cooking rack in place and set the food on the rack. Place an oven thermometer on the rack with the food (see figure 3, opposite). Cover the smoker with the lid and cook as directed in the recipes in this chapter. When turning the meat, adjust the smoker to maintain a temperature of 200 to 250 degrees. Do not open the smoker more than is necessary or you will slow down the cooking process.

Add more soaked wood chunks every 3 hours or more often for a smokier flavor (see figure 4, opposite). After 3 hours, check the water pan and refill as necessary. Use an instant-read thermometer to judge when food is done.

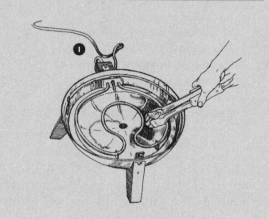

1. Place the soaked wood chunks in the hot smoker, avoiding direct contact with the electric coil so that they will burn more slowly.

Smoked Quail

SERVES 4

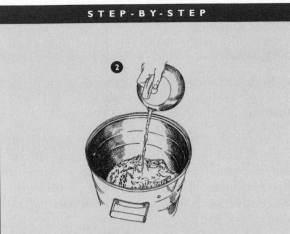

2. Fill the foil-lined water pan with hot tap water.

3. Place an oven thermometer on the rack with the food. (It's more accurate than a grill thermometer in the lid and heat loss is not a big issue when using an electric smoker.)

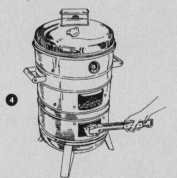

4. To add more soaked wood during cooking, slide open the door on the bottom of the smoker and use long-handled tongs to place the chunks around the electric coil.

T INY QUAIL ARE RUBBED with a mixture of brown sugar, cinnamon, ginger, and salt and then smoked until medium-rare.

1 tablespoon brown sugar
2 teaspoons ground cinnamon
2 teaspoons ground ginger
½ teaspoon salt
8 whole quail (about 5 ounces each),
   rinsed and patted dry

1. Combine the brown sugar, cinnamon, ginger, and salt in a small bowl. Rub the quail all over with the spice rub. Cover and refrigerate for at least 2 hours. (The quail can be refrigerated overnight for a stronger flavor.)

2. Following the instructions for grill or smoker (see "How to Smoke-Cook with a Kettle-Style Grill," page 462, or "How to Smoke-Cook with a Water Smoker," opposite), soak the wood chunks and set up the grill or smoker.

3. Smoke the quail until a meat thermometer registers 140 degrees (quail will be medium-rare), 40 to 50 minutes. Remove from the grill or smoker and let rest at least 15 minutes, then serve.

Smoked Whole Chicken with Chile-Cumin Rub

SERVES 4

A S MIGHT BE EXPECTED, a whole chicken smokes in much less time than a turkey. There's no need to wrap the chicken in cheesecloth. Just coat with a spice rub and smoke. To smoke a Cornish game hen (weighing about 1½ pounds), use half the rub and reduce the smoking time to about 2 hours, or until a thermometer inserted into the thigh registers 180 degrees.

1 whole chicken (about 3½ pounds), giblets removed and reserved for another use, chicken rinsed and patted dry
3 tablespoons Chile-Cumin Rub (page 467)
1 teaspoon salt

1. Rub the chicken all over with the spice rub, then sprinkle with salt. Cover and refrigerate for at least 2 hours. (The chicken can be refrigerated overnight for stronger flavor.)

2. Set up the smoker and soak the wood chunks (see "How to Smoke-Cook with a Water Smoker," pages 468–469).

3. Smoke the chicken until a meat thermometer inserted into the thigh registers 180 degrees, 3½ to 4 hours. Remove from the grill or smoker and let rest at least 15 minutes. (The chicken can be cooled to room temperature, wrapped in foil and refrigerated up to 3 days.) Carve (see page 13) and serve.

Smoked Chicken Breasts with Mustard Rub

SERVES 4

SMOKED CHICKEN BREASTS rubbed with a spiced mustard mixture make a flavorful sandwich or, dressed simply with a little mayonnaise or oil and vinegar, an excellent chicken salad.

> 4 boneless, skinless chicken breasts, trimmed and tendons removed
> 2 tablespoons Mustard Rub (page 467)
> ½ teaspoon salt

1. Rub the chicken breasts all over with the spice rub, then sprinkle with salt. Cover and refrigerate for at least 2 hours. (The chicken can be refrigerated overnight for stronger flavor.)

2. Following the instructions for grill or smoker (see "How to Smoke-Cook with a Kettle-Style Grill," page 462, or "How to Smoke-Cook with a Water Smoker," page 468), soak the wood chunks and set up the grill or smoker.

3. Smoke the chicken breasts until a meat thermometer inserted into thickest part of each breast registers 165 degrees, 45 minutes to 1 hour. Remove from the grill or smoker and let rest at least 15 min-

utes. (The chicken breasts can be cooled to room temperature, wrapped in foil, and refrigerated up to 3 days.) Carve and serve.

◆

Szechwan Smoked Chicken Breasts

HERE, WE MARINATE THE CHICKEN BREASTS FOR 30 MIN-UTES IN A WET SPICE PASTE. SERVE WITH RICE OR NOO-DLES AND A SELECTION OF STEAMED VEGETABLES FOR A FLAVORFUL, LOW-FAT MEAL. SERVES 4.

> 2 scallions, white and light green parts, coarsely chopped
> 1 1-inch piece fresh gingerroot, peeled
> 2 garlic cloves, peeled
> 1 tablespoon grated orange zest
> 2 tablespoons fresh orange juice
> 1 tablespoon soy sauce
> 2 teaspoons ground Szechwan peppercorns
> 2 teaspoons chili oil
> 4 boneless, skinless chicken breast halves, trimmed of fat and tendons removed
> ½ teaspoon salt

1. Combine the scallions, ginger, garlic, zest, juice, soy sauce, peppercorns, and chili oil in the work bowl of a food processor. Process until smooth. Rub the chicken breasts all over with the spice paste, then sprinkle with salt. Place the chicken in a sealable bag and refrigerate for 30 minutes.

2. While the chicken marinates, follow the instructions for grill or smoker (see "How to Smoke-Cook with a Kettle-Style Grill," page 462, or "How to Smoke-Cook with a Water Smoker," page 468), soaking the wood chunks and setting up the grill or smoker.

3. Smoke the chicken breasts until a meat thermometer inserted into it registers 165 degrees, 45 minutes to 1 hour. Remove from the grill or smoker and let rest at least 15 minutes and serve. (The chicken breasts can be cooled to room temperature, wrapped in foil, and refrigerated up to 3 days.)

PREPARING A CHICKEN FOR SMOKING ON THE STOVE

1. Line a large soup kettle, Dutch oven, or wok with at least 2 long sheets of heavy-duty aluminum foil so that there are several inches of foil overhanging all the way around the top of the pot.

2. Spread the rice, sugar, tea, cloves, anise, and orange zest evenly over the bottom of the pan. Set the wire rack over these ingredients, making sure that there will be about 1 inch of space all around the chicken. (If there is any less space, the chicken will not brown well.) If you do not have a rack that fits in the pan, set 2 empty tuna fish cans (tops, bottoms, and labels removed) on opposite sides of the pot, and bridge them with 2 metal skewers.

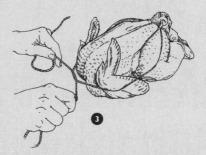

3. Use a 3-foot length of kitchen twine to tie the legs together. Run the twine around the thighs and under the wings on both sides of the bird, pull it snug, and tie a firm knot at the neck; snip off the excess twine.

4. Place the trussed chicken on the rack or skewers. Use another sheet of heavy-duty foil to make a tent shape over the chicken; crimp it together with the foil that lines the pot and work until you are halfway around the pot. Stick an instant-read thermometer through the foil lid and into the thigh.

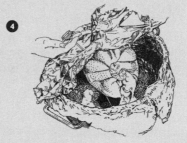

5. Finish crimping the top piece of foil to the bottom piece of foil to completely seal the smoker.

Tea-Smoked Chicken

WHILE MOST SMOKING IS best accomplished outside, it is possible to use a wok or large Dutch oven for stove-top smoking. We find this method is well suited to the classic Chinese technique of tea smoking. Instead of soaked wood chunks, tea and spices lend their flavor to a whole bird.

Traditionally, this recipe is prepared with a duck. Most recipes for tea-smoked duck involve five separate processes. The bird is first marinated in spices, next smoked, then steamed (to actually cook it), then air-dried (to improve the texture), and finally deep-fried (to crisp the skin). While each of these steps adds something to the finished product, few cooks today are able to spend the day and a half to six days that it takes to complete them all.

After much experimentation, we found that by making two adjustments it is possible to get the subtle flavors and textures of this dish with a relatively simple, one-step cooking process. First, the bird is smoked for a longer time over an aromatic mixture; this combines into one step the flavoring and cooking normally achieved by marinating, smoking, and steaming. Second, the duck is replaced by chicken, which makes it possible to eliminate the drying and deep-frying that were needed to deal with the layer of fat that lies under the skin of a duck.

In this shortened method, we cook the bird on an improvised smoker on top of the stove. The smoker is made from a foil-lined pot with a foil lid, and a rack that suspends the chicken over a smoking mixture.

Once you conquer any initial fears you may have about building a small fire on top of the stove, you can get a very juicy and flavorful bird with an absolute minimum of preparation and cleanup. And once you have done it a couple of times, the whole setup process, from pulling your bird out of the grocery bag to starting the cooking, will take no more than ten minutes. The cooking itself will take only one hour and twenty minutes if using a 4-pound bird.

The smoking mixture consists of brown sugar, rice, tea, and spices. Each plays an important role in the cooking and flavoring process.

As the brown sugar heats up, it begins to caramelize, forming various compounds, some of which are very volatile and enter the air as smoke. These give the bird a bittersweet, caramel flavor.

Like the sugar, the rice adds flavor. But it has an added function: it absorbs the moisture that the sugar creates as it caramelizes, as well as the moisture the bird gives off as it cooks. This is crucial—you want the smoking mixture to be as dry as possible so that you get smoke, not steam.

The tea provides most of the flavor in the smoke. Not only does it flavor the bird as the smoke is absorbed but also, as the bird releases moisture, the tea particles settle on the bird and actually make tea on the skin and in the cavity of the bird. The tea colors the skin a beautiful, glossy mahogany and also serves as a sort of marinade as the bird cooks.

To see what differences in flavor they might provide, we tried three different types of tea—regular Chinese black tea, orange pekoe, and a smoked Chinese tea called Lapsang souchong. While all three gave a good flavor, each had its advantages. Orange pekoe gave the best fragrance to the kitchen; Lapsang souchong gave the smokiest flavor to the meat. In the end we decided we liked Lapsang souchong best; when combined with the traditional Chinese flavorings of cloves, star anise, and citrus peel, it gave the chicken the strongest flavor.

We experimented with several combinations of spices and liked the sweet, aromatic combination of whole cloves, star anise, and orange peel best. However, other whole spices, including black peppercorns and cinnamon sticks, as well as lemon peel, may be used if desired.

For smoking, you will need a large Dutch oven or wok, some heavy-duty aluminum foil, and a rack to hold the bird.

The pot needs to be large enough to hold the bird, the rack, and the smoking material; it also needs to be fairly heavy. Only the aluminum foil protects the surface of the pot. Therefore, the pot needs to be able to withstand ninety minutes of high heat. A nonstick or glazed pan may be ruined. Most woks are sufficiently large and durable, and many come with a rack for steaming. The only potential problem with using a wok is that long exposure to high heat may burn away the embedded oil that seasons your wok. If, however, you regularly scrub out your wok after every use, the heat should not be a problem. Instead of a wok, you may use a cast-iron Dutch oven; we used a 12-quart pot successfully.

To seal the pot, use heavy-duty aluminum foil, preferably from an 18-inch-wide roll. By the end of the cooking time, the smoking mixture will have become a molten mass of sugar and burned rice; you simply let it cool, then remove the foil and throw this mess away inside the foil.

When placing the bird on a rack above the smoking mixture, the goal is to keep the bird suspended in the middle, with air on all sides. For most pots, this means the rack should stand up off the bottom of the pan by 1 inch and the chicken should have about 1 inch of room on the sides and top. Somewhat more crowded conditions will not affect the cooking time or flavor, but might lead to a splotchy color. Trussing the chicken helps to keep the bird compact and from touching the sides of the pot as it cooks.

Before sealing the chicken in the foil, stick a meat thermometer through the foil lid and into the leg or thigh. Other methods of checking doneness—such as looking at the juices or moving the leg—can't be used because they require unsealing the smoker.

The most critical part of cooking the chicken is being sure that you are cooking it at the right temperature. The smoking mixture should be giving off a steady amount of smoke without going out or burning too quickly. The best way to judge this is to take a look at the hole through which the thermometer is inserted. You should see a thin, steady stream of smoke coming out. If the smoke is billowing out, turn the heat down slightly.

◆

Stovetop Tea-Smoked Chicken

BE AWARE THAT THE POT GETS QUITE HOT, AND THAT YOU WILL HEAR A LOT OF SIMMERING AND HISSING. THE FINISHED CHICKEN SHOULD HAVE AN ATTRACTIVE BRONZE OR BROWN COLOR, BUT IT WILL BE A BIT SOFT. IF YOU ARE A FAN OF CRISP SKIN, SIMPLY COAT THE BIRD WITH SESAME OIL AND PLACE IT IN A HOT OVEN FOR SEVERAL MINUTES AS DIRECTED. SERVES 4 TO 6.

½ cup rice (any kind)
⅓ cup packed light brown sugar
⅓ cup loose tea, preferably Lapsang souchong
6 whole cloves
3 star anise pods
1 strip orange zest
1 whole chicken (3½ to 4 pounds),
   rinsed and patted dry
Salt and pepper
Sesame oil (optional)

1. Line a large, heavy soup kettle, Dutch oven, or wok with at least 2 long sheets of heavy-duty aluminum foil so that there is a 2- to 3-inch rim of foil all the way around the pot (see figure 1, page 472).

2. Spread the rice, brown sugar, tea, cloves, anise, and orange zest evenly over the bottom of the pan. Set the wire rack over these ingredients, making sure that there will be about 1 inch of space all around the chicken. (If there is any less space, the chicken will not brown well.) Alternatively, set 2 empty tuna cans (tops, bottoms, and labels removed) on opposite sides of the pot, and bridge them with 2 metal skewers (see figure 2, page 472).

3. Rub the chicken cavity and skin with salt and pepper to taste. Use a 3-foot length of kitchen twine to tie the legs together. Run the twine around the thighs and under the wings on both sides of the bird, pull it snug, and tie a firm knot at the neck; snip off the excess twine (see figure 3, page 472).

4. Place the trussed chicken on the rack or skewers (see figure 4, page 472). Use a large piece of heavy-duty foil to make a tent shape over the chicken; crimp this foil to about halfway around the rim of the foil lining the wok or pot. Stick an instant-read thermometer through the foil lid and into the leg or thigh and finish crimping the top piece of foil to completely seal the smoker (see figure 5, page 472).

5. Heat the pot over high heat until the tea mixture begins to smoke. Once the smoking starts, reduce the heat to medium-high. Smoke the bird, making sure a

thin, steady stream of smoke emerges from the opening made by the meat thermometer, until the chicken registers 170 degrees, 45 minutes to 1½ hours, depending on the size of the bird. Once the chicken is done, carefully remove the pot from the heat, unseal the foil, and remove the chicken. (If you want to crisp the skin, simply coat the cooked chicken with a little sesame oil and roast it in a 450-degree oven for about 5 minutes.)

6. Let the chicken rest 10 minutes, carve, and serve. For cleanup, let foil cool (molten sugar will burn, so cooling is essential), then fold it back on itself to reseal and discard.

Smoked Duck Breasts

SERVES 4

WE REMOVE the skin from the breast before smoking rather than steaming away the fatty layer underneath the skin beforehand. These breasts are coated with a spice rub and then brushed with a glaze of maple syrup, orange juice, and honey right before smoking to protect the breast meat from drying out as it cooks.

1 teaspoon salt
2 tablespoons dark brown sugar
1 tablespoon grated orange zest
1 teaspoon ground cinnamon
1 teaspoon pepper
2 whole boneless duck breasts, about 12 ounces each, skin and fat removed, split, rinsed, and patted dry
¾ cup fresh orange juice
½ cup maple syrup
2 tablespoons honey
1 teaspoon ground ginger
1 teaspoon ground coriander
1 teaspoon cracked black peppercorns
1 teaspoon finely chopped fresh thyme leaves

1. Combine the salt, brown sugar, orange zest, cinnamon, and pepper in a small bowl. Rub the mixture all over the duck breasts, cover, and refrigerate for at least 2 hours. (The duck breasts can be refrigerated overnight for stronger flavor.)

2. Combine the orange juice, maple syrup, honey, ginger, and coriander in a small saucepan over medium-high heat. Bring to a boil and cook until thick and syrupy, about 10 minutes. Remove from heat, stir in the peppercorns and thyme, and cool.

3. Following the instructions for grill or smoker (see "How to Smoke-Cook with a Kettle-Style Grill," page 462, or "How to Smoke-Cook with a Water Smoker," page 468), soak the wood chunks and set up the grill or smoker.

4. Brush the duck breasts thickly with the glaze. Smoke the duck breasts until a meat thermometer registers 140 degrees (breasts will be medium-rare), about 40 minutes. Remove from the grill or smoker and let rest at least 15 minutes and serve.

INDEX

Note: Page numbers in *italics* refer to illustrations.

CONVERSION CHART
Equivalent Imperial and Metric Measurements

American cooks use standard containers, the 8-ounce cup and a tablespoon that takes exactly 16 level fillings to fill that cup level. Measuring by cup makes it very difficult to give weight equivalents, as a cup of densely packed butter will weigh considerably more than a cup of flour. The easiest way therefore to deal with cup measurements in recipes is to take the amount by volume rather than by weight. Thus the equation reads:

1 cup = 240 ml = 8 fl. oz.   ½ cup = 120 ml = 4 fl. oz.

It is possible to buy a set of American cup measures in major stores around the world.

In the States, butter is often measured in sticks. One stick is the equivalent of 8 tablespoons. One tablespoon of butter is therefore the equivalent to ½ ounce or 15 grams.

LIQUID MEASURES

Fluid Ounces	U.S.	Imperial	Milliliters
	1 teaspoon	1 teaspoon	5
¼	2 teaspoons	1 dessertspoon	10
½	1 tablespoon	1 tablespoon	14
1	2 tablespoons	2 tablespoons	28
2	¼ cup	4 tablespoons	56
4	½ cup		110
5		¼ pint or 1 gill	140
6	¾ cup		170
8	1 cup		225
9			250, ¼ liter
10	1¼ cups	½ pint	280
12	1½ cups		340
15		¾ pint	420
16	2 cups		450
18	2¼ cups		500, ½ liter
20	2½ cups	1 pint	560
24	3 cups		675
25		1¼ pints	700
27	3½ cups		750
30	3¾ cups	1½ pints	840
32	4 cups or 1 quart		900
35		1¾ pints	980
36	4½ cups		1000, 1 liter
40	5 cups	2 pints or 1 quart	1120

SOLID MEASURES

U.S. and Imperial Measures		Metric Measures	
Ounces	Pounds	Grams	Kilos
1		28	
2		56	
3½		100	
4	¼	112	
5		140	
6		168	
8	½	225	
9		250	¼
12	¾	340	
16	1	450	
18		500	½
20	1¼	560	
24	1½	675	
27		750	¾
28	1¾	780	
32	2	900	
36	2¼	1000	1
40	2½	1100	
48	3	1350	
54		1500	1½

OVEN TEMPERATURE EQUIVALENTS

Fahrenheit	Celsius	Gas Mark	Description
225	110	¼	Cool
250	130	½	
275	140	1	Very Slow
300	150	2	
325	170	3	Slow
350	180	4	Moderate
375	190	5	
400	200	6	Moderately Hot
425	220	7	Fairly Hot
450	230	8	Hot
475	240	9	Very Hot
500	250	10	Extremely Hot

Any broiling recipes can be used with the grill of the oven, but beware of high-temperature grills.

EQUIVALENTS FOR INGREDIENTS

all-purpose flour—plain flour
baking sheet—oven tray
buttermilk—ordinary milk
cheesecloth—muslin
coarse salt—kitchen salt
cornstarch—cornflour

eggplant—aubergine
granulated sugar—caster sugar
half and half—12% fat milk
heavy cream—double cream
light cream—single cream
parchment paper—greaseproof paper

plastic wrap—cling film
scallion—spring onion
shortening—white fat
unbleached flour—strong, white flour
zest—rind
zucchini—courgettes or marrow